THE PRAEGER HANDBOOK OF ADOPTION

THE PRAEGER HANDBOOK OF ADOPTION

Volume One

Edited by
Kathy Shepherd Stolley
and Vern L. Bullough

Westport, Connecticut
London

Library of Congress Cataloging-in-Publication Data

The Praeger handbook of adoption / edited by Kathy Shepherd Stolley
   and Vern L. Bullough.
     p. cm.
   Includes bibliographical references and index.
   ISBN 0-313-33335-1 (alk. paper) — ISBN 0-313-33336-X (v. 1 : alk. paper) —
ISBN 0-313-33337-8 (v. 2 : alk. paper) 1. Adoption—History—Encyclopedias.
I. Stolley, Kathy S. II. Bullough, Vern L.
   HV875P694 2006
   362.734—dc22   2006025919

British Library Cataloguing in Publication Data is available.

Library of Congress Catalog Card Number: 2006025919
ISBN: 0–313–33335–1 (set)
     0–313–33336–X (vol. 1)
     0–313–33337–8 (vol. 2)

First published in 2006

Praeger Publishers, 88 Post Road West, Westport, CT 06881
An imprint of Greenwood Publishing Group, Inc.
www.praeger.com

Printed in the United States of America

The paper used in this book complies with the
Permanent Paper Standard issued by the National
Information Standards Organization (Z39.48-1984).

10   9   8   7   6   5   4   3   2   1

Family: *a unit formed by marriage, blood or fictive kinship ties, or adoption*
From us, to our families . . . . . .

From Kathy—
To my "childhood" family: Mama, Daddy, Jerry, Mit-Maw, Paw-Paw, Gracie,
Margaret; and to my husband Billy

From Vern—
To my children: James, Steven, Susan, and Michael, and to their mother,
Bonnie; as well as my granddaughter Jamie

In memory of Vern L. Bullough, 1928–2006

Table of Contents

Table of Contents

General Topical List of Original Content

Adoption in Culture:

Literature:

Abandonment and Adoption in European Folk Tales
Adoption Literature Sampler: The Best in Children's Literature for Adoptees
Children's Literature as a Resource in Adoptee's Lives
Orphans and Adoption in Adult Literature
Rapping about Adoption: "Just Like Me" (Sidebar)
Superman (Sidebar)
Textbooks on Marriage and Family: How They Include Adoption

Other:

Little Orphan Annie
Oedipus
Popular Culture and Adoption

Adoption Practice/Services and Child Welfare:

Child Protection and Adoption
Child Welfare League of America (CWLA)
Children's Home Society/National Children's Home Society Movement
The Cradle Society
Ethical Issues in Adoption
Facilitators, Adoption
Family Preservation
Lifebooks
Nineteenth Century Changes in American Adoption
Permanency Planning
Post-Adoption Services
Reunification
(Also see: *International Adoption Agencies; Social Work Perspectives on Adoption;* entries categorized under *Types of Adoption* heading)

Advocacy Surrounding Adoption Issues:

Adoptees' Liberty Movement Association (ALMA)
Adoption Search Movement
Adoptive Families of America
Advocacy and Adoption (Overview)
American Adoption Congress
Bastard Nation: The Adoptee Rights Organization
Concerned United Birthparents (CUB)
Human Rights and Adoption
Mutual Consent Registries
Reunion

Awareness:

> *Cultural Socialization*
> *Culture Camps*

Perspectives/Practices:

> *Africa and Adoption*
> *Australia and New Zealand: The Experience Of Indigenous Populations*
> *Canadian Adoption Practices*
> *China and the Change in Adoption*
> *Chinese Orphan Adoption by Foreign Families and the Development of Adoption in China*
> *Hanai and Adoption in Hawaii*
> *India and Child Adoption*
> *Indonesia: Permanency Planning post-December 26, 2004 Southeast Asia Tsunami: A Case Study*
> *Irish Adoption: A History*
> *Iroquois Adoption Practices*
> *Japan and Adoption*
> *Korea and Adoption*
> *Latin America and Adoption*
> *Mexico and Adoption*
> *Native Americans and Adoption: Defining Who is "Indian"*
> *Romania and Adoption*
> *Russia and Adoption*
> *South African Changes in Adoption: A Case Study*
> (Also see: entries categorized under *International Adoption* heading)

Dealing with Illegitimate, Unwanted, Needy, and/or Orphaned Children:

> *Baby Farming*
> *Baby-Selling*
> *"Binding-Out" Children*
> *Illegitimacy*
> (Also see: *entries categorized under Orphanages and Other Intitutional Settings*)

Disciplinary Perspectives on Adoption:

> *Feminism and Adoption: Changing Feminist Perspectives on Adoption*
> *Social Work Perspectives on Adoption*
> *Sociological Perspectives on Adoptive Families*
> (Also see: *Psychological Perspectives on Adoption*)

Financial Issues:

> *Adoption Insurance*
> *Employment Benefits and Adoption*
> *Financial Assistance for Adoption*
> *Financial Costs of Adoption*
> *Subsidy Programs for Adoption*
> (See also: *Interstate Compact on Adoption and Medical Assistance*)

First Person Original Accounts:

Growing Up in a Transracial Adoptive Family: Two Narratives
Myths and Realities of Adopting an Older Child
Operation Babylift: A First Person Narrative

Foster Care Issues:

Family Foster Care: British Perspectives
Foster Care in the United States
Foster Care: Transitioning Out of Care
Foster Parent Adoption

Gay/Lesbian and Same – Sex Adoption Issues

Foreign Adoption and Same-Sex Parents
Gay and Lesbian-headed Adoptive Families
Homosexuals and Adoption: The Case of Florida (Sidebar)
Lesbian Adoptions in Canada (Sidebar)
Same-Sex Adoption and Heirs
Same-Sex Couples and Religiously-Affiliated Agencies

Historical Perspectives: Adoption in Antiquity through Pre-U.S. History:

Ancient Babylonia and Adoption
Ancient China and Adoption
Byzantine Charities and Abandoned Children
Canon Law and Adoption
Child Donation
Classical Greece and Rome and Adoption
English Common Law
Foundling Wheels
Janissary
Medieval Europe and Adoption
Medieval Orphanages
Orphans' Court
Political Adoption
Roman Law and Adoption
Twins and Adoption in Medieval Europe (Sidebar)

International Adoption:

The Blumenfeld Case (Sidebar)
The Hague Convention on Protection of Children and Co-operation in Respect
   of Intercountry Adoption
International Adoption (Overview)
International Adoption Agencies
Operation Babylift
"Professional" Searchers
The United Nations and Adoption
U.S.-Born Children Adopted by Non-U.S. Parents
The Vietnamese Who Did Not Get Adopted
(Also see: *Foreign Adoption and Same-Sex Parents*)

Medical Issues in Adoption:

Acquired Immune Deficiency Syndrome (AIDS) and Adoption
Adoption Medicine (Overview)
Biology of Attachment and Adoption (Sidebar)
Developmental Assessment
Drug Exposed Infants and Adoption
Health Issues in Adoption
Human Immunodeficiency Virus (HIV)-Positive Infants
Infertility and Adoption
Medical Research Involving Orphans and Foster Care
(See also: entries categorized under the *Science and Adoption*
    Issues heading)

Orphanages and Other Institutional Settings/Issues:

Arizona Orphan Abduction
Florence Crittenton: National Florence Crittenton Mission/Crittenton Services
Group Homes
Institutionalizing Parentless Children: The Current Debate
Neighborhood Houses
Orphanages
Orphanages and "Mental Illness" (Sidebar)
Orphan Trains
Residential Treatment Centers
Soldiers' Orphans' Homes

Psychology of Adoption:

Adopted Child Syndrome
Adoptive Identity
Adult Adopted Persons' Psychosocial Adjustment
Attachment and Bonding in Adoption
Boundary Ambiguity in Adoption
Children's Understanding of Adoption
Counseling and Adoption
Gender and Mental Health Issues
Mutual-Aid
Outcomes of Adoption
Parenting and Adoption: Nature versus Nurture (Sidebar)
Postpartum Depression and Adoption
Psychological Perspectives on Adoption

Recruitment/Encouraging Adoption:

Advertising Adoption
Photographs and Advertising
Recruitment, Adoption
Wednesday's Child

Religious Perspectives:

Buddhism, Infanticide, and Adoption
The Catholic Church and Adoption: Lessons from Ireland
Catholicism and Adoption
Islam and Adoption
Judaism and Adoption
Mormons and Adoption
The Orthodox Church and Adoption (with special emphasis on Serbia)
Protestant Perspectives on Adoption
Religious Differences in Addressing Illegitimacy (Sidebar)

Science and Adoption Issues:

Assisted Reproductive Technologies and Adoption
DNA, Adoption, and Locating Biological Kin
Embryo Adoption
Eugenics and Adoption
Genetic Testing
Genetics and Adoption: Language and Ideology
Surrogacy and Adoption
(Also see: entries categorized under the *Medical Issues in Adoption heading*)

"Special Needs" Adoptions/Categories:

Adolescent/Teen Adoption
Large Special Needs Adoptive Families (Sidebar)
Older Children Adoption (Ages Five-Twelve)
Sibling Adoption
Special Needs Adoptions

Statistics/Data/Research Issues:

Census 2000 and Adoption
Longitudinal Adoption Studies
Public Opinion on Adoption
Statistics on Adoption

Stress and Crises in Families:

Children after Disasters and Crises
Disruption and Dissolution of Adoptions
Divorce and Adoption
(Also see: *Indonesia: Permanency Planning post-December 26, 2004 Southeast Asia Tsunami: A Case Study entry*)

Transracial Adoption:

Institute of Black Parenting (Sidebar)
Matching

Preface

The editors of this handbook and the many contributors have documented the history of adoption through recorded history. Entries cover the most ancient adoptions recorded to current events occurring as the completed manuscript goes to the publisher. Attitudes have changed over time, but the most radical changes at this writing have taken place in the United States. It is estimated that there are now more than 1.6 million adopted children in the United States and the circumstances surrounding their adoptions are not just discussed openly, but are often celebrated and honored, no longer kept secret and hidden.

In this new age of adoptive openness, if both the birth and adoptive parents agree, they can stay in touch with each other, and children—as they become adults—can also get records of their adoption and trace their birth mother and often their birth father. Races are often mixed in family composition, children are adopted in growing numbers from foreign countries, and single and same-sex adoptive parents abound. Some families have adopted dozens of children and these large families have replaced the old orphanages and transient foster care system. Many of these changes in the United States have often taken place without deliberate planning although, increasingly, rules and regulations are being issued to deal with some of the worst abuses which have occurred.

Certainly there are more social service agencies to help adopted parents through any difficulties they might encounter and to offer assistance to the adopted children. Most studies, however, emphasize the love that adoptive parents have for their children and the lengths to which they are willing to go to give them a wholesome, love-filled childhood. There are still many children with physical or other handicaps who need adoption and older children often pose special concerns, though many of these are also adopted. On the whole, adoption has become institutionalized in the United States.

The contributors to this handbook approach the topics of adoption and fostering from a variety of backgrounds. Among the disciplines represented here are history, sociology, psychology, anthropology, women's studies, social work, child welfare, family sciences, business, theology, medicine, and law. The majority of authors are based in the United States; however, contributors also participated from the nations of Canada, China, Ethiopia, Serbia and Montenegro, South Africa, Spain, Taiwan, and the United Kingdom. Reprints and excerpts from a number of primary documents are included to enrich the resource by providing additional information. These documents have also been selected to illustrate particular perspectives as well as to highlight notable events (e.g., legislation) in the history of adoption in the United States. We believe that this is the most comprehensive overview of adoption available, and we hope that it will be a basic reference for anyone interested in the history and practice of adoption or involved in the adoption process.

Kathy Shepherd Stolley and Vern L. Bullough

Acknowledgments

We wish to thank the many people who were instrumental in the creation of this handbook. It has been a true labor of love for many involved. We are grateful to our team of advisors (Drs. E. Wayne Carp, Priscilla Ferguson Clement, Trudy Festinger, Harold D. Grotevant, and Penelope L. Maza) who provided gracious and generous amounts of time, talent, and effort in suggesting topics, addressing various questions, critiquing, assisting in locating contributors, and writing entries—in general, doing what an expert team of advisors do, advising. We also appreciate the fine work of our contributors, many of whom assisted in ways well beyond writing entries to include locating other contributors and injecting humor throughout the lengthy process of producing this handbook. We also thank our editors at Greenwood and Praeger (Marie Ellen Larcada and, later, Deborah Adams and Elizabeth Potenza) who guided this process from the publisher's perspective, Erin Ryan who provided expertise on copyright permissions, and the additional staff who handled other issues. Plus, a special thanks to Christopher Lantz, who handled interlibrary loans in the Virginia Wesleyan College Hofheimer Library, for his efforts in locating the numerous primary documents from which many of the reprints and excerpts in the handbook are selected. Finally, we thank our families who provided inspiration and support in immeasurable ways throughout this process. May the final results be a positive contribution to the field of adoption studies and for those who are touched by adoption.

Kathy Shepherd Stolley and Vern L. Bullough

The Praeger Handbook of Adoption

Introduction: Adoption in History

Vern L. Bullough

As the entries in this handbook demonstrate, adoption in one form or another has long been part of the history of the human family. In many nomadic and tribal societies, motherless children were simply taken care of by other women in the group. Often, in many societies, children were part of the group and there was little effort to distinguish which woman had been the birth mother. This casual incorporation of a motherless child by other family members has continued throughout history. Sometimes there was an actual abandonment of unwanted infants as in ancient Greece, where those finding such infants might take them and raise them without any formal adoption procedure. However, most of these infants probably died from exposure since to survive they had to be found by a lactating woman or, in the case of Oedipus, by a sheepherder who probably had the infant nourished by a ewe.

For the most part in the past, the majority of individuals formally adopted were adults, not children. They were adopted to continue a family lineage or even to cement a friendship relationship between different families. Though there are exceptions, infants were rarely formally adopted, if only because of the difficulties of feeding and caring for them and the high rate of infant mortality. Abandoned and neglected children also were not widely adopted before the nineteenth century. Instead, institutions such as orphanages developed to take care of them. Still, gangs of homeless children are not uncommon in history. Often, in many areas of the world such as England, laws did not specifically address the question of adoption. Interestingly, however, in most of the European countries where the civil law had been based on Roman law, adoption was accepted as it was in canon law.

English common law did not recognize adoption until a formal statute on adoption passed in 1926, although earlier, a private bill of adoption could be authorized by parliamentary action. A variety of causes have been advanced for this lack of a general legal provision in English law. These range from a desire to protect property rights of blood relatives in cases of inheritance, to a moral dislike of illegitimacy, to the availability of other alternatives for abandoned children such as apprenticeship and voluntary transfers of custody. In the United States, where English common law served as the original basis of the law codes, Americans seemed less concerned than the British about the aforementioned issues, although adoption of children remained an informal affair rather than a formal one in the American colonies.

Things began to change in the nineteenth century, and these changes coincided with a changing attitude towards children. Jonathan Edwards, the Puritan evangelical preacher of the first part of the eighteenth century, for example, held that "children were not too little to die" and "not too little to go to hell." His extreme views were opposed by most of the religious believers in the United States and, in fact, Edwards was dismissed by his own congregation as their minister because of his extreme views. Still, his attitude towards children as more or less responsible individuals was not uncommon. Challenging these views and encouraging a change in attitudes was the influence of the eighteenth century movement known as the Enlightenment. In many ways, this was a continuation of the scientific spirit of the previous century, especially of the thought of René Descartes, John Locke, and Isaac Newton. The Enlightenment philosophers and writers, such as François Marie Arouet de Voltaire, distrusted all authority and tradition in matters of intellectual inquiry, holding that truth could only be attained through reason, observation, and experiment. Generally, they were socially committed individuals who sought to diffuse knowledge as much as to create it and, where possible, to use their scientific method in the service of their humanitarian ideals of tolerance, justice, and the moral and material welfare of human kind. Particularly important in challenging traditional views of children were Jean Jacques Rousseau and Johann Pestalozzi, both of whom stressed the "naturalness" of children and their lack of innate depravity.

During the nineteenth century, such views had begun to be accepted by increasing numbers of individuals. Once considered as miniature adults and the bearers of original sin, children increasingly came to be viewed as sweet innocents. Americans were less and less inclined to believe that predestination, which led to the belief that there was little anyone could do to change one's circumstances and character, decided life's outcome. Such a belief held that the purpose of education was to focus on the repression of the great evil that lurked in each soul. With the changing views, the innocence and purity of children became an increasingly powerful theme in American as it was in European thought.

Allied with this change was a changing view of motherhood, emphasizing that the mother's duty within the family setting was to protect a child's innocence with lessons of virtue and wisdom. Children were regarded as dependent upon adults around them for direction and instruction. This meant that child-rearing was a demanding and extremely important task in which the mother was all important in setting an example for the child to follow. Included in this was the job of teaching deference to the father whose role as breadwinner gave behind-the-scenes support to the family. Still, though the father might have the final word, the wise father left the teaching and management of children to the mother and her gentle nurturing. Everyone, it was believed, could succeed if they worked hard, and those who failed were regarded as having defects in their character, although these were not so much inherent as due to poor child-rearing or unusual circumstances which doomed such education to failure.

There was a widespread assumption that if children in troubled and disorganized families could only be placed in better environments where they could learn the necessary skills, they would be able to escape the hazard of their existing family life. The importance of escaping hazards was folded in with a growing belief among nineteenth century Americans, that though the United States had a vast store of natural resources, it was much too under-populated to exploit them. Even to begin to do so meant that Americans could only succeed if they could act in socially productive ways. That poverty existed in the United States, despite such potential riches, was explained as being due to defects in character and intent that afflicted the poor, something which was thought could be overcome. Thus, children who existed in poor families were, by definition, defective (although deserving families could also become poverty-stricken by tragedy or death). Children in such a situation could only overcome the problems of a defective family if they were placed in institutions where they could be taught moral lessons and right conduct. They could then be indentured into families or apprenticed during adolescence where they would learn the skills that would enable them to succeed.

This could more easily take place in rural families where there was a persistent shortage of workers. Large families in this situation were assets since children could be part of the labor force and learn the importance of labor and the interdependence of each other. Children of the urban poor, whether abandoned or not, were visualized as a source both of laborers and family members. At the same time, the developing urbanization—with the growth of larger and larger cities—made it more difficult for the poor to support large families. Further adding to the poverty was a mass migration of poor from Europe to American in the nineteenth century. Many who arrived penniless settled in the slums of the growing cities. Large numbers of children from poor families spent their youths living in homes other than their own as indentured servants or apprentices. Parents could rationalize this "farming out" of their children as providing their children with occupational skills to enable them to survive in the future. In their minds, farming out their children was not just a means of reducing household expenses, but was done for the child's benefit.

While indenture and apprenticeship helped move poverty-stricken adolescents into the community at large, it still left the children under eleven, not technically eligible for apprenticeship or indenture, mired in their poverty. It was for this group that the first orphan asylums developed in the United States. Almost all the early orphan asylums were established by women who believed they could improve the lot of children by indenturing them in families similar to their own. The first orphan asylum was the Boston Female Asylum founded in 1800 by Hannah Stillman, the wife of Boston's most prominent Baptist minister. She became convinced of the need to protect young girls and decided that an orphan asylum could serve as home and school. Soon after, orphan asylums were established in New York, Philadelphia, Norfolk, Virginia, and elsewhere. The women who established these institutions were, in a sense, pioneers in extending the role of women by stepping out on their own and making their own mark, a radical change that could be justified by their concern with children. As a group, they were also determined to demonstrate they could be good managers while managing to serve as mother figures for the poor and dissolute. While most of the early institutions took girls under eleven, who were seen as particularly vulnerable, some also took in boys, usually in coeducational institutions. The women managers saw themselves as providing not only assistance but solutions to the problems of the children, including placements when they were ready to leave.

Many children were temporarily placed in these developing asylums by parents unable, for some reason, to care for their offspring and with the assumption that they could return to get them when, and if, their conditions improved. Many of the early orphanages agreed with this hope, although the parents often failed to return for their children. To cope with the increasing numbers of children, the women running these orphanages tried to place children in homes of relatives, and failing that, with individuals of the same class and standing as the women who ran the asylum. They soon learned that neither birth parents nor elite families guaranteed a child's happiness or security. Slowly they turned to adoption, that is, to families who wanted to bring children up as their own. At first, most such adoptions were informal, and probably were not always recorded. They were also, in a sense, indentured contracts because the woman managers of the homes retained the same responsibility for the "adopted" children as for the rest of their wards. Gradually special individual adoptions were approved through private bills in the state legislature. As the numbers of these adoptions increased, Massachusetts—as the leader in this movement—enacted an adoption act in 1851, an action gradually followed by other states.

It is important to remember that during the nineteenth century, the United States was a frontier country, where settlers from both within the United States and from outside of the country began to come in increasing numbers. Many of them first settled in the growing urban centers of the East coast where slums grew larger. Yet there were vast stretches of scarcely populated areas that needed and wanted workers, and it was accepted that children could become workers. Urban reformers, worried about the increasing number of abandoned children, saw a market in the frontier, if it can be called that, for a product, namely children. The beginnings of this took place in Boston where, in 1826, the Boston Children's Mission began placing children with rural families within the state of Massachusetts in a form of indenture. Other states followed.

By the middle of the nineteenth century, the numbers of the poor as well as the numbers of abandoned children were rapidly growing in areas like New York City, Baltimore, Boston, Philadelphia, and other seaport cities. The Irish potato famine, for example, led to thousands, if not tens of thousands, of people fleeing Ireland for the United States, most of them poor and with few resources. Many were children without parents, and even those children who accompanied their families often turned to the streets to survive. What had been a trickle of children sent westward by the asylums became a mass movement in 1853 through the efforts of Charles Loring Brace and his New York-based Children's Aid Society.

The end of the American Civil War saw still another increase in the flow of immigrants, many of whom were also poverty-stricken, from German territories, Scandinavia, Italy, and, in fact, from all over Europe, as well as the British Isles. The majority of these immigrants first settled in the growing slums of America's large cities since they lacked resources to go elsewhere, and the numbers of children sent west rapidly increased. As nearby rural areas, which were once the destination of the children being placed out of the growing slums, reached a saturation point, children were sent farther and farther west. Some of the areas where children had once been sent even sent their surplus children on to other areas. Initially, Brace's movement organized and sent little companies of between five to thirty children, with an adult Aid Society agent, to rural communities. Increasingly, they went by train to the ever-expanding frontier. As the numbers increased, families or employers along the pre-selected route chose from among the group of children, and those remaining were taken to the next stop. Sometimes requests for children had been made in advance. While, in theory, the children were available for adoption, most were probably not, but they were given a home and work. Many of the older ones were still indentured. The Society relied upon correspondence for the most part to keep track of them, but between 1853 and 1893, a reported 84,328 children were placed out, and it was almost impossible to keep track of them. Many abandoned the homes they were sent to and sought others. Undoubtedly many also died.

Gradually, rules were added as the place-outs continued. One new regulation stated that if boys under fifteen were not adopted, they still had to be retained as members of the family until they were eighteen years of age. They were also to be sent to school regularly. Boys who were over fifteen when they arrived were to be treated as members of the family and kept until seventeen when they would be allowed to make their own way. The emphasis on boys in the regulations was deliberate since the majority of placements, in fact, were boys, with girls accounting for only 39 percent of the placements. One reason for this is that Brace himself, who regarded himself as a Christian missionary, felt uncomfortable about prepubescent and teenage girls, many of whom he felt displayed an overt sexuality and knowledge of worldly ways unbecoming a "lady." Interestingly, these urban to rural placements continued until well into the twentieth century. To meet the obligations of the influx of children, the states involved passed adoption laws. Kansas passed its law in 1864, and Illinois in 1867, although it had been possible to secure guardianship through private laws earlier in many of the states. By 1929 when the New York Children's Aid Society ceased to place children, they had sent out at least 150,000 individuals. Other groups also joined in the enterprise of sending out squads of children.

The youngest children, for the most part, did not participate in these movements westward, but instead were kept in institutions until they were considered old enough for adoption. There was almost no adoption of infants until the twentieth century. It was the invention of the nursing bottle with a rubber nipple, coupled with the development of special formulas for infants, that ultimately made infant adoption a plausibility in the twentieth century. There was, however, much stigma attached to children born to unwed mothers, which discouraged many people from adopting them. Not only did they suffer the stigma of being illegitimate, but the growing eugenics movement of the early twentieth-century emphasized the inheritability of criminality and feeblemindedness. Studies claimed to have found that unmarried mothers were more prone to be feebleminded and the would-be adopted parents were warned about the risk of bad heredity. The result was that many preferred to wait to see how a child would begin to turn out before they were willing to adopt.

As social work began to develop as a profession in the twentieth century, the early social workers, concerned with serving the best interests of the child, attempted to match physical, ethnic, racial, religious, and intellectual characteristics of would-be adopted children and the adoptive parents. This practice simply excluded large numbers of what eventually came to be called special needs children; those who were physically handicapped, belonged to racial minorities, were deformed, or had other difficulties, were simply excluded from any possible adoption. Social workers also tended to set income standards, housing conditions, neighborhood locations, psychological status, marital quality, and any number of other factors on would-be adoptive parents that simply discouraged adoption. The implementation of such stringent and artificial standards not only continued the trend of independent adoptions, but resulted in the growth of them as would-be adoptive parents sought to find children through physicians, lawyers, and others to avoid the red tape often imposed by the developing agencies. For example, in 1940, it is estimated that more than half of the adoptions were independent ones, an indication of the unwillingness of many Americans to deal with the agencies. Encouraging private adoption was the growing belief among child welfare advocates of the importance of trying to keep children with their biological parents even though this was increasingly unlikely. The result was that large numbers of children were kept in orphanages or remanded to the care of foster parents rather than made eligible for adoption. In fact, it seemed to many observers that professional social workers rarely recommended adoption of any kind of child who had long histories of living in foster homes or orphanages.

On a more positive note, the United States government began to extend its influence on adoption as the twentieth century progressed. The U.S. Children's Bureau established in 1912, among other things, gave out information on adoption and encouraged the setting of standards for adoption agencies. It was not until the Social Security Act of 1935, however, that funding was provided for child welfare services, including special provisions for the ill and the handicapped. The newly established government agencies worked to strengthen existing adoption programs and encouraged the establishment of state welfare departments where none had previously existed. Private, non-profit agencies, such as the Child Welfare League of America (CWLA—a private, non-profit agency founded in 1921), became important in setting standards for adoption in both private and public organizations. In 1938, the CWLA published a single page set of adoption standards, setting out the rights and responsibilities for the adopted children, for the would-be parents, and for the state. These became a model guide for agencies and failure of adoption agencies to conform to them could lead to their suspension from the organization.

The gradual recovery from the depression of the 1930s and changing demographics helped change the nature of adoption in the 1940s. The dislocations caused by World War II and the massive movement of men into the military services led to an increase in births to unmarried mothers and a growing number of children available for adoption. The number of new births each year began to rise as demobilization and the baby boom of the late 1940s and early 1950s took place. The media, in the words of Wayne Carp, "romanticized babies, glorified motherhood, and identified fatherhood with masculinity and good citizenship." Those unable to have children, fearful of being looked down upon for their childlessness, turned to adoption as a solution. The numbers of adoptions increased from about fifty thousand annually in 1945 (which in itself was more than double the number of ten years earlier) to ninety-three thousand in 1955 and one hundred forty-two thousand in 1965. It should be noted, however, that at least half of these were adoptions by relatives.

Adoption agencies also slowly began to change their definitions of those who were adoptable and even of those who could be classified as adoptable parents. In cities like Los Angeles, a special county adoption agency was formed to place special needs children; this example also occurred in other areas of the country. African-American children, regarded as more or less un-adoptable, also began to be placed for adoption in greater numbers, and a few pioneering agencies began placing such children with Caucasian families when there were not enough available applicants from the African-American community. Though transracial adoptions remained a small part of the adoption picture, in 1972 a high of 2,574 children were involved in transracial adoptions by 468 agencies. The numbers then began to decline, in large part because of the reaction of black social workers who, in 1972, denounced such adoptions as cultural genocide. By 1975, only 831 transracial adoptions took place. This meant that black children increasingly were kept in foster care, even though studies had indicated that children in transracial adoptions were overwhelmingly successful. The Howard B. Metzenbaum Multiethnic Placement Act of 1994 (MEPA) prohibited adoption agencies from denying any person the opportunity to adopt based solely on the person's race, color, or religion. Before that time, some black social workers had dropped their open opposition to such adoptions and went so far as to offer training sessions for would-be parents on how to care for the hair of black children or how to recognize fevers in black children; they even provided a number of helpful hints that the newly adopting parents might not have known. However, preserving families of African ancestry remains a contentious issue to others.

While most of those wanting to adopt were of European backgrounds, the number of American-born white infants available for adoption declined radically in the 1960s due to a variety of factors. These factors included the development of the birth control pill as well as a variety of other contraceptive devices, the legalization of abortion, and the change brought about by the sexual revolution, which lessened the stigma on unmarried mothers and resulted in increasing the numbers of unmarried women keeping their babies rather than turning them over for adoption. White babies seemed to be in such short supply that some agencies ceased to take requests for healthy white infants, while others established wait lists of three to five years.

One alternative that an increasing number of individuals sought was adoption of infants from other countries. The original impetus came from the number of children left behind by American troops in Europe, particularly in occupied Germany and Japan. In Germany, mixed-race children were most in need of adoption, as it was in Japan and later in Korea. The war also had left many abandoned children in China and other places, and agencies—such as those established by Pearl Buck, Jane Russell, and Henry and Bertha Holt—began to place children from abroad with American parents. Later, the emphasis by the Chinese government on the one-child family led to the widespread abandonment of infant girls who also were sought out by Americans, either through private adoptions or through agencies. For a time, Romania became a source of children when its government, which had banned contraceptives, fell and large numbers of children in the orphanages became available. Other countries also became sources for babies including Guatemala and, for a time, even Russia.

There were still infants and children available in the United States but in 2003, of the five hundred and twenty thousand children in foster care, only one hundred seventeen thousand (about 20 percent) were technically available for adoption, meaning parental rights had been either relinquished or terminated, and the child was also eligible for adoption by a non-related adult. It is assumed that the majority of children residing in foster care will eventually be returned to their parents or placed with an extended family member, although whether this is the case is sometimes questionable. Many of those eligible are classified as special needs children, a category which includes older children; more than half of the children available in that year were over five, members of a sibling group where it would be desirable to have the adopter(s) adopt more than one child to keep brothers and sisters together, members of minority racial groups, or individuals having physical, mental, or behavioral impairment, or a combination of factors. Less than 2 percent of those available were infants. For those parents desiring infants, international adoptions became an increasing source, although many international adoptions were also of older children. Nearly twenty thousand foreign-born orphans were adopted in the first year of the twenty-first century, constituting roughly 15 percent of all adoptions.

The U.S. government has increasingly entered into the regulation of adoption and foster care, some of it necessitated by the complications inherent in international adoption, which involves getting passports for the adopted child and all sorts of red tape. The Adoption Assistance and Child Welfare Act of 1980 mandated that child welfare agencies provide pre-placement preventative services, take steps to reunify children with their biological parents, and regularly review cases of children in long-term foster care. It also encouraged states to establish adoption subsidy programs for special needs children, with the U.S. government reimbursing the state 50 percent of the subsidies. The 1980 Act was amended by the Adoption and Safe Families Act of 1997. This Act resulted from Congressional concern over the continuing existence of large numbers of children in foster homes. The result was a de-emphasis by agencies on family reunification and the encouragement of adoption as quickly as possible.

A more recent development in adoption has been that of open adoption where birth parents (or parent) and adoptive parents (or parent) meet one another, share identifying information, and often agree to communicate directly over the years. There is considerable debate over this practice, and so far experience indicates that relatively few continue the contact after the adoption is finalized. In some of the cases, the would-be adoptive parents make contact with an expectant mother before she delivers and offer monetary support to her. This has become controversial when the mother has several solicitors to choose from, and there are many professionals opposed to such practices.

The adoption rights movement has also become increasingly influential. The impetus for this movement was a twice-adopted formal social worker, Jean M. Paton, who mounted a campaign in the 1950s to provide adopted persons with a voice. Her campaign received a major impetus from Florence Fisher, who spent twenty years searching for, and ultimately finding, her birth mother, and who, in 1971, founded the Adoptees' Liberty Movement Association (ALMA) to assist those hunting for birth families. ALMA urged the repeal of laws that sealed adoption records in order to help adoptees find their birth parents. Several states have established formal mutual-consent adoption registries where both birth parents and adoptees can register their names and if both agree, they can meet; other states simply release identifying information with the consent of both parties. This is important to both those adopted and those who adopted them because not all birth parents want to meet the child they gave up for adoption, and many adoptees are not necessarily interested in meeting their birth parents.

In sum, adoption has a rich and varied history, and though this handbook concentrates on the United States there is a tremendous amount of both information and understanding of family history through the ages by examining the entries in it. Adoption history is complicated but it is interesting and we think worthwhile. Hopefully, the reader will become convinced of the importance of the role that adoption has played in history.

Further Reading

E. Wayne Carp. *Adoption in America*. Ann Arbor: University of Michigan Press, 2002.
    Most of the information here is derived from articles in the handbook itself.

A

Abandonment and Adoption in European Folk Tales

Gwen Brewer

Formal adoption of children by the general public is more or less a modern phenomenon, but orphaned or abandoned children have always existed. Historical records often disclose only adoptions of powerful, important people, such as the Roman emperors, therefore the status and number of most homeless children from the past remain unknown. But glimpses into the situations of, and attitudes toward, homeless children can be found in folktales, which have been told in every culture during all periods of human history, largely among poor, illiterate people. Part of an oral tradition passed down from generation to generation, the stories reveal much about the values and living patterns of the people. Stories of orphaned or abandoned children are plentiful.

Folktale collection was begun in the nineteenth century by the Grimm Brothers, Wilhelm and Jacob, and soon scholars were collecting tales all over Europe and then all over the world. Stith Thompson and Antti Aarne sorted these thousands of world folk tales by type in *The Types of the Folktale: A Classification and Bibliography*, which lists many stories that deal with foundlings, changelings, and abandoned or mistreated children.

Such stories are still being collected by folktale scholars from today's non-literate areas of the world. Modern literate society has fewer folktales than any time in the past, most likely because most of our stories are recorded and published, often after considerable editing. The folktales that most people know today are stories they heard as children, and the source was probably a book, not an oral storyteller. Significantly, even the Grimms, the most famous of folktale collectors, adapted and polished the tales so they are really literary adaptations of true folktales. Each succeeding edition of their *Household Tales* (or *märchen*) was more obviously directed toward children. Today, children usually read or hear "Hansel and Gretel" from a beautifully and perhaps humorously illustrated book. This most famous story of abandoned children deals with the poverty and desperation of adults and the natural goodness and resourcefulness of children, who are ultimately rewarded with security.

These "literary" folktales told early in the nineteenth century give clues about the treatment of unwanted children in earlier times. The stories often begin with a brief description of a child being abandoned or orphaned. Survival is the immediate problem, and in folktales the child always survives. The plot deals with challenges or problems the child must face. The orphan in "The Spindle, the Shuttle, and the Needle" (Tale 188) is taken in and taught to sew by a kindly neighbor, but then the neighbor dies and she is left alone. The little girl in "The Star Talers" (Tale 153) is alone and penniless when her parents die. Rapunzel (Tale 12) is given to a witch by her parents to save themselves. Ashputtle (Cinderella, Tale 21) and Snow White (Tale 184) are young girls whose mothers die and whose fathers marry women who mistreat the girls. The parents in "Brier Rose" ("Sleeping Beauty," Tale 50) neglect to invite an important guest to the Christening, so the child is condemned to die from a spindle prick. The Goose Girl loses the protective handkerchief of her mother ("The Goose Girl at the Spring," Tale 179) and falls prey to a bully servant. All these unfortunate children are girls, but some boys are also in this helpless position.

The Fledgling (Tale 51) is carried to the top of a tree by an eagle and found by a forester. In "The Devil with the Three Golden Hairs" (Tale 29), a fortuneteller prophesies that the baby of poor parents will grow up to marry the king's daughter, so the king takes the child, puts him in a box, and throws him in a river to die. In "The Juniper Tree" (Tale 47) a stepmother chops off a boy's head by slamming the lid of a heavy chest on it. In all these stories, the baby, child, or adolescent is helpless and usually mistreated by adults in the larger world.

After this beginning, the orphan must face a problem or challenge that results in a change of fortune. Frequently, the innocent child is helped by a benevolent person, sometimes one with magical powers. Goose Girl (Tale 179) is taken in by a wise woman, but both the girl and the young count she will marry must work hard to help the wise woman. The boy in the box (Tale 29) is helped by a kind miller, by compassionate thieves, and by the devil's grandmother so he does grow up to marry the king's daughter. A good and powerful king marries Little Sister and sees that justice is done to her and Little Brother whom the wicked witch has turned into a fawn (Tale 11). When the wicked witch/stepmother turns siblings into a lamb and a fish (Tale 141), a cook saves them and a wise woman returns them to their human form. A good old woman performs the impossible tasks given the True Bride (Tale 186).

The innocent child is often helped by magic unrelated to another person. In Tale 51, Fledgling and Lenchen are changed into Rose and Rosebush, Church and Crown, then Pond and Duck. The innocent and beautiful Goose Girl is helped by a talking handkerchief and a talking horse's head. The natural order seems to protect the innocent.

In most of these stories, the innocent child tends to be passive, accepting cruelty and misfortune with patience. The Goose Girl complains only in private when her aggressive servant takes her place. Ashputtle sleeps in the ashes because her wicked stepsister tells her to. These passive, innocent children, however, are always diligent, obedient workers. The orphan in "Spindle, Shuttle, and Needle" diligently works hard spinning, weaving, and sewing. The mistreated but good daughter in "Mother Holle" (Tale 24) cheerfully helps overfull Apple Tree and Baker's Oven and then keeps house for Mother Holle, as Snow White did for the dwarfs. Only occasionally do the orphans act. The Duck (the sister) in Tale 51 pulls the evil cook into the Pond (the adopted brother) who drowns her. Hansel and Gretel also go beyond being passive, obedient workers. They are smart and aggressively take action to trick and kill the wicked witch. Here they are like the heroes of a different kind of tale—that of the clever hero who attains success in life through his or her own wits.

The denouement of every story involves punishment for those who are cruel to the innocent children. The mildest punishment comes to the Lear-like King in "The Goose Girl at the Spring" (Tale 179) who sends his youngest daughter away because she loves him "as much as salt." His punishment was being without her for three years. Most folktale punishments are more cruel and violent. The lazy sister in Mother Holle has black pitch poured on her. Ashputtle's sisters not only lose the part of their foot that they cut off to fit into the small shoe, but have their eyes pecked out by doves on Ashputtle's wedding day. A most cruel and violent punishment comes to the Goose Girl's aggressive servant, who is "shut up stark naked in a barrel studded with sharp nails" and dragged by horses until she is dead. Equally terrible is the end of Snow White's stepmother who is forced to put her feet in red-hot iron shoes and dance to her death.

More important, in the denouement, the innocent child is rewarded. The reward of Hansel and Gretel is living as children in a secure, loving home. More often, the reward occurs with puberty, a common time for marriage. Sexual overtones sometimes pervade the plot, as in Rapunzel. The reward to the innocent child is marriage to royalty and wealth and then "living happily ever after."

There are many kinds of folktales—droll, clever hero, animal tale—but orphaned or abandoned children as protagonists usually occur in these *märchen* kinds of tales. The natural order rewards innocence and goodness. Such tales occur all over the world. The kind that enter popular culture are increasingly the written, literary versions that are captured in books, usually books written for children with profuse illustrations.

See also Adoption Literature Sampler; Children's Literature as a Resource in Adoptees' Lives; Orphans and Adoption in Adult Literature; Popular Culture and Adoption.

Further Reading

Aarne, Antti. *The Types of the Folktale: A Classification and Bibliography.* Translated and enlarged by Stith Thompson. 5 vols. Helsinki: Suomalainen Tiedeakatemia, 1961.

Briggs, Katharine M. and Ruth L. Tongue, eds. *Folktales of England.* In *Folktales of the World,* edited by Richard Dorson. London: Routledge and Kegan Paul, 1965, Chicago: University of Chicago, 1965.

Grimm, Jacob and Wilhelm. *The Annotated Brothers Grimm.* Edited and translated with a Preface and Notes by Maria Tatar. NY: Norton, 2004.

Grimm, Jakob and Wilhelm. *Grimms' Tales for Young and Old: The Complete Stories.* Translated by Ralph Manheim of the Winkler-Verlag Edition of *The Complete Kinder- und Hausmärchen of 1819.* Garden City, NY: Doubleday, 1977.

Noy, Dov. *Folktales of Israel.* Translated by Gene Baharov. In *Folktales of the World,* edited by Richard Dorson. London: Routledge and Kegan Paul, 1963.

O'Sullivan, Sean, ed. and trans. *Folktales of Ireland.* In *Folktales of the World,* edited by Richard Dorson. London: Routledge and Kegan Paul, 1966.

Pino-Saavedra, Yolando, ed. *Folktales of Chile.* Translated by Rockwell Gray. In *Folktales of the World,* edited by Richard Dorson. London: Routledge and Kegan Paul, 1967.

Ranke, Kurt, ed. *Folktales of Germany.* Translated by Lotte Baumann. In *Folktales of the World,* edited by Richard Dorson. London: Routledge and Kegan Paul, 1966.

Thompson, Stith, ed. *One Hundred Favorite Folktales.* Bloomingdale and London: University of Indiana, 1975.

Acquired Immune Deficiency Syndrome (AIDS) and Adoption

Judith M. Saunders

Few people realized in 1981, when the new illness that we now know as Acquired Immune Deficiency Syndrome (AIDS) was first described among homosexual men, that it would become one of the largest killers of women in the world. This illness is the major contributor to an exploding population of orphans and vulnerable children. Although the Human Immunodeficiency Virus (HIV) that causes AIDS was isolated in 1984, and treatment options have converted HIV/AIDS into a chronic illness, no cure has been found. In this third decade of AIDS, major shifts have occurred in the geographic distribution of this disease and the characteristics of those who are infected. At the same time many challenges, such as stigma and ignorance, remain unchanged. HIV/AIDS has become a global epidemic, with adoption issues for children affected by HIV/AIDS growing much more complex.

According to the *2004 Report on the Global AIDS Epidemic*, almost 38 million people are living with HIV. Women account for nearly 50 percent of all people living with HIV worldwide, and a majority of these women are located in sub-Saharan Africa. While most children orphaned by HIV/AIDS also live in sub-Saharan Africa, the number of children orphaned by this disease has begun to grow in other regions, such as Asia, Latin America and the Caribbean, and Eastern Europe. AIDS has killed one or both parents of over 11 million children in sub-Saharan Africa alone, with another 2 million children orphaned throughout the rest of the world. Almost 3 million children are themselves infected with HIV/AIDS. *The Framework for the Protection, Care and Support of Orphans and Vulnerable Children Living in a World with HIV and AIDS* reported that, by 2010, the number of children orphaned globally by HIV/AIDS is likely to exceed 25 million. Now should be the time to develop infrastructures and resources needed to cope with the anticipated doubling of children orphaned by HIV/AIDS in 2010, but few countries are expected to meet this urgent challenge.

The epidemic has expanded most rapidly in Africa and Asia where treatment resources are most scarce and education programs have not been effective in reaching the population. Many become ill without knowing they have been at risk for infection. In high-income countries, an estimated 1.6 million (nine hundred fifty thousand in the United States) people are living with HIV/AIDS, but the majority of these people have access to effective education and treatment.

Adoption Issues

Tracking the scope of problems associated with the impact of HIV/AIDS on adoption is far more complex than tracking prevalence of the illness. Infected parents do not always tell their children about their illness or its serious nature. Counseling is not always available to assist parents in thinking ahead to make plans for their children. Inadequate funding and bulging caseloads plague foster care systems and hinder timely adoptions. Adoption processes are often inflexible and do not accommodate the particular needs imposed by HIV/AIDS on parents and potential guardians.

Sometimes other kin have absorbed orphaned children into their own homes without formally adopting them. We have learned little about who looks after children when they have lost their parents or even before their parents die, although most are taken informally into family networks. In the United States, the 2000 Census showed a striking increase of children living in grandparent-headed households, with additional children living in households headed by other relatives. Often, these family caregivers face unnecessary barriers and do not receive adequate help in overcoming these barriers. Given adequate support, such as access to health insurance, respite care, financial assistance, etc., family caregivers of orphaned children can prevent the child from entering the foster care system and could provide their orphaned relatives with permanent homes.

Parental HIV/AIDS and Family Responses

When one or both parents are infected with HIV/AIDS, emphasis is often directed toward treatment designed to retard disease progression. Often, parents receive no counseling on how to discuss their illness with their children and other relatives. Additionally, they receive too little counseling, or none at all, directed toward helping them make long term plans for their family and children. Health care providers' narrowly focused patient care of the parent must give way to family-oriented care for solutions that benefit children as well as their parents. When planning and discussions are postponed until too little time remains for adequate exploration of available options, decisions are then made in the midst of emotional crisis and turmoil. This delay is not always voluntary, such as when one parent only learns the cause of her/his illness late in the disease progression with no awareness that she or he has been placed at risk by their spouse.

Once a family is affected by HIV/AIDS, resources must be mobilized to strengthen the family by prolonging the lives of the parents, introducing succession planning, providing psychosocial support to the entire family, ensuring adequate child care resources, and when necessary, improving the economic capacity of the family as noted by *The Framework*. The family is the first line of defense to protect children affected by this epidemic, so strengthening family resources is the first step in protecting children. Sometimes families facing HIV/AIDS also struggle with drug addiction, poverty, and conditions that promote the disintegration of communities, such as armed conflict. Under extreme conditions of family and community disintegration, children will need added protection from sexual violence and exploitation by profiteers waiting to take and exploit children for their personal gain.

Community resources at local, regional, and international levels need to increase their effectiveness in providing as healthy a childhood as possible for children affected by HIV/AIDS. Resources also should be directed toward facilitating as smooth a transition as possible for children whose parents succumb to HIV/AIDS who need new homes and parents through adoption by the child's extended family or a new family.

Potential adoptive parents of children from homes affected by HIV/AIDS can take steps to make the transition to the new home smoother for the child and for themselves. Stigma and confidentiality pose challenges in learning if HIV/AIDS was involved in the death of the child's biological parents. Adoptive parents will want to ascertain what the child knows about the biological parent's illness/death in order to help the child know that he or she was not responsible for the death. Ideally, the adoptive parents would plan this transition with the birth parents before the adoption, but this rarely happens. If there are several children from the same family who have lost their parents to HIV/AIDS, potential adoptive parents can consider adopting all the children to keep their family as intact as possible. When this is not possible, adoptive parents will need to try to learn where the other siblings have been placed so their new son or daughter can stay in touch with their siblings.

With any adoption, parents need to ensure that the child is as healthy as possible. A good pediatrician will want to assess the child's physical and mental health to determine what resources are needed to assist the child in making the best adjustment possible. If the child has not been tested for HIV exposure, this test should be included in the physical assessment.

See also Adoption Medicine (Overview); Africa and Adoption; Health Issues in Adoption; Human Immunodeficiency Virus (HIV)-Positive Infants; South African Changes in Adoption: A Case Study.

Further Reading

Geballe, Shelley; Janice Gruendel, and Warren Andiman, eds. *Forgotten Children of the AIDS Epidemic*. New Haven: Yale University Press, 1995.

HIV/AIDS Unit of UNICEF Programme Division. United Nations Children's Fund. *Fighting HIV/AIDS: Strategies for Success, 2002–2005*. UNICEF Web Site. http://www.unicef. org/publications/HIVAIDS_strategies_for_success_English.pdf.

Joint United Nations Programme on HIV/AIDS (UNAIDS). *2004 Report on the Global AIDS Epidemic*. UNAIDS Web Site. http://www.unaids.org/bangkok2004/ GAR2004_pdf/UNAIDSGlobalReport2004_en.pdf (accessed January, 2006).

UNAIDS and UNICEF. *The Framework for the Protection, Care and Support of Orphans and Vulnerable Children Living in a World with HIV and AIDS*. July 2004. UNICEF Web Site. http://www.unicef.org/aids/files/Framework_English.pdf (accessed January, 2006).

Adolescent/Teen Adoption

Sara E. Valentino

Children adopted in their adolescence present their own unique set of issues. For those prospective adoptive parents who feel the urge to adopt an adolescent, the rewards are many and life changing. These children, in particular, need loving homes. Persons inclined to adopt adolescents should be encouraged to do so, assuming they are well advised of the cautions such as those briefly identified here.

Adolescent Adoptees

The majority of adolescent children in the adoption system have been in and out of their birth homes and/or foster homes, and many have come from previously failed adoptions. Consequently, their histories often include social instability, neglect, and abuse. These tattered histories often impede their ability to mature and socialize in a manner consistent with other children who have faced less adversity. Research demonstrates that the age at the time of adoption is generally positively correlated with a number of behavioral and emotional disturbances, meaning that as age at adoption increases, so do these disturbances.

Specifically, children adopted in middle and late childhood are more susceptible than their age-matched peers to substance abuse, delinquency, conduct disturbances, depression, and attention deficit hyperactivity disorder. Additionally, they may evidence developmental delays, attachment disturbances, and signs of Post Traumatic Stress Disorder. Although adolescents with insecure and unstable pasts may have suffered emotional trauma, the damage is not necessarily irrevocable. Despite the many emotional problems that may characterize adolescent adoptees, their strengths should not be overlooked.

Typically, adolescents in the adoption system are those who have clearly demonstrated a strong desire to be adopted and are willing to accept a new family structure. Adolescents in the adoption system have "been around the block," so to speak, and are often quite savvy, with clear conceptualizations of adoptive parents and what they hope to get out of being a part of a family. Adolescents who want to be adopted tend to make conscious efforts to make the placement work, fearing that it may be their last chance to have a family.

Issues of Adolescence

The World Health Organization (WHO) defines adolescence as the period of life between ten and twenty years of age. It is the transitional period between childhood and adulthood during which children undergo tremendous physiological and psychosocial development. Although this time is tumultuous for most adolescents, it is particularly challenging for adolescent adoptees.

Overt signs of physiological development are evidenced by the onset of puberty, bringing about tremendous physical changes. Adolescents become hyperconscious of their bodies and often display evidence of insecurities and issues of low self-esteem regarding their physical appearance. These psychological responses to physical change are often exacerbated in adolescent adoptees who, in addition to the normal insecurities about their bodies, may also be extremely cognizant of the differences between their own appearance and that of their adoptive parents. Furthermore, concerns regarding early or late onset of puberty questions related to heritability of physical traits may be issues adoptive parents cannot adequately address without knowing the details of the biological parents' developmental histories.

Unlike puberty, psychosocial growth is not demarcated by any physical characteristic; rather it is the existential struggle to form an autonomous identity. During this developmental stage, most adolescents' thinking processes mature as they begin to critically evaluate themselves, their families, and their peers, searching to find their own unique place in the world. In so doing, they work toward defining personal values, belief systems, gender-role identifications, and life goals. The process of identity formation is more difficult for adopted adolescents because, in most cases, they have been juggled between homes often characterized by differences in values and belief systems, and these differences are typically not readily assimilated by the adolescent.

For most children, adolescence is a time to test boundaries, challenge authority, and eventually grow away from their families, but adolescent adoptees are faced with an incredible inner conflict. They have an intrinsic need to define their autonomy versus a fundamental desire to secure a familial attachment. Consequently, psychosocial development and issues of control and autonomy may be delayed for adopted adolescents, in many cases persisting into the 20s. In fact, once adolescent adoptees establish familial bonds, they are often less likely to be driven by the compulsion to leave home than many other adolescents. As a result, children adopted in their adolescence may put off making decisions about career choices or college plans. These children need to first feel a part of the family before they can be ready to assert their independence from it.

Transition Issues

Although adolescent-aged children in the adoption system are typically those who have expressed an explicit desire to be adopted and have demonstrated motivation to adjust to the adoptive situation, they are usually fearful and anxious of impending changes. Likewise, adoptive parents are likely to be nervous about the addition to their family and concerned about the disruption that a new child will cause to the familial structure that is already in place. Thus, it is necessary that both the children and the parents be introduced to the upcoming changes gradually and that they both be provided with careful guidance along the way.

Adolescent adoptees should be encouraged to take an active part in the adoption process. They should be given several opportunities to meet their potential parents in non-threatening environments and to express their needs and concerns in an open forum. This will help to alleviate some of the fear of rejection and helplessness that adolescents may feel.

Just as adolescents should be well prepared for the transition, so should parents. Adoptive parents should be thoroughly educated about the unique needs of adolescents and given the most comprehensive history of their adopted adolescent as possible. Parents must be warned that the transition will be challenging. Realistic expectations are essential for both adolescent adoptees and parents.

The initial phase of the transition usually progresses smoothly, with adolescent adoptees typically eager to please their adoptive parents by demonstrating their ability to fit in. This period is known as the honeymoon period, in which adolescents tend to be extremely compliant and agreeable. But soon conflict sets in, and as the hurt and pain of the adolescents' past surfaces, they may begin to take their anger out on their new family or turn it inward—withdrawing from the socialization process. Behavioral misconduct such as breaking rules, stealing, using drugs or alcohol, or engaging in sexually promiscuous behavior is often evidenced during this phase.

True secure attachment between parents and adolescent adoptees is difficult to attain. Adolescent adoptees struggle to balance their desire to be accepted with their fears of loss, abandonment, and rejection. In many cases, their behavioral misconduct is an effort at self-preservation; it is an attempt to push their new families away before they have a chance to be pushed away themselves. Additionally, adolescents may thwart attachment with their new parents because they have concerns of being disloyal to their previous caretakers, or they may simply be unable to express intimacy due to lack of secure attachment from a very young age. Hostile behavior directed toward the adoptive parents in particular may be the result of transference issues, in which the children are acting out their anger with previous caretakers on their current parents.

Parenting Issues

The inner turmoil of adolescent adoptees and the chaos they can introduce into new homes often disrupts the attachment process. Adoptive parents of adolescents need to assure their children that they will not give up on them like the adults in their past may have done. It is important that the family "stick it out" through these rough times, accepting the child's faults, setting boundaries, and rewarding desired behaviors.

Families characterized by open communication and sincere expression of feelings are more likely to establish healthy relationships with their adopted children. Parents should not be afraid to bring up adolescent adoptees' past, and should even encourage them to talk about their memories, both the good and the bad. Often, contact with previous caretakers is warranted and can help foster a sense of continuity for adolescents.

This is particularly true for adolescent adoptees who have different cultural, religious, or ethnic backgrounds than their adoptive parents. These differences in backgrounds should be embraced by adoptive parents. In addition to teaching adolescent adoptees about the customs of their new family, adoptive parents are encouraged to learn about and celebrate their children's customs. Whenever possible, parents should help their adolescent adoptees to meet and interact with others who have similar heritages or backgrounds.

One last note on parenting issues: the social milieu of every living situation is different. Adolescent adoptees are likely to have deeply engrained habits of behavior or patterns of speech that may seem unacceptable to the new adoptive parents. For example, refusing to eat vegetables, exemplifying poor manners, or the overuse of profanities are behaviors adoptive parents of older children have cited as disconcerting. It is necessary that adoptive parents ease their adolescent adoptees into their family's particular social milieu gradually, demonstrating flexibility of standards and tremendous patience. Too much change can be overwhelming for adolescents. If they begin to feel they will never fit in, they may give up trying.

Advantages and Disadvantages

Indeed, age is to be considered when adopting children, but one thing is clear: all children deserve a fair chance at a happy and healthy family. There is no age at which a child becomes "too old for adoption." Infancy and childhood are relatively transient periods in a person's development, comprising just a fraction of the total time spent with, and bonded to, families.

Most parents of adolescent adoptees rate the experience as both frustrating and satisfying. The frustrating aspects associated with adopting adolescents include: 1) the emotional and behavioral baggage inherent in the adoption of older children; 2) the deeply entrenched bad habits often instilled by previous caretakers; 3) the difficulty understanding adolescents adoptees' emotional responses due to lack of knowledge about their previous experiences; 4) missing out on the joys of bonding during infancy and young childhood; 5) greater difficulty establishing a relationship due to the lack of enthusiasm often characteristic of adolescents; and, finally, 6) the limited time remaining to spend with adolescent adoptees in the home.

Some of the major advantages cited by parents of adolescent adoptees include: 1) adolescents understand the adoption process and are eager to be a part of a family; 2) gradual transitions into the family increase the likelihood of well matched personalities; 3) adolescents can be talked to, reasoned with, and understood through conversation; 4) adolescents are largely self sufficient, therefore requiring less displacement of the existing family schedule; 5) adolescents are old enough to participate in family activities upon entry into the home; and perhaps the most poignant advantage, 6) parents have the knowledge they are performing a needed humanitarian service.

See also Adoptive Identity; Myths and Realities of Adopting an Older Child: First Person Narrative; Special Needs Adoption.

Further Reading

Child Welfare Information Gateway. "Parenting the Adolescent." 1995. National Adoption Information Clearinghouse Web Site. http://www.childwelfare.gov/pubs/f_adoles/ (accessed August, 2006).

Kadushin, Alfred. *Adopting Older Children.* New York and London: Columbia University Press, 1970.

Keck, Gregory and Regina Kupecky. *Adopting the Hurt Child.* Colorado Springs: Pinon Press, 1995.

Nickman, S.L., A.A. Rosenfeld, P. Fine, J.C. MacIntyre, D.J. Pilowsky, R.A. Howe, A. Derdeyn, M.B. Gonzales, L.M. Forsythe, and S.A. Sveda. "Children in Adoptive Families: Overview and Update." *Journal of the American Academy of Child and Adolescent Psychiatry,* 44 (2005): 987–995.

Quinton, David, Alan Rushton, Cherilyn Dance, and Deborah Mayes. *Joining New Families.* Chichester, New York: John Wiley and Sons, 1998.

Myths and Realities of Adopting an Older Child: First Person Narrative

Lin S. Myers

We each have our own story of why we chose to pursue the adoption of a child. Mine had to do with infertility and, at the age of forty-three, I decided it was time to give up on biology and try adoption. Thus began a strange and frustrating journey that took me into the world of agencies—the adoption agency, medical services, governmental offices, county rules and regulations—and lots of paperwork, but little helpful information. I should mention that I am trained as a psychologist and had even recently gotten my clinical license when I started the adoption process. I was a professor and did consulting work to various foster family and group home agencies in my area. I didn't think I was naïve to "the system." But, every system has its quirks and even I wasn't really prepared to navigate and coordinate among all these different groups for my own needs.

As a single woman, I was told I could adopt a California-waiting child (those currently in foster care) or I could do a foreign adoption in certain countries. A foreign adoption would most likely mean a great deal of money and time, neither of which I had. Further, at my age, I didn't really want an infant, but thought someone four to eight years old would be ideal.

I was assigned a social worker, who was new to the job, through the private nonprofit agency I used. For the initial screening process, I had to have my original birth certificate, divorce decrees, a medical exam, personal references, and $1,000. After requisite background checks, I was approved to begin the search and began to be called about children who were available.

I had been asked numerous times about the characteristics of the child and/or the child's parents that I would, or would not, accept. I had specified that I only wanted one child to start as I would be a single parent with a full-time job and I had been able to say what kinds of psychological issues/medical conditions I would rule out. A lunch with a psychologist colleague of mine had yielded the admonition to consider staying away from children who had been in multiple placements as they would be more likely to have attachment issues or behavioral problems. I had been to three orientations with families who had adopted before. I read a number of books on adoption (mostly geared toward those adopting infants and unfailingly positive). I felt ready to proceed. My family and friends were supportive, but I was essentially on my own to make decisions.

What do I wish I had known in the initial selection process? First, to take my time. My social worker was new and put a lot of pressure on me to accept the children she was presenting to me. Adoption workers have their own agendas and they probably don't really match with yours. After I had said I wasn't interested in the first three sibling pairs she had called me about (remember I had only wanted one child), she actually got a bit hostile and told me I couldn't be so picky. I worried that I was being too picky and the next sibling pair she told me about, I agreed to go see. They were sisters, aged 10 and 11, with two other siblings in another foster home. I didn't stick to my own requirements and let myself be pushed into a meeting.

Second, don't believe the all information given by the various agencies. They may not have all the records and they may actually downplay the details. According to the information the social worker provided, the children I was to meet had only had two major placements, and while there had been abuse and neglect involved, they were in good health and ready to be adopted. Later I found out, mostly from the girls, that they had been in and out of various placements their entire lives. For some people, this may not be an issue, but in my case it really did translate into poor attachment. Ask for school records, therapy summaries, social work reports and any other information you can get. Maybe you are up to the challenge, but be prepared for a long period of adjustment (and I mean years' worth).

Third, spend time getting to know the children. Some people I know in the adoption process were actually expected to make a decision or take children after a meeting or two. Do normal things like going to the store, visiting friends, watching the children around other children—anything to get insight into what problems might present themselves later.

Fourth, if it doesn't feel right don't do it. Don't feel guilty—this is your life and such an important decision. There are other people out there who might be perfect for a given child.

After I got the two girls, there were innumerable problems. The younger one ended up leaving our house after four and a half months. Unfortunately, while we tried joint therapy to see if we could reconcile, the therapists the county had available were usually students in training and often some of my former students! With my remaining daughter, I did not receive the right kind of help to deal with the issues she came with and the trauma she suffered from having her sister leave. It was truly a nightmare for the first year.

So, fifth, be aggressive in getting support in any form you need. That may mean demanding social workers come to your house to actually see the kinds of things the children are doing. Some counties allow for respite care (a temporary break in another foster home for a weekend to de-escalate). Mine didn't, and I really felt trapped at times. Seek a psychiatric consultation earlier rather than later. While I am always cautious about medications, some children need temporary help to handle the adjustment (and you might, too!). You may need to reread what a particular agency or county will do for you.

After two and a half years of constant turmoil, I really felt at the end of my rope. It turns out that the county would not send my child to a foster placement, but would support group home placement for a period of time—if I had only known earlier. It is simply the case that some children need more contained environments to heal and be ready to live in a family setting. Again, don't feel guilty as your own mental and physical health may be at risk.

My daughter just graduated from high school and I wish I could say that it is all smooth sailing now, but I, too, get to deal with the typical teenage rebellion and search for independence and identity. Yet, I do love my daughter and realize that all parents are vulnerable to any number of problems with their children, biological or not.

My cautionary tale is that those of us who seek children need to be better prepared by hearing the reality of others' experience. We need to make those in the business of placing adoptive children more accountable to let us more knowingly engage in this process, and then we need to receive the support that is necessary to deal with the problems that older children typically bring to their new families.

It is important to remember that while there are challenges to adopting older children, being more realistic and prepared can only help the process. As with all children, we need to remember that there are joys and sorrows.

Adopted Child Syndrome

E. Wayne Carp

In 1978, David Kirschner, a Long Island clinical psychiatrist and consultant and/or expert witness in fourteen murder cases involving the defense of adoptees, coined the term, "adopted child syndrome." Kirschner claimed that the adopted child syndrome was marked by a cluster of behaviors such as theft, pathological lying, learning disabilities, fire setting, promiscuity, defiance of authority, preoccupation with excessive fantasy, lack of impulse control, and running away from home. As late as 1990, Kirschner qualified his findings as atypical of adoptees in general and observed that millions of adopted children grew up normally and did not become mass murderers. However, in 1992, Kirschner abandoned his scientific objectivity and published a paper that without a random or representative sample implicated all adoptees in the so-called adopted child syndrome and made no mention of the atypicality of his subjects.

Kirschner published in esoteric academic journals. But his theory also had legal implications. In 1986, it was used for the first time as part of the defense in a murder case involving Patrick DeGelleke, an adopted fourteen-year-old boy, who set fire to his house and murdered his adopted parents. His lawyers argued that the adopted child syndrome was a contributing factor to DeGelleke's psychotic rage. The defense failed. DeGelleke was found guilty of second-degree murder and arson.

The adopted child syndrome was given wide dissemination by adoption activist Betty Jean Lifton who, a month after the DeGelleke trial, popularized the concept. Drawing on Kirschner's work, she asserted in a *New York Times* op-ed article that most adoptees exhibit some of the traits of the so-called adopted child syndrome because they were confused over the origins of their birth. Lifton publicly linked confidential adoption records with the most infamous adopted serial killers in American history, citing the likes of David Berkowitz ("Son of Sam"), Kenneth Bianci ("the Hillside Strangler"), Joseph Kalinger ("the Philadelphia Shoemaker"), and Gerald Eugene Stano (who killed 32 people in Florida). Her effort to gain access for adoptees to the confidential adoption records by suggesting the harmful psychological effects of sealing them inadvertently stigmatized all adoptees as serial killers.

Kirschner's work found little acceptance in the psychoanalytic community and the "disorder" is not found in the standard reference of psychiatry, the *Diagnostic and Statistic Manual of Mental Disorders* (DSM-IV). In 1996, Kirschner attributed the failure of his theory to be accepted by the psychiatric profession to the adoption establishment, which, he claimed, denied the reality that adoptees may suffer from a predisposition to adoption-specific pathology. Kirschner suggested that the adoption establishment feared that the entire issue of violence-prone, antisocial adoptees might stigmatize adoption and adoptees in general. However, research from other social scientists and psychiatrists has demonstrated that adopted children are no different from non-adopted children for exhibiting serious pathological disorders.

Further Reading

Carp, E. Wayne. *Family Matters: Secrecy and Disclosure in the History of Adoption.* Cambridge, MA: Harvard University Press, 1998.

Kirschner, David. "Understanding Adoptees Who Kill: Dissociation, Patricide, and the Psychodynamics of Adoption." *International Journal of Offender Therapy and Comparative Criminology* 36 (1992): 323–333.

Adoptees' Liberty Movement Association (ALMA)

Vern L. Bullough

The Adoptees' Liberty Movement Association (known as the ALMA Society) is a non-profit, tax-exempt corporation set up to put adopted children in contact with their birth parents and/or siblings or to put birth parents in contact with children who were placed for adoption. It was founded in 1971 by Florence Fisher in Denville, New Jersey. Its budget is funded by donations and registration fees of those seeking information. As of 2005, the registration fee was $50, which is regarded as a lifetime membership and provides lifetime assistance with searching. ALMA claims to have the largest database of any adoption registry, but the data is private and not available online. Matching assistance is provided by the agency based on the information submitted by the registrants.

See also Adoption Search Movement; Fisher, Florence.

Further Reading

The Adoptees' Liberty Movement Association (ALMA Society) Web Site. http://www.alma-society.org. Email: manderson@almasociety.org

Adopting after Age Forty

Elizabeth Kelly

Older couples and singles are becoming parents more often today and are joining a group of middle-aged families, either through waiting and first establishing careers, through second marriages, or even through tiring of an empty nest and wanting little ones back in the home. Sometimes, however, parents are finding that having waited has diminished their chances of conceiving biologically, and adoption becomes their alternative for having a family or adding a baby to their current family.

Adoption agencies have taken note of the growing occurrence of couples in their late thirties, forties, and even fifties wanting a child, and adoption rules have changed to allow for older parents to adopt. However, parents may find that some adoption agencies refuse to work with couples over forty, especially those seeking white American infants. Concurrently, some international guidelines are changing. For example, China lowered the minimum age to thirty from thirty-five; yet Russia and Guatemala have raised the maximum age for adoptive parents. Some age requirements are broad, including a range between eighteen and sixty. Agencies concerned that the adoptive parent is young enough to see the children reach maturity may specify a minimum age difference (no less than fifteen years), and a maximum age difference (no more that forty years) that can separate parents and children.

Adoptive older parents are often more settled, more financially secure, more mature, and ready to accept the challenges of raising a child or infant. By the time the child arrives, the couple may own their own house, have worked for a company ten to fifteen years, and may be able to afford quality child care if necessary, or even have one parent stay at home. The strengths of older parents often include restraint and discipline, competence, enjoyment of a growing child, and being able to divide their time more easily between their children, work, and social lives. Some of today's fathers, especially older ones, tend to be more involved in family life than work life, helping more than their own fathers helped their mothers.

With longer and healthier life expectancies, as J. C. Branberger notes, the "family clock has been recalibrated." Many parents will face raising a child while dealing with ailing parents or while not having grandparents around to share their wisdom with their new grandchildren. Yet many older parents feel rejuvenated; having a child late in life can help one "feel younger," more intuitive, and better able to handle any crisis in a calm, confident fashion, as compared to someone in their 20s who is beginning to experience life. Keeping up with fashions and pop culture ensures that older adoptive parents do not act like grandparents. A lower energy level, which occurs naturally with aging, can be dealt with by preparing for these needs, for example, by starting exercise regimens. For aging mothers, there are hormone fluctuations, menopause, and the inevitable questions: "Are you the grandma?" Older mothers may also be asked, "What were you thinking?" Ironically, a teenager having a baby is often asked this same question.

As with any older parent, adoptive parents must plan for the future. For example, will college tuition be paid for with social security payments, or will the adoptive parents ever be able to retire? Estate planning with children is important regardless of the parents' ages; however, with adoptive parents over age forty, this is even more important as the parents may not live to see the child graduate from high school or college, and it is also important to ensure that the child is not forced to care for the parents. A projected time of life reflection may have to be postponed indefinitely. Parenting is a big step for a twenty-year-old or a forty-year-old; however, for those who decide to become a parent, regardless of age, it can be a rewarding experience.

See also Adoptive Parents.

Further Reading

Branberger, Joanne Cronrath. "Older, Wiser, and Warming Bottles." *Adoptive Families* Magazine Web Site. www.adoptivefamilies.com/articles,php?aid=1004 (accessed November, 2005).

Frankel, S.A., and M.J. Wise. "A View of Delayed Parenting: Some Implications of a New Trend." *Psychiatry* 45 (1982): 220–225.

Gilman, Lois. *The Adoption Resource Book*, rev. ed. Harper and Row: New York, 1987: 23–24.

Kaufman, Sharon. "Older Single Parent Adoption from China." Adopting.org Web Site. www.adopting.org/adoptions/older-single-parent-adoption-from-china.html (accessed November, 2005).

Morton, Carol Cruzan. "The Golden Age of Parenting." February 28, 2005. Sage Crossroads Web Site. http://www.sagecrossroads.net/Default.aspx?tabid=28&newsType=ArticleView&articleId=104 (accessed December, 2005).

Moses, Lucia. "Special Circumstances." *Adoptive Families 2005 Adoption Guide. Adoptive Families* Magazine Web Site. http://www.adoptivefamilies.com/articles.php?aid=1029 (accessed November, 2005).

Recker, Nancy. "In Praise of Older Parents." *Ohio State University Extension Fact Sheet: Family and Consumer Sciences.* The Ohio State University Extension Web Site. http://ohioline.osu.edu/hyg-fact/5000/5306.html (accessed December, 2005).

The Adoption History Project

Ellen Herman

The Adoption History Project is a digital public history resource. It was launched on June 1, 2003, and has continued to grow since then. It can be found online at http://www.uoregon.edu/~adoption.

The Adoption History Project was created, is maintained, and will be developed in the future by Ellen Herman, Department of History, University of Oregon. The website reflects the belief that history is an indispensable resource for understanding the personal, political, legal, social, scientific, and human dimensions of adoptive kinship. The Internet offers an avalanche of material about adoption—legal information, guides to agencies and support services, personal testimonials, updates on reform and legislation, and practical tips and opinions on anything and everything adoption-related. However, almost no historical information about adoption exists in cyberspace. The Adoption History Project aims to fill this gap. By documenting in words and pictures the many ways that adoption has changed over the course of modern U.S. history, The Adoption History Project makes adoption history accessible to visitors who may not be aware that adoption has a history at all.

The website is designed primarily for people with personal and professional ties to adoption, but it will also be relevant to students and teachers with interests in social welfare, human development, children, families, and the human sciences. The website offers a wealth of information on how adoption has been shaped and changed by the professions of social work, psychology, and medicine as well as law and government. It tracks the adoption research industry, which first appeared in the early twentieth century and continues unabated today. It includes descriptions of significant nature-nurture studies, clinical studies, outcome studies, and field studies that were conducted during the twentieth century and provides citations for the published findings of many adoption-related research projects. It follows the stories of adoption reform, regulation, and representation over time while also telling stories of particular children and adults whose lives were permanently changed by adoption.

The website is divided into areas that cover people and organizations, studies, and topics—all devoted to presenting the theory and practice of adoption in historical context. It contains hundreds of images and excerpts from published and unpublished primary documents including such topics as the orphan trains, infertility, sealed records, eugenics, baby farming, telling, as well as transracial, international, and special needs adoptions. Numerous links display interconnections between various pages on the website as well as external resources. A timeline, bibliography, and site index are included. The website is also equipped with a search engine that allows visitors to enter terms of their own choosing and locate pages on which those terms appear.

Pages consist of short biographical or topical essays. Each is accompanied (in a box at the bottom of the page) by links to a number of primary documents as well as a short list of suggestions for further reading. For example, visitors interested in Arnold Gesell will read not only about his career and contribution to developmental norms, but about his ties to such important governmental and service organizations as the U.S. Children's Bureau and the Child Welfare League of America. Both of these organizations are also described and documented on the website. Documents linked to the Gesell page include an important 1926 statement on "Psychoclinical Guidance in Child Adoptions" (drawn from a government pamphlet) and the text of a 1939 speech Gesell gave to Connecticut judges about the importance of adoption standards (located in the Gesell Papers at the Library of Congress). The "Further Reading" link on that page connects visitors to a selected bibliography of Gesell's own publications as well as articles and books about Gesell's life and work.

Biographical sketches include well-known figures, such as novelists Pearl S. Buck and father-daughter psychoanalysts Sigmund and Anna Freud. Lesser known individuals, such as Jessie Taft, are also included. Taft was the first and most articulate advocate of therapeutic approaches to adoption, which are ubiquitous today. Taft and her life partner, Virginia Robinson, who was also a well-known social work educator, adopted two children in the 1920s in Flourtown, Pennsylvania, where they raised them in a community of like-minded women, many of whom were also deeply involved in the world of social welfare. Documents linked to the Taft page include family photos, an excerpt from her 1916 dissertation, a 1919 manifesto about the importance of personality study, and a 1921 report from the Children's Aid Society of Pennsylvania about the role of mental testing and testers in child placement. With the click of a mouse, one can move from the sketch of Jessie Taft to sketches of related figures, including Sophie van Senden Theis, another understudied pioneer in the world of professional adoption services and research. (Theis worked for the New York State Charities Aid Association for forty-five years, from 1907 until her retirement in 1952, and served as the Executive Director of its Child Adoption Committee for thirty-six of those years.) Related topics, such as "feebleminded" children, child welfare, and minimum standards can also be easily accessed from within the pages devoted to biographies.

A visit to the area of the website called "Topics in Adoption History" turns up pages about matching, birth parents, search and reunion, and the Indian Adoption Project of the 1950s and 1960s, among many others. Like the pages about people and organizations, pages in this part of the website contain links to primary sources and further reading. Visitors interested in the documentary record itself can go directly to the part of the website titled "Document Archives." All texts excerpted and linked to various pages on the website are also linked and listed alphabetically there.

The Adoption History Project received a small seed grant from the Center for History and New Media, George Mason University. It was based upon work supported by the National Science Foundation and has also been funded by the Viola Bernard Foundation. Ellen Herman has published a number of articles about adoption history and is currently completing a book about adoption during the twentieth century, *Kinship by Design*.

Further Reading

The Adoption History Project Web Site. http://www.uoregon.edu/~adoption

Adoption Insurance

Kathy Shepherd Stolley

Adoption insurance, also sometimes called adoption cancellation insurance, is insurance for would-be adoptive parents in the event that the birth parent changes his or her mind, that the birth mother miscarries/the baby is stillborn, or that the adoption is disrupted before being finalized. Reimbursable expenses can include such things as the birth mother's maternity related expenses, travel expenses, and some social service and advertising fees under certain circumstances.

At this writing, this insurance is offered through Markel, underwritten by Tangram Insurance Services. It is sold online and is available only to those living in a handful of states, working though approved attorneys and/or agencies, and covers only domestic adoptions of children under two years old.

During the 1990s, adoption insurance was variously offered by Lloyd's of London, the Fireman's Fund, and MBO Insurance Brokers through Kemper Insurance. However, it disappeared from the marketplace. Although considered a good idea according to Art Adams, an insurance company executive who conceptualized the original insurance in the United States and was involved with the earlier and current product, it was not profitable for the insurers. Adoption insurance has only recently again become available. The current policy guidelines have been reformulated to be less risky for the insurance carriers.

Further Reading

AdoptingAssurance. Insurance for Adoptions. http://www.adoptionassurance.com/home. aspx

Duxbury, Sarah. "Insurance Can Remove One Risk From Adoption." *San Francisco Business Times*. April 24, 2006. http://sanfrancisco.bizjournals.com/sanfrancisco/stories/2006/04/24/focus2.html (accessed June, 2006).

Adoption Literature Sampler: The Best in Children's Literature for Adoptees

Helen Lodge

Books for adopted children can assure the child that adoption is an accepted way of forming a family, that love is the most important element in a family, and that a sense of identity comes partly from being a valued member of a family that allows the adoptee to discover and develop his or her own interests and abilities. If the early years are crucial in developing all these building blocks for later independence, then the books for early and middle childhood are of key importance in nurturing the adopted child. Older adoptees will also find satisfying experiences here. Children's literature is a treasure trove for the adopted child, a trove that grows yearly.

One picture book that succeeds in meeting all expectations discussed in this handbook in "Children's Literature as a Resource in Adoptee's Lives" (a companion piece to this entry) is *Tell Me Again About the Day I Was Born*, by Jamie Lee Curtis and illustrated by Laura Cornell. The narrator, a young girl, apparently knows this love tale by heart, but, like other children, wants to hear it told (or read) again and again. The story with its rhythmic repetition, "Tell me again how you got on an airplane with my baby bag and flew to get me and how there was no movie, only peanuts," or "Tell me again about the first time you held me in your arms and called me your baby sweet," are reassuring, easy to memorize, and suited to the egocentricity of the young listener. The father is included also in the recollections of "firsts." As he holds her, he talks to the tiny newcomer about baseball. The illustrations are childlike, colorful, and humorous; they achieve everything good illustrations should in a picture book. They enable the child to follow the narrative and to go beyond the text of the story. They enrich the story with details that the child will note particularly on rereading and help set the tone of lighthearted humor. The child can turn the pages to retell the story and will want to return to the pictures, which reinforce the text.

Another tale, easily understood and thus available to very young listeners, is *The Day We Met You*, by Phoebe Koehler. Simple and straightforward, it describes the momentous day when a baby becomes part of a family. Unlike the previous tale, the narrator here is a grownup, a parent who speaks of the preparations "we made" to get "you." The items necessary would be familiar to even a very young child—a car seat, bottles and formula, diapers, pajamas, a quilt, a teddy bear, even flowers for the baby's room. The focus is on the child whose adoption this day celebrates. The final illustration shows both parents gazing affectionately at the baby they hold and saying, "You felt like the sun shining inside us." Again the illustrations enrich the text and aid the child in retelling the story through identifying objects in the pictures that accompany the text. The story concludes with an affecting picture of parents beginning the bonding of a new family.

Stories about children adopted from faraway lands demand, for the most part, a longer attention span and, thus, a somewhat older child "reader" or listener than the earlier picture books. A central concept of these stories is acceptance of being part of a biracial family and of another culture that will inevitably be part of this child's heritage. *Through Moon and Stars and Night Skies*, by Ann Turner, is narrated by a little boy who wants to retell to his mother the tale often told to him of how he came to his new family. He tells of his journey for a night and a day from a faraway land in the care of a woman of whom he seems to know little, and of how he recognizes his parents from the pictures they had sent to him. The illustrations identify the boy as Asian, and though the country from which he comes is clearly Asian, it is never identified. Again the pictures reveal much—the little boy in a group home, a father and mother eager to meet him at the airport, a loving mother, and a father who rocks his son and puts him to bed. The final picture shows the new family—the child asleep in his bed, with both parents and the family dog nearby.

In *I Love You Like Crazy Cakes*, by Rose Lewis and illustrated by Jane Dyer, the narrator is a young woman who goes to China to adopt a baby girl. She finds her baby well cared for in a "big room with lots of other babies." Along with other prospective parents, she meets and falls in love with her child, plays with her, even puts her to bed, and then takes her on the long airline flight to her new home. In the baby's new home, the new mother sheds some tears for the Chinese mother "who could not keep you." With its soft water colors, the tale is affecting and effective. However the focus of the tale is on the mother, her experience in adopting a child from another land, another culture. There is no father in this story.

Our Baby from China, by Nancy D'Antonio, is a true tale, written and narrated by parents of a daughter adopted from China. There are elements repeated: the tale of the journey to China, this time by two prospective parents, to adopt a baby girl; again the getting acquainted and then the long airline journey home to a welcoming extended family. The illustrations are charming photographs of China, of the orphanage, of the prospective parents with other prospective American parents, and of the actual adoption signing and name change giving the baby dual citizenship. There is more of the Chinese heritage here. Both tales give a favorable impression of China and the care it gives children eligible for adoption.

Over the Moon: An Adoption Tale, by Karen Katz, relates the adoption of a baby girl from a faraway land, probably Central or South America. Again the story recounts the announcement of the birth, the long airline journey, the couple's first glimpse of the baby, their first day together as a family, the return home, and the welcome. The tale explains the adoption process in language suitable for a three or four-year-old. The tale concludes with the promise of the permanence of adoption. The folk art illustrations, while colorful, may prove difficult for a young child trying to follow the tale.

Pablo's Tree, by Pat Mora and illustrated by Cecily Lang, tells of the yearly visit that five-year-old Pablo makes to his grandfather's house. His grandfather, his "Abuelito," planted a tree the day after Pablo was born, as a celebration of Pablo's birth. Grandpa tells Pablo about the careful preparation he and his daughter had made for this baby to come, this promised child. After the much awaited phone call, "Come for your baby," actually takes place, Abuelito plants the tree. Pablo and his grandfather together recount the decorations placed on the tree on each of Pablo's birthdays. The colorful cut-paper illustrations depict the close, loving relationship among the three.

Picture books with more text are suited either for adults reading to children or for independent reading by children six to eight years of age. These books give more information about birth and adoption and often deal much more with the ambivalent feelings of adoptees. *A Koala for Katy*, by Jonathan London, begins with a young child's thoughts about babies and pregnancy. Katie questions her mother about why she did not come from her "real" mother's belly and why her "real" mommy did not want her. She is reassured by the answer that her first mother loved her but was too young to care for her. Her adoption of a toy koala baby after her trip to the zoo helps her entertain a fantasy that the baby koala's situation paralleled her own at the time of her adoption. The tale reassures the child that loving, protective parents are the most important element in establishing a family. Although the tale does not make a careful distinction between "birth" mother and "real" mother, it is a comforting tale for adopted children beginning to ask questions.

How I Was Adopted, by Joanna Cole, is a sunny tale narrated by a young girl, Sam, with all the egocentrism of a young child. She tells the reader all about herself and her home. She knows about the circumstances of her adoption when she was one week old and about the growth of the fetus and the birth process. She thinks of adoption as a normal way of forming a loving family. *Abby*, by Jeannette Cairns, is also a sunny tale, this time of adoption within a black family. Abby, a child of four or five, seeks to hear again from her mother about her age at adoption. She seeks attention and finally receives it and reassurance from her brother, Kevin, who is about seven or eight. The story is told completely in dialogue and through the illustrations, charcoal-like representations of active children. The illustrations carry much of the text and show the loving relationship among the three.

Two books by Linda Walvoord Girard deal directly with the questions adopted children are likely to ask in middle childhood. Both books have illustrations of angry children confronting their mothers. *Adoption Is for Always* conveys the feelings of sadness and aloneness that Celia, a child of about six, experiences when she really understands the word "adopted" that she has so often heard about herself. She feels that she was rejected by her birth parents. Her parents deal with her confrontation calmly and sensibly. Celia comes to understand that adoption is "for always" and that her birth parents gave her life but that her adoptive parents, who love her dearly, are her real parents and will raise her and always be there for her. She is an integral part of her family.

In *We Adopted You, Benjamin Koo*, Benjamin Koo Andrews tells his story of adoption from an orphanage in Korea, his airline flight to America, and the joy of his parents when they meet him. But in second grade, Benjamin looks in the mirror and sees that he is Korean and physically unlike his parents or the people he meets. He learns from a school counselor and from his parents that a mom and dad who love him and support him are his real parents. At age nine, Benjamin has a small sister adopted from Brazil. He remembers the final adoption ceremony for her in front of the judge, who "does not care where any of us were born." His family celebrates the Korean New Year and Brazilian carnival time. He feels he can take the mean comments from kids at school and the "dumb" comments of strangers in grocery stores. He is a good runner and hopes eventually to become an engineer. He has learned that promises are what make a family, that love is the important ingredient in a family, and that looking different from the rest of your family has nothing to do with love.

The focus of *Allison*, by Allen Say, is on a little girl of Japanese descent, still in preschool, who discovers that she does not resemble her Caucasian mother and father. After a period of anger during which she destroys toys, even keepsake toys from her parents, Allison is reconciled with her family when she is permitted to adopt a stray cat "who doesn't have a mommy or a daddy." The realistic water color illustrations convey Allison's feelings of aloneness and resentment, her parents' controlled exasperation at what she has done, and their reconciliation as all three agree to add the cat to a loving and once again harmonious family household.

Two picture books break new ground for lesbian and gay families. The first, *Heather Has Two Mommies*, by Leslie Newman, now in a ten-year anniversary edition, is the story of Heather, a preschooler, who discovers that her friends have different kinds of families, some including fathers or stepfathers, some including brothers and sisters. She has two mommies, one a doctor and the other a carpenter. The teacher comforts Heather and has the children draw pictures of their families. She assures them that each family is special and that the important quality a family must have is love for one another. In *Daddy's Roommate*, by Michael Willhoite, a young boy recounts his parents' divorce and then his weekend experiences with his father, who now has a gay roommate. The story emphasizes the seeming ordinariness of the relationship of the two men: "They live together, work together, eat together, sleep together." He recounts his own relationship with the two—going to the zoo, the movies, the beach. Again the important quality in the relationship is mutual affection and love. These books will reassure the children of parents in alternative lifestyles that these relationships can be nurturing for children. The books will also help children in heterosexual families understand differences in familial relationships.

Emma's Yucky Brother, by Jean Little, deals with another familiar situation for adoptees—the adoption of another child in the family that already has a child. Emma, who is about six or seven, is in the process of getting acquainted with Max, the four-year-old boy her parents plan to adopt. Emma becomes aware of Max's fears and insecurities while she learns a sister's responsibilities and the rewards of helping Max become a member of the family. The tale with its illustrations is deceptively simple. The story attempts much and succeeds.

Stories for preadolescents and adolescents often convey the feeling of aloneness and abandonment that adoptees feel at times, but also the tremendous sense of achievement of youngsters who win against the odds. One story that children remember reading in the middle grades is Marguerite Henry's *Justin Morgan Had a Horse*. At the center of the tale is Joel Goss, a sturdy but undersized boy of eleven bound out for "seven long years" to Miller Chase by an unloving father. But, like the little horse he befriends, Joel works hard and succeeds. Miller Chase calls him "son." He becomes the Miller's heir and a respected member of the community.

Two novels intended for older children and young adolescents offer an interesting contrast between an older kind of fiction and a psychologically sounder kind of novel. *Anne of Green Gables*, by L.M. Montgomery, originally published in 1908, has been much read over the years and is still much read by adolescents. Indeed, a simplified version of the novel is available in paperback in many libraries. Anne, an eleven-year-old orphan, is adopted by an older couple (brother and sister), living in rural Prince Edward Island, Canada, in the very early 1900s. Although she has had little schooling and has known hard work taking care of younger children, Anne is friendly, talkative, and an outstanding student in school. Children love her escapades—trying to dye her carrot-red hair black and succeeding in dyeing it green, or cracking her slate over the head of the boy who teased her in school. At the end of the novel, sixteen-year-old Anne is ready to teach and will stay with her adoptive mother in order to save the family farm.

The Great Gilly Hopkins, by Katherine Paterson, written seventy years later, is also the story of an eleven-year-old, a foster child. The tale covers only four momentous months in her life. Born out of wedlock, the child of one of the "flower children" of the 60s, rejected by numerous foster parents, Gilly regards herself as tough. She makes friends with no one, though she is a high achiever in school. She lies, she fights, and she steals. But in her last foster home placement, she meets a slovenly, uneducated foster mother who loves this troubled child and has real insight into her needs. This foster parent enables Gilly to accept love and to give it. Gilly finds a permanent home with her grandmother, her mother's mother, who is alone and needs this child to form a family. Gilly is a fully realized character in a tale that is as interesting for adults as it is for children.

In Lois Lowry's *Find a Stranger, Say Goodbye*, Natalie Armstrong, a bright, good looking teenager just graduated from high school and already admitted to college in the fall, seeks to answer the question: Who is my mother? When she finds the answer, a mother who is a stranger and who does not share her values, she returns to her loving family, assured that she can now move on with her life.

A recent historical novel, *Rodzina*, by Karen Cushman, is the story of a twelve-year-old girl, the child of Polish immigrants, who is orphaned and must take the orphan train with some twenty other children in the year 1881. Orphan trains took orphans from the streets and orphanages of major cities to be adopted by some family along the route to California. Many of these families were looking to these orphans as sources of cheap labor. Rodzina manages to team up with a young woman physician, near penniless and alone in the world, who is accompanying the orphans. She and Rodzina will form a family and Rodzina will get an education. Like the girl in Mary Zisk's *The Best Single Mom in the World: How I Was Adopted*, which is intended for younger children, this is the story of a single parent adoption likely to be successful.

We Rode the Orphan Train, by Andrea Warren, gives an historical account of the orphan trains which ran from the major cities of the East to the western United States between the years 1854 and 1929. Here are accounts of older children who rode these trains as children, were adopted, became successful adults, and married and raised their own children. Their accounts stress their difficulties in separating from siblings, their longing for loving adoptive parents, and their desire for stable loving families of their own. The photographs of these children reveal appealing, hopeful looking children. Older children and adults will find this book absorbing.

How It Feels to be Adopted, by Jill Krementz, reveals the feelings and attitudes toward adoption of nineteen adoptees ranging in age from eight to sixteen whom the author interviewed. All of these adoptees saw their adoptive parents as their true parents. Most of these children expressed some interest in their birth parents, particularly their birth mothers. But there was no consensus on wanting to meet their biological parents. These interviews seem to attest that there is no general adoptive experience. These children appeared to represent different socio-economic backgrounds, though most were probably middle class. There were some differences in racial background and some differences in age at which the children were adopted. Some were adopted out of foster care. The book can serve as a reference, or as a resource for older children who want to know the feelings and experiences of other adoptees, and who want to look at the pictures of these adoptees with their parents. It can also serve as a resource for adoptive parents seeking to know how some adoptees view adoption and parenting, and the difference adoption has made in their lives.

See also Abandonment and Adoption in European Folk Tales; Orphans and Adoption in Adult Literature; Children's Literature as a Resource in Adoptees' Lives; Popular Culture and Adoption.

Further Reading

Burnett, Frances Hodgson. *The Secret Garden*. Illus. Tasha Tudor. Philadelphia: Lippincott, 1962.

Cairns, Jeannette. *Abby*. Illustrated by Steven Kellogg. New York: Harper Collins, Children's Books, 1973.

Cole, Joanna. *How I Was Adopted*. Illustrated by Maxie Chambliss. New York: William Morrow and Co, 1995.

Curtis, Jamie Lee. *Tell Me Again about the Night I Was Born*. Illustrated by Laura Cornell. New York: Harper Collins, 1996.

Cushman, Karen. *Rodzina*. Boston: Houghton Mifflin, 2003.

D'Antonio, Nancy. *Our Baby from China: An Adoption Story*. Photographs by author. Morton Grove, IL: Albert Whitman and Co., 1997.

Girard, Linda Walvoord. *Adoption is for Always*. Photographs by Judith Friedman. Morton Grove, IL: Albert Whitman and Co., 1991.

Girard, Linda Walvoord. *We Adopted You, Benjamin Koo*. Illustrated by Linda Shute. Morton Grove, IL: Albert Whitman and Co., 1992.

Henry, Marguerite. *Justin Morgan Had a Horse*. Illustrated by Wesley Dennis. New York: Simon and Shuster, 1954.

Katz, Karen. *Over the Moon*. Illustrated by author. New York: Henry Holt, 1997.

Koehler, Phoebe. *The Day We Met You*. New York: Simon and Schuster, 1990.

Krementz, Jill. *How It Feels to be Adopted*. New York: Alfred A. Knopf, Inc., 1982.

Lewis, Rose. *I Love You Like Crazy Cakes*. Illustrated by Jane Dyer. Boston: Little Brown and Co., 2000.

Lifton, Betty Jean. *I'm Still Me*. New York: Alfred Knopf, 1981.

Little, Jean. *Emma's Yucky Brother*. Illustrated by Jennifer Plecas. New York: Harper Collins, 2001.

London, Jonathon. *A Koala for Katy*. Illustrated by Cynthia Jabar. Morton Grove, IL: Albert Whitman and Co., 1997.

Lowry, Lois. *Find a Stranger, Say Goodbye*. Garden City, NJ: Bantam Doubleday Dell Books for Young Readers, 1978.

Montgomery, L.M. *Anne of Green Gables* (orig. 1908). Pleasantville, NY: The Reader's Digest Association, 1992.

Mora, Pat. *Pablo's Tree*. Illustrated by Cecily Lang. New York: Simon and Schuster, 1994.

Newman, Leslie. *Heather Has Two Mommies*. Illustrated by Diane Souza. Los Angeles: Alyson Wonderland, 1990.

Paterson, Katherine. *The Great Gilly Hopkins*. New York: Crowell, 1978.

Rowling, J.K. *Harry Potter and the Sorcerer's Stone*. Illustrated by Mary GrandPre. New York: Scholastic, 1998.

Say, Allen. *Allison*. Illustrated by author. Boston: Houghton Mifflin, 1997.

Spyri, Johanna. *Heidi*. Illustrated by Agnes Tait. Philadelphia: Lippincott, 1948.

Turner, Ann. *Through Moon and Stars and Night Skies*. Illustrated by James Graham Hale. New York: Harper Trophy, 1992.

Warren, Andrea. *We Rode the Orphan Train*. Boston: Houghton Mifflin, 2001.

Willhoite, Michael. *Daddy's Roommate*. Illustrated by author. Los Angeles: Alyson Wonderland, 1999.

Zisk, Mary. *The Best Single Mom in the World: How I Was Adopted*. Illustrated by author. Morton Grove, IL: Albert Whitman and Co., 2001.

Adoption Medicine (Overview)

Dana E. Johnson

Focused interest in medical issues facing children without permanent homes and the specialty of adoption medicine are both rooted in the work of activist pediatricians in the early twentieth century responding to the high mortality rate in children who were abandoned or orphaned. As conditions improved in congregate care settings during the first half of the twentieth century, the focus of health care professionals shifted from the struggle to survive to the recognition that institutional care inhibited normal growth and development. These observations were instrumental in ending orphanage care in favor of placing of children within foster families.

Heightened current interest in medical issues in adoption can be traced to two developments with parallel time courses: a dramatic expansion of the foster care system, and a marked increase in the number of international adoptions from countries with high levels of poverty and poor health care. As research has advanced, there is recognition that commonalities exist in the backgrounds of children placed for adoption, irrespective of origin, that put them at risk for adverse outcomes. Practitioners in adoption medicine counsel potential adoptive parents on the health care needs of children prior to arrival, assure appropriate screening for health risks following placement, and coordinate assessment and care for long-term medical, developmental and behavioral problems.

Roots of Adoption Medicine

Well into the modern era, placement of an infant in an orphanage was essentially a death sentence. Henry Dwight Chapin, Chairman of Pediatrics at Columbia University Medical School, was among the first to note that malnutrition within infant orphanages lead to decreased ability to fight infections, inevitably resulting in fatal pneumonia. At the beginning of the twentieth century, Chapin and colleagues in New York and Chicago championed a boarding-out, or fostering, system where institutionalized infants were placed in the homes of private families, and developed programs where breast milk was provided by professional wet nurses or by birth mothers who were required to remain with their infants rather than abandon them. By the 1940s, mortality had dropped to ten percent, primarily through introduction of artificial infant formulas, suppression of infectious diseases through strict isolation techniques, and the development of antibiotics.

The negative effects of environmental and social deprivation on the well-being of institutionalized children could not be carefully studied until survival through infancy was assured. Consequently, it was not until the late 1930s and early 1940s that investigators reported on developmental delays and suppressed growth within congregate care settings for infants and children. Through the next three decades, investigators documented an increasingly wider array of problems in children institutionalized during infancy, including: delays in emotional, motor, social, speech and physical development; abnormal attachment; severe behavior and emotional problems with aggressive or antisocial behavior; and a variety of learning problems. It was during this era that it became clear to all that depriving a child of a family had global effects on health, behavior and development. In response in large part to these studies, institutional infant care in the United States ended in favor of foster placement.

The Health Care Provider's Role in Adoption

Aside from a handful of committed investigators, the role of health care providers in adoption prior to the mid-1970s was minimal and generally limited to providing a well-child examination prior to placement. While risk factors existed, little or no medical history was available because of the common policy of sealing court records. The legalization of abortion in the United States in 1973, increased availability of financial assistance for single mothers, and greater societal tolerance for single parenting all united to dramatically reduce the number of adoptable infants, the age group most desired by adoptive parents. At the same time, the number of families seeking to adopt increased, principally due to delayed child bearing and resultant decreased fertility. Consequently, the decrease in the number of children available through private adoptions generated increased placements through public agencies and from abroad.

Reports detailing physical and/or mental health issues in children within the foster care system and those adopted internationally increased concurrently with the expansion of the foster care system and the increase in international placements. Most children entered the foster care system because of abuse or neglect occurring within the context of parental substance abuse, mental illness, homelessness, extreme poverty, or HIV infection. Changes in the cohort of children adopted from abroad since the late 1980s mirrored the increase in risk factors seen in adoptees from the foster care system. The opening of Romania in 1990, followed shortly after by the ascendance of Russia and China as major placing countries, heralded a serious deterioration in the general health of the majority of international adoptees due to institutionalization, poverty, parental substance abuse, epidemics of HIV, syphilis, and hepatitis C, and an inadequate system of medical care. Therefore, it is not surprising that children placed for adoption from either the foster care system or from abroad are at risk for a variety of medical, developmental, emotional, behavioral and cognitive problems.

Infectious Diseases

Initially, health concerns in international adoptees focused on infectious diseases. Tuberculosis, hepatitis B, intestinal parasites, syphilis, hepatitis C, and HIV were disorders that placed a child's well-being in jeopardy and could, in some conditions, afflict family members as well. A number of studies identified latent tuberculosis as the most common infectious disease in international adoptees, afflicting children worldwide, followed by hepatitis B, particularly in children from East and Central Asia, India, and Eastern Europe. Intestinal parasites, particularly waterborne organisms, afflict children of all ages, while round- and tapeworm infections are found more commonly in older children. Though maternal syphilis is very common, particularly in Eastern Europe, few international adoptees arrive with untreated or partially treated syphilis. HIV infection, of grave concern to families because of long-term morbidity and mortality, is very rare—probably due to exclusion of HIV-infected children from the pool of potential adoptees. Since 1991, the Committee on Infectious Diseases of the American Academy of Pediatrics has recommended screening for these five conditions. Since 2000, hepatitis C screening has been recommended for children from China, Russia, Eastern Europe, and Southeast Asia. Due to backgrounds of poverty and sexual abuse, the spectrum of infectious diseases observed in children within the foster care system is strikingly similar to that observed in international adoptees.

Immunizations are often poorly documented in adoptees from abroad and from the foster care system. A child from the foster care system should not be considered immunized unless complete health records are available. International adoptees often have such records, but many children have been found to lack immunity to the vaccines received. In situations where data are limited, the American Academy of Pediatrics recommends either serologic testing to determine whether protective antibody concentrations are present or reimmunizing the child.

Physical Growth

Physical growth is often impaired in adopted children due to a combination of low birth weight, malnutrition, and an altered endocrine state caused by neglect or abuse. Height, weight, and head size (brain growth) can all be affected in early childhood. In older children, height is often the most impaired parameter. While dramatic catch-up growth following placement is common, the issue of growth failure prior to placement has long-term consequences. Not only can adult height be impaired by pre- and postnatal growth failure, but also by the development of early puberty. This phenomenon is best described in internationally adopted girls, and tends to affect those who are most growth impaired at placement and have the greatest degree of catch-up growth in the immediate post-arrival period.

Other Common Medical Problems

Hearing and vision are commonly impaired in international adoptees and in children within the foster care system. One out of eight has a permanent or temporary hearing problem and one out of four has an abnormality in vision. Dental care is neglected and most older children require extensive restorative work. Children in the foster care system often have elevated lead levels, as do international adoptees—particularly from China. Deficiencies in micronutrients such as iron are commonly seen in both groups, while iodine and vitamin D deficiencies have been described most commonly in international adoptees.

Evolution of Adoption Medicine as a Medical Specialty

In the mid-1980s, only a handful of medical practitioners concentrated on the needs of international adoptees or children within the foster care system. Today, there are scores of clinics and practices throughout North America, Western Europe, and Australia that focus on the needs of these children. The importance of this area of child care was recently emphasized by the establishment of the Section on Adoption and Foster Care by the American Academy of Pediatrics.

Practice in adoption medicine is focused in three areas. The first is to educate both adoption professionals and parents on the medical issues in adoption. This process is particularly important when a family receives the referral of a specific child. Using written records, videos, and photographs, adoption medical professionals play a key role in assessing the health and developmental status of the child, interpreting cryptic medical terminology and identifying risk factors that have long-term consequences for the child and adoptive family. The ultimate goal of this review is to help families determine if they have the resources to meet the needs of a particular child.

Following placement in the adoptive home, adoption medical professionals coordinate appropriate screening for medical problems, developmental delays, and mental health issues. In addition to a comprehensive physical examination and routine health screening tests, key issues include: identifying common infectious diseases; ensuring up-to-date immunizations; identifying vision, hearing and dental problems; assessing growth and development; and determining whether the child has been exposed to drugs or alcohol. As a rule of thumb, adopted children should be seen as frequently as are infants during the first year of life. The complete medical evaluation takes several visits, and developmental trajectories must be carefully plotted to ensure that growth and motor and language skills are catching up.

Behavioral and emotional concerns require constant attention, as few children arrive unscathed from foster or institutional care. In younger children, a number of post-arrival transitional problems are common, such as self-stimulation (e.g., rocking), sleep difficulties, feeding issues, temper tantrums, and being withdrawn. As these problems dissipate, parents may become concerned about attachment, attention, learning disabilities, depression, and anxiety. Ideally, parents adopting older children from institutional or foster care should be paired with a mental health professional prior to the child's arrival to learn strategies for handling the inevitable behavioral issues that put placements at risk.

Finally, professionals in adoption medicine act as long-term advocates for adopted children and their families. The needs of children neglected and abused in early life are complex and the true etiology of a problem is not always apparent. In these situations, practitioners act as coordinators of care, ensuring that evaluations are focused on the likely roots of the problem, and the family has the opportunity to avail themselves of all medical and educational services to which their child is entitled.

See also Acquired Immune Deficiency Syndrome (AIDS) and Adoption; Health Issues in Adoption; HIV-Positive Infants; International Adoption (Overview).

Further Reading

Chen, L.H., E.D. Barnett, and M.D. Wilson. "Preventing Infectious Diseases During and After International Adoption." *Annals of Internal Medicine* 139 (2003): 371–378.

Frank, D.A., P.E. Klass, F. Earls, and L. Eisenberg. "Infants and Young Children in Orphanages: One View from Pediatrics and Child Psychiatry." *Pediatrics* 97 (1996): 569–578.

Johnson, D.E. "Medical and Developmental Sequelae of Early Childhood Institutionalization in International Adoptees from Romania and the Russian Federation." In C. Nelson, ed. *The Effects of Early Adversity on Neurobehavioral Development.* Mahwah, NJ: Lawrence Erlbaum Associates, Inc.; 2000, pp 113–162.

"Medical Evaluation of Internationally Adopted Children for Infectious Diseases." In *2003 Red Book: Report of the Committee on Infectious Disease.* Elk Grove Village, IL: American Academy of Pediatrics, 2003, pp 173–180.

Takayama, J.L., E. Wolfe, and K.P. Coulter. "Relationship Between Reasons for Placement and Medical Findings among Children in Foster Care." *Pediatrics* 101 (1998): 201–207.

Task Force on Health Care for Children in Foster Care. *Fostering Health: Health Care for Children and Adolescents in Foster Care.* 2nd ed. Elk Grove Village, IL: American Academy of Pediatrics District II, New York State, 2004.

Adoption of Adults

Vern L. Bullough

Many, if not most, of the adoptions in the past were adoptions of adults or near adults. Adoption was a way of passing power on to a chosen successor as several of the Roman Emperors did. It was also a way of preserving lands and rights in a family where there were no suitable biological heirs. (Often female children could not inherit.) It was also used by many homosexual individuals to bind themselves together. Some courts have denied such petitions for adoption on the grounds that the petition was not in the best interest of society in general or because of the lack of a genuine parent-child relationship. However the court usually did not interfere.

Adoption is also a way of making official a long standing informal parent-child relationship. The adopted adult voluntarily consents to adoption, as does the adopter. In some states, notice of adoption to the birth parents might be required despite the adult status of the adopted person. Some states also require permission from the adopted person's spouse.

It is legal in every state in the U.S. and in most parts of the world for adults to adopt other adults if no fraud is intended. Laws vary from state to state and many require the adopting party to be older than the person adopted. In Illinois, for a time, the law required that persons to be adopted had to have lived with the prospective adopter for at least two years. Adult adoption usually does not involve any home study since the adult to be adopted can manage his or her own affairs and does not need the protection of a social worker's analysis of the adopter. Still, some states might require a social worker's report for all adoptions.

See also Adoption of an Adult: A Case Study.

Further Reading

Hollinger, Joan H., ed. *Adoption Law and Practice.* New York: Matthew Bender, 1988.

Adoption of an Adult: A Case Study

Vern L. Bullough

Regina Louise's mother left her as a toddler with a "woman who took in kids," in Austin, Texas, and then took off. Her father was only vaguely aware of her existence. Mistreated by her informal foster mother, Louise heard periodically from her mother and, at 11, ran off to rejoin her in North Carolina where her mother was then living. Her mother refused to accept her and, instead, sent her off to her father in Richmond, California. When he rejected her, Louise ended up in the foster care system.

In a Bay area shelter, she met a woman, Jeanne Taylor, who worked at the shelter and became her supporter. Taylor applied to adopt Louise, but the adoption petition was denied mainly because Louise was black and Taylor was white; the National Association of Black Social Workers who were opposed to interracial adoptions, opposed the adoption and the judge listened to them. In the aftermath, Louise went through more than thirty foster homes and spent a period in a restricted treatment facility for severely disturbed youth. Taylor tried to keep in contact with her but her visits to the girl were restricted. When she could not visit her any longer, she sent a series of letters to her that the authorities never forwarded. Taylor later married and moved from the Bay area. She lost contact with Louise because the agency never kept her informed of the child's situation.

Louise finished pubic school and enrolled at San Francisco State to study both social work and theater but she did not graduate. At twenty-three, she had a son, then married, divorced, and worked at various odd jobs until she entered cosmetology school. After graduation and an apprenticeship in a Vidal Sasson salon, she and a friend opened a salon of their own and this was soon followed by another.

Still her past continued to dog her, and she decided at age thrity-seven that the best way to confront it was to write a book about it. To do so, she got her files from the social services department and found the undelivered letters from Taylor who had written, among other things, that Louise would always be in her heart. Louise then began to hunt for Taylor but was unsuccessful until after her book, *Somebody's Someone,* was released. She was interviewed by a Bay area television station where she used Taylor's real name. A woman who had worked at the shelter when Louise was there traced down Taylor who was living in Alabama.

Taylor read the book and wrote Louise an email saying, "I am so proud of you sweetheart," and provided a telephone number. Taylor told Louise that she regarded her as "her first child," and that she had never stopped loving her. Gradually, the two women filled in the missing decades and met finally at LaGuardia Airport while Louise was between flights. Taylor handed her a photo album which brought back all sorts of pleasant memories. Since Louise looked upon Taylor as her mother, Taylor consented to adopt her. In the same Contra Costa County court where a judge had originally denied Taylor's request to adopt Louise, Taylor, then fifty-nine, adopted Louise who was then forty-one. The judge explained to Taylor's husband, and to her son, Christopher, then twelve, and to Louise's son Michael, then seventeen, that they were all family. And they have continued to grow closer.

Though adoptions of adults are not rare, it most often occurs to bequeath an estate or inherit money. This adoption was more than that and how typical it might be is unknown. This late adult adoption finally resolved an unfair turndown of adoption when social workers were blinded by their own prejudices.

See also Adoption of Adults

Further Reading

Louise, Regina. *Somebody's Someone: A Memoir.* New York: Warner Books, 2003.
Stewart, Jocelyn, "Memories Shrouded in Doubt." *Los Angeles Times,* Dec. 30, 2005, A 1, A22–23.

Adoption Search Movement

E. Wayne Carp

Before World War II, adoption records in the United States—court, adoption agency, and birth certificates—were open to adoption triad members (birth parents, adoptees, and adoptive parents). In the case of birth certificates, some states did not seal them until the 1980s. When in 1917 the first state, Minnesota, required its court adoption records be kept confidential, it did so to shield the adoption proceedings from public scrutiny, not to preserve anonymity between biological parents and adopters or to prevent adopted adults from accessing the records later in life. Other states followed Minnesota's example. However, as a result of complicated demographic changes and the influence of social work theory and practices after World War II, adoption records began to be sealed first from birth mothers and later from adopted adults.

In response to the closing of the adoption records, opposition emerged. Jean M. Paton, a twice-adopted ex-social worker, single-handedly pioneered the adoptee search movement. In 1953, Paton founded the Life History Study Center as well as the first adoptee search organization, Orphan Voyage, which attempted to locate adoptees' original family members. But Paton had little effect on state legislatures; adoption records remained sealed and, in fact, an increasing number of states sealed their birth and adoption agency records during the 1950s and 1960s.

By the early 1970s, the focus of the adoptee search movement changed. First, a critical mass of adopted adults had grown up in a world of sealed adoption records. Unlike their pre-World War II counterparts, this group of adopted adults was denied easy access to their adoption records. Second, 1960s protest and land-mark decisions on voting, school prayer, criminal rights, libel law, pornography, and school and housing segregation signaled that a "Rights Revolution" was in the making. By the late 1960s and early 1970s, "identity politics" overshadowed earlier liberal movements, as ethnic and racial self-interest groups organized to gain political legitimacy, economic power, and cultural authority. Of particular importance to the origins of the new adoptee search movement was the sexual revolution, which successfully challenged many of the 1950s sexual taboos, including the stigma of illegitimacy. By the beginning of the 1970s, many adopted adults viewed their adoptive status in terms of liberation and rights, not shame and fear.

Finally, in 1971, the new adoption search movement's most vocal and visible leader emerged, Florence Fisher, a New York City homemaker. After twenty years of searching for her mother, Fisher's tremendously difficult quest led her to found the Adoptees, Liberty Movement Association (ALMA). In addition to helping adopted adults contact their original birth parents, ALMA's mission was to abolish the laws that prohibited adult adoptees from obtaining identifying information about their birth parents. Fisher believed that adopted adults had a "right to know" at the age of eighteen their personal information, and she was determined to let the public, press, and adoption agencies know of her militant position. In 1973, Fisher published a book, *The Search for Anna Fisher*, recounting the dra-matic story of her success in reuniting with her natural family.

By 1974, Fisher had become the undisputed leader of the adoption rights movement and the head of the nation's largest and most influential adoption search group. ALMA's example started a movement that led to the creation of hun-dreds of other adoptee search groups across the United States, Canada, and the United Kingdom. By 1975, over three thousand adopted adults and fifteen hundred mothers had returned to 155 adoption agencies searching for information about their families and children. The first generation of the adoption rights movement was, thus, characterized by small isolated groups involved in personal search and reunion activities with charismatic leaders like Jean Paton and Florence Fisher, whose ideology revolved around adoptee rights.

A second generation of the movement began in 1978, when Jean Paton founded a national umbrella organization, the American Adoption Congress (AAC). The AAC soon supplanted ALMA as the pre-eminent adoptee activist orga-nization in the adoptee search movement, though it would be a very different type of organization. In fact, the AAC differed from the first generation of adoptee search movement groups in organization, composition of its membership, mission, style, and ideology. Rather than being led by a charismatic leader, the AAC was a demo-cratic, bureaucratic, hierarchical organization with an elected president at the top and a large board of directors. In addition to adopted adults, the AAC admitted to membership social workers, educators, birth mothers, and adoptive parents. It was dedicated to educating the public's attitudes toward sealed adoption records and lobbying legislators to repeal sealed records laws. Leaders of the AAC began calling the movement, whether out of tactical advantage or sincerity, the "adoption reform movement."

Thwarted in the state and federal courts in their effort to gain adoptee rights, second generation leaders began converting social workers to their world view and lobbying state law makers to pass legislation to unseal adoption records based on the idea that all adoptees were psychologically damaged and needed to find their roots. Consequently, during the 1980s and 1990s, a small revolution occurred among social workers, adoption agencies, and state legislatures. Individual adoption agencies, as well as the Child Welfare League of America, established more liberal disclosure policies and standards. Adopted adults increasingly encountered sympathetic attitudes. State lawmakers also began to pass statutes, which both facilitated searches and preserved the privacy of triad members. Initially, the most common legislative reform lawmakers embraced in order to satisfy the privacy rights of adoptees and birth mothers was the mutual-consent voluntary adoption registry, where both parties register their names with the state, consent to a meeting, and are informed of a match. Increasing in popularity was the confidential-intermediary system, in which a court-appointed intermediary acted as a neutral go-between for the adopted adult and the birth parents. By 2000, twenty-five states had established formal or informal voluntary adoption registries and an additional twenty-six states had confidential-intermediary systems in place.

On paper, these laws seemed to be the perfect solution to the problem of privacy for birth mothers and justice for adoptees. In practice, the adoption registries and confidential intermediary systems have proven to be cumbersome, expensive, and ineffective. Moreover, many adopted adults remained frustrated by what they considered "conditional access" or "compromise" legislation—voluntary adoption registries and confidential intermediary systems—and the ineffectiveness of adoption activism.

Thus was the "third generation" of the adoption reform movement born in 1996, represented by the radical adoption activist organization, Bastard Nation, which opposed the American Adoption Congress's leadership and ideology. Bastard Nation represents a turn away from a psychologically-based movement and a return to the adoption-rights movement. In 1997–1998, Bastard Nation successfully launched in Oregon Measure 58, a grassroots ballot initiative that restored the legal right of adopted adults to receive their original birth certificates. Oregon joined Alaska and Kansas, which had always allowed adopted adults to acquire their birth certificates. Today, these three states have been joined by Alabama and New Hampshire, in which adopted adults may receive their birth certificates unconditionally. In addition, in Tennessee and Delaware, adopted adults may also access their birth certificates, but birth parents may prohibit contact with other parties to the adoption through registering their nonconsent with state authorities. Failure to honor a contact veto carries criminal and civil consequences.

See also Adoptees' Liberty Movement Association (ALMA); American Adoption Congress (AAC); Ballot Initiative 58; Bastard Nation: The Adoptee Rights Organization; Fisher, Florence; Mutual Consent Registries; Paton, Jean; Professional Searchers; Social Movements and Adoption.

Further Reading

Carp, E. Wayne. *Family Matters: Secrecy and Openness in the History of Adoption.* Cambridge, MA: Harvard University Press, 1998.

Hollinger, Joan H., ed. "Aftermath of Adoption: Legal and Social Consequences." *Adoption Law and Practice.* 2000 Supplement, Vol. 3. New York: Matthew Bender, 2000.

Samuels, Elizabeth J. "The Idea of Adoption: An Inquiry into the History of Adult Adoptee Access to Birth Records." *Rutgers Law Review* 53 (2001): 367–436.

Primary Document

Making Adoption Records Confidential: The 1917 Minnesota Adoption Law

As recounted by E. Wayne Carp in *Adoption Politics: Bastard Nation and Ballot Initiative 58* (Lawrence, KS: University of Kansas, 2004), the 1917 Minnesota Children's Code was "the first law containing a clause making adoption court records confidential. The law was not intended to, and did not, prevent adoptees from viewing their records. Rather, lawmakers stated explicitly that the goal of Minnesota's sealed adoption law was to keep the *public* from viewing the records. Because of the stigma of shame and scandal that surrounded adoption and illegitimacy during the first quarter of the twentieth century, Minnesota lawmakers wished to prevent access to adoption records by potential blackmailers, who might threaten adoptive parents with telling the public about the child's adoption, or nosy neighbors, who might discover the child's illegitimacy. Sealing court and adoption agency records was never meant to exclude members of the adoption triad from examining their adoption records" (p. 6). The Oregon law challenged by Ballot Initiative 58 was "probably like that of Minnesota's Children's Code of 1917 and others whose motive was to prevent the public, especially those with a criminal intent, from having access to this information, and to protect children whose lives could be ruined by the social stigma of illegitimacy and adoption" (p. 7). However, later, generally well-intentioned efforts led to sealing the records from the members of the adoption triad as well.

Text of the Minnesota Children's Code, 1917

Adoption; petition and consent. Any resident of the State may petition the district court of the county in which he resides for leave to adopt any child not his own. If the petitioner be married the spouse shall join in the petition. All petitions for the adoption of a child who is a ward or pupil of the State public school shall be made jointly by the person desiring to adopt such child and the superintendent of the State public school. The State board of control may determine by resolution that the joinder of the superintendent in the petition shall be its consent to the adoption of the ward or pupil, as prayed for in the petition. A person of full age may be adopted [Gen. Stat. 1913, sec. 7151, as amended by Laws of 1917, ch. 222, p. 335.]

Investigation by board of control. Upon the filing of a petition for the adoption of a minor child the court shall notify the State board of control. It shall then be the duty of the board to verify the allegations of the petition, to investigate the condition and antecedents of the child for the purpose of ascertaining whether he is a proper subject for adoption, and to make appropriate inquiry to determine whether the proposed foster home is a suitable home for the child. The board shall as soon as practicable submit to the court a full report in writing, with a recommendation as to the granting of the petition and any other information regarding the child or the proposed home which the court shall require. No petition shall be granted until the child shall have lived for six months in the proposed home: *Provided, however*, that such investigation and period of residence may be waived by the court upon good cause shown, when satisfied that the proposed home and the child are suited to each other. [**Ibid., sec. 7152, as amended by Laws of 1917, ch. 222, p. 335.**]

Consent, when necessary. Except as herein provided, no adoption of a minor shall be permitted without the consent of his parents, but the consent of a parent who has abandoned the child, or who can not be found, or who is insane or otherwise incapacitated from giving such consent, or who has lost custody of the child through divorce proceedings or the order of a juvenile court, may be dispensed with, and consent may be given by the guardian, if there be one, or, if there be no guardian, by the State board of control. In case of illegitimacy, the consent of the mother alone shall suffice. In all cases where the child is over fourteen years old his own consent must be had also. [**Ibid., sec. 7153, as amended by Laws of 1917, ch. 222, p. 335.**]

Notice of hearing. When the parents of any minor child are dead or have abandoned him, and he has no guardian in the State, the court shall order three weeks' published notice of the hearing on such petition to be given, the last publication to be at least ten days before the time set therefore. In every such case the court shall cause such further notice to be given to the known kindred of the child as shall appear to be just and practicable: *Provided*, That if there be no duly appointed guardian, a parent who has lost custody of a child through divorce proceedings, and the father of an illegitimate child who has acknowledged his paternity in writing or against whom paternity has been duly

adjudged shall be served with notice in such manner as the court shall direct in all cases where the residence is known or can be ascertained. [**Ibid., sec. 7155, as amended by Laws of 1917, ch. 222, p. 336.**]

Decree; change of name. If upon the hearing the court shall be satisfied as to the identity and relationship of the persons concerned, and that the petitioners are able to properly rear and educate the child, and that the petition should be granted, a decree shall be made and recorded in the office of the clerk, setting forth the facts and ordering that from the date thereof the child shall be the child of the petitioners. If desired, the court, in and by said decree, may change the name of the child. [**Ibid., sec. 7156, as amended by Laws of 1917, ch. 222, p. 336.**]

Status of adopted child. Upon adoption such child shall become the legal child of the persons adopting him, and they shall become his legal parents, with all the rights and duties between them of natural parents and legitimate child. By virtue of such adoption, he shall inherit from his adopting parents or their relatives the same as though he were the legitimate child of such parents, and shall not owe his natural parents or their relatives any legal duty; and in case of his death intestate the adopting parents and their relatives shall inherit his estate as if they had been his parents and relatives in fact. [**Ibid., sec. 7157, as amended by Laws of 1917, ch. 222, p. 336.**]

Annulment. If within five years after his adoption a child develops feeble-mindedness, epilepsy, insanity, or venereal infection as a result of conditions existing prior to the adoption, and of which the adopting parents had no knowledge or notice, a petition setting forth such facts may be filed with the court which entered the decree of adoption, and if such facts are proved the court may annul the adoption and commit the child to the guardianship of the State board of control. In every such proceeding it shall be the duty of the county attorney to represent the interests of the child. [**Ibid., sec. 7158, as amended by Laws of 1917, ch. 222, p. 336.**]

Records of adoption. The files and records of the court in adoption proceedings shall not be open to inspection or copy by other persons than the parties in interest and their attorneys and representatives of the State board of control, except upon an order of the court expressly permitting the same. [Ibid., sec. 7159, as amended by Laws of 1917, ch. 222, p. 337.]

Placing out; surrender of parental rights. No person other than the parents or relatives may assume the permanent care and custody of a child under fourteen years of age unless authorized so to do by an order or decree of court. Except in proceedings for adoption no parent may assign or otherwise transfer to another his rights or duties with respect to the permanent care and custody of his child under fourteen years of age, and any such transfer hereafter made shall be void. [Laws of 1919, extra session, ch. 51, sec. 2.]

Penalty. Every person who violates any of the provisions of this act, or who shall intentionally make any false statements or reports to the board of control with reference to the matters contained herein, shall, upon conviction of the first offense, be guilty of a misdemeanor. A second or subsequent offense shall be a gross misdemeanor. [Ibid., sec 9.]

Guardianship; adoption. In any case where the court shall award a dependent or neglected child to the care of the State board of control or of any association or individual in accordance with the provisions of this act, the child shall, unless otherwise ordered, become a ward, and be subject to the guardianship of the State board of control or of the association or individual to whose care it is committed; but such guardianship shall not include the guardianship of any estate of the child, except as provided in section 17 of this act. Such board, association, or individual shall have authority to place such child in a family home, with or without indenture, and may be made party to any proceeding for the legal adoption of the child, and may by its or his attorney or agent appear in any court where such proceedings are pending and consent to such adoption: *Provided, however,* That when adoption proceedings for any such child are commenced in any other court than the court which originally committed such child, then notice of the filing of the petition in such adoption proceedings shall be filed in the office of the clerk of the court which originally committed such child, at least thirty days before any final decree of adoption shall be entered. [Laws of 1917, ch. 397, sec 12.]

Source

As reprinted from U.S. Children's Bureau, *Adoption Laws in the United States: A Summary of the Development of Adoption Legislation and Significant Features of Adoption Statutes, With the Text of Selected Laws*, edited by Emelyn Foster Peck, Bureau Publication No. 148. Washington, DC: Government Printing Office (1925): 27–28.

Adoptive Families of America

Susan A. Freivalds

Adoptive Families of America (AFA) was a national support and advocacy organization for adoptive and prospective adoptive families. The group originated in 1966 and served its progressively larger and more diverse membership from that time until it was disbanded in 2000.

The AFA organization originated with six families who met at the Minneapolis-St. Paul airport while awaiting the arrival of their children from Korea. Realizing that the children would benefit from maintaining their ties, the group arranged to meet again. Word of the emerging group, which called itself OURS, spread to other families who had adopted or were awaiting international children.

Betty Kramer, one of the original six adoptive mothers, was the group's founding leader. A newsletter was initiated with information about how to adopt, how to raise adopted children, and how to access local resources for raising international children. As membership expanded to include families adopting children from the U.S. and other countries, the focus of the group expanded as well. In addition, families who moved away from Minnesota established local parent groups and affiliated them with OURS. A national network of adoptive parent support groups began to form.

By the mid-1970s, the newsletter had grown to an 80-page bimonthly magazine, also called *OURS*. Affiliated families formed some of the first culture camps for international children, and OURS board members established an adoption agency that focused on non-traditional parents and children.

In the early 1980s, paid staff was hired to respond to the ever-increasing requests for information, to process memberships, and to handle sales of books and cultural items. In 1986, the first professional Executive Director was hired, and in 1987 the editor of *OURS* magazine became a paid position.

In recognition that OURS had outgrown its local roots and focus with ten thousand members, with members in every state, the name of the organization was changed to Adoptive Families of America in 1989. The scope of the organization was officially expanded to include families formed through all types of adoption.

In the late 1980s, national advocacy efforts were stepped up, particularly in regard to inequitable treatment of adoptive families in federal law. One problem of particular concern was the difficulty many families had in obtaining appropriate medical insurance for newly adopted children. Due to AFA efforts, mandated coverage for adopted children from the time adoptive parents became financially responsible for them, along with coverage for preexisting conditions, was included in the Omnibus Budget Reconciliation Act of 1993.

In 1991, a national conference for adoptive parents was initiated, attracting approximately 1,200 attendees every year through 1995. In 1994, AFA launched *Adoptive Families* magazine, a newsstand-quality bimonthly, as the successor to *OURS* magazine. Membership reached a peak of twenty-five thousand, with 350 affiliated adoptive parent support groups.

In 2000, *Adoptive Families* magazine was sold and AFA disbanded. Its support group role was being challenged by online groups and specialty organizations like Families with Children from China. Disappointing membership growth made its financial position untenable. The magazine's mission of education and support continues to be fulfilled by its current publisher, New Hope Media of New York City.

Adoptive Identity

Harold D. Grotevant

Adoptive identity addresses the question, "Who am I as an adopted person, and what does adoption mean in my life?" The process of adoptive identity development involves meaning-making when some aspects of one's life story may be unknown or unclear. Persons adopted under different circumstances may have different questions which are part of this meaning-making process. Children adopted as infants may wonder who their birth parents were or why they were placed for adoption. Children adopted at older ages may wonder whether they have siblings or whether their birth parents think about them. Children adopted from other countries may wonder why they were abandoned and placed in an orphanage. The process of constructing an identity narrative, or story, allows the person to make sense of the past, understand the self in the present, and project himself or herself into the future.

Identity development is a life long process, but it is especially intense during adolescence and young adulthood. Beginning in adolescence, young persons' emerging cognitive abilities allow them to think beyond the present to what might have been in the past or might be in the future. Identity is also about similarity and difference, so adolescents are challenged to think about what it means that they are different from their adoptive parents and siblings genetically, physically, and/or culturally. In young adulthood, adopted persons encounter life situations that raise questions relating to identity and adoption. Such situations often revolve around relationships and sexuality, such as a first intimate relationship, sexual debut, marriage, or birth of a child.

Changes in identity may be evoked by experiences that challenge a person's current thinking about adoption. Such encounters may include teasing, embarrassment at being asked to complete a family history assignment in school (when their family history is unknown), or disappointment at being turned down for a date by a classmate whose racial group matched their adoptive family's but not their own. These situations can also lead adolescents to question fundamental aspects of themselves, how they fit in their adoptive family, or even how they fit into the world.

Adoptive identity involves three important aspects: self-definition (how one defines oneself and is recognized by others); coherence of personality (how adoptive identity fits with other aspects of one's life); and continuity over time (linking past, present, and future). The intrapsychic, core component of identity is embedded within the network of one's intimate relationships as well as in the broader societal, cultural, and historical contexts in which one lives.

The process of identity development is a gradual one which adolescents and young adults navigate in different ways. A recent study of adoptive identity in a group of adolescents adopted as infants into families with confidential, mediated, or open adoptions revealed at least four identity types. The first group, those with *unexamined identity*, included adolescents who had not thought much about adoption issues and felt that, in general, adoption was not very central in their lives. Adolescents with *limited identity* had begun to explore ideas about adoption. Some talked with their friends about adoption or answered other peoples' questions about being adopted. In general, however, they did not view adoption as particularly salient in their lives.

In contrast, adolescents with *unsettled identity* had thought quite a bit about adoption, had explored its meaning in their lives, and felt that it was very significant for them. However, moderate to high levels of negative affect were associated with their feelings about adoption. The negative affect sometimes involved anger or resentment toward their birth parents or adoptive parents; occasionally it involved feeling bothered that there were certain things about their past that they did not know. Many of these adolescents felt "different" from their adoptive families. Those who had had contact with birth parents tended to be dissatisfied with the contact, wishing for more contact than they were able to bring about. Finally, adolescents with *integrated identity* had thought a great deal about adoption and felt clear and resolved about its meaning in their lives. Their adoption narratives tended to be expressed in positive terms. Although they felt that adoption was important to them, they were not preoccupied with it. They generally viewed themselves as fortunate and their family situation as positive. They regarded their birth parents with sympathy, compassion, and understanding.

This typology provides a snapshot of the diverse ways in which adolescents articulate a sense of self as an adopted person. The degree to which these types are stable is still under investigation, although it is likely that the unexamined and limited identity groups will show more exploration as they move through adolescence and young adulthood.

Factors from multiple sources influence adoptive identity development. Some are related to early experience, some to the fit of the child within the family and community, and others to societal attitudes about adoption. The complexity of adoptive identity itself underscores the challenge of how this aspect of identity is to be woven together, across the life span, with other aspects of identity, such as one's career path, religious or spiritual beliefs, values, and ways of relating to others.

See also Adolescent/Teen Adoption; Children's Understanding of Adoption.

Further Reading

Dunbar, Nora, and Harold Grotevant. "Adoption Narratives: The Construction of Adoptive Identity during Adolescence." In Michael Pratt and Barbara Fiese, eds. *Family Stories and the Life Course: Across Time and Generations*. Mahwah, NJ: Erlbaum, 2004.
Erikson, Erik. *Identity: Youth and Crisis*. New York: Norton, 1968.
Grotevant, Harold, Nora Dunbar, Julie Kohler, and Amy Lash Esau. "Adoptive Identity: How Contexts Within and Beyond the Family Shape Developmental Pathways." *Family Relations* 49 (2000): 379–387.
Lifton, Betty Jean. *Journey of the Adopted Self: A Quest for Wholeness*. New York: Basic Books, 1994.
McAdams, Dan P. *The Stories We Live By: Personal Myths and the Making of the Self*. New York: Morrow, 1993.

Adoptive Parents

Jerica M. Berge

Adoptive parents are people who lawfully adopt children that are not biologically theirs. This term can be used to describe parents who are seeking to adopt and parents who have already adopted.

Historical View and Demographics of Adoptive Parents

Several changes have occurred historically concerning trends in adoption for adoptive parents. Thirty years ago, most people thought the main reason that people adopted was infertility. Today, research has shown that, while some adoptive couples state infertility as the main reason for adoption, many more adoptive parents report that the reason they adopt is because they love children and feel something is missing in their lives.

Most adoptive couples range in age from their early twenties to early forties. Some adoption agencies will not accept applications from prospective adoptive parents under the age of twenty-five, while others have an upper age limit of forty-five. The current age policy is less strict than historical restrictions, which placed the age cutoff much lower than forty-five. Parents who adopt internationally may have an even more lenient age cutoff due to the fact that, in many countries, numerous babies and toddlers are residing in orphanages and need parents. As a result, the need for adoptive parents sometimes overrides considerations such as parental age. Another reason age may be viewed as less important in international adoptions is because of differing cultural attitudes toward age. Some countries view older parents as esteemed because they have more life experience. For example, Latin American countries may accept adoptive parents up to age fifty-five. Adoptive parents that adopt children with special needs usually range in age from around twenty-five to late forties or even sixties. Age limits may also be relaxed when a child is considered to fall into a special needs category by virtue of race, ethnicity, age, sibling group membership, or handicap.

Many agencies limit adoption of healthy infants to couples and may even require that they have been married at least two to three years. Single adults wishing to adopt are frequently referred to waiting children, or special needs adoption. Many single adults have turned to adopting internationally in order to have healthy infants.

Some adoptive parents may have previously been foster parents to the children they adopt. In many states, 50% or more of the children adopted through the state social services department were adopted by their foster parents.

Data from the National Center for Health Statistics 1999 report found that 9.9 million women had ever considered adoption, representing over a quarter of all ever-married women in this age range. Additionally, 15.9% (almost 1.6 million) had taken steps toward adoption and 31% of these had actually adopted a child.

The majority of the adoptive mothers were married; only 4% were not married. One-third were college graduates or higher; less than a quarter did not graduate from high school. Income data showed that over half of adoptive mothers have incomes level well above poverty level. These results also match other statistics measured by individual states. For example, a study by R. P. Barth, D. Brooks, and S. Iyer examining adoptions in California found that most adoptive parents were two parent families and most had attended or completed college.

The data from these reports overall indicate that the frequency of adoption increases with age, education, and income of adoptive parents and that adoption by black women has remained relatively stable, but adoption by white women has declined.

Research Findings About Adoptive Parents

Although there are numerous research studies looking at adopted child outcomes and birth parent outcomes in adoption, fewer studies have looked at adoptive parent outcomes with adoption. Of the studies conducted on adoptive parents, the main topics researched include adoptive parents' overall experience with adoption and adoptive parents' adjustment to adoption.

Studies have looked at adoptive parents' overall satisfaction with adoption. L. Raynor researched adult adopted persons and their adoptive parents. Of the adoptive parents interviewed, 85% reported that their overall experience with their adopted child was "very satisfactory" or "reasonably satisfactory." The other 15% of adoptive parents who had been "disappointed" with their adoptive experience reported that one of the main reasons was because of the severe health problems experienced by their adopted child. Another finding from Raynor's study was that the adoptive parent's perceptions of the similarities between themselves and the adopted child were vitally important for parental satisfaction. For example, 97% of adoptive parents who thought their child was similar to them in appearance, interests, intelligence, or personality were more likely to be happy with the adoption, while only 62% of adoptive parents were satisfied with their adoption experience when they perceived their adopted child as different from themselves.

Other research has looked into adoptive parents' adjustment to adoption. A common theme in the adoption literature is that adoption can be a stress-inducing experience for adoptive parents. The same studies also suggest that added social support may reduce the stress felt by adoptive parents. B. Priel, S. Melamed-Hass, A. Besser, and B. Kantor compared adoptive versus non-adoptive parents' functioning by measuring "self-reflectiveness." Self-reflectiveness was identified as a meta-cognitive capacity to understand ones' self and others in terms of feelings, beliefs, intentions, and desires. Results suggested that there was a difference in relation to self-reflectiveness between adoptive mothers and non-adoptive mothers, and between adoptive mothers who adopted small children (i.e., infancy to five years) and those who adopted older children (i.e., five years and older). The significant difference between adoptive and non-adoptive mothers on self-reflectiveness was that adoptive mothers reported that they believed they had moderate to lower parenting skills and that they had moderate to higher levels of feeling more helpless in disciplining their adopted child. The mothers that adopted older children reported lower parenting skills than mothers who had adopted younger children. The authors suggest that the adoptive mothers' perceptions about themselves as parents may contribute to a specific vulnerability factor in adoptive families that may lead to more difficult parental and child adjustments in adoption.

Another study by G. W. Bird, R. Peterson, and S. H. Miller also found that parents who adopted older children experienced more distress than those who adopted younger children. The authors hypothesized that the source of the distress may come from problems stemming from feeling responsible for solving problems that originated in the adopted child's previous placement history. This same study further found that the adoptive parents experiencing distress also reported adopting more children, having a lower sense of mastery, and receiving less support from family members.

A literature review by M. Ward examined the effects of adoption on the new adoptive parents' marriage. The review found a general decline in marital satisfaction. This decline was related to the partners' inability to balance marital and parental roles; their expectations about the division of housework, child care, and time demands with the addition of their adopted child. Adoption, especially of older children, added strains such as differing responses between parents to the adopted child's acting-out behavior. The review also indicated that several studies found that social support, including parent relief, enhance the adoptive parents' marriage.

K. M. O'Brien and K. P. Zamostny conducted an integrative review of 38 empirical studies on adoptive families. They found that adoptive parents reported several positive outcomes with regard to satisfaction with the adoption, familial functioning, and parent-child communication. The authors concluded that the studies form the foundation for future research that provides support for viewing most adoptive families as resilient.

Further Reading

Bachrach, C.A., P.F. Adams, S. Sambrano, and K.A. London. "Adoption in the 1980s." *Advanced Data from Vital and Health Statistics of the National Center for Health Statistics* (1990): 181.

Barth, R.P., D. Brooks, and S. Iyer. "Adoptions in California: Current Demographic Profiles and Projections Through the End of the Century." *Executive Summary*. Berkeley, California: Child Welfare Research Center, 1995.

Bird, G. W., R. Peterson, S.H. Miller. "Factors Associated with Distress Among Support-seeking Adoptive Parents." *Family Process* 51 (2002): 215–220.

Chandra, Anjani, Joyce Abma, Penelope Maza, and Christine Bachrach. "Adoption, Adoption Seeking, and Relinquishment for Adoption in the United States." Advance Data No. 306, May 11, 1999. Vital and Health Statistics of the Centers for Disease Control and Prevention/ Natl. Ctr. for Health Statistics, http://www.cdc.gov/nchs/data/ad/ad306.pdf

Freundlich, M. "Supply and Demand: The Forces Shaping the Future of Infant Adoptions." *Adoption Quarterly* 2 (1998): 13–42.

National Vital Statistics System Data. *National Center for Health Statistics (1999)*. National Center for Health Statistics Web Site. http://www.cdc.gov/nchs (accessed December, 2004).

O'Brien, K.M., and K.P. Zamostny. "Understanding Adoptive Families: An Integrative Review of Empirical Research and Future Directions for Counseling Psychology." *Counseling Psychologist* 31 (2003): 679–710.

Priel, B., S. Melamed-Hass, A. Besser, and B. Kantor. "Adjustment Among Adopted Children: The Role of Maternal Self-reflectiveness." *Family Relations* 49 (2000): 389–396.

Raynor, L. *The Adopted Child Comes of Age*. London, England: George Allen and Unwin, 1980.

Smith, S.L., and J.A. Howard. *Promoting Successful Adoptions: Practice with Troubled Families*. Thousand Oaks, CA: Sage, 1999.

Ward, M. "The Impact of Adoption on the New Parents' Marriage." *Adoption Quarterly* 2 (2000): 57–78.

Parenting and Adoption: Nature versus Nurture

Vern L. Bullough

The effect of parenting on adoption is part of the ongoing controversy about the importance of nature over nurture or vice versa. The economist Bruce Sacerdote attempted to answer this question by taking a long-term quantitative look of the effect of parenting on adoptive children. He used three adoption studies, two American and one British one, all of which contained in-depth data about the adopted children, their adoptive parents, and their biological parents. Sacerdote found that parents who adopted children were more intelligent, better educated, and more highly paid than the biological parents. But the adoptive parents' advantage has little bearing on the child's school performance.

For a comparison group, he used the data gathered by National Center for Education Statistics in their ongoing *Early Childhood Longitudinal Studies (ECLS)*, based on twenty thousand schoolchildren from birth to fifth grade. Sacerdote found, as did the ECLS data, that adopted children test relatively poorly in school; any influence the adoptive parents might exert is seemingly outweighed by the force of genetics, at least in the early school years.

By the time adopted children became adults, however, they had changed direction. Compared to similar children who were not put up for adoption, the adoptees were far more likely to attend college, have a well-paid job, and to wait until they were out of their teens before getting married. Sacerdote concluded that this was due to the influence of parenting on the children. Obviously, there is as yet no definitive answer, but Sacerdote's research raises interesting questions.

Further Reading

Sacerdote, Bruce. "The Nature and Nurture of Economic Outcome." *American Economic Review* 92 (2002), 344–347.

Primary Document

Must Adoptive Parents Profess a Religious Belief?

Religion is one of the many issues that may be encountered in placing children for adoption. As explained by James B. Boskey and Joan Heifetz Hollinger, "[r]eligious factors are not controlling in adoptive placements, but may be considered in determining what will serve the best interests of a particular child. Two separate issues may be considered. First is the desirability of matching the religious beliefs of the prospective adoptive parents with those of the child or the biological parents; and second is the presence or absence of any religious belief on the part of the prospective adoptive parents" (42). The legal arguments in regard to both of these factors can be complex and are touched on here only in brief.

The first factor, religious matching, according to Laura J. Schwartz, "has undergone a transformation similar to that of racial matching – from a mandatory to a discretionary policy" (178). This may be considered in the adoption process to some

extent in all states, with some states (e.g., New York) having stronger traditions and more explicit laws than others (179).

The second factor regarding prospective adoptive parents' religious belief has been addressed in the context of the moral character of the prospective adopters. In the past, the absence of prospective adoptive parents' religious belief may have been "a factor in determining the overall qualifications" of the parents. Nonetheless, courts and many agencies came to recognize that because of their first amendment right of free exercise of religion, prospective parents may not be disqualified solely on the basis of their religious beliefs if they are otherwise of "good moral character" (Boskey and Hollinger, 43).

In 1971, the Supreme Court of New Jersey addressed this second factor. In reversing a lower court decision, the court held that "absent special circumstances, adoption cannot be denied solely on ground that prospective adoptive parents lack belief in a

Supreme Being or lack church affiliation, and that agencies may not constitutionally require of applicants for adoption membership in established religion; but that ethics and beliefs of applicants, including religion, may be considered as bearing on issue of moral fitness." An excerpt from their decision below briefly lays out the background of the case and some of the pertinent testimony.

Source

Boskey, James B., and Joan Heifetz Hollinger. "Chapter 3: Placing Children for Adoption." In *Adoption Law and Practice*. (3 vols.) Hollinger, Joan H., ed. New York: Matthew Bender, 2003: 1–84.

Schwartz, Laura J. "Religious Matching for Adoption: Unraveling the Interests Behind the 'Best Interests' Standard." *Family Law Quarterly*. 25 (1991): 171–192.

IN RE ADOPTION OF "E"

Cite as 279 A.2d 785

59 N.J. 36

In the Matter of the Adoption of "E", a child,

by John P. Burke and Cynthia D. Burke, Plaintiffs-Appellants.

Supreme Court of New Jersey.

Argued May 11, 1971.

Decided July 1, 1971.

Proceeding on application to grant adoption. The Essex County Court, probate Division, 112 N.J.Super. 326, 271 A.2d. 27, denied application because prospective adoptive parents did not believe in Supreme Being, and parents and adoption agency appealed. The Supreme Court, Proctor, J., held that, absent special circumstances, adoption cannot be denied solely on ground that prospective adoptive parents lack belief in a Supreme Being or lack church affiliation, and that agencies may not constitutionally require of applicants for adoption membership in established religion; but that ethics and beliefs of applicants, including religion, may be considered as bearing on issue of moral fitness. The Court further held that where the sole ground for denying the adoption was the beliefs of the prospective

adoptive parents regarding religion and it was clear from the record that they were otherwise fit, Supreme Court would grant the adoption in the exercise of its original jurisdiction.

Reversed and rendered.

Weintraub, C.J., concurred in the result and filed opinion and Jacobs, J., concurred in the result. . . .

The opinion of the Court was delivered by PROCTOR, J.

The county court denied plaintiffs' application for a final decree of adoption. The court held that plaintiffs' lack of belief in a Supreme Being rendered them unfit to be adoptive parents. The plaintiffs appealed to the Appellate Division, and prior to argument there, we certified the case on our own motion. We reverse.

On June 27, 1969, the plaintiffs, John and Cynthia Burke, received custody of the baby girl "E" from the Children's Aid and Adoption Society of New Jersey (Society). On May 23, 1970, the Burkes, having received the consent of the Society, filed an application for adoption with the county court. The Society filed a report with the court recommending that the application be granted.

On August 25, 1970, a hearing was held and the Society was permitted to intervene. On November 2, 1970, the court denied the plaintiffs' application and ordered the return of the child to the Society. 112 N.J.Super. 326, 271 A.2d 27. Final judgment was entered on November 24, 1970, but was stayed to give the parties an opportunity to appeal.

Both the Burkes and the Society filed appeals from the judgment denying the adoption. Mark F. Hughes, Esq., was appointed by the Appellate Division on its own motion as amicus curiae "for the purpose of reviewing the law on both sides of the controversy" on appeal. Subsequently, the New Jersey Bureau of Children's Services, represented by the Attorney General, the Council on Adoptable Children, the New Jersey Council of Churches, the Department of Church in Society, Division of Homeland Ministries of the Christian Church (Disciples of Christ) in the United States and Canada, and Division of Human Relations, Board of Christian Social Concerns, United Methodist Church, all requested and were granted leave to file briefs amici curiae.

The facts are undisputed. Cynthia Burke, holder of a Ph.D. in Psychology, is a past Associate Professor at Seton Hall University. Her husband, John, holder of a Master's Degree in Speech Pathology, is currently working toward his Doctorate at Southern Illinois University. In 1965, the Burkes applied to the New Jersey Bureau of Children's Services for assistance in the adoption of a child. They were informed that, pursuant to a department regulation, they would be required to demonstrate some church affiliation before they could be considered suitable applicants. Since they could not demonstrate such an affiliation, they were denied the opportunity to adopt a child, and they instituted a suit for declaratory judgment seeking resolution of the question whether such "a religious qualification" might properly be required as a prerequisite to an adoption. The suit was dismissed by stipulation, however, when the Bureau of Children's Services revised its regulations which now provide in pertinent part:

Opportunity for religious or spiritual and ethical development of the child should receive full consideration in the selection of adoptive homes. Lack of religious affiliation or of a religious faith, however, should not be a bar to consideration of any applicants for adoption.

In July of 1967, after the regulations had been amended, the Society placed a baby boy (David) with the Burkes. With the recommendation of the Society, the county court granted final adoption on September 28, 1968. David has been living with the Burkes ever since and there is no dispute that he has been well cared for.

On June 27, 1969, the Society placed a three week old baby girl, "E", with the Burkes and she has been with them continuously since that date. On May 23, 1970, plaintiffs filed a complaint seeking adoption of the child. After conducting an investigation, the Society compiled and filed a report recommending the adoption. The report noted that both Cynthia and John Burke were in excellent health, intelligent, well educated, attentive to their children, and able to provide a physically suitable home. The report also noted that "* * * the Burkes' attitude toward the children is one that is healthy, and one that is full of warmth and love * * *. Mr. and Mrs. Burke have no church affiliation; however the agency has found them to be people of high moral and ethical standards."

At the hearing, the trial judge focused on the area of religion. He directed almost all of his questions to the plaintiffs' lack of church affiliation and their lack of belief in the existence of a Supreme Being. John Burke testified that he had had formal religious training as a Catholic and Cynthia testified that she had been raised as a Protestant. Both said they were now unaffiliated with any church and did not believe in a Supreme Being. Both articulated their humanistic views of morality and ethics, and their views of the type of ethical training they thought necessary to proper child rearing. The following colloquies with John Burke are illustrative:

THE COURT: Let's see now, an atheist doesn't believe in God at all and an agnostic does what? Can you tell me what you are? Are you an agnostic or an atheist, Mr. Burke?

MR. BURKE: Labels such as these have connotations that are unpalatable to some people. I wouldn't call myself an agnostic or an atheist.

THE COURT: Well, tell me what you are.

MR. BURKE: I am a humanist, I suppose. I believe in people. I believe in the goodness of morality in that what we need to learn in life is being good to one another and that the perception, the true perception of the Juda-Christian way of life are what make us good and this is the morality that obviously I haven't been able nor did I desire to throw off the teaching of my childhood.

* * * * * *

THE COURT: * * * [B]asically you have a good moral life and you believe in a code of morals, sir.

MR. BURKE: Yes, but I think that this code of morals while we have a tradition that brings it down to us the perception of the teachings of Jesus Christ. For instance, not the christians of christianity, but the teachings of Jesus Christ, love thy neighbor. We have those but we have something better, we have an intellect and we have examples from the people who are alive today, my grandfather, for example, my own parents, which leads you to be able to interpret a moral way of life that is your own, that is your own morality and it isn't exactly making up your morals as you go along, it isn't that at all.

* * * * * *

MR. BURKE: I do not believe in the existence of a Supreme Being.

THE' COURT: I am a little perturbed * * * the man is outspoken. He could have lied about it and the fact that he didn't lie about it is so much in his favor.

Cynthia Burke, who said her views were the same as her husband's, responded similarly to inquiries by the court:

THE COURT: Well, tell me your views about a Supreme Being.

MRS. BURKE: It would be very difficult for me to give you a description of what I believe a Supreme Being to be. I believe in the power of life. I am very much in awe of the creating of power of life. But, I do not believe in a Supreme Being who is in any way personified.

THE COURT: All right. You don't believe in religion as such, do you?

MRS. BURKE: I do not believe that any one religion is anymore preferable to any other.

THE COURT: Do you believe in any religion?

MRS. BURKE: I do not subscribe to any religion, no. I am not a practicing member.

THE COURT: What was that?

MRS. BURKE: I am not a practicing member of any religion.

* * * * * *

THE COURT: Mrs. Burke, do you have any definite plans as far as raising these children in reference to a particular religious training or religious training per se?

MRS. BURKE: Well, religious training involves, as far as I am concerned, a great many things. It involves standards of morality or a way of life which I feel involves honesty, regards of others, responsibility for one's own faith. I have already begun to teach my child [David] these things, both by teaching him the things that I think a three-year-old boy is capable of learning and I expect to teach him these things by example. As far as philosophy and the more abstract ideas involved in religion and philosophy, I suspect that my children will end up knowing more about Christianity than the average child who goes to Sunday School.

John Burke's testimony regarding his views led the judge to comment, "1 have heard some

Catholics who were unable to express the Christian view as well as you expressed it." Nevertheless, the court indicated that church affiliation was of critical importance:

THE COURT: Maybe I am old-fashioned, Mr. Burke, maybe I am old-fashioned. If you are Jewish, you are a good Jew. If you be a Protestant, you be a good Protestant. If you are Catholic, you be a good Catholic. It doesn't mean that people are good or that people are as good as you are.

In his written opinion, the trial judge recognized that a court should be loathe to intervene in matters of religion. 112 N.J.Super. at 329, 271 A.2d 27. Nevertheless, reasoning that the "child should have the freedom to worship as she sees fit and not be influenced by parents or exposed to the views of prospective parents who do not believe in a Supreme Being," he held that the best interests of the child "E" would not be served by granting the application. Id. at 331, 271 A.2d at 30. In effect, he held that the plaintiffs were unfit to assume the responsibility of adoptive parents. Accordingly, he denied the adoption and ordered that the child "E" be returned to the Society.

The trial court's decision rested solely on the grounds that plaintiffs, through their own testimony, did not believe in a Supreme Being or belong to a church of a recognized religion. There is nothing in the opinion to indicate that the Burkes were in any other way unfit or that E's "best interests" would be impaired by some other factor. In fact, the agency found them to be morally fit, and its report contained abundant evidence supporting this finding. Thus, the single issue before us is the propriety, under state and federal law, of the denial of an adoption solely on the basis of an absence of religious affiliation and a lack of belief in a Supreme Being.

No one appearing before this Court argues in favor of the trial court's determination. Attorneys representing numerous religious groups and adoption agencies and

organizations have submitted briefs and appeared before us. They unanimously urge us to reverse the trial court and to make it clear that, in the future, our courts may not deny persons the right to adopt a child solely because of their religious beliefs or non-beliefs. Only the court appointed amicus curiae takes a variant position. He urges that the adoption in this case should be permitted because the child has formed important ties with the Burkes and separating her from them at this point would be psychologically damaging. Although he suggests that the trial court should be reversed for this reason, he urges us to make a prospective ruling that an agency may require membership in an established religion as a prerequisite to adoption.

For the reasons to follow, we believe the trial court erred in denying the adoption. Moreover, we cannot accept the suggestion of the court appointed amicus curiae that adoption agencies should be free to refuse to place children with non-believers who are otherwise worthy. We believe that the trial court's decision and the suggestion of the court appointed amicus curiae both run counter to state and federal law....

[The decision continues with a discussion of various legal points. Highlights of these points are excerpted below.]

[1] The "best interests of the child" standard is flexible and leaves a great deal of discretion to the trial judge.... In the present case, the question is whether the trial court misused its discretion in denying an adoption solely because the applicants did not believe in a Supreme Being and were not affiliated with a church....

Although there are no decisions in this state which are directly on point, the cases demonstrate that generally our courts have been most reluctant to intervene in religious matters....

[2] On the other hand, religion has in some circumstances been one of the factors considered in determining the best interests of the child in both custody disputes and

adoption proceedings ... None of these factors operate against the adoption in this case.

It is implicit in our decisions as well as those of other states that religion may be viewed as a relevant factor in determining custody or adoption but, without other factual support, the religious factor is not controlling. . . .

[3, 4] By basing his decision *solely* on the absence of the Burkes' belief in a Supreme Being and their lack of church affiliation, the trial court relied on a factor which cannot alone be determinative of the "best interests" of the child "E". . . .

[5] The lower court's decision is also defective in that it runs afoul of the First Amendment of the United States Constitution. . . .

[6] The First Amendment provides in pertinent part:

Congress shall make no law respecting an establishment of religion, or prohibiting the free exercise thereof. * * * This freedom of religion provision is applicable to the States through the Fourteenth Amendment...The Establishment Clause bars a state from placing its official support behind a religious belief, while the Free Exercise Clause bars a state from interfering with the practice of religion by its citizens. . . .

[7] The United States Supreme Court has consistently held that government must maintain a posture of "wholesome neutrality" on the question of religion. . . .

... a court cannot disqualify someone from adopting solely on religious grounds without violating that person's rights to free exercise of his religious beliefs. . . .

[8] The trial court's reasoning does not confront the fundamental constitutional problem. The issue is not whether an individual has a right to choose religion or nonreligion, but whether the government has the power to impose religion or to place a burden on one's beliefs regarding religion. Burdening the opportunity to adopt with religious requirements does both and if, as we believe, the government lacks such a power,

religious requirements violate the Establishment Clause and the Free Exercise Clause of the First Amendment ... If judges are to have the power to deny adoptions on the basis of the applicants' lack of religious beliefs, the door is opened to other judicial intrusions into this sensitive field. . . .

[9, 10] ... adoptions should be dealt with in a highly individualistic manner rather than on the basis of speculative and sweeping generalizations; they should not be denied because the applicants belong to a class which statistically shows a greater propensity for some unfortunate trait. To deny an adoption, the court must find evidence of that trait or find some other damaging evidence in the individual applicants. Applicants for the adoption of children stand before the judge as individuals and must be judged on their own merits.

[11] Finally, the court appointed amicus curiae suggests that the likelihood that a child of nonbelievers will be ostracized serves as a valid secular reason for denying adoptions to them. Even assuming that nonbelievers are shunned by some elements of the populace, most minority groups suffer or in the past have suffered the same penalty. Yet, absent special circumstances, no one would contend that members of a minority group should be denied the opportunity to adopt a child on that basis.

One other point deserves mention. The concurring opinion finds our holding that religion may be a factor in adoption proceedings as objectionable on constitutional grounds as the trial court's holding that it may be the sole factor. That conclusion, of course, rests on the premise that the entire area of ethics and beliefs is irrelevant in adoption proceedings. If it is relevant, as we firmly believe it is, then questions concerning religion as it bears on ethics are not constitutionally forbidden because they serve a valid secular purpose. As stated above, such questions may be evidential of moral fitness to adopt in relation to how the applicants will conduct themselves as adopting parents. . . .

[12] The judgment of the trial court is reversed. Since the sole ground for denying the adoption was the Burkes' beliefs regarding religion and it is clear from the record that they are otherwise fit, we grant the adoption in the exercise of our original jurisdiction....

Judgment is entered in accordance with this opinion....

Adult Adopted Persons' Psychosocial Adjustment

Barbara J. Pierce

The term "adult adopted person" is used to describe an adult who was adopted prior to the age of eighteen. Another term, which many adopted persons do not like, is "adult adoptee." Many studies of child and adolescent adopted persons have taken place over the years. Fewer studies have documented the progress of adults who were adopted as children. The impact of adoption on a person's later functioning depends on many factors and may include: genetics; adoptive family stability; previous child maltreatment; and age at placement. Some researchers find that gender plays a role and think that women may fare better than men. Additionally, some researchers suggest that adopted people are at an increased risk for mental illness, school problems, and relationship problems while others suggest that there are sampling problems with these studies and argue that, in the general population, adopted people fare well.

Adjustment and Identity Formation

In order to understand issues of adjustment to the knowledge that one has been adopted, it is important to understand attachment theory. At its most basic, attachment theory explains how people develop trust in others and learn to form positive relationships with significant others. Typically, when children are born, they are cared for by their parents and get their needs met on a regular basis by the same one or two people, their birth parents. Over time this caring leads to the development of a sense of trust in knowing that their needs will be met in a timely fashion by those who love them.

If children are adopted as newborns, they are able to develop a primary attachment to their adoptive mother and father and are able to develop that first trusting relationship in an unimpeded manner. If children have had multiple foster placements, lived in orphanages overseas, or were adopted as older children because of abuse or neglect, they had one or more primary attachments disrupted. This disruption can cause problems with trust and psychosocial functioning over time. Adults who were adopted from newborn to 6 months of age tend to experience fewer adoption related complications than those adopted at older ages. One study by David Howe documented whether adults felt as if they belonged in their adopted families and found that those persons adopted as infants felt more a part of their adopted families than those adopted at older ages. Some people adopted as older children remember their birth mothers, grieve that loss, and may yearn for her. There has been some evidence, though, that even if adopted at older ages, children placed with consistent and loving adoptive parents can overcome the effects of discontinuity and realize good psychosocial outcomes.

Many of the problematic psychosocial issues related to adoption may be attributed to disruption in primary attachment. There have been problems related to anxiety and depression, and, especially in adolescence, identity issues. While identity and independence issues typically arise for all adolescents, adopted persons may have a more difficult time establishing an identity. Adolescents may begin to question their adoptive parents about the circumstances of their adoptions and try to find information about their birth families. In an attempt to grapple with the typical issues of who they are, and where they came from, adopted adolescents may begin to experience the feelings of loss of their birth parents or wonder about why they were relinquished. Some adopted persons believe they were relinquished because there is something wrong with them. In coping with loss issues, some people experience the very normal symptoms of anger, anxiety, or depression. This may lead to acting out behavior or adoptive parent-adolescent relationship issues. Adopted children and adolescents have idealized fantasies about their birth families and, in normal displays of rebellion, may tell their adoptive parents that they do not love them or want to go live with their birth families. Sometimes this rebellion can lead to problems of crime, addictions, or even mental health which can follow an adopted person into adulthood.

Many adopted people who are adults today were adopted prior to the trend of open adoption. When they were adopted, their adoption records were sealed by the courts. They may or may not have received a comprehensive medical history from their birth mothers and birth fathers. Therefore, we do not know if the resultant problems of coping with identity issues in adolescence and young adulthood (for example, depression) are a result of adoption or attachment issues, or if there was a history of depression in the birth family which may have predisposed them to depression. The same is true for problems with learning, addictions, or other mental illness diagnoses.

This issue of genetic identity is also important because many adopted people want to know if there are people in the world who look like them. They may question, for example, where they got their hair color or body type. Many adults who have searched and found their birth mothers comment on the physical resemblance. Genetics also becomes an issue in young adulthood when adopted adults decide to marry and have children. They may be concerned that there are genetically transmitted disorders in their birth family tree that are unknown to them. This can produce fear of having one's own children. Pregnancy and childbirth, two typical developmental tasks of young adulthood, also re-open grief and loss wounds when adopted persons realize the impact of parenting on their own lives and again wonder how their birth parents could have chosen to place them for adoption.

Even though most adopted adults do well psychosocially, some do report continuing to feel as if there must be something wrong with them because they were placed for adoption. Issues of low self-esteem can remain problematic throughout adulthood. While most adopted adults do fare as well as adults in the general population, some studies suggest that adult adopted people may score, on average, lower on measures of self-esteem and self-confidence.

For persons adopted internationally, the issues of identity may be exacerbated. Much research documents the success of people adopted internationally and transracially. Some researchers and social workers, however, remain unconvinced and point out the loss of cultural identity in these persons. Another issue of great importance is how transracially adopted people learn to cope with discrimination or oppression within the majority society. (An extended discussion of transracial and international adoption issues is included in this handbook.)

The issue of openness in adoption has been studied in relation to how adopted adults function. In general, it is thought that when adoptive parents are open and honest, provide as much information as they have, share letters and pictures at appropriate times, and avoid euphemisms and secrets, the adopted person does well psychosocially. Open and honest communication is especially important when the adolescent is searching for identity or when the adult chooses to search for birth parents.

Searching for Birth Families

Adult adopted persons choose to search for many different reasons. Some search just to obtain access to needed medical records, and others search because they want to establish contact with a birth parent. Some adults never feel the need to search. Accessing medical records has become a relatively simple task in many states now. Several states are allowing adults to have access to their original birth certificates, as well. Finding a birth mother or birth father can be a more cumbersome process and can take years to complete. Some birth parents have already died while others have moved away. Some birth parents do not want contact with the adopted person while other birth parents want to be found. Birth parents who are open to contact can register with state registries that have been established for this purpose. In these instances, many are found and reunions can occur.

Reunions can be joyful, comforting, and healing. They can also be confusing and hurtful. The motivations of the adult adopted person and the birth parent can affect the outcome. Some studies suggest that when the adopted person wants to meet a birth mother in order to place blame, the reunions are negative. Likewise, when a birth mother searches to allay her own guilt, reunions can be negative. However, if both people choose to meet because of an honest desire for contact, the reunion can be positive. Both participants will have emotional reactions to the process and will need to express their emotions openly and honestly. Disappointment may occur as a result of different socioeconomic status, educational attainment, or level of relationship desired. Some adopted people are shocked to find that they have full siblings that were raised by their birth parents. Others find that they have half-siblings. Reunions can and do occur with siblings, as well. Adults who choose to search for their birth parents must be emotionally prepared for all possibilities.

Overall, adult adopted persons fare well but when psychosocial issues arise, they can be assisted either by qualified mental health practitioners who are knowledgeable about adoption issues or by community support groups.

See also Adolescent/Teen Adoption; Adoption Search Movement; Adoptive Identity; Attachment and Bonding in Adoption; Open Adoption; Psychological Perspectives on Adoption; Reunion; Transracial and Intercountry Adoption.

Further Reading

Bastard Nation Web Site. www.bastardnation.org

Collishaw, S., R. Maughan, and A. Pickles. "Infant Adoption: Psychosocial Outcomes in Adulthood." *Social Psychiatry and Psychiatric Epidemiology* 33 (1998): 57–65.

Feigelman, William. "Adjustments of Transracially and Inracially Adopted Young Adults." *Child and Adolescent Social Work Journal* 17 (2000): 165–183.

Howe, David. "Age at Placement, Adoption Experience and Adult Adopted People's Contact with Their Adoptive and Birth Mothers: An Attachment Perspective." *Attachment and Human Development* 3 (2001): 222–237.

Levy-Shiff, Rachel. "Psychological Adjustment of Adoptees in Adulthood: Family Environment and Adoption-Related Correlates." *International Journal of Behavioral Development* 25 (2001): 97–104.

Lichtenstein, Tovah. "To Tell or Not to Tell: Factors Affecting Adoptees' Telling Their Adoptive Parents About Their Search." *Child Welfare* 75 (1996): 61–72.

Maughan, Barbara, Stephan Collishaw, and Andrew Pickles. "School Achievement and Adult Qualifications among Adoptees: A Longitudinal Study." *Journal of Child Psychology and. Psychiatry* 39 (1998): 669–685.

Moran, Ruth. "Stages of Emotion: An Adult Adoptee's Postreunion Perspective." *Child Welfare* 73 (1994): 249–260.

National Committee on Adoption. *1989 Adoption Factbook.* Washington, DC: NCFA, 1989.

Rosenberg, E. B. *The Adoption Life Cycle.* Free Press: New York: 1992.

Advertising Adoption

Beth Brindo

The nature of recruiting adoptive parents has been changed by recent developments in advertising. Though adoption agencies have long been listed in the yellow pages of telephone directories, the only supplement to this was word of mouth. Now web sites, newspaper and magazine ads, family profiles, direct mail, and various professional listings sell adoption products and services.

Advertising that includes educational components has increased accessibility of adoption information and resources for agencies, adoptees, and adoptive and birth parents. Professionals who offer adoption and related services may promote their adoption business to attract potential clients and increase adoptive placements. A range of products and professional services have gained wide-spread availability due in part to advertising. Books, tapes, videos, and note cards have become available to interested consumers. Availability of materials such as these helps disseminate information about pre-placement and post-placement adoption challenges and transitions.

Families waiting to adopt see advertising as a way to get information and adopt faster. Adoptive parents are able to identify needed services and information through advertising and network with agencies and individuals to identify a child to adopt. Adoption advertising often includes informative material that benefits not only adoptive parents but also birth parents and community members. Birth parents access service resources through print and Internet advertising. The birth parent benefits through access to information about adoption and questions they may have when considering making an adoption placement plan.

All of these methods can be exploited by those more concerned with making a profit than finding a suitable home for the adoptee. Those interested in adoption should be cautious and try to find out more about the agency or individual involved.

Print, Media, and the Internet

Waiting children benefit from adoption recruitment advertising that includes photo-listing books, child-specific recruitment, and advertising in venues such as televised waiting child features, newspaper columns, and Internet sites.

Photo-listing is an effective way to present actual children waiting for adoption to the community and interested adoptive parents. Books and newspaper inserts include a photograph of the specific child with a short biographical sketch. The information that is provided about the children that are shown on the Waiting Child photo-listing has been compiled and provided by the agencies and exchanges that have the responsibility of caring and planning permanent placements for the children. Prospective adoptive parents are able to meet with custodial agency representatives to obtain complete and up-to-date information about any child that they may be interested in adopting. Photo-listing is, however, frowned upon by some adoption professionals as misleading and exploitative.

The interests of families and children alike are best served when honest and complete information is provided to prospective parents. A child's photo-listing should include standard information as a minimum. A complete photo-listing should state any specific placement needs and whether the child has siblings or other meaningful contacts that should be maintained. In the case of older children, the child's likes and dislikes, personality, hobbies, special talents, health history, and educational standing should also be included.

Care should be used when writing narrative summaries about waiting children in need of adoptive homes. It is important to describe the child as a whole person, not a list of characteristics or diagnoses. Yet factual information related to any special need or circumstances should be sensitively explained and not misrepresented. Adoption recruitment advertising should be conducted with the child's consent and participation whenever possible. For example, advertising with a photo may need to be conducted outside the area in which a child lives or attends school. Keeping the specific child's information narrative information current will require regular updates. Sensitivity to the child's feelings and perspectives will necessitate the availability of support for the child by significant adults in their life.

Adoption recruitment posters and brochure materials represent children needing adoptive families. This recruitment advertising is positioned in key locations in communities such as community centers, recreation areas frequented by youth and families, and places of worship/religious gatherings. Information booths at community events and other locations help distribute information and identify prospective applicants. Picture buttons of specific waiting children with contact information on the back worn and distributed at businesses, social events, and at adoption-specific events is an example of innovative recruitment advertising.

The Internet is a particularly helpful way of communicating information. The use of waiting family photo-listings or text advertising on the Internet or in print media such as newsletters helps birth mothers who are considering placing a child for adoption. The birth parent consumer should use caution when looking at waiting family sites or listings in the newspaper since such listings do not guarantee that every single person or couple listed have satisfied all pre-adoption certification requirements in their state or are qualified to adopt. "Begging for babies ads" can sometimes be the result of such advertising. Birth parents that see such advertising as looking for a "family for their child" will fare better than those who are convinced that they are providing a "child to a family." Unless the site is directed by a licensed agency, waiting family sites are usually unable to certify that all the families on their page are qualified to adopt. Users of any advertising venues are usually recommended to contact several sources before selecting an adoption service or professional. The Internet has an advantage to birth parents because it is a confidential source of information for birth mothers and fathers who are thinking about making an adoption plan for their baby.

Word of Caution

As mentioned earlier, in the hands of some less ethical individuals and groups, adoption advertising has been the weapon of flesh-peddling and heartbreak. Ethical child welfare considerations avow that children should not be the subject of advertising efforts by unlicensed individuals or intermediaries who are in search of adoptable children, and children are not for sale. Advertising should be restricted to only those properly authorized and/or licensed adoption agencies that have professional services available in accordance with uniform standards. Attempts to permit unlimited advertising are opposed by many professionals in the adoptive field as a danger to children. These ethical boundaries that govern adoption advertising protect children, families, and larger society.

Legal considerations should be made when considering adoption advertising. Each state has laws and regulations that govern acceptable and legal adoption advertising. Some states uphold the restriction on advertising by unlicensed intermediaries to the adoption process as stated in the Civil Code. For example, within some states, a birth parent or prospective parent may advertise through the public media for the adoptive placement of a child. Conversely, in other states, no person may advertise for the placement of a child unless the State Division of Social Administration has certified them. Unlawful advertising may apply to advertising in a periodical, newspaper, or by radio that a person or group will accept, place, or provide children for adoption. Laws regarding the Internet and adoption advertising vary considerably depending upon the state.

In some regions across the country, the emergence of a "middle person" sometimes called an adoption intermediary or facilitator has opened the market to advertise services that once were the exclusive function of agencies. These people often serve as a link between birth and adoptive families and children. When considering an adoption intermediary (who operates apart from the child welfare system), their motivating factors should be considered.

See also Internet and Adoption: Difficulties and Rewards; Photographs and Advertising; Recruitment, Adoption; Wednesday's Child.

Further Reading

National Clearinghouse on Child Abuse and Neglect Information/National Adoption Information Clearinghouse. Use of Advertising and Facilitators in Adoptive Placements. State Statutes Series 2004. Child Welfare Information Gateway Web Site. http://www.childwelfare.gov/systemwide/laws_policies/statutes/advertisingall.pdf (accessed August, 2006).

Primary Document

Adoption Advertisements

Adoption advertisements have a long history in the United States. The following examples illustrate such ads during three distinct time periods—print ads from the early 1900s and the 1950s, and current ads available on the Internet as of this writing, 2006. The 1950s ads included here were included among the exhibits submitted during U.S. Senate hearings investigating illegal trafficking in interstate adoption practices.

1919–1921:

Adoption Advertisements from the *Chicago Tribune**

Personal — Wanted to Adopt Baby girl up to 4 years. Will furnish ideal home and best refs. Address M476, Tribune.

Personal — Wanted — Healthy Twins or Baby girl under 6 months, by couple able to give children wonderful home and future. Address KH 385, Tribune.

Personal — Wanted for adoption by wealthy Chicago couple, infant girl or boy. Address KH 386, Tribune.

Personal — Wanted to Adopt Baby month old, by responsible couple; good home. Address B 599, Tribune.

Personal — Want Home. 7 Year old boy, adoption. Call 2932 Indiana Av., Chicago.

1950s:

Adoption Advertisements**

Oklahoma City, Oklahoma *Advertiser*

Baby wanted – Loving home for baby of unfortunate circumstances. Will pay bill. Write Box J43, c/o The Advertiser or phone ME2-1419.

COUPLE wants to adopt baby, no questions asked. Box 1 3 c/o The Adv., or call.

WANT to adopt baby. Will be responsible for hospital and doctor bills. Write Box T55 c/o The Advertiser.

FOR ADOPTION – Boy 2; girls 3 and 8 years old. Box G83 c/o The Advertiser.

Wichita, Kansas, *Wichita Beacon*

ADOPTION – Young professional couple wishes to adopt child. All medical expenses guaranteed. Seclusion provided. Replies absolutely confidential. Eagle Box 187F.

YOUNG – Christian couple with fine future and home wishes to adopt child. All expenses of pregnancy and delivery guaranteed. Replies absolutely confidential. Reply to Eagle Box 287F.

2006:

Adoption Advertisements from the Norfolk, Virginia *Virginian-Pilot*** (Accessed online March 2006.)

A BABY TO LOVE: A loving couple wishes to give your newborn a lifetime of our love, care and happiness. Will comply with all state/federal adoption laws. Please call . . .

ADOPT: A truly loving married couple longs to share our hearts with a newborn

and offer security and endless love. Expenses paid. Will comply w/State and Fed. Adoption Laws. Please call

ADOPTION: A loving, young couple wishes to adopt a newborn. Know your child's life will be filled with lots of love, happiness and security. Please call Toll Free: . . . Will comply with all State and Federal adoption laws.

Source

Chicago Tribune, 1919–1921; re-printed in Robert H. Bremner, ed., *Children and Youth in America: A* *Documentary History. Volume II: 1866–1932.* Cambridge, MA: Harvard University Press, 1971,

p. 139; **Juvenile Delinquency (Interstate Adoption Practices). Hearings before the Subcommittee to Investigate Juvenile Delinquency of the Committee on the Judiciary. United States Senate. S. Res. 62. 84th Congress. 1st Session. Washington, D.C.: Government printing Office, 1956, *Advertiser* ads in exhibit insert following p. 24; *Wichita Beacon* ads in S. Res. 62 as extended version, following p. 50. ***The Virginian Pilot*, Norfolk Virginia. HamptonRoads.com Pilot Online Web Site. http://www.hamptonroads.com/pilotonline/ (accessed March, 2006).

Advocacy and Adoption (Overview)

Beth Brindo

There have always been non-professional advocates for adoption, and this is still true. Spanning levels from grassroots to legislation, advocates continue to influence and change attitudes and beliefs concerning adoption. The talents and dedication of individual advocates (including adoptive parents, foster parents, adopted people, birth parents, and social workers) have helped to shape public policy and to impress their mark on the lives of foster and adoptive families. Others who have effected change are allied professionals and groups with similar interests (e.g., non-profits, adult adoptee groups, consumer associations) and people who care about children and families (e.g., adoptive parent groups, professional associations, Parent Teacher Associations, volunteer organizations).

United voices are effective to help bring about and sustain change. By building a coalition of like-minded groups, an advocate can describe a strong case to decision-makers. These groups and individuals have advanced efforts to help guide the public attention of social service administrators and policy-makers to be more responsive to the needs of children, as well as foster and adoptive families, birth parents, and adopted adults. They work to ensure that the needs of their constituencies will be a priority and that services will receive the advantage of necessary funding, today and in the future. Policymakers have gained knowledge about adoption and special children's issues through the efforts of advocates. These efforts have led to the improved appropriation of resources, improvement of effective services, and assessment of social problems that impact children and families while shaping social policy, laws, and administrative rules.

See also Social Movements and Adoption

Further Reading

Babb, L.A. *Ethics in American Adoption*. Westport, CT.: Bergin and Garvey, 1999.
Babb, L.A., and R. Laws. *Adopting and Advocating for the Special Needs Child: A Guide for Parents and Professionals*. Westport, CT.: Bergin and Garvey, 1997.

Africa and Adoption

Alice K. Johnson Butterfield and Tenagne Alemu

War, disease, and the HIV/AIDS crisis in Africa have resulted in millions of orphaned children. The United Nations Children's Fund (UNICEF) reports that 11

million children under the age of fifteen have lost one or both parents to HIV/
AIDS in sub-Saharan Africa. By 2010, 20 million children, about half the total
orphans in this region, are likely to be orphaned from HIV/AIDS.

The orphan crisis in Africa has exceeded the ability of families and communities to provide informal, alternative care for orphaned children. In response, many
state governments have set up special government offices and developed specific
policies to guide the care of orphans. These national orphan programs, however,
do not list adoption as a part of the solution to the orphan problem.

The absence of adoption efforts on behalf of orphaned African children is due,
in part, to cultural mores which do not define the concept of "orphans" as it is typically defined in western societies. For example, prior to social disruption caused
by a thirty-year war in Eritrea, children who had lost both parents would be raised
by members of the extended family, or if no family members could be found,
friends of the family would take responsibility for the children. The new children
would, as noted by Wolff, "automatically become members of the new family and
have all the rights and responsibilities of other children in the same family" (p. 1).
There were no formal agreements or legal documents. In traditional Eritrean society, adoption and foster care were foreign notions.

Traditional African kinship systems may follow either matrilineal or patrilineal
lines, and these practices vary by tribe and country. The principles guiding orphan care
in Uganda begin with the responsibility of the father's clan—the father's sisters and
brothers, followed by the mother's sisters and brothers, paternal and maternal grandparents, and non-relatives. Step-mothers and their families may also participate in orphan
care. In Cameroon, grandmothers sometimes identify a male member of their family as
the child's father so as to keep their grandchildren in the maternal line.

Religious taboos also impede formal adoption processes. In Zimbabwe, taking
an unrelated child into a new family may have negative consequences. It is
believed that the failure to perform family-specific religious rites at death opens
the family to evil spirits from the adopted person's totem. However, due to children's rights education and some religious teachings, black families in Zimbabwe
are beginning to adopt. Formal adoption by Muslim families is constrained
because the Quran doesn't address the formal practice. Consequently, there are
few adoption agencies in Muslim countries in Africa.

Response to the Orphan Crisis in Africa

Orphans in Africa experience repeated psychological trauma. Trauma often starts
with the illness and death of their parents, and is exacerbated by poverty, malnutrition, stigma, exploitation, and often, sexual abuse. When alternative care is not available, the trajectory may lead to begging, child prostitution, and life on the streets. In
these cases, orphans develop harmful behaviors that endanger the community and
negatively affect economic development as discussed by Matshalaga and Powell.

To deal with the orphan crisis, African governments have established official
policies and programs. Types of programs include both in-kind and cash assistance, including direct subsidies (cash transfers) and indirect subsidies (education
vouchers and food supplements). Systems of care range from foster care to orphanages and children's villages. The most prevalent method of alternative care is fostering, which fits more closely with social and cultural customs than other types of
group care.

Foster care can be either temporary or permanent. Typically, temporary foster care occurs when children are waiting to be placed for adoption. This type of foster care is funded by international adoption agencies. Once a family has agreed to adopt a specific child, and during the time that in-country legal processes are taking place, the cost of foster care is added to the overall cost of the adoption. More permanent types of foster care include child sponsorship programs sponsored by international aid organizations such as Save the Children, World Vision, and other large private voluntary organizations (PVOs). The need for foster care and income subsidy is so great that it is not uncommon for poor families to approach aid organizations with a request to sponsor a specific child or children. These potential foster parents may include relatives of the children who may or may not disclose their kinship ties. Informal foster care is also common. In this case, poor and non-poor families take in orphan children and make them a part of their family. However, children from Benin, Gabon, Nigeria, and Togo have reportedly been bought or sold in neighboring countries. In cases in which orphans have no ties to family or community, fostering models tend to give way to other forms of group care.

There are also country-specific differences in how national orphan programs are organized. Botswana's National Orphan Programme works in partnership with government departments, non-governmental organizations (NGOs), community-based organizations, and the private sector. NGOs lead the effort to provide alternative care for orphans in Burundi and Uganda. As noted by Subbarao, Mattimore, and Plangeman, particularly in Uganda, NGOs report some success with orphanages. Eritrea's unsuccessful experiences with international adoption led the government to develop a system of state-run orphanages and children's villages. International responses, also known as sector-wide approaches, have included funding from the World Bank for developing community-based approaches to the orphan problem.

International Adoption

Most countries in Africa do not allow international adoption or do not have the legal and social service structures in place to allow children to be adopted outside the country. Four countries—Ethiopia, Liberia, Sierre Leone, and South Africa—have laws and some type of system in place to allow children to be adopted internationally.

Policies and laws regarding international adoption vary by country. For example, under the Child Care Act, No. 74 of 1983, South Africa did not allow international adoption unless one parent was a resident South African citizen. Although a court ruling in 2000 allowed American citizens to adopt South African children, there are no government-approved agencies or attorneys. Those wishing to adopt children from South Africa may work through a U.S. adoption agency or directly with the South African government. In contrast, Ethiopia has official agreements with three U.S.-based adoption agencies, including Americans for African Adoptions and Adoption Advocates International.

Ethiopia and Adoption

Overall, African adoptions are on the rise. Ethiopia is the lead country and ranks among the top twenty countries sending children to the U.S. In 2002, 114 children were adopted from Ethiopia, followed by 190 children in 2003, and 116 in the first six months of 2004. Since children from Ethiopia comprise the majority of international adoptions from Africa to the U.S., the orphan crisis and adoption process in Ethiopia is briefly reviewed.

Ethiopia is one of the poorest countries in the world, with an estimated per capita income of about $100. The country is largely an agricultural economy prone to droughts and famine. Various social, health, and economic needs have contributed to falling life expectancy from forty-five years in 1990 to forty-two years in 2001. In particular, HIV/AIDS is creating a tremendous burden on health care, social structure, and child survival. Ethiopia has an estimated 3 million people with HIV/AIDS, the third largest number of people living with HIV/AIDS of any country in the world, and an estimated 1.2 million Ethiopian children have been orphaned by HIV/AIDS.

Currently, there is no state-sponsored child welfare system in Ethiopia. Some small orphanages are operated by indigenous non-governmental organizations and international organizations. Most orphan children are cared for by their extended families through informal arrangements, or as part of a foster care program with funding through international aid and child sponsorship organizations. In cases in which informal foster care by extended family members or child sponsorship is not possible, child-headed households are common. For example, in Dessie, a town in Ethiopia of one hundred thousand, the Organization for Social Service for Aids (OSSA), in partnership with Save the Children, provides financial support and school uniforms for 150 children, but there are five thousand more orphaned children who need help. Typically, older siblings, often young girls, will drop out of school in order to support and manage the household. As aging and impoverished grandparents and caregivers decline over the next generation, child-headed households will become more common. Because of their limited economic capacity, child-headed households are at great risk of illiteracy, prostitution, and drug and alcohol abuse.

Permanent foster care—by far the most common type of community support— is also in crisis due to the fear and stigma associated with HIV/AIDS. Potential foster families prefer to avoid fostering children whose parents have died of AIDS. Those interested in foster children often want to know the child's HIV status. However, Ethiopian law prohibits HIV/AIDS testing before the age of eighteen, so unless biological parents give legal consent before their death—or a legal guardian is appointed through court processes—orphan children cannot be tested.

Although silent about the state's responsibility for orphans, Ethiopia's new Revised Family Code provides the legal framework for guardianship and adoption through the courts. The legal definition of adoption in Ethiopia, however, differs from its definition in the U.S. In Ethiopia, the relationship of the biological parents is not permanently severed, and adopted children, including their future spouses and dependents, are allowed to retain bonds with their family of origin. Still, whenever a choice has to be made between the family of origin and the family of adoption, the law states that the family of adoption will prevail. In cases of international adoption, the adopting parents must submit an annual report to the Ethiopian government about their adopted child until the child reaches the age of eighteen. Married couples wishing to adopt children from Ethiopia must submit a home study and other types of adoption papers to the Ministry of Labor and Social Affairs for approval before the courts will rule on the adoption.

Despite the recent legislation guiding adoption in Ethiopia, widespread poverty and deplorable health conditions create a "system" in which some children placed for international adoption are not true orphans, but have a parent or parents, and/or siblings still living in Ethiopia. Adoptive families from abroad only become aware of this fact as their older adopted children become secure in their new life and begin to talk about the family members that were left behind. One network of adoptive families in France has responded to this situation by providing sponsorship funds for family members remaining in Ethiopia.

See also Acquired Immune Deficiency Syndrome (AIDS) and Adoption; Human Immunodeficiency Virus (HIV)-Positive Infants; South African Changes in Adoption: A Case Study.

Further Reading

Barnett, Tony, and Piers Blaikie. *AIDS in Africa: Present and Future Impact*. New York: The Guilford Press, 1992.

Kalipeni, Ezekiel, Susan Graddock, Joseph R. Oppong, and Jayati Ghosh, ed. *HIV and AIDS in Africa: Beyond Epidemiology*. Malden, MA: Blackwell Publishing, 2004.

Matshalaga, Neddy Rita, and Greg Powell. "Mass Orphanhood in the Era of HIV/AIDS." *British Medical Journal* 324 (2002): 185–186.

Subbarao, K., Angel Mattimore, and Katherine Plangeman. *Social Protection of Africa's Orphans and Other Vulnerable Children*. Africa Region Human Development, Working Paper Series. Africa Region: The World Bank, 2001. http://info.worldbank.org/etools/docs/library/108875/toolkit/other/links.htm (accessed June, 2005).

United Nations Children's Fund (UNICEF). *Africa's Orphaned Generation*. New York, UNICEF, 2003. www.unicef.org/publications/africas_orphans.pdf (accessed June, 2005).

Whyte, Susan R., Erdmute Alder, and P. Wenzel Geissler. "Lifetimes Intertwined: African Grandparents and Grandchildren." *Africa* 74 (2004): 1–5.

Wolff, Peter H. "Eritrea: Collective Responsibility for War Orphans." Africa Regions Knowledge and Learning Center. IK Notes 50 Web Site. www.worldbank.org/afr/ik/default.htm (accessed November, 2002).

Albee, Edward (1928–)

Vern L. Bullough

Edward Albee, regarded by many as the most important American playwright of the last part of the twentieth century, was an adopted child. The play which made him famous, *Who's Afraid of Virginia Wolf?*, opened in 1962. He continued with a number of significant plays which won Pulitzer and other prizes.

His own hostile reaction to his adoption has been a major influence in his life. He was adopted shortly after his birth in 1928 by Reed and Frances Albee, a well-to-do couple who resided in Larchmont, New York. Albee felt he was pampered but unloved as a child and, like many upper middle class children, he was sent away to boarding school and in the summers, to camp. He responded by conceiving of himself as completely separate from his family. He became shy and secretive, and he reports that when he was told at age six or so that he was adopted, his only feeling was one of relief. Still today he refers to his adoptive parents as "those people." He complained to his biographer that his adopted parents "bought me" for $133.30.

Albee had a troubled youth and was kicked out of two schools for failing to attend class, but managed finally to graduate from Choate and briefly attended Trinity College before being expelled. Shortly afterward, following a fight with his parents about his coming home late, leaving the car covered in vomit, and failing to turn the lights off in the driveway, he left home in a taxi and never went back. When his father died, he did not attend the funeral, and he did not see his mother again for seventeen years.

He moved to Greenwich Village and fell in with a group of homosexual intel-lectuals and clearly identified himself as gay. When he turned twenty-one, Albee came into a small trust fund from his grandmother, and he supplemented this with various odd jobs.

It was not until ten years after he left home that Albee wrote the play that started his career. Most of his plays deal with brutal intra-familial wars or detached absurdism, but he has also created plays that deal with loving and affec-tionate couples. One critic has said that the problem with marriages in Albee plays is not necessarily that the husband and wife are at odds, but that they are too little at odds. The result is that, over the years, they build themselves a reassuring collec-tion of habits and understandings and forget how to be alive.

What is clear from Albee's life is that not all adoptions result in happy and pleasant family relationships, and while Albee's reaction might have been extreme, such reactions do happen.

Further Reading

Gusso, Mel. *Edward Albee: A Singular Journey: A Biography*. New York: Simon and Schuster, 1999.

MacFarquhar, Larissa. "The Making of Edward Albee." *New Yorker*. April 4, 2005, pp. 68–76.

American Adoption Congress

E. Wayne Carp

Founded in 1978, the American Adoption Congress (AAC) was the brain-child of Jean Paton, the pioneer leader of the adoption search movement, who despaired over the lack of coordination among the hundreds of adoptee search groups and their ineffectiveness in changing sealed adoption records laws. Paton hoped that a large, centralized organization composed of adopted adults would be more effec-tive. The AAC that emerged from the initial meeting held in Denver, Colorado, was a national organization, composed not solely of adopted adults as Paton envi-sioned, but also of search/support groups and individuals, such as adopted adults, birth parents, adoptive parents, and adoption social work, mental health, and legal professionals. The inclusion of professions into an organization that Paton believed needed to be run by adopted adults for adopted adults was a source of bitter disap-pointment to her for the rest of her life. In 1982, the AAC incorporated itself as a nonprofit organization. Since then, it has divided the U.S. into eleven regions and reports that it has 1,500 members.

The AAC's mission is to educate the public's attitudes toward sealed adoption records and to lobby legislators to repeal sealed records laws in order to guarantee access to identifying information to all adopted adults, their birth parents, and adoptive families. From its founding, AAC leaders de-emphasized the use of argu-ments based on constitutional rights, and instead highlighted those based on psy-chological theory: that knowledge of one's birth parents was crucial to the adopted person's self-identity and that searching for one's biological family is of great therapeutic value. It advocates for the right of birth family reunification for all adults, without prior restraint, through search and support group networking and/ or social service assistance.

Each year, the AAC holds one national conference; regional and local conferences are also held. Members receive a quarterly newsletter, *The Degree*, as well as the AAC *Annual Report*.

See also Adoption Search Movement; Paton, Jean; Reunion.

Further Reading

American Adoption Congress. "About the American Adoption Congress: An Overview." American Adoption Congress Web Site. http://www.americanadoptioncongress.org/ (accessed December, 2004).

Carp, E. Wayne. *Adoption Politics: Bastard Nation and Ballot Initiative 58*. Lawrence: University Press of Kansas, 2004.

Ancient Babylonia and Adoption

Vern L. Bullough

Hundreds of clay tablets dealing with adoption in the period around 1800 BCE have survived from ancient Nippur. So far, however, only twenty-five have been studied in detail. Several kinds of adoptions appear: (1) a man alone adopts one or more sons; (2) a man and his wife adopt one or more sons; (3) the sons of a previous marriage are adopted by a new spouse; and (4) a woman alone is probably the adopter, although it could also be interpreted that a woman is being adopted.

Records also exist from other ancient sources and it seems adoption served several needs. Adoption of children from a previous marriage by the new spouse and the adoption of children (in one case, a suckling infant) by a childless couple emphasize that adoptions filled the largely social needs of providing orphans with parents and childless couples with children and heirs. In some cases, adoption provided the adoptee with the chance for upward social mobility that had been denied by birth, while the adopter received a measure of security. Interestingly, economic gain was also a motivation for both adopter and adoptee. Sometimes natural sons (most adoptions are of sons) lost security and, in at least one instance, these sons saw their inheritance fall into the hands of a stranger who had been adopted.

The varied types of adoption implied that adoption could bring about needed social change. As Sir Henry Maine argued in the nineteenth century, although adoption also served traditional functions, without the fiction of adoption which permits the family tie to be artificially created, it is difficult to understand how society would ever have escaped from its swaddling clothes and taken its first steps toward civilization. Certainly adoption appears in some of our earliest records.

Further Reading

Stone, Elizabeth C. and David I. Owen, with a contribution by John R. Mitchell. *Adoption in Old Babylonian Nippur and the Archives of Mannum-mešu-lissur*. Winona Lake, IN: Eisenbrauns, 1991.

Ancient China and Adoption

Fang Fu Ruan and Vern L. Bullough

Adoption was not unusual in Chinese history. Even as late as the late nineteenth century and throughout the twentieth century, adoption was practiced fairly frequently, much more frequently than in the West. A major reason for such widespread adoption was the belief in Chinese culture that to die childless was a moral, religious, and social problem. So important was the need for heirs that the state early on recognized the plight of those who died without descendants and attempted to offer them solace by erecting special altars. Adoption became an alternative.

In the male-centered Chinese society, reproduction was not just a matter of simple biology, but a judgment of a man himself. Since offspring were regarded as a kind of reward in life, a man's childlessness could be seen as due to transgressions committed by his father, other ancestors, or himself. In turn, children could be looked upon as a reward for meritorious conduct. Men who had no children by age forty were encouraged to take a concubine or, failing that or in addition to it, to adopt.

Particularly influential in forming Chinese ideas was Confucius (Kongzi or Master Kong, 551–479 BCE). His idea of *xiao*, literally filial piety, was amplified by his disciples, especially Mencius (Mengzi, or Master Meng, 372–289 BCE). Mencius wrote that there were "three things that are unfilial, and to have no posterity is the worst of them" (Waltner, 1990: 2, 13n). It was essential for a man to have an heir. The most common form of adoption by a man without heirs (*guo ji*) was to adopt a child of a relative, preferably the son of a brother, and establishing him as an heir (*li shi*). An adoption could be carried out even after the adoptive father was dead if he did not have a son.

An alternative to adopting the child of a relative was to adopt a child with a different surname. Although a child thus adopted could inherit, he (and they were always boys), might not technically become a family member. This was because, even though the adopted son assumed the rights and duties of a son to his adopted parents, he did not necessarily terminate his relationship with his biological family. The adopted child could also be the son of a sister, therefore already having some relationship with the adopted family. The child of a woman by one husband who later married another man could be adopted by the new husband. This implies that adoption was rigidly controlled, but this was not necessarily the case.

There were also political reasons for adoptions. A good example of this is the case of Li Keyong (856–905 CE), a Tartar prince important in repelling an invasion by the Tufan (Tibetans). He was rewarded by the Emperor Yi Zong who gave him the imperial surname Li and the personal name of Gouchang. Keyong himself adopted others including Tan Li Shiyuan (867–903 CE) who became one of the best known emperors in Chinese history. Keyong also adopted thirteen warriors known as the "Thirteen Taibao," who became his devoted supporters. Adoption, in fact, became a way of cementing supporters since, in spite of oaths, duties, loyalties, and even kinship, ambitious warriors were always ready to try to wrest power from others above them. By adopting key subordinate warriors, Keyong and other warlords strove to make their relationship with them a familial one.

Success of such adoptions depended on having a strong ruler. Historians, in dealing with Li Keyong, often refer to his army of adopted sons as the key to his success. One emperor, Wu-tsung (1505–1521), adopted 127 men on a single day.

Adoption, at times, was a subterfuge. During the Ming Dynasty (1368–1644), commoners were not allowed to own serfs or indentured workers. To escape this restriction on serfs, many turned to adopting and registering them as adopted sons.

Sometimes adoption took place in an effort to change a child's environment. A sickly child might be adopted by another family or even a religious institution in the hope that the change in kinship configurations might improve his or her health. There were also uxorial marriages in which the groom joined the family of the bride, took her father's surname, and offered his offspring to serve as heirs to her father.

The Chinese also often engaged in child marriages which were a kind of adoption since the child was raised as an adopted daughter, although she was designated to marry her "brother" when they reached maturity. This was the most common form of female adoption. If a man died without an heir, a brother might assign a son to his name and he, thus, gained the right to inherit from his father's brother.

Adoption of infants also took place in China, many of them adopted as newborns. In any case, infants (whether newborn or older infants) were turned over to wet nurses until they were weaned. Wet nursing was common in ancient China, not only for adopted children but for children of the rich and powerful. Some indication of its extent is illustrated by the variety of terms such as *rummu, yuyu, ruao*, all of which can be roughly translated as "milk mother." Also frequently used as terms were *naim* and *nainiang*, literally "breast mother." Among large families, there were also informal adoptions by sisters, brothers, cousins, and similar relatives.

There were also wide local variations in adoption. In some areas and in different periods, even strangers were adopted. There were occasional outbursts against adoption in the Ming period but these were not universal and did not last. Adoption was important in China because the traditional family was seen metaphorically, legally, and ritually as the basis of the state, and so it was essential that the concept of family be retained. Adoption was a means of doing this. Both marriage and adoption were also viewed as means by which families could manipulate their composition, solve immediate problems, and achieve long-term goals. In the words of Anne Waltner, an expert on Chinese adoption, adoption mediated an array of tensions in Chinese society—the conflict between the principles of heredity and merit, between human emotion and the prescriptions of classical texts, between the dictates of heaven and the realities of life. It allowed them to tamper with the "natural" order for their own benefit.

Further Reading

Freedman, Maurice. *The Study of Chinese Society*. Stanford: Stanford University Press, 1979.
Goody, Jack. *The Oriental, the Ancient and the Primitive: Systems of Marriage and Family in Pre-Industrial Societies of Eurasia*. Cambridge: Cambridge University Press, 1990.
Waltner, Ann. *Getting an Heir: Adoption and the Construction of Kinship in Late Imperial China*. Honolulu: University of Hawaii Press, 1990.

Arizona Orphan Abduction

Vern L. Bullough

The so-called orphan abduction took place in October, 1904, when a train carrying forty orphans, several Roman Catholic nuns, and an agent from the New York Foundling Hospital arrived in Clifton-Morenci, two mining towns on the Mexican border of the Arizona Territory. Adoption arrangements had been made for the children before they had left New York and each of the adopted families had been investigated and approved by the priest before the orphans arrived.

Clifton was the first stop where a crowd of onlookers gathered to greet the orphans who were to be adopted by individuals there. The local priest took sixteen of the orphans to the local parish church where they were to be claimed by their new parents. As the children went off, some of the Clinton "Anglo" residents became upset over the fact that the children seemed to be blond haired and "white" and were to be adopted by Mexican parents. They then persuaded the Clifton deputy sheriff to prevent the rest of the children from being unloaded at Morenci. By the time the sheriff arrived, an angry crowd had gathered, some with tar, feathers, and rope in hand. The deputy demanded that the children be reassigned to white families but the Foundling Hospital's agent refused. The nuns and their agent were then told if they did not reclaim the children themselves the mob would. At gunpoint, the nuns agreed to have all the children collected and take them back to New York.

After the orphans had been returned to New York, the Foundling Hospital filed a suit against one of the abductors at the Territorial Supreme Court in Phoenix. The court ruled that the best interests of children had been served by the rescue of the orphans. On appeal, the case ended up in the U.S. Supreme Court which ruled that, because the adoptive parents were Mexican Indian, they were unfit by "mode of living, habits, and education ... to have the custody, care and education" of white children.

This decision, however, did not stop the so-called Catholic orphan trains of which this group of orphans were a part, but organizers were more cautious in their placement. Such trains were a Catholic reaction to the orphan trains established earlier by the New York Children's Aid Society which had resulted in many Catholic orphans being sent to Protestant homes. The court decision was one of the factors complicating adoption and set back the adoption movement.

See also Catholic Church and Adoption: Lessons from Ireland.

Further Reading

Linda Gordon. *The Great Arizona Orphan Abduction.* Cambridge, MA: Harvard University Press, 1999.

Assisted Reproductive Technologies and Adoption

Yvette V. Perry

Description of Assisted Reproductive Technology

Assisted Reproductive Technology (ART) refers to procedures performed to initiate conception by manipulating eggs, sperm, or both outside the human body. The term covers a wide range of medical procedures, such as *in vitro* fertilization (IVF), donor sperm insemination (DI), and gestational surrogacy. The term is also used to refer to techniques that are not currently possible with humans, such as reproductive "cloning" (somatic cell nuclear transfer), and it is sometimes used to refer to techniques that may be attempted in non-clinical contexts (e.g., "self-insemination"). ART usually does not refer to either the administering of ovulation-inducing drugs or corrective surgery in the reproductive system followed by pregnancy attempts through sexual intercourse.

Many writers mark 1978 as the birth of ART. This was the year that physicians in the United Kingdom reported the birth of the first "test tube" baby born through in vitro fertilization (IVF). However, donor insemination (DI) using intended fathers' or donors' sperm has been used since at least the 1940s.

Today, ART is employed by people in a wide range of circumstances, such as single adults wishing to parent without a partner, gay and lesbian couples wishing to co-parent, and people with medically complicating conditions such as HIV/AIDS and cancer. Use of ART has been increasing. V. C. Wright and Colleagues in a Centers for Disease Control report, note that in 2000 there were 35,025 infants born in the United States as a result of ART.

Relationships Between Art and Adoption

Many researchers and writers have compared ART with the older form of "alternative" family building, adoption. No consensus has been reached regarding the appropriateness of such comparisons—some advocate for the similarity of the two means of family building, some for the marked dissimilarity, while others note areas of overlap and areas of distinction. Separate from whether or not the two are similar are discussions about whether or not adoption and ART should be treated similarly in law, policy, or practice. Following are the main areas in which ART and adoption have been compared and contrasted.

Terminology

Similar to the adoption field, the use of terminology has been a contentious issue in the assisted reproduction field. The word "assisted" is used now to describe the general area and more specific techniques rather than the previous term "artificial." Persons intending to raise the children resulting from the procedures are often called "intentional" or "social" parents. However, making matters more complicated than in the adoption context, these intentional parents may or may not also be the biological or genetic parents. Further, in the case of female parents, a "biological" parent may be the one who gestates and gives birth to the child, but she may not be the genetic mother if the egg has been provided by an egg donor. The word "donor" has been particularly contentious, as some note that in many cases gamete providers are provided with money of varied amounts and, thus, cannot be said to be "donating" their genetic material.

Prospective Parents

Similar social forces regarding parenthood are often observed to be operating in ART and adoption contexts. For example, many ART patients are seeking treatment due to infertility or subfertility as are many persons seeking to adopt. Of these prospective parents, many undergoing ART treatments have also undertaken, or have considered undertaking, adoption procedures. In many cases persons concurrently pursue both adoption and ART, or cycle through periods of active ART treatments and active attempts at adopting. Also, some ART patients are those who may experience or perceive barriers to adoption, for example, because they are viewed to be less successful candidates for adoptive parenthood due to advanced age, health status, sexual orientation, or marital status.

Because of the similar motivation of infertility, parenthood through both ART and adoption are thought to often involve issues of loss and grief. However, unlike in the adoption context, prospective parents pursuing ART often have not been subject to assessments related to these psychological issues or other aspects of parental "fitness" as a precondition to, or component of, the ART process.

Children of ART

Children born as a result of ART are often thought to have similar needs as those adopted, such as the need to develop a coherent sense of identity, sometimes in the face of unknown or incomplete information about their genetic heritage. A difference in the two means of family formation is the fact that children born through ART, even in cases of donor gamete or surrogate use, are raised by the intentional parents from gestation or from birth. Less clear, then, about possible similarities between children born through ART and children adopted is whether or not this difference entails different issues regarding identity development, searching for genetic/gestational parents, and accessing birth records and other information.

One of the main differences in the ART and adoption contexts regarding children has been the policy and legal stance taken: adoption has been driven by the "best interests of the child" standard while ART has had no such child welfare mandate. One development, however, has blurred this distinction. During IVF procedures, there are often "excess" embryos created; that is, more eggs are successfully fertilized than can be safely or pragmatically used to try to initiate pregnancy in the intending mother. With better cyropreservation abilities, embryos that are not chosen by patients to be discarded can be stored for future pregnancy attempts by intended parents, used in research, or transferred to other patients undergoing infertility treatments. In this latter option, adoption language is increasingly being applied to the practice of transferring embryos from one patient or patient-couple to another. As of 2004, there was at least one fully operational agency specializing in "embryo adoption," with many of the same child welfare practices (e.g., home studies, post-placement services) as in traditional child adoption agencies.

"Birth" Parents

As already discussed, there is more complexity in the ART context than in the adoption context regarding the adult parties who are not the intended, or rearing, parents. In some cases, this adult may be genetically related to resulting offspring; in some surrogacy cases the woman may not be genetically related, although she is the gestating mother. The genetic parent may even be the deceased spouse of an intended parent as is the case in so-called posthumous reproduction. All of these cases have introduced legal challenges by adults related to children by birth, intention to rear, and genetics, analogous to cases between adoptive and birth family members in adoption.

Economic, Legal, Social, and Ethical Issues

As previously noted, one area of concern that overlaps both adoption and ART is that of the increasing "commodification" in family issues that have arisen in both contexts. Some have noted the increasing amounts of money involved in private adoptions of healthy white infants and in adoptions by Americans of children born in other countries. Similarly, some ART situations with donors and surrogates have involved various sums of money, and many of the medical procedures involve expensive fees. In both adoption and ART, this issue of money raises concerns about access to services and potential exploitation.

Very different legal and policy environments exist for ART and adoption in the United States. Adoption is regulated by state, national, and international laws as well as practice instituted by adoption agencies. Assisted reproduction in the United States began with very little or no legal and policy guidelines outside of those already existing in the medical fields in which these procedures occur. Over time, policy structures have emerged, most notably nation-wide reporting and data gathering efforts regarding such things as clinics' procedures performed and their "live baby" rates. All of these regulatory efforts still are broad and less structured than those found in other countries, such as Great Britain's Human Fertilisation and Embryology Authority.

Both ART and adoption have been discussed as variously challenging, broadening, or endangering social and cultural conceptions of such ideas as *family*, *relatedness*, and *parent*. Research and discussions in all of these areas have often involved questions about ethical issues related to both ART and adoption.

See also Embryo Adoption; Genetics and Adoption: Language and Ideology; Infertility and Adoption; Surrogacy and Adoption.

Further Reading

American Society for Reproductive Medicine (ASRM) Web Site. http://www.asrm.org/
Burns, Linda Hammer, and Sharon N. Covington. *Infertility Counseling: A Comprehensive Handbook for Clinicians*. New York: Parthenon, 1999.
Freundlich, Madelyn. *Adoption and Assisted Reproduction*. Washington, DC: Child Welfare League of America, 2001.
RESOLVE: The National Infertility Association Web Site. http://www.resolve.org/main/national/index.jsp?name=home
Shanley, Mary Lyndon. *Making Babies, Making Families: What Matters Most in an Age of Reproductive Technologies, Surrogacy, Adoption, and Same-Sex and Unwed Parents*. Boston: Beacon Press, 2001.
Shapiro, Vivan B., Janet R. Shapiro, and Isabel H. Paret. *Complex Adoption and Assisted Reproductive Technology: A Developmental Approach to Clinical Practice*. New York: Guilford Press, 2001.
Wright, V.C., L.A. Schieve, M.A. Reynolds, and G. Jeng. "Assisted Reproductive Technology Surveillance United States, 2000." In *Surveillance Summaries*, August 29, 2003, *Morbidity and Mortality Weekly Report*, 52 (No. SS-9).

Attachment and Bonding in Adoption

Tami W. Lorkovich

One of the most frequent concerns of prospective or new adoptive parents is whether an adopted child will attach or bond to them—or they to the child—as strongly as with a child who joined their family through birth. Additionally, adoption and mental health professionals frequently debate the effectiveness and legitimacy of treatments for children diagnosed with attachment disorders.

Attachment and bonding is the process by which caregivers and children create a lasting, reciprocal relationship that serves the basic human needs of safety and security. This process begins during pregnancy and continues throughout childhood. Attachment also refers to the physical, social, and psychological connection between a child and his or her caregivers. The strength and quality of an attachment is generally regarded as the basis for all future relationships, the foundation of a child's sense of identity, and the mode by which parents transfer core values and promote resilience in their children.

The concept of attachment was first introduced by British psychiatrist John Bowlby during the mid-twentieth century. Bowlby described the process by which infants form healthy attachments to their mothers. Bowlby's attachment cycle includes four basic stages: 1) the infant senses a need (hunger, wet diaper, too hot or cold, etc.); 2) the infant becomes aroused and expresses displeasure via crying or stirring; 3) the caregiver meets the need and offers comfort (eye contact, rocking, patting, feeding, changing a diaper, talking softly); and 4) the infant relaxes and feels relief. In healthy attachment relationships, this cycle is repeated continuously until the infant develops trust that his needs will be met and is able to wait longer periods of time to be gratified. Bowlby theorized that problematic attachment occurs when this cycle is disrupted. Subsequent research has included information about attachment patterns in children beyond infancy—but not much beyond early childhood.

Patterns of attachment are classified into four main categories: secure, anxious-resistant (ambivalent), anxious-avoidant, and disorganized/disoriented. Secure attachments are characterized by proximity seeking behavior (looking for and seeking the caregiver when absent or distant) and ability to be calmed by caregivers. Anxious-resistant attachment behaviors include proximity seeking behavior while simultaneously lacking the ability to be comforted when distressed. Anxious-avoidant attachments are characterized by displaying minimal affect or distress and avoiding interaction with caregivers in situations where securely attached children seek them out. The disorganized/disoriented pattern of attachment frequently results from maltreatment and blends contradictory and sometimes incoherent strategies for dealing with separation and getting their needs met.

In addition to classifying patterns that describe the strength and quality of attachment, researchers have also developed diagnostic criteria—included in the Diagnostic and Statistical Manual of Mental Disorders – Fourth Edition (DSM-IV)—for reactive attachment disorder (RAD). The DSM-IV breaks attachment disorder into two major types. While both types require a history of maltreatment and developmentally inappropriate social behavior beginning before age five, the inhibited type of attachment disorder is also characterized by ambivalent and inhibited responses to comforting and caregivers. The disinhibited type, by contrast, includes indiscriminate and over-familiar interactions with strangers which can make some children appear unusually charming or sociable and can place children at risk.

Although our knowledge about attachment issues has increased, more research needs to be conducted to develop more standardized diagnostic criteria and better understand biological or neurological contributions to attachment. Because attachment cannot be measured directly, researchers rely on widely varied behaviors, techniques, and caregiver reports to measure attachment security or diagnose attachment disorder.

Likewise, more formal scientific research could help identify the most effective treatments for attachment disorder or most promising activities to help strengthen attachment between adoptive parents and their children. Early treatments for attachment disorder like holding and rebirthing therapies have been highly modified or discredited—and in some extreme forms outlawed—to be less invasive and decrease the opportunity to re-traumatize children. Newer treatments include adaptations to cognitive and behavioral therapies and the use of play and group therapies.

In addition, therapists are beginning to use a family systems model of interaction to incorporate multiple attachment relationships instead of focusing only on the primary caregiver relationship. A leading proponent of this approach is Kirsten von Sydow who proposes five positions to complete her integrated model of attachment: 1) attachment is both intrapsychic and interpersonal instead of either a personality trait or an attribute of a relationship; 2) internal models and interpersonal relationships influence each other; 3) normative and competence orientation are used instead of deficit-based descriptions and definitions (i.e., careful attachment versus dismissing); 4) present and future relationships are the focus, instead of past relationships; and 5) losses and "inherited trauma," or unresolved losses and separations from the past, are treated sensitively by using genograms.

While adoptive parents frequently worry about attachment security or disorders in their children, the prevalence of severe RAD cases is extremely low even in adopted children who have higher rates of early maltreatment. In addition, growing evidence shows that most adopted children are highly resilient and can overcome early maltreatment and neglect if parents engage in attachment enhancing activities like limiting caregivers early in the adoption, playing games, reading while holding or sitting next to the child, and involving the child in chores or other activities. Finally, children who have been able to form significant attachments with other caregivers are generally able to transfer those relationship and attachment behaviors to new parents. More research in this arena could help support or clarify the methods that would be most effective for adopted children.

Further Reading

Ainsworth, M.D.S., M.C. Blehar, E. Waters, and S. Wall. *Patterns of Attachment*. Hillsdale, New Jersey: Erlbaum, 1978.

Atkinson, L., and K. J. Zucker, eds. *Attachment and Psychopathology*. New York: The Guilford Press, 1997.

Bowlby, John. *A Secure Base: Clinical Applications of Attachment Theory*. Routledge, London: A Tavistock Professional Book, 1988.

Von Sydow, Kirsten. "Systemic Attachment Theory and Therapeutic Practice: A Proposal." *Clinical Psychology and Psychotherapy*. 9 (2002), 77–90.

Biology of Attachment and Bonding

Vern L. Bullough

Attachment of the adopted child to its parents might be easier with newborns than with older children. This is because emotional deprivation early in life can permanently change people's brains. A study in 2005 by a group at the University of Wisconsin, Madison, led by Seth Pollak, found that children who suffered early neglect in orphanages or foster homes had deficiencies in hormones related to attachment.

Two hormones seem to be involved, oxytocin, the level of which increases with warm physical contact with a familiar person, and vasopressin, which plays a role in recognizing familiar people. The hormones are, however, hard to measure. Pollak and his colleagues devised a way to get measurements from urine, making it possible to test small children.

Eighteen tots who had spent an average of sixteen months in orphanages before adoption were compared with twenty-one children raised by their biological parents. Each child, over a two-week period, had a cuddly 30-minute play session with his or her mother and one with an unfamiliar woman. The researchers found that in the family-reared children, oxytocin levels increased after contact with the mother but not with the stranger. Oxytocin levels never went up in orphans, who also had lower baseline vasopressin levels. In commenting on the study, Thomas Insel, director of the National Institute of Mental Health in Bethesda, Maryland, said the report is consistent with not only animal evidence but also evidence that children with autism—who avoid social interactions—lack oxytocin responses. The research would seem to demonstrate that emotional deprivation early in life can permanently change people's brains. The question is how to overcome this.

Further Reading

"Attachment Chemistry," *Science*, 310 (December 2, 2005): 1421.

Australia and New Zealand: The Experience of Indigenous Populations

Dennis Miller

Australia

During the twentieth century, thousands of Aboriginal and mixed-race children were removed from their homes and institutionalized under the auspices of individual States. Rather than forced removal and adoption by private individuals, the predominant policy in Australia was removing children to compounds as foster wards of the States. Estimates of the number of children involved vary widely (ranging from thirty-five thousand to two hundred thousand in various reports) and have been the subject of debate between governments and those affected by the policy. They have been referred to as the "Stolen Generation."

By 1911, every state in mainland Australia had a functioning Protectorate that exercised control over the indigenous population, including the guardianship of children. By this time, indigenous people had been re-settled and concentrated on land that had been designated specifically for their use, facilitating control and the enforcement of governmental policies. Those policies included the anticipated assimilation of indigenous populations through the removal and acculturation of children. Of special interest were children of mixed Aboriginal and European descent.

Prevailing thought in the early twentieth century was that the Aboriginal population was in decline and would eventually disappear, while the number of children of mixed descent was increasing. Removing these half-caste children from the influence of Aboriginal culture and placing them in non-Indigenous foster care would integrate them into European society with the hope that their Aboriginal heritage would eventually be bred-out. The Protectors of both the Northern Territories and Western Australia were committed to this policy and its enforcement. At the first conference of Aboriginal affairs in Canberra in 1937, administrators took the initiative in promoting the policies of forced removal and assimilation. This was the first conference at which the issues of dealing with the Aboriginal problem had been discussed as a national issue.

A. O. Neville, Aboriginal Affairs Protector for Western Australia, believed that half-caste children must be removed from their homes by age six if they were to be effectively integrated into non-Indigenous society, as noted by author Robert Manne. He felt that he had the statutory power to remove them and place them under State-controlled foster care, and he did so. In Western Australia, children were separated from parents in relocation centers and sent to work within the mainstream population when they reached adolescence. Neville believed that this system would result in mixed-race adults marrying partners of European rather than Aboriginal descent. Children of these unions would have lighter skin color and would be accepted into non-indigenous society. As a result of the conference in 1937, the other States began adopting policies that included the assimilation, rather than the integration of indigenous populations. Government funding was provided to achieve those ends. When, as a consequence of increased removal of children, institutions reached capacity, children were placed with foster families of European descent in the hope that this would expedite their acculturation.

The intended goals of the policy of removal and assimilation were not realized. It became clear that reluctance by indigenous populations to abandon their Aboriginal heritage and lack of acceptance by mainstream society were responsible for the failure of the policy. In 1967, following a national referendum on the Commonwealth, the national government gained authority over indigenous populations with the establishment of the federal Office of Aboriginal Affairs. This was followed in 1972 by a policy of self-determination for indigenous people promoted by a new Labor government. Thus a legal mechanism was provided for indigenous people to challenge the administrative removal of their children.

During the 1980s, indigenous activists and their supporters demanded that the nature and consequences of Indigenous child placement policies be investigated. Of particular concern were the high number of indigenous children being placed in the homes of non-indigenous families. In 1981, the Secretariat of National Aboriginal and Islander Child Care was formed as a coordinating entity for Indigenous childcare services. In the 1990s, indigenous people and their supporters were demanding not only increased self-determination, but an inquiry into the public policies that had led to the policies of removal and assimilation.

In 1995, the national government initiated an inquiry into the separation of Indigenous children from their families. The findings of the inquiry were published in *Bringing Them Home: Report of the National Inquiry into the Separation of Aboriginal and Torres Strait Islander Children From Their Families.* As Antonia Buti notes, the report described and condemned the widespread racism and mistreatment of the indigenous population that resulted from social welfare efforts to deal with the "Aboriginal problem." The report made several recommendations, including compensation and rehabilitation. Following the publishing of the report, a "National Sorry Day" was held on May 26, 1999, and Prime Minister John Howard issued a statement of regret over the removal of Indigenous children from their parents.

The extent of the removal and relocation of indigenous children remains a source of friction between the indigenous community and some government officials at this writing. In 2000, the Minister for Aboriginal Affairs, John Herron, produced a report that was leaked to the public. The report claimed that there was no "stolen generation", since only 10 percent of indigenous families were affected. As noted by Sonny Inbaraj, indigenous activists vehemently disputed that figure, which they claim to be approximately 30 percent. Prime Minister Howard stood by the report while apologizing for any harm it might have caused. The issue of the removal and attempted assimilation of Indigenous children has received increased attention in the recent past as one component in the review and investigation of the treatment of Indigenous populations since the time of European settlement.

New Zealand

Unlike Australia, assimilation through removal of children in indigenous communities was not the policy in New Zealand. Maori society was organized on a tribal basis with extended family units. Children were considered to be the collective responsibility of that family, which took precedence over the parental rights as individuals. Adoption was informal and communal. When parents were not able to take care of children, or when families became too large, children were distributed among other family members. An adopted or foster child was referred to as *tamaiti whangai,* and the arrangement could be either of a temporary or permanent nature. The number of children in temporary or permanent custody could be as high as 20 percent in some areas.

New Zealand was the first Commonwealth country to formalize the adoption process by a statute in 1881. (England did not enact such a statute until 1926.) This statute allowed for a measure of self-determination by granting jurisdiction over adoption by a Maori to a Maori Land Court. This jurisdiction continued until the 1960s, when, as noted in the *Encyclopaedia of New Zealand*, oversight by a Magistrate became the standard in all of New Zealand.

As the Maori began moving away from their traditional tribal lands, the government became increasingly involved in the welfare of their children in need of adoption. This resulted in conflict between public social welfare policies and traditional Maori attitudes and customs. Maori social workers objected to the decreasing influence of the extended family in decisions made concerning Maori children in need of care. As noted by Terri Libesman, activists within the Maori social service community considered government policies to be racist. The result of this criticism led to passage of the Children, Young Persons and Their Families Act in 1989. This statute recognized the importance of the extended Maori family in determining the best situation for a child in need of assistance, and recommended that children be placed within their family unit when feasible. If placement within the family unit was not feasible, then "racial matching" in a home with the same tribal or ethnic background should be given first consideration. While the legal system in New Zealand has taken action to accommodate the self-determination desires of the Maori, some activists propose additional measures to insure that Maori culture and customs receive additional regulatory protection.

Further Reading

Buti, Antonia. *Bringing Them Home the ALSWA Way.* Paper presented at the 23rd Annual Australia and New Zealand Law and History Society Conference, Murdoch University, Western Australia (2–4th July, 2004). E LAW | Murdoch University Electronic Journal of Law Web Site. www.murdoch.edu.au/elaw/issues/v11n4/buti114text.html (accessed February, 2006).

Cameron, Bruce James. "Adoption." In McLintock, A. H., ed., *An Encyclopaedia of New Zealand 1966.* Te Ara The Encyclopedia of New Zealand Web Site. www.teara.govt.nz/1966/a/adoption/adoption/en (accessed February, 2006).

Human Rights and Equal Opportunity Commission 1997, *Bringing Them Home: Report of the National Inquiry into the Separation of Aboriginal and Torres Straight Islander Children From their Families.* Human Rights and Equal Opportunity Commission, Sydney. Reconciliation and Social Justice Library Web Site. http://www.austlii.edu.au/au/special/rsjproject/rsjlibrary/hreoc/stolen/ (accessed February, 2006).

Inbaraj, Sonny. "Natives Furious After Australia Denies 'Stolen Generation'". *Albion Monitor,* April 2000 as re-printed on Albert Eissing's Native Home Page Web Site. http://members.home.nl/aeissing/00766.html (accessed February, 2006).

Libesman, Terri. *Child Abuse Prevention Issues: Child Welfare Approaches for Indigenous Communities: International Perspectives,* Australian Institute of Family Studies, no. 20, Autumn 2004. Australian Institute of Family Studies Web Site. http://www.aifs.gov.au/nch/issues/issues20.pdf (accessed February, 2006).

Manne, Robert. "Stolen Generations." Reprinted from Peter Craven ed., *Australian Essays,* 1998. Tim-Richardson.net Web Site. http://www.tim-richardson.net/misc/stolen_generation.html (accessed February, 2006).

PBS, First Person Plural, Adoption History, Transracial Adoption. PBS/UNCTV Web Site. www.pbs.org/pov/pov2000/firstpersonplural/historical/transracial.html (accessed February 2006).

"Tamaiti Whangai" Adoption.com Web Site. http://famous.adoption.com/famous/tamaiti-whangai.html (accessed February, 2006).

B

Baby Farming

Priscilla Ferguson Clement

Baby farming was a method of caring for babies, developed in the late nineteenth century in several western countries, which might or might not involve adoption. The practice was eventually regulated out of existence by the 1920s. A more modern form of baby farming refers to women who donate their eggs (and potentially their babies for adoption) for in vitro fertilization.

Baby farming emerged in Great Britain and the United States in the mid to late nineteenth century when having sex outside of marriage and giving birth to an illegitimate baby were highly stigmatized. For poor women, abortion, which was very expensive and penalized by law after the 1860s in the United States, was not a possibility. The families of unwed pregnant women might very well turn them out. At a time when most women delivered their babies at home in the care of midwives, single mothers had to enter public almshouses or private lying-in hospitals. Once they had their babies, such women could obtain little welfare outside of public institutions. Private orphanages admitted few infants and routinely rejected illegitimate children, as did private day care agencies. Needy mothers had to obtain work—often as domestic servants in private homes where their babies were not welcomed.

Thus, a single mother with a baby desperately needed to provide for the child in some way so she herself could find work. Baby farmers were women who offered to provide childcare to the babies of single mothers. Typically, the baby farmer agreed to take an infant only after the mother had paid her a lump sum in advance for the child's care, although sometimes the baby farmer accepted smaller sums paid weekly. Often the baby farmer advertised that she would adopt infants herself or find others to adopt babies. However, it was probably understood by most mothers that baby farmers would dispose of infants for a price. Some mothers visited their infants at the baby farmer's home on a regular basis, but even these mothers often saw their children die in the care of such women.

Babies died frequently when under a baby farmer's care because such infants were denied the protective qualities of their mother's breast milk. (Sadly, mothers who left their illegitimate children with baby farmers often found employment as wet nurses to babies in the homes of well-off parents.) At a time when milk supplies were often contaminated, water was often bacteria laden, and baby bottles were not routinely disinfected, infants who were bottle fed quickly perished from bacterial infection, diarrhea, dehydration, and malnutrition. Not until the germ theory came to be understood in the late nineteenth century and cities began to clean up their water supplies and require milk to be pasteurized in the early twentieth century, did bottle-feeding become safer for infants.

As for adoption of babies from baby farmers, it was rare. In the nineteenth century, the most valued child was the one who was old enough to work. Youngsters who were adopted were typically old enough to labor for their adoptive families. Baby farmers, who did secure persons to adopt the infants in their care, typically charged a single mother a fee for taking on her baby and then charged the adopting family much less to take the infant.

In the 1870s and 1880s in Britain and the United States, middle-class reformers, who valued their own children so much that they kept them out of the labor force and in school through their youth, began to worry about the poor care afforded children in the lower classes. As children of all social classes came to be valued not so much for their labor but for their emotional value, baby farming came under sharp attack. Britain passed the Infant Protection Act in 1897. Cities in the United States passed similar laws beginning in the late 1870s and 1880s that required registration of births and licensing and inspecting of childcare facilities. By the 1920s, in both countries, baby farming had disappeared.

In the late twentieth century, the term "baby farming" has been used to refer to a different practice and is associated in a different way with adoption. This new type of baby farming came with a treatment for infertility called in vitro fertilization, which involves the harvesting of a woman's eggs, fertilization of them outside the womb, and then re-implantation of the fertilized egg in a woman's uterus. Some fertile women donate eggs, often for a fee, and these eggs are then fertilized and implanted in the uterus of another woman. The woman who donates her eggs is sometimes called a baby farmer, and the woman who receives the fertilized egg is in a sense adopting someone else's infant.

See also Nineteenth Century Changes in American Adoption.

Further Reading

Broder, Sherri. *Tramps, Unfit Mothers, and Neglected Children: Negotiating the Family in Nineteenth-Century Philadelphia.* Philadelphia: University of Pennsylvania Press, 2002.

Herman, Ellen. "Baby Farming." Department of History, University of Oregon Web Site. http://www.oregon.edu/~adoption/topics/babyfarming.html (accessed November, 2005).

Zelizer, Viviana A. *Pricing the Priceless Child: The Changing Social Value of Children.* New York: Basic Books, 1985.

Primary Document

Legislating Against Baby Trafficking

As a result of an extensive investigation into baby-farming conducted by the Maryland State-wide Vice Commission (See Appendix B), Maryland passed the 1916 legislation below to address the practice. Legislation in other states was also passed that saw an end to the practice by the early 1920s.

Laws of Maryland 1916 (Chapter 210)

AN ACT to add five new sections to Article 27 of the Code of Public General Laws, subtitle "Crimes and Punishments," to be known as Sections 484, 485, 486, 487 and 488, and to follow immediately after Section 483 thereof, making it unlawful to separate or cause to be separated any child under six months of age from its mother for the purpose of placing such child in a foster home or institution, or to place, receive or retain such child in a foster home or institution, and to regulate the manner and circumstances under which it may be done, and to provide a penalty for violation of said Act; the same to read as follows:

SECTION 1. *Be It Enacted by the General Assembly of Maryland*, That five new Sections be, and the same are, hereby added to Article 27 of the Code of Public General Laws, sub-title "Crimes and Punishments," to be known as Sections 484, 485, 486, 487 and 488, and to follow immediately after Section 483 thereof, and to read as follows:

SECTION 484. *Be It Enacted by the General Assembly of Maryland*, That it shall be unlawful to separate a child under the age of six months from its mother for the purpose of placing such child in a foster home or institution for the maintenance of such child, or to assist or participate in such separation, or to place, receive or retain any child in a foster home or institution for the maintenance of such child, or to assist or participate in so placing, receiving or retaining such child; unless it be necessary for the physical good of the mother or of such child that they be separated or that such child be placed, received or retained in a foster home or institution for the maintenance of such child, and two physicians, qualified to practice medicine in the State of Maryland, and who shall have been engaged in active practice for at least five years, shall have signed a certificate setting out the reasons for such necessity, or unless a Court of competent jurisdiction shall have so ordered, or unless within the discretion of the Board of State Aid and Charities such separation is necessary, and said Board gives its written consent thereto.

SECTION 485. It shall be the duty of every person separating, or assisting or participating in separating, any such child from its mother, and of every person placing, receiving or retaining or assisting in placing, receiving or retaining any such child in a foster home or institution for the maintenance of such child, before so doing, to investigate whether the mother of such child be living and whether two physicians have signed the certificate above provided for or whether a Court of competent jurisdiction, or the Board of State Aid and Charities, has ordered such separation and the placing of the child in such foster home or institution.

SECTION 486. It shall be the duty of the person who shall receive any such child in a foster home or institution for the maintenance of such child to file forthwith the certificate above provided for with the Board of State Aid and Charities, and the duty of every person who shall retain, or assist or participate in retaining, any such child in a foster home or institution for the maintenance of such child, to ascertain whether said certificate has been so filed, and, if there be no such certificate, then to notify said Board forthwith of the facts concerning the separation of said child from its mother and the reception and retention of such child in said foster home or institution.

SECTION 487. Whenever it shall come to the notice of said Board that any such child has been separated from its mother or has been placed in an institution for the maintenance of such child, said Board shall cause an investigation to be made, and if it appear to the Board that this Act has been violated it shall make known the facts to the authorities charged with the enforcement of the criminal laws to the end that proceedings may be started for the punishment of the person or persons who may have violated the Act.

SECTION 488. Every person who violates or fails to comply with any of the provisions of this Act, and every physician who knowingly makes a false certificate as above provided for, shall be guilty of a misdemeanor and upon conviction thereof may be fined not more than One hundred dollars ($100.00) or imprisoned in jail for not more than one hundred days, or both, in the discretion of the Court.

SECTION 2. *And be It Further Enacted*, That this Act shall take effect from the first day of June 1916.

Approved April 11th, 1916.

Source

As reprinted in Walker, George. *The Traffic in Babies: An Analysis of the Conditions Discovered During an Investigation Conducted in the Year* *1914*. Baltimore: Norman, Remington, 1918: pp. 155–156.

Baby-Selling

Karen Balcom

Charges of "baby-selling" and of "black markets in babies" recur in historical and contemporary accounts of domestic and international adoption. Viviana Zelizer has argued (from the history of adoption in the United States), that "selling" children for adoption is a troubling affront to the twentieth century vision of the sentimental, sacred and, literally, "priceless" child. To buy or sell a child, then, is a moral outrage which seems worthy of public condemnation and stiff legal penalties. But it is difficult to pin down precise moral or legal definitions of baby-selling in adoption, to determine when, except in the most egregious cases, paying (what level of?) fees for professional services in connection with an adoption or paying (what kind of?) expenses to a relinquishing parent or intermediary becomes buying a child. Exploring the history of baby-selling means confronting, as well, the pervasiveness of market metaphors to describe the "adoption transaction" and asking how adoption practices which do not involve a direct transfer of money might also contribute to the commodification of children.

The selling of children has a history as old as slavery. References to the "baby trade" invoke the slave trade to condemn baby-selling, although the child "sold" and adopted does not become legal chattel. Historians date surging American interest in adoption from the 1930s and especially the immediate postwar period, but Julie Berebitsky has documented a "shortage" of the children most desired by adopting parents—young, healthy, white, fully and finally separated from the birth family—as early as the 1910s. By the 1950s, the figure of ten waiting couples for every available white baby was quoted frequently. Both the public media and professional literature on adoption regularly discussed the rising "demand" for, and inadequate "supply" of, those children preferred for adoption. Crucially, discussions of "supply," "demand," and "shortage" were always about specific kinds of children; while there was a "shortage" of healthy, white infants there was a concurrent over-supply of older, non-white children and children with mental or physical disabilities. In a situation of scarcity (for white babies), a variety of adoption entrepreneurs appeared, some hoping to make a profit from adoptive parents in a "seller's market" for children that continues to this day.

For many parents at mid-century, the first stop in the search for a child was a reputable social agency. Through the mid-decades of the twentieth century, social workers were developing an expanded professional vision of "sound adoption practice" which included extensive investigation and supervision of potential adoptive parents. Parents who tried to adopt the limited number of children available through professional agencies faced detailed and intrusive investigations from social workers who probed their physical and mental health, their finances, their religious practices, and their motivation for adoption. Potential parents accepted by adoption agencies might then wait years before a child was offered to them. At times, the wait took them beyond the agency's upper age limit (often forty) for parents adopting infants. In many cases, adoption agencies simply stopped investigating new families because their waiting lists were too long.

Parents who were frustrated by the delays, who disliked the intrusion, who were turned down by accredited adoption agencies or feared they would be, looked for various kinds of independent placements, or placements arranged without the intervention of a licensed adoption agency. Independent placements could include everything from an adoptive family advertising in a newspaper for a child, to a mother finding a home for her own child, to the local doctor finding a home for a child he or she delivered, to the adoption lawyer placing the child of one client (the unwed mother) in the home of another (the adoptive parents) and then arranging for a court approved adoption, to various kinds of black market transactions. These activities could be overt or covert, and more or less exploitative of birth parents, adoptive parents and children. They could be perfectly legal or, depending on how the placement was engineered, how much money changed hands, and in what jurisdiction the adoption occurred, they could violate adoption and child placement laws.

Placements by (seemingly well-meaning) doctors, lawyers, ministers, and even adoption brokers were often referred to as gray market placements. This term connoted a separation from both the agency adoption overseen by a professional social worker and from the black market adoption arranged by a (seemingly nefarious) baby-seller. The terms "black market" and "gray market" helped to define each other, but in practice it could be very difficult to draw a line between the black and the gray. In 1955, in their "Special Report on Independent Adoptions," the United States Children's Bureau defined baby black marketers as "unauthorized middlemen who offer babies for a price unrelated to legitimate services rendered natural and adopting parents." But what was a "legitimate service" and what might one reasonably pay to cover the expenses of an expectant mother, to compensate an intermediary who located a child, or to secure legal representation? Other definitions of the black market refer to placements where considerations of price and profit take precedence over the welfare of children and parents. Practices that were sometimes described as typical of the black market and a signal of baby-selling activity driven by profit included warehousing unwed mothers awaiting the birth of their children, offering children for adoption before they were born, paying women to relinquish their children, lying to birth mothers about the fate of their children, charging adoptive parents large fees to secure children, securing an adoption court order through the use of bribery or submission of fraudulent documents, or bypassing the court order entirely by falsifying birth records to indicate that the "adopted child" was actually "born to" the "adopting" parents.

Baby-selling scandals and journalistic exposés of the black market exploited the public's concern for defenseless children, its sympathy for desperate adoptive parents, and its fascination with the cultural violation of selling children. In the 1940s and 1950s, a series of sensational black market prosecutions made headlines in newspapers and magazines across North America. Among the most notable cases were those of New York lawyers Irwin Slater (1949) and Marcus Siegl

(1950), the "Butterbox Babies" scandal at the Nova Scotia-based Ideal Maternity Home (1945–47), and the Tennessee Children's Home Adoption Scandal (1950). In 1954, police and prosecutors in New York and Montreal uncovered a set of trans-border black market baby rings which sold hundreds of infants born to unwed French-Canadian and Catholic mothers in Montreal to Jewish families in New York City for prices said to range from $2,500 to $10,000. The rings had their own maternity boarding houses (where children were born) and a series of "baby depots" (where children were housed while they awaited parents). Ring-employed "spotters" trolled the city for pregnant women. "Contacts" approached women in Montreal, "salesmen" sought out potential parents in New York, and "phony mothers" posed as birth mothers to secure fraudulent birth certificates and fraudulent consents to adoption. Lawyers helped parents secure the documents (false birth certificates and/or adoption court orders) which allowed parents to take their children back to the United States. In some cases, children were simply smuggled across the border by "couriers" who, it was alleged, had connections to organized crime.

The social work approach to adoption assumed that adoption was a complex legal and social institution, which could—in the absence of skilled professional supervision—be very risky. Parents who adopted a young child whose background and potential had not been thoroughly investigated risked attaching themselves to a child who might develop significant mental or physical problems or who would not "fit" their family. If the adoption itself was of questionable legality, parents opened themselves to blackmail, or to the heart-wrenching possibility that their child might be reclaimed by its birth family. Social workers feared for the safety and well-being of children placed in homes which had not been investigated, or which had been investigated and then rejected as unsuitable for an adoptive placement. As one U.S. Children's Bureau official noted in 1945 (see Morlock in the "Further Reading" section), "price, profit and service fees are only symptomatic of the real evil, thoughtless handing around of babies who have no families." In this analysis, the independent or gray market adoption was just as dangerous as the black market adoption. And, indeed, the Children's Bureau regarded the "public interest in 'baby black markets' ... [as] a golden opportunity for conducting a campaign to obtain legal safeguards against [all] loose adoption procedures." In 1954, the Children's Bureau launched a special project on "Black Market Adoptions" but soon changed the project to "Unprotected Adoptions" because they could not develop a working differentiation between the black market and the gray market, and because they understood the most serious problem to be not the selling of babies, but the absence of professional supervision in adoption.

Social workers argued that the best ways to stop the black market in babies was to provide more extensive social services to unwed mothers. But most unwed mothers knew that help from public agencies came at the cost of extensive investigation and public exposure of their pregnancy. In a time when out-of-wedlock pregnancy was highly censured, this was a high cost. Some women found exactly what they needed—living expenses, medical care, secrecy and an adoptive placement for their children—in various kinds of black and gray market operations. However, as Ricki Solinger has noted, the potent combination of the high demand for white babies, harsh social condemnation, and the need for material support during pregnancy and birth put poor white women, in particular, at risk for exploitation and abuse. The black market investigations of the 1950s revealed many instances where women were housed in terrible conditions, given inadequate medical care, lied to about the fate of their children and given no chance to reconsider relinquishing their children after they were born.

Social workers were sometimes blamed for "causing" the black market by placing unreasonable restrictions on adopting parents and introducing unnecessary delays in the process; hence, parents who only wanted to give their love to a child were "forced" into the black market. Social workers were conscious of this critique and tried to streamline their work, but also countered that their obligation was to find the best possible home for a child, not to provide a child for parents.

In 1955, only fifteen U.S. states (and one Canadian province) had criminal laws that specifically outlawed baby-selling. In 2005, all U.S. states, and most jurisdictions elsewhere in the world have anti-baby-selling statutes, but it has proved very difficult to draft and enforce laws which can separate baby-selling from "legitimate" fee charging in adoption. Some laws place upper limits on adoption-related fees and on the expenses which can be paid to expectant mothers, but there is often an option for a judge to approve higher fees or expenses, and the entire system depends on a full reporting of fees to the court. Few jurisdictions have been willing to shut down all independent placements by allowing only state-run or state-licensed agencies to place children. Those which place some restrictions on independent placements usually allow a mother to place a child herself, and this loophole opens the way for adoption entrepreneurs who effectively sell access to birth mothers but can claim that the mothers make the actual placements. Even the most reputable adoption agencies charge adoption service fees to adoptive parents, though they are likely to be lower than those charged in independent adoptions and less likely to include the payment of expenses to birth mothers.

Differences in adoption laws and practices between jurisdictions make the situation more complex. From the 1940s, reformers recognized that most baby-selling operations were intrastate or international. Moving parents and babies between units of governmental jurisdiction was an effective way to avoid state oversight or evade existing regulations; what was illegal or difficult to accomplish in one state, province or country might be accomplished quickly and without question elsewhere. From the late 1940s, there were numerous unsuccessful attempts to pass a federal anti-baby-selling law drawing on the federal power to regulate intrastate commerce, but there was, and continues to be, strong resistance to impinging on state level jurisdiction in child welfare. The 1960 Interstate Compact on the Placement of Children (ICPC–to which all U.S. states are now signatories) established protocols for the movement of children for adoption between states, but the compact depends for its force on the content of state laws. Adoption lawyers and facilitators continue to exploit the differences between state laws by moving birth mothers to states which allow higher fees and expense payments and scheduling court hearings in states with the least stringent adoption laws. The increasing use of the Internet makes the border crossing the more complex and difficult to trace.

In a 1975 Senate hearing, the Executive Director of the Child Welfare League of America estimated that four to five thousand adoptions per year in the United States, or 2 percent of all adoptions and 25–30 percent of all non-agency, non-relative adoptions, might be classified as black market. The same hearings collected testimony of babies "sold" for $10,000–$25,000. In 2001, the *New York Times* reported parents paying adoption fees and expenses ranging up to $100,000 for the closed domestic adoption of a white infant. In both agency and independent adoptions inside the United States, there is a distinct fee or price ladder based on race and ability which helps set the cost of an adoption. The highest rates are paid for independently adopted white children, with lesser service fees and expenses in the case of non-white children, or children with disabilities (for whom agency fees might be waived). Many countries continue to host both a domestic and an international "market in babies" that is determined by local context but in which there is potential exploitation of parents and children.

International adoptions have become increasingly popular with U.S. parents looking for a way around the scarcity of (desired) children and the increasing costs, delays and bureaucratic intrusions associated with domestic adoption, though the costs for an international adoption can also be considerable. Many international adoptions are carefully managed by professional social agencies in both countries and are far removed from baby-selling, but examples of corruption and black market practices in international adoptions attract great media attention. This is, in part, because most children adopted internationally end up in the western industrialized world (especially the United States) and exposés of corrupt practices in international adoption feed an overall critique of international adoption as a colonialist transfer of children from poor nations to wealthy nations.

In the 1990s, evidence of corruption in international adoptions in Guatemala—including paying women to relinquish children and stealing children from their families—lead to violence against foreign visitors (assumed to be adopters) in Guatemala. In response, several nations prohibited their nationals from adopting in Guatemala. Rampant baby-selling and bribery in international adoptions from Romania in the 1990s led the Romanian government—in part at the behest of the European Union—to declare a moratorium on international adoptions in 2001. Also in 2001, the U.S. Bureau of Citizenship and Immigration took the unprecedented step of refusing entry visas to children adopted by U.S. citizens in Cambodia, pending an investigation of irregularities in international adoptions; individual visa applications from Vietnam were also refused or suspended. In each case, these suspensions and moratoriums left families with children they had already adopted but were unable to bring home. The 1993 Hague Convention on Protection of Children and Co-operation in respect of Intercountry Adoption is designed to establish standard minimum procedures and prevent international trafficking in children. Under the convention, all international adoptions are to be monitored through a central agency in the sending and receiving country. It is too early to determine how effective the treaty will be. The United States ratified the treaty in 2000, but has yet (as of 2005) to establish implementation mechanisms.

It is important to recognize the coexistence of both venal and humanitarian motivations in instances of baby-selling and baby-buying. If we could agree on a firm definition of baby-selling, few of the people involved would think of themselves (or admit to) buying or selling a baby. Most people are motivated by the best intentions when they adopt a child; they want to give love and they want to provide the best possible environment for a child. The legal and moral questions surrounding baby-selling are complex and not easily resolved. And these questions are likely to become still more complicated with the spread of new reproductive technologies that challenge definitions of parenthood and custody. Recently, some commentators have argued that surrogacy contracts with large fees—which are enacted as relinquishment and adoption of the child borne by the surrogate—constitute the new frontier of child-buying.

See also Hague Convention on Protection of Children and Cooperation in Respect of Inter-country Adoption; Interstate Compact on the Placement of Children (ICPC); State Adoption Laws: Overview of Contemporary Challenges.

Further Reading

Berebitsky, Julie. *Like Our Very Own: Adoption and the Changing Culture of Motherhood.* Lawrence, KS: University of Kansas Press, 2001.

Lewin, Tamara. "At Core of Adoption Dispute is Crazy Quilt of State Laws." *New York Times*, January 19, 2001, 14.

Morlock, Maud. "Babies on the Market." *Survey Mid-Monthly* LXXXI, no. 3 (March 1945): 67–69.

Solinger, Rickie. *Wake Up Little Suzy: Single Pregnancy and Race Before Roe v. Wade.* New York: Routledge, 1992.

United States Congress. Subcommittee on Children and Youth of the Committee on Labor and Public Welfare of the United States Senate. *Adoption and Foster Care, 1975.* Washington, DC: Government Printing Office, 1975.

United States National Archives. United States Children's Bureau of Records, RG102, Series 3B, 1953–57, Box 674, 7-3-1-3 (January 1953–April 1955), "Special Project on Independent Adoptions," April 1, 1955.

Zelizer, Viviana. *Pricing the Priceless Child: The Changing Social Value of Children.* New York: Basic Books, 1981.

Ballot Initiative 58

Kathy Shepherd Stolley

Measure 58, "The Adoptee Rights Initiative," is a law passed by voter referendum in Oregon in 1998 that allows adult adoptees (age twenty-one and over) to access their birth certificates. Amended by HB 3194, passed by the Oregon Legislature in 1999, allowing birth parents to file "contact preference" statements, and delayed by subsequent court challenges, the law went into effect on May 30, 2000, at 5:00 p.m. As of the end of 2005, only a handful of states provided similar access to adopted persons' birth records.

Allowing access to adoption records to members of the adoption triad (birth parents, adoptive parents, and adopted persons) has a long history in the United States. The 1917 Minnesota Children's Code marked the first time birth records were sealed. However, this law clearly intended that only the public be kept from viewing records that might reveal potentially scandalous details of illegitimacy, not that members of the adoption triad be denied access. Indeed, through the 1940s, the members of the adoption triad were generally not restricted from accessing records, with social workers often assisting adopted adults and birth parents by providing information.

The 1950s, however, saw a change in this practice as a result of a complicated convergence of on-going concerns about divulging illegitimacy, the changing postwar demographics of relinquishing birth mothers, and an emphasis in the social work field on psychoanalytic theories that saw unwed mothers as emotionally disturbed. A 1957 Oregon law sealed birth records in that state; by 1979, they were also sealed by almost every other state. Alaska and Kansas remained the only exceptions.

To re-open these records, Measure 58 was the result of grassroots activism by the radical adoption reform group Bastard Nation. Bastard Nation's drive to support the measure was led largely by Helen Hill and Shea Grimm. They fashioned an initiative (originally identified as Initiative 46) around the idea that access to original birth certificates was a matter of civil rights for adult adoptees. Inexperienced in the intricacies of the political system, and thus underestimated by the opposition, they managed to develop a campaign allowing them to get more than the seventy thousand required signatures to qualify the initiative (an effort for which experienced petition manager Donna Harris was hired). Hill, herself, contributed significant financial support to the effort. The debate over Measure 58 received national media attention and attracted opposition from some other groups including the National Council for Adoption. Voters, however, supported it by a solid margin.

Days before the measure was to take effect, attorney Franklin Hunsaker filed a lawsuit representing several birth mothers. They claimed that the measure was unconstitutional because it violated promised privacy and confidentiality, as well as the Fourteenth Amendment's equal protection. A court injunction delayed enacting the measure until a court could hear the case. Although the court challenge was ultimately dismissed by Marion County Circuit Judge Paul Lipscomb, Hunsaker's subsequent appeal to the Oregon Court of Appeals further delayed implementation of the measure. The Court of Appeals also upheld the constitutionality of the measure and the Oregon Supreme Court denied further review of the case. An emergency request filed by Hunsaker with the U.S. Supreme Court was rejected.

Measure 58 went into effect amidst extensive national media attention. Within a day, the Oregon Health Division's Center for Health Statistics had received well over two thousand requests from adult adoptees for their original birth certificates. Within six months, almost five thousand such applications had been filed. The five year anniversary report of the measure indicates that over eight thousand four hundred records had been ordered by May 31, 2005. A lengthy and detailed account of the initiative, from which this summary is largely drawn, is provided by E. Wayne Carp in *Adoption Politics: Bastard Nation and Ballot Initiative 58*.

See also Adoption Search Movement; Bastard Nation: The Adoption Rights Organization.

Further Reading

Carp, E. Wayne. *Adoption Politics: Bastard Nation and Ballot Initiative 58*. Lawrence, KS: University Press of Kansas, 2004.
"Measure 58 Update Significant Dates and Events." Oregon Department of Human Services, Center for Health Statistics Web Site. http://www.oregon.gov/DHS/ph/chs/58update.shtml

Primary Document

House Bill 3194

The text of HB 3194 follows.

_____

Chapter 604

An Act   HB 3194

Relating to adoption rights; amending chapter 2, Oregon Laws 1999.

Be It Enacted by the People of the State of Oregon:

SECTION I. Chapter 2. Oregon Laws 1999 (Ballot Measure 58, 1998), amended to read:

(1) Upon receipt of a written application to the state registrar, any adopted person 21 years of age and older born in the state of Oregon shall be issued a certified copy of his/her unaltered, original and unamended certificate of birth in the custody of the state registrar, with procedures, filing fees, and waiting periods identical to those imposed upon nonadopted citizens of the State of Oregon pursuant to ORS [432.120] 432.121 and 432.146. Contains no exceptions.

(2) A birth parent may at any time request from the State Registrar of the Center for Health Statistics or from a voluntary adoption registry a Contact Preference Form that shall accompany a birth certificate issued under subsection (1) of this section. The Contact Preference Form shall provide the following information to be completed at the option of the birth parent:

a. I would like to be contacted;
b. I would prefer to be contacted only through an intermediary; or
c. I prefer not to be contacted at this time. If I decide later that I would like to be contacted, I will register with the voluntary adoption registry. I have completed an updated medical history and have filed it with the voluntary adoption registry. Attached is a certificate from the voluntary adoption registry verifying receipt of the updated medical history.

(3) The certificate from the voluntary adoption registry verifying receipt of an updated medical history under subsection (2) of this section shall be in a form prescribed by the State Office for Services to Children and Families and shall be supplied upon request of the birth parent by the voluntary adoption registry.

(4) When the State Registrar of the Center for Health Statistics receives a completed Contact Preference Form from a birth parent, the state registrar shall match the Contact Preference Form with the adopted person's sealed file. The Contact Preference Form shall be placed in the adopted person's sealed file when a match is made.

(5) A completed Contact Preference Form shall be confidential and shall be placed in a secure file until a match with the adopted person's sealed file is made and the Contact Preference Form is placed in the adopted person's file.

(6) Only those persons who are authorized to process applications made under subsection (1) of this section may process Contact Preference Forms.

Approved by the Governor July 12, 1999

Filed in the Office of Secretary of State July 12, 1999

Source

As reprinted in E. Wayne Carp. *Adoption Politics: Bastard Nation and Ballot Initiative 58.* Lawrence, KS: University Press of Kansas, 2004, pp. 171–172.

Bastard Nation: The Adoptee Rights Organization

E. Wayne Carp

Bastard Nation (BN) took its name from one of its founders who signed her e-mail, "Marley Elizabeth Greiner, Citizen, Bastard Nation." The e-mail had appeared in the spring of 1996 on the Internet Usenet newsgroup, alt.adoption, the largest adoption-related discussion group on the Web, with thousands of subscribers. Greiner, an Ohio adoptee with a master's degree in history from The Ohio State University, believed that adoptees had been bastardized by society and that the adoption system refused to recognize their full humanity and citizenship because of their "illegitimacy." Members of BN decided to reclaim the stigmatized concept of "bastardy" by naming their organization after it, denouncing the secrecy surrounding adoption, and proclaiming that they saw nothing shameful in being born out of wedlock. Greiner was quickly joined by three co-founders: Damsel Plum, Shea Grimm, and Lainie Petersen.

Bastard Nation self-consciously differentiated itself from mainstream adoption groups by its style, radicalism, and refusal to compromise. The organization's leaders and membership were technologically savvy, well ahead of other adoption reform groups. They were, on average, younger than other adoption movement groups and shared a dark sense of a humor, which extended even to issues concerning adoption, a topic about which mainstream activist groups found nothing humorous. Bastard Nation also held more radical goals than the more established adoption reform groups. Members of BN were frustrated with the inefficiency of state legislation, such as mutual consent registries or intermediary systems that did not give adopted adults unconditional access to their adoption records. Bastard Nation's primary goal was to open all adoption records to an adopted adult.

In pursuit of this objective, BN launched a grassroots ballot initiative in Oregon in 1997 to restore the legal right of adopted adults to request and receive their original birth certificate. The idea for the initiative originated with adopted adult Helen Hill, who, with the aid of Shea Grimm, successfully ran the November 1998 electoral campaign for Measure 58: "The Adoptee Rights Initiative." However, the opposition challenged the constitutionality of Measure 58 on the grounds that it violated the right to privacy, equal protection of the law, due process, and freedom of religion. Measure 58 was victorious in the Oregon Courts. On May 30, 2000, the U.S. Supreme Court denied the opposition's emergency request for a stay of judgment of the Oregon Court of Appeals and Measure 58 finally became law.

In addition, BN has strongly lobbied against Safe Haven laws, the statutes enacted by state legislatures to prevent the abandonment of babies and neonaticide. Safe Haven laws permit a parent to anonymously drop off an "unwanted infant" at a Safe Haven center such as a hospital emergency room, fire station, or police station. Bastard Nation argues that these laws, although well intentioned, are unnecessary and inefficient, and deny the right of identity to infants who are abandoned "legally" by stripping them of all genetic, medical, and social history.

Bastard Nation holds one national conference each year. It offers members a quarterly newsletter, *The Bastard Quarterly*. Recently, BN changed its name to: Bastard Nation: The Adoptee Rights Organization.

See also Adoption Search Movement; Ballot Initiative 58; Safe Haven Laws.

Further Reading

Carp, E. Wayne. *Adoption Politics: Bastard Nation and Ballot Initiative 58.* Lawrence: University Press of Kansas, 2004.

Holub, Cynthia Bertrand, ed. "The Basic Bastard." Bastard Nation: The Adoptee Rights Organization Web Site. http://bastards.org/bb/ (accessed December, 2004).

"Binding-Out" Children

Kathy Shepherd Stolley

Before the advent of the orphanage, the practice of "binding-out" was commonly used for children who were poor, illegitimate, abandoned, orphaned, or otherwise in need of care. The practice involved both voluntary and involuntary binding or indenturing children, or apprenticing them, as soon as they were able to work, often at six or seven years of age. They were trained in various trades, husbandry, and domestic services. For poor families, this was a way to reduce child care costs and see that their children learned a skill. Providing children with a skill served a further function of helping to integrate them as productive members of the community. Thus, the practice of binding-out not only reduced the economic burden on some families and provided for children in need, but also eliminated any state burden of costs of their care—a central objective from the state's perspective.

Early binding-out laws in the United States were derived from Elizabethan poor laws intended to address vagrancy. In England, authorities sometimes removed children from poor families, placing them with families better able to provide for their support. Carp (1998: 6) reports that Henry VIII's Parliament even went so far as to pass an act ordering the arrest and apprenticeship of all vagrant children ages 5 to 14.

Putting this system in a historical and social context, Bremner (1970: 64) notes that the binding-out system was "well suited to the needs of a pioneer society in which life was hard and precarious, labor was scarce, and where even small children were expected and required to make themselves useful." He observes that binding-out was also "a means of social control. It was a way of finding foster homes for orphans and illegitimate children; and it was used by magistrates to secure new family situations for children of parents who were deemed incompetent..." This system meant that many children grew up in families other than those of their biological parents or relatives.

Although only a handful of orphanages existed in the U.S. in the early 1800s, the numbers of such institutions increased rapidly. Changing social conditions of urban poverty, illness, and the abuse and inadequacy of existing facilities such as almshouses spurred their establishment. In the first half of the century, these institutions also used indenture and apprenticeship as a means of providing for the welfare of children; placement for adoption was far more infrequent. Adoption became more widely practiced only as the managers of these institutions used it as a means of responding to problems they found with indenture.

Further Reading

Bremner, Robert H., ed. *Children and Youth in America: A Documentary History. Volume I: 1600–1865.* Cambridge, MA: Harvard University Press, 1970, pp. 64–71.

Carp, E. Wayne. *Family Matters: Secrecy and Disclosure in the History of Adoption.* Cambridge, MA: Harvard University Press, 1998.

Carp, E. Wayne, ed. "Introduction." In *Family Matters: Secrecy and Disclosure in the History of Adoption.* Cambridge, MA: Harvard University Press, 1998.

Porter, Susan L. "A Good Home." In E. Wayne Carp, ed., *Adoption in America: Historical Perspectives.* Ann Arbor: University of Michigan Press, 2002, pp. 27–50.

Primary Document

"Binding-Out" Statutes

The following statutes from Virginia address the binding out of children, emphasizing the practical aspects of the practice, rather than the emphasis on child welfare, which would not arise for some time.

The Workhouse at James City, 1646[*]

Whereas sundry laws and statutes by Act of Parliament established have, with great wisdom ordained, for the better educating of youth in honest and profitable trades and manufactures, as also to avoid sloth and idleness wherewith such young children are easily corrupted, as also for relief of such parents whose poverty extends not to give them breeding; that the justices of the peace should, at their discretion, bind out children to tradesmen or husbandmen to be brought up in some good and lawful calling. And whereas God Almighty, among many his other blessings, hath vouchsafed increase of children to this colony, who now are multiplied to a considerable number, who if instructed in good and lawful trades may much improve the honor and reputation of the country and no less their own good and their parents' comfort, but, forasmuch as for the most part the parents, either through fond indulgence or perverse obstinacy, are most averse and unwilling to part with their children: *Be it therefore enacted by authority of this Grand Assembly,* according to the aforesaid laudable custom in the kingdom of England, that the commissioners of the several counties respectively do, at their discretion, make choice of two children in each county of the age of eight or seven years at the least, either male or female, which are to be sent up to James City between this and June next to be employed in the public flax houses under such master and mistress as shall be there appointed, in carding, knitting, and spinning, etc. And that the said children be furnished from the said county with six barrels of corn, two coverlets or one rug and one blanket, one bed, one wooden bowl or tray, two pewter spoons, a sow shoat of six months old, two laying hens, with convenient apparel both linen and woollen, with hose and shoes. And for the better provision of housing for the said children, it is *enacted*, that there be two houses built by the first of April next of forty foot long apiece, with good and substantial timber, the houses to be twenty foot broad apiece, eight foot high in the pitch, and a stack of brick chimneys standing in

---

[*]Va. Statutes at Large, I (New York, 1823), 336–337 as reprinted in Bremner, pp. 65–66.

the midst of each house, and that they be lofted with sawn boards and made with convenient partitions. And it is further thought fit that the commissioners have caution not to take up any children but from such parents who by reason of their poverty are disabled to maintain and educate them. *Be it likewise agreed* that the Governor hath agreed with the Assembly for the sum of 10,000 lbs. of tobacco to be paid him the next crop, to build and finish the said houses in manner and form expressed.

"An act empowering county courts to build work houses," 1668[**]

Whereas the prudence of all states ought as much as in them lies endeavor the propagation and increase of all manufactures conducing to the necessities of their subsistence, and God having blessed this country with a soil capable of producing most things necessary for the use of man if industriously improved, *It is enacted by this Grand Assembly and the authority thereof* that for the better converting wool, flax, hemp, and other commodities into manufactures, and for the increase of artificers in the country, that the commissioners of each county court, with the assistance of the respective vestries of the parishes in their counties, shall be and hereby are empowered to build houses for the educating and instructing poor children in the knowledge of spinning, weaving, and other useful occupations and trades, and power granted to take poor children from indigent parents to place them to work in those houses.

"An act for suppressing of vagabonds and disposing of poor children to trades," 1672[***]

Whereas several wholesome laws and statutes have by the wisdom of several parliaments of England been made and are in force as well for the suppression of vagrants and idle persons as setting the poor on work, the neglect of which laws amongst us hath encouraged and much increased the number of vagabonds idle and disolute persons, Be it enacted, and it is hereby enacted and ordained by the governor, council and burgesses of this grand assembly, and the authority thereof, that the justices of peace in every county do put the laws of England against vagrant, idle and disolute persons in strict execution, and the respective county courts shall, and hereby are empowered and authorized to place out all children, whose parents are not able to bring them up apprentices to tradesmen, the males till one and twenty years of age, and the females to other necessary employments, till eighteen years of age, and no longer, and the churchwardens of every parish shall be strictly enjoined by the courts to give them an account annually at their orphans' court of all such children within their parish as they judge to be within the said capacity.

Source

Bremner, Robert H., ed. *Children and Youth in America: A Documentary History. Volume I:* 1600–1865. Cambridge, MA: Harvard University Press, 1970.

[**]Va. Statutes at Large, II, 266–267 as reprinted in Bremner, p. 66.
[***]Va. Statutes at Large, II, 298 as reprinted in Bremner, p. 66.

Primary Document

The Demise of Apprenticeship, Identure, and Binding-Out

A 1925 Children's Bureau publication noted that "In the latter part of the [1800s,] when the movement to take children out of the almshouses was in full swing, a tendency away from the harsh indenture laws was also evident. Objection is often raised to child placing, even when it has been carefully guarded by original investigation and subsequent oversight, because of the popular prejudice aroused long ago by the "little slaveys" of the old indenture system." (See Peck, Emelyn Foster. *Adoption Laws in the United States. A Summary of the Development of Adoption Legislation and Significant Features of Adoption Statutes*, with the Text of Selected Laws. Department of Labor, Children's Bureau. Washington, DC: Government printing Office, p. 3).

The following excerpts from an earlier publication on child saving, dated 1893, record various accounts of this changing practice.

From a report on child-saving in New York state:*

It is customary for the superintendents of the poor, in placing children in families, to indenture them. Owing to the frequent changes of officials, the duty of looking after them till maturity is theoretical rather than practical. Formerly the custom of indenturing[a] was more prevalent in placing out children than at present. It is now growing into disuse, it having been found that, where there was dissatisfaction existing on the part of the foster-parent or the child, it was better to change than to insist upon a relation which was irksome to both. The greater proportion of children leaving the asylums are returned to parents.

In 1873 a law, the principle of which was taken from the French statutes, was passed for the adoption of children, which is growing more and more into favor, and has been attended with very satisfactory results ... (p. 184).

From a report regarding Girard College of Philadelphia, Pennsylvania:**

With regard to binding children out, the president of the college, A.H. Fetterolf, LL.D., says: "Our experience with farmers has not been satisfactory. They are not considerate for the child's welfare, caring only to use him for their profit. We send our boys out between the ages of fourteen and eighteen...While I have no statistics on hand, judging from what I see of our graduates, I am inclined to think that they do better in life than the same number of boys picked from the public schools. If you give children industrial training as well as a good English education, you will undoubtedly do better by them by keeping them until they are able to earn their own living. This is what a judicious parent would do; and why not those who stand in a parent's stead?"

---

[a]The power of apprenticing or indenturing was conferred upon overseers of the parish in 1730. When the parish system was superseded by the town system, the town overseers of the poor were given the same power; and a like power was conferred upon county superintendents of the poor in the establishment of the county system.

The number leaving the college annually is about one hundred and fifty. Those who are bound out are looked after by an officer from the college, to see that they are well cared for. If not well treated, the child is taken back to the college.

. . .

The practice of binding-out boys has almost ceased. Only seventeen boys have been bound out in the last six years; though for many years, in the early history of the college, large numbers were so placed out in families. But it was found that after a boy had received his education, and had passed through the school of manual training, – a five years' course, – he could take better care of himself that the average family would give him. . .The average age of the boys on leaving the college is sixteen years, though many remain until eighteen years old (pp. 73–74).

. . .

From a report regarding the State Public School at Coldwater, Michigan:***

. . .

When a child is placed in a home, an indenture agreement is entered into by the Board of Control, represented by the superintendent or State agent of the school and the parties taking the child. The contract secures to the child kind and proper treatment in health and sickness as a member of the family, a term in school each year, and the payment of a small sum of money at the expiration of the indenture contract. After a term of trial this indenture contract becomes operative. A clause is always inserted providing for the return of the child on request, in case its interests should require such action. The board may consent to the adoption of children. This is desirable in many cases, and is encouraged when the relations between the family and child are shown to be mutually cordial, after they have lived together long enough to become well acquainted with each other (pp. 212–213).

. . .

Source

Excerpted From:

*Letchworth, William Pryor. "The History of Child-saving Work in the State of New York." Pages 154–203; ** Alden, Lyman P., "Non-sectarian Endowed Child-saving Institutions." Pages 68–88; *** Merrill, G.A., "State Public Schools for Dependent and neglected Children." Pages 204–232; In *History of Child Saving in the United States*. National Conference of Charities and Correction. Report of the Committee on the History of Child Saving Work to the Twentieth Conference, Chicago, June, 1893. Reprinted as Publication No. 111: Patterson Smith Reprint Series in Criminology, Law Enforcement, and Social Problems. Montclair, NJ: Patterson Smith, 1971.

Birth Fathers

Kevin M. Green

The term "birth father" has become commonly associated with the alleged natural, biological, reputed, or putative father of a child placed for adoption. The husband of a woman who makes an adoption plan is legally considered the presumed father, although he may not have any biological ties to the child. The impact of the decision making process around adoption can affect both a presumed and an alleged father.

Parental Rights and Responsibilities in the Adoption Process

Birth fathers, historically, have had very little involvement in the adoption process as noted by Eva Deykin, Patricia Patti, and Jon Ryan. Also, as Paul Sachdev adds, very little research exists concerning their legal rights or their role in the adoption plan. Adoption professionals and laws have focused primarily on the birth mother. Not until 1972, with the landmark case *Stanley v. Illinois*, did unwed fathers have legal claim on their child. Prior to this time, most states did not afford a single father parental rights in the adoption of his child. In 1973, as Harry D. Krause discusses, the Uniform Parentage Act was developed to ensure that a child had full equity in his or her legal relationship with both parents, regardless of the parents' marital status. Deykin and colleagues note that it also prompted adoption agencies to implement procedures that would assist in identifying birth fathers and in seeking birth fathers' involvement in the planning and care of their child.

As Eleanor W. Willemsen and colleagues explain, the mere existence of a biological relationship with a child does not automatically grant the birth father legal protection. In *Quilloin v. Wallcott*, the Supreme Court held that the father must act like a father and should take responsibility for the child in order for constitutional protection to be granted. The court has also maintained in *Caban v. Mohammed* that a father must establish more than a biological connection with the child in order for the unwed father to have a protected relationship with his child. In other words, a father must also demonstrate a full commitment to parenthood by coming forward immediately after the child's birth to help financially, emotionally, and otherwise, in the rearing of the child. However, many putative fathers are unable to come forward if they do not know of the birth of the child.

In the 1990s, two highly publicized adoption cases in the United States in which the birth mother failed to inform the birth father of the birth of the child have become known as "Baby Jessica" and "Baby Richard." In the Baby Jessica case, the mother had lied about the father's identity, and in the Baby Richard case, the father had been told that the child died shortly after birth. In both cases, upon learning the truth, the fathers came forward to assert their parental rights.

These legal cases, including the cases of Baby Jessica and Baby Richard, have prompted the development of putative father registries in many states. As of 2002, thirty-one states had legislation regarding the establishment of putative father registries. Putative father registries, as discussed by Denise Skinner and Julie K. Kohler, require that a man register with the state as a potential father to a particular child in order to receive notification from the court regarding any court action for the adoption of his child. By choosing to register, the putative father admits his paternity of the child and assumes financial responsibility of the child. Registering with the system also makes it impossible for fathers to evade their responsibility to provide child support for their children because their names and addresses are included in the registry. By choosing not to register, a putative father takes the risk of losing his ability to assert his rights in a hearing regarding the adoption of his child because it may relieve the state of the responsibility of notifying him, or make it more difficult for the state to locate him and provide him notice.

The putative father registries, although intended to help alleviate future contested adoptions, continue to remain controversial. Many putative fathers are unaware of their existence and some state statutes around putative fathers have been deemed unconstitutional. These conditions do not encourage putative fathers to become more involved in their child's life.

Additionally, the attitudes of adoption agencies towards birth fathers also do not motivate them to become more involved in the adoption process. As the trend for openness in adoption continues to grow, potential opportunities for contact between birth fathers and adoptees are becoming more likely. As Tai Mendenhall and colleagues report, many adolescent adoptees have indicated a desire for contact with their birth parents, including their birth father. Another potential advantage in registering with the state's putative father registry is the potential for contact once the child has reached the age of majority, given the fact that identifying information is part of the registration process.

One of the ways in which fathers can initiate responsibility in their child's life is by establishing a relationship early on and, as noted by Paul Sachdev, some have argued that agencies have not done an adequate job in including birth fathers in the adoption plans. Agencies can play a vital role in facilitating this process by encouraging birth mothers to consider permitting the birth father to participate in the decision-making process. The limited existing research on birth fathers has shown, as discussed by Kathy Zamostny and colleagues, that factors such as pressure from their families, poor relationship with the child's mother, financial issues, and the attitudes of the adoption agency all significantly affect the degree to which a birth father will be involved in the adoptive process.

Increased interest in adoption research and specifically birth fathers, along with current state statutes and legislation, as well as the growing number of advocacy groups, all work to ensure that birth fathers are given a fair treatment when it comes to making an adoption plan. Birth fathers have an opportunity to assert their parental rights, but must recognize those rights in a timely fashion and must establish their role in the adoption process. Providing them with appropriate resources, both legal and social, will enable them to face those responsibilities in a manner that benefits not only the child and mother, but also the adoptive parents and other members of the adoption process.

See also Custody Wars; State Adoption Laws: Overview of Contemporary Challenges.

Further Reading

Aizpuru, R. "Protecting the Unwed Fathers' Opportunity to Parent: A Survey of Paternity Registry Statutes." *The Review of Litigation* 18 (1999): 703–32.

Clapton, Gary. *Birth Fathers and their Adoption Experiences*. London and Philadelphia: Jessica Kingsley Publishers, 2003.

Deykin, Eva Y., Patricia Patti, and Jon Ryan. "Fathers of Adopted Children: A Study of the Impact of Child Surrender on Birthfathers." *American Journal of Orthopsychiatry* 58 (1988): 240–248.

Evan B. Donaldson Adoption Institute. "Putative Father Registries." Evan B. Donaldson Adoption Institute Web Site. http://www.adoptioninstitute.org/

Freundlich, Madelyn. "Adoption Research: An Assessment of Empirical Contributions to the Advancement of Adoption Practice." *Journal of Social Distress and the Homeless* 11 (2002): 143–166.

Gustafson, Je'Nell Blocher. "The Natural Father, I Presume: The Natural Father's Rights versus the Best Interests of the Child." *San Diego Justice Journal* 1 (1993): 489–501.

Krause, Harry D. *Family Law in a Nutshell*. 3rd ed. St. Paul, Minnesota: West Publishing Company, 1995.

Mason, Mary Martin. *Out of the Shadows: Birthfathers' Stories.* Edina, Minnesota: O. J. Howard Publishing, 1995.

Menard, Barbara J. "A Birth Father and Adoption in the Perinatal Setting." *Social Work in Health Care* 24 (1997): 153–163.

Mendenhall, Tai J., Jerica M. Berge, Gretchen M. Wrobel, Harold D. Grotevant, and Ruth G. McRoy. "Adolescents' Satisfaction with Contact in Adoption." *Child and Adolescent Social Work Journal* 21 (2004): 175–190.

Sachdev, Paul. "The Birth Father: A Neglected Element in the Adoption Equation." *Families in Society: The Journal of Contemporary Human Services* 72 (1991): 131–139.

Skinner, Denise, and Julie K. Kohler. "Parental Rights in Diverse Family Contexts: Current Legal Developments." *Family Relations* 51 (2002): 293–300.

Willemsen, Eleanor W., Marcus Boccaccini, and Dustin Pardini. "Factors Influencing Custody Decisions in Contested Adoption Cases." *Child and Adolescent Social Work Journal* 16 (1999): 127–147.

Zamostny, Kathy P., Karen M. O'Brien, Amanda L. Baden, and Mary O'Leary Wiley. "The Practice of Adoption: History, Trends, and Social Context." *The Counseling Psychologist* 31 (2003): 651–678.

Unwed Father Registry

Vern L. Bullough

Many states allow the unwed father, if he is known, to have some say in the adoption of his child. While women have the right to get an abortion or to have and raise a child without informing the father, courts have increasingly found that when birth mothers choose adoption, fathers who have shown a desire for involvement have rights also. To claim those rights, however, most states require a father to put his name on a registry. While approximately 30 states have registries as of this writing, they vary widely. In some states, fathers must actually claim paternity, in others, just the possibility of paternity. The deadlines for such filing ranges from five days after birth to 30 days, or any time before an adoption petition is filed. The legality of such registries was upheld by the United States Supreme Court in 1983, but most such registries have been started within the past decade to ward off late parental claims. Surprisingly few men register, probably because most young men have never heard of such registries. Some states, such as Indiana, notify men when a birth mother names them as father and it has a long list of fathers. Many mothers refuse to identify the father to forestall interference.

If the father does find out after the child is put up for adoption, there is some chance he can still have some place in the child's life. Erik L. Smith, an Ohio paralegal who fathered a son in Texas, fought for paternal rights after the baby's placement with an adoptive family. In an unusual resolution, the boy lives with the aodptive family, while Smith, a non-custodial father, has visiting rights.

Adoption authorities recommend that men interested in potential offspring might well register every time they have sex with a new partner. If they live with the woman who becomes a mother, he also has to register. Even if he does register, a registration means nothing if the father or mother have moved to a different state or if the baby was surrendered for adoption in a different state specifically to avoid a challenge. In one case, Frank Osborne of North Carolina challenged his five-month-old son's adoption in Utah. The Utah Supreme Court rejected Osborne's claim although a dissenting judge found it unfair that Osborne lost a child he had lived with and supported until the mother "unilaterally and clandestinely" took the boy to Utah where he was adopted.

Congress has discussed intervening in such cases and, as of this writing, Senator Mary L. Landrieu of Louisiana is working to introduce a Proud Father Act which would become a national registry.

Further Reading:

Lewin, Tamar. "Unwed Fathers Fight for Babies Placed for Adoption by Mothers." *New York Times*. [Online, March 19, 2006.] New York Times Web Site. http://www.nytimes. com/ 2006/03/19/national/19fathers.html

Birth Mothers

Barbara J. Pierce

The term "birth mother" is used to denote the woman who conceives and gives birth to a child who is later placed for adoption. Other terms for birth mother are *natural mother, first mother,* and *biological mother.* Some birth mothers place their children voluntarily and others have their parental rights terminated as a result of child maltreatment. In the United States, women voluntarily place children for adoption for reasons as varied as an inability to care for a child financially, inadequate support from either family or the child's father, illness or addiction, or because they desire to pursue other goals in their lives.

Statistics and Characteristics of Birth Mothers

In the United States, voluntary placement of children as a remedy for unplanned pregnancy has changed since the landmark *Roe v. Wade* Supreme Court decision legalizing abortion. According to the National Center for Health Statistics, prior to the 1970s, approximately 9 percent of all never-married women (and 19 percent of white never-married women) experiencing unplanned pregnancies placed their babies for adoption. But since the 1973 Supreme Court decision and because of changing societal attitudes about the legitimacy of single parenthood into the 1980s, fewer than 2 percent of unplanned pregnancies result in placing the child for adoption according to C. H. Bachrach, K. S. Stolley, and K. A. London. Some women, especially from African-American families, temporarily place their infants with kin while they complete educational goals or feel more ready to parent. According to the Administration for Children and Families of the U.S. Department of Health and Human Services, Black women's placement rates have been at or below 1.5 percent since 1952.

Many studies have shown that birth mothers placing infants for adoption in the United States are typically Caucasian, better educated, and from intact families of higher socioeconomic status than others experiencing unplanned pregnancies. Birth mothers who relinquish a child also express future life goals for career or education that those who choose to parent their babies do not. They also tend to be more religious than women who choose other options. Most birth mothers are unmarried, are placing first born children, and tend to be more mature and independent than their parenting counterparts.

Not much is known about the birth mother in international adoptions. She appears to be a forgotten part of the adoption triad. We do know that the experience of birth mothers internationally depends on the country and culture from which they originate. For example, in China, because of the one child policy, the U.S. Immigration and Naturalization Service reports that in 2003, 98 percent of the children available for adoption in China were female and became available because married couples wanted to attempt to conceive a male child. In other countries, many of the birth mothers are married and place because of poverty. Some have other children within the marriage. In other instances, the birth mother is young and places or abandons the child due to the cultural stigma evident in their country regarding out-of-wedlock pregnancy. Many live in repressive or war-ravaged countries. As in the United States, some place because of their own illness or the illness or disability of the child.

Emotional Reactions of Birth Mothers

Prior to the 1970s, women who became pregnant out-of-wedlock routinely went to live in a distant community either in a maternity home or with relatives. While some of these women did get pre-adoption counseling in order to know what to expect from the adoption process, many did not. Most gave birth to their babies and never got to see or hold the new baby. Some did not even know the sex of their child since the adoption then was a closed and secretive process. Birth mothers had no input into placement decisions since that was the role of the adoption agency. These women were sent home to "get on with their lives." Most of the women were able to resume their lives and pursue their goals, eventually marry, and have children within their marriage. But, many experienced trauma and grief reactions as a result of the pregnancy and placement experience, and the secret nature of these adoptions, according to a study by R. Winkler and M. van Keppel, may have had an influence on the continued experience of loss.

Birth mothers today have the option of participating in the adoption process. Open adoption affords the birth mother the opportunity to choose the couple with whom she will place her child and then choose how much contact she will have with the child. Some choose to remain very involved in the child's life by having visits and phone calls, while others exchange pictures, letters, and updates on anniversary dates such as birthdays, religious holidays, or placement date. Some women choose to have no contact with the child after birth. Prior to placement, many birth mothers hold and care for the baby. Others allow the adoptive couple to be in the delivery room to view the birth of the child and begin to care for the child immediately. Most birth mothers placing either privately or through agencies receive financial assistance with medical care and other necessities, and counseling.

There are different professional opinions about whether open adoption allows an easier emotional adjustment than closed adoption. Some researchers have found that open adoption affords birth mothers the opportunity to know that their children are doing well. They believe that the secret, closed process contributed to the trauma and grief experienced by the women who placed prior to the advent of open adoption. Opposing them are researchers who assert that birth mothers tend to adapt to the adoption in a healthier manner when they do not have continuing contact with the child.

The grief reaction experienced by birth mothers occurs as a result of relinquishing the child with whom they had begun to attach. Some birth mothers tend to experience grief and loss as an immediate reaction at birth and placement. They may experience anniversary reactions in which grief and loss issues arise each year at the time of placement. Some birth mothers may experience grieving when they marry and have other children. Birth mothers who have post-adoption counseling and have participated in the process of letting go appear to work through the grief reaction easier than those who do not. However, the grief reaction is real and usually requires counseling. When birth mothers cannot resolve their grief, they can experience extended anxiety, depression, addictions, or relationship difficulties.

Major issues for birth mothers who placed their babies before the open adoption trend are extended and complicated grief reactions, loss of control, and, in some cases, guilt and shame at having relinquished. In general, birth mothers must resolve their feelings of grief and loss, and come to terms with their decision so they can accept life as they presently live it. Many birth mothers report that their children live in their hearts and they do not forget them.

Searching for the Adopted Person

Some birth mothers search for their relinquished child using established state registries. Many states allow birth mothers to register their contact information in case the adopted person would like contact once he or she reaches adulthood. Some birth mothers desire contact in order to allay their guilt feelings about the relinquishment. In this case, it is important for birth mothers to understand the impact of their attitude on the adopted person. Other birth mothers want to establish an honest and open relationship with their now adult birth child.

Reunions for birth mothers and adopted people can be positive or negative. Positive reunions are those in which both people can have an honest exchange of emotion and information and get their mutual needs met. Negative reunions involve disappointment and hurt. Studies have indicated that, in some instances, one or both people are disappointed because, over the years, both people have engaged in fantasies about the other. The fantasies are almost never true so each person has to learn to cope with the real person that they have now met. Adopted people may want to know about their birth father, extended families, and siblings. Some just want to meet in order to obtain information, particularly medical information, and want no further contact. Birth mothers should be prepared for all possible scenarios.

Birth mothers should seek out social supports since some researchers (for example, Winkler and van Keppel) and clinicians believe that women who lack social support tend to have continued feelings of loss. Birth mothers may choose to join a support group or seek professional counseling services. They should look for a qualified mental health practitioner who has experience working with adoption issues. Many birth mothers cope well with the loss and believe that the decision to place their child was the most loving decision they could have made at the time.

See also Adoption Search Movement; Closed Adoption; Mutual-Aid; Mutual Consent Registries; Open Adoption; Recognition Events Regarding Adoption and Fostering; Relinquishment; Reunion.

Further Reading

Bachrach, C.A., K.S. Stolley, and K.A. London, "Relinquishment of Premarital Births: Evidence from National Survey Data." *Family Planning Perspectives* 24 (1992): 27–32, 48.

Blanton, T. L., and J. Deschner. "Biological Mothers' Grief: The Postadoptive Experience in Open versus Confidential Adoption." *Child Welfare* 69 (1990): 525.

Chandra, Anjani, Joyce Abma, Penelope Maza, and Christine Bachrach. "Adoption, Adoption Demand, and Relinquishment for Adoption." Washington, DC: National Center for Health Statistics, May 11, 1999.

Deacon, Sharon A. "Intercountry Adoption and the Family Life Cycle." *The American Journal of Family Therapy* 25 (1997): 245–260.

Resnick, Michael D. "Studying Adolescent Mothers' Decision Making About Adoption and Parenting." *Social Work* 29 (1984): 5–10.

Roles, P. *Saying Goodbye to a Baby. Volume 1: The Birthparent's Guide to Loss and Grief in Adoption.* Washington, DC: Child Welfare League of America, 1989.

Stolley, Kathy. S. "Statistics on Adoption in the United States." *The Future of Children: Adoption* 3 (1993): 26–42.

U.S. Citizenship and Immigration Service. *2003 Yearbook of Immigration Statistics.* U.S. Immigration and Naturalization Services Web Site. http://uscis.gov/graphics/shared/aboutus/statistics/2003Yearbook.pdf (accessed October, 2004).

U.S. Department of Health and Human Services, Administration for Children and Families Web Site. http://naic.acf.hhs.gov

Wilkinson, H. Sook. "Psycholegal Process and Issues in International Adoption." *The American Journal of Family Therapy* 23 (1995): 173–183.

Winkler, R., and M. van Keppel. *Relinquishing Mothers in Adoption: Their Long-term Adjustment.* Melbourne, Australia: Institute of Family Studies, 1984.

A "Natural" Mother: One Woman's Experience

Vern L. Bullough

What does the mother of a newborn baby feel when giving her child for adoption or foster care as an estimated five million American women did from the 1940s to the 1960s? Undoubtedly, the reactions differed from case to case, but none of them ever forget. One who wrote about her feelings was Margaret Moorman.

A fifteen-year-old student in Virginia, she was ignorant of birth control when, in 1964, she became pregnant by her boyfriend. He talked about marrying her but instead joined the Navy. She stood almost alone in enduring the stigma of a teenage pregnancy. The disapproval of her doctors, the behavior of her withdrawn mother, and recent death of her father from a heart attack imparted a shame and humiliation that induced her to give away her infant son in a "closed" adoption.

Moorman later wrote: "I believe there are climates that cloud or clear the moral weather of a time and place and make it possible or impossible to feel all right about certain actions." She felt, at the time, that when she gave up her child it was a result of an individual moral choice but, in retrospect, she felt that she and other women like her were "simply responding to the Zeitgeist." She became convinced that in most cases of infant "abandonment," it was the prevailing moral climate that made real reproductive choice possible or impossible for a pregnant girl or woman. She questioned the way individuals use words like "family" and "parent," and expressions like, "It's for your own good," or "for the good of the baby." She was convinced of that at the time but she concludes that, regardless of the reason, it is "something you never get over."

Further Reading

Moorman, Margaret. *Waiting to Forget.* New York: W.W. Norton, 1996.

Boundary Ambiguity in Adoption

Deborah Fravel

Boundary ambiguity is a condition, dealt with in adoption and other circumstances, that exists when someone is psychologically present in a family where they are not physically present, or vice versa. *Physical presence* is simply and literally the bodily presence of an individual in the family. *Psychological presence* is formally defined as "the symbolic existence of an individual in the perceptions of family members, in a way that, or to a degree that, influences the thoughts, emotions, behavior, identity, or unity of the remaining family members" (Fravel, 1995, p. 18). More informally, this type of psychological presence simply means the person is on the mind or in the heart of another family member. Numerous studies have demonstrated that boundary ambiguity is associated with or predicts a variety of manifestations of stress.

As a result of the incongruence between these two manifestations of the person's presence, P. Boss (1988) notes that the family may feel unable to determine who is inside and who is outside the family boundaries. Boundary ambiguity occurs in one of two circumstances. Type II Boundary Ambiguity occurs when physical presence combines with psychological absence. For example, it exists when a family member is in a coma: the unconscious person is there physically, but not psychologically.

In adoption, people deal with Type I Boundary Ambiguity. As D. Fravel notes, there is someone who is psychologically present, but physically absent. Typically, adoptive families will experience the birth mother's psychological presence. Birth parents, on the other hand, typically experience the psychological presence of the adopted child.

Recently, researchers studying adoption have been able to refine the way we look at psychological presence, making it somewhat more understandable and also more useful. Three primary improvements include the following:

First, there are *indicators*, or signs, of psychological presence, as noted by Fravel, that make it easier for the individual, adoption professional, or scholar to recognize psychological presence when it occurs. They include occasions when:

1. Someone actually states he or she "felt" someone present. For example, an adoptive mother in a confidential adoption might say she felt the

birth mother present at the child's christening ceremony, when she has never even met the birth mother.

2. There is some cognitive response—one party thinks about, is preoccupied with, or worries about the person. For example, a birth mother may wonder if her daughter is in a happy home where she is loved and cared for.

3. An emotional response indicates psychological presence. For example, an adoptive father may begin to weep when he speaks of his joy in teaching his son how to play ball, and wonder whether the birth father is thinking about that or missing the son.

4. A biological connection brings the person to heart or mind. This can include physical characteristics as well as personality traits, talents, and skills. For example, an adopted child has fingernails that have a distinctive shape, and wonders if his birth mother has those too.

5. Roles become an issue, with regard to the person's place in the family (or whether there is a place), or how the family identifies members. For example, a birth mother may wrestle with knowing she is *a* mother, but not *the* mother of the child she gave birth to.

6. Boundaries are brought to the fore. For example, an adoptive family celebrating Mother's Day may struggle with inclusion—which mother should they celebrate? Or should they celebrate both?

7. Psychological presence is revealed in supernatural or mysterious referents. For example, a birth mother might refer to the adopted child as a ghost in her family, or the adoptive family may speak of their relationship with this unknown person as "spooky."

8. Someone uses *minimizing, deprecating,* or *dismissing* as verbal strategies that seem designed to either get rid of the psychologically present person, or keep the psychologically present person at a safe distance. For example, an adoptive father may say, "Well, she has her own little family now," in a sarcastic tone.

9. Someone uses *generalizing* as a verbal strategy to get rid of or reduce influence of the psychologically present person. For example, if a birth mother is asked a question about her specific adopted child, she responds with, "Well, I think all children. . ." declining to speak specifically about the child to whom she gave birth.

10. Issues associated with information sharing, or the lack of it, reveal psychological presence. For example, when an adopted child gets a letter from the birth mother, the adoptive mother gets the "blues" for a few days, wondering how the birth mother is doing.

These categories are not mutually exclusive as shown above where the example for Indicator 10 also reveals an emotional response (Indicator 3). Knowing the ways psychological presence can occur is a research, clinical, and educational tool. (Descriptors have been condensed here for brevity.)

Second, psychological presence can vary in *degree* rather than being viewed as an either/or, present/absent phenomenon. It can be assessed on a scale from 1 (low) to 5 (high). Thus, psychological presence can be minimal, with low frequency and low intensity, and gradations along the way to maximal, with high frequency and high intensity (Fravel, 1995).

Third, psychological presence has some *valence*, across a spectrum, rather than being associated with negative outcomes as in other situations. The valence of psychological presence can range from very negative, moderately negative, moderately positive, to very positive, or it can be *neutral* (neither positive nor negative) or *mixed* (both positive and negative) (Fravel, 1995).

Research to date demonstrates that psychological presence does exist in adoption, regardless of whose perspective one takes (Fravel et al., 2000, 2005). Further, the degree to which a party is psychologically present may vary considerably according to levels of openness. Similarly, the valence of psychological presence may also vary with level of openness. This knowledge challenges the once-popular idea that people experience adoption and then just "get on with" their lives (Reitz and Watson, 1992, p. 4). However, it also provides resources for integrating this information for those involved in the adoption field, whether parties to adoption, adoption professionals, or scholars.

Further Reading

Boss, P. "A Clarification of the Concept of Psychological Father Presence in Families Experiencing Ambiguity of Boundary." *Journal of Marriage and the Family,* 39 (1977): 141–151.

Boss, P. *Family Stress Management.* Newbury Park, CA: Sage, 1988.

Boss, P., W. Caron, J. Horbal, and J. Mortimer. "Predictors of Depression in Caregivers of Dementia Patients: Boundary Ambiguity and Mastery." *Family Process*, 19 (1990): 242–272.

Fravel, D. *Rating Scale for Measuring Psychological Presence.* [Available from the author, for scales from the perspective of the birth mother, adoptive parents, or adopted child.] 1994.

Fravel, D. "Boundary Ambiguity Perceptions of Adoptive Parents Experiencing Various Levels of Openness in Adoption." (Doctoral dissertation, University of Minnesota, 1995). *Dissertation Abstracts International, 56/10,* (1995): 4160.

Fravel, D., R. McRoy, and H. Grotevant. "Birthmother Perceptions of the Psychologically Present Adopted Child: Adoption Openness and Boundary Ambiguity." *Family Relations* 49 (2000): 425–433.

Reitz, M., and K. Watson. *Adoption and the Family System.* New York: Guildford Press, 1992.

Brace, Charles Loring (1826–1890)

E. Wayne Carp

In March 1853, the Rev. Charles Loring Brace, a transplanted New Englander and graduate of Yale Divinity School, founded the most influential of all charity organizations, New York's Children's Aid Society (CAS). In the four decades following the founding of the CAS, Brace enjoyed such great success that most existing charity organizations switched over to the CAS's placing-out system, and imitators also appeared in Great Britain and Australia. Between 1854 and 1929, the CAS sent as many as two hundred fifty thousand children by train to farm families in the midwestern and western states as well as in Canada and Mexico.

Brace, born on June 19, 1826, in Litchfield, Connecticut, moved to Hartford at age seven and was strongly influenced by the Reverend Horace Bushnell, the "father of American religious liberalism," who ministered to the family in the town's North Congregational Church. Bushnell, author of *Christian Nurture* (1847), rejected the notion that children were born sinful; he encouraged parents to think of their children as innocent and pure. Most important, Bushnell introduced Brace to "unconscious influence," the idea that every minute of the day an individual infuses unconscious influences on the moral health of small children that would effect their mortal souls. The idea acted like an earthquake on Brace's mind and inspired him to spend his life working with children and families.

Brace began his much celebrated career as an evangelical missionary working with "street arabs" at New York City's Five Points Mission. Upon arriving in New York City, Brace was appalled at the thousands of impoverished immigrant children supporting themselves as beggars, prostitutes, and flower sellers. To him they seemed a threat to the city's social order. His major goal during his thirty-seven year tenure as secretary of the CAS was to remove poor and homeless children from New York City's crowded, dirty streets and place them out West in good Christian families where they would be cared for, educated, and employed. For Brace, "placing out" was superior to traditional antebellum institutional care in almshouses, orphanages, or reformatories because it promised to transform destitute ragamuffins into decent, industrious, children with a bright future.

When Brace quickly discovered that placing children individually in families was slow and expensive work, he turned to group placement by railroad, thus setting in motion the movement that became known as the orphan trains. In March 1854, the CAS sent the first large train of 138 children to western Pennsylvania. In the following twenty years, the CAS placed out twenty thousand Eastern children in the midwestern states of Michigan, Ohio, Indiana, Iowa, Missouri and Kansas; by 1890 the number had climbed to eighty-four thousand.

The boys and girls whom Brace placed out came under the authority of the CAS by a variety of routes. A small number of children were removed from asylums and prisons. Some came of their own volition to CAS headquarters and volunteered for resettlement. Others were brought by their poor, immigrant, working-class parents hoping to give them a better life.

Critics of the child-placing system accused the CAS of stealing children, and there was much truth in the charges. Brace or a "Visitor" frequently roamed working-class neighborhoods, going from house to house to recruit poor, destitute, and delinquent children for the program. The net result of such recruitment was that a high percentage of Brace's clientele—some 47 percent by his own calculations—were not, in fact, orphans, but had one or both parents living.

Brace broke families up to "rescue" the children from the "evils" of an urban environment. He assumed that a rural setting was morally superior and that the farm families desiring a child partook of this rural virtue and would treat the children well. Brace's romantic optimism was reflected in the way the CAS placing-out system differed from the traditional idea of binding out: Brace did away with the written contract of apprenticeship. The CAS relied on an oral agreement with the adult, while retaining custody of the child. Brace counted on the farmer's "sense of Christian duty and of affection" for his young charge to resist overworking or abusing the child. If farmers mistreated children, the CAS could reclaim them. If the children were unsatisfactory, they could be returned. Brace anticipated that the children would be not treated as servants, but as members of the family. This latter goal was sometimes achieved when bonds of affection sprang up between the family and child, which eventually led to some adoptions.

The large-scale placing-out movement inaugurated by the widely imitated CAS had enormous consequences for the history of adoption. The origins of America's first adoption laws can be traced to the increase in the number of middle-class farmers desiring to legalize the addition of a child to the family. The 1851 Massachusetts law, "An Act to Provide for the Adoption of Children," was path-breaking in this respect, and is commonly considered the first modern adoption law. Brace's reckless child-placing system was also indirectly responsible for initiating a fifty-year child welfare reform movement that culminated in the professionalization and bureaucratization of social workers and an expanded state role in regulating adoptions. Moreover, beginning in 1874 and continuing for the next half-century, Brace's methods ignited a heated controversy in the annual meetings of the National Conference of Charities and Correction over the relative merits of institutionalization versus family homes.

In the course of the long-running debate, the child-placement system came under attack from a variety of groups highly critical of Brace's methods. Representatives from mid-Western states accused Brace of dumping into their communities juvenile criminals, resulting in a steep increase in vagrants and the state prison population. Catholic authorities viewed the CAS child-placement system as an aggressive and covert form of Protestant proselytizing, equivalent to kidnapping. Eastern child welfare reformers voiced concern that their states were losing valuable human resources that were needed closer to home. Child-welfare reformers also criticized the CAS for failing to investigate the families the children were placed with or supervising them afterwards.

Child welfare reformers' criticism of Brace's unsound child-placement practices led to the emergence of a "second generation" of child-placing leaders who reformed the procedures surrounding the placing of orphaned, abandoned, and dependent children in families for adoption. This movement was initiated by Catholic leaders, state officials, and a new generation of child welfare reformers, who successfully advocated modifying or abolishing many CAS child-placing practices, particularly the unnecessary breakup of families, casual solicitation of parental consent, poor investigatory procedures, inadequate supervision of the children placed, and deficient recordkeeping. During the Progressive Era, professional social workers would continue to lobby state legislatures to enact these standards into law.

See also Massachusetts Adoption Act (1851); Orphan Trains; Protestent Perspectives on Adoption.

Further Reading

Holt, Marilyn Irvin. *The Orphan Trains: Placing Out in America*. Lincoln, NE and London: University of Nebraska Press, 1992.

Langsam, Miriam Z. *Children West: A History of the Placing-Out System of the New York Children's Aid Society 1853–1890*. Madison: State Historical Society of Wisconsin, 1964.

O'Connor, Stephen. *Orphan Trains: The Story of Charles Loring Brace and the Children He Saved and Failed*. Houghton Mifflin: Boston, 2001.

Buck, Pearl S. (1892–1973)

David Beimers

Pearl S. Buck was an American author and humanitarian who became famous for her novels of Chinese culture. Throughout her life, Buck was a prolific author and tireless advocate of cultural understanding.

Buck was born as Pearl Sydenstricker in Hillsboro, West Virginia, to missionaries on leave from China. When she was three months old, her family returned to China, where she lived for the majority of her childhood.

In 1910, Pearl returned to the United States and matriculated at Randolph-Macon Women's College in Lynchburg, Virginia. Following her graduation, she returned to China to care for her mother, who was ill at the time. While there, she met John Lossing Buck, whom she married in 1917. The Bucks lived in Nanking, where they both taught at the university. They had a daughter in 1921, but a uterine tumor discovered during the delivery resulted in a hysterectomy. In 1925, the Bucks adopted a Chinese girl.

Buck began writing in the 1920s. She published stories and essays in several popular journals. Her second novel, *The Good Earth*, was published in 1931. *The Good Earth* became the best-selling book of 1931 and 1932, culminating in Buck being awarded the Pulitzer Prize. In 1938, she also won the Nobel Prize in literature, the first American woman to do so. Over her career, Buck published more than seventy books.

In 1934, Buck moved back to the United States, coinciding with a divorce from John Lossing Buck. In 1935, She and her publisher, Richard Walsh, were married. They adopted six more children over the years.

Profoundly influenced by her upbringing in China, Buck was a resolute advocate of civil and human rights. She gained a reputation as a supporter of adoption and critic of the child welfare policies of matching and institutionalization.

The notoriety of Buck's views on adoption resulted in personal inquiries seeking assistance in placing children for adoption. In 1948, Buck received two multi-racial children, both of whose parents were seeking to place them for adoption. Following her indignation at not being able to find a single adoption agency willing to accept the children, Buck decided to create her own adoption agency.

The Welcome House, established at her Green Hills Farm in Bucks County, Pennsylvania, became the first agency in the United States to serve minority, international, and multi-racial children, groups frequently ignored by traditional child welfare agencies. Later, Welcome House expanded to serve other hard to place children, including older children, sibling groups, and children with physical disabilities.

Buck emphasized "Amerasian" children, a term she coined to describe a child born of an American service man and an Asian mother. Amerasian children faced substantial intolerance and abuse in their own families and countries. Over the decades, Welcome House has assisted in the adoption placement of over seven thousand children. The Welcome House currently operates as Pearl S. Buck International from her Green Hills Farm in Bucks County, Pennsylvania.

Further Reading

Conn, Peter. *Pearl S. Buck: A Cultural Biography.* New York: Cambridge University Press, 1996

Primary Document

"I Am the Better Woman for Having My Two Black Children" An Account from Pearl S. Buck

In the same year that the National Association of Black Social Workers articulated their position against adoption of black children by white parents, Nobel prize winner Pearl S. Buck published the following account of her life with her black daughters and her thoughts on whites parenting black children. Buck was founder of Welcome House, the first international inter-racial adoption agency focusing its services on children that other agencies of the day generally considered unadoptable. Today, Welcome House literature indicates that the organization has placed over seven thousand children.

The famous Nobel novelist, who has lived "where white is the undesirable color," tells what it is like to adopt across racial lines.

Pearl S. Buck's Account

This has been a pleasant week. Two of my daughters spent unexpected time with me. While we try to cross paths as often as possible, we are professional women, each with her life to live, her own work to do.

The two who met me this week are, I think, exceptional young women. Both are married. One lives with her professor husband on a Vermont college campus not far from me. They have been married four years but have no children. The other daughter lives in Pennsylvania and has a beautiful son now nearly two years old.

These two daughters are adopted. The older one, who is 25, met me in Boston this week and joined me in a television show. I did not urge her to come. I never urge my children. I know better. My family life and professional and business life have always been separate.

My children know what I do, where I am, where I go. They can always reach me. Since they are now grown men and women, I never ask them to call, to write, or to visit unless they wish. Our relationship is deep but never demanding. They know I love them

and I know they love me. If need comes, as sometimes it does, we get into instant communication, and help is there. Fortunately, we are all healthy and we all work, and communication is normally just for pleasure.

I was pleased, therefore, when my 25-year-old caught an early plane and appeared in my Boston hotel suite. She is a beautiful young woman, and she wore a new pants suit so striking that it might have overcome a person less handsome. Her hair, straight and dark, had red-gold glints and hung long over her shoulders, but was held back from her face. The clog-heeled high boots she wore with her modish outfit made her look taller. In she burst, in top form and high spirits as usual, gave me a hearty kiss, and joined me immediately at breakfast.

"Wonderful that you're here," I said, "but I thought you wanted to be what you always call 'private.'"

She laughed. "I thought it would be fun for once."

She is a cheerful soul, ebullient, charming, opinionated. I never argue with her, because I enjoy her opinions without agreeing or disagreeing. I had my turn when she was little and when she was growing up. Now she has a right to herself. She even advises me. I always listen with interest and then do what I like. She accepts this.

My husband and I thought our family of five adopted children was complete when she first came to us. Her birth mother was a girl in a small town in Germany. Her father was an American soldier who was killed. He was black. The German mother said his black child was despised in her town and had no future there. She begged his university president in Washington to find the father's family.

I was a trustee of the university. We tried to find the family, but they had disappeared without trace. What then should we do with the child? From experience we knew that the little black children from Germany had difficulty adjusting to black mothers.

The president looked at me. "Would you …"

"Of course I will," I said. "We'd love to have another child."

I lived in a white community. But I knew it would make no difference to me or to my husband that this child was black, and since it made no difference to us, it should make no difference to our white children. If it did, I wanted to know it and see to it that attitudes were changed. If there were wrong attitudes in the school or community, I would see to that, too. If the basic love was in the home, the child would be fortified enough to be a survivor.

At any rate, she would fare better in our home than she would where she was. That was the final argument.

She arrived at our house on Thanksgiving Day—five years old, bone-thin, weighing only 35 pounds, speaking only German. She had been airsick, she was unwashed, she was terrified, but she did not cry. Later, years later, she told me her German mother had simply put her on the plane without telling her where she was going. She had promised to return in a moment, but had never come back.

That plucky little thing, so alone, those enormous haunted eyes! Tears come to my eyes now when I think of her that day. I took her in my arms and held her. Her heart was beating so hard that it shook her small, emaciated frame.

I carried her upstairs and gently, slowly, gave her a bath. It was her first, and she was terrified all over again, scratching and clawing like a small, wild cat. I lifted her into a big soft bath towel and sat in a rocking chair and rocked her slowly to and fro, to and fro, until she relaxed. She did not cry. She was too frightened.

After an hour or so she fell asleep from exhaustion. I stayed with her all night. For days she never left my side and for nights I stayed with her until she could be left. The door between our rooms was always open until, months later, she could let it be closed and not mind.

She was our child. When my husband died, she was my child. I am glad he lived long enough to share in her adoption. The ceremony was a double one. I asked the judge to ask her, too, to adopt us. She was then old enough to understand. It was a beautiful and sacred little ceremony, just the four of us in his private chambers. It sealed our love.

The years passed. She went to public school, developed a strong personality, fearless, independent, sometimes difficult. She had to be rid of all fear before she gave up lying as a protection. The result today is a strong, outspoken, fearless woman with a mind of her own. And yet love, our love, has helped her to try to understand other people. She understands both black people and white. She is in the deepest, truest sense a bridge between two peoples, to both of whom she belongs by birth.

Of course there were problems. We met them head on. She was my child and I would not brook the slightest nonsense from ignorant, prejudiced, small-minded people.

When she encountered nasty remarks from white people or black, we talked about it frankly. I explained that when I was a little girl in China, the Chinese made strange remarks about me. In China, I was the wrong color, for my skin was white instead of brown, my eyes were blue instead of black, and my hair was light instead of dark. I taught my children to feel sorry for people who made rude or nasty remarks about such differences.

My daughter and I knew we understood each other. I was happy when, though she had not finished college, she married a fine young Jewish man and brought into my family yet another element. That he was able to marry two prejudices, so to speak, assured me of his own maturity and common sense. I am very proud of him as my son-in-law and, best of all, we are good friends. I do not doubt the marriage has its stormy moments, for he is an only and much-loved son, grandson and nephew in his own Jewish family, and my daughter has a strong, independent personality of her own. But there is understanding and love, and whatever their differences, they do not bring them to me, nor would I hear them if they did.

Adopting a black child into my white family has taught me much I could not otherwise have known. Although I have many black friends and read many books by black writers, I rejoice that I have had the deep experience of being mother to a black child. I have seen her grow to womanhood in my house and go from it to her own home, a happy bride and wife. It has been a rich experience and it continues to be. It has brought me into the whole world. I loved to hear the great singer, Marian Anderson, sing that song, *He's Got the Whole World in His Hands*. Now I know what it means.

"Mommy, please find me a little sister." It was a natural request at a time when the older children were growing up and off to college.

Being always in touch with the children of American servicemen and Asian women in Asia—those piteous lonely children whom no country claims—I found in a Japanese orphanage a little seven-year-old girl and brought her home with me. She, too, was of a black father. She, too, I adopted. At first

she spoke only Japanese, but her lively mind soon discovered English.

How my two brown children enlivened our household! They loved each other and at the same quarreled loudly. Born sisters could not have loved each other with more fervor and storm. Their temperaments were so alike that they disagreed constantly and made up with loud devotion. I was torn between laughter and distress.

As far as I knew—and I knew everything sooner or later from the articulate pair—there was no difficulty in the neighborhood because of race or color. They had friends in abundance, both black and white. They never belonged to a "black only" or "white only" group. Both girls were full of fun and inventiveness and carried laughter with them. Such rebuffs as they met, if any, they handled with spirit.

We have few blacks in our conservative neighborhood, although our household was—and is—an interracial and international one with color taken as a matter of course. We had Negro friends who came to our house and brought their children. We had Chinese friends, and Indian friends, but there was never an emphasis on color.

Of course I taught my daughters to stand up for themselves and to be proud of what they were—my daughters. As they blossomed into their teens, they had friends who were white or black. Both were equally welcome in our home. Good behavior and not color was the criterion.

Let me say here that the attitude of adoptive parents is most important. If the parents are doubtful, if they are fearful, if they are not strong enough, secure enough in themselves, to accept children of a race different from their own, they should not adopt such children. My black children knew and know that color means nothing to me. Whatever they might meet outside they could cope with because at home there was only love and acceptance.

Discipline, yes, but administered with reason and full explanation. As they grew into young womanhood, they had suitors of both races. They chose finally to marry white men and they married young, though not too young. Both young men are of good family. The families accepted the marriages. I am sure—or I feel sure—that they would have preferred white girls, but they have accepted warmly enough my daughters. I do not know how much the fact that they were my daughters influenced them. If it does, they do not show it.

Both my black daughters are quite beautiful, and as they were growing up, they became used to comments about how pretty they were. Never at any time did they say they would rather be white. Nor did either ever express a desire to see her natural parents or to live with black families.

The younger daughter has a little son, now about two years old. He is a winsome, merry, highly intelligent human being. He is one-quarter Negro, one-quarter Japanese, and half white. With his charm and beauty, he will dance his way through life.

His mother, now a competent, successful young designer of fashions, manages her own life surprisingly well. Yes, both she and her older sister experience occasional slights, but their childhood lives have been secure enough so they know how to handle such situations.

Recently I invited my elder black daughter to accompany me on a business trip to West Virginia. She accepted without thought and then reconsidered.

"You don't understand that everyone is not like you," she explained. "You have no feelings about race whatsoever, and you take it for granted that no one else does. I know better and I will not put myself into the position of being in an atmosphere where there is prejudice against my race."

I accepted this decision without comment or distress. She had faced her own self and made her decision wisely. She was secure in herself, she had her own pride, she would simply live her life among people who accept her as a person. I understood that from my own experience. I have lived in parts of the world where white is the undesirable color. I prefer not to live in those places. There are other places where white is acceptable.

In sum, should white people adopt homeless black children? My answer is yes, if they feel the same love for a black child as for a white one. It all depends on their own capacity for love. The community? Never mind the community if the parents accept the child wholeheartedly. There will be situations that need to be handled, but if the parents are free of prejudice the child will be secure enough to handle them without damage. He would face them anyway, and he can do so better if he has the experience of love at home.

In short, his chances are better with love than without. Love is color blind.

And love works both ways. Reared in a home where white people love him, a black child will not hate white people simply because they happen to be white. Love will not discriminate.

I would not have missed the interesting experience of adopting children of races different from my own. They have taught me much. They have stretched my mind and heart. They have brought me, through love, into kinship with peoples different from my own conservative, proud, white ancestry. I am the better woman, the wiser human being, for having my two black children. And I hope and believe they are the better, too, and the more understanding of me and my people because of their white adoptive parents.

At least I know that there is no hate in them. No, there is no hate in them at all.

Source

Pearl S. Buck. "I Am a Better Woman for Having Black Children." *Today's Health*. 50 (January 1972): 20–23, 64. Used by permission.

Buddhism, Infanticide, and Adoption

Vern L. Bullough

Buddhism taught the transmigration of souls or *metempsychoses*. This is the concept that life is a cyclical process and involves the passage of the soul through successive bodies different from each other. Under this view, children were not fully formed and, until the age of seven, children belonged to the gods. Infanticide, therefore, was not homicide but an act that returned children to the other world to receive a different body. So long as a soul had not freed itself from hatred, greed, and stupidity, it would inevitably be subject to rebirth. The souls of the truly virtuous achieve Nirvana and are reborn as gods. Some for their sins are reborn as animals, hungry ghosts, or denizens of hell. Adoption of infants and small children had little support with such a belief, although adults could be adopted for various reasons.

Byzantine Charities and Abandoned Children

Vern L. Bullough

As the Roman Empire began to decline, it remained strong in the East where a new capital had been established in Constantinople (today's Istanbul) in the fourth century. It was there that Christian concepts of philanthropy came to be institutionalized in hospitals, *xenones* (hospices or homes for strangers and travelers), *gerocemia* (homes for the aged), and *ptocheia* (homes for the poor, and orphanages for children). Orphanages were established, as were the other charitable institutions, by both the state and the Christian Church. However, it is very difficult to draw a line between church and state institutions since they were mainly a cooperative effort. Staffing these institutions were monks and nuns, as well as lay women such as deaconesses.

It is believed that there were numerous orphanages although we can not clearly identify the sites of many of them. They are mentioned in the laws of Justinian in the sixth century. These laws stipulated that the administrators of the orphanages protect the property of the orphans under their care. Many of them had schools for the education and training of orphans. The main evidence for the existence of such institutions is the continual updating of regulations about orphanages until the fall of Constantinople to the Turks in the fifteenth century. The adoptions that took place in the Byzantine Empire seem to have been independent of the orphanage.

Further Reading

Constantelos, Demetrios J. *Byzantine Philanthropy and Social Welfare*. New Brunswick, NJ: Rutgers University Press, 1968.

C

Canadian Adoption Practices

Michael P. Grand

Adoption in Canada is governed primarily by provincial and territorial legislation. Each of these thirteen jurisdictions is charged with the responsibility of providing for the health, welfare, and safety of children. As such, each has provisions in its statutes that determine who holds parental rights, and how these rights may be severed and reassigned to another party.

In addition to provincial legislation, there are a few federal laws that make mention of adoption and govern such issues as family leave policies and citizenship status for international adoptees. Considering the multiple sources of legislation governing adoption in Canada, it is not surprising that there is some degree of diversity in the praxis of adoption across the country.

Demographics

Unfortunately, the only reliable domestic adoption figures were gathered by M. P. Sobol and K. J. Daly for the period between 1981 and 1990. They demonstrated a marked linear decline in the total number of domestic adoptions for this period. In 1981, there were 5,376 domestic adoptions. By 1990, only 2,836 children were adopted. Of this cohort, a steeper decline was found for children adopted under the age of one. In 1981, 3,521 infants were adopted. By the end of the decade, this figure had dropped to 1,698. When these data are split by facilitator, it becomes readily apparent that the major portion of the decline in infant adoption has come about in public agency facilitation. In 1981, 2,736 children were adopted under public agency or provincial ministry auspices. In 1990, this figure had fallen dramatically to 698. However, private agency facilitated adoptions rose from 785 in 1981 to 1,000 in 1990. While no figures are available for the subsequent years, informal reports would suggest that this trend has continued, with falling rates of infant adoptions in the public domain and a steady rate in the private domain.

To best understand the dramatic drop in adoption of children less than one year of age, it is necessary to consider this decline within the context of decisions about responses to an unplanned pregnancy. Drawing upon figures presented in Statistic Canada Annual Reports (1983–1991), Sobol and Daly demonstrated that there was a 10.9 percent decrease in the number of abortions of unplanned pregnancies by single women under the age of twenty-four (the primary age cohort of mothers whose infants are placed for adoption). At the same time, the percentage of these pregnancies that resulted in an adoption showed a modest decline of 2.9 percent. Interestingly, the most striking change in alternative responses to an unplanned pregnancy was to be found in the percentage of pregnancies that resulted in the birth mother or a non-adopting surrogate raising the child, a gain of almost 14 percent. Thus, it is not abortion but single parenthood that has led to a decrease in the use of adoption in Canada as a response to an unplanned pregnancy.

Adoption of children older than one year of age may also be differentiated by agent of facilitation. In 1981, 1,705 children, representing 91.9 percent of older adoptees, were placed through public agencies. By 1990, the figures had dropped to 1,030, or 90.8 percent of older adoptions for that year. In the private domain, parallel figures were 8.1 percent and 9.2 percent respectively. While no figures are available for subsequent years, there are reported increases seen in the public domain, starting in the early 2000s. This increase in activity has been fueled by financial pressures that provincial governments have had to address to meet budgetary targets. Recognizing the higher costs of maintaining a child in foster care, ministries have looked for means to expedite the placement of older children and those with special needs who would have been seen to be un-adoptable a decade earlier. To this end, legislation has been enacted in some provinces to shorten the period during which a child may remain in foster care without a permanency plan in place.

A second response to increasing older children placements has been to place pictures and character descriptions of potential adoptees on the Internet as a means of attracting more adoptive parent applicants. The province of Alberta has taken the lead in this initiative. It has been argued by proponents of this strategy that many applicants seeking children have never considered older children or those with special needs. By actually having the opportunity to see these children, they will favorably reevaluate their motivation to adopt them.

Critics of this strategy have argued that the advertising of children does not compensate for the harm done through public exposure and humiliation. Provincial advocates counter by offering statistics that photo-listing has led to increased numbers of placements of children with special needs. While the motivational aspect of photo-listing has been offered as the explanation of this increase in older child placements, proponents have failed to recognize the dual effects of the shift of staff resources and the motivation to meet institutional goals directed at the placement of these children. Daly and Sobol described the bottleneck in services between applicants' interest in adopting older children and the placement of these children in adoptive homes. With an institutional goal of increasing the number of these placements, it is not surprising that older children are more easily finding their way to adoptive homes. It is not photo-listing per se, but the concomitant services that are currently being utilized that are responsible for this increase in older placements.

International Adoptions

While domestic estimates reflect a diminishing use of adoption as a form of permanency planning, international adoption by Canadian citizens remains an active pursuit. From 1993 to 2003, the federal ministry, Citizenship and Immigration Canada, has reported that there were 21,757 international adoptions, or an average of 1,978 children per year, with a low of 1,800 in 1997 and a high of 2,181 in 2003. Over this time period, a majority of these children have come from the People's Republic of China with a total of 7,353 (1,108 in 2003), India with 1,938 (70 in 2003), Haiti with 1,521 (149 in 2003), Russia with 1,490 (92 in 2003), the Philippines with 1,040 (56 in 2003), and the United States with 860 (74 in 2003). Yearly rates of origin vary by such factors as the country's political circumstances, public health status, changes in the legislative control of adoption, and difficulty in traveling to the child's home country.

Most children adopted internationally range in age between birth and four years old, and make up 84.4 percent of the cohort for 2003. The remaining 15.6 percent of the children are spread over the ages five to fourteen.

The number of girls adopted from abroad for the period 1993–2003 clearly outnumbers the boys by a ratio of 68.7 percent to 31.3 percent. This is the result of the highly differential sex ratio for the People's Republic of China. In 2003, 1,064 girls (97.2 percent) were adopted from China compared to only thirty-one boys (2.8 percent). However, when considering all children other than those adopted from China for 2003, there is an almost even distribution of 49.4 percent boys and 50.6 percent girls. Clearly the international adoption pattern of Canadian citizens is strongly shaped by the one child policy of the People's Republic of China. With girls being less favored in China, it is not surprising that they are so readily available to be adopted abroad.

Daly and Sobol found that the motivation to adopt abroad was strongly influenced by the difficulty of moving through the quagmire of domestic adoption policies and procedures. International adoption provided a much shortened time period between the decision to adopt and finalization of the adoption. Furthermore, adoptive applicants would go anywhere in the world where children were available for adoption. When one door closed, the applicants would go elsewhere to find a child. This meant that domestic children who came from less challenging backgrounds were ignored as adoptive applicants soon tired of the struggle to adopt within Canada. Perhaps the political need to lessen the financial burden of keeping children in foster care, along with the realignment of personnel resources to expedite placements will reverse the use of international adoption in the coming years.

Openness in Adoption

In Canada, as reported by Daly and Sobol, the most typical form of openness used (54 percent of adoptions) is that of the birth mother choosing the adoptive parents from pre-selected files not containing identifying information. In 34 percent of all adoptions, birth and adoptive parents exchange letters and information on a regular basis through the auspices of a facilitator. Eighteen percent of birth mothers meet the adoptive parents prior to the placement without any exchange of identifying information. In 13 percent of adoptions, birth and adoptive parents exchange names. These openness procedures are used predominately by independent agencies charging fees, followed by independent agencies not charging fees, licensed practitioners charging fees, public (governmental) agencies and, finally, independent licensees not charging fees such as physicians. As infant placements have declined over the years, more birth mothers are choosing not to use public agencies but private, fee-for-service ones. As discussed by Sobol, Daly and E. K. Kelloway, it would seem that they do so in order to take more personal control over the form and future direction of the adoption, as private agencies in Canada are more prone to use open procedures.

Search and Reunion

Legislation governing search and reunion is quite varied. All provinces and territories allow for access to non-identifying information by adult adoptees. As of 2005, there are three provinces, Alberta, British Columbia and Newfoundland, and two territories, North West Territories and Nunavut, that allow adult adoptees and birth parents to have access to identifying information in the form of birth registrations and adoption orders, as long as neither party has filed a disclosure veto prior to the request for information. In other words, the default option is that the file is open until requested to be closed. In the case of British Columbia, parties to the adoption are also entitled to obtain the adoption file containing information up to the point of finalization of the adoption.

As for the right to initiate a search, a few provinces do not offer any searching services. Instead, they use passive registries requiring both adult adoptee and birth parent to sign the registry before the jurisdiction will bring the parties together. A majority of the provinces use mixed registries. These are active for adult adoptees who have the right to request a search for birth parents. However, for birth parents, the registry is passive in that they have no right to initiate a search.

This is not the case for Alberta, British Columbia, Newfoundland, North West Territories, and Nunavut. In these jurisdictions, as long as either party to the adoption has not signed a contact or disclosure veto, then the ministry will undertake a search for the other party. They also have the provision that all adoptions, finalized after the passage of the law, are fully opened when the adoptee reaches the age of legal adulthood. C. Miall and K. March find that this move toward more liberal search and reunion policies is supported by a majority of Canadians.

Future Trends

Over the next decade, the following trends are anticipated: greater use of openness in adoption; federal tax relief for the costs of bringing a child into an adoptive home; more provincial support for single, gay and lesbian adoption; the automatic granting of citizenship to children adopted abroad; the removal of disclosure vetoes from search legislation; and intense debate on whether First Nations communities will continue to have the right to restrict the placement of Native children in non-Native homes.

See also Photographs and Advertising; U.S.-born Children Adopted by Non-U.S. Parents.

Further Reading

Citizenship and Immigration Canada (CIC). "International Adoptions." Citizenship and Immigration Canada (CIC) Web Site. http://www.cic.gc.ca/english/monitor/issue03/ 06-feature.html (accessed April, 2005).

Daly, K. J., and M. P. Sobol (Grand). *Adoption in Canada*. Ottawa: National Welfare Grants, Health and Welfare, Canada, 1993.

Miall, C., and K. March. "Social Support for Adoption in Canada." Carleton University Department of Sociology and Anthropology Web Site. http://www.carleton.ca/ socanth/ Faculty/News%20Release%20Adoption%20Survey.pdf (accessed January, 2004).

Sobol (Grand), M. P., and K. J. Daly. "Canadian Adoption Statistics." *Journal of Marriage and the Family* 56 (1994): 494–499.

Sobol (Grand), M. P., K. J. Daly, and E. K. Kelloway. "Paths to the Facilitation of Open Adoption." *Family Relations* 49 (2000): 419–424.

Lesbian Adoptions in Canada

Vern L. Bullough

The Ontario provincial government, based on a judgment by Judge James Paul Nevis, allowed four lesbian women to adopt their partners' children on May 11, 1995, the first time this happened in Canada and before it occurred in the United States. The judge based his ruling on "elected to read" in the then current Ontario law, interpreting that an adoptive "spouse" meant a person either of the opposite sex to whom a person was married, or a person of the same sex living in a conjugal relationship. Though his decision was not binding on other judges, it marked the beginning of same sex adoptions in Canada. Among the adopting parents were Dr. Miriam Kaufman and Chris Phibbs, and Nisa Friedman and Cheryl Pollock.

Further Reading

Girard, Daniel. "Lesbian Couples Can Adopt." *Toronto Star*, May 11, 1995, p. 1.
Toughill, Kelly. "Laws on Gay Right Inevitable." *Toronto Star*, May 12, 1995, pp. A1–A2.

Canon Law and Adoption

James A. Brundage

Roman adoption practices long continued to persist following the barbarian invasions in the fourth and fifth centuries in the Mediterranean regions that had formed part of the Western Empire, essentially in the areas that now comprise Italy, Spain, and the south of France. In northern and central Europe, where Roman rule had either been established late or not at all, however, adoption came to be recognized by law only gradually. In a few regions, notably England, secular law did not recognize adoption until quite recent times.

The Christian church encouraged the practice of adoption from early in its history. The *Constitutiones apostolicae*, written in the late fourth or early fifth centuries, for example, taught that the adoption of orphaned children was a praiseworthy act for pious Christian couples. While the barbarian migrations were still in process, the Christian emperor Justinian (r. 527–565) codified the Roman law. In so doing, he chose to retain traditional Roman adoption as a legitimate legal practice and made available procedures to facilitate the practice. Popes and church councils in their turn incorporated numerous features of Roman law, including adoption law, into canon law, the legal system of the Christian church. Although early canon law collections preserved many parts of Roman adoption law, such as the distinction between adoption and adrogation, canonists slowly altered or discarded others over the course of time, as social and religious circumstances changed.

Canon lawyers were especially concerned with problems posed by the marriages of adopted children. Church law adamantly opposed incestuous relationships, and the prevailing canonical rules throughout the early Middle Ages prohibited marriage between persons related to each other within seven degrees of blood kinship. This severely restricted the choice of potential marriage partners, not only in isolated villages, but also among royal and noble families, whose members were loath to marry outside the tightly-closed ranks of their social class. The Fourth Lateran Council in 1215 relaxed the older rule considerably by reducing the range of forbidden relationships to just four degrees. Despite this change, marriages that church law considered invalid because the parties were too closely related continued to cause numerous legal difficulties even under the modified rule.

Although adoptive children were seldom related to their siblings by blood, their legal relationship inevitably raised the question of whether they should be permitted to marry members of their adoptive families to whom they were legally related within the prohibited degrees. Pope Nicholas I (858–867) ruled that a man could not marry his adopted sister. Later popes extended the rule to much more distant relationships. Thus, for instance, Pope Gregory VII (1073–1185) held that the marriage between Duke William VI of Aquitaine and Hildegarde, daughter of Duke Robert of Burgundy, was invalid because William's maternal grandfather had been the adopted son of Hugh the Great, the first duke of Burgundy, which meant that William was related to Hildegarde within the forbidden degrees of kinship.

Canonists also grappled with other questions posed by adoption. Did an adoptive child, for example, have a legal right to support from his or her adoptive parents? If so, could the adoptee sue his or her adoptive parents if they failed to provide appropriate support? While questions of this kind may at first glance seem far-fetched, they represented real problems when parents, for example, adopted a child whom they then exploited as an unpaid servant. The consensus that emerged among medieval authorities came down on the side of the child and held that the act of adoption created a legally-enforceable liability for support.

Inheritance rights raised even more hotly-contested problems. These became especially acute when parents died intestate and were survived by both natural and adoptive children. After considerable discussion and some strenuous disagreements, canon law ultimately concluded that adoptive children were entitled to precisely the same inheritance rights as their natural-born siblings.

Strangely enough, despite all this, some writers on family history claim that the practice of adoption disappeared altogether during the early Middle Ages and only reappeared as a legal institution in the western world quite recently. The Cambridge anthropologist, Jack Goody, and others claim that medieval church authorities flatly prohibited adoption and that they did so in the hope that couples who died without direct heirs would leave their estates to monasteries, churches, and other ecclesiastical bodies. This conclusion rests on the evidence of a unique statement by a single writer, Salvian of Marseilles (ca. 400–ca. 480). Salvian unquestionably argued that Christians had a moral obligation to leave property to the church and he lamented that childless couples often preferred to adopt children as heirs rather than leaving all their property to religious institutions. But Salvian, an obscure Latin moralist, seems to have been alone in taking this position. His statement was not cited by later legal authorities, either in the Middle Ages or since. Mainstream Christian authorities, including St. Thomas Aquinas (1224–1274), treated the adoption of orphaned children as a meritorious practice and recommended it as a work of mercy, especially for childless couples who wanted offspring to cherish.

Ample documentary evidence, furthermore, attests that people did continue to adopt children in practice throughout the Middle Ages, especially in southern Europe where thousands of cases are known. In Spain, surviving evidence of adoption occurs primarily among wealthy and powerful families, who were presumably anxious to pass on their advantages to the next generation, even if they lacked children of their own to inherit.

It is true, however, that the frequency of the practice fluctuated considerably. Only a few adoption contracts survive from the south of France during the thirteenth century, for example, but became far more common during the fourteenth century, possibly as a result of child mortality during the Black Death. The numbers of adoptions diminished again in the sixteenth century and adoption records virtually disappeared after the beginning of the seventeenth century. Adoption resurfaced in law and practice in almost all European countries during the nineteenth century. Alone among west European societies, only England and Scotland failed to provide any method for legal adoption until the passage of the Adoption of Children Act of 1926.

See also Roman Law and Adoption; Medieval Adoption.

Further Reading

Aubenas, Roger. "L'adoption en Provence au moyen âge (XIVe–XVIe siècles)." *Revue Historique de Droit Français et Etranger*, 4th ser. 13. (1934): 700–726.

Aubenas, Roger. *Recuiel des Letters des Officialités de Marseille et d'Aix (XIVe–XVe siècles*, 2 vols. (Paris, 1937–1938).

Boswell, John. *The Kindness of Strangers: The Abandonment of Children in Western Europe from Late Antiquity to the Renaissance*. New York: Pantheon, 1988.

Brundage, James A. "Adoption in the Medieval *Ius Commune*." *Proceedings of the Tenth International Congress of Medieval Canon Law*. Vatican City, 2001, pp. 889–905.

McKnight, Joseph W. "The Shifting Focus of Adoption." In *Critical Studies in Ancient Law, Comparative and Legal History: Essays in Honour of Alan Watson*, edited by John Cairns and Olivia Robinson, 297–331. Oxford: Hart Publishing, 2001.

Roumy, Franck. *L'adoption dans le Droit Savant du XIIe au XVIe Siècle*. Paris: LGDJ, Bioliotheque de droit prive, 1998.

The Catholic Church and Adoption: Lessons from Ireland

Moira Maguire

Many western countries began to legislate in the area of adoption in the late nineteenth and early twentieth centuries. For the most part adoption was not all that controversial an issue and indeed it seemed to make good sense both socially and economically. Socially, it allowed for the transfer of parental rights from biological parents who were unwilling or unable to fulfill their parental duties, to adoptive parents who were only too happy to take on that role. This ensured that children who otherwise would have been institutionalized or farmed out to foster homes of dubious quality had the chance to grow up in a "normal" family and home environment. This, in turn, reduced the likelihood that such children would lapse into juvenile delinquency or become burdens on public resources as adults. It made good sense economically because children who were not adopted were cared for by the state and thus diverted precious public funds away from other services and programs.

The passage of adoption legislation did not spark significant debate in many countries, particularly those where the legislature was entirely secular. But in countries, like Ireland, where the Catholic Church exerted a formal or informal influence over the legislative process, adoption was a controversial issue because it potentially contradicted Catholic teaching. There is no evidence that an official statement for or against adoption was issued by the Vatican in the late nineteenth or twentieth centuries, and the church's response to the issue likely was left to the Catholic hierarchies in individual countries. An examination of the Catholic Church's response to adoption in Ireland gives some insight into the grounds on which the Catholic Church opposed the question based on Catholic teaching and doctrine.

Ireland is perhaps one of the best case studies of the church's opposition to legal adoption because the Catholic Hierarchy consistently blocked efforts, by social reformers and civil servants, to press the government to legalize adoption to enable the thousands of children living in foster homes and institutions the opportunity for a "real" home. Church and state finally compromised on the question of adoption in Ireland in 1952 after several embarrassing international "incidents" brought to light the fact that thousands of Irish children were being sent out of Ireland for adoption overseas, particularly to the United States, at the same time that church and state dragged their feet on legalizing adoption in Ireland.

The attitude towards adoption amongst lawmakers in Ireland is underscored by a comparison of the debates on adoption that occurred in the British Parliament in 1925–26, and the Dáil (Irish parliament) in 1952. The primary distinctions centered on differing perceptions of the state's responsibility for children who lacked the protection and care of "natural" or "normal" families, how far the state could and should go in protecting the rights of the natural mother, and the role of a religious test in assessing the fitness of prospective adopters. Unlike their Irish counterparts, British Members of Parliament highlighted the social and economic benefits that would accrue to the state as a result of legalized adoption. They argued that giving children good homes, rather than consigning them to an institutional existence, would enhance the children's lives while also ensuring that the children would not become burdens on the state's financial resources or become entangled in the host of state penal and charitable institutions. The British legislation did not discount the importance of religion, but neither did they place it at the center of adoption legislation as was the case in Catholic countries. They were concerned, first and foremost, with matching the right child to the right home, and British lawmakers did not believe that religion was the most important deciding factor in that equation.

By the time the Irish government undertook to legislate on adoption in 1952, lawmakers acknowledged that Ireland lagged behind other western countries. Although on the surface lawmakers suggested that the reason for this lag was that there was no pressing need for it, privately they acknowledged their reluctance to legislate in areas where the Catholic Church had a strong position, and the difficulty of convincing the Archbishop of Dublin, John Charles McQuaid, that they could implement safeguards to protect Catholic children from adoption by non-Catholic families. And herein lies one of the Catholic Church's main objections to adoption: the fear that it would open the door to legalized proselytism. Catholic writings consistently emphasized the dangers of proselytizing, and one of the reasons that female religious orders sought to create a monopoly on caring for illegitimate children was to prevent them from coming under the sway of proselytizers. When they finally agreed to legalized adoption, the hierarchy acknowledged the state's right to provide for children, and in particular to ensure that "unwanted" children were given good homes, but not at the expense of their Catholic faith and birthright. Hence, their insistence on the legal proviso that Catholic children could only be adopted by Catholic parents.

So concerned were Catholics in some countries with this imperative that they adopted seemingly extreme measures to ensure that Catholic children did not fall into the hands of Protestants who, no matter their true intentions, were regarded as nothing more than proselytizers. Linda Gordon writes about the "abduction" of Irish Catholic children by Protestants in Arizona mining towns in the first decade of the twentieth century. The children had been sent there from New York by the Sisters of Charity, who believed that the Mexican miners living in those towns were suitable adoptive parents simply because they were Catholic. However, when the children arrived by train in Arizona, white Protestant families believed that they should have "first dibs" on the children because of their race. The abduction of these children from the Mexican Catholic homes reveals the racism that was prevalent in Arizona at the time, but the fact that the children were even sent there in the first place reflected the desire on the part of Catholic charitable agencies to keep children firmly within the fold, no matter what measures were necessary to effect that outcome.

In Ireland, charitable agencies were so intent on keeping children out of the hands of Protestants that they sent thousands of illegitimate children out of the state for adoption in America between the early 1940s and the mid-1960s, with no follow up to ensure their safety and well-being on arrival, at the same time that they refused to allow families from Britain or Northern Ireland to adopt Irish children. The main fear was that British and Northern Irish families were Protestant and would, therefore, wrest the children from their Catholic faith.

The Catholic Church opposed adoption for other reasons as well. In addition to proselytism, members of the hierarchy feared that legalized adoption might encourage the widespread use of contraception. When Irish Archbishop McQuaid began to play a personal role in approving American parents to adopt Irish children, he insisted that they prove that they were not "shirking natural parenthood." The Catholic hierarchy never intended that the "artificial" families created by adoption compete with or supplant "natural" families, nor did they want to facilitate or promote the use of artificial birth control measures.

Members of the Catholic Hierarchy occasionally expressed veiled concerns about the possibility that adoption might give rise to incest or other forms of sexual perversion. They recommended against the placement, in the same adoptive homes, of unrelated children of the opposite sex. They feared that such children, because they were adopted and therefore not biologically related, would not feel "natural" sibling bonds and might stray into dangerous territory sexually. There were similar fears that biological siblings not raised in the same home, and therefore not knowing one another, might meet as adults and unwittingly marry, thereby giving rise to any number of unnamed catastrophes. These fears were not expressed often, but given the Catholic Church's concern with a wide variety of sexual perversities and threats, such fears likely formed a small part of the Catholic Church's resistance to adoption.

Although never explicitly stated, the Catholic Church may have opposed legalized adoption for another reason: the fear that it would undermine, or indeed make obsolete, the work of the thousands of male and female religious orders throughout the world who engaged in a host of "good works" as part of their mission. The Catholic Church, through its hundreds of male and female religious orders, was at the forefront of education, social welfare, philanthropy, and medicine from the late eighteenth century, when the number of Catholic religious orders and communicants began to increase significantly, into the mid-twentieth century when most western governments began to assume responsibility for the medical, educational, and social welfare work once undertaken by them. Female religious orders were particularly active in the care of children, especially young children who for one reason or another did not have the care and protection of their natural parents. Religious orders provided institutions, fostering agencies, and "adoption" societies to provide the basic care for orphaned, abandoned, and unwanted children that they could not get from their biological parents.

Religious orders engaged in this work for a variety of reasons: it was part of their sense of mission or calling, and there is no doubt that they were genuinely motivated by the humanitarian impulse to care for children who could not be cared for by their own loving and protective parents. But they also regarded the care they provided—whether through institutions, fostering agencies, or adoption societies—as superior to anything that could be provided by the secular state, including adoption. In fact, institutional care was preferred over foster or adoptive homes for providing for children who were orphaned, abandoned, or illegitimate because it enabled the religious orders to not only tend to children's physical needs, but also to ensure that they received proper religious education and training. More importantly, keeping children under the watchful eye of religious orders guaranteed that they would not lose their Catholic "birthright" no matter what their material circumstances might be.

See also Arizona Orphan Abduction; Catholicism and Adoption; Irish Adoption: A History.

Further Reading

Gager, Kristin Elizabeth. *Blood Ties and Fictive Ties: Adoption and Family Life in Early Modern France*. Princeton: Princeton University Press, 1996.

Gordon, Linda. *The Great Arizona Orphan Abduction*. Cambridge: Harvard University Press, 1999.

Whyte, John. *Church and State in Modern Ireland*. Dublin: Gill and Macmillan, 1971.

Catholicism and Adoption

Vern L. Bullough

Institutions for abandoned children were established in many monasteries and convents in the Catholic parts of Europe. Babies were abandoned on infant wheels in trap doors in many religious institutions so the mother could escape detection. Until the nineteenth century. Probably most of the abandoned infants died because feeding them was a major problem since they needed a mother's milk to survive. The main purpose, in a sense, was to save their souls by baptizing them before they died. Still, some did live.

Older children who were abandoned were often institutionalized. Many of the larger Italian cities established special institutions in the thirteenth and fourteenth centuries, many of which continued to exist into the twentieth century. Most individuals placed in the various hospitals and asylums, however, were never adopted since the main purpose of adoption was to preserve the male line, and relatives in this line were preferred.

In the United States, Catholic orphanages appeared in most of the major cities in the late nineteenth century, in part as a reaction to the threat of the Protestant adoption system and as a reaction to Reverend Charles Loring Brace's massive move to send abandoned children out of New York City to rural areas where they would either be adopted or indentured by local farm families who needed workers. Both Catholics and Jews were upset at Brace's activities in sending Catholic and Jewish children to Protestant homes and began to seriously consider adoption policies of their own. Mostly, they believed in institutional settings instead of adoption, but by the end of the nineteenth century, they were reluctantly coming to believe in adoption as an important step to take.

Most of the reformers, however, regardless of religious affiliation and background, were interested in the cause of children collectively rather than appealing only to prospective adoptive individuals. Instead, they often favored binding the children out by indenture as apprentices or servants. In Chicago, where the Catholics established St. Vincent's Infant Asylum in 1881 as a home for foundlings and pregnant, unmarried women and their infants, the first infant placement for adoption took place in 1882. Other Catholic institutions slowly followed, but adoption was still comparatively rare.

This was because getting homes for would-be adoptees was difficult and the Catholics continued to support institutional settings where they could be assured of the children's religious training. They could also run orphanages cheaper than their Protestant or Jewish rivals because the use of unpaid sisters made their operations comparatively inexpensive. Catholic countries like France did not legalize adoption until 1923.

In the U.S., the various Catholic orders and reformers established orphanages, such as Father Baker did in Lackawanna, the industrial suburb of Buffalo. Other priests and religious interests established such institutions as Boy's Town. In fact, the orphanages in many parts of the country became a Catholic symbol since, in a sense, they were so comparatively inexpensive to operate compared to Protestant or Jewish institutions. Even Salt Lake City had an orphanage run by Catholics while the Mormons had no similar institution. Probably the commitment to orphanages by Catholic authorities held up the development of adoption practices among Catholics. The Catholic Church has continued to find such institutions invaluable in dealing with the problem of abandoned children as the example of the late Mother Theresa in India would indicate.

See also The Catholic Church and Adoption: Lessons from Ireland; Foundling Wheels; Orphanages.

Further Reading

Pfeffer, Paula F. "A Historical Comparison of Catholic and Jewish Adoption Practices in Chicago, 1833–1933." In *Adoption in America: Historical Perspectives*, edited by E. Wayne Carp. Ann Arbor: University of Michigan Press, 2002. pp. 101–123.

Census 2000 and Adoption

Kathy Shepherd Stolley

Although the decennial U.S. Census has been conducted since 1790, the 2000 U.S. Census was the first census to include "adopted son/daughter" as a response when determining relationship to the householder (the person who owns or rents the home being surveyed). This allowed the Census to provide information, for the first time, on adopted children separate from biological or step-children. The data are designed to assist agencies that serve adoptive families as well as policy-makers. Because there has long been a lack of comprehensive national adoption data, Census 2000 has provided needed, comprehensive data on adopted children and their households.

Among the highlights of the Census 2000 findings are the numbers of adopted children in households. The majority (82 percent) of the 1.7 million households with adopted children had only one adopted child. Only 15 percent had two adopted children and far fewer (3 percent) had more than two adopted children. Approximately 18 percent of these households consisted of members of different races; and approximately 13 percent of adopted children of all ages were foreign-born. For adopted children under age eighteen, there was little variation in geographic region or state of residence and somewhat more girls than boys were adopted. Compared with biological children of the householder, adopted children under the age of eighteen were reported to be more likely to have a disability. Adopted children lived in households with higher incomes and slightly older householder parents than biological children.

See also Statistics on Adoption.

Further Reading

Kreider, Rose M. *Adopted Children and Stepchildren: 2000*. Census 2000 Special Report. Washington, DC: U.S. Census Bureau, October 2003. U.S. Census Bureau Web Site. http://www.census.gov/prod/2003pubs/censr-6.pdf (accessed December, 2005).

Primary Document

Adopted Children and Stepchildren: 2000

The following excerpt from a Census 2000 Special Report provides statistical data on the numbers of adopted children in the U.S. The full report as cited below provides much more information on the demographics of these children and their families.

Although many data sources describe the living arrangements and characteristics of children in general, few are large enough to permit the analysis of children by whether they are the biological, adopted, or stepchildren of the householder. Census 2000 included "adopted son/daughter" for the first time in the decennial census as a category of relationship to the householder separate from "natural born son/daughter" and "stepson/stepdaughter." The adoption category includes various types of adoption, such as: adoption of biologically related and unrelated children, adoption of stepchildren, adoption through private and

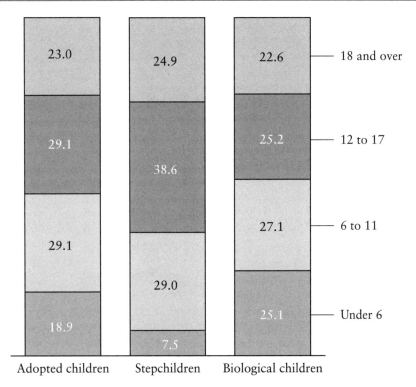

Figure 2. Percent Distribution of Children of the Householder by Type of Relationship and Age: 2000

(Data based on sample. For information of confidentiality protection, sampling error, non-sampling error, and definitions, see *www.census.gov/prod/cen2000/doc/sf3.pdf*)

Source: U.S. Census Bureau, Census 2000 special tabulation.

public agencies, domestic and international adoptions, and independent and informal adoptions. Census 2000 is the principal source of data on adopted children and their families on a national level.

[There are] 2.1 million adopted children and 4.4 million stepchildren of householders as estimated from the Census 2000 sample, which collected data from approximately 1 out of every 6 households. Together, these children represented approximately 8 percent of the 84 million sons and daughters of householders in 2000.

How Many Adopted Children and Stepchildren of the Householder Are There?

In 2000, 1.6 million adopted children of the householder were under age 18, making up 2.5 percent of all children of the householder under 18 (see Table 1). An additional 473,000 adopted children of the householder were aged 18 and over, again representing 2.5 percent of all children of the householder of that age group. In 2000, there were more than twice as many stepchildren (4.4 million) as adopted children (2.1 million), 7 with stepchildren representing 5 percent of children of the householder.

137

Census 2000 and Adoption

Table 1.
Number of Children of Householder by Type of Relationship and Age: 2000

(Data based on sample. For information on confidentiality protection, sampling error, nonsampling error, and definitions, see *www.census.gov/prod/cen2000/doc/sf3.pdf*)

Relationship	Total, all ages	Under 18 years					18 years and over		
		Total	Under 6	6 to 11	12 to 14	15 to 17	Total	18 to 24	25 and over
Total children of householder	83,714,107	64,651,959	20,120,106	22,803,985	11,200,237	10,527,631	19,062,148	11,185,934	7,876,214
Adopted children	2,058,915	1,586,004	389,296	598,326	316,638	281,746	472,911	273,957	198,954
Stepchildren	4,384,581	3,292,301	328,378	1,271,122	847,130	845,671	1,092,280	778,441	313,839
Biological children	77,270,611	59,773,654	19,402,432	20,934,537	10,036,471	9,400,214	17,496,957	10,133,536	7,363,421
Percent of age group	100.0	100.0	100.0	100.0	100.0	100.0	100.0	100.0	100.0
Adopted children	2.5	2.5	1.9	2.6	2.8	2.7	2.5	2.4	2.5
Stepchildren	5.2	5.1	1.6	5.6	7.6	8.0	5.7	7.0	4.0
Biological children	92.3	92.5	96.4	91.8	89.6	89.3	91.8	90.6	93.5

Source: U.S. Census Bureau, Census 2000 special tabulation.

The distribution of children in different age groups by type of relationship reveals marked differences associated with how the children became members of the household. The age distribution of biological children of the householder up to age 18 is primarily a consequence of the number of babies born each year, which has been relatively constant since the early 1980s. As a result, the proportions of biological children in each of the three 6-year age groups shown in Figure 2 differ slightly (25 to 27 percent). Percentages were smaller for both adopted children (19 percent) and stepchildren (8 percent) than for biological children (25 percent) under 6 years compared with the older age groups (see Figure 2). These differences probably reflect the time it takes to finalize the adoption process, as well as the decreasing number of infants in the United States in need of adoption, and the fact that children who are adopted by their stepparents would likely be at least several years old, having come from a previous marital union. For all three types of children, similar proportions were aged 18 and over, about 23 percent for adopted children and stepchildren and 25 percent for biological children.

. . .

Source

Excerpted from Kreider, Rose M. *Adopted Children and Stepchildren: 2000*. Census 2000 Special Report. Washington, D.C.: U.S. Census Bureau, October 2003. U.S. Census Bureau Web Site. http://www.census.gov/prod/2003pubs/censr-6.pdf (accessed December, 2005).

Child Citizenship Act of 2000

Suzanne B. Maurer

Public Law 106-395, better known as the Child Citizenship Act of 2000 and popularly referred to as the CCA, was enacted on October 30, 2000. It went into effect on February 27, 2001. The CCA established procedures for acquiring automatic citizenship or a certificate of citizenship by foreign-born children who meet specific criteria. Its passage and implementation are of interest to members of the international adoption community, including prospective parents in the United States.

Originating as a sixteen-page document in the House of Representatives, the CCA proposed significant amendments to Section 320 of Public Law 82-414, the Immigration and Nationality Act (INA). The INA was passed in Congress in 1952, long before issues such as international adoption and child citizenship became the subject of public attention in the United States. Also known as the McCarran-Walter Act, the INA was co-sponsored by Senator Patrick McCarran of Nevada and Representative Francis Walter of Pennsylvania. Established leaders in Congress (McCarran served a total of eleven terms while Walter served sixteen), the two men had joined forces to support legislation that would assemble an array of the existing immigration statutes into a single comprehensive piece of legislation.

Controversial at the time of its inception, the INA was vetoed by then-President Harry S. Truman and modified prior to its eventual passage in Congress. The final version of the Act comprised thirteen central provisions. Among these were revisions in the national origins quota system and the establishment of a central index of aliens living in the United States. The primary purpose of the Act was to address citizenship issues among adults. It did not directly consider the citizenship needs of minors.

Many changes have been made in the body of the INA since 1952. However, it was not until the enactment of the CCA in 2000 that extensive attention was paid to the question of citizenship status among foreign-born children. In response to the changing nature of migration flows, particularly the increase in the number of foreign-born children being adopted by American citizens, the CCA instituted a set of procedures that expedited the process of acquiring citizenship for children. Initially designated as the "Adopted Orphans Citizenship Act," the CCA was championed by legislators who had firsthand experience with international adoptions and were familiar with the delays that prospective American parents were likely to encounter as they sought naturalization for foreign-born children.

One set of provisions in Section 320 of the INA as amended by the CCA applies to foreign-born children who are living in the United States and have permanent residency status. The other specifies the provisions that apply to foreign-born children living outside the United States. Adopted children who fall into the first category are considered eligible for automatic citizenship; those who fall into the second category are not.

In order to become eligible for automatic citizenship, a child who is living in the United States and has permanent residency status must have at least one parent who is an American citizen. Additionally, the child must be less than eighteen years of age, be in the custody of a parent who is a citizen, and have lawful status as a permanent resident.

Under the CCA, the requirements for conferring citizenship upon foreign-born children residing outside the United States are more complex. These children can become naturalized citizens if a parent who is an American citizen completes an application for them and they live in the United States while completing the naturalization process. Other conditions set forth in the CCA, and consequently incorporated in the INA, call for taking an oath of allegiance if the child is old enough to understand the meaning and substance of the oath, having at least one parent who is a citizen, and being under eighteen years of age. The child must also reside outside the United States in the custody of a citizen parent, be temporarily present in the United States and have lawful status to do so, and have a citizen parent or citizen grandparent who has lived in the United States for a minimum of five years. Two of these five years of residency must have taken place after the age of fourteen.

Like other federal legislation, the CCA and INA continue to undergo revisions. Two years after enactment of the CCA, for example, another law was passed that had a far-reaching impact on the status of foreign-born children residing outside the United States. This law is Public Law 107-273, the 21st Century Department of Justice Appropriations Act. Enacted on November 2, 2002, the Justice Appropriations Act identifies a crucial change in naturalization procedures: either a citizen parent or a citizen grandparent could apply for naturalization on behalf of a foreign-born child residing outside the United States.

See also U.S. Naturalization Service and Foreign Adoptions.

Further Reading

"Agency Information Collection Activities: Proposed Collection; Comment Request." *Federal Register* 68 (2003): 6774–6775. U.S. Government Printing Office Access Federal Web Site. http://frwebgate1.access.gpo.gov/cgi-bin/waisgate.cgi?WAISdocID= 088308119206+1+0+0&WAISaction=retrieve (accessed November, 2005).

Aleinikoff, Thomas A., David A. Martin, and Hiroshi Motomura. *Immigration and Nationality Laws of the United States: Selected Statutes, Regulations and Forms.* Eagan, Minnesota: Thomson West, 2005.

Child Citizenship Act of 2000. H.R. 2883, 106th Congress, 2000. U.S. Government Printing Office Access Federal Web Site. http://frwebgate.access.gpo.gov/cgi-bin/useftp.cgi? IPaddress=162.140.64.21&filename=h2883enr.txt&directory=/disk3/wais/data/ 106_cong_bills (accessed November, 2005).

"Children Born Outside the United States; Applications for Certificate of Citizenship; Final Rule and Notice." *Federal Register* 66 (2001): 32137–32147. U.S. Government Printing Office Access Federal Web Site. http://frwebgate.access.gpo.gov/ cgi-bin/getdoc.cgi?dbname=2001_register&docid=01-14579-filed (accessed November, 2005).

LeMay, Michael and Elliott Barkan, eds. *U.S. Immigration and Naturalization Laws and Issues.* Westport, Connecticut: Greenwood Press, 1999.

O'Connor, Erin E. "Developments in the Judicial Branch: Automatic Citizenship Provisions in the Immigration and Naturalization Act, as Amended by the Child Citizenship Act of 2000, Do Not Apply Retroactively to Naturalized Citizens Over the Age of Eighteen." *Georgetown Immigration Law Review* 16 (2002): 539–541.

U.S. Citizenship and Immigration Services. "Fact Sheet: The Child Citizenship Act of 2000." U.S. Citizenship and Immigration Services Federal Web Site. http://uscis.gov/ graphics/publicaffairs/factsheets/chowto.htm (accessed November 2005).

U.S. Citizenship and Immigration Services. "Information for Adoptive Parents with Children Residing Abroad, January 2004." U.S. Citizenship and Immigration Services Federal Web Site. http://uscis.gov/graphics/services/natz/residing_abroad.htm (accessed November, 2005).

Child Donation

Vern L. Bullough

During the medieval period, children were often donated to a monastery. These oblates existed in both male monasteries and female convents. One of the more famous monasteries, St. Gall, had a special quarter for oblates. Most were well educated there and the stability of Benedictine monasticism was rooted in the child raising practices they established. Often passionate friendships developed among oblates and monks and as one author has argued, "transformed erotic into mystical impulses." It is not clear whether the oblates were obliged to remain in the monastery or were free at some point to leave, although large numbers became monks and nuns themselves. It also is not clear exactly what parents expected to get from giving their children to the monastery and what benefits the religious community saw in accepting such gifts. By the end of the medieval period, the practice had more or less ceased to exist.

See also Medieval Europe and Adoption; Medieval Orphanages.

Further Reading

Patricia A. Quinn, *Better than the Sons of Kings: Boys and Monks in the Early Middle Ages*. New York: Peter Lang, 1988.

Child Protection and Adoption

Zoë Breen Wood

The child welfare system has long seen safety as a primary justification for state intervention into the lives of families. The Child Abuse Prevention and Treatment Act of 1974 articulated identification and intervention in families where children were abused or neglected as a primary focus of child welfare. In those instances where children could not be safely maintained in their own families, it became the state's responsibility to remove them to the safety of foster care. As the number of children who "languished in foster care" increased, the state's responsibility to assure that children also achieved permanency was identified as well, sometimes in seeming contradiction to the goal of safety.

The Adoption and Safe Families Act (ASFA) of 1997 sought to address this dilemma. It clarified that a child's health and safety are paramount in making decisions about removing a child from their birth family or returning a child home. The ASFA specifies situations when the agency does not need to make reasonable efforts to reunify children with their birth parents and requires specific attention to safety in case planning, services, and case reviews. In this respect, the state's child protection role is emphasized. Child welfare systems increasingly use standardized risk and safety assessment tools to assist in determining whether a child can safely remain in his or her home or be safely reunited.

At the same time, the ASFA reinforces the concept that foster care must be seen as a temporary means of providing for safety, and requires states to make reasonable efforts toward achieving permanence for each child in care. The law establishes a shortened time for decision making for every child who comes into care. Unless there are compelling reasons to act otherwise, child welfare agencies must file for termination of parental rights when a child has been in foster care for fifteen months out of any twenty-four month period.

Thus, the number of older children needing adoptive placements is increasing. In 2002, a total of 127,942 children were in the custody of a public children's agency with the goal of adoption. Of those waiting children, 96.3 percent were age one or over, and 65.2 percent were age six or more.

In addition to being older than other children placed for adoption in more traditional settings, children whose parental rights are terminated through the child protection system are more likely to present with additional difficulties that make adoption more challenging. Children who have been abused or neglected are more likely to present with disorders of attachment, and with more severe behavioral and emotional difficulties. Children with documented prenatal drug and or/alcohol exposure are less likely to be successfully reunified with their birth families and may struggle with issues of learning and focus. Child protection agencies are often less able to obtain vital information about the child's medical and psychological background because the birth parent is not making a voluntary decision to relinquish custody and is less likely to cooperate with the agency. These additional challenges result in higher rates of adoption disruption than for children voluntarily placed as infants.

Many changes are being made in traditional adoption practice as it relates to placing children who become available through the child protection system. There is increasing emphasis on placing sibling groups together, placing children in the homes of relatives, recruiting and supporting non-relative adoptive families who are willing and able to take on more intense challenges, and developing and providing a variety of post adoption services and financial supports. No longer do child welfare agencies see their role as simply finalizing the adoption and closing the case. Instead they are recognizing their responsibility to partner with adoptive families to support a long-term healing process for their children.

Once a child is placed in an adoptive home, another question that arises is when and under what circumstances the child can be subsequently removed from that placement. In general, once an adoption is legalized, the adoptive family has the same responsibilities and rights regarding an adopted child as if the child had been born to them. That means that an adopted child could only be removed if the adoptive parents are found to be abusing or neglecting him or her. The same standards and procedures for removal should apply.

In some instances, the adoptive parents have argued that the child's behavior and/or disability is such that the only way to manage them is to engage in behaviors that would be considered abusive. For example, an Ohio family had their eleven adopted children removed when the children were found to be sleeping in enclosed beds characterized as "cages." The adoptive parents countered that this was their only way of controlling the children's behavior and that they had been counseled to do so by a therapist specializing in working with children with reactive attachment disorder. Another family in Tennessee had eighteen adopted children removed under similar circumstances. In general, the courts have continued to hold adoptive parents of troubled children to the same standards as those used for birth parents.

There have been numerous instances in which adoptive parents have requested that a child that they have adopted be removed from their home or "returned" because the adoption is "not working out." Agencies vary in the way in which they respond to these requests. At one end of the continuum, if the agency assumes custody of the adopted child, the adoptive parents can be charged with neglect and ordered to pay child support. At the opposite end, some agencies agree to take the child and try to find another placement. A recent phenomenon reported in the popular press involves underground networks of adoptive parents that find other families to take their unwanted child without the assistance of an agency.

See also Disruption and Dissolutions of Adoption; Permanency Planning.

Further Reading

Frame, Laura. "Maltreatment Reports and Placement Outcomes for Infants and Toddlers in Out-of-home Care." *Infant Mental Health Journal* 23 (2002): 517–540.

Koch, Wendy. "Underground Network Moves Children from Home to Home." *USA Today* January 18, 2006. USAToday.com Web Site. http://www.usatoday.com/news/nation/2006-01-18-swapping-children_x.htm (accessed February 2, 2006).

Pecora, Peter J., James K. Whittaker, Anthony N. Maluccio, and Richard P. Barth. The *Child Welfare Challenge: Policy, Practice, and Research*, 2nd ed. New York: Aldine De Gruyter, 2000.

Primary Document

"Discovering" Child Abuse and Protecting an Abused Child

Although child abuse did not become widely recognized as a social problem until the 1960s, the treatment of an illegitimate ten-year-old by her unrelated foster mother captured the public's interest almost a hundred years earlier. As Gene H. Starbuck (*Families in Context*, Wadsworth/Thompson Learning, 2002: 373–378) summarizes: in 1874 New York City, after neighbors' repeated complaints about the particularly bad treatment by the woman toward young Mary Ellen, legal action was finally taken to remove her to another foster home. Newspaper accounts generated widespread interest in Mary Ellen's case. As a result, a Society for the Prevention of Cruelty to Children was formed in several American cities. Although the Societies were modeled after the Society for the Prevention of Cruelty to Animals, a popular myth that Mary Ellen was removed under animal cruelty laws is not correct. She was actually removed under an old English writ, *de homine replegando*, that "allowed a magistrate to remove one person from the custody of another" (p. 375). Mary Ellen lived to be 92. The following excerpt provides a brief account of Mary Ellen's "legacy," the formation of the Society for the Prevention of Cruelty to Children.

Little Mary Ellen's Legacy

On a thriving farm up in Central New York a happy young wife goes singing about her household work today who once as a helpless, wretched waif in the great city through her very helplessness and misery stirred up a social revolution whose waves beat literally upon the farthest shores. The story of little Mary Ellen moved New York eighteen years ago as it had scarce ever been stirred by news of disaster or distress before. In the simple but eloquent language of the public record it is told: "In the summer of 1874 a poor woman lay dying in the last stages of consumption in a miserable little room on the top floor of a big tenement in this city. A Methodist missionary, visiting among the poor, found her there and asked what she could do to soothe her sufferings. 'My time is short,' said the sick woman, 'but I cannot die in peace while the miserable little girl whom they call Mary Ellen is being beaten day and night by her step mother next door to my room.' She told how the screams of the child were heard at all hours. She was locked in the room, she understood. It had been so for months, while she had been lying ill there. Prompted by the natural instinct of humanity, the missionary sought the aid of the police, but she was told that it was necessary to furnish evidence before an arrest could be made. 'Unless you can prove that an offence has been committed we cannot interfere, and all you know is hearsay.' She next went to several benevolent societies in the city whose object it was to care for children, and asked their interference in behalf of the child. The reply was: 'If the child is legally brought to us, and is a proper subject, we will take it; otherwise we cannot act in the matter.' In turn then she consulted several excellent charitable citizens as to what she should do. They replied: 'It is a dangerous thing to interfere between parent and child, and you might get yourself into trouble if you did so, as parents are proverbially the best guardians of their own children.' Finally, in despair, with the piteous appeals of the dying woman ringing in her ears, she said: 'I will make one more effort to save this child. There is one man in this city who has never turned a deaf ear to the cry of the helpless, and who has spent his life in just this work for the benefit of unoffending animals. I will go to Henry Bergh.'

"She went, and the great friend of the dumb brute found a way. 'The child is an animal,' he said, 'if there is no justice for it as a human being, it shall at least have the rights of the stray cur in the street. It shall not be abused.' And thus was written the first bill of rights for the friendless waif the world over. The appearance of the starved, half-naked, and bruised child when it was brought into court wrapped in a horse-blanket caused a sensation that stirred the public conscience to its very depths. Complaints poured in upon Mr. Bergh; so many cases of child-beating and fiendish cruelty came to light in a little while, so many little savages were hauled forth from their dens of misery, that the community stood aghast. A meeting of citizens was called and an association for the defence of outraged childhood was formed, out of which grew the Society for the Prevention of Cruelty to Children that was formally incorporated in the following year. By that time Mary Ellen was safe in a good home. She never saw her tormentor again. The woman, whose name was Connolly, was not her mother. She steadily refused to tell where she got the child, and the mystery of its descent was never solved. The wretched woman was sent to the Island and forgotten."

John D. Wright, a venerable Quaker merchant, was chosen the first President of the Society. Upon the original call for the first meeting, preserved in the archives of the Society, may still be read a foot-note in his handwriting, quaintly amending the date to read, Quaker fashion, "12th mo. 15th 1874." A year later, in his first review of the work that was before the young society, he wrote, "Ample laws have been passed by the Legislature of this State for the protection of and prevention of cruelty to little children. The trouble seems to be that it is nobody's business to enforce them. Existing societies have as much, nay more to do than they can attend to in providing for those entrusted to their care. The Society for the Prevention of Cruelty to Children proposes to enforce by lawful means and with energy those laws, not vindictively, not to gain public applause, but to convince those who cruelly ill-treat and shamefully neglect little children that the time has passed when this can be done, in this State at least, with impunity."

. . .

Source

Excerpted from Riis, Jacob A. *The Children of the Poor*. New York: Charles Scribner's Sons, 1902: 142–144.

Child Welfare League of America (CWLA)

Elizabeth S. Cole

The Child Welfare League of America (CWLA) is the nation's oldest and largest membership-based child welfare organization. Its mission is to engage people everywhere in promoting the well being of children, youth, and their families, and protecting every child from harm.

History and Mission

Founded in 1920 by sixty-eight private child welfare agencies, its membership base has grown to over one thousand organizations and includes hundreds more private agencies as well as city, county, and state public child welfare agencies. Headquartered in Washington D.C., the organization has six regional offices: Baltimore, Boston, Chicago, Denver, Los Angeles, and Reston, Virginia. These offices are affiliated with the Child Welfare League of Canada, which they launched as a separate entity.

The majority of CWLA members provide one or more of the full range of child welfare services, which includes adolescent pregnancy and parenting, day care, protective services, family preservation, kinship care, adoption, family foster care, and group and residential care. After 1990, as its mission expanded to include the well-being of children, youth, and their families, CWLA added to its membership groups providing health and behavioral health services, juvenile justice, and housing and education programs. Although it is a membership organization, CWLA provides leadership to the entire field, not just to its affiliates.

Since its inception, CWLA has had a particular interest in improving adoption as it is considered a basic and essential child welfare service. To promote excellence in policy and practice in adoption, the League has many roles. It sets standards, does research and data analysis, tests innovations and prototypes, educates, influences public policy, and collaborates with other groups towards shared goals. It was an early leader in improving the adoption of infants and then in moving the field solely from the placement of infants to include those with special needs and in securing federal funding and incentives for these services.

The CWLA Adoption Standards of Excellence

The CWLA Adoption Standards of Excellence, first published in 1930 and revised thereafter, are the only adoption standards that are nationally recognized. Originally conceived as guidelines to show best agency practice and policy, they are now also used for other purposes, such as formulating state and tribal regulations and laws governing adoption agencies, and by courts in cases to determine what agency practice should be, or should have been. Over the years, the standards have reflected the many issues and changes in all types of adoption—domestic, tribal and intercountry. Debates on determining what should be in these standards mirror the wide range of opinions within the field and the general public. The subject matter of the standards is occasionally determined by a combination of both public and professional concern. The content of these standards and the CWLA's other practice and policy positions flow in large part from the products of the Leagues's other activities, research and data collection, innovative projects, and educational and collaborative efforts with service-providing agencies and other organizations. The content is added to over the years as issues and practices emerge that need to be addressed.

The standards are a major method of signaling to the field changes in direction in the values, practice, administration, and policy of adoption. Always an important document, the standards take on added influence during times when there are many radical changes occurring in the field. For example, from the mid-1970s to 1990 there was a major shift in adoption values and practice from the placement of white infants to those children with special needs. At the same time, the conceptualization of who were acceptable adoptive parents and the role of the birth parents and the agency both during and after the adoption was significantly altered. Agencies and courts were being asked if previously sealed adoption records should be opened, and to whom and under what circumstances.

Additional CWLA Activities

Research and data analysis have always played an important role in CWLA adoption policy and practice recommendations. The CWLA staff conducts its own studies and collaborates with other researchers. Research in combination with information from practitioners and advocates sometimes has led to the creation of time-limited projects to focus needed effort on an issue or to test innovative practices and policies. In 1958, the League convened a conference of adoption practitioners to discuss the growing number of children in foster care and obstacles to their adoption placement. One of the recommendations coming out of the group was that agencies should consider financially subsidizing the adoption placement of these difficult-to-place children in much the same way their foster care was subsidized. CWLA became the first national organization to suggest the concept of subsidized adoption that is now present in all states and has federal financial participation.

In the 1970s, a study showed that people who lived near Indian reservations were less likely to adopt Indian children than prospective adoptive parents who lived at a distance from reservations in other states. CWLA started a project that kept records on the Native American children in one location who needed adoptive families as well as information on families in other locations who were willing to adopt them. Waiting children were linked with waiting parents. The project was called the Adoption Resource Exchange of North America (ARENA).

Because of its success in placing Native American children, the exchange began to list any other children that states were unable to place. This experience proved the need and benefit of a national adoption exchange cooperating with a network of state and regional exchanges. A much broadened exchange concept, which is technologically enhanced with children's pictures and utilizes the Internet, is still in existence. It is now part of the federally funded Collaboration to AdoptUSKids in which CWLA participates. The Collaboration's purpose is to devise and implement a national adoptive family recruitment and retention strategy. CWLA's role in the partnership is to facilitate and report on the National Advisory Board, to convene and conduct an annual partnership summit, and to perform evaluations.

Running the exchange in the early 1970s gave CWLA additional insight into the serious inadequacies in local agency provision of adoption services to children in foster care who were from minority groups, were older, were members of sibling groups, or who had physical, intellectual or emotional disabilities. Contemporaneous research and the clamor from vocal and newly-organized adoption advocates also pointed to the growing numbers of children in foster care and identified the obstacles to their adoption. At the time, most CWLA member adoption agencies only placed white infants for adoption, as did most of the other private adoption agencies in the United States. With funding from the Edna McConnell Clark Foundation, the North American Center on Adoption was created in 1975 within CWLA to refocus the entire field on the adoption of children with special needs and to identify and remove obstacles that prevented their placement. In partnership with other national organizations, the Center was instrumental in the passage of the Adoption Opportunities Act of 1978 and the Adoption Assistance and Child Welfare Act of 1980, which was the forerunner of the current National Center on Special Needs Adoption.

CWLA also seeks to improve adoption through leadership in policy making at the national level. It influences the legislative process through its Congressional testimony and lobbying efforts. In addition to being a major player in urging Congress to focus attention—resulting in the two pieces of landmark legislation just noted, as well as the Adoption and Safe Families Act of 1997—the CWLA also worked to have adoption expenses included as a credit against Federal income taxes due. Other accomplishments include increasing appropriations for the legislation and having workable rules and regulations accompany them.

The adoption standards and the information and knowledge gained through research, data collection, and projects are transmitted to the field through CWLA's educative efforts—training, consultation, and publications. CWLA hosts annual regional child welfare conferences at which adoption content is generally presented. It also sponsors special national adoption training events. Consultation and training are available to local, state, and national agencies and organizations. CWLA is the largest and oldest publisher of professional child welfare materials and, therefore, adoption-related materials. Its academic juried journal *Child Welfare* is issued several times a year and has often featured entire issues devoted to adoption topics. *Children's Voice* is a bimonthly periodical. *Children's Monitor* is an online newsletter on public policy and advocacy issues. During the 1970s and 1980s, the period of rapid and turbulent adoption change, the North American Center on Adoption issued the monthly *Adoption Report*. In 1996, the League established Child and Family Press, which specializes in children's and parenting books. Aside from its own publications, League staff also contribute articles to books and periodicals published by other organizations.

CWLA's educative efforts are not just limited to professionals and advocates. Public education is of equal importance. Their News and Media Center reaches out to local and national media as well as responds to requests for comments on breaking adoption stories. For current or more comprehensive information on CWLA adoption activities, find them online at http://www.cwla.org.

Further Reading

Child Welfare League of America. *Standards of Excellence for Adoption Services*, Revised Edition. Washington DC: Child Welfare League of America, 2000.

The Child Welfare League of America Web Site. http://www.cwla.org (accessed June, 2005).

Martin, Deborah L. *An Annotated Guide to Adoption Research*. Washington DC: Child Welfare League of America, 1998.

Children after Disasters and Crises

Vern L. Bullough

Natural disasters, wars and invasions, and other such crises often result in the breakup of families through the death or disappearance of parents and other adults known to children, as well as dispersal of siblings. Society is ill-equipped to cope with such crises; children often become victims through fake adoptions, or even real ones, by adults who are not concerned about the fate of the child involved, but primarily about how much income they can derive from the abandoned children. The abandoned children, often at a loss of what to do, turn to neighbors or even total strangers for help, protection, and psychological support, and they can easily be victimized again.

For example, only a few days after the tsunami struck Southeast Asia on December, 26, 2004, UNICEF estimated that there were 1.5 million children affected by the catastrophe; that is, they were now orphans or separated from their families. In Sumatra only a few days after the tsunami, UNICEF reported that they intercepted a message transmitted to cell phone users in the region offering three thousand orphans for sale. This was only the "tip of the iceberg" of mass trafficking in children from these beleaguered countries. Many children will be legally or informally adopted, but in a crisis there is little investigation of would-be adopters and many children are adopted to serve as cheap laborers or, in many cases, as sex slaves. These would-be adopters, called by a UN spokesperson "vultures in human form," seem to appear at every kind of crisis in which masses of people are dislocated.

Orphanages and other child caretakers become overburdened and even the most dedicated often fail. One of the major controversies in the aftermath of the surviving children of the holocaust of World War II was what to do with the Jewish children who were given refuge in Catholic convents. When relatives, and even parents in some cases, tracked them down after the war, official Catholic policy prevented their release to anyone but Catholics since the children had been baptized in the convent. Some convents and the cardinal archbishops in one or two countries deliberately violated this official policy, but many did not. Many of those Jewish parents or relatives who tried to reclaim their children utilized various subterfuges including even faked conversions to get the children, but many of those children could not leave the convent until they reached the age of consent.

In Mexico, a different kind of crisis resulted in separation of children from their parents when, in 1975, police rounded up what they believed were known guerillas and agitators with little concern for what happened to children of those arrested. The children involved were often taken in by friends or relatives, but many siblings were separated. It was only as a result of the development of DNA testing that some children separated from each other began to find and locate their siblings. This task was made somewhat easier by the opening of formerly secret Mexican archives by President Vicente Fox at the beginning of the twenty-first century. Some stories of recovered siblings made it into newspapers. In 2005, Aleida Gallangos, for example, who had been adopted by friends of her parents after her parents were arrested and disappeared, found her long-lost younger brother who had been sent to an orphanage and later adopted by another couple. Similar stories appear periodically about adoptions of Chilean and Argentine children who became orphans when their parents disappeared and who were separated from their siblings during the political crises in these countries.

Many children in such situations are neither sent to orphanages nor adopted, but manage to survive as street children. War and military occupation evidenced in areas such as post-war Vietnam, Korea, or Germany, which involved large numbers of American troops, led to the birth of vast numbers of mixed race children who often were abandoned by their mothers and placed in orphanages. Many were adopted by Americans, but large numbers were not. In countries like Romania, which under a communist dictatorship had criminalized contraceptives and abortion, thousands and thousands of unwanted children were abandoned. When the government was overthrown in 1990, the new government—in order to cope with so many children in its orphanages—more or less sold them for adoption on the international market. As the uproar grew both internationally and nationally over such practices, the government in early 2005 passed a law preventing any further international adoptions except to biological relatives.

The problem with adoption in any of these areas is that finding dedicated would-be parents and separating them from the vultures is no easy task. Failing this, the task is to protect the children from exploitation, and children's homes or orphanages or foster homes are only a second-best alternative.

See also Indonesia: Permanency Planning post-December 26, 2004 Southeast Asia Tsunami-Case Study; Operation Babylift; Romania and Adoption.

Further Reading

Boudreaux, Richard. "Woman Finds Lost Brother." *Los Angeles Times*, Jan 7, 2005, A5.

Coping in the Aftermath of a Disaster. Adoption.com Web Site. http://library.adoption.com/articles/disaster.html (accessed December, 2005).

Watson, Paul. "Amid Disaster's Wave of Misery, Orphans Are Cast Adrift." *Los Angeles Times*, Jan.5, 2005, A1.

(Similar post-tsunami stories, of which the ones included here are only a sampling, appeared in *Newsweek, New York Times*, and in most media.)

Children's Home Society/National Children's Home Society Movement

Roger W. Toogood

The National Children's Home Society was organized in 1883 in Illinois by Rev. Martin Van Arsdale, a Presbyterian Minister. He was motivated to spend his life helping children after a chance encounter with a little girl at a poor farm who asked him if he would try and find a family for her where she would have a "forever" mother and father. It is important to realize that in 1883 there was a tremendous lack of services. Most poor families and orphan children ended up in "poor farms." Many children were exploited as child slavery to work in factories.

Van Arsdale's first vision was to have a National Association with each state under his agency's charter. In the beginning, all of the societies were controlled by the central organization and originated under its charter. The first name was the American Educational and Aid Association. That was quickly changed to the Children's Home and Aid Society.

The first five years were spent establishing units within Illinois and setting up the National Charter. In 1888, Iowa was organized and then Minnesota in 1889. By 1895, twenty states had developed independent Children's Home and Aid Societies. They received support and direction from the National Children's Home Society organization that had become a Federation in 1897. By 1906, twenty-six states were members.

It was particularly significant when, in June 1906, the New York Children's Aid Society joined the Federation. The New York Children's Aid Society had been founded in 1853 by Charles Loring Brace, the pioneer of the placing-out system in America. Mr. Brace had previously started the Orphan Train Movement which occurred thirty years before the Children's Home Society Movement. Brace's effort was at a time when the population of New York City was some four hundred thousand people and there were four thousand orphans. Between 1853 and 1921, over one hundred twenty-one thousand children were shipped west on the orphan trains. Many of the Children's Home Societies formed between 1883 and 1920 cared not only for children in their own states but also for children who came by train.

By 1916, thirty-six states had developed Children's Home Societies including Ohio, Kansas and Nebraska (joining in 1893), Washington State and Kentucky (1895), Montana and West Virginia (1896), Florida and North Carolina (1902), Idaho (1908), Mississippi (1912), and Arizona, Utah, New Mexico, and Maine (1918).

In 1918, the name of the Federation was changed to the National Children's Home and Welfare Association. As the organization grew, a decision was made to set up four National Regions who held their own conferences. After 1921, the information becomes sketchy because of the merger into the Child Welfare League of America, which had been formed in 1920. The decision, however, to officially dissolve the National Children's Home and Aid Association did not occur until June 18, 1939.

The Children's Home Society Movement had a profound impact on the development of child welfare service and laws in America. The early founders had a keen sense of the value and importance of sharing their experiences and learning from each other. Being on the cutting edge of developing something new and important led to the leaders initiating annual meetings. National annual meetings were held starting in 1902 through 1939 when the final meeting of the National Children's Home and Aid Association was held in Buffalo, New York, on June 18. These annual meetings were held all over the country, even when the only method of transportation was by train or horse and buggy. Meeting places included Sioux Falls, South Dakota (1902), St. Paul, Minnesota (1905), Des Moines, Iowa (1909), Seattle, Washington (1913), Indianapolis, Indiana (1916), Milwaukee, Wisconsin (1921), and Memphis, Tennessee (1928).

Ideas for improving services were presented and discussed at all of the annual Children's Home Society National Meetings. In 1916, there was a major discussion about the concept of sterilization of the insane and feebleminded. The proceedings of the Joint Annual Meeting of the National Children's Home and Welfare Association and the Child Welfare League of America in Washington, D.C. on May 14–16, 1923, indicated that about one hundred agencies were members. Rev. J. V. Hawk, President of the National Children's Home and Welfare Association from Helena, Montana, spoke on "Paying Our Debt to Humanity." Other keynote speeches were given on the topics of investigation and reception work, the supervision and care of placed-out children, and the utilization of local resources by field workers in rural communities.

At these meetings, the "superintendents" and others shared their personal experiences on what worked, what was needed, what laws needed to be enacted and *how to raise money*. From the very beginning funds were raised chiefly through voluntary contributions in the form of membership fees. A 1905 National Children's Home Finder newsletter states that the National Society had received $276,794 and expended $274,687 during that year. At that time, Friends of the Children's Home Society also indicated a desire to endow the National Society. By 1923, the total Endowment had reached $4,000,000 and the annual operating income was at $2,000,000. In 1924, some counties began paying for part of the care of children they referred. In 1935, the first community chests—United Ways—began to donate to the agencies.

Although it is impossible to find all of the statistical data for all thirty-six agencies from 1883 through 1920, the available information indicates the significant amount of assistance provided. For example, in the founding year, Van Arsdale placed fifty-two children with families, one each week. From 1883 to 1933, the Illinois Children's Home and Aid Society ministered to one hundred thousand children. From 1883 to 1895, the combined twenty state societies had placed sixty-six hundred children. A report dated in 1923 indicates that, in forty years, the total number of children served by all of the societies was 153,784.

An excellent, detailed summary of the growth of child welfare services is contained in "History of the Illinois Children's Home and Aid Society" (1960), written by Marjorie Flint, an employee of the that organization. Some of the key child welfare items covered include the following: developing receiving homes; finding children who needed homes; supervising children after placement in suitable homes; hiring trained social workers; beginning use of boarding or foster homes in the 1890's; accepting care, starting in 1883, for children of all races, nationalities, and creeds; creating the first juvenile court in the world in 1899 in Chicago; describing how boarding homes became a well-defined service by 1902; and expanding focus in 1911 on work with parents to enable them to keep their children.

Early materials on the founding of the National Children's Home Society Movement pinpoint several key elements. They highlight that a tremendous need existed for improving the lives of children in 1883. There was almost a total lack of programs or laws relating to children's needs or rights at that time. Leadership of wise and compassionate people who were willing to give of themselves in an unselfish way to help children was still untapped. Also, the potential existed for new and creative solutions such as adoption, foster care, receiving homes, and financial help for single mothers and others. The very successful history of the Children's Home Society Movement—and the fact that many of the original thirty-seven agencies that formed the National Children's Home and Welfare Association in 1919 are still in existence and still serve children and their families in new and exciting ways—speaks strongly to the validity of their missions and the ability to adapt to major changes in the child welfare area.

See also Brace, Charles Loring; Child Welfare League of America.

Further Reading

The Minnesota Children's Homefinder Newsletter, Children's Home Society of Minnesota, 1899–1939.
The National Children's Home Society Newsletter, Annual Meeting Proceedings, National Children's Home Society, 1902–1939.

Children's Literature as a Resource in Adoptees' Lives

Helen Lodge

Interest in orphans and what becomes of them has long engaged readers. Nineteenth century readers and listeners, often children, enjoyed Charles Dickens'

Oliver Twist, David Copperfield, and *Great Expectations,* novels about children who somehow made their way without parents but with the timely intervention of kind, loving adults at important points in their lives. Later child readers, British and American, may have read Frances Hodgson Burnett's *The Secret Garden* and marveled at the change in orphaned and rather disagreeable Mary Lennox as she helps restore the invalid boy Colin to physical and mental health through the cultivation of the secret garden. *Heidi,* first translated into English in 1884, continues to interest children partly because it is the story of an unwanted, neglected child with a rare capacity for love who triumphs over obstacles. She loves her grandfather, the goats, and the Swiss mountains, with their restorative powers for Heidi and her friend Clara. Harry Potter, the latest orphan to hold children's attention, lives part of the year with a thoroughly unlikable aunt and uncle and a loathsome cousin, but has magical powers to transport himself from this mundane world into a parallel universe that is dangerous and exciting.

Twentieth century readers, adult and child, like to read about children abandoned, orphaned, or left with social service agencies because parents could not care for them. However, recent twentieth century fiction about children either in foster care or adopted is likely to be realistic and psychologically sounder than earlier fiction about such children. Tales for very young children focus on the necessity for love and the sense of security that love brings within a family or household. Tales for children in middle childhood or older broaden the focus to include development of a sense of identity. True accounts of adoption, historical and contemporary, available particularly to older children and adults, have the same focus and reassure readers that, despite hardships, adoptees can make it, can survive, do well, become successful parents, and raise their own families.

In a nation where there are a half million children in foster care (and millions more available for adoption in Central America, Eastern Europe, and Asia), it is well that American readers continue to read about adoption. The books considered here dispel the myth that adopted children are somehow inferior to children born into a family. All of these stories point to the sensitivities of children, their resilience, and their longing for sympathetic adults willing to become parents. Though there is much discussion and some disagreement over what constitutes a family and what kind of person a parent must be, the answer to the second question, in children's fiction about adoption, seems to be an adult capable of giving to children love, emotional and financial security, and the opportunity to grow into caring, empathetic adults whose interests and abilities are cherished and nourished during childhood and adolescence.

Stories for children in early and middle childhood can reinforce the child's sense of belonging to a loving family and of being a vital part of that family. Stories concerned with middle childhood emphasize that physical resemblance to parents is not the glue that holds families together. Instead, shared experiences, a valuing of aptitudes and abilities often different from those of the parents, and, in the case of biracial families, an appreciation of another culture matter most in the context of complete honesty about the circumstances of adoption. From a wealth of good material, certain stories stand out as suited to children as young as three, and other stories as better suited to children seven or older. For older children (sixth graders and older), there are many stories involving adoption or, perhaps, apprenticeship. For this older group, the readership is broader, but adoptees will be able to identify with some of the characters and the situations portrayed. All of these stories in which adoption is central present children seeking answers to persistent questions: Who really loves me? Who will be my friends? What do I do well? Where do I fit in? Responses to these queries help shape the answer to "Who am I?" These stories will help children understand adoption and, it is hoped, broaden their understanding of other children and adults.

The earliest stories that children will hear or "read" to themselves about adoption are picture books. The most successful picture book is one that the child asks for, especially at bedtime. Often the child will retell the story from the pictures and will repeat some of the more memorable phrases. Interest in reading begins with the picture book and extends to stories about older children as the child develops. An understanding of adoption as an accepted way of completing a family begins here.

Modern picture books for the youngest take care to distinguish the terms "real mother" and "birth mother" if the terms are used. If the book gives an explanation of the circumstances of adoption, it is an honest explanation of the circumstances under which the birth mother gave up the child. Some of the best stories about adoption for young children have been written by women who are themselves adoptive parents.

Stories for middle childhood deal with the persistent questions that children in this age group ask themselves and trusted adults. These tales take into account children's feelings of aloneness because they do not physically resemble their adoptive parents and because their biological parents gave them up. These tales counter their fears of rejection by peers and adults because these children may be, in some sense, outsiders or may not even be of the same racial background as others in the community. Children in the latter group find themselves inheritors of two cultures. Stories for this age group must be convincing and satisfying to the child reader.

Stories for older children, preadolescents and adolescents, are realistic depictions of soon-to-be adults still seeking answers to questions about their biological parents, their heritage, and their futures. These tales deal with the loneliness and abandonment that these children often feel. The best of the tales can give hope and a sense of achievement often against the odds. Children's literature can give children worthwhile vicarious experience while it allows them to explore in private the persistent questions: Who am I? What can I hope to achieve? Who are the people I would like to be like? The best of these stories have strong appeal to all children facing the developmental tasks of childhood and adolescence.

See also Adoption Literature Sampler; Abandonment and Adoption in European Folk Tales; Orphans and Adoption in Adult Literature; Popular Culture and Adoption.

Further Reading

Burnett, Frances Hodgson. *The Secret Garden.* Illustrated by Tasha Tudor. Philadelphia: Lippincott, 1962.

D'Antonio, Nancy. *Our Baby From China: An Adoption Story.* Photographs by author. Morton Grove, IL: Albert Whitman and Co., 1997.

Girard, Linda Walvoord. *Adoption is for Always.* Photographs Judith Friedman. Morton Grove, IL: Albert Whitman and Co., 1991.

Girard, Linda Walvoord. *We Adopted You, Benjamin Koo.* Illustrated by Linda Shute. Morton Grove, IL: Albert Whitman and Co., 1992.

Henry, Marguerite. *Justin Morgan Had a Horse.* Illustrated by Wesley Dennis. New York: Simon and Shuster, 1954.

Krementz, Jill. *How It Feels to be Adopted*. New York: Alfred A. Knopf, Inc., 1982.

Lewis, Rose. *I Love You Like Crazy Cakes*. Illustrated by Jane Dyer. Boston: Little Brown and Co., 2000.

Lowry, Lois. *Find a Stranger, Say Goodbye*. Garden City, NJ: Bantam Doubleday Dell Books for Young Readers, 1978.

Paterson, Katherine. *The Great Gilly Hopkins*. New York: Crowell, 1978.

Rowling, J.K. *Harry Potter and the Sorcerer's Stone*. Illustrated by Mary GrandPre. New York: Scholastic, 1998.

Say, Allen. *Allison*. Illustrated by author. Boston: Houghton Mifflin, 1997.

Spyri, Johanna. *Heidi*. Illustrated by Agnes Tait. Philadelphia: Lippincott, 1948.

Warren, Andrea. *We Rode the Orphan Train*. Boston: Houghton Mifflin, 2001.

Children's Understanding of Adoption

M. Elizabeth Vonk

Understanding adoption involves a life-long process for adoptees. At each developmental stage, the adoptee gains new understanding of complex core issues related to adoption, including loss, grief, identity and intimacy. Awareness of these issues is essential also for adoptive parents in order to assist their children's psychosocial adjustment.

During infancy, from birth to one year old, children are unaware of differences between adopted and non-adopted children. During this first year, all babies need consistent care and nurturance in order to establish a secure attachment that later can become the foundation of trust and intimacy. For adopted infants, this will involve adjustment to a transition from the biological to the adoptive parents. Even at this young age, adoptive parents can begin to practice and become comfortable with talking about adoption through acknowledgment of the way the child joined the family.

Toddlers and preschoolers, from one to five years old, experience enormous growth in their motor, cognitive, emotional, and relational abilities. They become aware of themselves as separate from their parents, begin to develop a sense of who they are, and begin to notice physical differences among people. Naturally curious, children of this age ask many questions, some of which are related to birth, reproduction, and their own "story" that explains where they came from. Recounting the details of their adoptions often becomes a favorite story that children of this age want to hear from their parents. Although often able to retell their own adoption story, preschoolers think concretely and are not yet able to understand the concepts underlying adoption. This may result in confusion for some children who may think that all children are adopted, or that some children are born while others are adopted—without first being born. Also due to concrete thinking, preschoolers are very accepting of adoption because they do not yet view their families as being different from others.

Cognitive development and exposure to other children and families during middle childhood, from six to eleven years old, allow children to understand the concept of adoption more clearly. At this point, children generally begin to realize that, in order to have adoptive parents, they must also have had biological parents who made a decision to place them for adoption. Adopted children at this stage wonder why their biological mother did not keep them. They begin to grieve the loss of their biological families, sometimes worrying about themselves and other times worrying about the sadness they imagine in the biological family members. They may wonder if they were placed for adoption because something about them is wrong or bad. In addition, children of this age begin to understand that they are "different" due to adoption, sometimes wishing they looked more like their adoptive parents, and sometimes fantasizing about life with their biological families. At the same time, they begin to receive and must learn to handle questions from peers about adoption, their biological parents, and differences in appearance between their adoptive parents and themselves.

Adolescence, from twelve to nineteen years old, brings further cognitive, physical, and emotional maturation, all of which contribute to adoptees' deeper understanding of adoption and its meaning in their own lives. As they work toward identity development and independence, adolescent adoptees experience a wide array of feelings from grief, anger, and confusion, to love, joy and gratitude toward both the adoptive and biological parents. Adoption-associated losses continue to be grieved during adolescence and may be heightened by identity issues and questions about belonging. In addition, the ability to think abstractly allows adolescent adoptees to try on alternative perspectives. For some adoptees, this allows for greater understanding of the complexity of their birth mothers' decision to make an adoption plan.

Questions related to identity development, an important task of adolescence, also are complex for adoptees. Fantasies about the biological family may continue well into adolescence as adoptees try to understand who they are in relation to both their adoptive and biological families. For example, adoptees may wonder about their biological potential in terms of their appearance, talents, and values. Some adoptees may begin to think about searching for their biological family in an attempt to better understand who they are. In short, the adoptees' emerging identity must include both the fact and the personal meaning of their adoption.

See also Adoptive Identity; Psychological Perspectives on Adoption.

Further Reading

Brodzinsky, David; Marshall Schechter, and Robin Henig, *Being Adopted: The Lifelong Search for Self*. New York: Random House, 1992.
Melina, Lois. *Making Sense of Adoption*. New York: Harper and Row, 1989.

China and the Change in Adoption

Vern L. Bullough

Beginning in the late 1980s, an increasing number of Chinese children were placed for adoption and available to the world at large. The result was a change in Chinese adoption practices. The change was a direct result of the Chinese effort to limit most families to having only one child. The Chinese used a "carrot and stick" approach—the women who already had one child were encouraged to be sterilized with all kinds of benefits given to them and their child, including a guaranteed place in the Chinese educational system. A new method, which allowed quick sterilization of the female, was often used because women could be sterilized in ten minutes without undergoing anesthesia. This involved inserting a catheter into each of the ovarian tubes and injecting an acid solution which scarred and burned the tube, effectively closing it to transportation of the ova. The effect was the same as if the tube had been cut or ligated.

Enforcing the one child family policy was not easy, and it was particularly difficult in rural areas. In fact, in many such areas, there was a modification, which has been labeled as a one son, or two child, family policy. This allowed rural families whose first child was a girl to try again for a son. (Some other families also received special permission.) If, instead of a son, a second daughter was born, the child was often abandoned and the couple tried again for a son. When found, the abandoned girl babies were put in an orphanage for possible adoption within China or by same-race families overseas.

There were more infant girls than this adoption market could handle, so the Chinese officials turned to a lesser favored alternative, adoption by a foreign Caucasian family or individual. American, Canadian, and European adoption agencies helped Chinese orphanages expand their facilities and modernize them to meet the growing crisis of abandoned female babies. In return, they were allowed to find adoptive homes outside of China for the children. China became a major source for international adoptions and remained so at the beginning of the twenty-first century.

See also Chinese Orphan Adoption by Foreign Families and the Development of Adoption in China.

Further Reading

Bullough, Bonnie, and Vern Bullough. "Sterilization in China." *American Journal of Public Health 75* (1985): 689.

Johnson, Kay Ann. *Wanting a Daughter, Needing a Son.* St. Paul, MN: Yeong and Yeong, 2004.

Chinese Orphan Adoption by Foreign Families and the Development of Adoption in China

Yue-mei He

Since the revised Law of Adoption of the People's Republic of China was passed in 1998, China has been involved in the international adoption market. The law, which took effect on April 4, 1999, led to increasing numbers of adoptions of Chinese orphans by foreign parents and families, especially by Americans. According to statistics issued by the U.S. government, 206 Chinese orphans were adopted by American families in 1992, and 330 in 1993. The numbers have continued to climb. In 2005, 7,906 were adopted, resulting in a total of over 55,000 adopted children going to the United States over this period. Among all the transnational adoptions taking place in China, those by Americans ranked eighth in 1993 but have remained number one from 2000 until this writing.

Researchers have given various reasons for the growing American preference for Chinese children. Probably the major reason is that China has a systematic and detailed national legislation for foreign adoptions. Although this has also been supplemented by provincial and municipal governments, the whole procedure is much simpler and easier in China than in most of the rest of the world. Another reason is that it takes much less time to adopt from China—only forty-five days for transnational adoption of children from China. In addition, it costs far less money for Americans to adopt Chinese children than to go through a domestic adoption in the United States or to adopt in most other foreign countries. Moreover, there is little chance of a lawsuit to later claim the child by its biological parents, which sometimes occurs in domestic American adoptions.

Information about the fate of the Chinese children adopted by many foreigners is occasionally reported by the Chinese media. From what Chinese know, they believe that, although the children are brought up in western cultures, the adopted parents try to also acquaint them with Chinese culture. The hope of the Chinese people is that these children will not forget their ancestors and traditions when they grow up. The Chinese currently believe that transnational adoptions will result in the building of strong bridges of love and friendship between the United States and China.

Generally speaking, Chinese think it legal and beneficial for foreigners to adopt Chinese orphans. With the development of industrialization throughout the world, increasing numbers of nations have begun to put more emphasis on the welfare of people in general, and those of women and children in particular. More and more people from different parts of the world have realized the importance of protecting children so they can reach their greatest potential. The Chinese believe that the main purpose of adoption, as the UN declared in 1986, is to provide an orphan with a permanent home rather than to adopt a child simply for kinship or to pass on family traditions from generation to generation. This new concept has become so widespread in many nations that the laws of adoptions have been modified to ensure a maximal benefit to the transnational adopted children.

Even regarding domestic adoptions, China has worked to upgrade its own program. For example, since 2003, social workers in Shanghai have supervised the whole process of adoption, both in domestic and transational adoptions. The Shanghai program, which is being adopted by other areas of China, involves procedures long used by Americans and others such as evaluation of the adoptive parents before adoption and regular follow-ups afterwards. Evaluations not only include the economic and social qualifications of the adoptive parents, but also their well-being: psychologically, morally, and ethically. The family background of the would-be adopted child is also examined including his or her family medical history and similar issues. If anything is discovered unfavorable to the growth and development of the child, the proposed adoptive relationship can be terminated or, at least, the would-be adoptive parents can decide whether to proceed further. Benefits to the adopted children of a sound psychological, as well as physical, development are considered the most important.

Transnational adoptions of Chinese orphans have been largely welcomed in China by institutions such as Children Welfare Centers or orphanages because of the crowded accommodations and limited funds and helpers. Most social welfare centers are overcrowded, although deserted disabled children and orphans keep coming in every day. The Shenzhen Social Welfare Center, originally designed to hold 200 children, has been forced to add 100 extra beds, and this is still insufficient space to meet an anticipated increase. This domestic failure has led China to encourage foreign adoptions.

From the Chinese data, it appears that most foreign adoptive parents are economically well off, with better living conditions and higher educations than the norm for the countries from which they come. The Chinese believe the children adopted by these parents can enjoy a better life and have greater opportunities than they could in China. This is particularly true for those who are physically disabled, although not many of them have been adopted so far. Adoption can enable these children to receive better medical treatment, and sometimes even remedy their disabilities as their biological parents or the Chinese orphanages could never do.

In sum, the Chinese believe that transnational adoptions not only help the welfare centers in China reduce the pressures of accommodations and shortage of funds, but also provide previously homeless children with better living conditions and even a better future. The ideas of mutual care, passions, humanity, and helpfulness so common among adoptive families will hopefully encourage more people from different nations to get together as a big family. They will love and respect each other more.

China certainly needs help to deal with its vast number of orphans. It is estimated that, as of 2005, there were more than two million orphans in China, 70 percent of whom were disabled with inherited heart diseases, cleft lips, or other physical defects. It would be unlikely for them to be adopted by Chinese families, mainly because of the costs of medical treatment and special education requirements. China has, however, taken some beginning steps. In 2004, China recognized a national funds committee, under the leadership of the Chinese Social Work Association, to aid orphans and the deserted disabled children in China. With these funds, it has been anticipated that, each year, 300 orphans can be sent to schools, 300 can find families to keep them, and another 300 can receive medical treatment. There are also some other local and personal organizations and funds to help support such huge armies of orphans and disabled children. Though these developments represent a beginning, China still has a long way to go.

There are, of course, other factors besides economic considerations that prevent Chinese families from adopting Chinese orphans or abandoned disabled children. These include traditional moral perspectives about the family, stereotypes of family development, and other traditional ways of thinking. Still, changes are taking place in China. In Guangdong Province, for example, new policies have been established to encourage local families to take more orphans into their homes in order to provide them with a family-like surroundings. This, it is believed, will help the orphans develop better physically and mentally. In return for participating, the families will be given small grants and the children can enjoy free medical care and free education. It is expected that such policies will encourage Chinese organizations and families to show greater love, care, and concern for their orphans and disabled children, and help them to live a happier life.

In a sense, this is a gamble by the Chinese since there is no certainty that these adopted children will be well-integrated into a new family setting and no certainty as to how long it will take them to get used to the new environment. There have already been a few reports about child abuse in such families. Questions have been raised as to whether these children's emotional personalities will be affected and twisted by such experiences. Another question involves what should happen if those placed in what Americans might call foster homes try to seek their biological parents when they become adults. These are developments the Chinese are just beginning to experience. In 2004, for example, a story appeared in the Chinese newspapers about an eleven-year-old Chinese orphan girl who went to Nanjing to seek her family roots. She was unsuccessful, but the question arose as to what would have happened if she had found her family. Obviously, many more problems will emerge as China wrestles with its problems. Still, with the development of new legal standards and concentration on nurturing children's needs, whether adoptive or genetic, children will live better lives.

Due to the major problems with orphans and handicapped children that China faces, it appears that transnational adoptions of Chinese orphans will increase each year. This will surely have effects on the adopted children, their adoptive parents, and even the nations where they are born and where they will be raised. Those adopted children will grow to be teenagers or will be in their twenties in the next decade. What will they be? What will their lives be like? Further research should be done regularly to improve the welfare of these adopted children, to better their benefits, and to strengthen the international friendly ties between nations.

See also China and the Change in Adoption.

Further Reading

China Internet Information Center Web Site. http://www.china.org.cn/english/index.htm

Collections of Laws of PR. China. *Law of Adoption:* Shanghai: Law Press, 2004.

Government documents. *The 15th Order Issued by Ministry of Civil Affairs of the People's Republic of China on the Enforcement of Law of Adoptions.* 1999. Ministry of Civil Affairs of the People's Republic of China Web Site. http://www.Mca.gov.cn

Immigrant Visas issued to orphans coming to the US. [Online, February 2006]. US Dept. of State Web Site http://travel.state.gov/family/adoption/stats/stats_451.html

Jiang, Xinmiao. *Research on the International Law System of Adoption.* Shanghai: Law Press, 1999.

Lin, Yuzhi. *Research on Kinship Laws.* Taiwan: Wunan Press, 1985.

Nanfang Daily Web Site. www.Nanfangdaily.com.cn./southnews

News reports by Wang, Xin: *Universal Times.* January 21, 2005, and the *Nanfang Daily,* December 2, 2003 and July 6, 2004.

People's Daily Web Site. http://www.people.com.cn

Zhang, Xuejun. "On the Essentials of Child-Adoption for Chinese Citizens." *Laws in China,* Vol. 6, 1998.

Classical Greece and Rome and Adoption

Vern L. Bullough

Both Greek and Roman civilizations recognized adoption, mainly to guarantee a male heir. This meant adoption was mostly limited to boys and it was the man who adopted, not the woman. There are references to adoption in the Homeric poems, so it would seem to have existed from earliest times.

Infants were usually not adopted, although this did happen. Rather, the custom in many parts of Greece was exposing unwanted infants. In Sparta, this was done on Mount Taygetus but, as the story of Oedipus indicates, other sites were also used. Usually the children were exposed in large clay vessels which would indicate that it was hoped others would find them. Often necklaces or rings were left, or distinctive marks were made, from which the child could later be identified by their biological parents if the need arose. Such identifications play an important part in Greek comedy. Sometimes new infants were informally sold to wives apparently unable to have children and desirous of deceiving their husband by presenting the infant as their own.

In Athens, the earliest adoption legislative regulation was attributed to Solon (c. 640–559 BCE). The purpose of this legislation was apparently to prevent a wealthy man from being post facto adopted in order to obtain the estate of another wealthy man. Athenian law provided that all sons succeeded their father without question or possibility of argument about shares of inheritance since all shared alike, even adopted sons. However, sons adopted outside of the family (i.e., by other families) were disinherited.

For a father with a daughter and no sons, the simplest method of preventing her becoming an *epiclerus* (a woman who went with the estate) was for the father to adopt a son and have him marry the daughter while the father was still alive so she could get part of the inheritance. If the father died intestate before such arrangements could be made, her nearest male relative might claim her in marriage but he could not inherit, although his sons by her might.

Adoption was not difficult and it could be done either *inter vivos* (formal presentation of the adopted son to the relatives and followers of the parent) or by will. Adopted sons were usually chosen from within the larger family unit (i.e. nephews, cousins, even brothers). Adopted sons differed from other sons in that they could not make an independent will. However, the sons of the adopted son could succeed him. Only citizens could be adopted by private individuals, and only citizens could own and pass on to his children the family possessions. Plato, however, makes it clear that the purpose of adoption in his mind was not only to provide a successor to an otherwise vacant inheritance, but also admission to a family since he implies that adopted sons could have brothers and sisters as a result of the adoption.

In Rome, adopted sons were given the position of a son in the new family with all the duties and rights of biological sons, especially regarding inheritance. They received the adoptive father's name and rank. (A plebeian adopted by a patrician became a patrician and vice versa.) While adoption in Republican Rome was limited to males, in Imperial Rome, women could be adopted as well.

Adoption was a powerful political weapon. During the second century of the modern era, it was a way of assuring succession. For over a hundred years, several emperors adopted their successor: Nerva adopted Trajan, who adopted Hadrian. Hadrian adopted Antoninus Pius and Antoninus Pius adopted Marcus Aurelius. Marcus Aurelius, however, had a son named Commodus who he designated as heir. The tradition of imperial adoption of successor never regained the influence it had during the second century. Adoption, however, remained engrained in Roman law. Under the Emperor Justinian in the sixth century, a declaration of the biological father before the magistrate and also in the presence of the adopter and the child was sufficient to recognize an adoption.

See also Oedipus; Political Adoption; Roman Law and Adoption.

Further Reading

Lacey, W.K. *The Family in Classical Greece*. Ithaca: Cornell University Press, 1968.
Oxford Classical Dictionary. Eds. Simon Hornblower and Anthony Spawforth. New York: Oxford University Press, 2000.
Pomeroy, Sarah. K. *Families in Classical and Hellenic Greece*. Oxford: Clarendon Press, 1997.

Closed Adoption

Betsie L. Norris

A closed adoption is defined as one in which no identifying information (defined as names, addresses and phone numbers) is shared between the birth and adopting parents. Current practice, however, in closed adoptions is to give at least some non-identifying information to the adopting parents about the child's and birth family's medical history. Other non-identifying information about the adopting family (such as age, interests, talents, religion, family history, occupation, medical history, and other background information) may or may not be shared with the birth parents.

History of Closed Adoption

Although closed adoption is often referred to as "traditional adoption," closed adoption was really a twentieth century development. Before that time, there was little effort to keep information about the birth parent or parents from the adopting parents. Many children, in the 1800s for example, were sent out to rural areas either as foster children or as adopted children on the orphan trains since there was a shortage of workers in many parts of the country. In the twentieth century, adoption increasingly became more formalized. Often strict rules were implemented emphasizing such things as placing children in a home of the same religion as that of the child's birth family, and adoption agencies became increasingly professionalized as social work developed as a profession. One part of these reforms was an attempt to shield the child from the stigma of being illegitimate or having the father listed as unknown. When birth certificates began to be issued by various governmental units, children of unmarried mothers often had "illegitimate" stamped on their birth certificate or the father was listed as unknown. Sometimes the certificates had a different color paper for children born out of wedlock.

"Shield" from Stigma

Advocates lobbied in state after state to change the birth record of a child being adopted by removing the birth parents' names and substituting the adoptive parents as the parents by birth. In addition, there was momentum to close these personal records to the public, making the fact that someone was adopted, and the circumstances of their birth, private. In most states, these laws closed access to the original birth record to the parties to the adoption, including the adopted person, as well as to strangers, reporters, or other curious members of the general public. These records were not closed due to beliefs that adult adoptees should not have access to their birth information, although that is what many believe today. The laws were meant to shield the child being adopted from a life of stigma.

Secrecy Flourishes

At the time these developments were taking place, infants were often regarded by both professionals and parents as being a "blank slate" who could be molded by their environment. Social workers promoted the "clean break" theory, encouraging birth parents who relinquished a child to tell no one and go on with their lives as if nothing had happened, and encouraging adoptive parents to live as if their children were born to them. Adoption professionals took pride in matching an infant with a family in which they felt there would be similar physical characteristics, and counseled adopting parents that their children would not have questions or concerns about adoption if they grew up in a happy family. Birth parents and adoptive parents were served separately and many agencies went so far as to have separate entrances and waiting areas for the parties involved so that there would be no chance they might meet. As a result, closed adoption was commonplace from the 1950s through the 1980s.

In the 1980s, open adoption practices began gaining in popularity, in part because of research challenges to the concept of a blank slate, in part because of American society's greatly relaxed attitude about sexual mores and ex-nuptial birth, and also in part as a result of now-adult adoptees searching and speaking out about the ill-effects of secrecy in their lives.

Spectrum of Openness

The result was a spectrum of openness by which adoptions could be redefined. Several alternatives appeared. Adoptions could be fully closed (no contact or information shared between the birth parents/family and the adoptive parents); semi-closed (limited, usually written, contact shared through the adoption agency but direct identifying information not shared); semi-open (information more fully shared but not full disclosure on both sides and no ongoing direct contact); and fully open (the birth parents/family and adoptive parents share full identifying information, have ongoing contact, and the child is included in that contact).

Adoptions may fall anywhere on this spectrum, and sometimes may move from one level of openness to another over time. Levels of openness are most often guided by factors which include the adoptive and birth parents' perception of, and comfort level with, each other and the real or perceived best interests of the child.

Pros and Cons of Closed Adoption

Adoption experts agree that adoption decisions should be made with the best interest of the child being held paramount. With that being said, however, there can be a variety of opinions on what is, in fact, in the best interest of a child. The adults involved, often with input from the adoption services provider, are the ones making the choices about the degrees of openness, if any, which will be included in an adoption.

Today, openness in adoption is generally viewed as a way to minimize the losses for the child that are inherent in adoption. The degree of openness is determined on a case-by-case basis depending on the wishes of the birth and adoptive parents, the circumstances involved, and the philosophy and practice of the adoption professionals involved. Closed adoption is in the best interest of the child in cases where the child's safety clearly would be in danger if there were direct open contact.

Pros of Closed Adoption

When compared to an open adoption, a closed adoption gives birth parents the choice for privacy, which some feel offers a sense of closure and ability to move on with life. For the adoptive parents, a closed adoption provides no need to physically share the child with birth parents, and no danger of birth parent interference or co-parenting. For the adoptee, closed adoption provides protection from unstable or emotionally disturbed birth parents.

Cons of Closed Adoption

For the birth parents, closed adoption provides less grief resolution due to lack of information about the child's well-being, and it may encourage denial of the fact that the child was born and placed with another family. For the adoptive parents, a closed adoption may allow for denial of "adopted family" or fertility status, which can result in increased fear and less empathy for birth parents. Closed adoptions prevent access to additional medical information about the birth family, and there is less control because the information is agency-controlled. For the adoptee, there is possible adolescent identity confusion because the child is unable to compare physical and emotional traits to his or her birth families; limited access to information that others take for granted; and the potential for preoccupation with adoption issues.

Shift in Professional Standards

Today, in their *Standards of Excellence for Adoption Services*, the Child Welfare League of America has adopted a number of recommendations. One set of recommendations deals with the adopting parents and the biological parents, and stipulates that all parties to the adoption (the agency, those placing the child, and those adopting) should recognize the value of openness to all members of the adoption triad, permitting those involved to determine the degree of openness on an individualized basis. Such a decision should be based on respect for the rights of all individuals involved and arrived at by mutual agreement. A second set of recommendations deals with the adopted child who later in life wants to find out something about his biological parents. These recommendations state that the agency providing adoption services should support efforts to ensure that adults who were adopted have direct access to identifying information about themselves and their birth parents. These records, it is now believed, have critical psychological importance as well as importance in understanding the health and genetic status of the adoptee. It is essential that agencies promote policies that provide adopted adults with direct access to identifying information. Because such information is essential to adopted adults' identity and health needs, the agency should promote policies that provide adopted adults with direct access to identifying information.

Access to Adoption Records

One result of these changes has been a groundswell of adult adoptees seeking to open their closed adoptions. At the same time, birth parents are becoming more visible and often initiating the search for their now-adult child as well. These adoptees and birth parents have spoken out about the perceived harmful effects of secrecy in adoption and have advocated for change in adoption practices and laws to allow for more information to be shared both at the time of the adoption, and later when the adoptee becomes an adult. As a result, many states have changed, or are considering changing, their adoption laws and opening records regarding adult adoptees' origins.

See also Open Adoption.

Further Reading

Adoption Network Cleveland Web Site. www.adoptionnetwork.org (accessed May, 2005).
Brodzinsky, David, and Marshall Schechter, eds. *The Psychology of Adoption*. New York: Oxford University Press, 1990.

Child Welfare Information Gateway. U.S. Department of Health and Human Services, Administration for Children and Families Web Site. http://childwelfare.gov (accessed May, 2005).

Child Welfare League of America. "Standards of Excellence for Adoption Services." Child Welfare League of America Web Site. www.cwla.org (accessed May, 2005).

Sachdev, Paul. *Unlocking the Adoption Files, reprint ed.* Lexington, MA: Lexington Books, 1990.

Schooler, Jayne, and Betsie Norris. *Journeys After Adoption: Understanding Lifelong Issues.* Westport, CT: Bergin and Garvey Trade, 2002.

Sorosky, Arthur, Annette Baran, and Reuben Pannor. *The Adoption Triangle: Sealed or Opened Records: How They Affect Adoptees, Birth Parents, and Adoptive Parents, reissue ed.* New York: Corona Publishing Co. 1989.

Birth Certificates and Adoption

Vern L. Bullough

In most countries, the birth certificates of adopted children record their adopted parents. Since most states in the United States now allow adoptees to seek out their original parents, there has been a demand by adoptees to have access to their original birth certificate. Several states as of this writing—Alabama, Alaska, Delaware, Kansas, New Hampshire, Tennessee—have passed laws allowing adult adoptees born in their states to have access to their original birth certificates. Often, however, the birth certificates fail to give the name of the father.

Concerned United Birthparents (CUB)

Kathy Shepherd Stolley

Concerned United Birthparents (CUB) is a national, non-profit organization. Founded in July 1976, CUB grew out of a meeting held in Cape Cod and organized by birth mother Lee Campbell, who served as the organization's first president. Members were inspired by Jean Paton and others who were giving voice to the experiences of adult adoptees. Although not opposing adoption outright, CUB's position (as recounted on the Adoption History Project) was that most adoptions could, and should, be prevented by a focus on family preservation aimed young, vulnerable birth families.

CUB originally focused on being a mutual support group for birth mothers and is still largely associated with their cause. It has, however, expanded to include not only birth parents (according to CUB the long forgotten people of the adoption community), but also adoptive parents, adoptees, and spouses/family members, as well as adoption professionals.

The organization's mission, at this writing, is to provide support for all family members separated by adoption; to provide resources to help prevent unnecessary family separations; to educate the public about the life-long impact on all who are touched by adoption; and to advocate for fair and ethical adoption laws, policies, and practices. Support is offered through various means including group meetings, letters and email, telephone, workshops, retreats, literature, and the organization's newsletter, the *CUB Communicator.* CUB is headquartered in San Diego, California with branches in several other U.S. cities. It maintains an online presence at the Web Site listed below.

See also Mutual-Aid; Paton, Jean.

Further Reading

Concerned United Birthparents, Inc. Web Site. http://www.cubirthparents.org/
"Concerned United Birthparents." The Adoption History Project Web Site http://www.
    uoregon.edu/~adoption/people/CUB.htm (accessed June, 2006).

Counseling and Adoption

Angela K. Fournier

Adoption counseling is counseling provided to any of the adoption triad before, during, and after the adoption takes place. The needs for counseling services may differ depending on the age of the child at the time of adoption. Counseling services can be provided by trained experts in the fields of clinical psychology, counseling, and clinical social work. Although one's social support network, consisting of supportive family and friends, may be available and willing to help, the understanding and support of a warm, objective, nonjudgmental third party can be very helpful in making the difficult decisions and experiencing the intense emotions associated with adoption. These counseling services will differ for the birth parents, the adoptive parents, and the adopted child.

Counseling for Birth Parent(s)

Sometimes called pregnancy counseling, individuals with unplanned pregnancies who are contemplating adoption may benefit from adoption counseling. These services involve receiving guidance and support from a mental health professional who is knowledgeable in issues related to adoption. Services are available at adoption agencies, family planning clinics, medical centers, schools, and private practice firms. Counseling may focus on educating the birth parent about the adoption process and providing practical information. Most importantly, adoption counseling will provide to birth parents help with emotional distress related to the pregnancy and adoption decision.

Counseling can include helping birth parents make the difficult choice of parenting or adoption. This may include helping birth parents analyze financial and emotional resources to determine readiness and ability to parent. Once adoption has been decided, counseling may be necessary to help birth parents process and manage emotions they have about the adoption. Feelings can include, but are not limited to, sadness, grief, guilt, and anger. Birth parents will likely experience a feeling of loss and may benefit from counseling to help them accept their decision and the consequences of that decision. Although grief and loss may be strongest at the time immediately surrounding the adoption, birth parents may experience psychological distress at various times. Many birth parents experience emotional distress on annual occasions, such as the child's birthday or the anniversary of the adoption. For these reasons, counseling may be beneficial at different points throughout the lifespan for birth parents.

Counseling for Adoptive Parents

Adoptive parents may benefit from counseling even before deciding to adopt. Parents choosing adoption because of infertility experience a significant loss. Although they will experience parenthood through adoption, adoptive parents will not experience the rich thoughts, feelings, and behaviors that coincide with biological parenthood, such as contributing to the family genealogy, pregnancy, and delivery. Seeking counseling from a professional in the mental health field can help those struggling with infertility accept these losses and grieve in a psychologically healthy way. In addition, counseling can help infertile couples cope with pressure, whether intentional or not, from family and friends who are having children or who are anxious for the infertile couple to have children. Beyond providing support with issues surrounding infertility, counseling may help infertile couples with the decision to adopt, support them through the stressful adoption process, and provide social support and education during their transition to parenthood.

Adoptive counseling needs for parents who have completed adoption may differ depending on the age of the adopted child. In addition to adjusting to parenthood, those who adopt older children may experience stress in the home as the child adjusts to a new environment. Older children may have psychological distress and subsequent behavior problems, which are discussed below. Family therapy can help in understanding what psychological issues are resulting in behavior problems and what the adoptive parents can do to manage the child's behavior and facilitate healthy adjustment. These difficulties in adjustment of older adopted children are related to the different adoption process for older children, compared to infants, and psychosocial history. For these reasons, there are significant differences in the counseling services that may be needed for children adopted as older children compared to those adopted as infants.

Counseling for the Adopted Child

Counseling for the adopted child may occur before, during, or after adoption, depending on the age and psychosocial history of the child. Regardless of the age at adoption, all adopted children experience feelings of abandonment and loss with regard to their biological parents. Some experts suggest children adopted as infants suffer a greater loss than older children because, although they experienced distress and abandonment when relinquished by their biological parents, they were incapable of expressing the loss. Children adopted as infants experience these feelings during childhood.

The feeling of loss can carry into childhood and adolescence, with the child still unable to verbalize what he or she is feeling, resulting in acting out behaviors. Counseling can help children adopted as infants understand these feelings and develop language to express their distress and accept feelings of abandonment and loss. Although children may experience many different feelings, adopted children may experience a feeling of low self-worth related to being "unwanted," in addition to possible anger toward birth parents. Adopted children may experience psychological distress throughout the lifespan as they cope with demands of different developmental stages, including struggling with identity formation in adolescence, forming intimate relationships as young adults, and becoming parents themselves.

In addition to loss, both infant and older adopted children are at-risk for problems related to attachment, including emotional and behavioral problems as children and adolescents, as well as difficulties developing healthy relationships and intimacy as adults.

Older adopted children face some particular struggles in addition to those described above for adopted infants. The adoption process is often different for older children, in that they have experienced relationships with the biological parent(s). In addition to the loss or interruption of relationships with biological parents, they will likely experience disruption of relationships with grandparents, extended family and friends, and siblings. The adopted child may require counseling services to process the intense emotions of grieving these relationships.

Further complicating matters, older children often enter the adoption process because of abuse or neglect. Suffering physical or sexual abuse or neglect is traumatic for any child and may result in significant psychopathology. Although not all children develop clinical disorders, common problems may include symptoms of disturbed mood, anxiety, and conduct problems, in addition to more severe signs of mental illness. Even children who do not demonstrate clinical symptoms can benefit from counseling services to process feelings of responsibility or guilt related to the abuse/neglect. Children with known histories of abuse or neglect should receive services from clinicians with specific experience treating child victims of abuse and neglect. In a similar vein, older adopted children may have been exposed to substance abuse in utero and/or in the family environment, putting them at increased risk for medical and psychological complications. Children with this family history should be assessed in order to determine any physical or cognitive complications (e.g., Fetal Alcohol Syndrome; developmental delays) and to counter any maladaptive behaviors they may have developed through vicarious experience.

In addition to traumatic experiences, older adopted children often reside in several transitional environments prior to adoption. These environments may include living with biological parents, extended family or friends of biological parents, foster homes, and group homes. Children with this background may experience different relationships, rules of conduct, and styles of discipline in each setting. Such differences can result in significant confusion, disobedience, and poor decision-making skills in the child, complicating the transition to the adoptive home and the parenting style of the adoptive parents. In this context, counseling can benefit the child by providing warmth and support while adjusting to a new home and may include psychoeducation in skills related to adjustment and problem solving.

Counseling in Open Adoptions

The adoption triad may have a different set of counseling needs in an open adoption, in which the biological parents' identity is open to the child and adoptive parents. The adoptive parents and child may maintain various degrees of contact with the biological parents. In such cases, counseling can be beneficial to the biological parents, adoptive parents, and adoptive child separately or as a group/family. Counseling may help with common difficulties such as respecting parenting boundaries and roles for the biological and adoptive parents, as well as conflicts the child may experience (e.g., maintaining loyalty to adoptive parents while satisfying curiosity about biological parents). As with other counseling issues, services may be needed at various points in time throughout the child's life, as each piece of the adoption triad may experience distress or confusion in their role as the child experiences various developmental milestones (e.g., schooling, romantic relationships, career choice, etc.).

General Information on Counseling

For individuals who have not experienced counseling or psychological services, it may be helpful to have some basic information. As noted above, counseling can be received from clinicians with various backgrounds, including counseling, psychology, and social work, and with various levels of education, including bachelor's, master's, or doctoral degrees. The clinicians' training determines their interpretation of the etiology (i.e., cause) of the presenting problem, which then leads to the suggested treatment approach.

Clinicians may have various views on etiology and treatment, often referred to as their therapeutic or clinical orientation. For example, a professional with a cognitive perspective may see the cause of a child's oppositional behavior as the result of distorted thoughts or interpretations about themselves and the world. The subsequent treatment might include helping children become aware of their thinking, including self-image, and accept more realistic views of themselves and the world. Conversely, a clinician with a behavioral perspective might attribute oppositional behavior to consequences of the behavior (i.e., increased attention) that maintain the behavior. The subsequent treatment would include advising the parents to respond differently to the oppositional behavior in order to shape more desirable behavior.

In addition to the clinician's orientation, counseling can vary in regard to length and focus. Counseling services can vary in length from one session to an unlimited number of sessions, depending on the treatment plan. Services may be directive, in which the clinician has a specific agenda and direction to move the patient/client, or may be nondirective and more passive, in which the patient/client decides the direction and the clinician's role is mainly to provide social support. In addition to these factors, clinicians vary in their experience with adoption cases. Therefore, prospective counseling recipients should research clinicians and determine who has the perspective and experience that may best help with the issues at hand.

See also Adolescent/Teen Adoption; Child Protection and Adoption; Older Child Adoptions (Age 5–12); Open Adoption.

Further Reading

Brodzinsky, David M., Daniel W. Smith, and Anne B. Brodzinsky. "Children's Adjustment to Adoption: Developmental and Clinical Issues." *Developmental Clinical Psychology and Psychiatry*, Vol. 38. Thousand Oaks, CA: Sage Publications, 1998.

Brodzinsky, David M., and Jesus Palacios, eds., *Psychological Issues in Adoption: Research and Practice*. Westport, CT: Praeger, 2005.

Groza, Victor, and Karen F. Rosenberg. *Clinical and Practice Issues in Adoption: Bridging the Gap Between Adoptees Placed as Infants and as Older Children*. Westport, CT: Praeger, 1998.

Primary Document

Serving Needs

In April of 1977, under the administration of then-President Jimmy Carter, a hearing called by the newly designated Child and Human Development Subcommittee of the U.S. Senate's Committee on Human Resources addressed the proposed Opportunities for Adoption Act of 1977. During the summer of 1975, hearings had been called by the former Subcommittee of Children and Youth to address "problems and policies affecting adoption" (p. 1). The 1977 hearing re-focused Federal attention on adoption. The hearing record contains numerous statements and an extensive appendix of information including letters of support, various

articles, and other background material. The following excerpt is from a prepared statement by Elizabeth S. Cole, who was at the time Director of the North American Center on Adoption. Hers was one of several prepared statements provided to the subcommittee. Together, the statements provide a snapshot of why and how the Federal Government should be involved in adoption and foster issues. This excerpt from Cole's statement focuses on client services, arguing that subsidies and improved services are crucial, and would be money and resources well spent.

. . .

Who Is the Client?

Adoption, today, is described as being child-centered–that is, it focuses on meeting the needs of children rather than answering the needs of applicants who yearn to be parents. The child, then, is the client.

But what about the biological mother (typically, a confused, very young teenager who understands little about her own body, drinks soda pop sooner than orange juice, and exists on a diet of hot dogs and potato chips?). If the child is the client, are we not to involve ourselves in caring for the mother—even before the child is born—to educate her to proper prenatal care and nutrition so that the child is born healthy? Is it not our duty to help her as she battles the confusion of what to do once she becomes a mother—give the child up? continue her own schooling? attempt to keep and raise the child? We must help her to understand herself and the possible consequences of each of these decisions. The biological mother of the child must be seen as the client.

What of the biological father? In 1971, the Supreme Court, in Stanley v. Illinois, recognized some rights of the fathers, or of the alleged fathers, of the children. Agencies, in

many cases, have used up much time in seeking the father (while the children wait). If found, must he not also be counseled? If he comes forward, is he not legitimately the client?

And now we come to the adoptive parents, people who have expressed interest in adopting youngsters who bring with them problems of medical assistance, therapy, the psychological traumas inflicted by impermanence, the defenses they've created in order to grow up in the system, and so on. To be effective parents to the children, these adoptive applicants need support and counseling before they agree to have a child placed with them. Even more, they need the caseworkers' support post-placement, if they are to successfully parent the child. Certainly, they are the clients.

We need more workers, who are better trained, who can spend more time on more complex caseloads if we are to be successful in placing the child—our client and the country's concern—in a supportive, loving environment.

* * *

Source

Cole, Elizabeth S. "Prepared Statement," excerpted from "Opportunities for Adoption Act of 1977." Hearing before the Subcommittee on Child and Human Development of the Committee on Human Resources, United States Senate. 95th Congress. First Session in S. 961. April 4, 1977. Washington, DC, U.S. Government Printing Office, 1977: pp. 51–52.

The Cradle Society

E. Wayne Carp

The Cradle Society is a private, not-for-profit, 501(c)3, non-sectarian, state licensed adoption agency located in Evanston, Illinois. It has placed more than fourteen thousand infants in its more than eighty years of existence. Founded in 1923 by Florence Dahl Walwrath, with financial backing from five prominent Chicago-area businessmen, the Cradle was one of the first private adoption agencies in the United States to place infants with families.

Florence Dahl was born in Chicago, Illinois, on October 18, 1877, of Norwegian parents and married William Bradly Walrath, a lawyer. The couple had four children. In 1914, Walrath became involved in adoption work by finding a baby for her older sister, who lost her first child at birth and was told that she would never be able to have another child. Walrath did not plan to start an adoption agency, but her career was thrust upon her as news of her ability to locate adoptable children spread among her upper-class neighbors and beyond. At first, she kept the infants at Evanston Hospital, which provided three beds, and paid for the costs out of her own pocket. By 1918, she needed the help of her friends to defray her mounting expenses. Soon thereafter, the Evanston Hospital voided the agreement with Walrath on the grounds that its charter prohibited the care of healthy babies. It was then that Walrath decided to establish a separate, permanent adoption agency and incorporate the Cradle Society.

From 1923 to 1945, the Cradle Society stood outside of established social work practices and philosophy. Run by volunteer workers from the upper-classes, it was opposed to career social workers and professional standards. The Cradle encouraged unmarried mothers to relinquish their infants, failed to investigate the background of adoptive parents, and did not keep written records on its clients. In the 1930s it became famous for providing babies to Hollywood celebrities such as Bob Hope, Al Jolson, Ruby Keeler, and Donna Reed. The Cradle's national reputation also rested in part on its pioneering scientific methods in health care, which drastically reduced infant mortality.

After World War II, the Cradle Society began to incorporate professional social work practices and evolved into a comprehensive adoption agency. In the 1990s, the agency once again reevaluated its policies and philosophy, incorporating "open adoption" (in which birth families remain in contact with adopted children) into its program and founding an African American Adoption Center (renamed the Ardythe and Gale Sayers Center for African American Adoption), which annually places more than 250 black and biracial infants with adoptive families.

Further Reading

Carp, E. Wayne, *Family Matters: Secrecy and Disclosure in the History of Adoption.* Cambridge, MA: Harvard University Press, 1998.

Pfeffer, Paula F. "Homeless Children, Childless Homes." *Chicago History* 16 (1987): 51–65.

Cross-Cultural Perspectives on Adoption

Suzanne Frayser

A cross-cultural perspective of adoption involves understanding three concepts: 1) adoption, 2) culture, and 3) cross-cultural. It begins with a definition of adoption that is broad enough to identify the process and interpret its meaning in a variety of cultural contexts.

Adoption means to take someone voluntarily into relationship, whether formally (through a socially established procedure) or informally (by behaving as relatives). Derived from the Latin word *optare*, *"to choose,"* adoption centers on choice and is a social process guided by cultural criteria.

Culture specifies the meaning of adoption by defining it in context. Realizing its influence depends upon recognition of its basic attributes. Culture is: 1) patterned (ideas, behaviors are connected in a consistent way), 2) explicit (articulated) and implicit (unarticulated) in its expression, 3) symbolic (synthesizes many meanings in language, behavior, material objects), and 4) traditional (passed down from one generation to the next).

A cross-cultural perspective of adoption accounts for its variability of form, function, and meaning across time periods, geography, social groups, and individuals. It relies on an identification of patterned ideas and behaviors that span cultural boundaries. Not confined to ethnic or international adoptions that are identified by language, physical appearance, and geographical location, it includes adoptions into subcultures (e.g., homosexuals, religious groups) as well as historical comparisons of adoption within the same culture.

A cross-cultural perspective of adoption highlights issues that are often submerged when adoption is viewed within one cultural context. What follows is a cultural framework that can be used to develop an awareness of cross-cultural similarities and differences in why and how adoptions occur, as well as who participates in them and what the consequences are both for the individuals and groups to which they belong.

Language: A Key to the Cultural Meaning and Social Impact of Adoption

Language, one of the major symbol systems in all societies, provides an entrée into the cultural significance of adoption. Kinship terms are cultural guides to who is related and who is not. They also channel social expectations for appropriate behavior. Is there a different category for someone who is adopted and someone who is not?

Kinship terminology distinguishes between relationships with a social or biological basis. In the United States, "step" and "in-law" refer to socially acquired relationships. "Half" refers to the degree of the relationship that is established biologically. Half brothers and sisters share one biological parent. These linguistic distinctions have meaning; they imply that biological ties are primary, because terms for socially acquired relationships qualify biologically-based ones (e.g., mother). Informal language also reflects this emphasis when biological parents are referred to as the "real" parents. Adoptive relationships have no special terms. Why?

Although kinship terminology (a cultural construct) and the social relationships to which they apply usually correspond, they may be "out of sync" as social relationships change faster than cultural concepts. Kinship terminology has not changed as quickly as marriage and the family. Increasing numbers of births outside of marriage, divorces, remarriages, blended families, and adoptions have created new relationships for which there are not adequate terms of reference and address. Therefore, individuals develop ways to frame relationships until adequate, culturally shared terms emerge. Without the compass of kinship terminology, it can be difficult to know how to position relationships in one's life or how to behave. For example, how do step-children address their parent's spouse if s/he has not adopted him/her? Using the first name of the step-parent has become a way of dealing with this. When children are legally adopted, how do they address their adoptive parents and refer to their biological parents? "Birth" mother and father are relatively new terms that provide a way to talk about these relationships.

Kinship terminology varies widely across cultural contexts and provides a structure to understand the meaning of blood ties, social relationships, and the place of adoption. Kinship systems are another culturally universal way that societies frame the significance of parenthood, children, and adoption.

Kinship Systems: A Guide to the Meaning of Parenthood, Children, and Adoption

Consistent links between kinship systems, the importance of children, and the significance of being a parent shape the meaning of adoption in different societies. They express the cultural patterning of kinship relationships and influence the acceptance or disapproval of adoption.

Unilineal kinship systems include as kin only the descendents of a common ancestor traced through one gender. The continuity of a patrilineal system depends on the birth of males, and a matrilineal one, the birth of females. Biological descent in a male or female line prescribes not only proper behavior toward different categories of kin but also rights to authority, inheritance, political positions and succession, and religious roles. Being a mother, father, or child has more than personal significance; it affects one's standing in society and the continuity of the lineage, i.e., social groups of kin.

Membership in a unilineal group depends upon descent through specific males and females. Blood ties determine the distribution of resources and status to children. Patrilineal systems emphasize establishing paternity, because the biological connection between a man and a child is not clear. Matrilineal systems do not grapple with the issue of validating maternity since the biological connection between a mother and child seems obvious at birth. Consequently, patrilineages use cultural beliefs and social rules to clarify a man's paternity. Restriction of a woman's sexual relationships to one man in marriage is common; it implies that the children she bears result from her relationship with her husband. Non-marital sexual relationships for women are generally prohibited and severely punished.

Groups that adhere to these beliefs and practices are particularly prevalent in the Circum-Mediterranean area, where punishments for premarital or extramarital sex may include death of the offending woman at the hands of her father, brother, or husband. When the kinship group places a premium on being a father and having male children, adoption is an unlikely option. Rather, a man may marry an additional wife to produce children and/or divorce the barren one.

In contrast, matrilineal systems, particularly prevalent in the Insular Pacific, support adoptions and use them to solidify their matrilineages. Since maternity takes precedence over paternity, cultural beliefs (e.g., women should confine sex and having children to marriage) and social practices (e.g., divorce of a barren wife) for verifying paternity in patrilineal systems are usually absent. Because the biological link between mother and child is clear, so, too, is the inclusion of the child into the matrilineage. Therefore, a woman's adoption of one of her female relatives' children does not create questions about whether the child belongs in the matrilineal group.

In this context, the importance of adoption extends beyond dealing with barrenness. Adoptions between matrilineal relatives occur readily and serve a variety of social purposes. Brothers and sisters are members of the same matrilineage, since they are both descended from a female link (their mother) in a matrilineal line. When brothers adopt sisters' children, they reinforce ties with their sisters and establish their positions in localized matrilineages. When sisters adopt each other's children, they strengthen their ties with each other. Adoption can also create ritual and economic bonds between birth and adoptive parents. "Real" parenthood is defined more in social terms (e.g., caring for children) than biological ones.

In non-unilineal kinship systems, social imperatives recede in emphasis and individual decisions and preferences come to the fore as reasons for adoption. The bilateral system of the United States, where descendents of a couple are regarded as kin, regardless of their line or gender, illustrates how this cultural trend developed. As market economies became more prevalent in Europe and the United States, family forms shifted from extended families to nuclear (mother, father, their children) ones. Increasing industrialization and mobility fostered a cultural emphasis in the United States on independence, achievement, and individuality. Motherhood, love, and the "self" became particularly important concepts around the turn of the nineteenth century. The traditional division of labor segmented along gender lines—women in the domestic sphere and men in the public arena. Therefore, children became important as the focus of a woman's role, the expression of her love, and a way to manifest her "self"; and the basis for a man's role as a provider of his family and testimony to his virility. In the absence of children, adoption became a desirable and necessary way to create a family so central to the personal meaning of people's lives and a society organized around nuclear units.

The Process of Adoption: Principles for Understanding Cross-Cultural Variations

Kinship terminology and kinship systems are universal cultural frameworks for understanding the significance of parenthood, children, and social support for adoption. The specific social processes used to effect adoptions in different cultural contexts highlight the significance of culture itself in shaping the meaning of these transactions. The participants and rules for securing an adoption vary cross-culturally. What follows is an annotated outline of factors that can be compared and contrasted to develop a cross-cultural perspective of adoption practices within and across cultures.

Intra-Cultural or Cross-Cultural?

When adoptions occur within the same cultural context (e.g., ethnic subcultures, economic classes, homogeneous geographical regions), participants share similar assumptions about the meaning of adoption. Indicators of shared cultural systems are: a common language, shared kinship terminology and systems, consistent beliefs about gender roles, the meaning of marriage, parenthood, children, and adoption. Cross-cultural adoptions exacerbate questions of adjustment for both parents and children.

Participants in, and Triggers for, Adoption

Why do people give someone for adoption and why do they want to adopt some-one? At one end of the spectrum are adoptions that are freely embraced and encouraged by those who give and receive an adoptee. As described previously, adoptions in the Insular Pacific occur for a variety of personal and social purposes—developing ties in the local community, developing social bonds, reinforcing the kinship group. Likewise, the frequent practice in the U.S. of adopting a spouse's chil-dren serves to reinforce the collective identity of a new family. Also in this category are people who fervently desire to have a child due to involuntary childlessness, who are child-centered and want to care for children, and prospective parents who feel socially responsible for children without homes.

At the other end of the spectrum, social factors prevail over the personal desire or consent of the parent(s) to provide a child for adoption. Such adoptions usually involve the intervention of a social agency or group (e.g., the state, social services, a kinship, or ethnic group) that monitors the treatment of children. If the child is born into socially unacceptable circumstances (e.g., outside of marriage), or to socially unacceptable parents (e.g., too young, mentally ill, abusive, "wrong" class or ethnicity), social influences can pressure the parent to place the child for adop-tion into an acceptable context (e.g., with a married couple). In extreme cases (e.g., abuse), the social group may forcibly remove the child from the parent and terminate parental rights.

Abandoned and orphaned children often become the responsibility of social groups rather than individuals. They are the main sources of cross-cultural adop-tions. For example, after World War II, in the 1940s and early 1950s, Americans adopted children from Germany, Greece, and other war-torn European countries as well as from Asia, particularly Japan. Political policies and social upheaval make it difficult for families to stay together, and parents may reluctantly agree to give up their children for adoption. In 2003, the People's Republic of China and Russia were the top two countries from which Americans adopted. China's one-child population control policy and the break-up of the Soviet Union sparked these trends.

Criteria for Adoption

Socially explicit rules for who can be adopted, who can give people for adoption, and who can receive someone in adoption are clues about cultural expectations for parenthood, childhood, and relationships with others. Preferences of adoptive parents in the United States for young, healthy children make it difficult to place children who are older, have physical handicaps, or suffer from emotional difficulties. In addition, ethnic groups may resist adoptions of their members by outsiders because they fear the erosion of their group's identity and power.

The primacy of biology in defining parenthood in mainstream U.S. culture provides salient clues for why some traditional adoption practices in the United States are so significant. For example, the longstanding practice of trying to match the physical characteristics of the child with that of the adoptive parents reinforces an emphasis on biological connection and parenthood. Explicit laws protect those who have a biological relationship with a child. Adoption procedures require the consent of the biological parent(s) to an adoption and formal termination of parental rights. If the biological parent is not known or able to be located, some form of search and notification to that parent is usually instituted.

Biological connection, kinship position, marital status, gender orientation, and economic circumstances are often critical criteria for assessing the suitability of adoptive persons. Until the 1980s in the United States, it was difficult for unmarried couples, singles, and gays to qualify as adoptive parents. This implied a cultural belief that children should be raised by a married, heterosexual couple.

The standards for becoming adoptive parents are often more stringent and precise than for parents in general. A study of foreign adoptions in Scandinavia found that adoptive families are not representative of parents in general; they are more stable (less divorce and mobility), humanistic, and have more economic and educational resources.

Consequences of Adoption

The ramifications of adoption range from the intensely personal to the broadly social. Do family members treat adopted children differently than their biological kin? What effect does this have on the identity, adjustment, and self-confidence of the adopted child? How do members of the new family adjust to differences in appearance, language, and familiar behaviors? What social ties between individuals and groups does the adoption create? Are there different social rights and privileges given to adopted persons than to blood relatives? For example, what rights of inheritance do adopted children have?

Interpretation of Research on Adoption

More research on adoption has been conducted intra-culturally rather than cross-culturally. Research on foreign adoptions began in the 1970s in the United States and Sweden, among the first countries to institute international adoptions. Issues for study vary according to cultural context. For example, where there is more ethnic homogeneity in the researchers' countries, the research emphasis is on psychological problems, e.g., separation, attachment, adjustment. Where there are a number of ethnic subcultures, researchers focus on the self-confidence, sense of belonging, and identity of those adopted.

The Significance of a Cross-Cultural Perspective

Given changing sexual, marital, and family patterns in the United States, an increase in the proportion of ethnic groups in the population, greater contact between cultures worldwide, and increased acceptance of cross-cultural adoptions, the importance of a cross-cultural perspective toward adoption is critical. The frameworks and questions posed in this discussion can orient those who wish to enter this complicated, cross-cultural world in a systematic way.

Further Reading

Coughlin, A. and C. Abramowitz. *Cross-Cultural Adoption*. Lifeline: Washington, D.C., 2004.

Dalen, M. "The State of Knowledge of Foreign Adoptions, 2001." Comeunity Web Site. www.comeunity.com/adoption/adopt/research (accessed October, 2004).

Frayser, S.G. *Varieties of Sexual Experience: An Anthropological Perspective on Human Sexuality*. HRAF: New Haven, CT, 1985.

Cultural Socialization

Richard M. Lee

Cultural socialization is defined as the transmission of cultural values, beliefs, customs, and behaviors primarily between parents and the child, and the extent to which the child adopts these cultural norms and expectations to become a functional member of society. Specific goals of cultural socialization include the development of a positive racial and ethnic identity, an awareness of racism and discrimination, the acquisition of coping strategies to manage racism and discrimination, and competent participation in different cultural milieus. In transracial and international adoptions, cultural socialization is not as inherent or natural a process as it is for same-race biological and adoptive families due to the apparent and immutable racial and ethnic differences between parent and child. Consequently, transracial and international adoptive parents must make a more explicit effort at cultural socialization.

Two distinct approaches to cultural socialization, particularly relevant to transracial and international adoptive families, are *enculturation* and *racial inculcation*. *Enculturation*, also known as ethnic socialization, refers to the belief in, and practice of, providing children with educational, social, and cultural opportunities that instill ethnic awareness, knowledge, pride, values, and behaviors. These ethnic-specific experiences are believed to promote a positive ethnic identity, including a sense of belonging and pride in one's ethnic group. It is important to note, however, that enculturation does not specifically address the ways in which children are taught to respond to unfair treatment, discrimination, and racism. *Racial inculcation*, by contrast, refers to the belief in, and practice of, making children aware of racism and discrimination and having them develop coping skills to deal effectively with racism and discrimination. Other researchers have referred to racial inculcation as preparation for bias and racial socialization. Instilling children with this type of race-specific knowledge and skill is believed to protect them from the deleterious effects of racism and discrimination.

These approaches to cultural socialization—enculturation and racial inculcation—additionally may be expressed directly and indirectly by parents. Direct enculturation practices include having the child develop ethnically similar friendships, celebrate cultural holidays, and learn the language of the birth culture.

Parents who participate equally in these cultural opportunities or engage in parent-specific cultural activities, such as a post-adoption support groups, indirectly engage in enculturation. Direct racial inculcation practices include educating children about the history of racism in society, talking with the child about negative racial encounters, and teaching effective race-related coping strategies. Parents also may indirectly promote racial inculcation by modeling appropriate coping skills when discrimination takes place and proactively working to minimize future instances of racism or discrimination in their communities.

It is important to recognize, however, that not all transracial and international adoptive parents believe or engage in the practice of cultural socialization. Parents who are unaware of the prevalence and deleterious effects of racism in society are unlikely to engage in cultural socialization. R. G. McRoy and L. A. Zurcher, for example, made this observation in a seminal study of African American children adopted domestically into white families. They noted that adoptive parents who exhibited a sense of colorblindness were less likely to live in racially integrated neighborhoods and to make an effort at teaching their adopted child about what it means to grow up as black in the United States. Transracial and international adoptive parents with a more colorblind racial attitude, instead, are likely to engage in parenting behaviors that promote cultural assimilation. *Cultural assimilation*, also known as acculturation, refers to the belief in and practice of downplaying racial and ethnic differences between parents and the child and encouraging the child to adopt the norms and expectations of the host culture. In these instances, transracially adopted children are more likely to identify with the dominant and mainstream culture in their environment.

Cultural socialization is viewed as an important aspect of transracial and international adoption because issues of race, ethnicity, and culture are known to affect the well-being and adjustment of children. A Swedish study by A. Hjern, F. Lindblad, and B. Vinnerljung, for example, found that international adoptees were two to three times more likely to have serious psychiatric and social maladjustment problems than their Swedish siblings and the general Swedish population. But adoptees were not much more likely to have problems than non-European immigrants, suggesting racism and discrimination are contributing factors to their psychological problems. Other research confirms the impact that negative racial and ethnic experiences, such as perceived discrimination and identity confusion, can have on behavioral and emotional problems.

Cultural socialization also is believed to help transracial and international adoptees come to terms with the inherent loss of their birth culture and heritage. This type of loss is relatively unique to adoptees because they are not raised by their birth parents who are natural transmitters of the birth culture. The actual and perceived loss of birth culture and heritage consequently can have a profound impact on the development of a child, particularly on the formation of identity and a sense of place in society. Cultural socialization aims to mitigate these developmental challenges by instilling in the child an understanding of and pride in the birth culture's history and traditions, as well as preparing the child for life as a racial and ethnic minority in society.

There is a need for further research on the process and outcome of cultural socialization, as most empirical studies tend to focus on only specific aspects of culture and provide limited descriptive information about cultural socialization.

Research is necessary that addresses the complexity of relationships associated with cultural socialization and its impact on well-being and adjustment.

See also Culture Camps; International Adoption (Overview); Transracial and Intercountry Adoption.

Further Reading

Hjern, A., F. Lindblad, and B. Vinnerljung. "Suicide, Psychiatric Illness, and Social Maladjustment in Intercountry Adoptees in Sweden: A Cohort Study." *The Lancet* 360 (2002): 443–448.

Lee, R.M. "The Transracial Adoption Paradox: History, Research, and Counseling Implications of Cultural Socialization." *The Counseling Psychologist* 31 (2003): 711–744.

McRoy, R.G., and L.A. Zurcher. *Transracial and Inracial Adoptees.* Springfield, IL: Charles Thomas, 1983.

Culture Camps

Kim Park Nelson

Culture camps, also called heritage camps, are experiences for transnationally adopted children (and sometimes for adoptive parents) intended to provide cultural familiarity to the adoptee's birth culture. The first culture camps were started specifically for Korean adoptees to introduce Korean language, customs, crafts, food, and history. Dozens of culture camps have sprung up for transnationally and transracially adopted Chinese, Vietnamese, Asian Indian, Latino/a, Russian, Eastern European, Filipino/a, African American, and Korean adoptees. Some provide programs and services for a single ethnic or national group, while others serve a multicultural population. Culture camps generally state their goals are to promote ethnic and national pride for adoptees' birth cultures and to provide the opportunity for transnationally adopted children to meet other adoptees of a similar racial or ethnic heritage.

Like most children's camps, culture camps generally take place in the summer for several days or weeks. Both day camps and overnight camp programs are available. Camp activities typically include exposure to material culture such as food, crafts, clothing, and housing; instruction in national history, physical and human geography, and language; and cultural activities, such as music, games, storytelling, holiday celebration, and observed traditional customs. Sometimes sessions on adoption experience, self-esteem, and racism are also included. A typical camp schedule might include classes and hands-on workshops during the day, an ethnically appropriate meal, and social activities incorporating elements of birth country culture in the evening.

Culture camps are considered to be one tool in a suite of post-adoption services for adoptees and their families. Camps are sponsored by a variety of post-adoption service organizations, including adoption agencies, adoptive parents organizations, and cultural organizations. Camp staff may include adoption agency social workers or other educators, adoptive parents, and/or adult adoptees.

Though it is unknown how many transnational and/or transracial adoptees have attended them, culture camps are generally touted by adoptive parents as positive experiences for their transnationally adopted children, necessary as one element of a multi-level strategy of effective parenting of a child of a different race or culture. Because of the minority status of transnational adoption as a family-building practice, culture camps are a location in which being a transnational adoptee or family is "normal." Camps can provide a foundation for community among families or adoptees, especially if campers attend yearly.

Adoptee alumni have given mixed reviews of their camp experiences. Some adoptees say that their camp experiences were good opportunities to learn about their birth cultures and feel they benefited from spending time with other adoptees, while others say they had little or no interest in camp experiences. Many say that their camp experience was key in their understanding of themselves as members of a racial minority.

Parents have criticized some culture camps as lacking substantive content or for promoting sales of motherland tours or birth parent search services through the hosting organization. Some adoptees have criticized camps for presenting an "orientalized" (in the case of Asian homelands), materialist, simplified, or pre-modern version of birth cultures. This critique stems from the emphasis on folk arts and crafts and simple material articles as cultural tokens at camps, and the general lack of instruction about birth countries' contemporary politics, economies, or societies. In addition, because culture camps are usually run by parents, adoption agency workers, or adult adoptees (as opposed to nationals of birth countries), there are also sometimes concerns about the cultural illiteracy of camp staff. Specific concerns about orientalist depictions of birth countries are raised in response to current Asian American racializations as foreign, passive, and commoditized. No matter how well-intentioned camp staff are, concerns remain that racial stereotypes are reproduced rather than undone at culture camp.

Other detractors doubt the effectiveness of teaching subject matter as complex as "culture" in a brief summer camp setting and see this practice as a gross over-simplification of cultural beliefs, practices and norms. For transnational adoptee youths, there is a general lack of useful curriculum that addresses the position of adoptees with respect to the complex and intersecting characteristics of class, race, culture, gender and sexuality.

See also Cultural Socialization; Post Adoption Services; Transracial and Intercountry Adoption.

Further Reading

Adoption.com. *Adoption Camps: Summer Culture Camps and Adoption Camps for Kids and Families.* Adoption.com Web Site. http://camps.adoption.com (accessed October, 2004).

Cunningham, Susan and Jeanette Wiedemeier Bower, compilers. *Transracial Parenting Project: Parenting Resource Manual*, NACAC (North American Council on Adoptable Children). July 1998.

Freundlich, Madelyn and Joy Kim Lieberthal, Joy Kim. *The Gathering of the First Generation of Adult Korean Adoptees: Adoptees' Perceptions of International Adoption* Evan B. Donaldson Adoption Institute, 2000. Evan B. Donaldson Adoption Institute Web Site. http://www.adoptioninstitute.org/proed/korfindings.html (accessed October, 2004).

Custody Wars

Vern L. Bullough

Custody wars came to public recognition with the case of Baby Jessica in 1993. That case involved a Michigan couple, the DeBoers, who had raised toddler Jessica from birth, but the adoption had never gone through. Jessica had been turned over by Cara Clausen, an unmarried mother, who had given birth in Iowa and signed an agreement to let Jan and Roberta DeBoer adopt her baby. She also lied about paternity, listing her then boyfriend, who also signed a release, as the baby's father. Clausen, however, changed her mind shortly thereafter when she reconciled with the baby's actual biological father, Daniel Schmidt.

Both biological parents filed for custody of the child. In the ensuing lawsuit, the right of Daniel Schmidt was affirmed by Iowa courts. The DeBoers appealed to the Michigan courts, which ultimately, after appeals, declined to overrule the Iowa court. The U.S. Supreme Court also refused to stay an order to return the child to her biological parents who, by then, had married. Baby Jessica, renamed Anna Jacqueline Schmidt, was transferred to the Schmidts in August of 1993. To aid the DeBoers in their struggle, Joan Pheney Engstrom of Ann Arbor, Michigan, had founded the DeBoer Committee for Children's Rights. Other counter groups were also organized such as the National Association of Birth Fathers.

Another case getting national publicity was that of Baby Richard. Baby Richard, who was legally adopted, had lived with a family since he was four days old. At age three and a half, he was removed and turned over to his birth father. Illinois law—the state where Baby Richard had been born—required a father to demonstrate an "interest" within the first 30 days of a child's birth. Otakar Kirchner, the father, did not start legal action for 80 days. He claimed he was living under the impression that the child was dead. He had left Daniella, the birth mother, when she was eight months pregnant to go to Czechoslovakia to tend to his critically ill grandmother. While he was away, Daniela was told he had run off with another girlfriend, and she fled to a shelter. By the time Daniela gave birth in 1991, she decided to give up the infant, and refused to contact Kirchner or reveal his name to the adoptive family. She also told Kirchner on his return that the baby had died. Eventually, when she told him the truth, after they had married, Kirchner moved to recover his child. Two lower courts agreed that Kirchner had abandoned his rights, but the Illinois Supreme Court chastised the adoptive parents (who preferred to remain anonymous) for going ahead when they knew that a father might be out there. The court ordered Baby Richard removed from the family who had legally adopted him.

Another contentious court decision, not in an adoption case but in a case of switched babies at birth, involved Kimberly Mays. When Kimberly's birth parents became aware of the switch, they wanted, if not to gain control of the child, to have visits with her, something that the girl did not want to do. The Sarasota, Florida, circuit court ruled that children are entitled to privacy and pursuit of happiness and that she had a right to bring to the court her desire to be free of her birth parents. To consolidate this victory, the Mays applied to formally adopt Kimberly. This decision was regarded as a victory for children's rights. However, the ultimate victory was the Florida decision in 1992 allowing Gregory K., then age twelve, to server ties with his birth mother. He was backed in his suit by a court-appointed guardian.

See also Birth Fathers.

Further Reading

In re Baby Girl CLAUSEN. 502 N.W.2d. 649 (Mich. 1993).
Ingrassia, Michele and Karen Springen. "A Bitter New Battle in the Custody Wars." *Newsweek*, July 11, 1994: 59.
Seligmann, Jean, with Susan Miller and Carolyn Friday. "Stirring Up the Muddy Waters." *Newsweek*, August 30, 1993: 58.

What Makes a Family?: A Case Study from the Courts

Kathy Shepherd Stolley

In 1993, American televisions, newspapers, and magazines were filled with pictures of the two-year-old child who had come to be known to the nation as "Baby Jessica." Photos showed a tearful child being transferred from the custody of her would-be adoptive parents, Jan and Robert DeBoer, to her biological parents, Cara and Daniel Schmidt, at the conclusion of a lengthy and highly emotional court battle that had been fought through eight legal cases in two different states. The "Baby Jessica" case culminated in a decision by the Michigan Supreme Court that provided a microcosm of larger social issues about the meaning of "family" that were, and still are, being debated throughout society. (See "Culture Wars" in this volume for a brief description of the case.) An examination of the perspectives expressed in the court documents provides telling evidence in this debate.

Over twenty briefs and expert opinions were submitted to the Michigan Supreme Court, most in an attempt to convince the justices that Jessica should remain with the DeBoers or be transferred to the Schmidts. For the DeBoers, the goal was to convince the Court that parenthood and family are more than biology; for the Schmidts, the heart of their case was that biological ties take precedent over other relationships because biology creates a parent.

The DeBoers and their supporters argued that the "modern" and appropriate view, "knowing what we know about children and their needs" was for Jessica to stay with them, who were her "psychological" rather than biological parents. Conversely, sprinkled throughout the Schmidt briefs were comments that "biology does matter" and that a "child's very identity is linked to his biological family." They framed biological families as "natural" institutions in which children are entitled to participate.

Interestingly, both sides argued that they formed a "natural" family. The DeBoer camp argued that, from Jessica's point of view as the only parents she had ever known, they were her "natural, if not biological" parents. The Schmidts claimed that, but for the DeBoers' interference, "this child undoubtedly would have developed the bonds of love and affection that naturally exist between a child and biological parents." They referred to themselves as her "natural parents."

The DeBoers and supporters also argued that children are not property but are treated as such by outdated court notions. They accused the Schmidts of claiming "ownership" based on biological ties, and that "it takes more than copulation to establish a parental relationship from a child's perspective." The Schmidt's arguments framed children as property by virtue of their being a biological product. They, in turn, accused the DeBoers of seeing the child as property and trying to apply the "most ancient principle of personal property known to matters affecting child: 'Possession is 9/10ths of the law.'"

Positions favoring the DeBoers argued that Jessica would experience "intense trauma and possibly permanent emotional damage" from losing the only parents she had ever known. Any transfer of the child was likened to a "tragedy of great magnitude ... amounting to court-mandated child abuse." Their attorney mused that if this abuse were to be apparent physical abuse such as a broken leg, the court would not consider ordering a transfer and that, from Jessica's point of view, a transfer would be equivalent to kidnapping. The Schmidts, in turn, accused the DeBoers of using "inflammatory language" and emphasized the importance of following existing laws and legal precedents that would return Jessica to them. Ultimately, these legal precedents held.

The case provided a reflection of society trying to work out some complicated issues. If one supports the DeBoers's position, the case was a tragic example of culture lag in which laws had not caught up with life's realities about the increasing numbers of non-traditional families and a slowly growing recognition of children's rights. If one supports the Schmidts, then the case was an example of the strength and preeminence of the biological family on which America was founded. Although this case was the "final word," so to speak, on "Baby Jessica's" custody (now Anna Jacqueline Schmidt), it spawned a number of similar cases in a society wrestling with the sorting out of family-related values. It was also not the final word for society, and succeeded in raising more difficult questions about psychological versus biological ties and what comprises a family than it provided satisfactory answers.

Further Reading

In re Baby Girl CLAUSEN. 502 N.W.2d. 649 (Mich. 1993). And all briefs submitted in this case. (This brief examination of the "Baby Jessica" case is based on a longer unpublished paper.)

D

Developmental Assessment

Bob L. Herman

Although many adopted children exhibit typical development, as a group they are at higher risk for developmental problems than non-adopted children. Developmental delays are to be expected in children who have been institutionalized, neglected, abused, or severely malnourished. While many of these children eventually achieve typical development, some do not. Because they are known to be at higher risk for developmental problems, adopted children should be closely monitored through periodic developmental assessments.

Developmental problems are usually defined as lags in major skills areas compared to other children of the same age. A child may exhibit developmental problems in only one area or in several areas. Furthermore, the levels of delay may vary from mild to severe in each area affected. The term "developmental delay" is typically used when the condition is believed to be temporary, whereas the term "developmental disorder" is used when the child's condition is believed to be a permanent limitation. Disorders are difficult to diagnose reliably in children under the age of five because developmental change occurs so rapidly in the younger years. Consequently, many professionals prefer to use the term developmental delay for adopted preschoolers with lags in development.

A developmental assessment is a close examination of various skills areas that are important to daily functioning. They include motor, speech, language, self-help, cognitive, or social-emotional skills. Children under the age of five usually benefit most from an assessment that examines each of these areas. As children near the age at which they begin formal education, specific skill areas can be targeted for assessment depending on the needs of the child. For school-age children, this usually involves an intelligence test performed by a licensed psychologist.

Some pediatricians perform developmental screenings as part of their routine examinations; however, an assessment is a more comprehensive examination of development that occurs over time. While screening performed by many physicians helps to identify areas in which an assessment should focus, assessment is more in-depth and helps to clarify whether intervention for delays is warranted. Assessments typically occur more than once—usually every six to twelve months for preschool children and annually for school-age children until early adolescence. This is because some milder forms of learning problems are not evident until later childhood.

Some pediatricians who specialize in services to adopted children have staff that can provide these assessments, but this is more the exception than the rule. There are also private assessment providers in many communities. These specialists are usually psychologists or certified special education specialists, though other specialists such as physical therapists and speech-language pathologists may perform the assessments depending on the needs of the child.

Health insurers do not usually cover the costs of developmental assessments. However, any parent in the United States with concerns about their child's development can obtain these free of charge. Locating assessment and intervention programs may require some research on the part of the parents, though the pediatrician's office should also have local contact information. While the pediatrician can be helpful in offering referral information about these assessments, a medical referral is <u>not</u> required.

For children aged three and older, assessments are available through local public school systems. Many school systems are struggling to keep up with demand for these assessments, resulting in long waits; therefore, referrals should be made as soon as possible post-adoption. Children under the age of three also have access to free developmental assessments through publicly funded early childhood intervention programs. As mandated by the Individuals with Disabilities Education Act, assessments for children under the age of three must be completed within forty-five days of the referral. Early intervention programs are available in each state, but they are administered through different departments, such as public health, mental health, and school systems. Pediatricians should have contact information for these local resources. Other adoptive parents may also be willing to share contact information.

Information for developmental assessments is usually obtained in two ways. The first is by gathering information from parents about the child's current and past skills. Information from parents is usually gathered through a structured interview. Parents of recently adopted children may have little information about the child's birth, medical, and developmental histories. This is especially true in situations in which the child was abandoned by birth parents or when institutions did not keep adequate records. Furthermore, at the first assessment point, the parent and child may still be getting to know each other. Sharing what is known about the child's medical history, social environment, and skills demonstrated thus far, even if this information is limited or incomplete, can be helpful in understanding the present needs of the child.

The second way that assessors gather assessment information is through the use of standardized developmental tests. On standardized tests, a child is given a particular task to do, for example stacking blocks or naming pictures. Testing instructions require the assessor to provide instructions in the same way and use the same materials each time the test is administered. Because the test is administered in the same way, the child's performance with these tasks can be compared to a representative sample of children of the same age and culture.

While standardized tests may be used as part of a comprehensive assessment, they should not be the sole basis for a diagnosis or treatment planning for any child. The usefulness of standardized assessment with recently adopted children has not been well-researched; however, this does not mean that they cannot be utilized. Adopted children do have unique characteristics that demand changes to the usual assessment process.

All children's development must be understood in the context of a child's prior experiences. Children adopted from institutions, especially younger children, may be extremely difficult to engage for structured assessment with someone they do not know. Assessors should never demand that adopted children under the age of five be separated from their parents for an assessment. The parent should be careful not to assist the child, because this will alter the test results. However, parents can be very helpful in helping the assessor elicit the child's best independent performance by being available and by indicating when the child is engaged, performing well or passively resisting. Some children may not exhibit all the skills they possess until they have spent more time with the assessor. If so, the assessment should occur over more than one visit.

Children who are internationally adopted present special challenges for developmental assessment. First, most do not speak or understand English well. These children can be assessed through the use of an interpreter using their native language if the interpreter is willing to stay as close as possible to the instructions administered in English. Even when this is the case, results obtained through an interpreter can only be considered an approximation of the child's true abilities. Language skills are especially difficult to assess because the translation may not match the content of the test item precisely. A better alternative is to use tests that do not require spoken language. For example, instructions for the *Leiter International Performance Scale*, which assesses learning skills, are administered through pointing and pantomime. Parents should be sure that assessors are not making predictions about the internationally adopted child's skills based on an assessment designed for English speakers only, at least until is it clear that the child is using and responding to English in his or her everyday life.

Keeping in mind the caveats described above, developmental assessment is valuable as a point of reference from which progress can be measured. As a rule of thumb, young children who are delayed as a consequence of institutionalization or neglect should make about two months of developmental progress in one month. Ongoing assessment can assist parents in evaluating whether the child is making adequate progress toward age appropriate development. Additionally, assessment offers an opportunity for parents to think about normal development and consult with a professional about their questions. Perhaps most importantly, assessment results can be useful in accessing developmental services if they are needed. Regardless of the child's developmental skills at an initial assessment, there is evidence that early intervention can make a difference in eventual outcomes for all children with developmental problems.

Further Reading

Barnett, D.W., and G.M. MacMann. "Early Intervention and the Assessment of Developmental Skills: Challenges and Directions." *Topics in Early Childhood Special Education* 12 (1992): 76–89.

Individuals with Disabilities Education Act Amendments, 20 U.S.C. §1400 *et seq.* (2004).

Juffer, F., and M.H. van Ijzendoorn. "Behavior Problems and Mental Health Referrals of International Adoptees: A Meta-analysis." *JAMA: The Journal of the American Medical Association* 293 (2005): 2501–2515.

Disruption and Dissolution of Adoptions

Trudy Festinger

Adoption disruption refers to an adoptive placement that does not continue. It generally involves a child that has been formally placed for adoption with an adoptive parent(s), who usually has signed an adoption placement agreement or similar paper. For some reason the adoption does not become final (is not legalized), resulting in the child returning to foster care and possibly thereafter to another set of adoptive parent(s). Adoption dissolution refers to a situation in which a child has been returned, usually to the custody of the child welfare system (foster care), following legal adoption.

Although there are many kinds of adoption, there is no systematic collection of information on independent or private adoptions in the United States, and no data on disruption or dissolution are available on international adoptions. There fore, the focus here is on children placed into foster care in public or private (voluntary) agencies, and in unrelated foster or related kinship families who wished to adopt.

Background

Over the years, there have been widespread changes in policies, practices, and attitudes toward foster child adoption in the United States. One of the more noticeable changes in recent years has been in the volume of adoptions. For instance, according to federal estimates, the number of adoptions of children in public out-of-home care between 1983 and 1995 remained quite flat, between seventeen and twenty thousand (Maza, 2000). Since then, the numbers have risen considerably in response to various federal legislative initiatives. For example, the Adoption Assistance and Child Welfare Act of 1980 (P.L. 96-272) mandated permanency planning for all children in state custody. Courts and agencies were directed to pursue the goal of adoption for children who were unlikely to return to their birth families. The legislation also required states to establish an adoption subsidy program (monthly payments to families who were eligible), and provided federal funds to be used as part of the state's adoption subsidies for children adopted from foster care.

The rise in adoptions most recently has been in response to the Adoption Incentive Program (also known as the Adoption Bonus Program) of the Adoption and Safe Families Act of 1997, which provided both policy and fiscal incentives to states for increasing adoptions. It was the first outcome-oriented incentive program, as explained by Penelope Maza of the U.S. Children's Bureau, as it authorized payments to states for increasing the number of children adopted from public out-of-home care. Thus, by fiscal year 1998, there were roughly thirty-six thousand adoptions (Maza 2000). A fiscal year 2001 report by the Children's Bureau estimates that there were fifty thousand children adopted from the public child welfare system nationwide.

Along with the national increase in foster care adoptions, there was a rise in professional concerns that more adoptive placements would disrupt, and more adoptions would fail. More recently, the concern has been intensified as a result of the focus on increasing adoptions and on speeding the adoption process. It has been noted by Richard P. Barth and Julie M. Miller that part of the concern has been based on the assumption that more adoptive placements and increases in adoption would be a function of speedy and inadequate home selection. Concern has also been kindled by guesses and rumors about high rates of disruption. Such concerns are not surprising, because disruptions are painful for all involved—the children, the adoptive parents, and the caseworkers.

Rumors and guesses sometimes fill the void when there is a dearth of knowledge. In this regard, however, there is quite a sizable amount of empirical literature on rates of disruption, showing that it is not such a frequent occurrence. In contrast, very little is known about the frequency of dissolution following legal adoption because it is so difficult to obtain accurate data. As noted by Trudy Festinger (2002), the limited data that are available show dissolution to be a rather rare event.

Disruption Rates

Richard P. Barth and Marianne Berry (1988), as well as Festinger (1990), note that it is difficult to arrive at an accurate estimate of the rate of disruption because of the many approaches used in numerous reports. Some focused on new adoptive placements, while others used all children already in an adoptive placement at a particular point in time (thus losing their history), following the children until an outcome was known. Most focused only on disruptions, but a few included dissolutions, impossible to disentangle. Some did not differentiate between single child and sibling group placements, although the inclusion of the latter can affect the rates reported and can result in problems of independence (duplication) with respect to some data such as adoptive parents' characteristics. Finally, with the exception of the study by Robert Goerge and colleagues, which used administrative data to track cases forward over an eighteen-year period, studies have used shorter follow-up periods, thus probably missing some cases that may have disrupted at a later time.

Nevertheless, what can one say about all these reports? For one, the figures show that the proportion of disruptions has risen since the 1970s. This appears to be the case in spite of problems of methodology and precision, and in spite of probable variations in the definitions used. The general rise in disruption rates is not terribly surprising, in view of the fact that adoptive homes were increasingly sought for older children, for those with other special needs, for instance sibling groups, or children with physical, educational, or emotional handicaps. It must be kept in mind as one thinks about rates that a global rate is really a composite of many rates that may differ depending on which particular group or subgroup is examined.

Furthermore, the focus on disruption, while dramatic, distorts the picture. It is best not to think of such rates in isolation, but to view them in conjunction with completed adoptions. Worries and rumors about disruption rates appear to have exaggerated the extent of the problem. It is indeed impressive that the rates reported since mid-1980, despite some variations here and there, do not differ substantially. Excluding studies that singled out small groups of older children, disruption rates have mostly varied from about 9–15 percent. Among older children, the reported rate has reached roughly 25 percent. Such rates hardly need to arouse astonishment, or be viewed in a negative light. One must not lose sight of the fact that in the long run the vast majority of children will have been adopted.

Factors Related to Disruption

It is difficult to arrive at a neat summary statement about factors that predict disruption because the picture is so complex, involving the children and their histories, the adoptive families and their circumstances, as well as service elements. Factors in all these areas have distinguished between past adoptive placements that did or did not disrupt, leading one to ask whether the group of disrupted placements is really composed of several subgroups that could be separately reviewed. For instance, there would be benefit in separating the analyses of foster parent adoptive placements and "new" (sometimes called legal risk or stranger) placements. The former, for example, has consistently been shown to have lower rates of disruption, most likely because the child and family have, in many instances, been together for some time. If problems in these placements arose, they would have "disrupted" before they became adoptive placements, and, thus, were not part of an adoption disruption group.

The other two factors that have most commonly been predictors of disruption are the older age of the child at adoptive placement and the psychological and behavioral problems exhibited by the child. Older children bring more of a history of past experiences, possibly including more prior placements and more families, more psychological links to birth families, more wariness about entering into new relationships, and perhaps less adaptability with respect to new family constellations and situations. The problems that some children exhibited were more difficult for adoptive families to manage, and presented these families with major challenges to their patience and skills.

Interviews by Richard P. Barth and Marianne Berry, and by Dolores M. Schmidt, James A. Rosenthal, and Beth Bombeck with adoptive parents following disruption, although based on small samples of volunteers, provide some clues about their disappointments, their sense of failure, their guilt and sorrow, and their perspective on what they felt went awry. Important themes concerned the attachment problems of the children and the parents' expectations for a less difficult child, a difference between what they imagined and the reality. Other themes concerned such things as children's difficulty "letting go" of birth families, and gaps in information about a child's background. Parents felt the information about the child was neither accurate nor complete; they felt that they were given a sales pitch and were ill prepared to handle the problems presented by the youths placed in their homes. Some felt the children were not ready to be adopted. They also spoke of little support from agencies following the placements.

Practice Implications

Studies point directly to the importance of extensive and accurate pre- and post-placement preparation of all parties—the children and the prospective adoptive parents—and to the parents' recognition that children adopted when older have greater adjustment difficulties than infants. Furthermore, prospective parents need to be given as much accurate information as possible about the children and their backgrounds, in order to avoid being enticed into stretching beyond their comfort level with regard to the kind of child they had in mind.

At the same time, families may need help in altering idealistic notions that their love and acceptance are sufficient to overcome the children's sense of deprivation and loss. In this regard, as noted by Michael Rutter, adoptive parents can be helped to recognize that many children come from high-risk backgrounds that include genetic vulnerabilities in addition to adverse past environmental experiences. At the same time, it is important to emphasize that there is much individual variation in children's responses to such past conditions, possibly due to various protective influences, including factors related to resilience.

S. L. Smith and J. A. Howard note that numerous recommendations of approaches to adoptive family preparation have been set forth amid an absence of any evaluation of their effectiveness. For the child, constructing a life-book, establishing a child's level of commitment to adoption, and contacting other adoptees, individually as peer mentors or as a support group, have been recommended. For the adoptive family, full disclosure of a child's background and difficulties, the availability of medical records of the birth parents and the child's birth records are considered very important. Adoptive parents have also suggested that child-specific information from sessions with a child's current or previous caretaker can be very helpful.

Support groups, including another family as mentor and meetings with other adoptive families, warm lines (telephone support services), and respite care, as well as online support groups, have been mentioned. Assigned readings, providing factual information about adoption, and discussions regarding subsidy contract negotiations and relevant tax laws have been suggested. Also, as discussed by Harold D. Grotevant and Ruth G. McRoy, if the intended adoption is a so-called "open" one with some level of links maintained with the birth parents, there are additional considerations for support.

Following any adoptive placement, social worker contact with the family is vital so that the family can discuss whatever questions and concerns may arise, and workers can assist families to develop plans and strategies, or provide referrals, if needed. Finally, adoptive parents need information about accessing various community supports and services so that they know where to turn in the future in case the need arises.

Adoption dissolution, although few in numbers, does point to the critical need for post-adoption supports and services as discussed by Madelyn Freundlich and Lois Wright. A study based on 450 post-adoption interviews by Festinger (2001) showed that many families who adopted children from foster care felt abandoned and felt they did not know where to turn for information and support when the need arose. Most, having been foster parents for quite some time, had been accustomed to a variety of agency supports until the day they adopted. They expressed an urgent need for informational assistance in general, as well as substantial needs in numerous substantive areas: after-school services, educational services, home assistance, clinical services, health services, housing assistance, vocational services, and legal assistance. It is essential that post-adoption services, when developed, address the variety of needs voiced by families.

See also Counseling and Adoption; Lifebooks; Mutual-Aid; Post-adoption Services.

Further Reading

Barth, Richard P. and Julie M. Miller. "Building Effective Post-adoption Services: What is the Empirical Foundation?" *Family Relations* 49 (2000): 447–455.

Barth, Richard P. and Marianne Berry. *Adoption and Disruption: Rates, Risks and Responses.* New York: Aldine De Gruyter, 1988.

Festinger, Trudy. "Adoption Disruption." In David M. Brodzinsky and Marshall D. Schechter, eds. *The Psychology of Adoption.* New York: Oxford University Press, 1990, pp. 201–218.

Festinger, Trudy. *After Adoption: A Study of Placement Stability and Parents' Service Needs.* New York: New York University, School of Social Work, 2001.

Festinger, Trudy. "After Adoption: Dissolution or Permanence." *Child Welfare* 81 (2002): 515–533.

Freundlich, Madelyn and Lois Wright. *Post-Permanency Services.* Washington, DC: Casey Family Programs, 2003.

Goerge, Robert M., Ebony C. Howard, David Yu, and Susan Radomsky. *Adoption, Disruption, and Displacement in the Child Welfare System, 1976–94.* Chicago: University of Chicago, The Chapin Hall Center for Children, 1997.

Grotevant, Harold D. and Ruth G. McRoy. *Openness in Adoption: Exploring Family Connections*. Thousand Oaks, CA: Sage Publications, 1998.

Maza, Penelope L. "Using Administrative Data to Reward Agency Performance: The Case of the Federal Adoption Incentive Program." *Child Welfare* 79 (2000): 444–456.

Rutter, Michael. "Children in Substitute Care: Some Conceptual Considerations and Research Implications." *Children and Youth Services Review* 22 (2000): 685–703.

Schmidt, Dolores M., James A. Rosenthal, and Beth Bombeck. "Parents' Views of Adoption Disruption." *Children and Youth Services Review* 10 (1988): 119–130.

Smith, S. L. and J. A. Howard. *Promoting Successful Adoptions—Practice with Troubled Families*. Thousand Oaks, CA: Sage Publications, 1999.

U.S. Children's Bureau. *The AFCARS Report: Preliminary FY 2001 Estimates as of March 2003(8)*. Washington, DC: U.S. Department of Health and Human Services, Administration on Children, Youth and Families, 2003. U.S. Children's Bureau Web Site. http://www.acf.hhs.gov/programs/cb/stats_research/index.htm (accessed September 2004).

U.S. General Accounting Office. House of Representatives. *Foster Care: States Focusing on Finding Permanent Homes for Children, but Long-Standing Barriers Remain*. Testimony before the Subcommittee on Human Resources, Committee on Ways and Means. Washington, DC: Government Printing Office, 2003.

Divorce and Adoption

Elizabeth Embry

When examining divorce and adoption, three key areas of interest arise: divorce during adoption, divorce after adoption, and the adoption of stepchildren after remarriage following a divorce. Each has legal implications for the adoption process, as well as emotional implications for the child and the family affected by the divorce.

Divorce During Adoption

A couple considering adoption, or in the process of adopting, who decide to divorce must look at the consequences that this decision may have on the adoption proceedings. When the decision to adopt is made, the Department of Social Services makes an initial investigation of the child's potential household—the household of the adoptive family. In this interview, if the couple is planning to divorce, they must disclose this information. Withholding this decision from the Department of Social Services, the adoption agency, or the birth parents is fraud, and the birth parents may withdraw their consent based on this misinformation. The birth parents make their decision based on the information gathered in this initial interview, and misleading information could lead them to make a decision that is against their personal desires for the child they are placing for adoption. There is the chance the birth parents will not have an objection to the divorce, and will allow the adopting parents to hold either joint custody, or one of the parents to hold sole custody, of the child. If the child is adopted in a joint custody agreement, both adopting parents are responsible for the child, including the payment of child support. If one parent adopts the child, typically the mother, the other parent is not legally tied to the child, and has no visitation rights or financial obligations as noted by Michelsen and Winchester.

Divorce After Adoption

When divorcing long after an adoption is finalized and the child has been living with the family, special considerations should be made. Legally, the child is treated in the same way as the biological child of the couple would be, with the same custody rights applying. However, Laws and Ashe note that an adopted child, by definition, has already suffered a loss, and so stands to be impacted more by the emotional implications of the divorce.

It is often reported that children from divorced homes tend to have trouble adapting to different situations in their lives. When a divorce occurs, Eagan notes that children lose part of the important attachment that they hold with one of their parents. As Blakeslee and Wallerstein (1989: 55) state: "They fear betrayal. They fear abandonment. They fear loss. They draw an inescapable conclusion: Relationships have a high likelihood of being untrustworthy; betrayal and infidelity are probable."

If this is the case with the biological children of the divorcing couple, the circumstances tend to be even worse with adopted children who can remember the sense of loss they felt at losing their biological parent. These children may have an even more difficult time forming meaningful attachments, an essential element of any childhood. A study of adopted children reported by Juffer, Stams, and van Ijzendoorn shows that those who form secure attachments to their parents, whether those parents are biological or not, have a better chance of leading a well-adjusted, happy, and fulfilling life. It is essential, then, that the needs of an adopted child be taken into account when proceeding with a divorce.

Adoption after Divorce or Remarriage

When adopting after a divorce, the proceedings depend on whether the adoption is by a single parent, or a couple who has remarried after previous divorces. The Department of Health and Human Services reports that, in the U.S., 33 percent of children adopted from foster care are adopted by single parents. Most of these adoptions are by single women who are more likely to adopt an older child than an infant (U.S. Department of Health and Human Services, 2004). However, there are still some agencies whose policy is to not allow single parents to adopt children, or who will move non-married adopters farther down on the list than those who are married. Yet, while single parenthood is not a cause for refusing adoption in the United States, there are some foreign countries that will not allow single parents to adopt children from their countries.

Provided that the adoptive parent is remarried, a previous divorce should not hinder the adoption process. The Department of Social Services will again come to investigate the potential home life of the adopted child, and will include in the investigation questions about why previous marriages dissolved, why the current marriage is different, and the stability of the parent relationship. The birth parents must also be consulted, but barring any objections from them, the adoption should proceed as it would with a non-divorced married couple.

Stepparent Adoption

The most common form of adoption in the United States is stepparent adoption, where a stepparent adopts the biological children of his or her spouse. According to data from the 2000 U.S. Census, 42 percent of those children who are adopted were adopted by their stepparent (U.S. Census Bureau, 2003). When this occurs, the child is legally separated from the non-custodial biological parent. That parent is no longer financially or legally obligated to care for the child—he or she signs over all legal and financial rights and obligations to the child's other biological parent and his or her new spouse. While each state has different guidelines for stepparent adoption, most states have an efficient process for adoptions by stepparents in which the judge can dispense with the state requirements for home visits and allow the adoption. There are some states, however, that require the custodial parent to be married to the stepparent for one year or longer before the adoption can proceed. These adoptions are covered more in-depth in the entry on "Stepparent Adoption" in this handbook.

See also Stepparent Adoption.

Further Reading

Blakeslee, S., and J.S. Wallerstein. *Second Chances: Men, Women, and Children a Decade after Divorce.* New York: Ticknor and Fields, 1989.

Eagan, Cristina E. "Attachment and Divorce: Family Consequences." Dr. G. Scott Acton's Great Ideas in Personality—Theories and Research Web Site. www.personalityresearch.org/papers/eagan.html (accessed December, 2005).

Juffer, F., G.J.J.M. Stams, and M.H. van Ijzendoorn. "Maternal Sensitivity, Infant Attachment, and Temperament in Early Childhood Predict Adjustment in Middle Childhood: The Case of Adopted Children and their Biologically Unrelated Parents." *Developmental Psychology* 38 (2002): 806–821.

Kreider, Rose M. *Adopted Children and Stepchildren: 2000.* Census 2000 Special Report. Washington, DC: U.S. Census Bureau, October 2003. U.S. Census Bureau Web Site. http://www.census.gov/prod/2003pubs/censr-6.pdf (accessed December 2005).

Laws, Rita, and Nancy Ashe. "Divorce After Adoption: Practical Tips for Parents." Adopting.org Web Site. www.adopting.org/adoptions/divorce-after-adoption-practical-tips-for-parents.html (accessed October, 2005).

Michelsen, Diane, and Colleen Winchester. "Divorce During Adoption." Adoption.com Web Site. http://library.adoption.com/Hoping-to-Adopt/Divorce-During-Adoption/article/335/1.html (accessed October, 2005).

U.S. Department of Health and Human Services. *How Many Children Were Adopted in 2000 and 2001?* Washington, DC: National Adoption Information Clearinghouse, 2004.

DNA, Adoption, and Locating Biological Kin

Vern L. Bullough

DNA has made it much more possible to trace the biological parents of adopted children than was possible in the past. The ease with which this is possible was demonstrated by a fifteen-year-old English boy who was not adopted, but whose mother had used a sperm donor to father her child. The mother herself did not know the name of the sperm donor since many men who donate sperm do so under conditions of anonymity and expect their identity to remain secret forever. Such guarantees are no longer possible.

The boy, using nothing more than a swab of saliva and the Internet, tracked down his anonymous sperm donor father. After taking the swab from the inside of his cheek, the boy sent it off to an online genealogy DNA-testing service in England known as FamilyTree DNA.com. The firm charged him $289 (173 English pounds) to give him his genetic code. Although the boy's genetic father had never supplied his DNA to the site, two men were on the database with Y chromosomes matching the boy's. The two men did not know each other, but shared a surname, albeit with a different spelling. The genetic similarity of their Y chromosomes suggested there was a 50 percent chance that the two men and the boy shared the same father, grandfather, or great grandfather.

The surname was the clue the boy needed. His mother had been told his father's date and place of birth. With the growing pile of information, the boy turned to another Internet service, Omnitrace.com, which he used to buy information on everyone born in the same place and on the same date as his father. Only one man had the surname he had obtained earlier and, within ten days, the teenager had made contact, fortunately, amicably so, with his genetic father. Bernard Sykes, a geneticist at the Oxford University and chairperson of Oxford Ancestors .com, a company that offers genetic testing for ancestry research, said this was the first time he knew of such ancestor tracing being done, but he added that the practice will soon become quite common.

There can be no anonymity in sperm banks any more according to Wendy Kramer, founder of Donor Sibling Registry.com, a web based service that matches donor children with their siblings. What has been done in terms of a donor parent can also be done for adopted children who seek to find their biological parents. Adoption agencies will no longer be able to prevent a determined seeker from tracing them down. Recognizing this, a number of agencies in the U.S. already are at work on making this somewhat easier.

DNA has also proven to be a useful tool in locating biological kin in international adoptions. For example, two families in Arizona and Alabama learned that their adopted children from China, both born with cleft palates, were at least biological half-siblings. (Children adopted from foreign countries such as China have often been abandoned and could possibly be adopted by different families.) Other adoptive parents who noted similarity between their own adopted child and another adopted child have turned to DNA to find out if there is a relationship.

In 2004, a family from Florida and one from California at a ten-year reunion of parents and their children adopted from a Chinese orphanage found their two daughters were very similar to each other, even displaying the same kind of birthmark. They turned to DNA testing for an answer to whether the girls were biologically related. The lab reported that their daughters were probably at least half-siblings. All such results are ambiguous because, to fully confirm the relationship, it is essential to have genetic material from the biological parents. Some full-siblings might not share any of the tested markers and, to complicate matters, even biologically unrelated individuals might share a number of markers by chance. Identical twins, however, who have been separated can be more easily confirmed. An email group known as Sister Far, started by Susan and Jim Rittenhouse of Lisle, Illinois, has been involved in testing 60 suspected or confirmed twins and other siblings before the end of 2004, most from China, but also from Cambodia, Russia, and Nepal.

The practice is controversial in adoption circles, with some adoption specialists and bioethicists fearful that unscrupulous labs will exploit parents eager to fill in the missing piece of their children's lives. Others worry that adopted children could find the sudden discovery of a sibling profoundly unsettling. Some have advised waiting until children reach adulthood and letting them decide whether, and how, to seek out potential long lost siblings. Still others feel that DNA testing goes against a central assumption of adoption: that families created through the adoption process are just as authentic as those based on blood relationships. Increasingly, however, regardless of expert opinion, DNA testing is being used by adoptive parents who want to know more about their children than the orphanages from where they were adopted knew or were willing to tell them.

Further Reading

Groves, Martha. "Sisters Linked in the Lab." *Los Angeles Times*. Nov. 2, 2004, p. 1.
Sample, Ian. "Teenager Finds Sperm Donor Dad on Internet." *The Guardian*, Thursday, Nov. 3, 2005. The Guardian Unlimited Web Site. www.guardian.co.uk/science/story/0,3605,1607434,00.html (accessed December, 2005).

Drug-Exposed Infants and Adoption

Tillman Rodabough

Prevalence of the Problem

Each year 11 percent of all newborns, or nearly half a million infants, are exposed to illicit drugs, and about 2.6 million infants are exposed to alcohol in utero. Of these three million infants prenatally exposed to alcohol and drugs, an estimated three hundred seventy-five thousand newborns have been exposed to serious health hazards due to their mother's prenatal drug use. A larger proportion of adopted children may have drug difficulties because of the age and economic characteristics of parents who either have their children taken from them or who relinquish them voluntarily, thinking that others could give their child a better life than they would be able to provide.

Over five hundred thousand children in the United States currently reside in some form of foster care, and these placements have been increasing over the past decade. At least one hundred thirty thousand children are adopted each year in the United States. Moving from the number of adoptions in a single year to all of the adopted children in the United States under 18, the size of the potential drug hazard rises into sharp relief. In 2003, the U.S. Census Bureau released the results to its first ever questions on adopted children, revealing that 1,586,000 (2.5 percent) of the 65 million children under 18 are adopted. That extrapolates to approximately one hundred sixty thousand adopted children under 18 who were exposed to illegal drugs in utero—a significant problem in American society.

The census revealed that 12 percent of adopted children under 18 have a disability, compared to 5 percent of biological children. Offsetting these disabilities is the fact that adoptive parents tend to be older with higher incomes and more formal education than other parents. This supports the notion of birth parents that their child will have a better environment if placed for adoption and means that adoptive parents may have more resources to combat the effects of drug-exposed infants.

Consequences of Prenatal Exposure to Drugs

A drug of choice for many pregnant mothers is alcohol—a major cause of preventable mental retardation. About one thousand two hundred children born each year are exposed to alcohol in the womb and later suffer from Fetal Alcohol Syndrome (FAS). Associated with FAS are premature births and low birth-weight babies, mental retardation, heart defects, poor muscle coordination, and other assorted disabilities. Although FAS can sometimes be difficult to diagnose, adoptive parents should know that children so diagnosed are eligible for assistance under the Individual with Disabilities Education Act. There is no cure for FAS, but these children can be helped by receiving good medical and dental care, eyeglasses or hearing aids as needed, and being placed in special school programs. Moreover, cases of Alcohol Related Birth Defects outnumber cases of FAS by a ration of 2–3 to 1.

Cocaine receives the most attention in the media relative to birth defects. Pregnant women using cocaine are more likely to have earlier contractions, premature labor, and a premature separation of placenta from the uterus, which endangers the fetus. Infants prenatally exposed to cocaine or to crack cocaine, an instantly addictive and cheap drug, stay in the hospital longer and at a higher cost than do non-exposed infants. Cocaine-exposed infants are more likely to have urinary tract infections, to be more irritable, and to have trouble sleeping for weeks after birth. They have trouble tracking a moving object and exhibit jerky eye movements. As they grow older, they are characterized by an insecure attachment style to their adoptive parents, are hyperactive, have a low frustration tolerance and are easily aroused or startled.

Newborns exposed to cocaine have been subject to the popular myth that they will always have lowered social and academic functioning, but research has found other factors more important to the child's outcomes, including interaction between mother and child and the number of moves experienced while in foster care leading up to adoption. Many of these children are less helpless than originally thought because the degree of their handicap is determined by such factors as the time during her pregnancy when the birth mother abused drugs and the length of that abuse. The exposed children's futures can be improved through proper care if the adoptive parents know what to expect and are able to respond to the child's lack of responsiveness with patience and love.

Cocaine-exposed infants seem no more likely to have birth defects, although they are smaller at birth. One problem for these infants, as for infants exposed to alcohol, is that their mothers may continue to drink or abuse drugs, which hinders care of the infant. Cocaine can be transmitted to infants through breast feeding by mothers who have used cocaine within sixty hours prior to feeding. These mothers may also smoke and use other drugs detrimental to their child's health. If the mother used needles to abuse drugs, some infants are also exposed to AIDS and hepatitis. Drug-exposed infants range across economic strata, with no detectable differences across social class, race, and whether they use public or private medical care.

Drugs cause problems when the birth parents are so involved with drugs that they neglect their children, resulting in removal of the children for their own protection. Children not removed as infants or young children are exposed to a model that increases their likelihood of abusing drugs themselves. Children born into drug homes may develop mental and emotional problems that require years of counseling and that discourage families from adopting them because of their need for constant attention.

Richard Barth, a professor and researcher at the University of California, Berkley, conducted two large surveys to determine the differences that parents raising drug-exposed children are likely to face that other parents will not. These surveys, encompassing 1,396 children who had been adopted in the first study and 581 children in foster care in the second, used good samples and comparison groups to provide reliable data on the problems in care for drug-exposed foster and adopted children. Parents who did adopt drug-exposed children felt that it was either their best chance for adopting a child or that the child would not do as well without them. Adoptive parents of drug-exposed children felt better prepared to deal with the children than did adoptive parents of non-exposed children; they were also less likely to work full-time. Of the parents of drug-exposed children, most (96 percent) were "very satisfied" or "satisfied" with their children—similar to the satisfaction of those who had adopted non-drug-exposed children. The same proportion of both sets of parents said that their children either "cried less than average" or "cried about average." There were no significant differences between the two sets of children on the Problem Behavior Inventory or in school performance. The researcher concluded that, although there is great concern that a large percentage of children available for adoption have been exposed prenatally to drugs, the experiences of their adoptive parents do not appear significantly different from the norm.

However, further research did find some differences between exposed and non-exposed foster children. Drug-exposed children were slightly, but statistically significantly, more likely to have behavior problems and to be enrolled in special education classes—although most drug-exposed and non-drug-exposed children were equally likely to be making either A's or B's. The researchers warn these differences in performance could be confounded by the difference between foster care by relatives or non-relatives—drug-exposed foster children in the care of relatives do not fare as well as those in non-relative care. These differences between foster and adoptive children may also indicate that children with more problems in foster care are simply not adopted as frequently. Most drug-exposed children can, with the proper care, do as well as non-exposed children.

Government Initiatives to Address Drug Abuse and Adoption

Several efforts are being made to address the problems related to drug-exposed infants and adoption. One example, on the national level, is the Adoption and Safe Families Act of 1997. Major changes implemented by this Act are directed at protecting children by speeding the adoption process. Facilitation is accomplished in several ways: by not requiring states to make reasonable efforts to keep children in their own homes prior to foster care and adoption if there are aggravated circumstances; by terminating parental rights if children under age ten have been in foster care under State responsibility for eighteen months; by making incentive payments for adoption in states with disproportionate numbers of children in foster care; by requiring states to provide notice and opportunity to be heard for foster parents, preadoptive parents and caretaker relatives; and by providing earlier and more decisive permanency in residence for these children.

Another example, on the state level, is Rhode Island's Vulnerable Infants Program (VIP-RI), an attempt to prevent potential problems for drug-exposed infants by intervening early in the baby's life with medical and educational care. In 1998, the nation spent an additional $352,000,000 on special education for children of school age with prenatal cocaine exposure. Rhode Island spends $800,000 per year that VIP advocates suggest could be cut in half if all cocaine-exposed children were placed in the already proven VIP program. The purpose of this program is to keep families together, get people into treatment, and prevent destruction of the children's emotional life.

Suggestions to Families Considering Adoption of Children Prenatally Exposed to Drugs and Alcohol

Parents thinking of adopting a drug-exposed child must get a realistic idea from the social worker of the birth parent's life style, obtain written summaries of the child's diagnoses and medical complications, and determine what kind of services have been provided and what will be needed in the future. The child's eligibility for adoption subsidies and Medicare health coverage must be explored along with ways to reduce the child's biological risks through a healthy care-giving environment. The pre-adoptive parent should be prepared to tolerate the uncertainties that are a part of adopting a child exposed to drugs. Finally, prenatal exposure should not be used as a label for all of the children's problems while neglecting other contributing environmental and social factors. These children must be raised with an understanding of the birth parents' past, the children's past, and the current factors that affect them, all imbedded in their total social, educational, medical, and familial system.

See also Health Issues in Adoption.

Further Reading

American Academy of Family Physicians. "Fetal Alcohol Syndrome: Why Pregnancy and Alcohol Don't Mix." *Familydoctor.org*, Reviewed and updated, April, 2005. Familydoctor.org Web Site. http://familydoctor.org/068.xml (accessed January 2006).
Barth, Richard P. "Revisiting the Issues: Adoption of Drug-exposed Children." *The Future of Children: Adoption* 3 (1993): 167–175.
Brooks, Devon, and Richard P. Barth. "Characteristics and Outcomes of Drug-Exposed and Non Drug-Exposed Children in Kinship and Non-Relative Foster Care." *Children and Youth Services Review* 20 (1998): 475–501.
Chasnoff, Ira J. "Drug Use in Women: Establishing a Standard of Care." *Annals of the New York Academy of Science* 562 (1989): 208–210.
Chasnoff, Ira J., Dan R. Griffin, Scott MacGregor, Katheryn Dirkes, and Kaytreen A. Burns. "Temporal Patterns of Cocaine Use in Pregnancy." *Journal of the American Medical Association* 261 (1989): 1741–1744.
Edelstein, Susan. *Children with Prenatal Alcohol and/or Other Drug Exposure: Weighing the Risks of Adoption.* Washington, DC: CWLA Press, 1995.
Fiango, V. and C. Fiango. *The Flow of Adoption Information from the States.* Williamsburg, VA: National Center for State Courts, 1994.
Grand Parent Again, Legal: Safe Family Act, 1999. Grandparent Again Web Site. http://www.grandparentagain.com/legal/family.html (accessed January, 2006).
Jenista, Jerri Ann. "Fetal Alcohol Syndrome (FAS) Diagnostic Dilemma." *Adoption/Medical News* 4 (1998). Adoption.com Web Site. http://encyclopedia.adoption.com/entry/fetal-alcohol-syndrome-FAS/140/1.html (accessed January 2006).

Lester, Barry M., and Jeremiah S. Jeremiah Jr. "Our Choice: V.I.P. or R.I.P." *George Street Journal* 27 (2003). George Street Journal at Brown University Web Site. http://www.brown.edu/Administration/George_Street_Journal/vol27/27GSJ23e.html (accessed January 2006).

Myers, B.J., H.C. Olson, and K. Kaltenback. "Cocaine-Exposed Infants: Myths and Misunderstandings." *Zero to Three* 13 (1992): 1–5.

Streissguth, A., and C. Giunta. "Mental Health and Health Needs of Infants and Preschool Children with Fetal Alcohol Syndrome." *International Journal of Family Psychiatry* 9, 1988: 29–47.

Taggart, Cynthia. "Substance Abuse Frays Kids' Safety Net; Adoption Proving Less an Option for Kids Born into Drug Homes." *Behavior Health News*, 2005. *The Spokesman–Review*, Coeur d'Alene, Idaho. Mount Regis Center Web Site. http://www.mtregis.com/display_article.asp?article=7004

E

Embryo Adoption

Vern L. Bullough

One result of test tube pregnancies is the production of thousands of human embryos, microscopic clusters of cells, frozen in tanks in laboratories around the nation. These embryos, consisting of two to a hundred cells, are potential babies. The cells are the basis for stem cell research, and many of them have been used in this. But when such research was forbidden by the U.S. Government, labs sought other alternatives.

One alternative was adoption of the cells by others. One such special program was developed, Snowflake Embryo Adoption, run by Nightlight Christian Adoptions in Fullerton, California. Established in 1998, this was one of the pioneer programs. By 2001, the agency had paired twenty-six sets of genetic parents with twenty-one adopting families. Not all the transfers result in the birth of a baby. Nationally, only 19 percent of the women who attempt pregnancy with frozen embryos give birth. The Snowflake program was somewhat more successful: of the first fourteen women to have embryos implanted, six became pregnant, and eight babies resulted, including two sets of twins. Often, those putting their embryos up for adoption set standards for the users of their embryos. One couple offering embryos insisted that the recipient of their embryos be Christian, be married for at least seven years, and have bachelor's degrees. Some have treated the whole process as an open adoption and want to maintain contact with any children who might result from their donated embryos.

One physician involved is Dr. Robert T. Scott, Jr., of the Reproductive Medicine Association of New Jersey who has had several embryo adoptions. He screens the genetic parents for AIDS and other diseases, and provides psychological counseling to both sides. The adoptive parents can experience pregnancy and control prenatal care. They also have a good idea of the genetic background of their child.

While embryos can be sold—and some have been for as much as $15,000—most of those involved in the program encourage donations, in part because they are fearful of being accused of selling babies. Adoption of embryos is a legal procedure, just as is adoption of a born child. As of this writing, several states have enacted laws to regulate embryo adoptions.

See also Assisted Reproductive Technologies and Adoption; Infertility and Adoption.

Further Reading

Stolberg, Sheryl Gay. "Clinics Full of Frozen Embryos Offer a New Route to Adoption." *Los Angeles Times.* Feb. 25, 2001, p. 1.

Employment Benefits and Adoption

Carrie Lacey Boerio

Workplace adoption benefit plans offer financial assistance and paid or unpaid leave for employees who adopt. Adoption benefit plans vary, ranging from $1,000 to $10,000 in financial assistance and/or from one to six weeks of paid or unpaid leave. Since the late 1980s, the number of employers offering adoption benefit plans has increased dramatically. These plans benefit the employer, the employee, and children waiting for permanent homes. They are not difficult to administer and are an inexpensive addition to existing plans as they are generally used by less than 1 percent of eligible employees.

Advantages of Adoption Benefits

For employees, workplace benefits make adoption more affordable and give them time to bond with their child. Financial reimbursement can remove a barrier for employees who are considering adoption but feel they cannot afford it.

For employers, adoption benefits can enhance a family-friendly environment, which helps inspire loyalty and increase retention. They also provide a competitive edge in recruitment by attracting employees who may be considering adoption, and make benefits equitable for adoptive and biological parents. More than one hundred twenty-nine thousand children are waiting in America's foster care system to be adopted, according to the U.S. Department of Health and Human Services. Workplace benefits may increase their likelihood of finding a permanent adoptive family.

Financial Assistance

Most adoption benefit plans offer between $1,000 and $10,000 in financial assistance. Some companies provide increased aid for the adoption of a special needs child, for example, a physically, medically or emotionally challenged child; a sibling group; or an older child. Employers may require proof of adoption expenses and reimburse only for that amount, or may provide employees with the maximum benefit regardless of actual expenses.

Covered expenses may include costs incurred for home studies, attorneys, court proceedings, foster care placement, parental counseling, medical expenses not covered under group insurance, transportation, lodging and immigration. Most companies pay benefits after the adoption is finalized. Adoption benefits can be excluded from the employee's taxable income.

Paid Leave

Adoption benefit plans generally offer from one to six weeks of paid leave. Use of adoption leave varies, but often requires that the employee first use all earned vacation and personal days. Eligibility requirements usually involve length of time employed by the company and/or hours worked.

Unpaid Leave

Some employers offer unpaid leave instead of, or in addition to, paid leave. Larger employers and public agencies must grant twelve weeks of family leave for the placement of a child for adoption or foster care and to care for the newly placed child in accordance with the Family and Medical Leave Act of 1993 (FMLA). This may be paid, unpaid, or a combination of both, depending on each company's policy. FMLA also stipulates that the employee be able to return to an equal or similar position. Employees must have worked at least 1,250 hours in the previous year, and the unpaid leave must be offered to both males and females for companies with fifty or more employees.

History

Only a small number of organizations offered adoption benefits prior to 1990. Their growth is due, in large part, to the efforts of Dave Thomas. Thomas was an adopted child and the founder of Wendy's restaurants. His passion for the issue led him to create the Dave Thomas Foundation for Adoption and to address every audience of decision-makers possible. Thomas served as spokesperson for the White House "Adoption Works for Everyone" initiative, addressed legislative and judicial leaders, encouraged other CEOs to offer benefits, promoted adoption in Wendy's stores, and made the adoption-friendly workplace a primary focus of the Dave Thomas Foundation for Adoption. He also involved the W. K. Kellogg Foundation in 1992, which then provided a grant to the National Adoption Center to promote workplace benefits.

Adoption benefits also increased as more employees began requesting them. In an annual survey of one thousand major U.S. employers conducted by Hewitt Associates, the number offering financial adoption benefits rose from 12 percent in 1990 to 36 percent in 2003. According to the 2003 Hewitt Associates survey, one third of employers offering benefits provide up to $5,000 or more in financial assistance.

A Corporate Profile

Wendy's International is representative of an adoption-friendly workplace. Their adoption assistance program was established in 1990. In the following fourteen years, there were fifty-seven adoptions, which represented a utilization rate of about 1 percent of eligible employees.

In Wendy's adoption assistance program, employees are eligible for adoption benefits if they have completed one year of continuous service, work a minimum of twenty hours per week, and are employed at the time any financial assistance payments are made. Financial assistance includes up to $5,000 of reimbursement per adopted child and up to $7,000 for the adoption of a special needs child. Payments are made directly to the employee after the adoption is final. A written request for reimbursement must be submitted along with itemized bills. Covered expenses include licensed adoption agency fees, legal costs, medical expenses not covered under the group insurance plan, charges for temporary foster care, and domestic transportation costs for both the adoptive parents and the adoptive child. A paid leave of absence, which must be taken immediately upon assuming physical custody of the child, is also offered. Six weeks of paid leave is offered at 60–100 percent of earnings, depending on years of service. Leave is available to both male and female employees, and may be shared if both adoptive parents are employees of Wendy's International.

Technical Assistance

Information and technical assistance is available to both employers and employees interested in adoption benefits from the Adoption Friendly Workplace program online at http://www.adoptionfriendlyworkplace.org, or by telephone at 1-877-777-4222.

See also Financial Assistance for Adoption; Financial Costs of Adoption; Subsidy Programs for Adoption; Thomas, Dave.

Further Reading

Dave Thomas Foundation for Adoption. "Beginner's Guide to Adoption." Dave Thomas Foundation for Adoption Web Site. http://www.davethomasfoundationforadoption.org (accessed November 2004). 1-800-275-3832.

Dave Thomas Foundation for Adoption. "Bringing Adoption-Friendly Benefits to Your Organization." Adoption Friendly Workplace Web Site. http://www.adoptionfriendlyworkplace.org (accessed November 2004). 1-877-777-4222.

Family and Medical Leave Act. U.S. Department of Labor Web Site. http://www.dol.gov/esa/whd/fmla (accessed November, 2004).

Internal Revenue Service. *Publication 968, Tax Benefits for Adoption.* 2003.

English Common Law

Vern L. Bullough

Adoption was not recognized in English Common Law. Why this was the case is uncertain. Several reasons have been advanced: the need to protect the property rights of blood relatives in case of inheritance; a moral dislike of illegitimacy; and the availability of other semi-adoptive alternatives such as apprenticeships and voluntary transfers through wills or similar documents. It was not until 1926 that the first adoption statute was enacted.

Further Reading

McCauliff, C.M.A. "The First English Adoption Law and Its American Precursors." *Seton Hall Law Review* 16 (1986): 656–77.

Ethical Issues in Adoption

Madelyn Freundlich

Given the many interests and needs that individuals bring to the adoption process, it is inevitable that ethical issues will arise. Resolution of these issues involves an articulation and application of clearly identified values and principles. These values and principles guide how adoptions should take place and how the individuals served through adoption—children, birth parents, prospective adoptive parent, and adoptive families—should be supported and served. There has not been consensus about the specific values and principles that should form the foundation for adoption nor how these values and principles should translate into adoption practice and policy. Nonetheless, certain values and principles have gained acceptance as important to adoption policy and practice. There is considerable debate, however, about how these values and principles should be applied in designing and providing adoption services.

Values in Adoption

The values that can guide the resolution of ethical issues in adoption flow from a recognition that adoption represents a fundamental decision in the lives of children, birth parents, and adoptive parents and that adoption has life-long effects on children and adults alike. These values can be organized into two categories: values that inform the services provided to children, birth parents, prospective adoptive parents, and adoptive families; and values that inform the way in which adoption services are developed, provided, and evaluated. The values that inform direct services include: respect (a recognition of the inherent worth and dignity of each individual); beneficence (a focus on promoting "good" for each individual served); knowledge (access to and an understanding of information that is important to the individual on a personal level); and autonomy (the ability to make informed decisions on one's own behalf). The values that inform the development, implementation and evaluation of adoption services include: fairness (a just approach to service development and delivery); equity (comparable services for those who need them); and accountability (knowledge of and responsiveness to the impact of services on those individuals who are served).

The Core Principle: The Best Interest of the Child

Based on an understanding that the child is the principal concern in adoption, law and practice direct that adoption be based on a child's "best interest" and respect for the child's rights. Although "the best interest of the child" has emerged as the core principle governing adoption, its exact meaning has been subject to considerable debate. A value-based perspective, however, can be used to clarify the principle of "the best interest of the child." On the basis of the values of respect, beneficence, knowledge, autonomy, fairness, equity and accountability, "the best interest of the child" can be defined as requiring that the child be the starting point in the adoption process; adoptions be undertaken because children need adoptive families, not because adults wish to adopt children; adoption be available for all children who need adoptive families, irrespective of the child's physical or mental health disabilities, age, social situation, or race, color, or ethnicity; children be consulted on the adoption plan, taking into account the child's age and degree of maturity; and adoptions evidence respect for children's ethnic, religious, cultural, and language backgrounds.

Children's Rights to Family

The principle of the "best interest of the child" can be interpreted as placing priority on children's connections with their families of origin and as requiring the selection of appropriate adoptive families for children who cannot remain with their birth families. Both the United Nations Convention on the Rights of the Child (CRC) and the Hague Convention on Intercountry Adoption (the Hague Convention) state that the primary right of a child is to remain with his or her family of origin. These international documents, consistent with ethical practice, place priority on ensuring that children remain with their parents or extended families whenever possible. In some situations, however, birth families cannot provide for their children's safety, well being, and healthy development, and decisions must be made to separate children from their families of origin. Ethically, children's relationships with their families should be terminated only when a parent lacks the ability to care for his or her child. An issue of serious ethical concern is the separation of children from their families of origin solely because of poverty. Economic factors, standing alone, are not an ethically acceptable basis for separating children from their birth families.

The separation of children from their families of origin should take place only when appropriate information has been provided to, and legal protections are in place for, children's birth parents. Children should be separated from their families of origin only when (1) their birth parents voluntarily consent to adoption based on a clear understanding of the meaning of adoption and its impact on their children and themselves and with adequate time to make the decision, or (2) there has been a governmental determination of parental unfitness, with legal protections in place for birth parents. Unless one of these processes has led to a child being freed for adoption, birth parents' rights have been violated and the child improperly separated from its family of origin.

When families of origin cannot raise their children, ethical practice directs that they be raised by other families and not placed in long-term institutional care. Children require the stability of permanent families, and provisional care for indeterminate periods of time is not an appropriate alternative for children. These principles make clear the ethical duty of adoption professionals to actively seek adoptive families for all children who have been permanently separated from their families of origin.

In international adoption, a critical ethical issue is whether adoptive families should be sought for children within children's own countries of origin. Should intra-country adoption be given priority over international adoption? Though not uniformly embraced, there is a growing ethical consensus that whenever possible, children should be placed with adoptive families in their own countries or, alternatively, with families in communities that are similar to the culture, religion, and language of children's original communities. In this view, international adoptions should take place only after timely efforts to find adoptive families in a child's country of origin have proven unsuccessful.

Adoptive families selected for children who will not be raised in their families of origin must have the ability to meet the physical, developmental, social, and emotional needs of the child. Adoption law and practice have recognized that family studies must be conducted of anyone seeking to adopt, and families must be officially approved to adopt before children are placed with them and adoption proceedings begin. Nonetheless, it has become clear that children continue to be placed with families without approved home studies by governmental or duly licensed private adoption agencies. This practice raises serious ethical concerns about children's safety and well-being and represents a serious breach of professionals' ethical obligations.

Family Preparation and Support

If adoption is to offer children the legal and social protections it is designed to provide, children, birth parents, and prospective adoptive parents must be well prepared for adoption. From an ethical perspective, birth parents and prospective adoptive parents must be provided with information that assists them in understanding the short- and long-term impact of adoption on their lives. Prospective adoptive parents must receive health and social background information on the child whom they are considering for adoption in order to make informed decisions about the adoption. When birth parents are involved in selecting an adoptive parent for their child, they must receive information on each prospective family in order to make a fully informed family selection. Children of appropriate age and degree of maturity also must be provided with information about the impact of adoption on their lives and, whenever possible, with information about the families that have expressed interest in adopting them.

Once the child-family "match" decision has been made, ethical adoption practice requires that the child and adoptive family receive support as they meet, get to know one another, and begin their lives together. Services and supports should be made available for adoptive parents, their adopted children and, when relevant, biological children in the adoptive family. Although there is a growing recognition of an ethical obligation to support adoptive families after the adoption, there has not been an equivalent recognition of an ethical duty to support birth parents after they voluntarily place their children for adoption or their parental rights are involuntarily terminated. This disparity raises important ethical issues.

One aspect of adoption professionals' ethical duties in connection with post-adoption services relates to greater openness in adoption and the growing interest in search and reunion. Increasingly, there has been a recognition of professionals' obligations to prepare birth and adoptive families for open adoption and support them in their ongoing relationships. Likewise, there has been a recognition that adopted persons and birth families need support when they search for one another, seek to reconnect and, when possible, form a relationship.

Identity Issues

The CRC and the Hague Convention endorse as a key ethical principle the right of a child to know his or her origins, including the identity of his or her parents. Although there is consensus that adopted children/adults should have access to non-identifying information about their birth parents and siblings, the right of adopted persons to obtain identifying information about their birth parents has been hotly contested in the United States. On both sides of this debate, ethical principles and values have been advanced. Proponents of adopted persons' access to identifying information focus on the values of respect for adopted persons' rights as independent individuals, their knowledge and autonomy interests, fairness, and equity. Opponents of adopted persons' access to identifying information about their birth parents focus on the values of respect for birth parents' desires to remain anonymous and fairness to birth parents who may have relied on promises of confidentiality. As this debate has continued, an ethical consensus has grown in support of adopted persons' access to identifying information regarding their birth parents, although the issue remains controversial.

Market Forces in Adoption

Of growing ethical concern in the field of adoption is the powerful role that money has come to play in the international adoptions of children in developing nations and of newborns in the United States. Of great concern internationally are trading and trafficking in children by adoption "brokers" or "facilitators" who have no professional adoption credentials. These individuals often realize significant sums of money by paying impoverished, often ill-informed parents extremely minimal sums of money or stealing their children outright, and then charging affluent and desperate prospective adoptive parents excessive fees. There are other market forces of ethical concern in international adoption, including adoption professionals' counseling of prospective adoptive families in the United States to carry large sums of money with them to other countries in order to bribe public officials to complete adoptions. In domestic adoptions in the United States, market forces likewise have presented ethical issues. Of growing concern has been the exchange of excessive sums of money (reported to range as high as $100,000) for children considered to be particularly desirable to prospective adoptive parents: healthy, white newborns.

These activities in the United States and internationally reflect a growing business dimension to adoption in an environment that is not well-regulated. Because these practices are seen as divorced from the principle of "best interest of the child," they have raised serious ethical concerns. They may negatively impact children who, in effect, may be treated as commodities; birth parents who may be maneuvered into placing their children for adoption because of economic desperation or a failure to understand what adoption means; and adoptive parents whose urgent needs to adopt are being exploited. The Hague Convention addresses many of these practices, but it remains to be seen to what extent they will be eliminated when the Hague Convention is implemented by the United States and other countries.

See also Adoption Search Movement; Facilitators, Adoption; Hague Convention on Protection of Children and Cooperation in Respect of Intercountry Adoption; United Nations and Adoption; Wrongful Adoption.

Further Reading

Babb, L. Ann. *Ethics in Contemporary Adoption Practice.* Westport, CT: Bergen and Garvey, 2001.

Freundlich, Madelyn, and Rena Phillips. "Ethical Issues in Adoption." *Adoption and Fostering*, 24 (2000), no. 4: 7–17.

University of Chicago School of Social Services Administration and Office of the Inspector General, Illinois Department of Children and Family Services. *Ethical Child Welfare Practice.* Washington, D.C.: CWLA Press, 2002.

Eugenics and Adoption

Vern L. Bullough

A major force in discouraging adoptions in the United States and much of the western world during the first part of the twentieth century was the widespread belief in eugenics. The concept was developed by Sir Francis Galton, a major figure in nineteenth century science. Galton, through his studies of gifted individuals, came to believe that heredity played an essential part in the development of individuals of unusual competence (i.e., geniuses). To gather evidence for his thesis, he founded what he called the science of eugenics—the study of forces under social control that enhance or impair the inborn qualities of future generations. He also founded an organization to carry the message of the eugenic science, the purpose of which was a deliberate attempt to increase from one generation to another the proportion of individuals with better-than-average intellectual endowment.

The major spokesperson for the movement in the early twentieth century was Karl Pearson, the founder of the science of statistics, who believed that the high birth rate of the poor held a major threat to civilization. He held that it was essential that the "higher races," i.e. European Caucasians, supplant the "lower." Although the English Eugenic Society founded by Galton eventually opposed Pearson's racist views, large sections of the eugenicist movement held racist and anti-poverty views, and the American eugenics movement founded in the early 1900s initially adopted Pearson's views wholeheartedly.

As a group, the American eugenicists believed that the "white race" was superior to other races and that within the white race, the Nordic white was superior to others. It was also assumed that upper-class people had superior hereditary qualities that justified their being the ruling elite. To document this assumption, eugenicists gathered all possible evidence supporting their interpretation, including the results of intelligence tests, which had been introduced by Alfred Binet in the early 1900s. In spite of the opposition of Binet himself to what he regarded as a misuse of his tests, the eugenicists held that such tests measured the innate, genetic intelligence of individuals. They classified all people whose IQs were labeled as being below the mental age of twelve as feebleminded or morons, without regard to the educational backgrounds or deprived environments that might have led to such results. Criminality was also considered a concomitant of feeblemindedness.

One of the strongest advocates of eugenics in the United States was H. H. Goddard who argued that the chief determiner of human conduct is intelligence, which is inborn, and that it is little affected by later influences, except such serious accidents that could destroy part of the mechanism. He became the intellectual spokesperson in the United States for a movement that felt justified to limit immigration into the country, to enact laws against interracial marriage, and even in the south to justify segregation. Widespread sterilization of mental defectives was advocated and most states in the United States adopted such laws. Ultimately, Goddard's doctrine was carried to its extreme conclusion by Nazi Germany which, holding Jews, homosexuals, Poles, mental "defectives," and many others as inferior, tried to eliminate them through mass executions or through sterilization. Americans never went to the extreme that Hitler did, but eugenic ideas did have a significant effect on discouraging adoptions since family heredity became all important. And while adoptions still existed, they most often took place among family members or from families whose mental "inheritance" was known. Nature was all important and nurture was overwhelmed.

In the post World War II period, the realization of what the Nazis had done in the name of eugenics forced a rethinking among Americans. Most eugenic laws were gradually repealed and a renewed attention was given to nurture and environment, although eugenic ideas still have considerable influence on some segments of the American population. With the decline of eugenics, adoption was seen more and more as an attractive alternative for those who could not have children of their own or who wanted to enlarge their families, and for numerous other reasons that led to adoption becoming so widespread.

Further Reading

Galton, Frances. *Memories of My Life*. New York: Dutton, 1908.
Goddard, H. H. *Psychology of the Normal and Subnormal*. New York: Dodd, Mead, and Company, 1919.
Gould, Stephen Jay. *The Mismeasure of Man*. New York: Norton, 1981.

Primary Document

"Three Generations of Imbeciles are Enough."

In 1924, in the midst of the eugenics movement, Virginia enacted the Eugenical Sterilization Act that authorized compulsory sterilization of the "feeble-minded." Under the statute, the superintendent of the Virginia State Colony for Epileptics and Feeble-minded sought to sterilize eighteen-year-old patient Carrie Buck (1906–1983), a resident at the institution. Although later scholars have found the claim to be highly suspect, Carrie was claimed to have a child's mental age. She had given birth to an illegitimate child (now known to be the result of a rape). Carrie's mother had also been "immoral" regarding her sexuality. This case made its way to the U.S. Supreme Court where, in the 1927 *Buck v. Bell* decision, the statute was upheld in the interest of public welfare. Carrie Buck was sterilized and the statute remained on Virginia's law books until 1974. During that time period, over 8,000 other Virginians were also sterilized. In 2002, on the seventy-fifth anniversary of the historic *Buck v. Bell* decision, a Virginia General Assembly bill honored Carrie Buck and the governor of Virginia issued an apology for the state's participation in the eugenics movement. A historic marker near Charlottesville, Virginia, commemorates the decision near Carrie Buck's burial site. The opinion of Justice Holmes rendered in this case is a telling reflection of the period in its now infamous declaration that "Three generations of imbeciles are enough."

U.S. Supreme Court

274 U.S. 200 (1927)

BUCK v. BELL, Superintendent of State Colony Epileptics and Feeble Minded.

No. 292. Argued April 22, 1927.—Decided May 2, 1927.

Mr. Justice HOLMES delivered the opinion of the Court.

This is a writ of error to review a judgment of the Supreme Court of Appeals of the State of Virginia, affirming a judgment of the Circuit Court of Amherst County, by which the defendant in error, the superintendent of the State Colony for Epileptics and Feeble Minded, was ordered to perform the operation of salpingectomy upon Carrie Buck, the plaintiff in error, for the purpose of making her sterile. 143 Va. 310. The case comes here upon the contention that the statute authorizing the judgment is void under the Fourteenth Amendment as denying to the plaintiff in error due process of law and the equal protection of the laws.

Carrie Buck is a feeble-minded white woman who was committed to the State Colony above mentioned in due form. She is the daughter of a feeble-minded mother in the same institution, and the mother of an illegitimate feeble-minded child. She was eighteen years old at the time of the trial of her case in the Circuit Court in the latter part of 1924. An Act of Virginia approved March 20, 1924 recites that the health of the patient and the welfare of society may be promoted in certain cases by the sterilization of mental defectives, under careful safeguard, &c.; that the sterilization may be effected in males by vasectomy and in females by salpingectomy, without serious pain or substantial danger to life; that the Commonwealth is supporting in various institutions many defective persons who if now discharged would become a menace but if incapable of procreating might be discharged with safety and become self-supporting with benefit to themselves and to society; and that experience has shown that heredity plays an important part in the transmission of insanity, imbecility, &c. The statute then enacts that whenever the superintendent of certain institutions including the above named State Colony shall be of opinion that it is for the best interest of the patients and of society that an inmate under his care should be sexually sterilized, he may have the operation performed upon any patient afflicted with hereditary forms of insanity, imbecility, &c., on complying with the very careful provisions by which the act protects the patients from possible abuse.

The superintendent first presents a petition to the special board of directors of his hospital or colony, stating the facts and the grounds for his opinion, verified by affidavit. Notice of the petition and of the time and place of the hearing in the institution is to be served upon the inmate, and also upon his guardian, and if there is no guardian the superintendent is to apply to the Circuit Court of the County to appoint one. If the inmate is a minor notice also is to be given to his parents, if any, with a copy of the petition. The board is to see to it that the inmate may attend the hearings if desired by him or his guardian. The evidence is all to be reduced to writing, and after the board has made its order for or against the operation, the superintendent, or the inmate, or his guardian, may appeal to the Circuit Court of the County. The Circuit Court may consider the record of the board and the evidence before it and such other admissible evidence as may be offered, and may affirm, revise, or reverse the order of the board and enter such order as it deems just. Finally any party may apply to the Supreme Court of Appeals, which, if it grants the appeal, is to hear the case upon the record of the trial in the Circuit Court and may enter such order as it thinks the Circuit Court should have entered. There can be no doubt that so far as procedure is concerned the rights of the patient are most carefully considered, and as every step in this case was taken in scrupulous compliance with the statute and after months of observation, there is no doubt that in that respect the plaintiff in error has had due process at law.

The attack is not upon the procedure but upon the substantive law. It seems to be contended that in no circumstances could such an order be justified. It certainly is contended that the order cannot be justified upon the existing grounds. The judgment finds the facts that have been recited and that Carrie Buck "is the probable potential parent of socially inadequate offspring, likewise afflicted, that she may be sexually sterilized without detriment to her general health and that her welfare and that of society will be promoted by her sterilization," and thereupon makes the order. In view of the general declarations of the Legislature and the specific findings of the Court obviously we cannot say as matter of law that the grounds do not exist, and if they exist they justify the result. We have seen more than once that the public welfare may call upon the best citizens for their lives. It would be strange if it could not call upon those who already sap the strength of the State for these lesser sacrifices, often not felt to be such by those concerned, in order to prevent our being swamped with incompetence. It is better for all the world, if instead of waiting to execute degenerate offspring for crime, or to let them starve for their imbecility, society can prevent those who are manifestly unfit from continuing their kind. The principle that sustains compulsory vaccination is broad enough to cover cutting the Fallopian tubes. *Jacobson v. Massachusetts*, 197 U.S. 11. Three generations of imbeciles are enough.

But, it is said, however it might be if this reasoning were applied generally, it fails when it is confined to the small number who are in the institutions named and is not applied to the multitudes outside. It is the usual last resort of constitutional arguments to point out shortcomings of this sort. But the answer is that the law does all that is needed when it does all that it can, indicates a policy, applies it to all within the lines, and seeks to bring within the lines all similarly situated so far and so fast as its means allow. Of course so far as the operations enable those who otherwise must be kept confined to be returned to the world, and thus open the asylum to others, the equality aimed at will be more nearly reached.

Judgment affirmed.

F

Facilitators, Adoption

Vern L. Bullough

Adoption facilitators, sometimes called adoption intermediaries or "go-betweens," are individuals (usually women) who make connections between a birth parent, or parents, to locate a child for a client. The use of intermediaries began to take hold in the 1980s as birth parents began seeking more control and adopting parents began to look for financial savings.

Facilitators can only locate babies, not finalize adoptions. Though they are legal in some states, they are banned in others. In California, they were licensed by the Adoption Facilitation Law in 1997, which regulates advertising by facilitators, mandates disclosure to clients about fees and services, and forbids facilitators from engaging in counseling. Facilitators need to obtain a business license and post a $10,000 bond. Most facilitators work closely with individual adoption lawyers. In California, there is a small organized facilitator group, the Academy of California Adoption Professionals. They can charge fees for their services individually or share their fee with a lawyer.

Further Reading

"Adoption Go-Betweens." *Los Angeles Times*. March 12, 2001, Section E, 1, 4.

Family Foster Care: British Perspectives

Gillian Schofield

In Britain, children who are in the care of the state are referred to as being "looked after." As in other European countries, the term "foster care" relates only to children looked after in families and does not include, for example, children in residential care. Family foster care in Britain is the major resource for children who cannot be looked after in their birth families and who become the responsibility of the state. Of the 69,857 children looked after by local authorities in England, Scotland and Wales on 31st March 2003, 47,403 (68 percent) were in foster families. A proportion of those foster placements (around 12 percent) were placements with relatives, but for the majority, family care will be provided by foster carers recruited by the local authorities or, for around 17 percent of fostered children, by foster carers employed by independent fostering providers (Department for Education and Skills 2004).

The foster care service in Britain is highly regulated. All foster carers are assessed according to set procedures, approved by fostering panels using criteria laid down by government, reviewed annually, expected to attend training, and required to work alongside agency social work staff to promote the welfare of the children for whom they care. Independent fostering providers are also inspected to ensure they conform to the same standards.

However, in contrast, terms and conditions of employment for foster carers vary widely between agencies across Britain, ranging from foster carers who only receive a very modest financial allowance that barely covers the expenses incurred by caring for the child to carers who are paid a professional salary and generous allowances. Levels of support also vary widely, with those receiving least financial support often also receiving the least practical and emotional support and training.

Although the professionalization of the foster care service is widely endorsed as necessary in terms of enhancing skills to meet the needs of the increasingly troubled children now looked after in the care system, the continued lack of resources and local variation has led to a very uneven provision for children and for carers. The general picture is of a foster care workforce that is required to be professional, but is often treated as "volunteers." It is only recently, for example, that there is some provision for pensions for foster carers. This generally low level of resourcing is felt to be a key factor affecting recruitment. In England alone, there is reckoned to be a shortfall of more than eight thousand carers (Fostering Network 2004), which affects placement choice and may indirectly affect a range of other issues discussed below, for example the willingness of local authorities to promote adoption by foster carers.

Children come into foster care in England and Wales (Scotland has different legislation) either under a voluntary arrangement with parents, known as "accommodation" (Section 20 Children Act 1989), or as subjects of a care order made by a court (Section 31 Children Act 1989). The legal obligation to safeguard the children's welfare is the same, but for the 33 percent of looked-after children who are accommodated, only the birth parents will have "parental responsibility" in law, whereas for the 67 percent under a care order, the local authority will also have parental responsibility and indeed can limit the birth parents' exercise of their parental responsibility (Department for Education and Skills 2004). In neither case will foster carers have parental responsibility in law; nevertheless, their role will be to promote the physical, emotional, educational, and social development of children in just the way that competent parents do.

The major concerns within the looked-after children system generally, and within family foster care in particular, have been around stability of placements and, in particular, the need to achieve secure permanent families for looked-after children. It is here that we meet the closely interconnected relationship between the worlds of foster care and adoption. In the British context, foster care is of most relevance to adoption policy and practice in three major areas. First, most children adopted from care will come from foster families which have provided a *bridge* to the new adoptive family. Secondly, many children will have a permanence plan for *long-term foster care* when, as an alternative to adoption, foster care must become a family for childhood and for life. Thirdly, children may be *adopted by foster carers*, changing the status of the child, the family, and their relationship with the local authority.

Foster Care as a Bridge to Adoption

The foster carer's contribution to assessment and planning for permanence through adoption is a significant one. For example, they are often asked to keep a diary of the child's developmental progress, and good practice would be to include them as professional colleagues in planning and review meetings. Alongside this is the equally important task of helping children to cope with the sense of separation and loss that they may feel. Being available to offer the child a secure base in attachment terms is a necessary part of the carer's role, even when it is known from the outset that the child will need to move to a new permanent family. At the same time, foster carers are also actively involved in promoting successful and safe contact with birth family members (as required by the Children Act 1989), whether the plan is for reunification or for permanence through a new family.

Where adoption becomes the plan, foster carers are actively involved in preparing the child. For example, many carers work alongside social workers or independently in undertaking life story work. Foster carers are also involved in the decision about the match, as foster carers prepare a report for, and attend, the Adoption Panel that makes the decision to match the child with particular prospective adoptive parents. (Adoption, too, is highly regulated.) As the foster carer is likely to know the child best, his or her role in the introduction and placement for adoption period is often critical. During the process of introductions to the new family, foster carers need to manage their own feelings of happiness and anxiety for the child, mixed often with a personal sense of loss. The importance of the child's relationship with the foster carer is generally well-recognized where there is good practice, and the foster carer may be asked, for example, to accompany the child to the new family home for one of the visits in order to offer his or her approval for the plan and to "give permission" emotionally for the child to move on. It is also quite common for children to have contact with their former foster carers once in their new adoptive placement and, to a limited extent, after the adoption order is made.

Although the bridging process is recognized as an essential part of helping children into adoption placements, there has been a lack of British research on what is "good practice" and on the appropriate nature of emotional relationships and practical arrangements for supporting children, foster carers, and adopters during this phase. Concerns often swing between foster carers who are deemed to be "too close" to children, to those who may not be offering enough emotional warmth because of concerns about the difficulty of "letting go." Incorrect use of attachment theory has sometimes led to fears that children forming an attachment to a foster carer may not then be able to go on to form an attachment to the new adoptive parents. The message that children can form multiple attachments, that they need close emotional support through this period, and that increasing a child's sense of felt security, self-esteem, and self-efficacy will help them in their new families has still not entirely percolated through to all practitioners.

Foster Care as a Permanence Option

British Government policy on achieving best outcomes for children in care, as in the United States, has since the 1980s focused on achieving stable *permanent* family placements, with the birth family being the placement of first choice. Where this is not in the interests of the child, adoption is promoted as the positive alternative. The value of adoption for children who would otherwise remain in the care of the state has been reinforced by the introduction in England and Wales of the Adoption and Children Act (2002) and a powerful policy steer from Government that rates of adoption from care must be increased (as they were from 4–6 percent between 1999 and 2003) (Department for Education and Skills 2004). However, unlike the United States but more like most of Western Europe (where adoption from care is rarely an option), British policy and practice has also retained the concept of *long-term foster care* as a legitimate permanence option.

Although long-term foster care lacks the legal permanence of adoption and has been rather eclipsed by the sense of adoption as the "gold standard" permanent placement, it is accepted that for some children, foster families can become a successful family for life. Studies of adults who grew up in foster families report that it is possible for children to continue to belong to their foster family, and that many foster carers do continue to see former foster children as members of their family and become grandparents to their children. Foster carers of children in current long-term foster placements talk of their commitment to children into adulthood. Legitimate concerns still remain about how this form of permanence can be achieved when long-term foster care has no formal or legal status and when there is a high level of skepticism, especially in government, about any option that leaves children "looked after." However, there is a gradual recognition that not all children who need a permanent new family can be or, indeed, should be placed for adoption. There is therefore some limited acceptance that long-term foster care needs to be made to work, since it will undoubtedly be many vulnerable children's only chance of a family for life. Ignoring it or treating it as a 'Cinderella' option causes distress to settled foster children and their foster families. The challenge is to ensure that long-term foster care is a planned permanence option and that it is supported and valued.

Adoption by Foster Carers

In Britain, adoption by foster carers can occur relatively early in a placement if the relationship rapidly develops, and the assessment of the child and the carers is conducted swiftly. Alternatively, it may occur after a variable period when other options (e.g. return home) have been tried and failed. It may also occur at the point that a young person who is fully part of their foster family is leaving care.

Attitudes to foster carer adoption and the associated practice and decision making vary significantly across the country—although this is an area in which we do not have useful statistics. Some foster carers who have adopted looked-after children report that they do not regret their decision, but have had a significant loss of income, because they lost allowances and were also not allowed to foster other children for an extended period. In contrast, other carers who adopted were receiving the same financial support as they had while fostering the children and could also have general support from their existing family placement worker. As pressure mounts to increase the numbers of children adopted from care (e.g. this is a key performance indicator for local authorities), it seems likely that in Britain, as in the United States, adoption by foster carers will be more actively encouraged than has been the case in the past.

Further Reading

Beek, M., and G. Schofield. *Providing a Secure Base in Long-Term Foster Care*. London: BAAF, 2004.

Department for Education and Skills. *Children Looked After by Local Authorities, 2003–2004*. London: Stationery Office, 2004.

Fostering Network. *Foster Care Survey*. London: Fostering Network, 2004.

Schofield G., M. Beek, K. Sargent, and J. Thoburn. *Growing up in Foster Care*. London: BAAF, 2000.

Schofield G. *Part of the Family: Pathways through Foster Care*. London: BAAF, 2003.

Sellick C., J. Thoburn, and T. Philpott. *What Works in Adoption and Foster Care*. London: BAAF/Barnardos, 2004.

Sinclair I., K. Wilson, I. Gibb. *Foster Placements: Why Some Succeed and Some Fail*. London: Jessica Kingsley, 2004.

Family Preservation

Elizabeth M. Tracy and Trista D. Piccola

The term *family preservation* refers to a philosophy as well as a particular model of service delivery that underscores the importance of restoring families to safe levels of functioning. As a philosophy, the basic premise underlying family preservation is that the physical, social, psychological, and emotional needs of adults and children are best met when their familial relationships are preserved. As a service model, family preservation programs share common features including intensive services delivered over a relatively short period of time, individualized to a family's needs, and offered in the family's home and community. Family preservation philosophy and services can be applied to many families: biological, blended, kinship (comprised of both extended biological and non-biological members), or families joined through adoption.

Background

The service orientation of family preservation can be traced to the roots of social work. Serving families in their communities was a trademark philosophy of the "friendly visiting" workers of the Charitable Organization Societies of the early 1900s. Also, one of the earliest documented family preservation programs was the St. Paul Family-Centered Project established in 1949, which provided intensive services to families facing multiple problems.

Much of the stimulus for the development of family preservation arose as a result of dissatisfaction with the conventional child welfare services that characterized the 1960s and 1970s. During this time period, several studies emerged that confirmed that large numbers of children were removed from their homes and placed in foster care for long periods of time. Many of these children experienced multiple moves and some never returned home. These lengthy, unstable separations had long-lasting detrimental effects on the well-being of parents and children.

The passage of the Adoption Assistance and Child Welfare Act (AACWA) of 1980 (P.L. 96-272) was a step toward recognizing the value of supportive services to prevent the potentially harmful effects of separation. Among other things, P.L. 96-272 called for *reasonable efforts* to be made to either prevent removal or support timely reunification. Subsequently, during the 1980s there was an increase in the number of family-based, home-based, and intensive service programs. In 1989, the Child Welfare League of America published standards for such services. At the same time family preservation programs were growing in number, the number of children in out-of-home placement was declining substantially.

Unfortunately, in some instances family preservation was inappropriately used with families that were not in a position to be maintained safely together. As a result, media stories of children who suffered serious and sometimes fatal injuries appeared. Critics attacked family preservation services as preserving families at the expense of child safety.

Since the 1990s, one response to these criticisms has been less focus on intensive service models and more focus on integration of "family centered" practice across all child welfare services. The Adoption and Safe Families Act (ASFA), passed in 1997, while supportive of family preservation, also placed a heavy emphasis on safety, well-being, and timely permanence for children through alternatives such as adoption and kinship care.

Essential Program Elements

Family preservation programs generally share an explicit value base, including the following beliefs: that families should be maintained together whenever possible; that children need continuity and stability in their lives and their families are the best source for this; and that separation has detrimental effects on both adults and children. This value base is expressed in service delivery models that capitalize on strengths of the family, mobilize formal and informal supports, and provide a variety of concrete and clinical services to meet individual family needs.

An exact prescription for family preservation service delivery has not been established, and, thus, models vary in typology. Most models include intensive, time-limited services delivered in the family home or community. The amount of time spent in the first several meetings has proven critical in establishing a rapport and trust with a family who might otherwise be resistant to, or lack confidence about, the possibility of change. Caseloads are typically small so that the worker can be easily accessible to the family, often available 24 hours a day for emergencies and crisis intervention. The period of time for service delivery varies usually from one month to several months depending on the model, and is time-limited in order to restore family functioning as soon as possible. As discussed by Mark Fraser, Kristine Nelson, and Jeanne Rivard, cross-cutting elements of successful programs are thought to be the "in vivo" focus in the home where skill-building can be directly applied, and there is the ability to respond to crises, the use of community resources and concrete services, and the empowering approach to family intervention.

What Works in Family Preservation?

When family preservation programs were first introduced, they were enthusiastically viewed by child welfare workers as a way to reduce out-of-home placements for those children and families at "imminent risk" of disruption. The mixed results of statewide evaluations of family preservation services, however, have tempered this enthusiasm as discussed in a recent U.S. Department of Health and Human Services report. Several research reviews have shown that children who receive family preservation services are placed about as often as children in control or comparison groups who do not receive such services, that the effects of family preservations services are often not long lasting, and that determining reductions in subsequent child maltreatment is problematic.

Part of the difficulty in evaluating family preservation programs lies in accurately measuring risk of placement, and ensuring that eligible families are appropriately referred for these services. There has also been dissatisfaction with relying on placement as the measure of program success. In some situations, placement is clearly indicated, or is indicated as part of an overall plan for permanency for the child, as in kinship care placements. When placements do occur, they do not automatically guarantee the child's development and safety. In addition, service models tend to "drift" over time such that it becomes unclear what types and amounts of services have actually been provided or if the model was implemented consistently across treatment sites.

In order to address these problems, more recent evaluations have examined changes in child behavior and family functioning following the provision of family preservation services. Studies have also explored the relationship between the type and intensity of services and outcomes as well as family characteristics which might predict better outcomes. Mark Fraser, Kristine Nelson, and Jeanae Rivard note that some types of family problems, such as child neglect, have been less amenable to family preservation. Concrete services, such as clothing, furniture, supplies, and housing assistance to families with economic problems, were associated with a reduced risk of subsequent maltreatment according to Joseph Ryan and John Schuerman. In a recent review of seventeen studies by Christian Dagenias, Jean Begin, Camil Bouchard, and Daniel Fortin, programs that targeted behavioral problems or delinquency were observed to yield better results. Overall, however, it has been difficult to determine with certainty which specific services are most effective.

Researchers have suggested that the client-worker relationship, family level of participation, and number of contacts between the family and the worker may be an important predictor of family outcomes (as discussed by Julia Littell and John Schuerman). Finally, some researchers have pointed out that as evidence-based practice techniques are established, these techniques should find their way into family preservation programs.

Future Practice Directions and Challenges

Much of what has come to be known as "family-centered practice" was first embodied in the family preservation movement. This includes forming a partnership with the family to assess strengths as well as needs and jointly developing a comprehensive flexible treatment plan. These programs have helped broaden the definition of family by including extended family members and natural helping networks. Service models have been adapted by increasing the length of service and by building in contacts with self-help groups and mentors in order to meet the needs of adoptive families and kinship care providers, and to help families become reunified. Many family preservation programs now work closely with community groups, neighborhoods, and natural helping networks as a means of fostering healthy communities. One of the more recent family-centered models in child welfare—Family Group Decision Making—makes use of a principle central to family preservation services, the ability of the extended family to make decisions regarding child safety. In addition, the use of concurrent case planning has meant that even while family preservation services are being delivered, planning continues "concurrently" for other forms of permanence for the child and family, either through kinship care or adoption.

Further Reading

Barth, Richard, Deborah Gibbs, and Kristin Siebenaler. "Assessing the Field of Post-Adoption Service: Family Needs, Program Models, and Evaluation Issues," 2001.

Office of the Assistant Secretary for Planning and Evaluation, U.S. Department of Health and Human Services Web Site. http://aspe.hhs.gov/hsp/PASS/lit-rev-01.htm

Dagenais, Christian, Jean Begin, Camil Bouchard, and Daniel Fortin. "Impact of Intensive Family Support Programs: A Synthesis of Evaluation Studies." *Children and Youth Services Review* 26 (2004): 249–263.

Evaluation of Family Preservation and Reunification Programs: Interim Report. Washington, DC: U.S. Department of Health and Human Services, 2001. http://aspe. os.dhhs.gov/hsp/fampres94

Fraser, Mark, Kristine Nelson, and Jeanne Rivard. "Effectiveness of Family Preservation Services." *Social Work Research* 21 (1997): 138–153.

Kinney, Jill, David Hapala, and Charlotte Booth. *Keeping Families Together: The Homebuilders Model.* Hawthorne, NY: Aldine de Gruyter, 1991.

Lindsey, Duncan, Sacha Martin, and Jenny Doh. "The Failure of Intensive Casework Services to Reduce Foster Care Placements: An Examination of Family Preservation Studies." *Children and Youth Services Review* 24 (2002): 743–775.

Littell, Julia, and John Schuerman. "What Works Best For Whom?: A Closer Look at Intensive Family Preservation Services." *Children and Youth Services Review* 24 (2002): 673–699.

National Family Preservation Network. http://www.nfpn.org

Ryan, Joseph, and John Schuerman. "Matching Family Problems with Specific Family Preservation Services: A Study of Service Effectiveness." *Children and Youth Services Review* 26 (2004): 347–372.

Schuerman, John, Tina Rzepnicki, and Julia Littell. *Putting Families First: An Experiment in Family Preservation.* New York: Aldine de Gruyter, 1994.

Walton, Elaine. "Family-Centered Services in Child Welfare." In *Social Workers' Desk Reference*, edited by Albert R. Roberts and Gilbert J. Greene, 285–289. New York: Oxford University Press, 2002.

Walton, Elaine, Patricia Sandau-Beckler, and Marc Mannes. *Balancing Family-Centered Services and Child Well-Being.* New York: Columbia University Press, 2001.

Feminism and Adoption: Changing Feminist Perspectives on Adoption

Katarina Wegar

Feminist analyses of adoption have highlighted the unequal treatment of birth mothers in the adoption system. Both domestic and international adoptions have been described as routes to family formation that benefit economically and racially privileged women and men, but punish women who lack resources and who violate patriarchal norms of sexuality, motherhood, and family life. Although adoption in public and professional discourse has been viewed as serving the best interests of both children and the mothers who cannot care for them, birth mothers, nevertheless, face social judgment because they fail to live up to the cultural expectation that mothers are the primary caretakers of their biological children.

Because the dominant North American family ideal posits that parents should be genetically related to their children, and presumes that "real" mothers give birth, adoptive mothers have also been socially marginalized. As Christine Ward Gailey has argued from a feminist point of view, adoption in the United States has traditionally derived from not only one but from two betrayals of the assumed "natural order" of motherhood: "Procreation without marriage, and non-procreation within marriage" (2000, p. 22).

Feminist researchers have stressed that both these mothering relationships and experiences are real. In Barbara Katz Rothman's words, the question "Who is the real mother?" is fundamentally misleading (1989, p. 126). Women who carry babies in their bodies and give birth are real mothers, but so are women who adopt children and have an intimate caring social relationship with them. (Although feminist researchers have generally focused on mothers and their children, their introduction of gender as a central structuring principle in society and in adoption expands our understanding of men, fatherhood, and adoption as well.)

Feminist Perspectives on Birth Mothers

The failure to conform to patriarchal parameters of motherhood has traditionally been regarded as a primary indicator of a woman's moral irresponsibility, her personal and social ineptitude. Historical studies of adoption and illegitimacy in the United States since the late nineteenth century have traced a transition from a view of the white unwed mother as a fallen woman to be saved, to a sexual delinquent to be controlled, to a neurotic girl to be cured. During the early Progressive Era, the social work literature typically portrayed adopted individuals as children of sin who had inherited the biological mental and moral weakness of their mothers.

As a response to the rapidly expanding demand for white adoptable infants and the rising rate of out-of-wedlock pregnancies among white women, adoption experts and social workers began after the Second World War to encourage adoptions and emphasize the psychological causes of illegitimacy. While white unwed mothers before the Second World War were expected to keep their babies and, thus, pay the wages of their sins, in the period after the war they were recommended to relinquish their babies for adoption. However, they had to adhere to a patriarchal model of feminine maturity that assumed a causal link between women's mental health, their sexual and reproductive behavior, and their capacity to mother. By relinquishing their babies for adoption, white unwed mothers were deemed worthy as future wives and mothers. Conversely, by adopting, childless married women were able to attain the dominant domesticity ideal.

For unwed mothers of color, different rules and assumptions applied. Rather than explaining illegitimacy as a neurotic symptom, child welfare professionals explained out-of-wedlock pregnancies among women of color in terms of cultural pathology. The post-war adoption mandate also channeled social welfare resources into adoption work, while simultaneously curtailing the resources available for single mothers who kept their babies. This trend had a particularly detrimental effect upon the lives of minority and poor single mothers, who mostly chose to keep their children and were encouraged to do so by social workers.

Contrary to the long-standing interest among adoption professionals in the mental health of adopted individuals, the emotional meaning and consequences of adoption for birth mothers received little attention until the 1980s. In the post-war years, about one-fifth of the unwed mothers who came into contact with social workers ended up raising their babies. According to the National Adoption Information Clearinghouse, it is estimated that less than one percent of children born to never-married women are currently placed for adoption. Although the adoption system still disadvantages women who lack economic resources and white racial privilege (birth as well as adoptive mothers), the influence of the women's movement on community attitudes toward single mothers has helped ease the stigma of unwed motherhood.

Encouraged by the equal rights movements of the 1960s and 1970s, and largely supported by the women's movement, birth mothers (and adopted individuals) formed interest groups and actively challenged traditional adoption practice. Some feminist critics argued that adoptions should be illegal, since most adoption papers are signed under some form of duress. This social change prompted adoption and mental health professionals to re-evaluate relinquishment and recognize birth mother's experiences. The psychological issues of grief and survival that Suzanne Arms addressed in her seminal book based on interviews with birth mothers, *To Love and Let Go*, are today acknowledged in most professional guides to adoption. The increased say of birth mothers in the adoption process (which also was due to the dearth of adoptable babies) encouraged a shift from closed towards more open adoptions—a more flexible and a less secretive and punitive form of adoption that allows birth mothers to stay in touch or receive information about the fate of their children.

However, as feminist critics of the child welfare system have pointed out, the overhaul of the United States welfare system in the 1990s further hindered the ability of many poor and minority women to care for their children. Although social attitudes toward pre-marital motherhood have become more accepting, empirical research on relinquishment still tends to emphasize the risks involved in becoming an unwed mother and support an optimistic view of relinquishment that emphasizes the positive social benefits. Adoption is also viewed as a practical private solution to providing homes for children in foster care that simultaneously upholds the traditional family ideal. The public and professional discourse emphasizes the inherent dangers in unwed motherhood. In contrast, the larger social context of adoption, such as the lack of quality sex education, the unavailability of contraceptives, and insufficient social support for disadvantaged women and their families, has been overlooked. Feminists have argued that the emphasis on relinquishment (court ordered or not) among minority mothers is particularly misleading since children of color stand a much lesser chance than white infants of being adopted. As long as adoption is not understood within broader systemic inequalities in the distribution of resources, adoption continues to reinforce class and race inequalities among women.

Feminist Perspectives on Adoptive Mothers

While gender inequality has been considered crucial to understanding how adoption practices have negatively affected birth mothers, feminists have been less likely to examine adoptive motherhood from a gender perspective. For example, the 1984 edition of classic feminist women's health treatise, *Our Bodies, Ourselves*, featured a lengthy discussion of the predicaments of birth mothers, but addressed adoptive motherhood only briefly. (The 2005 edition includes a somewhat greater focus on issues of adoptive parenting.) Since adoptive mothers tend to belong to a privileged socioeconomic stratum—in particular those who choose more expensive adoption options such as private, independent, or international adoptions—adoptive mothers' experiences have understandably remained, until recently, a comparatively neglected area of feminist inquiry.

For feminists, motherhood has traditionally provided a prime site for exploring and contesting the confines of nature and culture, biology and identity. Whereas some have regarded biological motherhood as a source of oppression, others have reasserted the "natural" and viewed motherhood as an important site of political praxis. In the late 1980s, some feminists began to emphasize the importance of acknowledging women's bodily, psychological, and social experiences of childbearing and rearing while trying not to lapse into biological essentialism. Other feminists interpreted this trend as a return to the essentialist view of women as defined by biology, by the ability to bear children. According to Diane Eyer, the idea that there are, and should be, biological underpinnings to the mother-infant relationship fits in with the growing feeling that everything should be "natural," and that feminists therefore have endorsed the "ideology of the natural" (1992: 181). These circumstances might explain why feminists initially were not interested in studying adoptive mothers.

Nevertheless, since the 1980s, an increasing number of feminist researchers have stressed the extent to which adoptive mothers have been affected by the negative stigma of infertility, and subjected to essentialist biological norms of motherhood. More than men, women are defined by their reproductive capabilities, and their social status depends on biological motherhood (within patriarchal parameters). Even recent studies of community attitudes towards adoptive and biological motherhood and fatherhood have shown that women's parenting is viewed as instinctual, whereas men's capability to father is more often viewed as learned.

Research on diversity among adoptive mothers has stressed that adoption practices historically have been, and to some extent continue to be, used to reinforce the two-parent heterosexual and racially homogenous family ideal. Consequently, women who do not fulfill this family ideal—such as single women and lesbian women—historically have been excluded from the option to adopt either by law or in practice. Critics of transracial adoption have argued that the adoption system primarily has served the white community, while not enough effort has been made to attract adopters from other ethnic groups.

While the prevailing economic, racial, national, and heterosexual privilege has allowed some women and men to gain from the adoption system, all adoptive mothers are vulnerable to cultural images of them as inadequate, less "real," second-rate mothers. Suspicions about adoptive mothers' parenting capabilities have also entered into the professional discourse on adoption. Since the mid-1940s, adoption experts have been concerned with risks in the adoptive environment, especially the risks posed by adoptive mothers. The first psychodynamic theories to appear in the adoption literature tied mature womanhood to biological motherhood, and emphasized the negative psychological effect of childlessness on an adoptive mother's capacity to fully afford her adopted child her maternal love.

In the 1960s, a host of psychiatrists argued that adopted children were at greater risk of suffering from emotional problems, and they identified adoptive mothers' presumed inability to conceive and her "feelings of inadequacy" as the primary cause of their children's psychological problems. (The early studies assumed that the adoptive mother was infertile while little if any attention was given to the possible infertility of the adoptive father.) By presuming that women's mental health is determined by their wombs, the clinical adoption literature has reflected and reinforced essentialist stereotypes of women as mothers. Many adoption workers still regard the adoptive mother's "resolution of infertility" as the most important precondition for the readiness to adopt.

As feminist critics have noted, the larger ideological and cultural context of adoption has remained relatively unexamined. Adoption professionals have tended to interpret problems in adoptive families as the consequence of individual psychopathology rather than as social reactions to the stigma of infertility and lack of social support. Still, many adoptive mothers and their families actively resist marginalization and challenge the assumption that the best and strongest families are based on blood. Some adoptive mothers develop mutually supportive relationships with their children's birth mothers (and vice versa). Examples from other cultures, as well as from our own, show that multiple caring relationships, with mothers (and fathers), can enhance, rather than complicate, a person's life. Adoptive families are in a unique position to shape cultural assumptions about family, identity, and diversity, and expand society's vision of human kinship and connectedness.

See also Genetics and Adoption: Language and Ideology; Surrogacy and Adoption.

Further Reading

Arms, Suzanne. *To Love and Let Go*. Berkeley: Celestial Arts, 1983.

Berebitsky, Julie. *Like Our Very Own: Adoption and the Changing Culture of Motherhood, 1851–1950*. Lawrence, KS: University Press of Kansas, 2000.

The Boston Women's Health Book Collective. *The New Our Bodies, Ourselves*. New York: Simon and Schuster, 1984.

The Boston Women's Health Book Collective. *Our Bodies Ourselves: A New Edition for a New Era*. New York: Simon and Schuster, 2005.

Chesler, Phyllis. *The Sacred Bond: The Legacy of Baby M*. New York: Vintage Books, 1989.

Child Welfare Information Gateway. U.S. Department of Health and Human Services, *"Voluntary Relinquishment for Adoption: Numbers and Trends."* Washington, D.C., 2005. Web Site. http://www.childwelfare.gov/pubs/s_place.cfm

Cornell, Drucilla. "Reimagining Adoption and Family Law." In *Mother Trouble: Rethinking Contemporary Maternal Dilemmas*, edited by Julia E. Hanigsberg and Sara Ruddick, 208–228. Boston: Beacon Press, 1999.

Eyer, Diane. *Mother-Infant Bonding: A Scientific Fiction*. New Haven: Yale University Press, 1992.

Gailey, Christine Ward. "Ideologies of Motherhood and Kinship in US Adoption." In *Ideologies and Technologies of Motherhood*, edited by France Winddance Twine and Helena Ragone, 11–55. New York: Routledge, 2000.

Kunzel, Regina G. *Fallen Women, Problem Girls: Unmarried Mothers and the Professionalization of Social Work, 1890–1945*. New Haven: Yale University Press, 1993.

Miall, Charlene. "The Stigma of Adoptive Parent Status: Perceptions of Community Attitudes toward Adoption and the Experience of Informal Sanctioning." *Family Relations* 36 (1987): 34–39.

Miall, Charlene. "The Stigma of Involuntary Childlessness." *Social Problems* 33 (1996), 268–282.

Miall, Charlene and Karen March. "A Comparison of Biological and Adoptive Mothers and Fathers: The Relevance of Biological and Adoptive Kinship and Gendered Constructs of Parenthood." *Adoption Quarterly* 6 (2003): 7–39.

Roberts, Dorothy. *Shattered Bonds: The Color of Child Welfare*. New York: Basic Books, 2002.

Rothman, Barbara Katz. *Recreating Motherhood: Ideology and Technology in a Patriarchal Society*. New York: W.W. Norton & Company, 1989.

Smith, Betsy, Janet L. Surrey, and Mary Watkins. "'Real' Mothers: Adoptive Mothers Resisting Marginalization and Recreating Motherhood." In *Adoptive Families in a Diverse Society*, edited by Katarina Wegar. New Brunswick: Rutgers University Press, 2006.

Solinger, Rickie. *Wake Up Little Susie: Single Pregnancy and Race before Roe v. Wade*. New York: Routledge, 1992.

Solinger, Rickie. *Beggars and Choosers: How the Politics of Choice Shapes Adoption, Abortion and Welfare in the United States*. New York: Hill and Wang, 2001.

Wegar, Katarina. "In Search of Bad Mothers: Social Constructions of Birth and Adoptive Motherhood." *Women's Studies International Forum* 20 (1997): 77–86.

Financial Assistance for Adoption

Vern L. Bullough

Some adopting parents spend thousands of dollars in the process while others who go through the public social service system may pay little if any cash out of pocket. Other costs are also involved such as time off work in ease the adjustment of the new family members.

There are, however, sources of financial aid for adoption. Many companies offer adoption assistance programs for their employees. Hewitt associates in Chicago in 2005 found that 39 percent of the large companies they surveyed offered adoption assistance, and that was an increase from 31 percent in 2000. Amounts of assistance varied by year but this too increased from an average of $3,100 in 2000 to $3,897 in 2005. The appeal of these payments for employers is that, like pensions or health benefits, they are tax deductible for the company. They are also not generally taxable for the employee. Some companies just offer simple information and referral programs while others provide cash grants for as much as $15,000. A program called the Adoption Friendly Workplace, sponsored by the Dave Thomas Foundation for Adoption, has a website with a listing of companies providing adoption assistance programs.

Tax credits for adoption have been available from the U.S. government since 1997 for adopting parents. The amount available has increased from a maximum of credit of $5,000 in 1997 to $10,630 in 2005. Credits are different than deductions since a tax credit is a dollar-for-dollar reduction in the tax paid, unlike a deduction which simply reduces the individual's taxable income. Credit can be used to offset "qualified" expenses, including legal bills, travel expenses, adoption fees, medical bills, and other payments necessary to complete a legal adoption. In the case of "special needs" children, the full credit can be taken regardless of how much the parents spent on adoption, even if it was less than $100. If an adoption fails or drags on the credits can be used to offset adoption related expenses in the year after the year the expenses were incurred. There are limits on credits, however. In 2005, families with more than $159,450 in adjusted gross income lost a portion of the credit while families with adjusted gross incomes above $199,450 could not claim the credit.

Parents who go through the public social service system not only have much lower fees but in many cases can qualify for other adoption assistance payments which include medical coverage. Moreover, adoption assistance payments can, in many cases, last until the child reaches age 18 depending on the child and the parents' need. In California, almost all children adopted through the state foster care system qualify for financial assistance. One of the reasons for these benefits in California is that the public system has a large number of children available but few of them are healthy babies or toddlers. Many are older children who have been taken from abusive or neglectful parents and many of these require more medical and psychological attention than babies adopted through private means. Services available in California for the special needs children include pediatricians, tutoring, psychological counseling, and pre- and post-adoption training. Other states also provide comprehensive services but not all do.

See also Adoption Insurance; Employment Benefits and Adoption; Financial Costs of Adoption; Subsidy Programs for Adoption.

Further Reading

Adoption Friendly Workplace Web Site. Dave Thomas Foundation for Adoption.
    http://www.adoptionfriendlyworkplace.org/
Adopt*US*Kids Web Site. US Children's Bureau. http://www.adoptuskids.org
California Kids Connection Web Site. The California Department of Social Services and
    Family Builders by Adoption. http://www.cakidsconnection.com/
Kathy M. Kristow, "Aid is Available to Help Ease Adoption Burden," *Los Angeles Times*,
    July 31, 2005, C2.

Financial Costs of Adoption

Sharon Valente

How much does it cost to adopt a child? Costs for the adoptive parents may vary depending on the type of child adopted and whether it is an agency or non-agency adoption, a public or private agency adoption, an international or U.S. adoption, as well as many other factors. As many public agencies place special needs children, initial cost may range from nothing to around $2,500. When a child with special needs is adopted, the adoptive parents are typically eligible for continuing Medicaid after the adoption is final. Adoption subsidies may also be available to help defray the cost of continuing medical care and counseling the child may need.

The costs are borne by the adopting parents when the adoption is through an agency or through an intermediary, such as an attorney. When a private agency brokers the adoption, the fees can range from roughly $6,500 to more than $20,000 depending upon where one lives and where the adoption takes place. The fee may also vary depending on the age and race of the child. Infants in high demand, such as healthy Caucasian infants, usually have the highest costs.

Adoptive parents also face other costs such as the attorney consultation or a home study. International adoptions may involve other fees. Adoptive parents will wish to make sure they clearly understand the fee schedule and fees that will be charged. In some instances, where an attorney assists by matching a pregnant woman with the adoptive parents, the adoptive parents usually give the attorney money for expenses, and these funds are put into a restricted account.

For an international adoption, the costs may depend on the country where the child is being adopted, but the adoptive parents may also need to travel to that country to arrange for, and pick up, the child and defray the travel costs. Costs range from $7,000 to $30,000 depending on the country and whether or not an agency is involved.

For adoptive parents, costs usually begin with the application fee which may start at about $50. Application fees in excess of $500 should be questioned. Although agencies often want the fees paid when the child is placed, some agencies will allow installment payments, and this is more likely for a child with special needs. Other costs may include a physical exam for the adoptive parents and children already in the home, photographs, and phone calls. When the parents spend funds to redecorate or furnish a room for the expected child, these are usually out of pocket. Those interested in adopting should fully investigate both the range of expenses as well as the various resources (e.g., tax credit, subsidies or reimbursements, employer benefits, and adoption loans and grants) that may be available to help defray costs.

See also Adoption Insurance; Employment Benefits and Adoption; Financial Assistance and Adoption; Subsidy Programs for Adoption.

Further Reading

Child Welfare Information Gateway, 2004. "Costs of Adopting: A Factsheet for Families" NAIC Web Site. http://www.childwelfare.gov/pubs/s_cost/s_cost.cfm

Committee on Early Childhood, Adoption, and Dependent Care: "Developmental Issues in Foster Care for Children." *Pediatrics.* 91 (1993): 1007–1009.

Erichsen, Jean Nelson and Heino Erichsen. *How to Adopt Internationally.* Fort Worth, TX: Mesa House Publishing, 2003.

Gilman, Lois. *The Adoption Resource Book, 4th ed.* New York: Harper Perennial, 1998.

National Endowment for Financial Education (NEFE). "How to Make Adoption an Affordable Option." NEFE Web Site. http://www.nefe.org/adoption/default.htm

Fisher, Florence (1939–)

E. Wayne Carp

In 1971, the adoption search movement's most vocal and visible leader emerged: Florence Ladden Fisher, the founder of the Adoptees' Liberty Movement Association (ALMA), a pioneer search and reunion organization. Fisher had been adopted as an infant, but that fact was kept from her until she became a young adult. During a long and frustrating search for her birth parents, Fisher was denied knowledge about the identity of her family by lawyers, doctors, social workers, the clerk of New York's Surrogate Court, and the nuns of St. Anthony's Hospital. She finally located her mother after twenty years of searching. Fisher's traumatic odyssey led her to founding ALMA. (Fisher deliberately chose the acronym ALMA because it is the Spanish word for "soul," and she believed that every adopted person's soul has been scarred by adoption.)

Along with aiding adopted adults searching for their birth parents, ALMA's principal goals were to abolish the sealed adoption laws and to make them available to adopted adults over the age of eighteen. Fisher added a completely different tone and emphasis to the movement, which clearly differentiated ALMA from earlier search groups, such as Jean Paton's Orphan Voyage. She was unabashedly defiant and militant. Her rhetoric was angry, and she refused to compromise when advancing the movement's goals. And the emphasis on adopted adults' rights and the demand to repeal sealed adoption record statutes were unprecedented.

With the popular success of *The Search for Anna Fisher* (1973), a book recounting the dramatic story of her success in reuniting with her birth family, Fisher became the movement's undisputed leader and the head of the nation's largest and most influential adoption search group. ALMA's example started a movement that spread like wildfire, leading to the creation of hundreds of other adoptee search groups across the United States, Canada, and the United Kingdom with names like Yesterday's Children (IL), Adoptees' Identity Movement (MI), and Reunite (OH). By 1975, over three thousand adopted adults and fifteen hundred birth mothers had returned to 155 adoption agencies searching for information about their families and children.

Initially, adoptee search organizations neither lobbied state legislatures nor filed "rights-based" lawsuits to repeal the sealed adoption records statutes. However, in May 1978, ALMA filed a class-action federal lawsuit in the U.S. District Court for the Southern District of New York against the state's sealed adoption records law (Fisher 1976). The District Court for the Southern District of New York dismissed ALMA's suit. On appeal, the United States Court of Appeals for the Second Circuit considered for the first time the constitutional arguments of adult adoptees in *ALMA Soc'y, Inc. v. Mellon* (1979). ALMA challenged the validity of New York's sealed adoption records law on the basis that without showing "good cause" adopted adults were constitutionally entitled to the information contained in adoption records. This constitutional right to information basic to their development, ALMA claimed, was to be found in the first, fourth, ninth, thirteenth, and fourteenth amendments. The Appeals Court for the Second Circuit rejected ALMA's claim, denying that there were any constitutional grounds for opening adoption records. The decision in *ALMA* would stand unchallenged by other Federal appeals courts or the U.S. Supreme Court for the next twenty years.

ALMA reached its peak in membership and power in the early 1980s. It has been in decline ever since, superseded by the American Adoption Congress and Bastard Nation in influence within the adoption reform movement. Throughout the 1990s, Fisher has remained out of the spotlight, though ALMA maintains a presence on the Internet (http://www.almasociety.org/).

See also Adoptees' Liberty Movement Association (ALMA); Adoption Search Movement; American Adoption Congress; Bastard Nation: The Adoptee Rights Organization; Paton, Jean.

Further Reading

Allen, Leslie. "Confirming the Constitutionality of Sealing Adoption Records." *Brooklyn Law Review* 46 (1980): 717–145.

Carp, E. Wayne. *Family Matters: Secrecy and Openness in the History of Adoption.* Cambridge, MA: Harvard University Press. 1998.

Primary Document

"Who's Anna Fisher?"

Florence Fisher remembers the day that, as a seven year old child, she found her birth certificate. Her later frustration in finding information about her biological roots led her to found the influential Adoptees' Liberty Movement Association (ALMA) in 1971.

[Florence's mother sent her to retrieve an item from mother's dresser drawer where, while feeling around in the drawer, Florence accidentally discovered the birth certificate.]

I can remember with the greatest clarity the day I found the paper . . .

. . . It was a black paper with white writing on it. I'd never seen a photostat before and it frightened me. I could read very well by now, but the small white printed letters were not what caught my attention first. I saw my parents' names, Rose and Harry Ladden. I saw a strange name, Anna Fisher. And I saw the word "adopted."

Adopted? I knew that word. It meant: not *really* someone's child. It meant you were someone else's.

I left the bedroom with the paper in my hand and headed for the kitchen, where my mother was preparing dinner. My name was Florence Ladden. Who was Anna Fisher?

My mother was standing beside the refrigerator . . .

I came up close to her, holding the paper out in front of me. "Who's Anna Fisher, mommy?" I asked.

She looked startled, frightened. Her soft pink skin flushed, her eyes grew wide. She reached out quickly and tore the paper out of my hand so roughly that a piece of it ripped off. I couldn't understand what was happening. Why was she so angry? I could see it in her eyes. I could feel her body tense up and she took the paper and, without looking at it, thrust it behind her back.

"Am I Anna Fisher?" I asked her, looking deep into her eyes.

"No, no," she said quickly now. "No, there's . . . well, there's another Rose and Harry Ladden in the family. Yes. They adopted a little girl . . . and we're holding this paper for them."

I wanted to believe her. But her eyes and her voice said that something was terribly wrong. My mother was not telling me the truth.

Source

Excerpted from Fisher, Florence. *The Search for Anna Fisher.* New York: Arthur Fields Books, 1973: pp. 29–31.

Florence Crittenton: National Florence Crittenton Mission/Crittenton Services

Katherine G. Aiken

Charles Nelson Crittenton, druggist, philanthropist, and evangelist, founded the National Florence Crittenton Mission (NFCM) in 1883, as a tribute to his daughter Florence who died of scarlet fever when she was four years old. Imbued with protestant evangelical notions of civic responsibility, Charles Crittenton's early concern was for prostitutes, who he viewed as helpless victims and pawns of men's lascivious tendencies. Florence Crittenton rescue homes provided former prostitutes with shelter as they sought to leave their former lives. The National Florence Crittenton Mission received a charter by a special act of Congress in 1893. The organization continues to administer endowment funds Charles Crittenton established and funded at his death in 1909.

Kate Waller Barrett, wife of an Episcopal clergyman and eventually a trained physician, joined Crittenton and their partnership coincided with the Progressive Era's reform obsession with saving prostitutes. However, soon the emphasis shifted to unmarried mothers and their children.

Dr. Kate Waller Barrett's essay, "Motherhood as a Means of Regeneration," captured the maternalistic element of Florence Crittenton work. Florence Crittenton homes were havens for unmarried mothers and other women facing difficulties. Women themselves were the primary operators of the homes, and the Florence Crittenton volunteers sought to inculcate their charges with their own attitudes towards motherhood. Early Florence Crittenton Homes encouraged residents to keep their children and therefore their status as mothers.

By 1906, there were seventy-three Florence Crittenton Homes located throughout the United States and by 1924, when Kate Waller Barrett died, one-third of all maternity homes in the United States were affiliated with the National Florence Crittenton Mission; it was the largest chain of maternity homes in the country.

One of the NFCM's greatest contributions was fostering public awareness of the problem of unmarried mothers and their children. Kate Waller Barrett and later Florence Crittenton activists realized they were dealing with more than the individual concerns of the unmarried mothers and their children. They brought to the fore the notion that this was a societal problem. Early Crittenton workers were determined that the so-called double standard of sexual behavior be abandoned and that fathers accept responsibility for their children. They worked for laws that raised the age of consent and that provided rights for children born to parents who were not married. Florence Crittenton Homes filled a significant social welfare services niche. Pregnancy could be a crisis in the lives of women and there were few options available for them. A hallmark of Crittenton efforts was an overarching concern for both the mother and her child.

By the 1930s, Florence Crittenton Homes were dealing almost exclusively with maternity cases. Most of the homes featured their own maternity ward and residents could receive prenatal, obstetrical, and postnatal care. Fewer Florence Crittenton workers were evangelically motivated volunteers and more of them were professional social workers. Adoption became an accepted strategy for dealing with unmarried mothers. The children involved were assured of loving families with the financial wherewithal to care for the children. At the same time, the mothers would be free to re-establish themselves in their own families and communities.

During the 1950s and 1960s, the name "Florence Crittenton" was almost synonymous with the term "maternity home," and most major cities had a Florence Crittenton Home. By the mid 1960s, Florence Crittenton establishments housed about ten thousand clients each year and a majority of those women gave their children up for adoption.

In 1950, the Florence Crittenton Homes Association was founded in Atlantic City, New Jersey, and in 1960 changed its name to the Florence Crittenton Association of America. In 1976, the organization merged with the Child Welfare League of America to become the Florence Crittenton Division of that organization. It continues its prominence in terms of services to unmarried mothers and their children, adoption services, and services to families and young children. In fact, the Florence Crittenton emphasis has returned to Kate Waller Barrett's viewpoint that it behooves society to prepare unmarried mothers to provide healthy home environments for their children.

See also Child Welfare League of America.

Further Reading

Aiken, Katherine G. *Harnessing the Power of Motherhood: The National Florence Crittenton Mission, 1883–1925.* Knoxville: University of Tennessee Press, 1998.
Child Welfare League of America Web Site. http://www.cwla.org
Kunzel, Regina G. *Fallen Women, Problem Girls: Unmarried Mothers and the Professionalization of Social Work, 1890–1945.* New Haven: Yale University Press, 1993.
Solinger, Rickie. *Wake Up Little Susie: Single Pregnancy and Race Before Roe v. Wade.* New York: Routledge, 1992.

Foreign Adoption and Same-Sex Parents

Vern L. Bullough

Adoption of children overseas for same-sex parents is not always a straightforward proposition. Many states do not recognize same-sex adoptions and, even in those that do, not all agencies in a particular state are willing to participate in such adoptions. Moreover, many of the agencies that do participate in same-sex adoptions usually do not advertise that they do so, since they are fearful that foreign agencies might be less willing to deal with them. Thus, it often takes some "detective work" to find out which agencies will cooperate. There are also problems in foreign countries since some are reluctant to participate in same-sex adoptions; some agencies advise bringing along a third person of the opposite sex to act as an adopting parent in cases where trouble is anticipated.

As of this writing, it is impossible to know how many gay and lesbian parents have successfully found children overseas since there are no statistics dealing with this information. One limitation that both same-sex parents and opposite-sex parents face in overseas adoptions is the expense; the agencies involved indicate that a gay couple could expect to pay at least $20,000 before the adoption takes place. Another of the difficulties (as noted above) with adoption by same-sex parents is that such adoptions are not fully recognized in all states. Oklahoma, for example, has a law as of this writing that disallows same-sex couples from being adoptive parents, even if they came from another state where they were legally recognized as such.

See also Gay and Lesbian-headed Adoptive Families.

Further Reading

Griffths, Kelly. "Gay Parenting, 2005." *The Advocate*, July 19, 2005, pp. 43–46.

Foster Care in the United States

Judith Schachter

Foster care, or fosterage, involves the transfer of a child from a biological parent to a substitute parent, who provides care, nurture, and safety for the child without assuming permanent parental rights. Foster care may occur at any time in childhood. The rights of the biological parent are not terminated, and the child remains a legal member of the birth family. Foster care may end in family reunification, permanent guardianship, or adoption. Legal prescriptions, customary norms, and interpretations of foster care reflect changes in economic, demographic, and social conditions. Foster care is also a barometer of cultural ideologies of parenthood, family, and kinship as well as of perceptions of the health and well-being of a child. In the United States, since the mid-nineteenth century, foster care has come under the purview of the state, a subject of child welfare policies that shift from decade to decade.

Foster care is found in virtually all societies of the world and in historical periods ranging from the ancient to the modern. While the following piece concentrates on contemporary American practices and policies, comparisons with other customs are introduced to illuminate distinctive aspects of the transaction in a modern, diverse society.

The functions foster care serves vary, both within and across societies. Even when the transfer is in the interests of the child, this includes different motivations. A child may be transferred in order to gain resources and privileges not available in the natal family. A transfer may raise the status of the child, whether in terms of rank or of material benefits. Foster care is also a form of rescue, of providing a safe place for a child who has been neglected, abandoned, or abused, however those concepts are defined. Adults, too, benefit from foster care arrangements. A parent may establish lasting bonds with another adult by exchanging a child. In times of trouble and poverty, parents relinquish children into foster care as a temporary remediation of circumstances. With a growing global economy in the twentieth century, adults leave children in fosterage arrangements in order to travel for economic and educational opportunities. These functions of foster care persist, either culturally sanctioned or conducted on a private basis.

The degree to which foster care comes under public supervision varies from time to time and place to place. In the Western tradition in which American practices are rooted, foster care has alternately been a private, individual transaction between adults and a highly-formalized exchange, supervised by institutions like the church, the court, and government bureaucracies. In modern Western societies, policies and laws have reduced the functions of foster care to child welfare. Deemed a transaction "in the best interests of the child," foster care is subject to partisan, often controversial interpretations of the phrase. Currently in the United States, foster care links to other aspects of child welfare policy, including aid for dependent children, medical subsidies for children with major health needs, and tax relief for caretakers of mentally challenged children.

From its founding until the present, American society has harbored variations of fosterage. In the seventeenth and eighteenth centuries, a foster care arrangement represented the decision by a parent to have a child raised by a sterner, more religious, or otherwise more upstanding community member. Foster care was a form of moral and educational training, performed by a godparent, a relative, or a neighbor. Within small and homogenous communities, foster care arrangements occurred between two adults who exchange a child guided by shared religious and cultural norms.

Nineteenth century urbanization and industrialization radically changed foster care. Increasingly, foster care served the purpose of rescuing a child from an unsafe or unhealthy environment and the arrangement fell under the purview of the state, which established laws and criteria for the transfer of a child. While a parent could still decide to give a child up to the temporary care of another, by mid-century, child welfare experts and legal officials stepped in to approve or to compel the arrangement.

The same period of time saw the growth of institutional care. With a rising number of children in need of substitute care, institutions became the convenient option for an overworked state bureaucracy. A parent retained parental rights to the child and the possibility of reunification after a period of time. During the Progressive Era, institutional care came under fire, and the push toward family foster care intensified. Foster *parent* became the operative concept, with connotations of kinship and family, as well as implications about the role of the adult. A 1909 Conference on the Child put family foster care into place in American child welfare policy.

The Progressive Era brought foster care under the control of social workers and agencies, whose policies and practices were increasingly regulated by states. (Foster care, like adoption, is regulated state by state.) While parents retained a degree of choice about transferring a child, experts determined the best placement. Criteria for a *fit* foster parent, though less stringent than those for adoptive parents, attended to contemporaneous literature on parenting and child development. By the second half of the twentieth century, foster care had become an arm of child welfare agencies, serving two functions: a temporary way station for infants awaiting adoption and a safe haven for children at risk. American child welfare policies, and the manifestation in federal and state law, struggle with the dual, often contradictory functions of fosterage.

Foster parents receive subsidies for their services. Payment transforms their roles into that of employees of a state or agency, contradicting cultural notions of the parent. Standards of performance restrict the pool of potential foster parents, while excluding applicants from the pool of adoptive parents. A sharp differentiation between foster and adoptive parents dominated practice, policy, and popular imagery during the decades following the Second World War. Studies initiated in the 1950s show that foster parents occupy a lower socio-economic status, have fewer years of schooling, and experience more marital instability than those selected for adoptive parenthood. The distinction between adoptive and foster parent is reiterated in instructions to foster parents to limit their attachment to the child, to recognize the "real" parents of the child, and to accept a temporary place in the child's life. This policy-driven framework for foster care is antithetical to understandings of parenthood in the United States and produces a negative stereotype of the person who temporarily cares for a child. The stereotype further shrinks the pool of prospective foster parents.

The 1980s saw efforts to break down the distinction between foster and adoptive parents, in response to the growing number of children who need placement. *Fostadopt* (or foster-adopt) programs encourage adoption by foster parents, transforming temporary care into permanent legal rights to the child. In the 1990s, too, parental subsidies were continued after adoption, in recognition of the difficulties many foster children face as a result of earlier neglect or abuse. Under some circumstances, the biological parent may retain visitation rights until, and even after, an adoption has been finalized.

Among industrialized nations, the United States has a record high number of children in foster care. Statistics kept by the Adoption and Foster Care Analysis and Reporting System (AFCARS) reveal that, in 2004, there were half a million children in foster care. Of these children, 37 percent are Black non-Hispanic; 17 percent are Hispanic; 39 percent White non-Hispanic, with the remaining of varying backgrounds. Boys make up slightly more than half (52 percent), girls slightly less than half (48 percent) of the foster care population. Sixteen percent of the children are over five years old and, as they age, are increasingly less likely to find permanent homes either in a biological or an adoptive family. For older children, foster care is not a transitory stage, preliminary to placement, but a permanent fact of life until adulthood.

The federal government tried to address this fact in the Adoption and Safe Families Act (ASFA) of 1997. The thrust of ASFA is to provide children with permanency, to ensure that no child "floats" through the system, and to insist on speedy placement. Family reunification is the first choice, adoption the second, and a permanent foster care arrangement the third choice in the "best interests of the child." The Act mandates that children not remain in temporary foster care for more than eighteen consecutive months.

The pool of foster parents in the United States does not fill the need for permanent homes for children who cannot return to a biological parent. This is not just a matter of numbers but also of fitness and of appropriateness for the child. Selection criteria and a lingering emphasis on *matching* restrict the placement of children into permanent foster homes. Although the 1994 Multiethnic Placement Act (MEPA) rules against delaying the placement of a child into foster care on the basis of the race, color, or national origin of the foster parent or the child, custom and practice still favor same race, same nationality placement. Statistically, the number of white foster parents exceeds that of parents of color, with the result that children of color remain in temporary foster care arrangements longer than do white children. The phrases *foster care drift* and *foster limbo* refer to the situation in which a child moves from one foster home to another, without finding permanency through reunification, adoption or legal guardianship.

The ASFA revises the customary practice of excluding foster parents from the adoptive parent pool. With new understandings of the importance of permanence, familiarity, and stability, ASFA encourages foster parent adoption, and provides for subsidies when needed. Currently, approximately one-half of all adoptions out of state are by foster parents; in urban areas, that rises to between 80 and 90 percent. The Act also supports placement with kin in order to keep the child in familiar surroundings and, often, in contact with a biological parent. *Kinship care* accounts for approximately 35 percent of foster care placements in the early twenty-first century. Kin who care for a foster child receive a stipend, as do all foster parents.

When foster care, adoption, and reunification are not possible, courts may appoint a legal guardian. The legal guardian acts as caretaker, seeing to the child's health and well-being. Not termed a parent, the guardian nevertheless represents a version of the meaning of parenthood in American culture, emphasizing the protective rather than the nurturing or loving aspects of being a parent. Like a foster parent, a legal guardian does not assume parental rights, which remain with the birth parent. Critics argue that any arrangement that leaves parental rights in tact keeps the child at risk. Supporters of the practices of kin-care and legal guardianship argue that a child should not be removed from a kinship network based on blood ties.

Cultural diversity within the United States results in differing forms and interpretations of fosterage, alongside those sanctioned by policy and law. Within the African-American community, the notion of "child swapping" means a child may spend part of childhood in several households. In religious communities, a child may be passed around for spiritual and secular upbringing. In Hawaii, many children are still transferred under the Hawaiian practice of *hanai,* or customary adoption. None of these arrangements is officially deemed foster care, while all share a recognition that different adults at different times may best serve the child's interests. Moreover, these arrangements resemble practices in other parts of the world, where foster care is not a response to crisis but a variation on parenting; this is true in many West African cultures. In Polynesian societies, well over half the children in a group or village may be fostered during their childhoods.

With rising cases of drug abuse, AIDS, and HIV, foster care in the United States is a form of crisis intervention. Providing a child with a healthy and safe environment, foster care responds to a public health need. At the same time, the transfer becomes more complicated, prompting questions about the return of the child if a parent is rehabilitated, the importance of bonding, and the developmental stage at which a child is moved. These questions bring an array of experts into the discussion of foster care who must examine the connection between foster parent and cultural notions of parenthood, family, and kinship. The use of the term "parent" keeps foster care in the realm of attachment and of love, while the practice increasingly responds to a social crisis. The ambiguous link with kinship and family renders foster care perhaps the most difficult issue in current child welfare policy.

See also Foster Care: Transitioning Out; Foster Parent Adoption; Informal Adoption; Kinship Care; Multiethnic Placement Act (MEPA); Permanency Planning; U.S. Children's Bureau and Adoption.

Further Reading

Adoption and Foster Care Statistics. Administration for Children and Families Web Site. http://www.acf.hhs.gov/programs/cb/stats_research/index.htm#afcars

Bartholet, Elizabeth. *Nobody's Children.* Boston: Beacon Press, 1999.

Bernstein, Nina. *The Lost Children of Wilder.* New York: Pantheon, 2001.

Modell, J. Schachter. *A Sealed and Secret Kinship.* New York, Berghahn Books, 2002.

Foster Care: Transitioning Out of Care

Donna Dea Holland

Transition out of foster care is also referred to as aging out of foster care. Both phrases refer to the process of individuals moving directly from foster care placement to independence. However, transition out of foster care is a much broader concept and might also include individuals who are in foster care and who are reunified with family or for whom an adoptive arrangement has been made. The information provided here refers only to aging out of foster care and none of the other possible applications of the transition out of foster care.

Aging out of foster care usually involves individuals who turn eighteen or the legal age of majority while still placed in foster care. It may also, however, include individuals with developmental disabilities transitioning to adult services from foster care after their eighteenth birthday and before their twenty-first birthday. It may also include individuals who are over eighteen years of age but who were still completing a high school educational program beyond the age of eighteen and then transitioning out of foster care to independence.

It is important to consider individuals aging out of foster care when seeking to fully understand adoption. While a small percentage of individuals aging out of foster care are in temporary custody and not permanent custody, the majority of individuals aging out of foster care have been in permanent custody. Many have been available for adoption and have not had permanent adoptive placements located for them. Thus, many who age out of foster care are the individuals who were not provided permanent adoptive families and who were never permanently reunited with their families of origin.

Over twenty thousand individuals age out of foster care every year according to the Adoption and Foster Care Analysis and Reporting System (2003). Aging out of foster care has been associated with lower levels of education, housing problems, unemployment and low wage jobs, lower levels of social support, difficulty making the transition to independence, and involvement in deviant behavior in young adulthood as well as other less favorable adult outcomes. There are several possible reasons individuals aging out of foster care have more negative adult outcomes than people who were never in foster care. These reasons involve the experiences prior to foster care placement, the experiences in foster care, the life skills training they received to prepare foster children for the aging out process and the level of social support after the transition out of foster care.

Experiences Prior to Foster Care Placement

Children are placed in foster care for a multitude of reasons. Child neglect, physical child abuse, child sexual abuse, emotional abuse, and dependency are the five main reasons for placement in foster care. Each type of abuse is, to some extent, associated with emotional upset and lower levels of self-esteem. The effects of child abuse and neglect are not uniform, but do tend to be negative. Some individual characteristics and social context issues are related to how well one recovers from child abuse and neglect. The negative effects of child abuse and neglect may create deficits for individuals aging out of foster care. For example, if individuals aging out of foster care have developmental delays due to the trauma experienced as a child, it is likely that these delays will negatively influence the skill acquisition needed to succeed in the transition out of foster care. Skill acquisition is also related to foster care experiences.

Foster Care Experiences

The vast majority of children placed in foster care are eventually reunited with their families of origin. Unfortunately, some of these individuals eventually reenter the foster care system. When children experience multiple occasions of being removed from their families of origin, multiple foster care placements, and reunification with families of origin, this is referred to as foster care reentry. Negative adult outcomes for individuals aging out of foster care are related to foster care reentry. While experiencing multiple foster care reentries, some individuals aging out of foster care may have missed important learning experiences that would have better prepared them for the transition to adulthood. Foster care reentry may result in children having interruptions in their formal education due to being moved from school to school. Foster care reentry occasionally results in children feeling as though they will fail because of the instability they experienced due to foster care reentry. There is another reason some foster children may experience instability in childhood.

Foster care drift is when a foster child is moved from one foster home to another. There are a few reasons foster care drift occurs. Some children display behaviors that foster parents are either unprepared to manage, that foster parents do not want to manage, or that places another child in the home at risk. When these situations arise, foster parents or caseworkers may decide moving the child to a different foster home is in the child's best interest. Sometimes foster children are harmed while in the foster care. When this happens, foster children are often placed into a different foster home in order to protect the child from additional harm. Another reason foster care drift takes place is due to the foster child requesting removal from the foster home.

So, although there are some legitimate reasons that foster care drift may occur, it is clear that the experience of foster care drift would cause additional instability in a child's life. This instability places more stress on the child who has already experienced other trauma from the child abuse experiences, foster care reentry, and multiple school changes. Each of these then complicate the acquisition of skills needed to make a smooth and successful transition to adulthood. Because professionals in the child welfare system have been aware of these connections between child abuse, neglect, and foster care drift with negative adult life outcomes for those who transition out of foster care, they developed independent living skills training to aid older children in the foster care system in the transition to adulthood.

Life Skills Training

Life skills training is often referred to as independent living skills training. It is offered to older teenagers in the foster care system. County custodial agencies and private child placing agencies offer a variety of training regimes. The general purpose of the independent living skills training is to compensate for inadequate preparation for the transition to adulthood for the older foster care youths.

The training takes a variety of forms. Some foster care youths are expected to work with the foster parents to gain these independent living skills; some are provided workbooks that have practical real life problems the youths are supposed to read about and learn to apply to their lives. Other independent livings skills trainings involve actually meeting in a group setting with other similarly situated children who then receive formal training from a trainer. The trainer is usually a caseworker but may be an otherwise contracted trainer from outside the custodial agency.

Depending upon the needs of the youths, the more formal trainings appear to better prepare young adults for the transition out of foster care. Adult foster children report various experiences and levels of satisfaction with the life skills training they received in foster care. Some indicate the trainings were inadequate and were not structured in a way that forced them to really appreciate the knowledge they needed. Others suggest that merely doing assignments in a workbook did not closely approximate the problems they encountered as they made the transition out of foster care. Some foster care experienced adults who previously aged out of foster care indicate that more real-life activities were needed in their independent living skills training to better prepare them for the aging out of foster care process. Some blame inadequate training and preparation for the negative life outcomes they experienced after aging out of foster care. For example, some suggest they needed training on how to have healthy romantic relationships because they did not have adequate role models in their childhoods and, as adults, they do not know how to maintain healthy adult romantic relationships. The level of social support also influences how individuals manage the transition out of foster care.

Social Support

Individuals who age out of foster care receive social support from various sources. Many return to their families of origin or extended families for social support after aging out of the foster care system. Some rely on support from friends known prior to foster care placement and some turn to peer friendships formed with other foster care experienced adults. At times, some who aged out of foster care maintain relationships with prior foster parents and caseworkers.

The type of social support needed by foster care experienced adults varies greatly. Some individuals age out of foster care and turn to their social support network for housing to avoid being homeless. The majority, however, use their social support system to have a sense of belonging and family relationships. Some may turn to caseworkers in order to have guidance on things like how to get a food voucher in the community as an adult, how to register their children for day care services, or how to acquire documents (such as a copy of a social security card) that might be on file at the county office. Caseworkers tend to be contacted for information that a case manager might provide if the foster care experienced adult had one.

A smaller percentage of individuals who aged out of foster care refuse to turn to families of orientation for social support or they limit the level of involvement with families of orientation. This is known as disidentification. Disidentification takes place when an individual decides not to emulate or accept certain people as role models or may involve cutting ties completely. Some foster care experienced adults indicate that they disidentify with some family members who caused them harm during their childhoods.

It is not clear if disidentification has more positive or negative consequences for foster care experienced adults. It may be that disidentification frees the foster care experienced adult to pursue more socially accepted goals in society. Or, it may be that disidentification reduces the level of social support available to the foster care experienced adult in the transition out of the foster care system thereby making the move to adulthood even more difficult.

Summary

Many who age out of foster care were available for adoption but never experienced a permanent adoptive placement. It is clear that individuals who age out of foster care face greater challenges than individuals who have never been in foster care. Some of the reasons for the greater difficulty moving to adulthood are due to experiences prior to placement in foster care, experiences during foster care, the type and amount of life skills training provided, and the level of social support following the move out of the foster care system to independence. It is important to remember that although individuals who age out of foster care face greater challenges and have less pro-social adult outcomes in general, many people who age out of foster care go on to become very successful adults.

See also Foster Care in the United States.

Further Reading

Blome, W.W. "What Happens to Foster Kids?: Educational Experiences of a Random Sample of Foster Care Youth and a Matched Group of Non-foster Care Youth." *Child and Adolescent Social Work Journal* 14 (1997): 41–53.

Buehler, Cheryl, John G. Orme, James Post, and David A. "The Long-Term Correlates of Family Foster Care." *Child and Youth Services Review* 22 (2000): 595–625.

Cook-Fong, Sandra K. "The Adult Well-Being of Individuals Reared in Family Foster Care Placements." *Child and Youth Care Forum* 29 (2000): 7–25.

Courtney, M.E., and I. Piliavin. *The Wisconsin Study of Youth Aging Out of Out-of-Home Care: A Portrait of Children About to Leave Care.* Madison, WI: School of Social Work, University of Wisconsin-Madison, 1995.

Courtney, M.E., and R. Barth. "Pathways of Older Adolescents Out of Foster Care: Implications for Independent Living Services." *Social Work* 1 (1996): 75–83.

Holland, Donna Dea. "A Life Course Perspective on Foster Care: An Examination of the Impact on Variations in Levels of Involvement in the Foster Care System on Adult Criminality and Other Indicators of Adult Well-being." Ph.D. Dissertation, Bowling Green State University, 2005.

Meyer, Harvey. "CASA Volunteers Offer Hope to Older Children Leaving Foster Care." National CASA Association Web Site. http://www.nationalcasa.org/htm/casa_news_article.htm (accessed March, 2006).

U.S. Department of Health and Human Services. Administration for Children and Families, Adoption and Foster Care Analysis and Reporting System (AFCARS). Preliminary Estimates for FY 2003 as of April 2005 (10). Children's Bureau Web Site. http://www.acf.hhs.gov/programs/cb/stats_research/afcars/tar/report10.htm (accessed March, 2006).

Foster Parent Adoption

Jeanne A. Howard

Foster parent adoption, sometimes called conversion adoption, is the term describing the transfer of parental rights from the State to the person who has served as the sanctioned caregiver of a child who was a ward of the State. When children are adopted from foster care, in the majority of cases it is foster parents who adopt them. For example, for fiscal year (FY) 2002 the U.S. Children's Bureau reported that 61 percent of child welfare adoptions were by foster parents. This compares to 24 percent by kin and 15 percent by non-kin, non-foster parent adopters. This percent has declined slightly from 65 percent in FY 1998 when data were first reported.

Adoption by foster parents typically serves the best interests of the child. Foster parent adopters have a relationship with the child, are experienced in providing care to the child, and have knowledge of a child's habits, interests, fears, and often his or her background. Because foster parents have cared for children over time, parent and child are likely to have an emotional connection. And because for most foster children the initial goal is to return home, foster parents are likely to have information about, and perhaps relationships with, the birth families of the child.

While foster parent adoption is now common, this was not always the case. Adoption by foster parents was rendered more possible by the Adoption Assistance and Child Welfare Act (AACWA) of 1980. Through AACWA for the first time, federal funds were made available to states to support adoption subsidy as well as Medicaid coverage for children with special needs. This removed a significant barrier for many foster parents whose income levels might otherwise prevent them from adopting children in their care or from adopting children's whose medical needs might overwhelm family income.

Background

Through much of the period where dependent or maltreated children were cared for in foster care, such care was a sort of de facto adoption. While the general intention was for children to return home, children were often provided for in foster care throughout their childhood. Even when such placements were stable, however, they lacked legal protection. Decision-making power about the child's life, including the decision to move the child to another home, remained in the hands of the entity who placed the child.

Foster care and adoption practice remained separate through much of the development of the field of child welfare. As adoption practice was formalized after World War II, the emphasis was on finding homes for infants, and finding infants for couples. In response to social stigma about both out of wedlock pregnancy and infertility, adoption practice involved careful matching of children and parents so as to render their adoption invisible.

Even when young children were placed into foster care and became available for adoption, their foster parents were often not considered as adoption resources. Despite the fact that many children remained in foster care for significant periods, foster homes were traditionally viewed as transitional, serving to protect the child until return home or adoption occurred. Adoptive homes were seen as permanent. Thus, potential adoptive families were subjected to a higher level of scrutiny than foster parents. Their desire to parent as well as their ability to do so (often judged by income level, education level, and even housekeeping standards) was carefully examined. In addition to concerns about foster parents being less suited for adoption, adoption professionals were concerned that foster parent adopters might allow the child contact with members of the original family or that foster parents might work against a child's reunification if they felt they could adopt. An additional concern was that when foster parents adopted, fewer slots would be available for children needing temporary care. The idea that foster parents were less than ideal adoptive parents was supported by the fact that foster parents were more likely to be older, single parents, and have lower incomes and educational levels than those coming to the child welfare system specifically to adopt. This view of foster parents as acceptable for temporary care but undesirable for permanent parenting held as late as the mid-1970s, when Trudy B. Festinger found that two in three states either prohibited foster parent adoption or warned against it.

As early as 1973, the Child Welfare League of America recognized the value of pursuing adoption by foster parents if this served the best interests of the needs of the child. By the mid- to late 1970s, a number of studies pointed out the large numbers of children in foster care and the risk that such children were unlikely to be adopted; they were at risk for permanent separation from their original families and multiple moves in care. In the landmark *National Study of Social Services to Children and Their Families,* Ann Shyne and Anita W. Schroeder found that over five hundred thousand children were in foster care across the U.S. Further, they estimated that over one hundred thousand children were free for adoption, but their care would be more costly than most parents (usually foster parents) wanting to adopt could provide. Other researchers (see David Fanshel and Eugene B. Shinn) identified the problems of long-term foster care: the risk that the child would lose contact with the family of origin; the risk of multiple moves in care, especially for African-American children; and diminishing likelihood that they would adopted.

Growing awareness of the negative impact of remaining in foster care, as well as foster parent advocacy, led to a push for increased permanency for children through adoption. For the first time, foster parents might be asked to assume a dual role—to be a supportive and nurturing foster parent to assist the child's return or, if return was ultimately deemed inappropriate, to adopt the child. A number of permanency planning demonstration projects found that adoption by foster parents was the primary means by which children in care could be moved to adoption. When permanency planning was codified in federal law with AACWA in 1980, foster parent adoption was encouraged in two ways. First, for the first time, the federal government provided after-adoption subsidy to children with special needs, removing one of the barriers to adoption for foster families who otherwise took on challenging children without financial or medical assistance. Second, the act exempted adoptions by foster parents of a child in their care from the requirement that a non-subsidy home be sought before a subsidy could be provided.

Since 1980, as Kathleen Proch notes, foster families have become an increasingly important resource for children needing adoptive homes and, early in the permanency planning era, became the preferred resource. Indeed, agencies began placing "legal risk" children with foster families. Such children were not legally free for adoption but the circumstances of their parents suggested that such termination was likely to occur. If it did, children could stay in the home into which they were first placed, minimizing breaks in emotional connection.

The Adoption and Safe Families Act (ASFA) of 1997 further encouraged adoption by foster parents. Its emphasis on concurrent planning (i.e. developing a plan for permanency outside the care of birth parents, while at the same time working for reunification or kin placement), assures that foster parents will continue to be important adoption resources. In addition, several studies have found that foster parent adoptions are less likely to disrupt than are "matched" adoptions where the child has no previous relationship with adopting parents. Most states now give preference to foster parents in adopting children in their care, or at least grant them first consideration when adoption becomes the goal. This policy is supported by research by Susan L. Smith and Jeanne A. Howard, and by Richard P. Barth and Marianne Berry that indicates that adoption by foster parents reduces risk of adoption disruption.

Practice in Foster Parent Adoption

Foster parent adoptions are by far the most common adoption type for children in foster care. Despite this fact, there has been surprisingly little research specifically on foster parent adoption, and most was conducted in the 1980s and 1990s. Research on adopting versus non-adopting foster parents, by William Meezan and Joan Shireman, points to aspects of agency practice that promote foster parent adoption. Exceeded only by the family's familiarity with adoption (usually through previous adoption), the continuity and quality of the family's relationship with the worker and family contact with the child's birth family were the two most potent predictors of a family's decision to adopt. (Other important, though less powerful, predictors of adoption were factors typically outside agency control: family socio-economic status; parent-child interactions, including the child's ability to form relationships; foster parents' belief that they are different from the birth parents; the degree of the child's special needs; and the parents' ages.)

In a more recent study of children adopted from the child welfare system, Jeanne Howard and Susan Smith examined 1,343 families, the largest group of which were foster parent adopters (44 percent). The study found just under half of foster parent adopters reported receiving specialized training on adoption issues, which 84 percent found very or somewhat helpful. In terms of child adjustment, foster parents consistently fell between kin adopters (who reported fewer problems and more satisfaction) and matched adopters. An important exception was their score on the Behavior Problem Index (where lower scores equal fewer problems), where kin adopters rated children with scores averaging 9.76 and foster and matched each averaged 13.12. Further, 47 percent of foster parent adopters identified barriers to receiving needed services after adoption. Finding medical professionals who accept the Medicaid payment was the most common, followed by finding affordable counseling professionals. Parents also identified the need for post adoption information, support, and services. The fact that foster parents are the largest pool of adopters, yet they receive training in less than half the cases and have children with significant needs, argues for re-examining practice with foster parent adopters.

Additional research on foster care practice and foster care adoption practice should consider several things. One is how to make the first placement the best placement. Since foster parents are the most likely resource for children, and adoption timetables under ASFA appear to be reducing the time before adoption, the field must assure that careful selection is made in the initial placement. Another is how to assess a particular family for its ability to meet the lifelong needs of a particular child. Careful and thorough preparation for foster parent adopters, including full information about the child and birth family's history and interpretation of the implications of that history for the child's lifetime development, is another consideration. Supportive work with foster parents to determine if they truly can commit to adoptive parenting—with careful work to avoid coercion and to involve the foster parent fully in helping the child adapt to a new adoptive home—is also important, as is the need for post adoption support and services across the child's life span.

Such findings highlight the need for specialized training for foster parents who adopt, even though they are familiar with the children in their care. In addition, the need for post adoption services is clear. Post adoption services have the capacity to not only strengthen foster families who adopt children with special needs, but to encourage current foster parents to take the "leap of faith" to adopt, with the understanding they will have continuing support.

Foster parent adoption is a critical part of the solution to the problem of children remaining in foster care without permanency. The bias against foster parents has been largely eliminated and their capacity to parent the most challenging children has been recognized by the field. The child welfare field needs to consider how to best promote such adoption and how to sustain families after it occurs.

See also Foster Care in the United States; Foster Care: Transitioning Out; Permanency Planning; U.S. Children's Bureau.

Further Reading

Barth, Richard P., and Marianne Berry. *Adoption and Disruption: Rates, Risks and Responses*. New York; Aldine de Gruyter, 1988.

Fanshel, David, and Eugene B. Shinn. *Children in Foster Care: A Longitudinal Investigation*. New York: Columbia University Press, 1978.

Festinger, Trudy B. "Placement Agreements with Boarding Homes: A Survey." *Child Welfare* 53 (1974): 643–652.

Howard, Jeanne, and Susan Smith. *After Adoption: The Needs of Adopted Youth*. Washington, DC: Child Welfare League of America, 2004.

Meezan, William, and Joan Shireman. *Care and Commitment: Foster Parent Adoption Decisions*. Albany, NY: State University of New York Press, 1985.

Proch, Kathleen. "Foster Parents as Preferred Adoptive Parents: Practice Implications." *Child Welfare* 60 (1981): 617–626.

Shyne, Ann, and Anita W. Schroeder. *National Study of Social Services to Children and Their Families*. Rockville, MD: Westat, 1978.

Smith, Susan L., and Jeanne A. Howard. "A Comparative Study of Successful and Disrupted Adoptions." *Social Service Review* 65 (1991): 248–261.

U.S. Children's Bureau. *The AFCARS Report: Preliminary FY 1998 Estimates as of August, 2004*. Washington, DC: U.S. Children's Bureau, 2000.

U.S. Children's Bureau. *The AFCARS Report: Preliminary FY 2002 Estimates as of August, 2004*. Washington, DC: U.S. Children's Bureau, 2004. Administration for Children and Families Web Site. http://www.acf.hhs.gov/programs/cb/stats_research/index.htm

Foundling Wheels

Vern L. Bullough

The foundling wheel was a common feature at convents and monasteries in Italy and much of Catholic Europe until the nineteenth century. The wheel, half inside the convent or hospital and half outside, allowed a mother to leave a baby without being seen. Staff could then turn the wheel and collect the newborn child when the mother rang the bell as she was departing. Santo Spirito Hospital near the Vatican, which had a wheel up until the nineteenth century, is said to have had approximately three thousand babies deposited every year.

There is now an attempt to revive such wheels. Concerned with the increase in the number of abandoned infants attributed to the growth of illegal migration to Italy, Grazi Passeri (head of the Civil Rights 2000 Association) launched a campaign in 2005 to reestablish them using modern technology, such as a heat sensor to alert the hospital staff to a new arrival, and still preserve the anonymity of the mother. Her effort to introduce the wheel follows several failed attempts at other methods to address the problem of abandoned newborns including a hotline for distressed pregnant mothers, a symbolic adoption of an abandoned Nigerian baby by officials of the city of Rome, and an effort to post multi-lingual stickers on rubbish bins with telephone numbers to call for desperate mothers, who were urged not to place their infants in the bins. This last proposal ran into opposition from local mayors who objected that the stickers gave a bad image to tourists. Moreover, the bins, even those close to a hospital, had not been regularly checked. Santo Spirito agreed with Grazi Passeri on the concept of the wheel, and she said that the first of a planned 100 such wheels would be placed there.

See also Medieval Orphanages.

Further Reading

Clarke, Hilary. "Saving Babies the Medieval Way." News.telegraph Web Site. http://www. telegraph.co.uk/news/main.jhtml?xml=/news/2005/09/09/wbaby09.xml&sSheet=/news/ 2005/09/09/ixworld.html (accessed September, 2005).

G

Gay- and Lesbian-Headed Adoptive Families

Scott D. Ryan

Adoptions by gay and lesbian individuals and couples, while not a new phenomenon, have been receiving great attention recently. With an estimated five hundred thousand children in foster care, and an increased focus on permanency options since the advent of the Adoption and Safe Families Act (ASFA) of 1997 (P.L. 105-89), all placement options are being explored—including those with gay men and lesbians.

Adoption Statistics

Approximately 33 percent of children adopted from foster care are placed with single parents. If this trend holds for all adoptions, approximately 64,549 children are adopted by single parents annually from all sources. Since most jurisdictions allowing gay men or lesbians to adopt children only do so for single parents (not recognizing the coupled relationship), these 64,549 adoptions annually constitute the potential population of adoptable children for gay men or lesbian prospective.

Dan Black, Gary Gates, Seth Sanders and Lowell Taylor estimate that 2.5 percent of the population are comprised of gay men and 1.4 percent lesbian women. If gay men and lesbians adopt at the same rate as their heterosexual counterparts, there are at least 229 and 199 adoptions by each group annually. However, it could be argued that the biological male/female coupled path to parenthood is not as easily available to these families; as such, adoptions for gay men and lesbians may occur at a higher rate. Although there are no clear data identifying the actual number of gay men or lesbians who are adoptive parents, the illustration above clearly shows that there are most probably many thousands of adopted children currently being parented by gay men and lesbians.

Laws and Policies

Despite the evidence that demonstrates that success in adoption is not related to family form, as noted by the Human Rights Campaign (2002), several states prohibit or restrict the adoption of children by gay or lesbian individuals or couples. Florida continues to be the only state that explicitly prohibits gay men or lesbians from adopting children. In 1977, it became the first state to enact a specific statutory ban on such adoptions. The statute (Florida Chapter 63.042(3)) states that, "No person eligible to adopt under this statute may adopt if that person is homosexual." This law has survived several court challenges, including the most recent ruling by the 11th Circuit Court of Appeals which found that the ban does not violate the United States Constitution. Furthermore, the United States Supreme Court subsequently refused to hear the case on January 10, 2005, and made no comment outlining its reason for this decision. The result is that the law continues to be in force at this writing, and is the only clear prohibition against single gay or lesbian persons adopting children in any state.

In general, individual states outline who may/may not adopt children, with relevant case law also setting the precedent. As such, it is often difficult to determine a particular state's position since many jurisdictions do not publish adoption decisions. The Human Rights Campaign (2005a) has identified three other states—Arkansas, Nebraska, North Dakota—where, due to this ambiguity, it is not clear whether or not single gay or lesbian persons may adopt a child.

There are many more states with either outright prohibitions or vagueness in their relevant statutes toward whether or not gay or lesbian couples may adopt. Obviously Florida, by default, leads the list of those prohibiting such adoptions. Mississippi passed a law in 2000 explicitly barring these couples from adopting. In 1987, the New Hampshire Supreme Court ruled that two unmarried adults may not jointly petition to adopt a child. Similarly, Utah passed a law in 2000 preventing any unmarried couple from adopting which, by default, restricts gay and lesbian couples from adopting. Again, there are numerous states that, while not specifically excluding such adoptions by statute, do not embrace such prospective adoptive families—who may be met with systemic and other biases. These states include Idaho, Maryland, Minnesota, Missouri, North Carolina, North Dakota, Pennsylvania, South Carolina, South Dakota, Texas, Washington, and Wyoming.

As a result of these laws, gay men and lesbians seeking to adopt children may choose to make no mention of their sexual orientation, and agencies do not ask—much like the military's 'don't ask, don't tell' policy. This assists them in becoming adoptive parents as a single parent, but allows society to continue its biased practices and attitudes—and precludes the prospective adoptive parents' ability, in many jurisdictions, from adopting jointly, thus undermining the adoptive parents' relationship.

Professional Policy Statements

For many years, the American Psychiatric Association, the American Psychological Association, and the National Association of Social Workers have, as Ricketts discovered, all followed official policy statements that explicitly address the placement of children with gay men or lesbians. The American Psychiatric Association's policy on adoptions by gay men or lesbians states that, "single factors such as homosexuality should not necessarily or automatically rule out the selection of a potential adoptive parent" (1986: 1506). The American Psychological Association, in 1974, after removing homosexuality from its list of mental disorders, adopted the following resolution, "homosexuality per se implies no impairment of judgment, stability, reliability, or general social and vocational capabilities" (1975: 1). They later adopted the following resolution, "sex, gender identity or sexual orientation of prospective adoptive parents should not be the sole or primary variable considered in placement" (1976: 1). The National Association of Social Workers' *Code of Ethics* states that, "social workers should not practice, condone, facilitate or collaborate with any form of discrimination on the basis of ... sexual orientation" (2000: 201).

More recently, the American Academy of Pediatrics (2002) released a policy statement endorsing not only adoptions by gay men and lesbians, but supporting adoptions by same-sex couples. They assert that children who are born to, or adopted by, one member of a same-sex couple deserve the security of two legally recognized parents. Similar positions have been taken by the American Academy of Child and Adolescent Psychiatry and the American Psychoanalytic Association.

In addition to the major professional discipline-focused organizations, other entities have also taken positions that support such adoptive placements. The Foster Family-based Treatment Association, an international child welfare association comprised of member agencies including Father Flanagan's Boys' Home, Spaulding for Children, The Casey Family Program, and numerous others, highlights those criteria needed to be a successful foster parent in their Program Standards for Treatment Foster Care. In order to adequately fill the parent role successfully, they identified the qualities of "commitment, positiveness, willingness to implement treatment plans and follow program philosophy, a sense of humor, enjoyment of children/youth, flexibility, tolerance and the ability to adjust expectations concerning achievement and progress to children's individual needs and capacities" (1991: 17). They do not indicate heterosexuality as a selection criteria or homosexuality as an exclusionary factor. The association embraces other family forms and states that, "single treatment parents should have access to a reliable back-up and network of support" (1991: 17).

The Child Welfare League of America, the Nation's oldest and largest child advocacy group, is more explicit in its assertion that lesbians and gay men seeking to adopt shall be judged by the same standards that apply to heterosexuals—stating, "All applicants should be assessed on the basis of their abilities to successfully parent a child needing family membership and not on their race, ethnicity or culture, income, age, marital status, religion, appearance, differing life style, or sexual orientation. Applicants should be accepted on the basis of an individual assessment of their capacity to understand and meet the needs of a particular available child at the point of the adoption and in the future" (2000: 50).

Lastly, the North American Council on Adoptable Children, founded in 1974 by adoptive parents, has as its mission that, "Every child has the right to a permanent family. The Council advocates the right of every child to a permanent, continuous, nurturing and culturally sensitive family." Toward that end, they adopted a policy on March 14, 1998 (and amended on April 14, 2000) stating that, "Children should not be denied a permanent family because of the sexual orientation of potential parents. Everyone with the potential to successfully parent a child in foster care or adoption is entitled to fair and equal consideration" (NACAC, 2000).

As can be seen, all of the major professional organizations within mental health, child health and child welfare take affirmative positions on allowing children to be adopted by gay or lesbian persons/couples. It is important to note that, as Kenneth Haller (2002) wrote, "[these] are not, after all, the Human Rights Campaign or the Lambda Legal Defense and Education Fund. [These are] apolitical organization[s] whose primary mission[s] [are] to advocate for the best interest of children" (p. 32).

Agency Receptiveness

Only one study, that of D. Brodzinsky, C. Patterson, and M. Vaziri, has empirically examined the openness of agencies to gay and lesbian prospective adoptive parents. Questionnaires were mailed to adoption agency program directors across the United States. A total of 214 useable surveys were returned from a mix of public and private placement agencies. At the time of the survey, only two states (New Hampshire and Florida) explicitly denied such adoptions by statute; however, respondents from six other states incorrectly reported that such adoptive placements were against the laws of their respective jurisdictions—with another twenty-nine respondents unsure of their state's legal position.

Approximately 63 percent of respondents did indicate that their agencies accepted applications for adoption by gay men and/or lesbian individuals and/or couples. There was a significant relationship between an agency's religious affiliation and its openness to applications from such prospective adoptive parents.

Of those agencies reporting, over the two years prior to the study, they had placed 22,584 children for adoption, with 371 known to have been placed with gay men or lesbians (approximately 1.6 percent). The study acknowledges that, due to the possibility of non-disclosure or other reporting biases, this figure most likely underestimates the actual number of placements made with gay men or lesbians. This figure, as estimated by the respondents themselves, is calculated to be 2.9 percent. In either case, it does illustrate that there are hundreds of such adoptive families created annually—and that the majority of agencies, at least in this sample, were open to working with gay and lesbian prospective adoptive parents.

S. Ryan, S. Pearlmutter, and V. Groza note that efforts to make agencies more receptive to such placements should occur on three levels. The first is intrapersonally, through which the individual adoption worker (at any level within the organizational structure) holding negative attitudes toward such families is addressed. The second level is interpersonally, or, more specifically, between the adoption worker and his/her supervisor. If the adoption worker holds a positive view of creating such adoptive families, but his/her supervisor does not, then it will be difficult to overcome such influences and support the placement. Third is the overall organizational climate. Agency policies, whether covert or overt, can be discriminatory and discourage the approval of gay and lesbian prospective adoptive parents. Adoptive placements can be derailed at each of the three levels described, and, as such, interventions must be devised for each level.

The Public's View

Although limited, research exploring public perceptions about gay men and lesbian adoptive parents has increased over the years. Gregory Herek found that heterosexual men were the least supportive group of same sex couples, stating their relationships should not be "officially recognized" nor should they be allowed to adopt children. However, Herek (2002) further found that "men and women alike were significantly more likely to endorse adoption rights for lesbians than for gay men" (pg. 50).

P. Leung, S. Erich, and H. Kanenberg found no negative effects for children adopted by gay or lesbian parents compared to the other adoption types. Families headed by gay or lesbian parents of older children, non-sibling group adoptions, and children with more pre-adoption foster care placements experienced higher levels of family functioning. The authors concluded that gay/lesbian headed families show promise as resources for children, particularly older children.

S. Ryan, L. Bedard, and M. Gertz, in their study of 413 randomly called super-voters (those persons who have voted in at least the last three out of four possible elections) in the state of Florida regarding the gay adoption ban, found that, on average, respondents fell into the placement range on the Attitudes Towards Gay Men and Lesbians as Adoptive Parent Scale. Those respondent characteristics that significantly predicted a higher score were race/ethnicity (Caucasian), religion (persons not of the Christian faith), gender (female), political ideology (Republicans scored lowest, Democrats significantly higher, and Independents the highest), and level of education (more than high school).

Child Welfare Worker's View

There have been only two studies, by M. Taylor and by S. Ryan, that assessed the opinions of child welfare workers and the impact on the placement recommendation. Taylor reports that his sample of 50 child welfare workers, overall, favored allowing adoptions by gay men and lesbians; although the sample mean score fell into the Index of Attitudes toward Homosexual's low-grade homophobic range. In addition, approximately one-third of respondents stated that gay and lesbian adoption applicants should not be able to adopt a child under the age of five, and 25 percent held this position until the child was fifteen. Utilizing a specially designed questionnaire to obtain attitudes toward gay men and lesbians as adoptive parents from social work respondents, Ryan found that social workers' attitudes are a function of both childhood/familial experiences as well as later professional indoctrination.

Current Research—What Do We Know?

The majority of the existing empirical research exploring gay and lesbian families has been cross-sectional design studies that utilized non-random, purposive sampling techniques that yielded responses from largely white and middle class respondents. This is also true of the few studies focusing on gay and lesbian adoptive families—with a literature review yielding only four empirical studies that specifically explored the experiences and well-being of gay and lesbian adoptive families.

S. Bennett explored the parental perceptions of attachment in fifteen lesbian couples who had adopted internationally. In this qualitative study, thirty mothers were interviewed to obtain information surrounding the hierarchy of parenting bonds, the division of labor in the household, time with the child, and the legal status of each of the mothers. The findings indicate that the children developed bonds with both adoptive mothers, but that 80 percent had primary bonds to one mother despite shared household and childcare responsibilities. The quality of maternal caretaking was found to be a contributing factor to the child's primary attachment. There was no significant relationship between legal status of the parent and the child's primary attachment figure.

In a study of lesbian adoptive parents, heterosexual adoptive parents, and lesbian parents using in-vitro fertilization, L. Shelley-Sireci and C. Ciano-Boyce found that the level of difficulty with the adoption process was relatively equivalent across groups. There were no significant differences in the length of time to adopt. Their *overall* experiences with the adoption process were also equivalent; however, the lesbian adoptive parents did perceive significantly more discrimination throughout the adoption process.

The third study—L. Peterson, J. Butts, and D. Deville—based on a small sample of three gay, adoptive fathers, sought to uncover the reasons that self-identified gay men decide to parent, their experiences of fatherhood, the relationships they have with their children, and the coming out process as a father. The researchers conducted qualitative interviews with participants to develop content and process themes from these data. The preliminary data analysis resulted in the identification of content themes in four areas: decision to parent, experiences with fatherhood, coming out as fathers, and what researchers need to know about gay fathers. Additionally, the researchers identified two process themes: expressing pride in adopted children and protecting the time they had with their children.

The largest study of gay or lesbian-headed adoptive families to date, by S. Ryan and S. Cash, included 183 families. Respondents were asked by agencies about their sexual orientation slightly over 43 percent of the time, and the parents generally disclosed such information. Virtually all couples wanted to be legally recognized as such—with most not having the opportunity to do so due to restrictive laws in their geographic area. Many reported having some type of religious or spiritual connection, as well as a high level of support from their extended families.

Conclusion

Although the studies described above contribute valuable knowledge to the small base of literature that exists, much more empirical work is needed to gain a complete understanding of adoptive gay and lesbian parents and their children. Future research should address some of the current gaps by obtaining a large representative sample, incorporating a comparison group of non-gay/lesbian adoptive parents, and, independent of parental reporting, collecting data from adoptive children on how they grow and develop within such families. While there is no evidence that such adoptions are harmful in any way, and growing evidence that such placements are as loving and supportive as adoptive families in general, more rigorous research will enable adoption practitioners and policy-makers to be more responsive and supportive to the needs of this all too often hidden adoptive family form.

See also Foreign Adoptions and Same-Sex Parents; Same-Sex Couples and Religiously-Affiliated Agencies.

Further Reading

Adoption and Safe Families Act (ASFA) of 1997 (P.L. 105-89). American Bar Association Web Site. http://www.abanet.org/ftp/pub/child/pl105-89.txt

American Academy of Child and Adolescent Psychiatry. (1999). *Policy statement: Gay, Lesbian and Bisexual Parents.* AACAP Web Site. http://www.aacap.org/publications/policy/ps46.htm (accessed December, 2004).

American Academy of Pediatrics. (2002). *Coparent or Second-parent Adoption by Same-sex Parents.* AAP Web Site. http://www.aap.org/policy/020008.html (accessed December, 2004).

American Psychiatric Association. "Position Statement on Discrimination in Selection of Foster Parents." *American Journal of Psychiatry 143 (1986):* 1506.

American Psychoanalytic Association. (2002). *Position Statement on Gay and Lesbian Parenting.* APA Web Site. http://apsa-co.org/ctf/cgli/parenting.htm (accessed January, 2005).

American Psychological Association. (1975). *Policy Statements on Lesbian, Gay, and Bisexual Concerns: Discrimination Against Homosexuals.* APA Web Site. http://www.apa.org/pi/lgbpolicy/child.html (accessed January, 2005).

American Psychological Association. (1976). *Policy Statements on Lesbian, Gay, and Bisexual Concerns: Child Custody or Placement.* APA Web Site. http://www.apa.org/pi/lgbpolicy/against.html (accessed January, 2005).

Bennett, S. "Is There a Primary Mom? Parental Perceptions of Attachment Bond Hierarchies with Lesbian Adoptive Families." *Child and Adolescent Social Work* 20 (2003): 159–173.

Black, D., G. Gates, S. Sanders, and L. Taylor. "Demographics of the Gay and Lesbian Population in the U.S.: Evidence from Available Systematic Data Sources." *Demography* 37 (2000): 139–154.

Brodzinsky, D., C. Patterson, and M. Vaziri. "Adoption Agency Perspectives on Lesbian and Gay Prospective Parents: A National Study." *Adoption Quarterly* 5 (2002): 5–23.

Brooks, D., and S. Goldberg. "Gay and Lesbian Adoptive and Foster Care Placements: Can They Meet the Needs of Waiting Children?" *Social Work* 46 (2001): 147–157.

Child Welfare Information Gateway. U.S. Department of Health and Human Services "Adoption Services." Child Welfare Information Gateway Web Site. http://www.childwelfare.gov/systemwide/statistics/adoption.cfm

Child Welfare League of America. *Standards for Adoption Service* (rev. ed.). Washington, DC: Child Welfare League of America, 2000.

Child Welfare League of America. National Data Analysis System, 2002. Child Welfare League of America Web Site. http://ndas.cwla.org (accessed January, 2005).

Florida Chapter 63.042(3) The Florida Senate Web Site. http://www.flsenate.gov/Statutes/index.cfm?App_mode=Display_Statute&Search_String=&URL=Ch0063/SEC042.HTM&Title=-%3E2004-%3ECh0063-%3ESection%20042#0063.042.

Foster Family-based Treatment Association. *Program Standards for Treatment Foster Care.* New York: Foster Family-based Treatment Association, 1991.

Groza, V., S. Ryan, and S. Cash. "Institutionalization, behavior and international adoption: Predictors of behavior problems. *Journal of Immigrant Health* 5 (2003): 5–17.

Haller, K. "The American Academy of Pediatrics Coparent or Second-parent Adoption by Same-sex Parents Policy Statement: Its Science, Its Implications." *Journal of the Gay and Lesbian Medical Association* 6 (2002): 29–32.

Herek, G. "Gender Gaps in Public Opinion About Lesbians and Gay Men." *Public Opinion Quarterly* 66 (2002): 40–66.

Human Rights Campaign. *The State of the Family: Laws and Legislation Affecting Gay, Lesbian, Bisexual and Transgender Families.* Washington, DC: Human Rights Campaign, 2002.

Human Rights Campaign. (2005a). *Adoption Laws: State by State.* Human Rights Campaign Web Site. http://www.hrc.org/Template.cfm?Section=Laws_Legal_Resources&Template=/TaggedPage/TaggedPageDisplay.cfm&TPLID=66&ContentID=19984 (accessed January, 2005).

Human Rights Campaign. (2005b). *Supreme Court Sidesteps Gay Adoption Case.* Human Rights Campaign Web Site. http://www.hrc.org/Content/ContentGroups/News3/2005_January/Supreme_Court_Sidesteps_Gay_Adoption_Case.htm (accessed January, 2005).

Leung, P., S. Erich, and H. Kanenberg. "A Comparison of Family Functioning in Gay/Lesbian, Heterosexual and Special Needs Adoptions." *Children and Youth Services Review* 27 (2005): 1031–1044.

Mallon, G. "Gay Men and Lesbians as Adoptive Parents." *Journal of Gay and Lesbian Social Services*, 11 (2000): 1–22.

National Association of Social Workers. *Code of Ethics of the National Association of Social Workers* (Section 4.02). NASW Web Site. http://www.naswdc.org/pubs/code/default.htm (accessed January, 2005).

North American Council on Adoptable Children. *Gay and Lesbian Adoptions and Foster Care* NACAC Web Site. http://www.nacac.org/pub_statements.html#gay (accessed January, 2005).

Peterson, L., J. Butts, and D. Deville. "Parenting Experiences of Three Self-identified Gay Fathers." *Smith College Studies in Social Work 70* (2000): 514–521.

Ricketts, W. *Lesbians and Gay Men as Foster Parents.* Portland, ME: National Child Welfare Resources Center for Child and Family Policy, 1991.

Ryan, S. "Examining Social Workers' Placement Recommendations of Children with Gay and Lesbian Adoptive Parents." *Families in Society* 81 (2000): 517–528.

Ryan, S., L. Bedard, and M. Gertz. "Florida's Gay Adoption Ban: What do Floridians Think?" *Journal of Law and Public Policy* 15 (2004): 261–283.

Ryan, S., and S. Cash. "Adoptive Families Headed by Gay or Lesbian Parents: A Threat … or Hidden Resource?" *Journal of Law and Public Policy* 15 (2004): 443–466.

Ryan, S., S. Pearlmutter, and V. Groza. "Coming Out of the Closet: Opening Agencies to Gay Men and Lesbian Adoptive Parents." *Social Work* 49 (2004): 85–96.

Shelley-Sireci, L., and C. Ciano-Boyce. "Becoming Lesbian Adoptive Parents: An Exploratory Study of Lesbian Adoptive, Lesbian Birth, and Heterosexual Adoptive Parents." *Adoption Quarterly,* 6 (2002): 33–43.

Sullivan, T., and A. Baques. "Familism and the Adoption Option for Gay and Lesbian Parents." *Journal of Gay and Lesbian Social Services* 10 (1999); 79–94.

Taylor, M. (1998). *Attitudes of Social Workers Toward Gay and Lesbian Adoption.* Unpublished master's thesis, California State University, Long Beach. (UMI No. 1390139).

Homosexuals and Adoption: The Case of Florida

Vern L. Bullough

Adoption of children by homosexuals and lesbians has become increasingly frequent in recent years in many states but, as of this writing, the issue is still controversial. Only one state, Florida, specifically singles out gays and lesbians as ineligible to be adoptive parents, although Mississippi has a broad ban against adoptions by same sex couples. The Florida law was enacted in 1977 as a result of a statewide campaign by the popular singer Anita Bryant's campaign against homosexuals.

Steven Lofton and his partner Roger Croteau challenged the law in the U.S. Supreme Court in a case known as *Lofton vs. Florida*, but on January 10, 2001, it refused to hear the challenge. It probably should be added that this was just one of the 426 appeals that were denied by the Supreme Court that day. The court gave no reason for its decision and it is not clear whether it will encourage other states to adopt similar laws. The major reason the case went to the court was that a federal judge had ruled to uphold the Florida ban, and his decision on appeal to the U.S. Court of Appeals in Atlanta had resulted in a 6-6 vote; it was this split decision that was being appealed before the Supreme Court.

It is also worthy of note that, in spite of the illegality of adoption by same sex parents, Florida law did not, and still does not, prohibit gays and lesbians from caring for foster children. This is how Lofton and Croteau became involved in the first place; they had taken in two special needs children in 1988 and raised them. Both infants had been diagnosed as HIV-positive. It was only when the two children reached seventeen that they tried to adopt them and the would-be parents ran into trouble.

Their lawyers for their court case pointed out that Florida permitted former drug abusers, felons, and even child abusers to become adoptive parents; that there was a desperate need in Florida to find people willing to adopt since at the time there were 3,400 children were in need of adoption; that homosexuality or lesbianism was not against the law; that gays and lesbians should have a right to adopt; and that the law as written meant "a beloved" lesbian aunt wanting to adopt her orphaned nieces or nephews could be passed over in favor of complete strangers for a child. The challenge to the law was supported by the Child Welfare League of America, which argued it was a mistake to exclude any group of willing parents. The American Civil Liberties Union also supported them. The president of the Liberty Counsel, a pro-family, anti-gay group, defended the law and praised the court's action. He argued that adoption was a privilege and that common sense and human history emphasize the need for a mother and father. The state's ban on same sex adoptions, he said, served to preserve the traditional models of the family.

A survey of state practices at the time of this writing indicates that, while most states seek married couples as the ideal for placing abandoned children, the emphasis is not necessarily on the marriage status of those wanting to adopt, but rather finding those whom they think will be good care givers. In a sense, the reason for the Supreme Court's unwillingness to act is unclear, since the justices in recent years, as exemplified by the case of *Lawrence vs. Texas*, have struck down state laws that discriminated against gays and lesbians. The last word has not been said on this issue.

Further Reading

Savage, David. "High Court Lets Ban on Gay Adoptions Stand." *Los Angeles Times*. January 11, 2005, p. A10.

Primary Document

Gay, Lesbian, and Bisexual Adoption-Related Concerns: Taking a Position

The following excerpts of policy statements from selected professional national organizations reflect their official positions on gay, lesbian, and bisexual adoption-related issues.

American Academy of Child and Adolescent Psychiatry (AACAP)

Gay, Lesbian, and Bisexual Parents

Policy Statement, Approved by Council June, 1999

The basis on which all decisions relating to custody and parental rights should rest on the best interest of the child. Lesbian, gay, and bisexual individuals historically have faced more rigorous scrutiny than heterosexuals regarding their rights to be or become parents.

There is no evidence to suggest or support that parents with a gay, lesbian, or bisexual orientation are per se different from or deficient in parenting skills, child-centered concerns and parent-child attachments, when compared to parents with a heterosexual orientation. It has long been established that a homosexual orientation is not related to psychopathology, and there is no basis on which to assume that a parental homosexual orientation will increase likelihood

261

of or induce a homosexual orientation in the child.

Outcome studies of children raised by parents with a homosexual or bisexual orientation, when compared to heterosexual parents, show no greater degree of instability in the parental relationship or developmental dysfunction in children.

The AACAP opposes any discrimination based on sexual orientation against individuals in regard to their rights as custodial or adoptive parents as adopted by Council.

Source

Quoted from: Gay, Lesbian, and Bisexual Parents. Policy Statement, Approved by Council June, 1999. American Academy of Child and Adolescent Psychiatry (AACAP) Web Site. http://www.aacap.org/publications/policy/ps46.htm (accessed February, 2006).

American Academy of Pediatrics

Coparent or Second-Parent Adoption by Same-Sex Parents

Committee on Psychosocial Aspects of Child and Family Health

Children who are born to or adopted by 1 member of a same-sex couple deserve the security of 2 legally recognized parents. Therefore, the American Academy of Pediatrics supports legislative and legal efforts to provide the possibility of adoption of the child by the second parent or coparent in these families.

Children deserve to know that their relationships with both of their parents are stable and legally recognized. This applies to all children, whether their parents are of the same or opposite sex. The American Academy of Pediatrics recognizes that a considerable body of professional literature provides evidence that children with parents who are homosexual can have the same advantages and the same expectations for health, adjustment, and development as can children whose parents are heterosexual. When 2 adults participate in parenting a child, they and the child deserve the serenity that comes with legal recognition.

Children born or adopted into families headed by partners who are of the same sex usually have only 1 biologic or adoptive legal parent. The other partner in a parental role is called the "coparent" or "second parent." Because these families and children need the permanence and security that are provided by having 2 fully sanctioned and legally defined parents, the Academy supports the legal adoption of children by coparents or second parents. Denying legal parent status through adoption to coparents or second parents prevents these children from enjoying the psychologic and legal security that comes from having 2 willing, capable, and loving parents.

Source

Quoted from: Coparent or Second-Parent Adoption by Same-Sex Parents. American Academy of Pediatrics Web Site. http://aappolicy.aappublications.org/cgi/content/full/pediatrics%3b109/2/339 (accessed February, 2006).

American Psychological Association (APA)

Policy Statement on Lesbian, Gay and Bisexual Concerns

Discrimination against Homosexuals

Adopted by the APA Council of Representatives on January 24–26, 1975.

... the APA urges all mental health professionals to take the lead in removing the stigma of mental illness that has long been associated with homosexual orientations....

[The APA] deplores all public and private discrimination ... against those who engage in or have engaged in homosexual activities and declares that no burden of proof of such judgement, capacity, or reliability shall be placed upon these individuals greater than that imposed on any other persons.... [and] supports and urges the enactment of civil rights legislation ... that would offer citizens who engage in acts of homosexuality the same protections now guaranteed to others on the basis of race, creed, color, etc.... [and] supports and urges the repeal of all discriminatory legislation singling out homosexual acts by consenting adults in private (Conger, 1975, p. 633).

Reference

Conger, J.J. (1975) Proceedings of the American Psychological Association, Incorporated, for the year 1974: Minutes of the Annual meeting of the Council of Representatives. *American Psychologist*, 30, 620–651.

Source

Excerpted from: Policy Statement on Lesbian, Gay and Bisexual Concerns. Discrimination Against Homosexuals. American Psychological Association Web Site. http://www.apa.org/pi/lgbpolicy/against.html (accessed February, 2006).

Child Custody or Placement

Adopted by the APA Council of Representatives on September 2 and 5, 1976

The sex, gender identity, or sexual orientation of natural, or prospective adoptive or foster parents should not be the sole or primary variable considered in custody or placement cases (Conger, 1977, p. 432).

Reference

Conger, J.J. (1977). Proceedings of the American Psychological Association, Incorporated, for the year 1976: Minutes of the Annual Meeting of the Council of Representatives. *American Psychologist*, 32, 408–438.

Source

Excerpted from: Policy Statement on Lesbian, Gay and Bisexual Concerns. Child Custody Or Placement. American Psychological Association Web Site. http://www.apa.org/pi/lgbpolicy/child.html (accessed February, 2006).

Child Welfare League of America (CWLA)

Position Statement on Parenting of Children by Gay, Lesbian, and Bisexual Adults

CWLA's Position on Same-Sex Parenting

The Child Welfare League of America (CWLA) affirms that gay, lesbian, and bisexual parents are as well suited to raise children as their heterosexual counterparts . . . .

As they pertain to GLBTQ children, youth, and families, CWLA's Standards of Excellence for Family Foster Care Services do not include requirements for adults present in the home to be legally related by blood, adoption, or legal marriage. Specifically, section 3.18 of the foster care standards establishes a policy of nondiscrimination in the selection of foster parents, stating: "The family foster care agency should not reject foster parent applicants solely due to their age, income, marital status, race, religious preference, sexual orientation, physical or disabling condition, or location of the foster home" (CWLA, 1995).

CWLA also articulates a strong position on the issue of nondiscrimination of adoptive applicants. Section 4.7 of the Standards of Excellence for Adoption Services states:

All applicants should be assessed on the basis of their abilities to successfully parent a child needing family membership and not on their race, ethnicity or culture, income, age, marital status, religion, appearance, differing lifestyle, or sexual orientation. Applicants should be accepted on the basis of an individual assessment of their capacity to understand and meet the needs of a particular available child at the point of the adoption and in the future (CWLA, 2000).

Thus, based on a preponderance of existing research substantiating the ability of gay, lesbian, and bisexual adults to serve as competent, caring, supportive and loving parents, and consistent with the Standards of Excellence for Child Welfare Services, CWLA commits its experience, its resources, and its influence to supporting GLBTQ children, youth, adults, and families involved in America's child welfare system.

Source

Quoted from: Position Statement on Parenting of Children by Gay, Lesbian, and Bisexual Adults. CWLA's Position on Same-Sex Parenting. Child Welfare League of America Web Site. http://www.cwla.org/programs/culture/glbtqposition.htm (accessed February, 2006).

The documents cited above as CWLA 1995 and CWLA 2000 are:

- Child Welfare League of America. *Standards of Excellence for Family Foster Care Services.* Washington, DC: Child Welfare League of America, 1995.

- Child Welfare League of America. *Standards of Excellence for Adoption Services.* Washington, DC: Author, 2000.

North American Council on Adoptable Children

Gay and Lesbian Adoptions and Foster Care

Position Statement, April 9, 2005

Philosophy

Children should not be denied a permanent family because of the sexual orientation of potential parents.

Practice and Policy Recommendations

All prospective foster and adoptive parents, regardless of sexual orientation, should be given fair and equal consideration.

NACAC opposes rules and legislation that restrict the consideration of current or prospective foster and adoptive parents based on their sexual orientation.

Source

Quoted from: NACAC Position Statements. Gay and Lesbian Adoptions and Foster Care. North American Council on Adoptable Children (NACAC) Web Site. http://www.nacac.org/pub_statements.html#gay (accessed February, 2006).

National Association of Social Workers

Code of Ethics

Approved by the 1996 NASW Delegate Assembly and revised by the 1999 NASW Delegate Assembly

4.02 Discrimination

Social workers should not practice, condone, facilitate, or collaborate with any form of discrimination on the basis of race, ethnicity, national origin, color, sex, sexual orientation, age, marital status, political belief, religion, or mental or physical disability.

Source

Quoted from: Code of Ethics of the National Association of Social Workers. Section 4.02 Discrimination. National Association of Social Workers Web Site. http://www.naswdc.org/pubs/code/code.asp (accessed February, 2006).

Primary Document

Positions on Controversial Gender and Custody Issues: Where the American Psychiatric Association Stands

As more "non-traditional" adopters seek to adopt, various organizations have been forced to address the controversies raised by issues including gay parenting, transracial adoption, and various custody issues. The text of the following document from the American Psychiatric Association (APA) summarizes one well-known organization's position on several such issues. The APA removed homosexuality as a disorder from the Diagnostic and Statistical Manual (DSM) in 1973.

APA Document Reference No. 970008

Controversies in Child Custody: Gay and Lesbian Parenting; Transracial Adoptions; Joint versus Sole Custody; and Custody Gender Issues

Resource Document

Approved by the Board of Trustees, December 1997

"Policy documents are approved by the APA Assembly and Board of Trustees ... These are ... position statements that define APA official policy on specific subjects ..."

—*APA Operations Manual.*

265

The purpose of this resource document is to provide information about several controversial issues related to child custody determinations. This document was prepared by members of the APA Subcommittee on Child Custody Issues under the auspices of the APA Council on Psychiatry and Law. Much of the content was presented as a component workshop at the 1997 APA Annual Meeting and a symposium at the 1997 APA Annual Meeting.

The following summary statements represent current knowledge based on a thorough review of the literature. The backup document contains a more detailed discussion of each issue including a critique of the literature, its limitations and a current bibliography.

Disclaimer: It is important to note that the research in this area is imperfect. There have been no longitudinal studies with controls. This document will need ongoing modification based on the results of further studies. Nevertheless, at this point in time, these statements represent what is supported by the literature and by our judgment.

Summary Statements on Controversies in Child Custody

Child Custody: Gay and Lesbian Parenting

1. Sexual orientation should not be used as the sole or primary factor in child custody determinations.

2. Gay and lesbian couples and individuals should be allowed to become parents through adoption, fostering and new reproductive technologies, subject to the same types of screening used with heterosexual couples and individuals.

3. Second parent adoptions which grant full parental rights to a second, unrelated adult (usually an unmarried partner of a legal parent), are often in the best interest of the child(ren) and should not be prohibited solely because both adults are of the same gender.

4. Custody determinations after dissolution of a gay relationship should be done in a manner similar to other custody determinations.

Child Custody: Transracial Adoption

(These statements, based on a literature review, apply to African-American children or Asian children adopted by white families. There is inadequate literature dealing with other transracial or transethnic situations such as the adoption of Native American children and international adoptions.)

1. The existing literature does not support the conclusion that transracial adoption should be prohibited or discouraged.

2. There does not appear to be any significant differences between transracial adoptees and intraracial adoptees on measures of family integration, self-esteem, school performance, or overall adjustment.

3. The existing literature supports that there may be significant issues related to racial identity that need attention by adoptive parents and adoptees (as they get older).

Child Custody: Joint versus Sole Custody and Custody Gender Issues

1. There is no single best custody arrangement for all children. Determinations about custody need to be made on a case by case basis.

2. In determining visitation with non-custodial parents, the benefit of having contact with both parents must be weighed against the harms associated with having contact with parents who have ongoing conflict.

3. The literature indicates that frequent visitation with the non-custodial parent is beneficial for children provided that there is

a low conflict post-divorce parental relationship.

4. Gender of the child and parent should not be used as the sole or primary factor in child custody determinations. Determinations about the best custody arrangement in terms of gender of child and parent should be done on a case by case basis related to factors such as the age of the child, the emotional/psychological health of the child, stability of the parents, and presence of extended family.

5. The literature provides some evidence that boys tend to do better in father custody families and girls tend to do better in mother custody families, provided all other custody determination factors are equal, e.g., parenting skills.

Source

Re-printed with permission from the American Psychiatric Association, 1400 K Street NW, Washington, D.C. 20005, Telephone: (888) 357- 7924, Fax: (202) 682-6850, Email: apa@psych.org.

Gender and Mental Health Issues

Vern L. Bullough

An early study of adopted persons and mental disturbances was by psychiatrist Marshall Schecter who concluded about 13 percent of his psychiatric patients over five had been adopted. Though the study continues to be cited, his sample was much too small to make any generalizations since it was based on a study of 16 adopted persons in his total sample of 120 mental patients. Moreover, many of the criteria he used such as not being toilet trained at fourteen months, do not seem particularly valid. Still Richard Barth and others believe that the older the child is at the time of adoption, the more likely there will be problems. Children adopted as adolescents have a disproportionate number of difficulties.

Some of the more recent studies conducted in Canada find adoptees overrepresented in referrals to child mental health clinics, but whether this reflects a genuine increase in behavioral difficulties or whether adoptive parents simply make better use of clinical services is unclear. A 1998 Canadian study examined some 238 boys referred to a gender identity clinic in Ontario. Between 1965 and 1989, 24,613 boys under the age of two, out of the 1,651,266 male live births in Ontario, were adopted. Of the 238 referred for gender identity problems, the percentage of youth with gender identity problems was 7.6 percent. Only 238 is a very small minority of this group. The percentage of boys adopted in the first two years of life was compared to the base rate of boys adopted in Ontario. The percentage of boys with gender identity problems who were early adoptees, 7.6 percent, was significantly higher than the rate of non-adopted males (1.5 percent).

Several explanations have been offered for this disparity. Some argue that pre-natal maternal stress was greater in the adopted children than in the non-adopted children, and this might lead to feminization. Others argue that the lack of attachment in the early development of the adopted child might predispose such a child to gender identity problems. In short, it is not certain what causes this, and the important point to emphasize is that most boys, whether adopted or not adopted, do not develop gender identity problems, and most boys with gender identity problems are not adopted. Obviously adoption, even early adoptions, might have some causal effects on development, but the how and why is uncertain.

Further Reading

Cohen, N.J., A. Coynd, and J. Duvall. "Adopted and Biological Children in the Clinic: Family, Parental and Child Characteristics." *Journal of Child Psychology Psychiatry* 34 (1993): 545–562.

Haugaard, J.J. "Is Adoption a Risk Factor for the Developments of Adjustment Problems?" *Clinical Psychological Review* 18 (1998): 47–69.

Jerome, L. "Over Representation of Adopted Children Attending a Children's Mental Health Center." *Canadian Journal of Psychiatry* 31 (1986): 526–531.

Kotosopoulos, S., A. Cote, K. Joseph, N. Pentland, C. Stavrakaki, P. Sheahan, and others. "Psychiatric Disorders in Adopted Children: A Controlled Study." *American Journal of Orthopsychiatry* 58 (1988): 608–612.

Zucker, K.J., and S.J. Bradley. "Adoptee Overrepresentation Among Clinic-Referred Boys with Gender Identity Disorder." *Canada Journal of Psychiatry* 43 (1998): 1040–1043.

Genetic Testing

Kathy Shepherd Stolley

Genetic testing, in brief, examines an individual's genetic diseases or conditions, or risk factors for disease. As explained by the Genetics Home Reference of the National Library of Medicine, "Genetic tests look for abnormalities in a person's genes, or the presence or absence of key proteins whose production is directed by specific genes. Abnormalities in either could indicate an inherited disposition to a disorder. Genetic testing includes gene tests (DNA testing) and biochemical tests (protein testing)." This testing is done by a variety of laboratory techniques. Widespread and perhaps increasing interest has been shown in genetic testing by adoptive parents and professionals in the field. Whether discussing adoption or genetic testing in a wider context, myriad contentious and often unresolved social, psychological, cultural, medical, scientific, emotional, financial, legal, and ethical issues abound.

As recounted by the National Institutes of Health, genetic testing is not a new idea, beginning as early as the 1960s when physicians began to urge that children be tested for inheritable genetic diseases. During the following decade, testing parents for the risk of having children with inheritable genetic diseases such as Tay Sachs (a genetic disease often found in Jews of Ashkenazi descent, resulting in death during early childhood) and sickle cell anemia (a genetic disease impacting the hemoglobin that is most common among people of African descent) arose. Prenatal genetic tests followed in the 1980s. Preimplantation genetic diagnosis (PGD) now even allows for diagnosis of genetic diseases in the embryo. The 1990s and beyond has seen the development of increasingly sophisticated testing including testing for "genetic predispositions" to diseases such as breast and colon cancer, as well as advances toward genetic profiling in which a large collections of a person's genetic makeup can be examined at once. Pharmacogenomics (tests that predict response to various drug therapies) are also available and of increasing interest.

Over 900 genetic tests are offered by laboratories, at this writing, and many more are in development.

Some genetic testing for children is now routine. For example, newborns in most states of the United States and numerous other nations undergo mandatory screening for treatable metabolic diseases such as phenylketonuria. Commonly known as PKU, the condition involves a liver enzyme deficiency resulting in an inability to metabolize the amino acid phenylalanine that, left untreated, generally results in mental retardation and other problems. However, with awareness of the condition, placing newborns on a special diet can avoid or mitigate these problems.

Medical examinations and family histories are commonplace for children placed for adoption. However, many questions involving genetic testing in adoption and foster cases continue to be raised and emotionally debated. As noted by the American Society of Human Genetics (ASHG) and the American College of Medical Genetics (ACMG), interests of the child, adoptive and birth parents, adoption agency, and the public are all involved in genetic testing. Their position is that the child's well-being should be the primary concern. Although retaining certain genetic information is important in the adoption process, protecting children from potential stigmatization is also necessary. According to their joint statement, these organizations "support genetic testing in the adoption process if it is consistent with preventive and diagnostic tests performed on all children of a similar age, if it is generally limited to testing for medical conditions that manifest themselves during childhood or for which preventive measures or therapies may be undertaken during childhood, and if it is not used to detect genetic variations within the normal range."

A colloquium on the Ethics of Adoption held at the University of Massachusetts Boston in March, 2000 addressed "The Ethics of Genetic Testing in Adoption." Drawing on experts from numerous disciplines (including several contributors to this handbook), the depth and breadth of complicated issues involved in genetic testing is illustrated by the range of questions addressed during that event. These included: What criteria should guide the application of genetic testing to children in foster and adoptive placement? How should competing interests of such things as rights to privacy and medical disclosure be handled in this context? Do prospective adoptive parents have the right to know more genetic information about an adoptive child than their biologic child? What legal issues need to be addressed and how? When and under what circumstances is genetic testing of a child appropriate? Who should be entrusted with overseeing the best interests of the child in the era of genetic testing? How will policies in this area impact fostering and adoption? The dialogue and debate on these and other issues surrounding genetic testing, adoption, and fosterage continue.

Further Reading

Freundlich, Madelyn, and Lisa Peterson. *Wrongful Adoption: Law, Policy, and Practice.* Washington, DC: CWLA Press, 1999.

"The Future of Genetic Testing: Telling Science Fact from Science Fiction" *News in Health.* National Institues of Health. February 2006. NIH Web Site. http://newsinhealth. nih.gov/2006/February/docs/01features_01.htm#feature01. (accessed June, 2006.)

Genetic Home Reference. "What is Genetic Testing?" National Library of Medicine, National Institutes of Health Web Site. http://ghr.nlm.nih.gov/handbook/testing/genetictesting. (accessed June, 2006.)

"Genetic Testing in Adoption." Joint Statement of the American Society of Human Genetics and the American College of Medical Genetics. American College of Genetics Web Site. http://www.acmg.net/resources/policies/pol-017.asp. (accessed June 2006).

Holtzman, Neil A., and Michael S. Watson, eds. *Promoting Safe and Effective Genetic Testing in the United States. Final Report of the Task Force on Genetic Testing.* September 1997. National Institutes of Health-Department of Energy Working Group on Ethical, Legal and Social Implications of Human Genome Research. National Human Genome Research Institute. National Institutes of Health. http://www.genome.gov/10001733. (accessed June 2006).

Lorandos, Demosthenes A. "Secrecy and Genetics in Adoption Law and Practice." *Loyola University of Chicago Law Journal.* Winter 1996: pp. 277–320.

National Adoption Information Clearinghouse. "Impact of Adoption on Adopted Persons: A Factsheet for Families." 2004. http://naic.acf.hhs.gov/pubs/f_adimpact.cfm. (accessed June 2006).

Smith, Janet Ferrell, ed. "The Ethics of Genetic Testing in Adoption." Transcript of the Proceedings from a Colloquium on the Ethics of Adoption held at the University of Massachusetts Boston. Friday, March 10, 2000. (September 2002.) John W. McCormack Graduate School of Policy Studies, University of Massachusetts BostonWeb Site. http://www.mccormack.umb.edu/dean/docs/GeneticTestingAdoption.pdf (accessed June, 2006.)

Genetics and Adoption: Language and Ideology

Barbara Katz Rothman and Amy Traver

In many ways, the notion of difference is inherent in the language we use to talk about adoption. For example, the word "adoption" typically implies the taking of something foreign—be that something a new textbook, a pet, a highway, or (alas) a child or young adult—and making it one's own. But, in the context of the family, what is it that makes an adopted child so different? Wherein lies the consistent, abiding foreignness of that child to his or her adoptive kin? In this era of genetic ideology, such difference is said to come from the child's unique genetic structure.

This is most clearly demonstrated in our use of the word "adoption" to describe the modern ability to transplant an embryo from one woman to another, or to create an embryo in vitro out of the ovum of one woman and place it in the body of another. Of significance is that it is the genetic material and very little else that is being "adopted." Interestingly, we never speak of a transplanted kidney or heart as "adopted"; that biological material becomes part of the "host," though of course it remains genetically distinct. A transplanted embryo, on the other hand, is understood as adopted because the child that grows remains, in contemporary ideology, always foreign. It does not, in our current talk, grow to be entirely one's own baby in one's own body, but remains adopted, someone else's child nurtured as if one's own.

If the nurturance of pregnancy, the growth of a human baby from a blastocyst, does not make a child one's own, then how can other, later nurturance offered to a born baby or child ever make that child one's own? This negation of the significance of nurturance, its relegation to the background as genetics is foregrounded, thus shapes our contemporary understanding of adoption.

Yet, it is important to distinguish the science of genetics from its function as an ideology for our time. Genetic scientists inform us that genes do not determine much of anything about us. Rather, genes are one factor in a multifactorial process; genes interact with other genes and with the environment, and complex processes cannot be reduced to simple discussions of genes for diseases, characteristics, or types.

Genetic ideology, on the other hand, tells us something different. Genetic ideology is the popular belief system that has grown up with, alongside, out of, and underpinning genetic science. According to this ideology, genes are fate; they are causal and determinative. If genes are the cause, the active force, the predictor of traits, then to read genes is to predict traits. But geneticists often cannot predict traits, and so they have introduced a useful distinction, noting the difference between genotype and phenotype. The genotype is the genetic reading. The phenotype is how it actually played out as the being before "you." Environment can then be understood as that which muddies the waters, that which interferes between the genotype and the phenotype. Geneticists themselves are very aware of the significance of the environment, from the environment of the rest of the cell outside of the gene-laden nucleus, to the environment of the rest of the body, to the environment that lies outside of the body. What we are is the product of the interactions of genes with each other and with the environment. But in popular thinking, in the dominant ideology of genetic determinism, genes are seen as the real and ultimate cause while environment is seen as a variety of contributing, or even complicating, factors.

Seeing fate this way—inborn, inbred, predetermined—has profound implications for parenting in general, and for adoption specifically. All parents are helpless bystanders as the child's fate plays out. They can nurture, supervise, and protect, but they are essentially powerless. They do not create children; they oversee them. This is true of all parents in this ideology; the child is what it is, and the parent cannot change that.

The old-fashioned word for what, in each of us, cannot be changed was "seed." In the history of Western society, that seed was something that men had, and women were part of the environment: the place where the seeds of men grew into babies, the children of men. In the current version, both men and women have "seeds"; each has a genetic essence that they pass on to their children. In this way, children are the embodiment of the genes of their parents, and it is genetic connection that defines parenthood.

This ideology has greatly contributed to the selling of new reproductive technologies, from in vitro fertilization to technologies that attempt to insert a single sperm of an otherwise infertile man into a harvested egg—all technologies designed to maintain genetic ties between parent and child. According to this belief system, which sees only the child of one's own genes as one's own child, the child of unknowable genes will be the foreign and unknown/unknowable child.

Thus, it is this deep sense of the unknown and perhaps unknowable that makes the adopted child different: if the child is the product of its genes, and the sources of those genes are not known, then the child is essentially unknown. In reality, of course, we are all unknown and unknowable. Which genes are inherited and which not; which genes are being passed along a family silently, not showing consequences until the right (or wrong) combination of genes and environment arises; which new genes have mutated for the first time—these are the genetic unknowables. Even if parents give birth to a child, they will still not know the genetic fate that child has been given.

271

In one interesting way, the ideology of genetics and genetic determinism becomes freeing for adoptive parents: the responsibility for passing on "bad genes" is removed. If all kinds of behavior and characteristics are seen as genetic, then not having produced the genes that go into the child frees the parent from responsibility. Is the child depressed, smart, hyperactive, mathematical, addicted, bulimic, absent-minded, or musical? Whatever the characteristic, good or bad, desirable or not, it simply is what it is, and the parents do not get the blame or the credit.

This may, in fact, be one understudied reason for the well-known fact that parents are more likely to make use of stigmatized mental health services for adopted children: the parents can be free of the stigma. If a child of one's own is in need of mental health services, counseling, therapy, or drugs, that says something about oneself. If an adopted child has such needs, then it can be read as an undesirable characteristic inherited by the child from its family of origin, something with which adoptive parents must cope. In this ideology, the adoptive parents switch from causative agents of their child's misery or problem to innocent victims of bad genes passed on, and perhaps martyrs for dealing with it at all.

This is one of the points of connection between genetic determinism writ small, or micro-eugenics (eugenics at the level of the individual), and genetic determinism writ large, or macro-eugenics (eugenics at the level of population). Adoption does not occur randomly across race and class lines. Adoption most often means moving a child up from its point of origin to a family higher in the social and economic hierarchy. Poorer women and families are put in the position of relinquishing children; wealthier women and families take those children in. The history of eugenics makes clear the connection between socioeconomic status and genetic status: better genes rose to the top. The very fact of adoption placement, or the factors that would lead to placement, were themselves often seen as proof or indication of bad genes or inferior genetic stock. Adoption was discouraged by this very belief that the children available for adoption were likely to have a history of mental illness or instability in their families, and thus in their genes.

While these eugenic ideas fell out of favor during the post-World War II era, they have not entirely left American society. In fact, they resurface periodically, especially in discussions of race and class. For example, the racial stereotype of the smart Asians undoubtedly influences both the decisions of Americans who adopt from Asia and feelings about those Asian children brought among us. Characteristics that are on the one hand explained with reference to culture (hard-working, studious, model immigrants) are at the same time racialized, or perhaps we should say geneticized, and seen as inbred in the baby, as independent of upbringing or cultural influence. Negative imagery, too, slides from culture to genes, from "culture of poverty" explanations to "genetic predispositions" for what are better understood as cultural outcomes: crime, school failure, teenage pregnancy, and the like. Consequently, there has developed a well-known hierarchy in adoption; this ranking of adoptability—or more crudely even a ranking of cost—reflects our racial climate and socioeconomic structure: white babies of middle-class college-educated women are the most costly; babies of poor women of color the least.

While macro-eugenics plays out in race and international marketing of babies for adoption, micro-eugenics is increasingly coming into play. By micro-eugenics we mean a eugenics of the individual, a valuing or disvaluing of specific characteristics believed to be genetic. Micro-eugenics was first seen in American life in the marketing of prenatal diagnostic technologies. By means of amniocentesis and a host of interrelated technologies, fetuses have been tested for genetic disorders or characteristics widely considered undesirable. Down syndrome and neural tube defects are the most common conditions for which testing is done, but a host of other conditions are also being tested for, including Tay-Sachs disease, sickle cell anemia, cystic fibrosis, and literally hundreds of others.

Thus, it should come as no surprise that genetic screening for newborns would be used as a form of pre-adoption screening, just as prenatal screening is used to avoid the birth of a baby with an undesirable genetic condition. In prenatal diagnosis, abortion is the only real option; if a fetus is found to have a condition such that the potential mother decides its life would be too burdensome—for the potential baby itself, actually, not necessarily for the family alone—the mother can decide not to continue the pregnancy, not to make a baby at all.

In pre-adoption screening, the issues are quite different: a baby exists. The testing is done after birth, on a baby someone is deciding to adopt or not. The question of "burden" shifts entirely to the potential adoptive family: Are they willing to take on this particular baby, with its projected problems? The ethics, as well as the legal and social ramifications, of this testing have been explored at length by Janet Farrell Smith. According to Smith (2002), the number of prospective adopters who consult medical geneticists for private physical or genetic testing is increasing. In most cases, these exams are conducted in addition to adoption agency screening procedures for use in adoption decisions by the prospective parents.

Although the facts of genetic science may not support the cultural image of genetics, it is genetic ideology that grounds the notion of difference in adoption. According to this belief system, an adopted child can never become "one's own" because he or she will always be the product of a foreign seed.

See also Assisted Reproductive Technologies and Adoption; Embryo Adoption; Eugenics and Adoption; Feminism and Adoption: Changing Feminist Perspectives on Adoption; Genetic Testing.

Further Reading

Benward, Jean and Adrienne Asch. "A Case for Cross-Fertilization: Adoption and the Reproductive Technologies." Workshop at the Evan B. Donaldson Adoption Institute Conference, Ethics and Adoption: Challenges for Today and the Future, Anaheim, CA, November, 1999.
Genetic Testing and Adoption American College of Medical Genetics Web Site. http://www.acmg.net/resources/policies/pol-017.asp (accessed June, 2005).
Lebner, Ashley. "Genetic 'Mysteries' and International Adoption: The Cultural Impact of Biomedical Technologies on the Adoptive Family Experience." *Family Relations* 49 (2000): 371–377.
Rothman, Barbara Katz. "Of Maps and Imaginations: Sociology Confronts the Genome." *Social Problems* 42 (2005): 1–10.
Rothman, Barbara Katz. *Weaving a Family: Untangling Race and Adoption.* Boston: Beacon Press, 2005.
Smith, Janet Farrell. "A Cautionary Tale on Genetic Testing: The Case of Foster and Pre-Adoptive Children." An Occasional Paper published by the John W. McCormack Institute for Public Affairs, University of Massachusetts at Boston, 2002.
Smith, Janet Farrell. "The Ethics of Genetic Testing in Adoption." A Transcript of the Proceedings, edited and with an introduction by Farrell Smith, from a Colloquium on the Ethics of Adoption, 2000 March 10.

Gesell, Arnold (1880–1961)

Ellen Herman

Arnold Gesell was the most famous childrearing guru in the United States during the era before Benjamin Spock. He profoundly influenced the way Americans thought about how children developed and how parents should raise them. Gesell also had a great deal to say about adoption, especially about reducing its risks. Few social operations required more purposeful planning, he insisted, neatly summarizing the central theme of adoption reform during the first half of the twentieth century.

A psychologist and physician, Gesell championed a process of family formation carefully overseen by authorities in the human sciences and government. To achieve that goal, he worked with the most important advocacy organizations of his day, including the federal Children's Bureau and the Child Welfare League of America. Gesell spoke and wrote widely on placement age, pre-placement testing, and clinical supervision. He favored the confidentiality of adoption records and worked to promote methods of scientific selection and matching. Like other reformers, Gesell believed that adoptions arranged by agency experts were far superior to those arranged privately through sentimental baby bureaus or commercial brokers. Professional design was, according to Gesell, the surest way to make families well and protect vulnerable children and adults from botched adoptions.

Gesell attended the University of Wisconsin, completed his Ph.D. at Clark University, and then moved to New York. There, he taught elementary school and lived in the East Side Settlement House before launching a long academic career at Yale. At New Haven, Gesell studied hundreds of ordinary children from the late 1910s through the 1930s. After posing mental and behavioral challenges ranging from bells and balls to stairs and strangers, he meticulously recorded their reactions in numbers, pictures, and films. Whatever more than half of the children of the same age did regularly was defined as "normal."

Gesell's ambitious goal was to standardize developmental norms beginning at birth. His research helped to bring into being an idea considered obvious today: development is a universal process that follows consistent patterns over time. The practical expression of this idea was a test that measured whether children were growing normally or deviating (either a little or a large amount) from expected patterns of mental, motor, linguistic, and social maturation. In adoption, the Gesell scales were used for two specific purposes: to determine if children were qualified for adoption in the first place, and to place them in families where a good "fit" promised a good outcome.

Gesell's technological optimism contrasted with the pessimism of professionals and eugenicists at the time who believed that most dependent children were unadoptable genetic "lemons." Gesell agreed that adoption was risky, but he also believed that risks could be predicted and minimized. With the aid of "intelligent social control," "every adoption makes a rich addition to human happiness" (Gesell n.d., p. 2). Adoption was good for children and good for adults who wanted children, and Gesell never hesitated to recommend it to strangers, friends, even people in his own family. Gesell trusted professionally-managed adoption to identify and eliminate "defective" children while also making adoption better for the children and adults who belonged in families. "The combined critical judgment of the social investigator, the court, the physician, and the mental examiner should enter into the regulation of adoption," he wrote. "Clinical safeguards can not solve all the problems of child adoption but they can steadily improve its methods and make them both more scientific and humane" (Gesell 1926, p. 204).

Further Reading

The Adoption History Project, http://www.uoregon.edu/~adoption

Gesell, Arnold. "Is It Safe to Adopt an Infant?" n.d., p. 2. Arnold Gesell Papers, Library of Congress, Box 45, Folder: "Subject File: Adoption [Law]."

Gesell, Arnold. "Psychoclinical Guidance in Child Adoption." In U.S. Children's Bureau, *Foster-Home Care for Dependent Children*, Pub. No. 136. Washington, DC: Government Printing Office, 1926, pp. 193–204.

Herman, Ellen. "Families Made by Science: Arnold Gesell and the Technologies of Modern Child Adoption." *Isis* 92 (December 2001): 684–715.

Gladney, Edna Browning Kahly (1886–1961)

Vern L. Bullough

Edna Browning Kahly was born in Milwaukee, Wisconsin. After marrying Sam Gladney in 1906, she spent much of her life in Texas working for the welfare of children. Early on, she concentrated on placing abandoned children with adoptive families, although she also focused on the welfare of unmarried mothers. Among other things, she lobbied the Texas legislature to have the word "illegitimate" kept off of birth certificates and urged the passage of legislation to give adopted children the same inheritance rights as other children. As a result of her efforts, Texas instituted a policy of issuing second birth certificates in the names of adoptive parents.

Edna Gladney acquired a national reputation for her work after the release of a 1941 film, *Blossoms in the Dust*, a fictionalized account of her life starring Greer Carson. In 1948, she began operating the West Texas Maternity Hospital, which soon became the Edna Gladney Home and is now Gladney Center. During her career, she placed over ten thousand babies with adoptive parents. She continued to direct the Center until shortly before her death.

Further Reading

McArthur, Judith N. "Edna Browning Kahly Gladney." The Handbook of Texas Online Web Site. http://www.tsha.utexas.edu/handbook/online/articles/GG/fgl11.html (accessed December, 2005).

Grandparent Adoption

Diahanna Roberson

Grandparent adoption occurs when grandparents becomes the parental figures to their grandchild(ren). They are physically, emotionally, financially, and legally responsible for the basic needs (i.e., food, shelter, clothing) and well-being of their grandchild. In the public child welfare arena, grandparents have become a viable resource to children coming into the public system. With a decrease in resources, public agencies have had to look outside their own system to provide stability and permanency to children in their custody.

Grandparents as their grandchildren's caregivers provide a form of kinship care. The Child Welfare League of America (1994, p. 2) defines kinship care as, "the full-time nurturing and protection of children who must be separated from their parents by relatives, members of their tribes or clans, godparents, stepparents, or other adults who have a kinship bond with a child." Kin is any person related to another person by blood, marriage, or specific designation. As Wornie L. Reed observes, kinship care may be either formal (when children are placed with relatives by public child welfare agencies) or informal (when there is not agency involvement).

Reed's examination of kinship care reveals the child welfare system has seen an increase in the number of children residing with formal grandparent caregivers, and there is an additional hidden population of children in informal care. In 2000, according to U.S. Census Bureau data, there were 5.8 million grandparents living with grandchildren under age eighteen. Over two million were "grandparent caregivers" who were responsible for their grandchild's basic needs: 1.5 million grandmothers and nine hundred thousand grandfathers. Almost 40 percent of the grandparents had been responsible for most of the basic needs of their grandchildren for at least five years.

Reasons for Grandparent Caregiving

James P. Gleeson and Creasie F. Hairston examine how, in many cultures, grandparents have assumed a role of caregiver to their grandchildren due to parental illness, unemployment, or single parenthood. Grandparents also become caregivers of their grandchildren due to their adult children's substance abuse and/or criminal behavior, or the abuse and neglect of their grandchild(ren). Complaints range from lack of supervision to lack of food and clothing, filthy conditions, or homelessness. The parent may become a danger to the child and can no longer provide basic care. Grandparents may also be providing care because of an adult child's incarceration. Many of the children of incarcerated mothers live with their grandparents. Social issues that include poverty, AIDS, and reductions in social services, as Reed explains, have also contributed to the increase in this aspect of kinship care.

Current Practice

Generally, when a child or children come into the custody of the child welfare system, the first contact is usually with relatives when attempting to find an alternate caregiver. Because of this, grandparents are, many times, the first family member contacted to provide care and stability for their grandchild. Children remain connected to someone they know and maintain a connection to their past. Grandparents are often more willing to deal with their kin's behavior and show a greater commitment to keep the child through the full range of behaviors. This greater tolerance often leads to the child's permanency and successful adoption. The child welfare system recognizes and honors kinship care within families. Tami W. Lorkovich, Trista Piccola, Victor Groza, Merri Brindo, and Jonnie Marks agree that kinship care-givers, grandparents especially, have become increasingly important in permanency options.

Since 1979, pressure has increased on child welfare agencies to make formal kinship care placements. The Adoption Assistance and Child Welfare Act of 1980 (Public Law 96-272) cleared the path for child welfare agencies to choose relatives as alternative caregivers to non-relative foster care. It also encouraged better permanency planning.

The foundation of relative placement is expressed in both welfare reform and child welfare reform via the 1996 Personal Responsibility and Work Opportunity Reconciliation Act (PRWORA). Carrie Jefferson Smith, Claire Rudolph, and Peter Swords recognize that under PRWORA, families are encouraged to take personal responsibility for their members and states are mandated, when relative caregivers meet the relevant child protection standards, to consider preferences for adult relatives over non-relatives in determining child placement.

In reaction to the continued problems in child welfare in general, and foster care in particular, the U.S. Congress enacted the Adoption and Safe Family Act (ASFA; Public Law 105-89) in 1997. The ASFA intended to address the problem of foster care drift—that is, children remaining in temporary foster care without a permanent family. As children continue to enter care, innovations in finding permanency for children became seriously needed.

A family member caring for their kin is consistent with the intent of ASFA. In fact, ASFA stipulates that relatives must be given consideration in all legal proceedings. Not only are there legal obligations to include relatives, there are many benefits to children to have relatives care for them. Benefits to the child include that the child is still connected to their family of origin, the child most likely knows the relative, and the disruption in the child's life may be reduced. For families, caring for a relative is consistent with many religious principles, offers them an opportunity to try to correct the mistakes of a family member, and follows a long tradition of families caring for each other in a time of crisis. For the child welfare system, promoting relative caregiving is consistent with family empowerment techniques.

Implications for Policy

There are many issues that grandparent adopters face. As Reed notes, grandparents have many needs including the need for help with finances, physical health, mental health, legal issues, housing, parenting skills, respite care, and accessing social services. These needs are more likely to be met in a formal kinship arrangement such as adoption than in an informal arrangement because of the higher level of monetary stipend (i.e., adoption subsidy) and other resources available to adopters. Informal relative caregivers may receive Temporary Aid to Needy Families (TANF) funds for the child only, but the amount of money given usually does not support the level of needs. In addition, many grandparents do not work outside the home and, therefore, do not have adequate income to support children in their home. Hence, it should not be surprising that some children's needs remain unmet and relatives do without to provide for their kin.

Currently, there is a debate concerning grandparent adoption. Grandparents are not given the appropriate services to maintain adoptive placements. Many grandparents are on fixed incomes (i.e., social security or retirement stipend), have no medical coverage for the children they will adopt, or need financial support to care for grandchildren. As of this writing, there are only a few states such as New Jersey that have subsidized guardianship which provides grandparents with a funding source to care for grandchildren. There is public assistance but the dollars are limited compared to the per diem (rate) that foster parents currently receive. Many adoption professionals argue that policies embracing grandparent adoption would enhance collaboration between grandparents and government entities and assist in achieving permanency for children.

See also Kinship Care: Informal Adoption.

Further Reading

Adoption.com Encyclopedia. "Grandparent." Adoption.com Web Site. http://encyclope-dia.adoption.com/entry/grandparent/156/1.html (accessed December, 2004).

Child Welfare League of America. *Kinship Care a Natural Bridge.* Washington, DC: Child Welfare League of America, 1994.

Danzy, Julia, and Sondra M. Jackson. "Family Preservation and Support Services: A Missed Opportunity for Kinship Care." *Child Welfare* 76 (1997): 31–45.

Gleeson, James P., and Creasie F. Hairston, eds. *Kinship Care: Improving Practice Through Research.* Washington, DC: Child Welfare League of America, 1999.

Hegar, Rebecca, and Maria Scannapieco. "From Family Duty to Family Policy: The Evolution of Kinship Care." *Child Welfare*, 74 (1996): 200–208.

Lorkovich, Tami W., Trista Piccola, Victor Groza, Merri Brindo, and Jonnie Marks. "Kinship Care and Permanence: Guiding Principles for Policy and Practice." *Families in Society; Journal of Contemporary Social Services*, 85 (2004): 159–164.

Reed, Wornie L. *Kinship Care in Cuyahoga County.* Cleveland, OH: Saint Ann Foundation, 2003.

Simmons, Tavia and Jane Lawler Dye. *Grandparents Living with Granchildren: 2000.* (October 2003.) U.S. Census Bureau: Washington, D.C., U.S. Census Bureau Website. http://www.census.gov/prod/2003pubs/c2kbr-31.pdf

Smith, Carrie Jefferson, Claire Rudolph, and Peter Swords. "Kinship Care: Issues in Permanency Planning." *Children and Youth Services Review* 24 (2002): 175–188.

U.S. Bureau of the Census. "Profile of Selected Social Characteristics: 2000." U.S. Bureau of the Census Web Site. http://factfinder.census.gov/servlet/QTTable?_bm=y&-geo_id=01000US&-qr_name=DEC_2000_SF1_U_QTP11&-ds_name=DEC_2000_SF1_U&-_lang=en&-redoLog=false&-_sse=on (accessed April, 2004).

U.S. Bureau of the Census. "Facts for Features: Grandparents Day 2003: Sept. 7." U.S. Bureau of the Census Web Site. http://www.census.gov/Press-Release/www/2003/cb03-ff13.html (accessed December, 2004).

Group Adoption and Shared Motherhood

Vern L. Bullough

Group motherhood is a term used by early researchers of the history of the family to explain the practice among many tribal groups for children to share mothers and siblings. Sometimes all male members of a clan of about the same age were recognized as brothers and all females as sisters. Older members of the tribe were called by terms that could mean either father or uncle, and females by words connoting mother or aunt without much distinction. In other groups, children were said to belong to all people of the group and the women tended to their own biological children as well as others. When a biological mother was otherwise occupied, other women who were capable of nursing satisfied the child's hunger needs. In some areas, the shared motherhood was emphasized by having every infant be suckled in turn by every nursing mother, a practice which some observers believe was done to strengthen tribal unity.

In some Polynesian settlements, it was obligatory that every child be suckled by several mothers. Often the child did not remain with its birth mother but was adopted into some other family, even losing contact with its biological mother. Many Polynesian and Melanesian groups had their biological children adopted by foster parents at their birth. In fact, in some areas it was considered a disgrace for a woman to raise her own biological child.

This was not only limited to Polynesian or Melanesian groups. Among the Nupe in North Africa, the first child was generally taken from its mother at birth and suckled by another woman. Subsequent children were taken over by relatives as soon as they were weaned, divorcing them entirely from their own parents, and distributing them among uncles and aunts who acted as foster or adopted parents.

Collective clan relationships have an old history but were still being observed in the twentieth century, not only in contemporary tribal society. In nineteenth century United States, the polygamous Mormons practiced sort of a group motherhood, with some women seemingly better qualified to be caretakers of infants than others who took on other tasks. In many societies where polygamous relationships still exist, including communities in the U.S., group motherhood and shared adoption is not uncommon.

Further Reading

Briffault, R. *The Mothers*. 3 vols., New York: Macmillan, 1927.

Group Homes
Vern L. Bullough

Group homes are residential facilities for children and are somewhat different from orphanages. Such homes may be funded by the state or other governmental units, by religious organizations, privately-funded, or a combination of funding sources. The children might be voluntarily placed in such a home by their parent or they may be foster children put there by the courts.

Group homes house children over five and provide temporary shelter for emergency situations or long-term shelter for hard-to-place children such as teenagers and large sibling groups. If an adoption is interrupted, the child might also be placed in such a home instead of a foster home.

In recent years, the group home has declined in importance as the emphasis has switched to foster homes, although many social workers prefer the group home to a foster home for many situations and individuals. This is particularly true of those children who have been physically or sexually abused who could benefit more from the available psychiatric and other services in the group home. The

Alliance for Children and Families is continuing the program of one of its predecessor organizations, the National Association of Homes and Services for Children, to improve services of children in such homes.

Further Reading

Alliance for Children and Families Web Site. http://www.alliance1.org/.

Guardian ad Litem

Sharon Valente

The United States legal system has recognized the child's need to have independent representation in court to protect a child's rights. Evidence shows that parents do not always act in the child's best interests. The Guardian ad Litem (GAL) serves as a special guardian with both legal and non-legal activities and is obligated to do everything within his or her power to ensure a judgment in the child's best interests. The GAL can act as an investigator, advocate, counsel, and guardian to protect the child.

Although most states had implemented laws for this purpose by the 1980s, the states varied in their interpretation, funding, use of volunteers, and evaluation of these services. At first, most judges appointed attorneys as GALs. More recently, models of representation include volunteers or specially appointed advocates with specific training. The GAL's duties may be precisely defined or vague depending on the state statutes. There are no uniform methods of representation or no clear guidelines across states.

When conflicts emerge among those who see themselves as advocates for the child, such as social workers, volunteers, and attorneys, the child's interest may be compromised. Attorneys who serve as GALs may also face ethical conflicts (e.g., the child's wishes versus best interests, privileged communication, and provision of testimony). For example, the attorney is bound to keep the child's communications confidential. If the child divulges information that would be relevant to the court's decision about adoption, the attorney must keep that information confidential. The older child may also communicate his or her wishes to the attorney—when these do not match with what is in the child's best interest, the attorney is torn between conflicting duties. In addition, the social worker may be working to reunite the child with the birth family while the attorney, who may not know about the reunification goal, is working to help a family adopt the child. When the conflict emerges, the child's best interests may not be well served.

Although there is no consensus about the actual role and functions of the GAL, general principles exist, which include the following: The GAL should be independent from other parties; have the freedom to explore options available to the child; have knowledge of the child's cultural and ethnic heritage; be carefully screened and have initial and ongoing training; and have immunity from liability when performing duties in the job description except for wrongful acts or gross negligence. Evaluation programs should also be in place to determine and assure the effectiveness of the GAL.

The GAL's role typically includes the following duties: conducting an independent investigation by reviewing all relevant documents and records; determining the interests of the child; seeking solutions, and acting as a mediator among conflicting parties (e.g., the birth and adoptive parents); providing written reports at hearings; appearing at hearings to represent the child's interests; explaining the court proceedings and the role of the GAL in terms that the child can understand; making recommendations for specific appropriate services for the child and the child's family (e.g., services for a developmentally disabled child or counseling for child and family if needed); monitoring implementation of service plans and court orders; informing the court of important developments; and advocating for the child's interests in the community.

Because children can often become invisible in the court system and in the overburdened agencies designed to protect them, the GAL exists to be the watchdog who takes steps to make sure that the child has quality representation in the legal system and to help all those concerned act together to protect the child's best interests.

Further Reading

Aitken, S. S., L. Condelli, and T. Kelly. *National Study of Guardian ad Litem Representation*. Washington, DC: CSR, 1990.

CASAnet Resources. Guardian ad Litem Advocate's Library. National Court Appointed Special Advocates (CASA) Association Web Site. http://www.casanet.org/library/guardian-ad-litem/index.htm (accessed March, 2005).

Davidson, Howard. "Collaborative Advocacy on Behalf of Children: Effective Partnerships Between CASA and the Child's Attorney." In American Bar Association, ed., *Lawyers for Children*, 17–42. Chicago, IL: American Bar Association, 1990.

Duquette, D. N. *Advocating for the Child in Protection Proceedings: A Handbook for Lawyers and Court Appointed Special Advocates*. Lexington, MA: Lexington Books, 1990.

Horowitz, R. M., and H. Q. Davidson, eds. *Legal Rights of Children*. Colorado Springs, CO: Shepard's/McGraw Hill, 1984.

The Hague Convention on Protection of Children and Co-operation in Respect of Intercountry Adoption

Joanne Selinske

The development of an international convention on intercountry adoption in the last half century reflects globalization's effect on private family matters and a general consensus regarding the principles and standards that should be applied in these circumstances. Prior to World War II, intercountry adoption was generally limited to children adopted by extended families residing in other than the child's country of origin. The war had a dramatic effect, transforming intercountry adoption into a relief effort for the thousands of children it orphaned. The mechanisms established to resettle and find permanent homes for these children indefinitely altered expectations and perspectives. National boundaries no longer limited the search to find new homes and permanent families for children unable to be reared by birth parents. The effects of overpopulation and severe economic problems, along with conflicts/wars of the second half of the twentieth century, further increased adoption across borders, but did not permanently resolve the matter of whether intercountry adoption is an option that is in the best interests of the child.

Each year thousands of children journey across international borders to new homes and adoptive families. Fortunately for the growing number of children involved in intercountry adoption, although slow, a consensus has been forming that international standards must be implemented to protect the child's best interest and fundamental rights. The Convention on Protection of Children and Co-operation in Respect of Intercountry Adoption was approved unanimously on May 28, 1993 after years of discussion, deliberation, and negotiation.

In 1957, the United Nations Technical Assistance Administration (UNTAA) and International Social Service co-sponsored a meeting of international experts and produced the UN publication, "Intercountry Adoption." This seminal work was the foundation for the basic principles of intercountry adoption articulated in the Proceedings of the European Seminar in Leysin, Switzerland in 1960; the 1967 European Convention on Child Adoption; 1967 Hague Convention on the Jurisdiction and Law Applicable to Cases of Adoption; the 1978 UN Group of Experts Meeting on Adoption and Placement in Foster Homes on National and International Levels; and the UN Declaration on Social and Legal Principles Relating to the Protection and Welfare of Children with Special Reference to Foster Placement and Adoption Nationally and Internationally, passed by the General Assembly in 1986. Finally, the convention takes into account the principles set forth on November 20, 1989, in the United Nations Convention on the Rights of the Child.

The convention affirms the role of the family in the child's development and nurturance, and the child's right to grow up in a family—affirming the primacy of the biological family over the subsidiary nature of an adoptive family, as well as the primacy of being raised in one's country of origin. The convention has three objectives. They are to: 1) establish safeguards to ensure that intercountry adoptions take place in the best interests of the child and with respect for his or her fundamental rights as recognized in international law; 2) establish a system of co-operation among contracting states (i.e., states that ratify the convention and enter it into the full force of law) to ensure that those safeguards are respected, and thereby prevent the abduction, sale of, or traffic in, children; and 3) secure the recognition in contracting states of adoptions made in accordance with the convention.

The convention's 47 articles cover only adoptions that create permanent parent-child relationships, and its provisions have been crafted to assure their veracity. It governs intercountry adoptions only when a child moves from one convention party country to another. It establishes norms and procedures to safeguard children in intercountry adoptions and their birth and adoptive parents. To achieve necessary cooperation, state parties to the convention must establish a central authority as the authoritative source of information and point of contact in that country, to ensure effective implementation of the convention, to carry out certain functions, and to cooperate with other central authorities including replying about a particular adoption. Emphasis is placed on preventing improper financial or other gain, and deterring all practices that are contrary to the objectives of the convention.

Adoption includes recognition of three essential elements: 1) the new legal parent-child relationship between the child and his/her adoptive parents; 2) the new parental responsibility of the adoptive parents for the child; and 3) the termination of the pre-existing legal relationship between the child and his/her mother and father. In this latter instance, the provision applies only if the adoption has this effect—that is, the termination of parental rights—in the contracting state where it was made. The convention does not bar a prospective adoptive parent from taking steps to adopt a child from another contracting state, but does stipulate limitations.

Adoption under the Hague Convention can take place only if the country of origin has established that the child is adoptable; that appropriate consideration has been given to the child's adoption in its country of origin; and an intercountry adoption is in the child's best interests. Further, the convention stipulates that the necessary consents to the adoption must be given freely and only after counseling has been provided regarding the effects of such consent and relinquishment. The child's wishes and consent are necessary when age and maturity make this a relevant factor. No payment, compensation, or other inducement can be used to secure the consent of the relevant parties. Where required, the consent of the birth mother can only be given after the birth of the child. A crucial provision is the stipulation that both prospective adoptive parents must be eligible and suited to adopt. Notable is the requirement that the child they wish to adopt will be authorized to enter and reside permanently in the receiving country. (A receiving state or country is the destination country for the adoptive child while the sending state is the country of origin or habitual residence of the child prior to the adoption.)

A key provision is that adoptions made pursuant to the convention will generally be recognized and given effect in other party countries, ensuring that the adopted child will qualify for immigration and automatic naturalization in the receiving state. Persons wishing to adopt a child resident in another party country must initially apply to a designated authority in their own country to obtain approval for intercountry adoption.

The convention requires that central authorities perform or delegate to other entities a range of activity to protect and safeguard the integrity of the adoption process. To perform designated functions regarding individual adoption cases, adoption agencies and individual providers of international adoption service must become Hague Convention accredited or approved. Among the most critical is the accreditation of public or private bodies to perform a wide range of adoption functions, including: collecting, assessing, preserving, and exchanging information about the situation of the child and the prospective adoptive parents; executing the adoption proceedings; and providing pre- and post-adoption counseling. Accreditation can only be granted to, and maintained by, entities with demonstrated competence to carry out the duties entrusted. Accredited bodies only pursue nonprofit objectives and are directed and staffed by qualified persons upholding ethical standards. It stipulates that only costs and expenses, including reasonable professional fees of persons involved in the adoption, may be charged or paid.

While the convention does establish norms and procedures, it does so without dictating explicit operational details or protocol. This enables contracting states to craft enabling legislation that respects the myriad structural and political differences that exist across national borders.

Conversely, while establishing internationally recognized rights and protections in contracting states, the convention has no capacity to regulate or influence unprofessional, unethical, nefarious, illegal or other harmful actions that violate the child's rights in states not party to the convention. While advancing the fundamental rights and best interest of the child—including to be raised in a family environment—guaranteeing these rights will only happen when all states become party to the convention. The values, principles and standards that the instrument delineates are the metaphorical clarion call to the other members of the global family of nations. In this regard, the Hague Convention on Protection of Children and Co-operation in Respect of Intercountry Adoption has made this here-to-fore private family matter an instrument of international cooperation and collaboration as well as a tool for advancing the child rights agenda.

See also United Nations and Adoption.

Further Reading

Convention on Protection of Children and Co-Operation in Respect of Intercountry Adoption. Hague Conference on Private International Law Web Site. http://www.hcch.net/index_en.php?act=conventions.text&cid=69 (accessed December, 2005).

Hanai and Adoption in Hawaii

Judith Schachter

Hanai is a Hawaiian word that refers to the permanent transfer of a child from a biological to another parent. A customary mode of child exchange, *"hanai"* is derived from the concepts of nurturing and feeding, indicating that care and affection, not blood or law, constitute the relationship between parent and child. Historically, the father gave his first-born son to his parents and the mother gave the first-born daughter to her parents. The *hanai* child became the favorite in her or his new setting, accorded lavish love and attention. Members of the royalty strictly observed the custom, while commoners made looser arrangements.

Over the course of the nineteenth century, American law and cultural views of the parent-child relationship relegated *hanai* to the domestic arena, denying it a legal standing equal to adoption despite the permanency of the transfer. Territorial status followed by statehood in 1959 institutionalized the perception of *hanai* as a transitory, casual, and unreliable custom compared with adoption. For the *kanaka maoli* (native Hawaiian), *hanai* remains comparable to adoption, representing a commitment made between persons that creates a new parent-child tie, rearranges kinship ties, and presumes permanency. However, customary interpretations do not hold up in cases of disputed inheritance rights, when American law prevails over the customary sanctions of *hanai*.

In the twentieth century, *hanai* acquired new meanings and forms. Though still the ideal *hanai* parent, grandparents are no longer the only recipients of a child; the *hanai* child is no longer necessarily the first born, but might be any child requested by, or freely given, to another adult. A child may become *hanai* at any stage of life, and, with rising crime and drug problems in the state, adolescents are frequently the subjects of the transfer. Increasingly, too, the chosen *hanai* parent has no prior membership in the *'ohana* (extended family), but is someone with whom a relationship is desired.

In court-determined *hanai*, an effort is made to choose existing kin, close friends, or neighbors in order to facilitate contact between the biological and the *hanai* parent. Changes in interpretation and in practice give *hanai* flexibility, and the arrangement currently addresses diverse problems of children at risk. Depending on need and on form, *hanai* may be analogous to foster care, with the possibility of a return to the biological parent and without permanent reconstruction of kinship ties. Alternatively, *hanai* can come to resemble court-approved adoption, according the child new parents and severing ties with the biological parent. Neither the foster nor the adoptive form of *hanai* has the secrecy that is typical of mainland American adoption, and the child is not denied knowledge of his ancestry. Finally, in recent decades *hanai* can be the choice of the child, who relinquishes one parent for another. As a mode of exchanging children, *hanai* is a culturally sensitive as well as efficient route to placing a child; *hanai* contrasts with adoption, which is often slow, surrounded by red-tape, and based on impersonal criteria of fitness.

Hanai varies across socio-economic lines. Upper-class Hawaiian families frequently practice *hanai* in its traditional form, perpetuating the origins of the custom: a gift of child to grandparent. Working-class Hawaiian families caught by economic constraints place a child with another adult as a pragmatic measure. In all instances, the contrasts with American legal adoption are evident: the *hanai* child knows the biological parents and members of the natal *'ohana*; the child can choose and construct the new parent-child relationship; the arrangement may be permanent or temporary, depending on the desires of the primary actors. Reflecting current changes in American adoption practice and policy, *hanai* has become an element in debates about open adoption, about the continuum between fosterage and adoption, and about the rights of individuals to determine the expectations and the endurance of a transfer from biological to other parent.

The symbolic significance of *hanai* as a marker of Hawaiian ways of conceptualizing family, love, and kinship unifies diverse forms and interpretations. Whatever the particulars, the term *hanai* always refers back to its roots in "feeding" and "nurturing" and thereby reiterates the constructed character of Hawaiian kinship. With the rise of movements for national sovereignty, *hanai*, like *aloha 'aina* (love of the land), becomes a symbol of Hawaiian cultural identity. In these new debates, *hanai* reiterates core cultural values: relationships are based on performance not blood, on love and not biology, and on care and not on American law.

Further Reading

Modell, J. Schachter. "Rights to the Children: Foster Care and Social Reproduction in Hawaii." In *Reproducing Reproduction*, edited by H. Ragone and S. Franklin. Philadelphia: University of Pennsylvania Press, 1997. pp. 156–172.

Health Issues in Adoption

Sharon Valente and Judith M. Saunders

Introduction

Adoptive parents need to be aware of important health issues and the steps to take to safeguard the adoptee's health. Adoptive parents should be concerned about getting information about the adoptee's health including such issues as immunizations, communicable disease (e.g., tuberculosis or sexually transmitted diseases), abuse and neglect, developmental disabilities, prior environmental risks (e.g., food or lead poisoning, and rabies), and epidemiology of diseases. The most common issues adoptive parents need to consider include health risks, health history information, child development and disability, and psychiatric disorders, among others. Health issues facing adoptive families also have public health implications.

Knowing Health Risk Information

Most adopted children, regardless of where they come from, arrive at their new home in relatively good health. It is important to know, however, that their geographic origins may influence their health resources, and the comprehensiveness of their medical exam may affect their health. Both national and international adoptees may have common health risks. Adoptive parents should know as much about the birth parents and adoptee's health as possible. This includes their record of immunizations and risk factors in the birth parent's history (e.g., prenatal smoking, drug or alcohol use). Adopted children's risks may parallel the reasons they are available for adoption: abandonment, poverty, war, displacement, parental illness or death, alcoholism, drug abuse, child abuse or neglect, inadequate pre- or post-natal care, nutrition, early neglect, and poor health care. Hence, a child may be at risk for a variety of developmental disorders or delays, or medical problems (e.g., anemia, rickets, malnutrition, lead poisoning, asthma, communicable diseases, or fetal alcohol syndrome).

When the adoptive parent knows of these risk factors, they can make sure the child is evaluated for the problem so treatment may be started early. Children with special needs with a troubled past that may have included abuse, neglect, or a history of trauma have successfully adapted to their new families. The best starting point for adoptive parents is to explore the adopted child's health history as thoroughly as possible.

Exploring The Health History

A pre-adoption health assessment, tests, and a comprehensive medical exam are important. The health history should include demographic data (e.g., age, ethnic background, education, occupation, height, weight, and medical condition of both parents); familial diseases or medical conditions; health condition of other children of the birth parents; parental lifestyle (e.g., prenatal smoking, alcohol or drugs, and nutrition); prenatal history (e.g., prenatal care, prescribed or other drugs; tests or problems during pregnancy, labor, or delivery); parents' sexual behavior and risk for sexually transmitted diseases; child's weight, height, head circumference, medical problems, medical tests, and immunizations; developmental milestones (i.e., sitting, hearing, walking, talking, motor skills); child's personality and relationships; and early childhood history (e.g., whether the child lived at home, in foster care, or an orphanage; any physical, sexual, or emotional abuse). Knowing the family history, familial illnesses, and the causes of death of parents or grandparents allows the health care provider to help educate parents about monitoring or reducing risks for some disorders. For instance, if a family had a history of asthma, cancer or diabetes, then specific testing of the child might be recommended. If a child has no obvious illness, parents should schedule the first visit to a health care provider after observing the child for a couple of weeks.

To protect the family, parents will want to take precautions by updating their own family's immunizations before the adoptee arrives. Because international adoptees may have some medical conditions poorly recognized in the United States, primary care providers need to know about medical assessments of children from foreign countries. Although agencies will give adoptive parents information about the child's background, this does not guarantee normalcy, and some parents may encounter medical or developmental problems. Some problems may be as easy to remedy as bringing a child's immunizations up to date or as complex as coping with a psychiatric, developmental, or serious medical problem.

Child Development and Disability

Infants are usually born with innate behavioral capacities that enhance interactions with caretakers, and with the building blocks for mastering developmental stages. Normally, infants relate well to their caretaker or adoptive parent and they elicit a caretaker's positive response. They can discriminate and imitate facial expressions and differentiate between a mother's and a stranger's face, and they can master physical, social, and psychological developmental tasks. When the child has an ongoing disability or condition before age twenty-two years, and limits in three or more of the following areas—self-care, language, learning, mobility, self-direction, potential for independent living and potential for economic sufficiency as an adult—it is called a developmental disability. Within these diagnoses (e.g., attention deficit disorder, attention deficit hyperactivity disorder, retardation, and pervasive developmental disability such as autism), problems range from mild to severe and may interfere with learning (e.g., retardation or autism). These problems are not always detected until the child begins school and must cooperate with age mates.

For children with a developmental disability, parents need to have flexible goals, learn about the disorder, and collaborate with multiple providers to improve the child's functioning, reduce symptoms, prevent negative outcomes, and improve the adoptee's education and skills. Coordination of care, a variety of services, and advocacy for the individual and family are essential. Education, social skills training, and behavior management techniques help improve functioning.

School achievement provides the foundation for occupational and life success for normal children and higher functioning autistic children. In school, the child learns to pay attention, cooperate, and complete tasks. Skills training for the child with autism focuses on social interaction, adaptive and functional skills (e.g., speech therapy), and skills for living and working. Health-care providers need to collaborate and communicate with school personnel. To meet these children's special learning, attention, and psychological needs, the parent needs to know that the school should have an individual educational program or education plan (IEP). This plan helps the parent, teacher, and child coordinate their efforts, measure progress, and enhance success. Psychiatric disorders are different from developmental disabilities and require different approaches.

Psychiatric Disorders

An adopted child might face issues related to rejection, adjustment to the new family, and self-esteem, but experts dispute whether adoptees experience more psychiatric disorders than do non-adoptees. Children from orphanages may have suffered nutritional and health care deficits, neglect, trauma, and loss. P. M. Brinich and E. B. Brinich reviewed 5,135 patients and found no significant differences in psychiatric diagnoses of adopted and non-adopted patients. D. W. Smith and D. M. Brodzinsky studied eighty-two adoptees and their parents. They found that adopted children who reported higher levels of negative affect about birth parent loss also reported higher levels of depression and lower self-worth. However, some case studies suggest that adoptees might face problems with anxiety, depression, fetal alcohol syndrome (FAS), and other consequences from prenatal exposure to drugs. Although they look physically normal, children born with FAS have physical and mental deficits. FAS can cause mental retardation, attention deficit disorder, developmental delays, learning disabilities, and behavior problems. These children can be difficult to nurture because their biological "brain wiring" is permanently faulty and they have central nervous system problems.

Parents need to know that an estimated 75–80 percent of the children who need mental health services don't receive them. Therefore, parents need to take a very active role in asking health care providers for evaluation of a child's problems and persisting in getting the child the services that are needed. In addition, as the Child Welfare League of America notes, the adopted child may have originally been placed with the child welfare system because of his or her original family's problems with substance abuse, mental illness, or violence. Overall, in order to safeguard their child's health, the adopted parents need to know the birth family's health history and risk factors so they can monitor potential risks and take broad preventive action.

Other Health Risks

Research suggests that children have an increased risk of developing several disorders if their birth parents have these disorders (e.g., substance abuse, family violence, or diverse types of abuse). Just as the adult with a family history of high cholesterol or cardiac problems can begin to reduce the risk by changes in lifestyle, diet, or exercise, perhaps the child who knows of a risk of substance abuse from the birth family can learn about the risk indicators and develop safer ways to manage stress and avoid substance use. Programs for families of alcoholics teach attendees to watch for early indicators of substance use and to take preventive action; they also teach stress management strategies. If the birth family had a high risk of a genetic disorder and several individuals with that disorder (such as Sickle Cell—a blood disorder common among African Americans, or Tay Sachs—common among people of Ashkenazi Jewish heritage), then genetic testing might be recommended to educate the individuals about the risk of passing this on to offspring when the adoptee plans for marriage and wants to evaluate familial genetic risks. However, if adopted children do not know their familial risk of early cardiac death, cholesterol, cancer, genetic disorders, or substance use, then they do not know how to reduce this risk. For instance, if adoptees know they have a familial risk of glaucoma, a serious but treatable eye disorder, preventive screening can detect the early onset of glaucoma. Early treatment can prevent complications such as blindness.

Some Public Health Implications for Research and Policy

In public health clinics, nurses commonly educate people about how to prevent communicable diseases, environmentally transmitted diseases (e.g., lead poisoning), and sexually transmitted diseases. Epidemiological data on health issues in adoptions and research on adoptions are needed so we know the characteristics of groups of adoptees in relationship to their health needs. Additionally, comprehensive national statistics are needed that would help policymakers and clinicians have reliable and accurate public health information to improve program planning, health care services, policies, and program evaluation data.

See also Acquired Immune Deficiency Syndrome (AIDS) and Adoption; Adoption Medicine (Overview); Developmental Assessment; Drug-Exposed Infants and Adoption; Human Immunodeficiency Virus (HIV)-Positive Infants; International Adoption (Overview).

Further Reading

Brinich, P.M., and E.B. Brinich. "Adoption and Adaptation." *Journal of Nervous and Mental Disease* 179 (1982): 489–493.

Child Welfare League of America Web Site. http://www.cwla.org

Feigelman, W., and A.R. Silverman. "Single Parent Adoption." In Hope Marindin, ed. *The Handbook for Single Adoptive Parents*. Chevy Chase, MD: National Council for Single Adoptive Parents, 1998: 128–129.

Groze, V.K. "Adoption and Single Parents: A Review." *Child Welfare* 70 (1991): 321–332.

Groze, V.K., and J.A. Rosenthal. "Single Parents and Their Adopted Children: A Psychosocial Analysis." *Families in Society: The Journal of Contemporary Human Services* 72 (1991): 67–77.

Smith D.W., and D.M. Brodzinsky. "Coping with Birthparent Loss in Adopted Children." *Journal of Child Psychology and Psychiatry and Allied Disciplines* 43 (2002): 213–23.

Weitzman, C.C. *Developmental Assessment of the Internationally Adopted Child: Challenges and Rewards*. Thousand Oaks: CA: Sage Publications, 2003.

Primary Document

Investigating the Child: A Physician Recommends a Practice for Avoiding the "Grave Injustice" of Placing a Mentally Defective Child

The following excerpt is from a 1934 article that appeared in the *Journal of the American Medical Association*. The author, a physician, considers adoption "in its purely human aspects as it concerns the medical profession" (403). Taking a progressive tone, he writes of the primacy of the child's interests even over that of the adoptive and birth parents, and the importance of individualization of placement, meaning selecting the most suitable homes for these children. The author argues the need to investigate the adoptive home previous to the adoption to ascertain such information as the would-be parents' motives for adoption, their health, and their ability to provide for the child. However, reflective of the concerns of the period regarding inherited mental deficits, the child, he argues, should also be investigated to avoid the "grave injustice" of placing a mentally defective child. Additionally, he advocates a probationary period after placement of a year or longer. At the end of this time period, he recommends that children be tested to ascertain whether they would be recommended for adoption. He then questions whether it would be proper, regardless of the foster parents' attachment to the child, to permit the adoption to be completed against expert opinion.

The following practice, based on a consideration of the relative unreliability of intelligence ratings of young children, is recommended as reasonably cautious in regard to the evidence of intellectual adequacy required before the consummation of adoption:

Each child should be tested before and at the completion of the probationary period of one year. It is desirable, particularly with children under 4 years, that each examination should include two tests. The tests should be administered by an adequately trained clinical psychologist.

In cases in which the results of the tests are discrepant with the rough estimation of the child's intelligence from the observation of his behavior, judgment should be withheld until the discrepancy is dissolved.

1. With children, aged 1 year or older, indication of very superior intelligence is adequate for adoption.

2. With children, aged 18 months or older, indication of superior intelligence (intelligence quotient 110 or above) is adequate for adoption.

3. With children, aged 2 years or older, indication of intelligence at or above the presumed mean (intelligence quotient 100 or above) is adequate for adoption.

4. With children, aged 3 years or older, indication of intelligence falling in the grouping "average" or above (intelligence quotient 90 or above) is adequate for adoption.

5. With children, aged 4 years or older, indication of intelligence falling at or above the middle of the grouping "dull and backward" (intelligence quotient 85 or above) is adequate for adoption.

6. With children, aged 5 years or older, indication of intelligence above "borderline defective" (intelligence quotient 80 or above) is adequate for adoption.

Adoptions of children with an intelligence quotient between 70 and 80 are advisable only under circumstances particularly favorable to the adjustment of such children (page 407).

Source

Excerpted from Jenkins, R.L. "Adoption Practices and the Physician." *Journal of the American* *Medical Association.* 103 (August 11, 1934): 403–408.

Holt, Harry (1905–1964) and Bertha (1904–2000)

E. Wayne Carp

Harry and Bertha Holt, born-again Baptists from Creswell, Oregon, became legendary figures in the history of intercounty adoption when they adopted eight multiracial Korean babies fathered by U.S. soldiers in 1955. They went on to found the Holt Adoption Program in 1956 (now Holt International Children's Services), responsible for placing more than two hundred thousand babies from overseas.

With the end of the Korean War (1949–1954), the Republic of Korea (South Korea) was devastated: half of the population of forty-one million was in need of relief, especially its one hundred thousand orphans, ten to twelve thousand of whom had been fathered by American soldiers. Most of these latter children had been abandoned because Koreans' staunchly patrilineal, "Confucian" society, which places primal importance on consanguineous relations, made it extremely difficult for "illegitimate" or mixed-race children to be accepted.

In 1954, after viewing the documentary *Other Sheep*, which graphically depicted the plight of the abandoned Korean children, the Holts were profoundly moved to financially support ten Korean orphans. Several months later, they decided to adopt eight multiracial babies fathered by U.S. soldiers, but discovered that the 1953 Refugee Relief Act limited families to the adoption of two foreign-born children. The Holts successfully adopted the eight Korean infants after the U.S. Senate passed a personal bill in 1955, which was signed by President Eisenhower. In 1957, Congress repealed the old Refugee Relief Act and, in 1961, put international adoption on a permanent footing in American law with a congressional amendment to the Immigration and Nationality Act, which ended proxy adoption.

When Harry Holt returned to Oregon with the eight adopted children, the national publicity was so great that hundreds of people asked the Holts to help them adopt their own Korean children. With evangelical zeal, the Holts set up the Holt Adoption Program in 1956 to bring abandoned and orphaned Amerasian babies to the United States. Between 1956 and 1960, the Holts' program brought some one thousand to fifteen hundred Amerasian children to the United States to be adopted. In these early years, the Holts were often criticized by Communist North Korea, which accused Holt of sending children to the U.S. to be child slaves for capitalists and plantation owners, and by a wide spectrum of American professional social workers, who noted that Harry Holt had no experience in the field of child welfare and disregarded minimum adoption standards, such as proxy adoption. Nevertheless, in 1958, the Korean government awarded Harry Holt its Medal for Public Welfare for his work in intercountry adoption. Harry Holt died of a heart attack in April 1964.

By the 1970s, the Holt program had found homes in America for four thousand five hundred abandoned and relinquished children, a large majority of them now fathered by South Korean men and South Korean working class, single women, a consequence of rapid economic growth and industrialization. The Holt program had also reacted to the criticism of the social work establishment and had begun adhering to professional adoption standards.

With the death of Harry, Bertha Holt assumed the leadership role of the Holt Adoption Program. She traveled endlessly, working to improve conditions at the Il San Center in Korea, built as an orphanage in 1958, which is currently home to three hundred disabled children. Bertha Holt received numerous honors in her long life. President Lyndon B. Johnson named her National Mother of the Year and, in 1995, she became the only non-Korean to receive the Korea National Merit Award.

See also Korea and Adoption.

Further Reading

Holt, Bertha. *The Seed from the East.* Los Angeles: Oxford, 1956.
Hübinette, Tobias. "Adopted Koreans and Development of Identity in the 'Third Space.'" *Adoption and Fostering* 28 (2004): 16–24.

Human Immunodeficiency Virus (HIV)-Positive Infants

Vern L. Bullough

Children born to Human Immunodeficiency Virus (HIV)-positive mothers carry their mother's antibodies to HIV, but it is not clear for up to eighteen months whether they will have HIV themselves. This is because up to that time it is possible for an HIV positive infant to sero convert. That means they are rid of their mother's antibodies and produce them on their own if needed. If they no longer have HIV antibodies, they do not have the disease. If new antibodies appear, however, it signals that the child has contracted HIV and is producing his or her own antibodies.

This means that those adopting HIV-positive infants are not certain whether their child will have AIDS. Whether they do or not is not a life or death matter, but if they test positive they will have to go on medications in order to continue to survive and will stay on them for the rest of their lives. HIV testing is standard for both American and foreign adoptions. To help parents of foreign born children with AIDS, Margaret Fleming established "Chances by Choice," which attempts to place them. Earlier, Fleming, a Chicago resident, had established Adoption-Link, a Chicago agency with a mission to help African-American birth mothers have their child adopted if they want to do so. Fleming has adopted several children herself, both those of racial minorities as well as those who have tested positive for AIDS.

See also Acquired Immune Deficiency Syndrome (AIDS) and Adoption; South African Changes in Adoption: A Case Study.

Further Reading

Adams, William Lee. "More than Adoption." *Newsweek,* June 30, 2005, p. 54.

Human Rights and Adoption

Sharon Valente

The adoption and child welfare system is challenged by a host of controversies regarding the rights of each individual stakeholder (e.g., the child as well as the biological and adoptive parents) and each nation. While adoption has benefits, many of the neediest children remain poorly served, particularly children with disabilities, stigmatized illnesses, or ethnic diversity. The foster and adoption systems may not serve all children equitably or preserve their rights, and some children may become transients in an overburdened foster system. Debates also rage about rights of gay and lesbian adoptive parents, surrogates, sperm donors, and parties in international adoptions.

Sexual Orientation

Adopting a child can be frustrating and challenging for potential parents, as B. Alder notes, because of the shortage of babies, the rigorous selection procedures, endless delays, and a confusing system, as well as human rights issues. Despite the research that shows that single, older, or gay individuals successfully raise children, barriers to parents who seek to adopt may include marital status, age, sexual orientation, previous medical history, or other social criteria. However, several professional organizations have advocated for policies that support same-sex parents. The American Academy of Pediatrics advocates for co-parent or second-parent adoption by same-sex parents. As K. Haller notes, their policy positively reflects the movement toward equal rights for gay, lesbian, bisexual and transgendered people. Since the 1970s, adoption policies have become more open about the process and consideration of the rights of multiple stakeholders with most legal systems asserting that the best interest of the child is paramount.

Children of Color

Children of color, as noted by L. D. Hollingsworth, account for 47 percent of those entering the foster care/adoption system, although they account for 35 percent of the nation's child population. Unfortunately, the number of these children far exceeds the available parents who desire a child of color. Over half a million children in foster care await reunification with their parents or hope for adoption. Although foster care was designed to provide temporary placement for children, children may stay in one or more foster homes for years. The laudable goal of adoption policy is to protect the child's health and safety, but it also can further disadvantage those poor families, cultural groups, and disabled or sick children who are politically and economically disenfranchised.

Culture and Worldview

The American child welfare and adoption system reflects assumptions based on Anglo-Saxon, Protestant ideals and beliefs that: (1) individuals cause poverty due to poor character, laziness, and immorality; (2) each religious group has the right to practice its faith; and (3) children should conform to Anglo-Saxon cultural developmental standards. However, minority groups may hold different world views and cultural development benchmarks. For instance, an African-American worldview reflects philosophical assumptions about: (1) the spiritual nature of humans; (2) reliance on a collective/communal orientation among people; and (3) interdependence and interconnectedness of all things. Without adequate training in cultural diversity, courts, legislators, and adoption workers may mistake the assumptions about poverty and culturally biased development standards for fact and this may disadvantage culturally diverse groups and interfere with social justice. In addition, if a professional evaluates a child's development by models such as the Denver Developmental Screening Test, then minorities and foreign born children may be disadvantaged because the test has American norms when questions are culturally biased.

Adoption Legislation and Initiatives

In open adoption, the birth and adopting parents know and maintain a relationship with each other. Benefits may include the increased feeling of control, open communication, and maintenance of self identify. However, the adoptive and birth parents may worry about whether openness could threaten their parental role and might divide children's loyalties. Since the 1960s, adoptees asserted their right to know their biological origins and to search for parents. Controversy concerns whether adoptees have a "need" versus a "right" to know about their biological parents. The adoptees' need to know might conflict with the rights of the adoptive parents (e.g., to avoid dealing with biological parents) and the biological parents' right to privacy. The law also requires that relatives who provide care for a child be notified of, and heard at, any review regarding the child, but they are not guaranteed the right to be a party in the review. Relatives who do not provide care have no such right, but pre-adoptive parents and certified foster parents have the right to be notified and heard.

Surrogacy

Heated debate surrounds the issue of whether surrogate mothers have the right to charge adoptive parents for their services. Another question is whether the childless couple has the right to have a binding contract with the surrogate as opposed to the surrogate's right to the fruit of her womb. A similar question is whether a sperm donor should be paid and whether the embryo has rights. Does the embryo have the right to live or can it be used for research purposes? Adults who were conceived by in vitro fertilization assert their right to know the details of their biological conception while their parents argue for their right to privacy.

Pre-Adoption Genetic Testing

Families and adoption professionals desire a child's genetic information prior to adoption, but an analysis of the child's rights is needed. Although genetic testing of adults aims to predict disorders of their future offspring, genetic testing can offer some information about the child's future health that may influence a family's decision to adopt. It also has important implications for adoption policy and practice. Genetic testing may include expensive procedures such as a chromosome analysis or DNA testing to determine the risk of a limited number of inherited medical conditions and diseases (e.g., sickle cell trait or disease or cystic fibrosis). Although genetic testing does not provide data about many common disorders such as diabetes, depression, or cancer, it could reveal the possibility of a serious disease that might influence an individual's educational goals, occupational choices, or adoptability.

International Issues

International adoption of children raises serious questions about the principles of social justice. As noted by L. D. Hollingsworth (2003), these adoptions ignore the child's social context (e.g., poverty, disenfranchisement of the child's biological family and of children with lower social status, gender oppression, and gender discrimination of female children). As American parents struggle to adopt children, many turn to third world countries where they can adopt a child more easily—and desired children from an economically impoverished country or family are moved to a wealthier environment while the undesired children remain. Outcome studies of these adoptions show few or no negatives and some benefits; however, the impact of removing a child from its native culture is difficult to measure. Follow-up studies of outcomes for these children are lacking, but in some instances, the adoptive family becomes unable to care for the child due to divorce or economic hardship.

International adoption has developed in several waves: 1) Post World War II American adoptions of European war orphans (e.g., from Germany and Greece); 2) Korean orphans after the Korean War, and then South Koreans; 3) Central and South American children; and 4) Central and Eastern European children. According to Hollingsworth (2003), this last group provided the first white children available to international adoption. The goals of the United Nations Convention on the Rights of the Child and the Hague Conference aimed to protect families, and the Hague Conference encouraged countries to take whatever measures were needed to help children remain in the care of their families, or at least with a family in the child's country of origin.

See also Foster Care in the U.S.; Gay and Lesbian-headed Adoptive Families; Genetic Testing; Hague Convention on Protection of Children and Co-operation in Respect of Intercountry Adoption; Surrogacy and Adoption; United Nations and Adoption.

Further Reading

Adoption and Safe Families Act of 1997. P.L. NO 105-89 111 Stat.2115.

Adoption 2002: The President's Initiative on Adoption and Foster Care. U.S. Children's Bureau, Administration for Children and Families Web Site. http://www.acf.hhs.gov/programs/cb/publications/adopt02/ (accessed October, 2004).

Adoption and Foster Care Analysis and Reporting System. U.S. Children's Bureau, Administration for Children and Families Web Site. http://www.acf.hhs.gov/programs/cb/systems/index.htm (accessed October, 2004).

Alder, B. "Reproductive and Gynecologic Issues: Volume 8, Health Psychology." In *Comprehensive Clinical Psychology*, edited by A. S. Bellack and M. Hersen, 393–394. Amsterdam: Elsevier, 1998.

Freundlich, M. D. "The Case Against Pre-adoption Genetic Testing." *Child Welfare* 77 (1998): 663–79.

Hague Conference on Private International Law: Final Act of the 17th Session. Including the Convention on Protection of Children and Co-operation in Respect of Intercountry Adoption (1993). *International Legal Materials* 32, 1134–1146.

Haller, K. "The American Academy of Pediatrics Coparent or Second-Parent Adoption by Same Sex Parents Policy Statement: Its Science, Its Implications." *Journal of the Gay and Lesbian Medical Association* 6 (2002): 29–32.

Hollingsworth, L. D. "Adoption Policy in the United States: A Word of Caution." *Social Work* 45 (2000): 1–5.

Hollingsworth, L. D. "International Adoption Among Families in the United States: Considerations of Social Justice." *Social Work* 48 (2003): 209–217.

Miller, O. A., and R. J. Gaston. "A Model of Culture-centered Child Welfare Practice." *Child Welfare* 82 (2003): 1–9.

United Nations Convention on the Rights of the Child. In *Children, Law and Justice: A South Asian Perspective*, edited by S. Goonesekere, 382–401. New Delhi: Sage, 1998.

Illegitimacy

Vern L. Bullough

Illegitimacy, also called bastardy, refers to a child being born out of wedlock, through adultery, or any other relationship not recognized by the law. Historically, illegitimacy has been dealt with harshly in western societies. Various punitive measures have been imposed on unmarried mothers, and their children have suffered both legal and social disabilities. Great Britain in 1576, for example, made it an offense to beget an illegitimate child who was likely to become a public charge.

There were, and are, however, wide variations in attitudes toward illegitimacy and the treatment of illegitimate children among different cultures and countries. For example, in 1968, Israel had only 0.6 births per hundred live births born out of wedlock; Jamaica, with 74.1, had the highest rates of countries keeping records. Panama was second highest with 70 percent in 1967. Quite simply, the Jamaicans and Panamanians had a different concept of marriage and child bearing which did not, and still does not, conceive illegitimacy to be a problem. This view is shared by many other Central American countries. Of the highly developed nations, Sweden had a high rate of 15.1 in 1967 where, by choice, many would-be mothers prefer not to get married. The United States, with 9.7 in 1968, was in the middle of those countries then reporting. Statistics vary somewhat over the years and are reported annually by the *Population Yearbook* published by the United Nations. Some of the Muslim countries such as Syria and Egypt rarely report illegitimate births, perhaps because the associated punishment and ostracism leads to hidden pregnancies and child abandonment, which are not counted as illegitimate births on the official reporting statistics.

In the not so recent past, similar actions were taken in Europe where large numbers of unwanted children were simply abandoned. Society as a whole was reluctant to deal with the issue. Where institutions did exist, such as the Foundling Hospital in London established in 1759, they could not begin to meet the need and, as a result, restricted their admissions and services. In the United States, one of the first institutions to deal with abandoned children (most of whom were probably illegitimate) was St. Vincent's Infant Asylum established in Baltimore in 1856. Other institutions soon followed, both private and public (usually county-run).

Adoption was not considered even as a partial solution to the problems of abandoned and illegitimate children until the nineteenth century. The United States pioneered in that area through such developments as orphan trains and changes in laws allowing adoption. In the twentieth century, the U.S. also extended equal rights to those children born out of wedlock. Increasingly, states in the U.S. as well as governmental units in other countries have abandoned the practice of recording illegitimacy on birth records. The major change in attitudes in the U.S. came when the Aid to Dependent Children section of the Social Security legislation of the 1930s included those who were born out of wedlock. This inclusion was not without controversy and there was considerable hostile reaction to this extension, particularly against women of color who were accused of having children to live off of welfare. Some states opposed to such legislation attempted to legalize compulsory sterilization for females who had more than one illegitimate birth, fearful that their fecundity would undermine social welfare legislation.

As the twentieth century progressed, however, the demand for adoptable children further lessened the stigma of illegitimacy. Adoption was increasingly seen as a solution to the problem because it brought together illegitimate children, a natural source for adoption, with adults who wanted children but for some reason could not, or did not, have children. Unfortunately, many children were considered un-adoptable by American adoption agencies because of their race or physical disabilities. It was only in the last half of the twentieth century that such adoptions occurred in any number.

Some countries, such as Great Britain, were slower to encourage adoption as a solution for abandoned and illegitimate children. Not until the passage of the Adoption of Infants Act of 1936 was it possible for a parent or parents to legally abandon their control over a child, making it eligible for adoption. Each country has its own rules, and there are wide variations. In Germany, for example, adoption is a civil contract between the biological mother and the child's adopting parents. Some countries, like Russia and France, were slow to establish adoption procedures for illegitimate children. Increasingly, however, adoption either by citizens of their own country or by outsiders (mainly from the U.S.) has come to be seen as at least a partial solution to the problem posed by illegitimate or abandoned children.

In the United States, it has not only been chartered institutions or agencies that encourage adoption, but many placements in homes are done privately by attorneys or physicians. Some have labeled these private individuals as engaged in "baby selling." The Child Welfare League of America has been outspoken in its desire to outlaw such practices. Many unmarried mothers, however, feel safer and more secure going the "private route" rather than through an agency. They also feel they have a real right to assist in determining who will adopt their baby.

According to figures compiled by the National Adoption Information Clearinghouse, one of the noticeable changes taking place in the U.S. is a steady and stable increase in the number of single parent adoptions during the last years of the twentieth and first years of the twenty-first century. The result is, in part, a redefinition of what constitutes a family. One effect of this is to make it easier for the mother of an illegitimate baby to keep her child since there is now much less stigma attached to being a single unmarried parent.

Ultimately, whether to have her child adopted by others is an individual decision by the unmarried mother. It is dependent on numerous factors including willing support by family members as well as the commitment of the biological father if he is known. It is worth noting that it was the opening up of adoption of vast numbers of illegitimate children that also made it easier for the unmarried mother to keep her baby if she wanted to do so without being as stigmatized as she once was.

Further Reading

Baker, Nancy. *Baby Selling: The Scandal of Black-Market Adoption*. New York: Vanguard Press, 1978.

Hartley, Shirley Foster. *Illegitimacy*. Berkeley: University of California Press, 1975. (*The statistics in this article come from this book. The best way to keep up with current rates is through the United Nations *Demographic Yearbook*, which updates the statistics yearly.)

Ludtke, Melissa. *On Our Own: Unmarried Motherhood in America*. New York: Random House, 1997.

Martin, Cynthia D. *Beating the Adoption Game: The Definitive Guide to Modern Infant Adoption.* San Diego: Harvest Books, 1988.

Teichman, Jenny. *Illegitimacy.* Ithaca: Cornell University Press, 1982.

Religious Differences in Addressing Illegitimacy

Vern L. Bullough

Protestants and Catholics historically adopted different paths in handling illegitimate birth. Protestants, for the most part, placed considerable emphasis on the individual, that the individual should be responsible for his or her actions and pay the price. They tried to force parents of illegitimate children to support them, and if the father was not identified, they still insisted that the mother nurse and care for the "bastards" they bore. In some Protestant areas, judicial officials administered oaths to unmarried women in labor as they were in their highest agony to name the father in order to involve him in the support of the child. What they tried to avoid by such tactics was the child becoming a burden to the state.

Catholics, however, held that society and the Church must take in babies, and presumably illegitimate babies, abandoned by mothers whom they did not attempt to find. By the sixteenth century, institutions for foundlings had been established in France, Spain, Portugal, and especially in Italy, the area which had the most abandoned infants in Europe. Such foundling homes became ever more ubiquitous throughout Catholic Europe but were much less common in Protestant areas. In the U.S., the first such homes were established by the Catholic Church and only later did other authorities, both secular and religious, become involved.

Further Reading

Kertzer, David. *Sacrificed for Honor: Italian Infant Abandonment and the Politics of Reproductive Control.* Boston: Beacon Press, 1993, pp. 10–17.

Watt, Jeffrey R. "The Impact of the Reformation and Counter-Reformation." In *Family Life in Early Modern Times, 1500–1789,* edited by David I. Kertzer and Marzio Barbagli, p. 149. New Haven: Yale University Press, 2001.

Independent Adoption

Vern L. Bullough

Independent adoption is the term used to describe non-agency adoptions, in which there is no genetic relationship between the child and parents, that are handled by attorneys, physicians, or other go-between individuals. It is estimated that about half of all adoptions of healthy infants are independent adoptions. Such adoptions are legal in most states and, even in those which it is not, birth parents may choose non-relative adopted parents.

Individual judges in some states sometimes refuse to finalize such adoptions, which are called by some as "gray market" adoptions, implying that baby selling might be involved, but this is not the case in most independent adoptions. Independent adoptions allow would-be parents to escape some of the restrictions on age, ability to have children (fertility or infertility), length of marriage, and similar criteria that most agencies have or had in the past such as race and nationality. Some adoption seekers also feel they have a greater sense of control in choosing whom they will adopt; birth parents also feel they can be more involved in the decision. The birth parents might get some monetary support before the child is born, and in some cases negotiate a high amount to be paid by the adopted parents.

Perhaps inevitably, agency workers often have a low opinion of independent adoptions, regarding it as a way to beat the system. Many feel it is a way to avoid the counseling, the emphasis on a proper home system, and other services which agencies feel are essential for successful adoptions.

Past studies of independent adoptions, however, have found that most independent adoptions had a good outcome, although many of the parents felt they lacked the extensive background information on their adoptive children which might have been available from an agency.

One major difference between independent adoption and private adoptions is that, in the agencies, prospective parents are not informed about a child until consent papers have been signed and there is usually only a few days delay in picking up the child. In the case of independent adoptions, sometimes the adoption begins fairly early in the pregnancy, and the would-be parents are never quite certain they will get a child until they actually do. Many birth parents who have agreed to adoption, and even agreed on the parents they feel their child should have, change their mind at the last minute and so the child the adoptive parents have been anticipating is not available.

When all is said and done, however, most independent adoptions are lawful and probably successful, and those intermediaries involved usually hold themselves to high ethical standards. However, as the entry about the Internet and Adoption indicates, serious problems can arise.

Further Reading

Meezan, W., S. Katz, and E. Manno-Russo. *Adoptions Without Agencies: A Study of Independent Adoptions.* New York: Child Welfare League of America, 1978.

Witmer, H., E. Herzog, Eugene A. Weinstein, and M. E. Sullivan. *Independent Adoptions: A Follow-up Study.* New York: Sage Foundation, 1963.

India and Child Adoption

Robert B. Tapp

Child adoption in India must be understood from several perspectives: religious, legal, historical, and sociological. The subcontinent has birthed several religions (Hindu, Jain, Buddhist, Sikh); welcomed communities of Jews, Christians, and Parsis; and been invaded by Aryans and Muslims. In most cases, differing from the West, these religions have not developed centralized authority structures. Changes, therefore, have come slowly and remained obdurate.

Among the indigenous religions, Hindu is the most ambiguous label, and the "classical" Sanskrit has no real term for "religion." We know nothing of the practices of the extinct Indus valley cultures that preceded the Aryan invasions and little of the earlier forms of the tribal religions that were invaded, downgraded, and yet still persist. The pervasive forms of mother-goddesses probably had local origins, and the shamanic-yogic strains within Indian religions may come from the Indus civilization.

Stratification by "color" goes back to early invasions of the subcontinent, and developed into a very complex system of caste—degrading large numbers of low-caste (currently known as "Dalit") and tribal peoples. Non-Hindu (Jaina, Buddhist) groups that were seeking new converts were open to Dalit groups, as were the invading Muslims. This multi-communalism generated varied marriage and inheritance patterns and these, in turn, affected adoption practices. A persistent preference for male children affected unwanted female children. Those stratifications were further entrenched in regional and linguistic differences.

Sociologically, several patterns must be recognized. The tendency of less powerful groups to adopt the practices and beliefs of upper groups has been termed Sanskritization (e.g., a tribe announces that "the real name of our mother goddess is Kali"). Resentments can lead to reordering the pantheons (e.g., Dravidians bring Hanuman into Shiva's circle). Reformist movements (e.g., Arya Samaj, Brahmo Samaj) within the mainstream have emerged to counter conversionist practices—first reacting to successions of Buddhists, then of Muslims, and most recently of Christians. Westernization, today perhaps better termed as globalization or modernity, inevitably produces both imitation and resistance.

The historic absence of any overarching political power left legal matters in local and communal hands. Islamic rule was confined to the northern areas, resulting in a diminishing of Buddhist populaces and a limiting of Hindu princely powers. Successful French, Portuguese, and especially British hegemonies further complicated matters with the introduction of quite different (and varying) legal codes (Napoleonic, common-law, Catholic).

Under British rule, separate legal codes were created that allowed for different regulations of many customs of marriage, divorce, and adoption. In 1890, the Guardian and Wards Act (GAWA) was passed. This provided for adoptive parents to establish a guardianship over available children. But a child in this ward status retained name, religion, and had no legal right to any inheritance.

The political independence of 1947 meant a separation of many northern areas (west and east Pakistan—the latter eventually separating as Bangladesh) and Bhutan, Sikkim, Nepal, and the southern island of Sri Lanka. Pakistan designated itself a Muslim state; India declared itself a secular state; and Sri Lanka declared itself Buddhist. Massive and violent population transfers, and their lasting aftermaths, further affected cultural identities. Within the republic, all of these communities remain, and this article will focus on the current situation there.

Declaring India to be a "secular state" meant tolerance of all religions, as opposed to Pakistan's mono-religiosity. The Congress Party came to power with this Gandhian pluralistic commitment, and Nehru, as a scientific humanist, implemented it. Presidents of the republic have been Muslim, Hindu, Sikh, and the first Minister for Law and drafter of the constitution was B. R. Ambedkar, born into the "untouchable" Mahar caste.

India's current adoption situation must be seen within this colonial background of qualified pluralism and the constitutional commitment to secularism. The term "Personal Law" covers historic rules within religious communities. In reference to adoption, this includes communal laws relating to marriage, divorce, bigamy, polygamy, widow remarriage, caste/*gotra* intermarriage, inheritance, dowry, bride-harassment, *sati*, adoption, and succession. This religious pluralism of the country, with its heavily Hindu majority, was kept in focus as the Hindu Adoptions and Maintenance Act (HAMA) was adopted in 1956. Prior to this act, only males could be adopted. This meant that Islamic prohibition of adoption and Hindu concerns of caste purity were still on the table, to be eventually labeled as personal issues. From 1984–2000, a series of directives of the Indian Supreme Court have extended guidelines along with the Central Adoption Resource Agency (CARA), established in 1990 under the Ministry of Social Welfare and Empowerment. Within India, "Hindus" may freely and legally adopt. Essentially that term extends throughout the citizenry for any who choose to claim it, whether actually Buddhist, Jaina, or Sikh. Other citizens—Christians, Parsis, Muslims, Jews—can only resort to "guardianship" under GAWA. This curious mix of Western and Indian laws has resulted in a hybrid and shifting political situation criticized by the smaller religious communities but supported by Hindus and Muslims.

The HAMA provisions apply not only to those who were born into the four religious communities, but to those who were raised within them regardless of birth or who are converts or reconverts to them. Re-conversion is an interesting concept referring historically to descendants of those families who had changed religion to Buddhism, Islam, or Christianity and then, at a later point in time, decided to become "Hindu" again. More recently many of Ambedkar's followers, frustrated by free India's failure to sufficiently remedy the status of "untouchable" castes, followed him into Buddhism. They, too, were eligible for re-conversion.

Under British rule, lists of "scheduled" tribes and castes were made, and in free India certain perquisites attached to this status in terms of employment, education, and reserved political offices. The president has the power to adjust this schedule that provides for affirmative action to disadvantaged groups. Hindu majorities in many cases ruled that converts to "other" religions lost this status.

Several features of Indian family life must be viewed against this historic background. Male hegemony, polygamy, and inheritance lead the list. In addition, the practice of men and some women to renounce the world raises special questions of inheritance. Legally, HAMA theoretically ended Hindu bigamy while leaving Muslim polygamy untouched. Reformers, and especially feminists, have continually called for a uniform civil code.

The HAMA gives the father the right to surrender a child for adoption, while the mother is supposed to give her consent unless she has renounced the world, is no longer mentally competent, or has ceased to be Hindu. A mother can surrender a child if the father is dead, has renounced the world, or has ceased to be a Hindu. In the case of relinquished children, adoption must wait three months until the relinquishment is irrevocable. In the case of abandoned children, after one month's investigation and advertising, adoption can proceed.

A child may be taken in adoption if not yet fifteen or married (in either case, the law provides exception when local "custom or usage" permits otherwise). However, in the case of boys, neither the adoptive father nor mother can have a Hindu son, or son's son, or son's son's son living. In the case of a girl, neither the adoptive father nor mother can have a Hindu daughter or son's daughter living. In the cases of a male adopted by a female, or a female adopted by a male, there must be age separation of at least twenty-one years. In case the adoptive father has more than one wife, the consent of all wives is normally required. The senior wife shall be considered the adoptive mother and any others wives become stepmothers. The adopted child becomes a full family member and cannot renounce this status. Inheritance provisions obtain unless prior restrictions existed.

Islamic prohibition of adoption goes back to a Quranic story when the Prophet wanted to marry his adopted son's wife, Ayesha. Allah said that adoption was invalid. This prohibition has remained strong in Muslim cultures and has been one of the reasons that India does not yet have a uniform code. Inheritance is based on blood relationship in *shari'a*. Guardianship, of course, is possible, as is also acknowledgement of paternity.

As in most countries, there is considerable gap between stated law and actual enforced practices in India's thirty-five states and union territories. Registrations of marriages range between 50 and 90 percent. India has the largest child population in the world, 400 million under eighteen according to the second report to the United Nations. Despite the announced standard of universal education, 60 million never go to school and only 60 percent stay more than five years. Fewer girls than boys are born, largely because of female fetal infanticide (better called "fetacide" to avoid Christian confusions), and female illiteracy is significantly higher. Four percent are orphaned.

The Juvenile Justice Act (JJ) from 1986 moved the country closer to uniformity. The 2000 enlargements remain to be worked out as they apply to states, but adoptions are now to be irrespective of sex or religion. The Act covers orphaned, abandoned, neglected, or abused children, and may eventually prevent children leaving the country before full adoption has occurred. The current rationale is the child's right to the protection of a family. In 1992, India signed on to the United Nations Convention on the Rights of Children (CRC). The first report was filed in 1997 and examined in 2000.

Changes in regard to India's children are, thus, the result of the awareness of international standards and national pressures for reform. In 2001, an Alliance for Child Rights was formed. A Constitutional Act of 2002 legislated the free and compulsory education of children up to age fourteen. The existence of laws and their implementation are different matters in India as elsewhere. And the resistance to change has often come from the varied religious communities. Recent opposition has been based upon *hindutva*, best translated as Hindu nationalism. This ideology privileges all who regard India as their motherland, essentially excluding Muslims.

Adoption is an answer to infertility, particularly for families and individuals who have moved beyond traditional beliefs in blood inheritance and caste purity, and this has been stressed by many reform movements. It is also a partial solution to many forms of child abuse, such as child labor and child trafficking.

Intercountry adoptions must follow a more circuitous course. Non-resident Indians do not need to use placement agencies in their foreign country of residence. Adoptive families where one parent is of Indian origin are next in line for preference, followed by totally foreign families. These last two groups must become guardians in India then follow "enlisted agency" rules in their resident countries, make regular reports to the Indian government, and complete adoption within two years. The clear aim here is to provide the advantage of a family for the adoptee and to avoid trafficking in children for illegal purposes. A 2002 ruling states that a child must be rejected by at least three Indian families before becoming available for intercountry adoption. There is no way to avoid considerable payments to the facilitators of these processes, both in India and in foreign countries.

Indian statutes prefer that the child be raised in the "natural social milieu." Given the cultural objections to adoption and the large number of children in need of adoptive families, this means intercountry adoptions will prevail in the foreseeable future. While not ideal, these are certainly preferable to situations of under-education, child labor, and child trafficking that are the alternatives. In the long-run, economic improvement will reduce birthrates and enlarge child opportunities reducing the number of unadopted children now released from state care as adults when they reach fifteen years of age.

Further Reading

Apparao, Hansa. "International Adoption of Children: The Indian Scene." *International Journal of Behavioral Development* 20 (1997): 3–16.

The Guardians and Wards Act, 1890. Helplinelaw Web Site. http://www.helplinelaw.com/bareact/index.php?dsp=guardians (accessed December, 2004).

The Hindu Adoptions and Maintenance Act, 1956. Sudhir Shah and Associates Web Site. http://www.sudhirlaw.com/HINADMAN.htm (accessed December, 2004).

The Hindu Marriage Act, 1955. Sudhir Shah and Associates Web Site. http://www.sudhirlaw.com/HMA55.htm (accessed December, 2004).

The Hindu Minority and Guardianship Act, 1956. Sudhir Shah and Associates Web Site. http://www.sudhirlaw.com/MINGUARD.htm (accessed December, 2004).

India Alliance for Child Rights (IACR). India's Girl Child: Early Childhood—or Early Disposal? Child Right's Information Network (CRIN) Web Site. http://www.crin.org/docs/resources/treaties/crc.37/India_Alliance_for_Child_ Rights%20_IACR_.pdf (accessed December, 2004).

The Juvenile Justice (Care and Protection of Children) Act, 2000. Department of Social Welfare, Govt. of Delhi Web Site. http://socialwelfare.delhigovt.nic.in/juvenilejustice1.htm (accessed December, 2004).

Report of the Steering Committee on Empowerment of Women and Development of Children for the Tenth Five Year Plan (2002–07). Government of India Planning Commission Web Site. http://planningcommission.nic.in/aboutus/committee/strgrp/stgp_woman.pdf (accessed December, 2004).

U.N. General Assembly. Convention on the Rights of the Child (1989). Human Rights Web Web Site. http://www.hrweb.org/legal/child.html (accessed December, 2004).

The Indian Adoption Project and the Indian Child Welfare Act of 1978

Dennis Miller

The Indian Adoption Project, begun in 1958, was funded by the federal government and administered by the Child Welfare League of America (CWLA) in conjunction with the Bureau of Indian Affairs. The project, as Marilyn Holt explains, was intended to address what was perceived as the extensive neglect and suffering of Indian children on reservations in the United States. It was an attempt to initiate the nationwide transracial and transnational adoption of Indian children, with a total of 395 Indian children adopted while the Project was active. Indians were not encouraged to adopt these children and most went to Caucasian families. In 1978, the Indian Adoption Project was replaced by the Indian Child Welfare Act.

Background

The issue of Indian child welfare has been as problematic as other long-standing conflicts between Native Americans and the federal government. At the center of these conflicts have been the issues of sovereignty, governance, shifting authority over Indian affairs between state and the federal governments, and the unique status of Indians in American society. From 1790 to 1871, C. Mathew Snipp reports that Indians were dealt with by the federal government as foreigners and were encouraged to exchange their native culture for that of European-Americans. This manifested itself most prominently in the removal of Indians from native lands and placement on reservations.

By the late nineteenth century, Indian military resistance had ceased, most Indians were on reservations, and the federal government saw full assimilation as the best solution to its Indian "problem." The widespread use of Indian boarding schools was implemented as an effort to enforce this assimilation by separating children from tribal influence while reinforcing mainstream American culture. The boarding school experience, as M. M. Slaughter notes, made it difficult for these children to subsequently return to tribal life. And as Kristen Kreisher reports, thousands of Indian children were sent to these schools for cultural and religious education while being allowed only minimal contact with their families.

The Indian Adoption Project

Efforts to assimilate Indians into mainstream America were recognized as unsuccessful by the 1930s and the boarding school system began to be phased-out, to be replaced by foster care and adoption. The prevailing attitude toward adoption at the time was to racially match adoptees with prospective parents. The Indian Adoption Project of 1958 was a unique departure from this concept, with almost all Indian adoptees placed in non-Indian homes. As the Adoption History Project notes, this was the first attempt at widespread transracial adoption of an entire child population from a single culture. It was estimated that in 1957 there were one thousand adoptable Indian children who were in foster care, but the wherewithal to move them to new homes did not exist. This was corroborated by a study conducted by The National Council of Protestant Churches. David Fanshel notes that children without appropriate guardianship were either sent to orphanages or passed from family to family on reservations.

During the 1950s, the federal government began delegating the management of Indian affairs to the states, which led to the increasing influence of professional social workers in the welfare of Indian Children. Their activities generated significant criticism among Indians and their supporters, who blamed the unwarranted removal of Indian children on the cultural ignorance of social workers who were not located on reservations. As noted by Holt, critics believed that situations were often incorrectly characterized as abusive or neglectful because those making determinations were ignorant of tribal society.

The Civil War and an increase in urban crime and disease in large east coast cities had created a substantial number of orphans and destitute children in America. The response to this problem was the proliferation of child protection agencies, an increase in regulatory activity, and greater influence in child welfare by the emerging disciplines of sociology and social work. Social workers, as Holt notes, attempted to professionalize the adoption process and to decrease the influence of religious institutions.

The extensive removal of Indian children was complicated by conflicting ideas about the nature of "family" between Indians and non-Indians. As Slaughter discusses, European-Americans traditionally embraced the notion of the nuclear family, with children "belonging" to a family. In Indian culture, children were members of a clan first and members of a nuclear family second. The clan represented an extended family with clearly defined lines of kinship that determined an individual's status and importance. The removal of Indian children by social workers and missionaries was so successful that Kreisher notes, between 1941 and 1978, 68 percent of all Indian children were placed in orphanages, foster homes, or were adopted.

As early as 1960, there was adverse tribal reaction to the Indian Adoption Project. In that year, the Navajo Tribal Council issued Resolution CN-60-56 that addressed the removal of children from tribal land. It prohibited "Removing or attempting to remove any Navajo minor from the Navajo Reservation without prior approval of the Advisory Committee of the Navajo Tribal Council, except for the purpose of attending school under a non-sectarian program approved by the Bureau of Indian Affairs." The Council resolved that "The Navajo Tribe looks with disfavor upon the adoption of Navajo children by non-members of the Tribe in cases where the parents of the children are living, in good health, and have not abandoned or continuously neglected said children."

The impact of the Indian Adoption Project has been the subject of some debate. At the conclusion of a five-year study in 1968, David Fanshel concluded that most adoptees were doing well, but, being aware of the controversy surrounding the Project, suggested that the continued adoption of Indian children would be an issue that the tribes would have to decide for themselves. The Adoption History Project notes that Indian activists in the 1960s and 1970s characterized the Project as a form of cultural genocide. In 2001, Shay Bilchik, Executive Director of the CWLA, formally apologized for the Indian Adoption Project at a meeting of the National Indian Child Welfare Association. Bilchik characterized the Project as well-intended, but hurtful and biased. Kreisher reports that, in May, 2001, the CWLA Board of Directors acknowledged the painful legacy of the Indian Adoption Project and gave its support to the Indian Child Welfare Act.

The Indian Child Welfare Act (ICWA) of 1978

The federal government ultimately recognized the shortcomings of the Indian Adoption Project. It was supplanted by Public Law 95-608, the Indian Child Welfare Act (ICWA), in October 1978. It was a de facto repudiation of the Indian Adoption Project and an acknowledgement of many of the problems and abuses carried out under its auspices since its inception in 1958. Title 1 of the Act declares that "it is the policy of Congress to establish minimum Federal standards for the removal of Indian children from their families (extended families) and for the placement of such children in foster or adoptive homes which will reflect Indian culture."

Passage of the ICWA was the result of recommendations made by the American Indian Review Commission and of congressional investigation into the welfare of Indian children. These investigations showed an alarmingly high rate of removal of Indian children by state welfare agencies. As Steven L. Pevar reports, most were removed and placed in non-Indian homes because they lived in poverty. And according to Holt, the ICWA re-asserted federal control over Indian child welfare, gave principal jurisdiction and decision-making to tribal councils, and established a hierarchy of preference in the adoption of children: family members first; tribal members second; other Indians third; non-Indians last.

The ICWA gave tribes jurisdiction over custody proceedings involving any Indian child who resides within a reservation. This had two principal effects: 1) it made it more difficult for non-Indians to adopt Indian children and; 2) it significantly raised the standard for removal of children from their families. When a child must be removed, the ICWA emphasized the importance of placing them in homes that were culturally familiar, which was left to the discretion of the Tribes.

While the ICWA has made it more difficult to remove children from their families, it has not achieved all of the goals originally envisioned. In testimony before the U.S. Senate in 1987, it was argued that adoption attorneys were circumventing the Law by instructing their clients to hide the Indian heritage of potential adoptees. As reported by Snipp, the American Humane Association estimated in 1997 that fifty thousand Indian adoptees were living with non-Indian families. A 1999 Nebraska study found that the burden of proving "clear and convincing evidence" for placing an Indian child outside the family (as mandated by the ICWA) was present in only 22 percent of cases.

The Indian Child Welfare Act was implemented to correct the abuses carried out under the Indian Adoption Project. It remains the strongest statutory device that Indian families and tribes have for retaining control of child adoption. While several attempts have been made to weaken the law by individuals and groups interested in promoting the transracial adoption of Indian children, none has been successful.

See also Native Americans and Adoption: Defining Who is "Indian".

Further Reading

Alexie, Sherman. *Indian Killer.* New York: Warner Books, 1996.

Bakeis, Christine D. "The Indian Child Welfare Act of 1978: Violating Personal Rights for the Sake of the Tribe." *Notre Dame Journal of Law, Ethics and Public Policy* 10 (1996): 543–586.

Benson, Robert, ed. *Children of the Dragonfly: Native American Voices on Child Custody and Education.* Tucson: University of Arizona, 2001.

Fanshel, David. *Far from the Reservation: The Transracial Adoption of American Indian Children.* Metuchen, NJ: The Scarecrow Press Inc., 1972.

Graham, Judith. "Adopted Indians Pine for Lost Lives." *Chicago Tribune*, May 9, 2001.

Hollinger, Joan Heifetz. "Beyond the Best Interests of the Tribe: The Indian Child Welfare Act and the Adoption of Indian Children." *University of Detroit Law Review* 66 (1989): 451–501.

Holt, Marilyn Irvin. *Indian Orphanages.* Lawrence, KS: University of Kansas Press, 2001, 1–5, 9, 10, 257.

Indian Adoption Project. The Adoption History Project Web Site. http://www.uoregon. edu/~adoption/topics/IAP.html (accessed September, 2004).

Indian Child Welfare Act—Title 1: Child Custody Proceedings. Public Law: 95-608, 1978. National Indian Child Welfare Association Web Site. http://www.nicwa.org/policy/law/icwa/index.asp

Jones, Sondra. "Redeeming the Indian: The Enslavement of Indian Children in New Mexico and Utah." *Utah Historical Quarterly* 67 (1999): 220–241.

Kingsolver, Barbara. *Pigs in Heaven*. New York: Harper Perennial, 1993.

Kreisher, Kristen. "Coming Home: The Lingering Effects of the Indian Adoption Project." *Children's Voice*. March, (2002): 1–2.

Lyslo, Arnold. "Adoptive Placement of American Indian Children with Non-Indian Families." In *Readings in Adoption*, edited by I. Evelyn Smith. New York: Philosophical Library, 1963.

Navajo Tribal Council. Tribal Policy on Adoption of Navajo Orphans and Abandoned or Neglected Children. In Steven Unger, ed., *The Destruction of American Indian Families*. New York: Association on American Indian Affairs, 1977: 85–86. Excerpted on the Adoption History Project Web Site. http://www.uoregon.edu/~adoption/archive/NavajoTPOA.htm

Pevar, Steven L. *Rights of Indians and Tribes: The Basic ACLU Guide to Indian and Tribal Rights*. Carbondale and Edwardsville, IL: Southern Illinois University Press, 2000, 333–335.

Slaughter, M. M. "Contested Identities: The Adoption of American Indian Children and the Liberal State." *Social and Legal Studies* 9 (2000): 227–229.

Snipp, C. Matthew. *American Indian and Alaska Native Children in the 2000 Census*. Washington, D.C. Population Reference Bureau with support from The Annie E. Casey Foundation, April 2002. Population Reference Bureau Web Site. http://www.prb.org/Ameristat.Template.cfm?Section=Children1&template=/ContentManagement/ContentDisplay.cfm&ContentID=5651

Unger, Steven, ed. *The Destruction of American Indian Families*. New York: Association on American Indian Affairs, 1977.

Indonesia: Permanency Planning post–December 26, 2004, Southeast Asia Tsunami: A Case Study

Joanne Selinske

[The following case study is informed by the author's post-tsunami visits to Indonesia.]

The enormity of loss and devastation caused by the December 26, 2004, Southeast Asia tsunami is difficult to comprehend. Likewise, it may be difficult for adoption professionals to fully appreciate the complexity of issues and the short-term and long-term interventions pursued by authorities in a nation with no recent history of adoption as a permanency planning tool. Legal, cultural, and religious mores exert dramatic influence in Indonesia. These values do not preclude adoption of the children orphaned by the tsunami by nonfamilial caretakers. However, attachment to family and cultural lineage, devotion to religious and cultural values, and connection to community affiliation are so strong that Indonesian children orphaned by the tsunami will most likely find permanence in familiar settings where heritage is preserved.

Estimates of the loss of life due to the tsunami range from one hundred thousand to four times that number. Exact figures are unknown due to a lack of nation-wide birth registry and the loss of governmental records in areas hardest hit by the tsunami. In Indonesia alone, more than six hundred thousand people were displaced from their homes. Belief is widespread that children were least capable of surviving given the power of the ocean surge that reached miles inland. A year after, the number of children separated from their primary caregivers in Indonesia ranges between two and three thousand. Exact figures are unknown given the scale of displacement and the dispersal of survivors. Two important questions remain unanswered: how many surviving children lost both parents but are safe in the care of relatives or family friends—in kinship care?; how many of these children are in other living circumstances that preclude guarantee of their safety and/or protection?

Social Context

Indonesia is the fourth most populous nation in the world. Its 242 million citizens (70 million under fifteen years of age) inhabit six thousand islands in the world's largest archipelagic state that straddles the equator in Southeast Asia along the major sea lanes between the Indian and Pacific Oceans. In 1945, the nation declared its independence—since the early seventeenth century it was colonized by the Dutch; in 1942, it was occupied by the Japanese. Eighty-eight percent of the population is Muslim, and Islam is recognized as the national religion (World Fact Book, 2005). National reforms in the 1990s prompted decentralization to the local level of public policy decision making. The net effect in this geographically dispersed, culturally diverse nation is a lack of centrality of solutions, even for problems as large as reconstitution of normalcy of daily life for orphans in post-disaster recovery.

Indonesia is an economically "developing" country, with 15 percent of its population living below the poverty line in 2004. In the last decade, Indonesia codified the child's right to access free public education. Notwithstanding, a decade later access is limited and not free. To overcome this deficit and the geographic distances separating the population, religious and other sectarian groups operate boarding schools that house several dozen to two thousand students each. Government officials have knowledge of seven thousand boarding schools, but acknowledge an incomplete count of both the number of schools and the numbers of children attending. No licensing nor accreditation system exists and registration of these institutions is voluntary. In addition to these institutional settings, an unknown number of orphanages accommodate children without parental care and protection. These factors underscore one of the most significant facts defining the care of orphans and other children who lack parental care and protections in Indonesia. It is currently institutionally focused.

Despite long periods of separation from parents, institutional care is valued and pervades Indonesian society. Care by extended family or kin is common; conversely, adoption is rare. Paradoxically, although child care may not be assumed by birth parents, ties to the biological family are seldom legally or socially severed. Viewed from a context where family is imagined to provide emotional security and safety, and adoption becomes an instrument to achieve this end, this approach is perplexing. Viewed through the social and cultural lens of Indonesian life, this approach demonstrates reverence of religious, cultural, and historical attachments and the belief that these connections provide the emotional security and safety that are illusory particularly given the harsh realities of life in a developing economy where natural disasters commonly redefine geography as well as life.

Legal Context

The Indonesian domestic legal system on child care and protection is rooted in the nation's 1945 Constitution (Articles 28 B (2) and 34 (1). In September 1990, the country ratified the United Nations Convention on the Rights of the Child (CRC). Article 20 of the CRC provides that a child deprived of a family environment shall be entitled to special protection and assistance. The same article details that alternate care for such children can "include, inter alia, foster placement, kafalah of Islamic law or adoption or if necessary placement in suitable institutions for the care of children." (Indonesia is not signature to The 1993 Hague Convention on Protection of Children and Co-operation in Respect of Inter-country Adoption.)

In 2002, efforts to strengthen the country's child protection and child welfare system culminated in the Parliament's adoption of *Law no 23 on Child Protection*, building upon the 1979 *Law no 4 on Children's Welfare* and the 1974 *Law no 6 on Basic Provisions of Social Welfare*. Article 39 articulates the legal framework for the adoption of children deprived of parental care. However, adoption does not "sever the blood relationship between the adopted child and his natural parents."

The primacy of biological ties is further underscored in Article 32 of Law 23. It stipulates that even when temporarily separated "there shall be no severance of relations between the child and his natural parents." Articles 33–36 delineate that an individual or institution may be appointed to serve as guardian; while Article 72 of the same law specifies that "the community shall be entitled to play as broad a role as possible in the effort to protect children." Community includes religious groups, neighborhood associations, and family foundations. They may assist by fulfilling the basic needs of children including providing social and financial support to families in difficulties. Law 23 emphasizes residential care as the alternative form of care for children deprived of family. Articles 37–38 exclusively regulates "fostering" that is "undertaken by an institution." Nonresidential forms of care are mentioned in Law 23 as a possibility, but no provision regulates the specifics. (For a more complete delineation of the legal framework on children deprived of family or at risk, the reader is referred to a report of International Social Service and UNICEF Indonesia, *Supporting the Development of the Alternative Care System at Regional (Aceh) and National Levels in Indonesia*, as listed in the "Further Reading" section below.

In late 2005, Regulation on Requirements and Procedures for the Appointment of Guardians was under government review. These regulations allow a guardian to be appointed when the parents' fail to fulfill their responsibilities and obligations, when they are legally incapable, or when their whereabouts is unknown. Among the provisions under review is decreasing from 24 months the time a child's parent or guardian could be missing (including deceased) before guardianship could be granted.

Within six weeks of the tsunami, the Indonesian Ministry of Social Affairs released a Policy on Separated Children, Unaccompanied Children and Children left with One Parent in Emergency Situations (February 2005). This policy stipulates that every effort be made to ensure that children are able to stay with their families and communities. Further it stresses that the priority must be to reunite unaccompanied or separated children with their parents or family relatives. The policy elaborates that adoption not be contemplated during the emergency and only considered once all search and family reunification efforts have failed. At that point, priority is given to adoption by relatives who are known to the children.

Finally, to overcome existing gaps in the legal framework to protect children lacking parental care, Indonesian authorities have developed a comprehensive set of guidelines covering a variety of circumstances and organizations. Not yet codified in law, at this writing these guidelines direct practitioners to adhere to high standards of care and protection of rights. Lacking the authority of law, they remain voluntary not compulsory.

Cultural Values Define Indonesian Response

Multiple challenges face Indonesian authorities seeking to guarantee child rights and extend protections, particularly those who are biased towards family-based solutions for children lacking parental care including those orphaned by the tsunami. Indonesia's legal and social values reflect respect for, and heavy reliance on, institutional solutions. This perspective is not likely to manifest in near future use of adoption as a permanency planning instrument. The singularity of adoption, albeit if it provides the promised emotional security and stability for an orphaned or abandoned child, does not weigh equally in the Indonesian framework. Consequently, contemporary solutions to the crises of orphaning will rely on attachment to family lineage, cultural heritage, religious, and community affiliation—even when they are precipitated by catastrophes of the proportion of the late 2004 tsunami. While its physical effects moved sea and land for thousands of miles, the shock of the tsunami was not so great as to dramatically shake or reshape the core values of Indonesian society.

See also Children after Disasters and Crises.

Further Reading

Supporting the Development of the Alternative Care System at Regional (Aceh) and National Levels in Indonesia. 18 November, 2005. International Social Service (ISS) Web Site. http://www.iss-ssi.org/Resource_Centre/Tronc_DI/documents/Indonesia-Report2005.pdf (accessed February, 2006).

United Nations Convention on the Rights of the Child. http://www.unhchr.ch/html/menu3/b/k2crc.htm (accessed February, 2006).

World Fact Book, 2005. Central Intelligence Agency Web Site. http://www.cia.gov/cia/publications/factbook/geos/id.html (accessed February, 2006).

Infant Adoption

Victor Groza and Frida Perales

Overview

About six million adopted individuals of all ages live in the United States according to U.S. Census Bureau data, comprising about 2.5 percent of the population. Since adoption data are not kept, we do not know how many of the adoptees were placed as infants. In separate works, R. P. Barth and K. S. Stolley estimate that infant adoptions account for approximately 15 percent of adoptions. However, V. Groza, L. Houlihan, and Z. B. Wood estimate that infant adoptions may actually comprise less than 5 percent of adoptions in the United

States. While the exact percent is not known, it is known that infant adoptions have decreased since the 1970s. Voluntary adoptive placements, a common practice of placing infants in the first half of the twentieth century, have become increasingly rare. It is not simply because of access to contraceptives and safe abortions that began in the early 1970s, but young unmarried women, for a variety of reasons, now often decide to raise their children. One major reason is that the stigma that once shadowed out-of-wedlock pregnancy and single parenthood has been lifted.

Most infant placements, as reported by T. Gilles and J. Kroll, are made through attorneys and private agencies. Historically in infant adoptions, as V. Groza and K. Rosenberg note, children were chosen for parents who were infertile, resulting in a process that was adoptive parent-centered. These adoptions were closed; that is, at no point in the adoption process was there contact between the birth parents and the adoptive family. Only non-identifying information was shared (age, occupation, general health) and the expectation was that birth mothers would "move on" with their lives. The adoptee would be treated as if he or she was born into the adoptive family. K. Rosenberg and V. Groze cover this issue. This mythology was challenged by all members of the adoption triad starting in the late 1970s.

Following these challenges, since the 1980s, infant adoptions have the option of being more open. Openness in adoption ranges from sharing information to complete and ongoing-contact between birth and adoptive families. As noted by R. Laws, they can be loosely structured or highly structured, involve an agency as an intermediary, or be navigated independently. In some way, infant adoptions are now more birth parent-centered; birth parents have an active role in choosing from a selection of adoptive parents for their child. Not only is identifying information shared, there is often contact between the birth and adoptive parents.

Studies have been steadily accumulating about open adoptions. Several are provided in the "Further Reading" section below and a summary article is also included in this handbook. Overall, these studies are positive about open adoptions, suggesting that many of the concerns and fears expressed about openness were unfounded.

Post-Adoption Issues

For families who adopt infants, there are few post-adoption support services, implying that these services are not necessary. With infant placements, lawyers and private agencies are more likely to perpetuate the myth that adoption is a one time legal event. Agencies tend to have developed more supports for families adopting older children. For families who adopt infants who later demonstrate difficulties, there is more of a tendency to scrutinize the family as if the family is the cause of difficulties with the child. That is not to say that there are not family system issues as part of the problems for infant adoptees, rather, as noted by V. Groza and K. Rosenberg, to highlight the different messages families receive and services available for adoptees entering the family as infants compared to older children.

From several studies, it is clear that birth parents, adoptive parents, and adoptees benefit from support services before, during, and after adoptions. Adoption support services must be available and accessible to all members of the adoption triad.

When adoption support services of all types are available, adoption outcomes—already very positive—will become even better. The few studies conducted about post-adoption services by J. A. Rosenthal, V. Groze, and J. Morgan, and by T. Reilly and L. Platz suggest that there are problems with the types of services and accessibility of services for adoptive families. To strengthen and support adoption, the service systems need to increase the number and type of adoption-sensitive services.

Search and Reunion

Stories and research about the reunion of adult adoptees with their birthmothers and extended biological families have been accumulating for several decades. L. Stiffler estimated that five hundred thousand adult adoptees seek, or had found, their birth families. As J. Schooler notes, the desire to locate their origins, once thought to be pathological, is now viewed more positively and a normative component of development for some adoptees.

Adoptees search for several reasons, as summarized by J. Schooler. These range from searching as an adventure, to searching as part of healing, to searching for concrete medical or other information, including searching for people who look like the adoptee. At the same time, there are significant numbers of adoptees placed as infants who choose not to search. Recent research in England by D. Howe and J. Feast has provided some of the best research on search and reunion issues, including a model for conceptualizing the search process. It is too early in this phenomenon to draw solid conclusions, but the evidence is accumulating that closed adoptions do not work for many members of the adoption triad. While outcomes from reunions are complex and may take many directions (from the members of the triad having an ongoing relationship to complete rejection), it is clear that search and reunion will be a significant component of the life cycle for members of the adoption triad.

Summary

Infant adoptions have moved from a closed system to more openness in recent years. The openness is manifested in birth parents choosing adoptive parents, birth and adoptive families maintaining relationships after the adoption, triad members searching for connections, and reunions between adoptees placed as infants with birth parents. Unfortunately, we do not know the number of infant adoptions, the number of adoptees who search, or the outcomes of searches and reunion, given the inadequacy of the management information systems in the United States and the lack of rigorous social science research.

See also Adoption Search Movement; Open Adoption; Post-adoption Services; Reunion.

Further Reading

Babb, L. A. and R. Laws. *Adopting and Advocating for the Special Needs Child*. Westport, CT: Bergin and Garvey, 1997.

Barth, R. P. "Adoption of Drug-exposed Children." *Children and Youth Services Review* 13 (1991): 323–342.

Barth, R. P., and M. Berry. *Adoption and Disruption: Rates, Risks, and Response*. New York: Aldine De Gruyter, 1988.

Berry, M. "The Effects of Open Adoption on Biological and Adoptive Parents and the Children: The Arguments and the Evidence." *Child Welfare* 70 (1991): 637–651.

Berry, M. "The Practice of Open Adoption: Findings from a Study of 1396 Adoptive Families." *Children and Youth Services Review* 13 (1991): 379–396.

Berry, M. "Risks and Benefits of Open Adoption." *The Future of Children* 3 (1993): 125–138.

Brodzinsky, D. "A Stress and Coping Model of Adoption Adjustment." In *The Psychology of Adoption*, edited by D. Brodzinsky and M. Schecter, 3–24. New York: Oxford University Press, 1990.

Gilles, T., and J. Kroll. *Barriers to Same Race Placement*. St. Paul, Minnesota: North American Council on Adoptable Children, 1991.

Groza, V., L. Houlihan, and Z. B. Wood. "Adoption." In *Child Welfare for the 21st Century: A Handbook of Children, Youth, and Family Services*, edited by G. Mallon and P. Hess. New York: Columbia University Press, In press.

Groza, V., and K. Rosenberg. "Treatment Issues of Adoptees Placed as Infants and as Older Children: Similarities and Differences." In *Clinical and Practice Issues in Adoption: Bridging the Gap Between Adoptees Placed as Infants and as Older Children, revised and expanded*, edited by V. Groza and K. Rosenberg. Westport, CT: Bergen and Garvey, 2001. pp. 1–21.

Henney, S. M., R. G. McRoy, S. Ayers-Lopez, and H. D. Grotevant. "The Impact of Openness on Adoption Agency Practices: A Longitudinal Perspective." *Adoption Quarterly* 6 (2003): 31–51.

Hollenstein, T., L. D. Level, L. V. Scaramella, R. Milfort, and J. M. Neiderhiser. "Openness in Adoption, Knowledge of Birth Parent Information, and Adoptive Family Adjustment." *Adoption Quarterly* 7 (2003): 43–52.

Howe, D., and J. Feast. *Adoption, Search and Reunion: The Long-Term Experience of Adopted Adults*. London: The Children's Society, 2000.

Laws, R. "The History, Elements, and Ongoing Need for Adoption Support." In *Clinical and Practice Issues in Adoption: Bridging the Gap Between Adoptees Placed as Infants and as Older Children, revised and expanded*, edited by V. Groza and K. Rosenberg. Westport, CT: Bergen and Garvey, 2001. pp. 81–104.

Mendenhall, T. J., J. M. Berge, G. M. Wrobel, H. D. Grotevant, and R. G. McRoy. "Adolescents' Satisfaction with Contact in Adoption." *Child and Adolescent Social Work Journal* 21 (2004): 175–190.

Neil, E. "Understanding Other People's Perspectives: Tasks for Adopters in Open Adoption." *Adoption Quarterly* 6 (2003): 3–30.

Reilly, T., and L. Platz. "Post-adoption Service Needs of Families with Special Needs Children: Use, Helpfulness and Unmet Needs." *Journal of Social Service Research* 30 (2004): 51–67.

Rosenberg, K., and V. Groza. "The Impact of Secrecy and Denial in Adoption: Practice and Treatment Issues." *Families and Society* 78 (1997): 522–530.

Rosenthal, J. A., and V. Groza. *Special Needs Adoption: A Study of Intact Families*. New York: Praeger, 1992.

Rosenthal, J. A., V. Groza, and J. Morgan. "Services for Families Adopting Children via Public Child Welfare Agencies: Use, Helpfulness, and Need." *Children and Youth Services Review* 18 (1996):163–182.

Schooler, J. "Search and Reunion Issues." In *Clinical and Practice Issues in Adoption: Bridging the Gap Between Adoptees Placed as Infants and as Older Children*, revised and expanded, edited by V. Groza and K. Rosenberg. Westport, CT: Bergen and Garvey. pp. 49–80.

Siegel, D. H. "Open Adoption of Infants: Adoptive Parents' Feelings Seven Years Later." *Social Work* 48 (2003): 409–419.

Stiffler, L. *Synchronicity and Reunion*. Hobe Sound, FL: FEA Publishing, 1992.

Stolley, K. S. "Statistics on Adoption in the United States." *The Future of Children* 3 (1993): 26–42.

U.S. Census Bureau. *Adopted Children and Stepchildren: 2000.* Washington, DC: U.S. Census Bureau, 2003.

Infertility and Adoption

Sun Yung Shin and Vern L. Bullough

Becoming pregnant is not unlike a game of chance; one must beat the odds by maintaining all components in good working order, and the timing must be correct. About 85 percent of the couples earnestly seeking to have a child conceive within a year, and another 5 percent do so within eighteen months.

Those who do not conceive within a year are now advised to seek help from the medical profession. Infertility is not a woman's problem, and it can be associated with either the male or female, or both partners. It is estimated that 30–40 percent of infertility problems involve males while 40–50 percent involve females. Between 5 and 10 percent involve both partners, and in many case the causes are simply not known. In a small minority of cases, probably less than 5 percent, infertility is related to psychological or emotional factors. For example, stress might increase the production of the gonadotropin releasing factor (GNRF) which may lead to a woman not being able to produce an egg.

A very common misconception about infertility relates to adoption. Many people seem to have heard of a couple who have adopted a baby and almost immediately thereafter became pregnant. The unfounded conclusion is that adoption somehow increases fertility. This is not true although if stress was a major factor, as it is in a number of couples, it is possible that the removal of the pressure to reproduce can have a positive effect. Inability to conceive might be caused by infection, anatomical defects, physical injuries, drugs, and many other factors including misunderstanding of the fertility cycle.

In the past, the only alternative for those couples who wanted children was to adopt them. This changed in 1978 when the world's first "test tube" baby was born in Manchester, England as a result of in vitro fertilization (IFV). The success rate for IVF is between 15 and 20 percent. Other technologies have developed such as *Gamete intrafallopian transfer (GIFT)* which uses surgically retrieved eggs and "washed" sperm. The success rate for this procedure is nearly twice as high as IVF since fertilization and beginning development take place in the fallopian tube and is later implanted in the uterus of the woman. There are other variations including *tubal embryo transfer* (TET) and *zygote intrafallopian transfer* (ZIFT). In both of these procedures, fertilization takes place outside the body.

Since these procedures are not always successful, the alternatives of adoption, surrogacy, or a decision to remain childless, remain. Surrogacy involves a woman who acts as mother in place of another. The surrogate gets pregnant, carries the infant for nine months, and then turns the child over to the social mother. Sometimes the biological father's semen is used in the pregnancy while, at other times, the semen of a donor is used. Surrogate motherhood first reached national consciousness in 1976 when a Michigan lawyer, Noel Keane, began recruiting potential surrogate mothers who, for a fee as well as altruistic feelings, would carry a child for someone else. Surrogacy often has complications and problems, and a number of lawsuits have developed.

The more traditional and still widely used way to parent in the face of infertility is adoption, although the number of newborns available began to decrease drastically after the legalization of abortion. Also important in decreasing the number of newborns was the increasing unwillingness of many mothers of illegitimate children to give up their babies for adoption; instead, they kept and raised the children themselves. One result of this was the growth of both international and transracial adoptions as well as the adoption of older children.

As families become smaller and as women increasingly enter the working force, childlessness (or remaining "child-free") has also become more acceptable. The lack of children is much less a social stigma, and a small but growing number of couples look to their families and friends to give them an opportunity to have contact with children and prefer not to have children of their own.

See also Assisted Reproductive Technologies and Adoption; Surrogacy and Adoption.

Further Reading

Freeman, Sarah, and Vern L. Bullough. *Fertility and Family Planning*. Buffalo: Prometheus Books, 1993.

Informal Adoption

Vern L. Bullough

Informal adoption has been an almost universal custom in history. Laws regulating adoption in fact only were enacted in fairly recent time. Although Roman law countries always recognized adoption, English common law did not, and it was not until the nineteenth century that some states began to legally recognize adoption. Usually the adoption was by relatives or friends, but in the case of abandoned children, it was by someone who was impressed by them or saw economic advantage in taking them in. During the time of Biblical Moses, on the contrary, infants were rarely adopted (even informally) because of the problem of feeding an infant. However, if a woman had lost her own infant and could, therefore, nurse a child or had enough milk to supply more than one child, informal adoption often took place. The abandoned children in ancient Greece were often adopted, and perhaps even passed off, by the mother as her own, although it was a matter in which the courts did not play a role.

The problem with informal adoption was that, unless arrangements had been made by the birth mother or birth parents, the "adopted child" had no legal rights to inheritance in the new family unless it was specifically specified in the will of the adoptive parents or had been negotiated by the mother giving up the child. Another difficulty with informal adoption was that birth parents could come back months, or even years, later to reclaim the child unless specific documents or agreements prevented them from doing so. If such documents were made, it was not really an informal adoption, although it did not take place in the courts.

Probably the most common informal adoption was between relatives and, even today, many states do not require a complete home study for such adoptions. In the nineteenth century, it was the preferred way to adopt a child. Often the adoption is concealed from the child if adoption took place early in life, although it was still often known by other adult family members. One advantage of adoption by relatives is that the birth parent(s) feels the child will be safe and loved by a family member (often the grandparents) and the birth parent(s) can perhaps have some influence on how the child develops and keep track of the child. The main disadvantage is that other family members, knowing of the adoption, might make it difficult for the adoptive parents to form a strong relationship with the child.

In a sense, the adopted child in an informal adoption is comparable to a step-child since the adoption is never fully completed for financial or other reasons. If the biological father had not been part of the decision, he might still be responsible for child support, and if the relatives formally adopted the child he would not have to contribute. Most informal adoptions in today's world take place at lower income levels in society and among blacks and Hispanics. Even here, however, informal adoptions have been decreasing as adoption practices in the U.S. and elsewhere have become more formalized.

Further Reading

Bachrach, Christine A., Kathryn A. London, and Penelope L. Maza. "On the Path to Adoption: Adoption Seeking in the United States, 1988." *Journal of Marriage and the Family* 53 (1991): 705–718.

Hamm, Maria Suarez. "Latino Adoption Issues." *Adoption Factbook III*. National Council for Adoption: Washington, DC, 1999: 257–260.

Hill, Robert. *Informal Adoption among Black Families*. Washington, DC: National Urban League, 1977.

Kalmuss, Debra. "Adoption and Black Teenagers: The Viability of a Pregnancy Resolution Strategy." *Journal of Marriage and the Family* 54 (1992): 485–495.

Stack, Carol. *All Our Kin: Strategies for Survival in a Black Community*. New York: Harper and Row, 1974.

Primary Document

Informal Adoption In an African-American Community

In the following excerpt from her book, *All Our Kin: Strategies for Survival in a Black Community*, Carol B. Stack explains the system of "child-keeping" in The Flats (a pseudonym for a community in which she lived and studied for several years). This form of informal adoption was an important part of the structure of life within the community and has been well-documented among African American and some other groups.

Examples of Child-Keeping

Violet did not have enough money with her to buy tickets to travel out of the state. In fact, she only had enough money to buy one-way tickets to Chicago. She and her daughters took the bus to Chicago and she called one of her closest girl friends, Samantha, to pick them up at the bus station. Violet and her daughters stayed with Samantha and her three children for nearly a month.

Violet and Samantha considered themselves kin. They lived down the street from one another while they were growing up, attended the same schools, and dated boys who were close cousins or best friends. Five years ago, just after Samantha gave birth to her second child, she became very ill. Violet insisted upon "taking" Samantha's year-old son in order to help her. Scene Six was told to me by Violet three years after the event.

Scene Six

That day I went over to visit Samantha, I don't know how the good Lord tell me, since I hadn't been seeing her for some time. The last old man she had didn't like me, so I stayed away. He sure was no good. Left her right before the baby come.

I went over to her place. She had a small, dark little room with a kitchen for herself and those two babies. The place look bad and smell bad. I knew she was hurting. I took one look around and said to her, "Samantha, I'm going to take your boy." I hunted up some diapers and left the house with her year-old son. She didn't come by my place for over a month, but her younger sister brought me a message that Samantha was feeling better. A week or two later she came by to visit. Her boy hardly knew her. She came by more often, but she still seemed pretty low. I told her one day, "Samantha, I don't have any sons, just daughters, so why don't you just give me this boy." She said that if he didn't favor his father so much she'd let me keep him, but she was still crazy over that man. Her boy stayed with me three or four months, then she came and got him. Soon afterwards she moved to Chicago with her two kids and her new old man.

When friends in The Flats have good social dealings with one another they often call each other by kin terms and conduct their social relations as if they were kinsmen. Close kin form alliances with one another to cope with daily needs. Close friends assume the same style of dealing with one another. Samantha and Violet shared an exchange of goods and services over the years and lived up to one another's expectations. They obligated, tested, and trusted one another.

The exchange of children, and short-term fosterage, are common among female friends. Child-care arrangements among friends imply both rights and duties. Close friends frequently discipline each other's children verbally and physically in front of each other. In normal times, and in times of stress, close friends have the right to "ask" for one another's children. A woman visiting a friend and her children may say, "Let me keep your girl this week. She will have a fine time with me and my girls. She won't want to come back home to her mama." This kind of request among kin and friends is very difficult to refuse.

Temporary child-care services are also a means of obligating kin or friends for future needs. Women may ask to "keep" the child of a friend for no apparent reason. But they are, in fact, building up an investment for their future needs. From this perspective it is clear that child-keeping in The Flats is both an expression of shared kin obligations toward children and an important feature of the distribution and exchange of the limited resources available to poor people in The Flats.

* * *

Close female kinsmen in The Flats do not expect a single person, the natural mother, to carry out by herself all of the behavior patterns which "motherhood" entails. When transactions between females over the residence, care and discipline of children run smoothly, it is difficult to clarify the patterns of rights and duties to which kin and non-kin are entitled. But scenes in which these rights and duties come into conflict show which behaviors may be shared.

* * *

These social positions represent the composite of typical parental behaviors which may be shared primarily among a child's close female kinsmen. They are categories of behavior which have predictable, non-legal rights and obligations.

Economic providers are expected to share in providing subsistence and scarce goods, daily meals, food stamps, a bed, a blanket, clothes and shoes. Discipliners (primarily women) are allowed to participate in the control of children. At their own discretion they may beat—usually with a green branch stripped of leaves—threaten, terrify, blame, or scare children for unacceptable social behavior. Trainers not only discipline but teach moral values and respect for adults. They instruct by example, teaching children the consequences of their acts. A girl is taught to sit like a lady—even a two-year-old would be slapped for sitting with her legs apart, or a three-year-old boy might be chastised for hugging or touching a two-year-old girl. The consequences are taught by trainers by harsh, clear example.... Curers provide folk remedies for physical ailments. They have the right to attempt

to heal rashes with a little lye or detergent in the bath water, remove warts, pull teeth, and cure stomach ailments of children with "persnickety"—a pungent brew made from tobacco and added to the baby's milk. A groomer has the obligation to care for the children, wash clothing, and check the children's bodies for rashes and diseases. In addition to eligible adults, older females are also expected to groom younger children.

Adult females who share parental rights in children are recruited from participants in the personal domestic networks of the child's mother. This includes cognatic kin to the mother, the child, and close friends. Social roles such as that of provider were often shared; thus, responsibilities were seen to have composite elements and the various parts could be assumed by more than one individual. For example, a woman who lived next door to Ruby left her three children with her sister. The sister fed and clothed the children, took them to the doctor, and made all the other necessary decisions with respect to their lives. But, the rights that eligible kinsmen or close friends share in one another's children are not equal. Other factors such as economics and interpersonal relationships within domestic networks come into play. In white middle-class families, on the other hand, few persons, not even kin, would be authorized or would feel free to participate in health care or disciplinary behavior with regard to children without specific permission or transfer (care of a child in case of a parent's illness), or except in the case of an emergency.

Source

Excerpted from Stack, Carol B. *All Our Kin: Strategies for Survival in a Black Community.* New York: Harper Torchbooks/Harper and Row, 1974: pp. 81–85. Reprinted by permission of Westview Press, a member of Persus Books, L.L.C.

Inheritance and Adoption

Naomi Cahn

When a child is adopted, she becomes the legal child of her adoptive parents. At the same time, all ties with her biological parents are terminated (aside from situations involving adoption-with-contact agreements). If her parents die intestate, or without a will, there is generally no distinction between her rights as an adoptee and the rights of biological children to inherit from their parents. If the parents have drafted a will, then her status is also irrelevant, and she inherits property based on the provisions of the will. This entry discusses the general rules of intestate inheritance, of what happens to adoptees when their parents die without a will. Although the general principles of adoption law support a "fresh start" for the adoptee in her new family, the laws of inheritance are not always consistent in providing this fresh start.

Inheritance Rights

Historically, under the common law approach to inheritance prior to the mid-nineteenth century, only a legitimate, blood-related child served as his or her father's heir. Indeed, this was so strongly embedded in the law that illegitimate children were deemed to have "no" blood, and were thus incapable of inheriting unless a will provided otherwise. To ensure that adopted children were treated as legitimate heirs, the early adoption statutes of the mid-nineteenth century often explicitly provided that the adopted child was, with certain exceptions, the heir of his [sic] adoptive parents, and not of the biological parents. Yet they also provided that the adoptive parents could not inherit from the child. In addition, there were a series of differences between the other inheritance rights of adoptees and biological relatives. While some early statutes provided that adopted children would have the same inheritance rights as "natural children," others distinguished between the rights of the two different types of children. First, some statutes specifically distinguished between the rights of adopted and biological children to inherit from their parents. Second, historically, under the "stranger-to-the-adoption" rule, an adopted child generally could not inherit through relatives who were not a party to the adoption. This meant that they could not inherit from relatives of their parents. Third, adoptive children could continue to inherit from their biological relatives in some states, and their biological relatives could inherit from them even after the adoption. Finally, even outside the general laws of intestacy and wills, some statutes allowed the adoption agreement itself to determine the adoptee's rights.

During the twentieth century, every state eventually amended their statutes to accord more fully equal treatment to biological and adopted children for purposes of intestacy, class gifts (such as gifts "to all my children"), and other donative dispositions. Nonetheless, the scope of adoptees' intestacy rights remained difficult throughout the century.

Even today, however, the intestacy rights of an adopted child remain complicated. Inheritance follows blood, stated the South Dakota Supreme Court in 1978. In Vermont, until the 1996 case of *MacCallum v. Seymour*, an adopted child could inherit from her parents, but, unlike biological children, could not inherit from any relatives of her adopted parents who had died intestate. In Mississippi, the right of adoptees to inherit from such collateral relatives is still unclear. In some states, depending on the phrasing of the will, an adopted child may not be able to inherit through a "class gift," or a gift that is phrased as, for example, to my "descendants" or to my "grandchildren" without specifically naming members of the class. In at least one state, an adoptee may inherit from her biological parents if there are no other heirs. In another state, when the biological relatives—other than the parents—have maintained a relationship with the adoptee, then she may inherit from those relatives. In other states, an adoption decree can itself protect the child's rights to inherit from her biological family.

Nonetheless, both the new Uniform Adoption Act, promulgated in 1994, and the Uniform Probate Code (2002 version), which is model legislation for inheritance purposes, treat adoptees as fully equivalent to biological children for purposes of intestacy and all donative dispositions, including class gifts, as well as for purposes of receiving wrongful death and other public or third party benefits from the estate of an adoptive parent or collateral adoptive relative. The Uniform Adoption Act provides what has become the standard rule in most states: "... each adoptive parent and the adoptee have the legal relationship of parent and child and have all the rights and duties of that relationship," (Section 1-104) including, as the Comments note, the rights to intestate succession and inheritance by, from, and through each other.

Adoptees and Stepfamilies

At the same time, many states provide an important exception for children adopted by stepparents from the now general rule that adoption severs the legal and economic ties between adoptees and their biological or former legal families. This is particularly important because the number of children who live in stepfamilies is rapidly increasing. Stepparent adoptions can only occur after the rights of one of the biological parents has been terminated: the adoption may take place after the death of one of the biological parents, or as a result of the relinquishment or involuntary termination of parental rights by the non-custodial biological parent. While the term "stepparent" may, in popular culture, refer to any partner of one of the child's biological parents, it has a different meaning within the law. A legal stepparent is someone who adopts when one of the biological parents relinquishes custodial rights, and that stepparent then becomes the second parent. It is estimated that more than 40 percent of all domestic adoptions are by a stepparent, and that 50 percent of all adoptions are by a person related to the child.

Stepparent adoptions raise two distinct legal issues for inheritance purposes: first, can a stepparent adopt without terminating the right of the child to inherit from the stepparent's partner who is a biological parent? And second, can the child inherit from the biological parent whose rights have been terminated? With respect to this first issue, most state statutes do allow a stepparent to adopt without terminating the rights of the biological parent who is the stepparent's partner. They create a specific exemption for this type of adoption. The Uniform Probate Code (UPC), the model statute that governs inheritance, explicitly protects the child's relationship with the existing legal parent who is the stepparent's spouse, stating that the adoption by the biological parent's spouse does not affect "the relationship between the child and that natural [sic] parent."

Turning to the second issue, some states allow the child to inherit from the biological parent whose rights have been terminated. According to this approach, adoptees can inherit from both biological parents as well as a legal stepparent. Under the UPC, a child adopted by the spouse of one of her legal parents (legal parents are either adoptive or biological parents) can still inherit from her other biological parent, even though all legal ties have otherwise been severed between that parent and the child. The purpose of the UPC intestacy statute, as with other intestacy schemes, is to determine the decedent's probable intent, in the absence of a valid will explicitly setting out that intent. These statutes may serve to protect a child's relationship with her biological kin, but seem to reflect an assumption that the decedent would prefer that her estate be left to a blood relative, even one that has been adopted by other parents, rather than to more distant relatives.

States have taken other approaches to the rights of a child adopted by her stepparent to inherit from her other biological or former adoptive parent. Some states do not address the issue at all; the assumption is that the adoption completely terminates the right of the child to inherit from the biological parent whose rights have been terminated. States that do address the issue have developed provisions that differ from those of the UPC.

Under one alternative model, the stepparent exception is limited to situations where the other parent has died. If the stepparent adoption occurs while the biological parent whose rights have been terminated is still living, then the adoptee does not inherit from that biological parent.

Under another model, the stepparent exception applies only if the biological parent and child had some relationship prior to the adoption. In California, an adoptee can inherit through a biological parent whose rights have been terminated if the adoption is by a stepparent and the child either lived with the biological parent in a familial relationship, or the biological parent was married to or cohabiting with the other natural parent at the time the person was conceived and died before the person's birth. California also allows the adoptee to inherit if the adoption occurred after the death of one of the biological parents.

As a result of these various provisions, an adoptee can inherit from and through three family lines: the biological parent with whom the child and the adoptive stepparent live, the adoptive stepparent, and the noncustodial biological parent. Among the purposes of these statutes are to address some of the complexities of "blended" stepfamilies, and specifically, to protect a child's relationship with her noncustodial former parent's relatives.

While the general rule is that children cannot inherit from family members unless they have been legally adopted, in some states, even without a formal adoption, adoptees have been able to inherit from their parents' partners. For gay and lesbian partners unable to adopt, these alternatives may allow the child to be treated like adoptees in stepparent adoptions. For example, a California statute provides that children can inherit from their foster or stepparents if the parent-child relationship began during the child's minority and continued throughout the lifetimes of both parent and child, and if there is strong evidence that the parent would have adopted the child if there had been no legal barrier to doing so. For gay and lesbian parents, the Uniform Adoption Act allows them to be treated as a stepparent if there is good cause to do so. Under such a circumstance, the adoptee would still inherit from the biological parent whose rights had been terminated.

Children who have not been legally adopted may also inherit from three lines if there has been an "equitable" adoption, a doctrine which is recognized in more than half of the states. In such cases, a foster parent or stepparent has agreed to adopt a child, but the adoption process has not been complete. Under the doctrine of equitable adoption, the child may be still able to inherit from the stepparent but in other states, has the same status as any other adoptee.

Regarding other relative adoptions, in some states courts can preserve a child's right to inherit from the biological parents, particularly where the adoption is by relatives of children whose parents have died. The adoption decree can thus specify the child's rights to inherit from and through the biological former parent. Nonetheless, under contemporary law, when their parents die without a will, adoptees are increasingly given the same inheritance rights as biological children.

Finally, it is important to note that parents can draft wills and other testamentary documents (such as trusts) to establish how they want their estates to be distributed. In that case, adoptees have no special rights.

See also Stepparent Adoption.

Further Reading

Cahn, Naomi. "Perfect Substitute or the Real Thing?" *Duke Law Journal* 52 (2003): 1077–1144.

Cahn, Naomi, and Joan H. Hollinger. *Families by Law: An Adoption Reader.* New York: New York University, 2004.

Hampton, Lawrence P. "The Aftermath of Adoption: The Economic Consequences—Support, Inheritances and Taxes." In *Adoption Law and Practice*, edited by Joan Heifetz Hollinger. New York: Matthew Bender, 2004.

National Conference of Commissioners on Uniform States Laws. Uniform Adoption Act (1994). http://www.law.upenn.edu/bll/ulc/fnact99/1990s/uaa94.htm

National Conference of Commissioners on Uniform States Laws. Uniform Probate Code (2003).

Institutionalizing Parentless Children: The Current Debate

Vern L. Bullough

In the past, institutionalizing parentless children in orphanages was standard practice in the United States. Federal law as it now exists favors foster homes and adoption for such children, but there are also advocates of orphanages. One of the major spokesmen for the reconstitution of orphanages is Richard McKenzie, an economics professor at the University of California, Irvine. Raised in an orphanage himself, he wrote of the experience in *The Home: A Memoir of Growing Up in an Orphanage.* Since then, he has spoken widely on the topic and has seen several communities adopt his ideas, although such institutions are no longer called orphanages but usually go by the name of "home," "community," or "center." One such institution under construction in 2005 in California has taken the name of "Children's Village."

McKenzie did a survey of two thousand five hundred people raised in orphanages and found that, for the most part, his respondents outpaced their counterparts of the same racial and age group in the general populations on practically all measures, not the least of which were education, income, and attitudes toward life. His survey findings, however, have been criticized because they came from people who attended orphanage reunions and left out the many thousands of those who did not enjoy orphanages, including his own brother who was raised in the same orphanage as he was and who disagrees with him. Still, McKenzie argues that the foster care system as it now exists in the United States is in difficulty and that the best solution is to recognize this and go to a new kind of orphanage institution.

Disagreeing with him are individuals like Madelyn Freundlich, a social worker and former policy director for Children's Rights, a national legal group that monitors foster care programs that, as of this writing, serves more than half a million children. Though the group has filed eleven lawsuits against state-run foster and child welfare programs claiming neglect and frequent abuse, she argues that it is better to fix the system than discard it in favor of new orphanages which she said disappeared for a good reason. Freundlich cites horror stories of foster care with children found starving in New Jersey and Texas, a five-year-old foster child suffocated with duct tape in Maine, and the list goes on, but emphasizes these cases have been dealt with and settled. She argues that research has concluded that orphanages do not provide greater safety than foster homes, and that they can deprive youngsters of long-term, caring relationships.

Some who support part of McKenzie's ideas, such as the Coalition for Residential Education, a non-profit organization that promotes boarding schools for at-risk children (including those in foster care), feel that "residential schools" are fitting only for adolescents who have been failed by foster care, as well as other neglected children, and are not at all suitable for younger ones. Freundlich argues that the family setting is best and, rather than building institutions, money should be spent to help families who need help to stay together. Even John Koppelmeyer, the administrator of the Barium Spring Home in which McKenzie was raised as an orphan and which is now a treatment center for abused and neglected children, argues that the best way to assure that children achieve a healthy, safe, and nurturing place to be is in the family setting. He, himself, is continually seeking foster parents for his recovering wards. Most authorities would agree that adoption, when there are no legal impediments to it, would be even better.

See also Orphanages.

Further Reading

D'Antonio, Michael. "The Upside of Orphanages." *Los Angeles Times Magazine*, November 27, 2005: 25–26, 48.

McKenzie, Richard. *The Home: A Memoir of Growing Up in an Orphanage*. New York: Basic Books, 1996.

International Adoption (Overview)

Anna M. Mandalakas and Victor Groza

International adoption has dramatically increased and changed over the past two decades. Since 1990, Americans have adopted roughly one hundred seventy thousand children from overseas according to the State Department, including twenty-one thousand children in 2003 alone. The 2000 Census estimates that there are over 2 million adopted children in the United States, 13 percent adopted from foreign countries.

During this same period, the demographics of international adoption have significantly changed. Prior to the 1990s, children typically came from Korea, India, the Philippines, and Latin America. J. A. Jenista reports that these children were generally less than one year of age and frequently came from foster care or small orphanage settings. Since 1990, as noted by V. Groza, K. Rosenberg and L. Houlihan, and the State Department, children have been primarily adopted from Asia (50 percent), former Soviet Republics (Russia and Eastern European countries, 30 percent) and Central/South America (<10 percent).

International adoption is fueled by a variety of social, political, and cultural pressures. Most countries that allow large numbers of children to be placed internationally are countries in transition. Many South American countries are developing democracies after ending military dictatorships. Former Soviet Republics are transitioning from state economies to private market economies after the fall of communism.

Of note, transition is not the major reason that children are available for international adoption in Asian countries. As noted by P. Selman and by J. W. Rojewski, M. S. Shapiro, and M. Shapiro respectively, family policy that limits the number of biologic children and strong cultural values favoring male children, coupled with a very weak domestic adoption program, results in thousands of abandoned Chinese female infants and toddlers each year. While initially developed to deal with the problem of orphans after the Korean War, Selman notes that the practice of placing children abroad for international adoption has continued despite the fact that South Korea has a large and affluent middle class living in relative peace. Cultural factors such as stigma against adopting non-related children also continue to influence international adoption policy in South Korea.

While sending countries may change, international adoption will likely continue to color the adoption mosaic in the United States. Although the impact of the U.S. implementation of the Hague Convention is unclear, U.S. families will likely continue to adopt children from overseas barring any major world event.

The pre-adoptive experience of domestically and internationally adopted children is markedly different and has significant life-long implications for children and families. The vast majority of sending countries have children residing in some type of group care before they are placed for adoption. South Korea is the only sending country that currently utilizes a family-based system of substitute care (i.e., foster care). Thus, it is imperative to understand the impact of institutional life on children subsequently placed for adoption.

Effects of Institutionalization on Children

As discussed by a number of sources available in the "Further Reading" section, institutionalization early in life delays emotional, social, sensory, and physical development. Institutionalization increases the likelihood that children will become adults with psychiatric impairments. In addition, learning problems such as poor reading ability and deficits in intellectual functioning have been reported. Children who have spent time in an institution are also at increased risk for various behavior problems. As age increases, the likelihood of emotional and behavioral problems increases.

However, some research such as that discussed by S. L. Judge suggests that institutionalization may not lead to emotional problems. W. Goldfarb (1945) found that some children from institutions were socially and emotionally well adjusted. M. L. Pringle and V. Bossio found that about one-third of previously institutionalized children were well adjusted. S. W. Wolkind found that most children were not antisocial. B. Tizard and J. Rees, and B. Tizard and J. Hodges found no difference in the prevalence of behavior problems in institutionalized children as compared to children from working class families. In a subsequent follow-up, Tizard and Hodges demonstrated that attachment behavior, cognitive development, and emotional difficulty are positively affected by the family after institutionalization. Recovery depends on family environment, social class, and parents' willingness to devote a significant amount of time to their children. C. Beckett and colleagues indicate that there are marked individual differences in response to early deprivation, including complete recovery from severe difficulties. These findings underscore the importance of re-evaluating linear cause-effect theories about the influence of early negative experiences after radical improvements in care. Additionally, these findings offer caution about examining international adoptees (abbreviated IAs) as a group since within group differences can be quite dramatic.

Nonetheless, early negative experiences place IAs at significant risk for a multitude of problems. It is critical that adoption professionals and mental health practitioners characterize the early history of the adoptee and recognize the potential impact of their experiences.

Health and Medical

The quality of care received by children prior to adoption varies. Many of these children have lived in institutional settings that are crowded and have poor resources with limited access to medical care. Orphanage directors are frequently challenged by the delivery of basic requirements including adequate nutrition and hygiene. Subsequently, children suffer from malnutrition, psychosocial deprivation and transmissible diseases. As a result of these insults, children have significant risk of developing a number of health problems.

From 1990 to 1993, Romania provided the greatest number of IAs. The complicated health issues of Romanian adoptees were well documented by D. Johnson and colleagues and included hepatitis, tuberculosis, syphilis, skin infections, and intestinal parasites. A longitudinal study of Romanian adoptees by C. Beckett and team found medical problems in 50 percent at adoption and persistent problems four years later including problems with hearing (17 percent), skin (35 percent), strabismus (12 percent) and, hepatitis B (6 percent). This led to a belief that *only* children from the former communist countries were medically-complicated children. L. C. Miller and N. W. Hendrie challenged this assumption when they demonstrated that children from China exhibited similar medical problems and patterns of developmental delay.

Regardless of birth country, IAs are now recognized to be at risk for a variety of problems and benefit from focused medical attention. The American Academy of Pediatrics (AAP) recommends careful screening of all IAs for hepatitis B and C virus, tuberculosis, intestinal parasites, HIV, congenital syphilis, and lead poisoning. However, according to L. C. Miller (1999), a surprising number of children do not receive appropriate evaluation. Although specialty clinics exist, most children receive their post-adoptive evaluation and care from primary care physicians who may not be aware of current recommendations.

Development

During the first half of gestation through the first three years of life, brain development occurs that is crucial to focusing attention and inhibition—skills that are critical for planning, problem solving, and sound critical judgment. IAs are at risk for exposure to a number of hazards to early brain development including malnutrition, lead poisoning, hyprothyroidism, infectious diseases, and pre-natal alcohol and drug exposure. Children who have lived in institutional settings are also at increased risk of severe abuse or deprivation, which have also been linked to poor brain development and cognitive function.

Recent research suggests that modifications in the quality of care may dramatically improve developmental outcomes. M. Rutter and colleagues found that four-year-old Romanian adoptees experienced dramatic recovery in cognitive development after two years in their adoptive homes despite months to years of early deprivation. Factors that appear to modify developmental outcomes include the length of institutionalization and quality of the pre- and post-adoptive environments.

Attachment and Psychosocial Functioning

Adverse pre-adoptive experiences have a direct impact on the psychosocial development of IAs as documented in material throughout the "Further Reading" section. In combination with potential genetic predispositions, social-behavioral characteristics of IAs can result in a pattern of relating and responding that is incongruent with the expectations and skills of adoptive parents. Such patterns of mismatched parent-child interaction further exacerbate these children's risk for developmental and socio-emotional problems.

Early parent-child attachment process tends to be more problematic in adoptive families than in birth families and is also well-documented. Such problematic attachment relationships are associated with a higher risk of later behavior problems. Conversely, sensitive responsiveness (the ability to observe and respond to a baby's signals adequately, appropriately, and promptly) is one of the key determinants of a secure attachment relationship. The association between parental sensitivity and infant-parent attachment has been empirically established. Adopted children who were more securely attached to their parents attained better social and cognitive outcomes; additionally, their parents displayed greater sensitive responsiveness.

Supporting Families That Adopt Internationally

Adoption is a life-long process. Families adopting internationally and domestically benefit from different pre-adoption preparation and post-adoption supports. To optimize long-term outcomes, families adopting internationally should be prepared for possible challenges and have realistic expectations. As covered by V. Groza, preparation should have formal educational components focusing on: (a) the adoption process; (b) issues unique to life as an adoptive family; (c) developmental, health, and behavior risks; and (d) services that strengthen their lives as adoptive families. Preparation should also be informal, allowing families to meet with other adoptive families, so they can cognitively process and prepare for the issues they might encounter. In addition, families benefit dramatically from post-adoption support and access to professionals aware of the unique health needs of IAs. Families often need case management to assist them in locating and accessing an array of services. While many complicated issues exist, international adoption offers a tremendous number of rewards. Most adoptions are successful, most children recover, and the quality of children's lives dramatically improves.

See also Adoption Medicine (Overview); Health Issues in Adoptions; Transracial and Intercountry Adoption.

Further Reading

Albers, L. H., D. E. Johnson, M. K. Hostetter. S. Iverson, and L. C. Miller. "Health of Children Adopted from the Former Soviet Union and Eastern Europe." *Journal of the American Medical Association* 278 (1997): 922–924.

American Academy of Pediatrics (AAP). "Medical Evaluation of Internationally Adopted Children." In *Red Book: 2003 Report of the Committee on Infectious Diseases*, edited by L. K. Pickering. Elk Grove Village: American Academy of Pediatrics, 2003. pp. 173–180.

Aronson, J. "Medical Evaluation and Infectious Considerations on Arrival." *Pediatric Annals*, 29 (2000): 218–223.

Beckett, C., J. Castle, C. Groothues, T. G. O'Connor, M. Rutter, and the E.R.A. "Health Problems in Children Adopted from Romania: Association with Duration of Deprivation and Behavioural Problems." *Adoption and Fostering* 27 (2003):19–28.

Bowlby, J. "Maternal Care and Mental Health." *World Health Organization Monograph No 2*. Geneva: WHO, 1951.

Carlson, M., and F. Earls. "Psychological and Neuroendocrinological Sequelae of Early Deprivation in Institutionalized Children in Romania." *Annals of the New York Academy of Sciences* 807 (1997): 419–428.

Cermak, S. and V. Groza. "Sensory Processing Problems in Post-Institutionalized Children: Implications for Social Work." *Child and Adolescent Social Work Journal* 15 (1998): 5–37.

Dalen, M. "School Performances Among Internationally Adopted Children in Norway." *Adoption Quarterly* 5 (2001): 39–57.

Dennis, W. *Children of the Creche*. New York: Appleton Century-Crofts, 1973.

Faber, S. "Behavioral Sequelae of Orphanage Life." *Pediatric Annals* 29 (2000): 242–248.

Frank, D. A., P. E. Klass, F. Earls, and L. Eisenberg. "Infants and Young Children in Orphanages: One View from Pediatrics and Child Psychiatry." *Pediatrics* 47 (1996): 569–578.

Freud, A., and D. T. Burlingham. *Infants without Families*. New York: International University Press, 1973.

Goldfarb, W. "Infant Rearing and Problem Behavior." *American Journal of Orthopsychiatry* 15 (1943): 249–265.

Goldfarb, W. "Effects of Early Institutional Care on Adolescent Personality: Rorschach Data." *American Journal of Orthopsychiatry* 14 (1944): 441–447.

Goldfarb, W. "Effects of Psychological Deprivation in Infancy and Subsequent Stimulation." *American Journal of Psychiatry* 102 (1945): 18–33.

Groza, V. "International Adoption." In *Encyclopedia of Social Work, 19th Edition, 1997 Supplement*, edited by R. L. Edwards. Washington, DC: NASW Press, 1997. pp. 1–14.

Groza, V., C. Proctor, and S. Guo. "The Relationship of Institutions to the Development of Romanian Children Adopted Internationally." *International Journal of Child and Family Welfare* 3 (1998): 198–217.

Groza, V., K. Rosenberg, and L. Houlihan. "International Adoptions." In *Clinical and Practice Issues in Adoption: Bridging the Gap Between Adoptees Placed as Infants and as Older Children, revised and expanded*, edited by V. Groza and K. Rosenberg. Westport, CT: Bergen and Garvey, 2001. pp. 187–206.

Groza, V., S. Ryan, and S. Cash. "Institutionalization, Behavior and International Adoption: Predictors of Behavior Problems." *Journal of Immigrant Health* 5 (2003): 5–17.

Hostetter, M.K. "Infectious Diseases in Internationally Adopted Children: Findings in Children from China, Russia and Eastern Europe." *Advances in Pediatric Infectious Diseases* 14 (1999): 147–161.

Jenista, J. A. "The Risks Are Many, But the Joys Are Great." *Pediatric Annals* 29 (2000): 208–209.

Jenista, J. A., and D. Chapman. "Medical Problems of Foreign-born Adopted Children." *American Journal of Diseases in Children* 141 (1987): 293–302.

Johnson D. "Post-Arrival Evaluation of International Adoptees." Sixth Conference of the International Society of Travel Medicine, Montreal, Canada, June 6–10, 1999.

Johnson, D., L. C. Miller, S. Iverson, S., W. Thomas, B. Franchino, K. Dole, et al. "The Health of Children Adopted from Romania." *Journal of the American Medical Association* 268 (1992): 3446–3451.

Johnson D. E. "Long-Term Medical Issues in International Adoptees." *Pediatric Annals* 29 (2000): 234–241.

Johnson, D. E., and K. Dole. "International Adoptions: Implications for Early Intervention." *Infants and Young Children* 11 (1999): 34–35.

Johnson, D. E., L. C. Miller, S. Iverson, et al. "The Health of Children Adopted from Romania." *JAMA* 268 (1992): 3446–3451.

Johnson, D. E., L. H. Albers, S. Iverson, et al. "Health Status of US Adopted Eastern European Orphans." *Pediatric Research* 1996; 39 (sup. part 4): Abstract 792.

Johnson, D. E., M. Traister, S. Iverson, K. Dole, M. K. Hostetter, and L. C. Miller. "Health Status of US Adopted Chinese Orphans." *Pediatric Research* 1996: Abstract 792.

Judge, S. L. "Eastern European Adoptions: Current Status and Implications for Intervention." *Topics in Early Childhood Special Education* 19 (1999): 244–252.

Kaler, S. R., and B. J. Freeman. "An Analysis of Environmental Deprivation: Cognitive and Social Development in Romanian Orphans." *Journal of Child Psychology and Psychiatry and Allied Disciplines* 35 (1994):769–81.

Kim, S. P., S. Hong, and B. S. Kim. "Adoption of Korean Children by New York Area Couples: A Preliminary Study." *Child Welfare* 63 (1979): 419–428.

Mapstone, E. "Children in Care." *Concern* 3 (1969), 23–28.

Miller L. C. "Caring for Internationally Adopted Children." *New England Journal of Medicine* 341 (1999): 1539–1540.

Miller L. C. "Initial Assessment of Growth, Development, and the Effects of Institutionalization in Internationally Adopted Children." *Pediatric Annals* 29 (2000): 224–232.

Miller, L. C., and N. W. Hendrie. "Health of Children Adopted from China." *Pediatrics* 105 (2000):1–6.

Pringle, M. L., and Bossio, V. "Early, Prolonged Separation and Emotional Adjustment." *Journal of Child Psychology and Psychiatry* (1960): 37–48.

Provence, S. A., and R. C. Lipton. *Infants in Institutions*. New York: International Universities Press, 1962.

Rojewski, J. W., M. S. Shapiro, and M. Shapiro. "Parental Assessment of Behavior in Chinese Adoptees During Early Childhood." *Child Psychiatry and Human Development* 31 (2000): 79–96.

Rutter, M., and the English and Romanian Adoptees Study Team. "Developmental Catch-up, and the Deficit, Following Adoption after Severe Global Early Deprivation." *Journal of Child Psychology and Child Psychiatry* 39 (1998): 465–476.

Selman, P. "The Demographic History of Intercountry Adoption." In P. Selman, ed., *International Adoption: Developments, Trends and Perspectives*. London: British Agencies for Adoption and Fostering, 2000: pp. 15–39.

Spitz, R. A. "Hospitalism: An Inquiry into the Genesis of Psychiatric Conditions in Early Childhood." *Psychoanalytic Study of the Child* 1 (1945): 53–74.

Tizard, B. "Intercountry Adoption: A Review of the Evidence." *Journal of Child Psychiatry and Psychology* 32 (1991): 743–756.

Tizard, B., and J. Hodges. "The Effect of Early Institutional Rearing on the Development of Eight-Year-Old Children." *Journal of Child Psychology and Psychiatry* 19 (1977): 99–118.

Tizard, B., and J. Rees. "A Comparison of the Effects of Adoption, Restoration to the Natural Mother, and Continued Institutionalization on the Cognitive Development of Four-Year-Old Children." *Child Development* 45 (1974): 92–99.

Tizard, B., and J. Rees. "The Effect of Early Institutional Rearing on the Behaviour Problems and Affectional Relationships of Four-Year-Old Children." *Journal of Child Psychology and Psychiatry* 75 (1975): 61–73.

U.S. Census Bureau. *Adopted Children and Stepchildren: 2000*. Washington, DC: U. S. Census Bureau, 2003.

U.S. Department of State. "Immigrant Visas Issued to Orphans Coming to the U.S." U.S. Department of State Web Site. http://travel.state.gov/family/adoption_resources_02.html (accessed November, 2004).

Wolkind, S. N. "The Components of 'Affectionless Psychopathy' in Institutionalized Children." *Journal of Child Psychology and Psychiatry* 15 (1974): 215–220.

Primary Document
Immigrant Visas Issued to Orphans Coming to the U.S.—1990–2005

Immigrant Visas Issued to Orphans Coming to the U.S. - 1990-2005
The U.S. State Department data for immigrant visas in this table shows the top countries of origin for orphans coming to the United States. The table indicates the number of visas and country of origin of the child for which those visas were issued in each cell.

	FY 2005	FY 2004	FY 2003	FY 2002	FY 2001	FY 2000	FY 1999	FY 1998
1	7,906 - CHINA (mainland)	7,044 - CHINA (mainland)	6,859 - CHINA (mainland)	5,053 - CHINA (mainland)	4,681 - CHINA (mainland)	5,053 - CHINA	4,348 - RUSSIA	4,491 - RUSSIA
2	4,639 - RUSSIA	5,865 - RUSSIA	5,209 - RUSSIA	4,939 - RUSSIA	4,279 - RUSSIA	4,269 - RUSSIA	4,101 - CHINA	4,206 - CHINA
3	3,783 - GUATEMALA	3,264 - GUATEMALA	2,328 - GUATEMALA	2,219 - GUATEMALA	1,870 - S - KOREA	1,794 - S - KOREA	2,008 - S - KOREA	1,829 - S - KOREA
4	1,630 - S. KOREA	1,716 - S. KOREA	1,790 - S - KOREA	1,779 - S - KOREA	1,609 - GUATEMALA	1,518 - GUATEMALA	1,002 - GUATEMALA	911 - GUATEMALA
5	821 - UKRAINE	826 - KAZAKHSTAN	825 - KAZAKHSTAN	1,106 - UKRAINE	1,246 - UKRAINE	1,122 - ROMANIA	895 - ROMANIA	603 - VIETNAM
6	755 - KAZAKHSTAN	723 - UKRAINE	702 - UKRAINE	819 - KAZAKHSTAN	782 - ROMANIA	724 - VIETNAM	709 - VIETNAM	478 - INDIA
7	441 - ETHIOPIA	406 - INDIA	472 - INDIA	766 - VIETNAM	737 - VIETNAM	659 - UKRAINE	500 - INDIA	406 - ROMANIA
8	323 - INDIA	356 - HAITI	382 - VIETNAM	466 - INDIA	672 - KAZAKHSTAN	503 - INDIA	323 - UKRAINE	351 - COLOMBIA
9	291 - COLOMBIA	289 - ETHIOPIA	272 - COLOMBIA	334 - COLOMBIA	543 - INDIA	402 - CAMBODIA	248 - CAMBODIA	249 - CAMBODIA
10	271 - PHILIPPINES	287 - COLOMBIA	250 - HAITI	260 - BULGARIA	407 - COLOMBIA	399 - KAZAKHSTAN	231 - COLOMBIA	200 - PHILIPPINES
11	231 - HAITI	202 - BELARUS	214 - PHILIPPINES	254 - CAMBODIA	297 - BULGARIA	246 - COLOMBIA	221 - BULGARIA	180 - UKRAINE
12	182 - LIBERIA	196 - PHILIPPINES	200 - ROMANIA	221 - PHILIPPINES	266 - CAMBODIA	214 - BULGARIA	195 - PHILIPPINES	168 - MEXICO
13	141 - CHINA (TAIWAN BORN)	110 - BULGARIA	198 - BULGARIA	187 - HAITI	219 - PHILIPPINES	173 - PHILIPPINES		151 - BULGARIA
14	98 - MEXICO	102 - POLAND	191 - BELARUS	169 - BELARUS	192 - HAITI	131 - HAITI		140 - DOMIN REP
15	73 - POLAND AND THAILAND (BOTH 73)	89 - MEXICO	135 - ETHIOPIA	168 - ROMANIA	158 - ETHIOPIA	106 - MEXICO		121 - HAITI
16	66 - BRAZIL	86 - LIBERIA	124 - CAMBODIA	105 - ETHIOPIA	129 - BELARUS	95 - ETHIOPIA		103 - BRAZIL
17	65 - NIGERIA	73 - NEPAL	97 - POLAND	101 - POLAND	86 - POLAND	88 - THAILAND		96 - ETHIOPIA
18	63 - JAMAICA	71 - NIGERIA	72 - THAILAND	67 - THAILAND	74 - THAILAND	83 - POLAND		84 - THAILAND
19	62 - NEPAL	69 - THAILAND and BRAZIL (both 69)	62 - AZERBAIJAN	65 - PERU	73 - MEXICO	79 - MOLDOVA		77 - POLAND
20	54 - MOLDOVA	57 - ROMANIA	61 - MEXICO	61 - MEXICO	51 - JAMAICA and LIBERIA (both 51)	60 - BOLIVIA		76 - LATVIA

	FY 1997	FY 1996	FY 1995	FY 1994	FY 1993	FY 1992	FY 1991	FY 1990
1	3,816 - RUSSIA	3,333 - CHINA	2,130 - CHINA	1,795 - KOREA	1,775 - KOREA	1,840 - KOREA	2,594 - ROMANIA	2,620 - KOREA
2	3,597 - CHINA	2,454 - RUSSIA	1,896 - RUSSIA	1,530 - RUSSIA	746 - RUSSIA	418 - GUATEMALA	1,818 - KOREA	631 - COLOMBIA
3	1,654 - S. KOREA	1,516 - KOREA	1,666 - KOREA	787 - CHINA	512 - GUATEMALA	404 - COLOMBIA	705 - PERU	440 - PERU
4	788 - GUATEMALA	555 - ROMANIA	449 - GUATEMALA	483 - PARAGUAY	426 - COLOMBIA	357 - PHILIPPINES	521 - COLOMBIA	421 - PHILIPPINES
5	621 - ROMANIA	427 - GUATEMALA	371 - INDIA	436 - GUATEMALA	412 - PARAGUAY	352 - INDIA	445 - INDIA	348 - INDIA
6	425 - VIETNAM	380 - INDIA	351 - PARAGUAY	412 - INDIA	360 - PHILIPPINES	324 - RUSSIA	393 - PHILIPPINES	302 - CHILE
7	352 - INDIA	354 - VIETNAM	350 - COLOMBIA	351 - COLOMBIA	331 - INDIA	309 - PERU	329 - GUATEMALA	282 - PARAGUAY
8	233 - COLOMBIA	258 - PARAGUAY	318 - VIETNAM	314 - PHILIPPINES	330 - CHINA	249 - HONDURAS	266 - CHILE	257 - GUATEMALA
9	163 - PHILIPPINES	255 - COLOMBIA	298 - PHILIPPINES	220 - VIETNAM	273 - UKRAINE	212 - PARAGUAY	234 - HONDURAS	228 - BRAZIL
10	152 - MEXICO	229 - PHILIPPINES	275 - ROMANIA	199 - ROMANIA	224 - PERU	206 - CHINA	190 - PARAGUAY	197 - HONDURAS
11	148 - BULGARIA	163 - BULGARIA	146 - BRAZIL	164 - UKRAINE	179 - HONDURAS	179 - CHILE	175 - BRAZIL	121 - ROMANIA
12	142 - HAITI	103 - BRAZIL	110 - BULGARIA	149 - BRAZIL	161 - BRAZIL	138 - BRAZIL	131 - THAILAND	112 - MEXICO
13	108 - LATVIA	82 - LATVIA	98 - LITHUANIA	97 - BULGARIA	133 - BULGARIA	121 - ROMANIA	123 - EL SALVADOR	105 - COSTA RICA
14	91 - BRAZIL	78 - LITHUANIA	95 - LITHUANIA	95 - LITHUANIA	124 - BOLIVIA	117 - EL SALVADOR	97 - MEXICO	103 - EL SALVADOR
15	82 - ETHIOPIA	77 - GEORGIA	90 - CHILE	94 - POLAND	110 - VIETNAM	109 - POLAND	92 - POLAND	100 - THAILAND
16	78 - LITHUANIA	76 - MEXICO	83 - MEXICO	85 - MEXICO	100 - ELSALVADOR	91 - BULGARIA	87 - JAPAN	66 - POLAND
17	78 - POLAND	68 - HAITI	67 - ECUADOR	79 - CHILE	97 - ROMANIA	91 - MEXICO	61 - CHINA	66 - TAIWAN
18	77 - BOLIVIA	64 - POLAND	63 - ETHIOPIA	77 - HONDURAS	91 - MEXICO	86 - THAILAND	60 - CAMBODIA	64 - HAITI
19	72 - HUNGARY	63 - CHILE	63 - JAPAN	61 - HAITI	70 - POLAND	73 - BOLIVIA	56 - COSTA RICA	59 - ECUADOR
20	66 - CAMBODIA	55 - THAILAND	59 - LATVIA	54 - ETHIOPIA	69 - THAILAND	68 - JAPAN	54 - TAIWAN	58 - DOMINICAN REP
		51 - ECUADOR,HUNGARY	51 - GEORGIA	49 - JAPAN	64 - JAPAN	64 - COSTA RICA	50 - DOMINICAN REP	57 - JAPAN

Source: Immigrant Visas Issued to Orphans Coming to the U.S. [Online, February 2006]. U.S. Department of State Web Site <http://travel.state.gov/family/adoption/stats/stats_451.html>.

The Blumenfeld Case

Vern L. Bullough

The Blumenfield Case was an important case that helped change the laws on international adoptions. Gloria and Myron Blumenfeld, who had a seven-year-old daughter, decided they would adopt a second child since it was unlikely they would have a second one biologically. Since they had a child, most adoption agencies were reluctant to consider them for any local adoption, so they turned abroad. The United States had, in 1961, passed a law stipulating that an adopted orphan could be brought into the United States as a non-quota entry.

In Greece, the Blumenfelds found an infant boy whom they intended to name Joshua. In going to the embassy, however, they found that adoption would not be approved until their suitability as parents was investigated, something that would take a month to six weeks. They began the process of adoption and, after a month, received clearance from the Justice Department to adopt.

When he went to the embassy to obtain a visa for Joshua, Blumenfeld found that questions on the forms asked the baby's race and ethnic classification. It also asked whether the baby had ever been a prostitute. When he returned home, he began a campaign to eliminate race and ethnic classification on the two forms (known as FS 510 and FS 497) and to have would-be adoptive parents investigated before they departed for a foreign country to adopt a child.

On the second issue, he was almost immediately successful. In May 1963 the government put into effect pre-investigations for adoptive parents. The matter of race and ethnicity was more complicated. Interestingly, Blumenfeld found that, in 1961, such questions had already been eliminated, and the bureaucracy in the State Department had not known about it. By 1965, the forms had been revised to reflect the new policy, previously ignored. An official of the American Civil Liberties Union (ACLU), reflecting on the issues Blumenthal raised, said that if anyone should get real credit for making international adoptions much easier, the credit should belong to Blumenfeld and that his perseverance "deserves an accolade."

Further Reading

Rogers, John G. "Man Fights U.S., Wins After Adoption Ordeal." *Los Angeles Times*, January 10, l965, F-8.

International Adoption Agencies

Susan Soon-keum Cox

Traditional Role of Agencies in International Adoption

Adoption agencies placing children internationally typically provide direct services to adoptive families in the United States (adoption study and post-placement) as well as working directly with the overseas side of the process. Some U.S. adoption agencies have individuals or organizations in the sending country representing them and facilitating the overseas process. This may include being the source of the children to be adopted, providing social work and legal services, and working with the families when they travel to the country to adopt their child.

International adoption agencies often collaborate with an existing private or public orphanage or institution overseas to place children for adoption. Generally, the U.S. agency will provide financial support for childcare and other related services. If the orphanage or institution overseas is a public facility under the jurisdiction of local government authorities, the U.S. agency has limited influence on the institution and how it is operated. Management of the overseas facility, how children come into care, access to information about the children, or access to the children is at the discretion of local authorities. While there are some exceptions, under these circumstances there is often minimal background or current information on children in care. Health, social and developmental assessments or progress reports on the children may be limited, and prospective adoptive families must be open and prepared for the uncertainties this could mean regarding the child they hope to adopt.

The responsibility of adoption agencies is to be truthful and frank with adoptive families about what they do and do not know about the children they are placing for adoption. Withholding information or misrepresenting information about a child or birth family is a serious violation of ethical adoption practice.

When an adoption agency in the United States works through a private orphanage rather than a government institution, the terms of agreement and working relationship are established between the United States and overseas agencies or individuals. Private overseas organizations generally have the latitude to give U.S. agencies unrestricted access to the children in care. This is critical in securing accurate and first-hand information on the health and well being of children to share with prospective adoptive parents.

International adoption agencies may choose to establish their own facility overseas to place children for adoption. This program model has the significant benefit of developing standards of how children come into care, direct access to the children in care, and the ability to monitor and provide for their well-being. Another benefit of this model is the U.S. agency's capacity to select and train orphanage staff and childcare workers. Their hands-on involvement can ensure adequate care for the children and that information on the children is more timely and accurate. This method of operation overseas also requires greater support, financial responsibility, and commitment to program sustainability.

When an international adoption agency does not have a local presence in a particular state or region in the United States, they can hire a licensed local adoption provider or agency to provide the direct service requirements of the home study and post-placement services to adoptive families. Local direct service agencies typically do not have an international adoption program. They work under the umbrella of the international agency that is considered the primary agency, with licensing and accountability for the overall adoption process.

How International Adoption Agencies Have Evolved

Within the general adoption community, there is growing awareness of the critical importance of adequately preparing adoptive families and the need for ongoing post adoption services. Race, culture and identity have emerged as significant issues in international adoption. To ensure a successful adoption and the long-term well being of adoptees, it is imperative that agencies thoroughly address these issues when they prepare families to adopt a child from another country.

Increasingly, it is the expectation of sending countries that there is a commitment to assisting adoptees to stay connected to their birth country and culture.

As more sending countries require adoptive families to travel to bring their child home, agencies must prepare families for travel overseas and the requirements necessary to complete the process. How agencies work with families regarding travel varies greatly. Some agencies send families overseas on their own with little preparation or support. Other agencies have staff overseas to be with the families until they return home.

It is difficult to measure the impact of electronic communication on intercountry adoption. Procedures that previously took months and weeks can now be completed in days or hours. Geography is less of a barrier in communication, especially as the Internet becomes available in less developed regions of the world. Photos and videos of children waiting for adoption provide a more objective profile, especially helpful in placing children with special needs.

The Internet has also created a virtual community of adoptive families who are in constant communication. This provides a network of support and information that is vital and timely. This unique community has broad range, tremendous force, and is devoted to adoption from the adoptive family perspective. Informally and effectively, they distribute information among themselves and to others regarding adoptive family experiences and agency practices, both good and bad.

Responsibilities and Obligations of International Adoption Agencies

International adoption is a complex and sensitive issue that is not universally accepted. As a consequence, even the most ethical and consistent adoption practices in any country can be profoundly affected by political, social, and economic circumstances. In countries or regions with suspected illegal and unethical adoptions, intercountry adoption is vulnerable to the general ambivalence and unease about international adoption in many sending countries.

The appropriate response when unethical, illegal, or questionable adoptions are taking place is to eliminate the unethical practice and prohibit the individuals involved from further adoption activity. Frequently, no evaluation or distinction is made between good or bad adoption practice, and good or bad adoption agencies. The unfortunate outcome is often the temporary or permanent closure of intercountry adoption with all agencies suffering the consequences. Sadly, it is the children who have the most to lose and directly suffer the greatest loss.

Under the best of circumstances, adoption is a complex and profoundly emotional experience with life-long impact on those personally involved. International adoption has the added complexity of working with a different country, culture, language, and nationality. It is the responsibility of agencies to understand not only the adoption laws and policies of their international programs, but also to know the nuances and cultural standards that affect both current and future adoption activity in a particular country. Adoption is both a social work and legal process. Agencies should be prepared to meet both the legal and social work obligations in the United States and overseas.

Adoption agencies should be committed to ethical standards of practice that are in the best interest of the child and also consider and respect both the birth and adoptive family. In addition to placing children abroad, agencies should consider the children who are not adopted by families but are left behind. While placing children with adoptive families overseas, agencies should also attempt to establish domestic adoption with families in the Sending Country. This demonstrates a commitment to keeping children in their birth country and culture rather than simply placing them only with families overseas. Some international adoption agencies develop humanitarian projects overseas, especially for children who age out of institutions, or have special needs.

In many countries, documents and data collected when a child comes into care have minimal, if any, detail, particularly any identifying information. Even the tiniest bit of information is a treasure that cannot be retrieved or created at a later time. Gathering and documenting information on children may seem like a simple extra step, but generally when a child comes into care there are many considerations, including the physical condition of the child, sensitivity to the birth family, the demands of other children who are already in the institution. Pausing to learn and record this precious information requires understanding of its immediate and long-term importance and a commitment to make it a priority. Adoption agencies can influence and improve this practice by providing support and training overseas to orphanage directors, social workers, and government officials.

It is necessary for adoption agencies to charge fees for the services they provide to families. However, there is an enormous range in fees from agency to agency and the amount of fees charged does not necessarily relate to the quality of service provided. An agency's fees should be reasonable and related directly to the cost of providing the service. Fees should be identified in advance, transparent, and easily understood. Hidden fees or "extra charges" are unethical. Most international adoption programs include an overseas adoption fee that is passed directly to the sending country. The practice of sending cash with families to personally deliver to overseas officials is troublesome and gives the appearance of adoptive parents handing over cash in exchange for their child.

The Hague Conference on Intercountry Adoption and Agency Responsibility

In the 1980s The Hague Conference on Private International Law convened sixty-six countries who negotiated the 1993 Hague Conference on the Protection of Children and Co-operation in Respect of Intercountry Adoption. The Hague Conference on Intercountry Adoption was in response to the global concerns of unethical and unregulated practices in intercountry adoption. The Conference on Intercountry Adoption sets out norms and procedures for the protection of children who are going from one country to another for the purpose of adoption. The Preamble to the Conference clearly elevates the role of intercountry adoption as an appropriate response for children without families—it is the responsibility of all international adoption agencies to ensure that intercountry adoption practices are consistent with the goals and intent of the Treaty.

"Recognizing that the child, for the full and harmonious development of his or her personality, should grow up in a family environment, in an atmosphere of happiness, love and understanding. Recalling that each State should take, as a matter of priority, appropriate measures to enable the child to remain in the care of his or her family of origin. Recognizing that intercountry adoption may offer the advantage of a permanent family to a child for whom a suitable family cannot be found in his or her State of origin ..."

—*The Preamble to The Hague Conference on Intercountry Adoption*

See also Hague Convention on Protection of Children and Co-operation in Respect of Inter-country Adoption; International Adoption (Overview).

Further Reading

Child Welfare Information Gateway Web Site. http://www.childwelfare.gov

Child Welfare League of America. *Standards of Excellence in Adoption Services.* Washington, DC: Child Welfare League of America, 2000.

Cox, Susan Soon-keum, ed. *Voices From Another Place, An Anthology of Korean Adult Adoptees.* Minneapolis, MN: Yeong and Yeong Publishing, 1999.

The Hague Conference on Private International Law Web Site. www.hcch.net

U.S. Department of State Web Site. http://www.state.gov

The Internet and Adoption: Difficulties and Rewards

Vern L. Bullough

The Internet has revolutionized adoption, but the result has been a mixed blessing. The problem is in finding what is, and what is not, legitimate. On the one hand, the Internet sometimes becomes a new form of baby or child selling. On the other hand, it has also fostered connections, bringing together children in need of a home with adoptive families.

One of the more notorious Internet cases involved Neal and Cilla Whatcott who found Inga, a "Russian" orphan through an online adoption agency in 1997. Twelve year old Inga was represented to them as "somewhat delayed because of her history of institutionalization but eager to have a family." Through the agency, they went to Russia to get Inga, who they then learned had been placed twice before and returned. The Whatcotts felt they had been misinformed but proceeded anyway. On their flight home, Inga ran away at a stopover, only to be returned by the police. When they took her home, she started fires in her bedroom, refused to learn English, and was very aggressive with other children. Among other things, she would wake up screaming in the night and crawl out her bedroom window.

At this point, they sent Inga to a Maryland family who had agreed to temporary custody; this soon ended and she was sent to still another family, and still a third before ending up in a psychiatric facility in Michigan. She was diagnosed there as having a reactive attachment disorder, major depression disorder with psychosis, and post-traumatic stress disorder. Soon after this, a Michigan court charged the Whatcotts with child abandonment, even though they said they were in regular contact with Inga and had "maxed out" their health insurance to help pay for her care. The court ordered Neal's wages garnished to help defray the costs of the institution, an action which the Whatcotts claimed cost him his job with a top secret defense agency. The Whatcotts convinced the court to place Inga with another foster family, promising to take her back if and when she was ready. She never was. Rejected by three more foster homes, she was again institutionalized, with the Whatcotts bearing part of the cost. The director of the online source from where they got the lead to Inga indicates that he could not have foreseen the difficulty and that it was a tragic case. Interestingly, the Whatcotts, who said they were nearly destroyed by the Inga affair, later successfully adopted another child, Lily.

A different kind of case occurred about the same time. A gay couple, Steven Levine and his partner, Lane Schickler, posted a letter on an independent adoption center web site and, after a sixteen-month search, brought home a healthy African American/Latino son, having been chosen by his nineteen-year-old birth mother after reading information about them. The two reported that many mothers had rejected them because they were gay, but several women seemed interested because they felt they would then be the only mother. Still, it took considerable time and energy and many missed opportunities before they brought home a child.

Some babies are actually auctioned to a highest bidder and there is a case of one attorney who was caught in a sting operation after being handed $60,000 for a child. One of the more notorious Internet adoption fraud schemes was devised by a Philadelphia "facilitator," Sonya Furlow. Operating as Tender Hearts Family Services, as well as other names, she duped at least forty-three victims between 1993 and 1997, netting more than $200,000 according to prosecutors in Philadelphia. She sent adoptive parents photos of babies who were not available for adoption and also sent e-mails by non-existent birthmothers seeking someone to adopt their child. Furlow pleaded guilty to mail fraud and was sentenced to serve time in a federal penitentiary.

Sometimes it is the birth mother herself doing the scamming, and Internet chat sites often recount tales about young women collecting money from three or four families while keeping all of them on a string. Others fake pregnancies and then suffer miscarriages after an initial payment has been given. This is possible to do in California since birth mothers are allowed to collect 'reasonable and necessary' pregnancy-related expenses from the adoptive parents and some do so before the would-be adoptive child is born. This can, and does, lead to abuses since some young women want under-the-table money for cars and college tuition as well.

The Internet, in sum, is a handy vehicle, not only for those operating a scam, but for adoptive parents doing their own search, as well as birth mothers doing their own placements. Would-be users, however, need to be aware of the difficulties and the rewards. The various search engines post a number of adoption advertisements and there are several Internet services that can be used for a fee. Information about most of them is available through the National Adoption Information Clearinghouse (http://naic.acf.hhs.gov/) which, as the name implies, is a clearinghouse for free adoption publications and other services.

See also Advertising Adoption.

Further Reading

Byett, Beverly. "A Tangled Web of Hope and Fear." *Los Angeles Times*. March 11, 2001, E1, E3.
Gilman, Lois. *The Adoption Resource Book*. New York: Harper Perennial, 1998.

Interstate Adoption (Overview)

Elizabeth (Liz) Oppenheim

An interstate adoption is an adoption that involves the placement of a child from one state with a family that resides in another state. There is no national data on the number of interstate adoptions that occur in the United States.

In 1997, Congress passed the Adoption and Safe Families Act (ASFA) which specifically mandated that states develop a plan for the effective use of cross-jurisdictional resources and prohibited the delay or denial of the placement of a child for adoption when a family was available outside the jurisdiction responsible for the case. The launch of the national photo listing of children waiting to be adopted, the AdoptUS-Kids web site (http://www.adoptuskids.org), and the increased use of state Internet-based adoption exchanges have exponentially increased the ability of families and state agencies to learn of waiting children living in jurisdictions across the country. As a result of the national and state web sites, ever-increasing numbers of children will be adopted across state and local lines.

Children born and living in the United States can be adopted independently or through private agencies by a family in another state. The same is true for children adopted from foreign countries. The agency working with the country of origin of the child may be in one state and the prospective adoptive family may reside in a different state. As with children who are adopted from the public child welfare system, the advent of the Internet has also revolutionized the ability of families to learn about children available for adoption in other states as well as other countries.

In interstate adoptions, differences in state law and policy make the process more difficult. Adoption law is the purview of state law, that is, each state enacts its own adoption laws. While there are similarities, and in some cases identical provisions, in state adoption laws, they are in no way uniform. Further, judicial interpretations of the laws can also be in conflict with one another. A range of differences exists between the states, which include the requirements for a valid consent or relinquishment for adoption; what is required in the home study to determine the suitability of the adoptive parents; the confidentiality of adoption proceedings and records; and the sanctions imposed for unlawful placements.

Because of differences in state adoption laws, issues regarding which law should apply may arise when there is a conflict. For example, problems may occur in finalizing the adoption in one state when the relinquishment was made in a different state. A voluntary relinquishment of parental rights obtained in one state may not be valid in another state. In adoptions that involve involuntary termination of parental rights, adoptive parents may have to await legal action in the state where the biological parents live, or where the custody of the child was first taken from the biological parents, before they can move forward with the adoption in their state of residence.

Finally, most adoptions across state lines must be made pursuant to the Interstate Compact on the Placement of Children (ICPC) which is state law in all fifty states, the District of Columbia, and the U.S. Virgin Islands. Unless the pre-adoptive placement is made entirely between close relatives of the child or by persons already having full guardianship responsibilities, ICPC must be complied with in order for the adoptive placement to be lawful. The Interstate Compact on Adoption and Medical Assistance (ICAMA) is another important compact that enables the states that are parties to it ensure that children who are adopted across state lines or move across state lines during the continuance of an adoption assistance agreement between the state and the adoptive family receive necessary benefits and services.

See also Interstate Compact on Adoption and Medical Assistance (ICAMA); Interstate Compact on the Placement of Children (ICPC).

Further Reading

Child Welfare Information Gateway. U.S. Department of Health and Human Services, Administration for Children and Families Web Site. http://www.childwelfare.gov (accessed December 2005).

Hollinger, Joan Heifetz. *Adoption Law and Practice.* New York: Mathew Bender, 2004.

Primary Document

Oversight of Interstate Adoption: Early Legislation

Early legislation addressing interstate placement of children is illustrated by the following laws from Kansas (dated 1901) and New York (dated 1930). Both laws reflect concerns about oversight and the characteristics of the children to be brought into the state, including a concern that the child not be a trouble-maker—in other words, of "vicious character" in Kansas or a "juvenile delinquent" in New York. The former also includes a concern with "feeble-mindedness" a prevalent concern during that time period.

Kansas Laws, 1901, Chap. 106, "To Provide For Dependent Children"

SECTION 15. *Foreign corporations.*—No association which is incorporated under the laws of any other state than the state of Kansas shall place any child in any family home within the boundaries of the state of Kansas, either with or without indenture or for adoption, unless the said association shall have furnished the state board of charities with such guaranty as they may require that no child will be brought into the state of Kansas by such society or its agents having any contagious or incurable disease, or having any deformity, or being of feeble mind or of vicious character, and that said association will receive and remove from the state any child brought into the state of Kansas by its agent which shall become a public charge within the period of five years after being brought into the state. Any person who shall receive to be placed in a home, or shall place in a home, any child in behalf of any association incorporated in any other state than the state of Kansas which shall not have complied with the requirements of this act shall be imprisoned in the county jail not more than thirty days, or fined not less than five dollars or more than one hundred dollars, or both, in the discretion of the court.

Cahill's Consolidated Laws of New York, 1930, Chap. 56, "State Charities Law"

SECTION 306. *Children imported from other states; bond required.*—It shall be unlawful for any person, agency, association, corporation, society, institution or other organization, except an authorized agency, to bring, send or cause to be brought or sent into the state of New York any child for the purpose of placing or boarding such child or procuring the placing of such child, by adoption, guardianship, or otherwise, in a family, a home or institution, except with an authorized agency, in this state, without first obtaining a license from the board. Application for a license shall be submitted on a form approved and provided by such board and be accompanied by proof that the applicant holds a license, or is approved by the state board of charities or similar body in the state where the applicant resides, or where its chief office is located, or where it has its place of business. Before bringing, sending, or causing to be brought or sent into this state any child, the person, agency, association, corporation, society, institution, or other organization, duly licensed as provided in this section must furnish to the board a blanket indemnity bond of a reputable surety company in favor of the state of New York in the penal sum of not less than one thousand dollars. Such bond must be approved as to form and sufficiency by the board and conditioned as follows: That such licensee (1) will report to the board immediately the name of each such child, its age, the name of the state, and city, town, borough, or village, or the name of the country from which such child came, the religious faith of the parents of the child, the full name and last residence of its parent or parents, the name of the custodian from whom it is taken, and the name and residence of the person or authorized agency with whom it is placed or boarded, released or surrendered, or to whom adoption or guardianship is granted, and the death of such child or any reboarding, replacement or other disposition; (2) will remove from the state within thirty days after written notice is given any such child becoming a public charge during his minority; (3) will remove from the state immediately upon its release any such child who within three years from the time of its arrival within the state is committed to an institution or prison as a result of conviction for juvenile delinquency or crime; (4) will place or cause to be placed or board or cause to be boarded such child under agreement which will secure to such child a proper home, and will make the person so receiving such child responsible for its proper care, education and training; (5) will comply with the provisions of section three hundred and two of this article; (6) will supervise the care and training of such child, and cause it to be visited at least annually by a responsible agent of the licensee; and (7) will make to the board such reports as the board from time to time may require. In the event of the failure of such licensee to comply with the second and third conditions of the bond hereinbefore mentioned, and to remove, after thirty days' notice so to do, a child becoming a public charge, such portion of the bond shall be forfeited to the state or the county or municipality thereof as shall equal the sum which shall have been expended by the state or such county or municipality thereof for the care or maintenance or in the prosecution of such child or for its return to the licensee. (Added by L.1930, ch. 590, April 18.)

Source

As re-printed in Abbott, Grace. *The Child and the State: Volume II The Dependent and the Delinquent Child. The Child of Unmarried Adults.* New York, Greenwood, 1968, p. 151, 155–153.

The Interstate Compact on Adoption and Medical Assistance (ICAMA)

Elizabeth (Liz) Oppenheim

The Interstate Compact on Adoption and Medical Assistance (ICAMA) was developed in response to a mandate in the Adoption Assistance and Child Welfare Act of 1980 (P.L. 96-272). This mandate requires that states take measures to protect the interests of children with special needs receiving adoption assistance when they are placed with adoptive families in another state, or subsequently move with their adoptive families to another state. ICAMA was adopted by nine states in 1986. At this writing, forty-seven states and the District of Columbia are party to the Compact. New York, Wyoming, and Vermont are not. However, Vermont's legislation for joinder is moving.

Background

Prior to 1980, states recognized that the extraordinary costs and demands of raising children with special needs posed barriers to many would-be adoptive parents. The adoption subsidy programs developed by the states helped to overcome those barriers. Following the states' lead, Congress passed the Adoption Assistance and Child Welfare Act in 1980 (P.L. 96-272). Among other things, P.L. 96-272 established a federally aided adoption assistance program under Title IV-E of the Social Security Act. Through this program, the federal government contributes to the states' cost of providing adoption subsidies and Medicaid for children who meet the program's eligibility criteria.

P.L. 96-272 also sought to encourage the adoption of children with special needs by mandating protections for children who are placed beyond the borders of a specific state. To ensure that children received necessary benefits and services across state lines, the states developed the ICAMA.

Consolidated Omnibus Reconciliation Act (COBRA)

In 1985, Congress passed a Consolidated Omnibus Reconciliation Act (COBRA) which made two changes in Title XIX Medicaid of the Social Security Act. These changes affected special needs adoption. First, COBRA mandated that the child's state of residence provide Medicaid to all children adopted under the Title IV-E federally assisted adoption subsidy program. While the mandate constituted a significant step, COBRA did not provide any administrative mechanism by which the provision of Medicaid across state lines would be facilitated. Each state's Medicaid program differs; the forms, information required, benefits, and coverage vary substantially. The ICAMA prevents these differences from becoming barriers to children and families receiving medical benefits in interstate situations.

In addition, this COBRA provided states the option of extending Medicaid coverage to children who do not receive benefits under Title IV-E but do receive subsidy through a state-funded adoption subsidy program, if those children meet the criteria outlined. ICAMA is the mechanism by which the provision of Medicaid for children receiving state-funded adoption assistance is facilitated.

How The Compact Works

ICAMA was established to ensure the delivery of medical and other services to children and their adoptive families on an interstate basis. ICAMA creates a framework for formalized interstate cooperation as envisioned under P.L. 96-272. The Compact, which has the force of law within and among the party states, provides for uniformity and consistency of policy and procedures when a family from one state adopts a child with special needs from another state, or the adoptive family moves to another state. The children covered by ICAMA are those adopted pursuant to adoption assistance agreements between states and prospective adoptive parents under the terms of Title IV-E of the Social Security Act. Through the Compact, states may also extend these protections to children adopted through state-funded adoption assistance programs.

Operation of the Compact is the responsibility of the designated Compact administrator in each state. The administrator coordinates with in-state and out-of-state officials to facilitate the provision of benefits and services for special needs adopted children, processes ICAMA forms, serves as an information resource, and assists adoptive families in identifying and accessing needed programs and services for their children. Although the designation of a contact person with responsibility for interstate adoption assistance activities and the establishment of an administrative structure is a simple concept, the value cannot be overstated because it prevents needless delays or denials of essential services and benefits.

Continuing adoption assistance payments are simple in interstate situations. Checks can be mailed to any address. Ensuring the delivery of other benefits and services across state lines (for example, medical assistance) is another matter. While it is true that the COBRA of 1985 mandated that residence states provide Medicaid services to children who have Title IV-E adoption assistance agreements with other states, ICAMA is the mechanism that allowed the states to develop the administrative structure for accomplishing this.

Every state's Medicaid program is unique. Without the Compact, the systemic differences could provide barriers to children and families receiving medical benefits in interstate situations. Standard forms, institutionalized procedures, and regular and reliable channels for information exchange make the process simple and efficient.

Although medical assistance is the most obvious interstate interest of families who adopt special needs children, the importance of post-adoption services cannot be overlooked. Adoption specialists agree that the availability of post-legal adoption services is directly related to the success of an adoption and the long-term health and stability of adoptive families. Geographic boundaries do not alter the need for these services. While the Compact does not mandate the delivery of these services by the residence state, it does foster a coordinated response to ensure that the child and family receive what they need. Compact administrators help families identify providers of these services if they are not provided by the public agency. In fact, the Compact declares that their personnel will assist the agencies of other Compact states in accomplishing interstate delivery of all types of services. This is not a matter of professional courtesy, but lawful obligation.

Compact Procedures

If an adoptive family is moving or is adopting a child from another state and has an adoption assistance agreement in effect, the state responsible for financing the adoption assistance agreement completes Form 6.01, Notice of Eligibility for Medicaid/Case Activation, and attaches to it a certified copy of the adoption assistance agreement. These documents are sent to the adoptive parents' residence state and take the place of an application for Medicaid. A copy of the Form 6.01 and the adoption assistance agreement is also sent to the adoptive parents. Form 6.02 notifies the parents that the adoption assistance state has taken the necessary actions to initiate Medicaid benefits in the new residence state. These documents identify the person in the new residence state who will serve as the point of contact for the family.

See also Interstate Adoption (Overview).

Further Reading

Association of Administrators of the Interstate Compact on Adoption and Medical Assistance (AAICAMA). *The Interstate Compact on Adoption and Medical Assistance Handbook for Administrators.* Washington, DC: AAICAMA, 2003.
Association of Administrators of the Interstate Compact on Adoption and Medical Assistance (AAICAMA) Web Site. http://aaicama.aphsa.org/ (accessed December, 2005).

Interstate Compact on the Placement of Children (ICPC)

Elizabeth (Liz) Oppenheim

The Interstate Compact on the Placement of Children (ICPC) was developed in the late 1950s to address states' concerns regarding their ability to assure that children placed across state lines are afforded the same protections and services as children placed intrastate. States recognized that their importation and exportation laws did not provide enough protection for these children and they knew that because a state's jurisdiction ends at its borders, necessary protections could not be compelled for a child placed beyond those borders. It was apparent that states needed to work together within a legal framework to protect children placed outside their individual jurisdictions. The states chose the proven framework of an interstate compact to provide this protection.

The ICPC has been enacted by all states, the District of Columbia, and the U.S. Virgin Islands. It is an agreement between the states that has the force and effect of statutory law. An interstate placement made in violation of the Compact is sufficient grounds for the revocation of a license to place children and, in some states, criminal sanctions may be mandated for noncompliance. The Compact provides protection to, and enables services for, children placed across state lines for foster care or adoption. The Compact establishes procedures that ensure placements are safe, suitable, and able to provide proper care and fixes the legal and financial responsibilities of those involved in interstate placements.

Type of Placements Covered

The ICPC applies to all interstate placements of children in foster care including: foster and group homes; residential treatment facilities and institutions; pre-adoptive placements; placements with a parent or relative when a parent or relative is not making the placement; and placements of adjudicated delinquents in out-of-state institutions. Not all placements of children outside their home states are subject to the Compact. The Compact does not include placements made in medical and mental health facilities or in boarding schools, or "any institution primarily educational in character." The Compact also excludes placements made entirely between close relatives of the child or by persons already having full guardianship responsibilities. Close relatives include parent, stepparent, grandparent, adult brother or sister, adult aunt or uncle, or guardian.

The ICPC Process

When a proposed foster or adoptive parent resides in a state different from the state responsible for the care and protection of the child, the comprehensive sharing of information generated by the home study must be coordinated between the child-placing agencies in the two states. The ICPC office in each state facilitates, administers, and oversees this process.

The process of placing a child pursuant to ICPC begins with sending the Form ICPC 100-A, the Interstate Compact on the Placement of Children Request. The 100-A is completed and sent by the "sending agency" to the Compact administrator in the state where the placement originates. "Sending agency" is defined as any individual or entity (including a court or public or private agency) that is making the placement.

The packet is reviewed for completeness and compliance with applicable laws and sent to the ICPC office in the state where the child's prospective family resides. The 100-A includes the following information about the child and the prospective placement resource: a social and case history including medical and educational reports; signed court order verifying jurisdiction; financial plan for meeting the costs of the child's care in the receiving state; and, if a home study has not already been completed, a request for one on the prospective foster or adoptive parents. Provision of this comprehensive information on a child's unique needs and strengths allows for an informed evaluation of how a prospective family will be able to provide a safe, nurturing environment.

Once the 100-A arrives in the receiving state, the receiving state will begin the process for assessing the suitability of the prospective placement. A home study will be done in the receiving state if one has not already been completed. This study involves: assessments of social and medical histories of the placement family; their backgrounds, parenting and discipline styles; employment and financial histories; personal and professional references; physical evaluation of their home; satisfactory criminal and child abuse background checks; completion of foster or adoptive parent training; and case worker recommendations. Based on the results of the home study and other information provided, the receiving state will make a determination as to whether the placement is "not contrary to the welfare of the child" and would be in compliance with receiving state law. In addition, any issues between the sending and receiving states on how services and supports for the child will be financed must be resolved. This process of ensuring how appropriate services are provided can be complex as it may involve cooperation of several systems within both states, including education, mental health, and education. At the conclusion of this process, the receiving state sends a written notice to the sending state approving, or not approving, the placement. No ICPC placement can be made without written approval.

Once placement is made, the receiving state becomes responsible for ongoing supervision of the placement, providing support services to the family and child, and sending regular reports to the sending agency. If adoption is the goal, these responsibilities continue until finalization. It is important to note that the sending agency retains legal and financial responsibility for the child. In addition, the sending agency maintains jurisdiction over the child and continues to have both the authority and the responsibility to determine all matters in relation to the "custody, supervision, care, treatment, and disposition of the child," just as the sending agency would have "if the child had remained in the sending agency state."

Rewriting the ICPC

At this time, the ICPC is being rewritten. Focus on safety and permanency for children in the public child welfare system placed across state lines brought the ICPC into the spotlight. While this focus confirmed the important role the ICPC plays in ensuring appropriate placements, it also highlighted concerns that ICPC processes cause unnecessary delays. In March 2004, dissatisfaction with the current ICPC among the states and other child welfare professionals and advocates prompted the American Public Human Services Association's (APHSA) state human services leadership to adopt a policy resolution directing a rewrite of the ICPC. While members agreed that there were interim steps that could be taken to improve the interstate placement process, true reform required revisions to the actual language of the ICPC. APHSA, in response to this resolution, assembled a diverse team composed of state human service administrators, child welfare directors, compact administrators, and representatives of national child welfare organizations to provide recommendations for addressing the issues in the Compact and its implementation. After intensive meetings and extensive communication with the states and outside stakeholders, APHSA disseminated two drafts of the rewritten Compact—the Interstate Compact *for* the Placement of Children—for review and comment. The comments and concerns of the states and stakeholders have been compiled and integrated by APHSA staff and the drafting team. The third and final draft is forthcoming upon resolution of several issues. It is expected that the states will have the new Compact to introduce in the state legislatures in 2006.

See also Interstate Adoption (Overview).

Further Reading

American Public Human Services Association (APHSA). Documents. APHSA Web Site http://icpc.aphsa.org/documents.asp (accessed December, 2005).

American Public Human Services Association (APHSA). *Guide to the Interstate Compact on the Placement of Children*. Washington, DC: APHSA, 2002.

Dunhem, Rebecca. *Understanding Criminal Records Checks*. Washington, DC: Association of Administrators of the Interstate Compact on Adoption and Medical Assistance (AAICAMA), 2002.

Oppenheim, Elizabeth and Ursula Krieger. *Understanding Delays in the Interstate Home Study Process*. Washington, DC: American Public Human Services Association, 2002.

Irish Adoption: A History

Moira Maguire

In March 1950, the *New York Times* published a photograph of six Irish children departing from Ireland's Shannon Airport for adoption by American couples. The photo was accompanied by a story about the children's origins and backgrounds and details of their adoption by American families. This press attention revealed what had, until then, been a well-kept secret in Ireland: that children were sent out of Ireland in the thousands from the late 1930s to the 1960s for no other reason than that they were illegitimate and thus "unwanted." This illicit trade in Irish children was conducted by unofficial "adoption" societies, mostly administered by religious orders, with the tacit approval of the Archbishop of Dublin, John Charles McQuaid, and the cooperation of the Department of Foreign Affairs, who issued passports enabling children to be removed from the state for the purposes of adoption overseas (and specifically in America). Until the 1952 Adoption Act provided for the legal transfer of parental rights from biological to adoptive parents, the only alternative for unwanted children to an institutional existence or an insecure boarding-out arrangement was adoption by foreign, primarily American, families.

American couples acquired illegitimate Irish children almost for the asking, earning Ireland a reputation, particularly among American servicemen stationed in Britain, as a "happy hunting ground" for healthy white babies. In some cases, American couples called on institutions in person to inquire about adopting a child; other hopeful adoptive parents wrote to adoption societies requesting that a child be sent to them. Preliminary transactions often occurred through the mail: the adopted child was accompanied to America by a paid attendant, no one in a position of responsibility ever met the adopting family or inspected their home and qualifications, and the adoptive parents did not meet the child until s/he actually arrived in their home. Adoption societies were so eager to secure adoptive families for the children in their charge that, at least until 1950, they required little or no information about an adopting couple's background, home life, or financial position. All they required was an affidavit whereby the adopting parents undertook to raise the adopted child as a Catholic, although the couple did not have to prove that they were practicing Catholics. These overseas adoptions carried on in virtual silence and secrecy from the early 1940s until 1951, when a high-profile incident involving the Hollywood film actress Jane Russell compelled the Irish government to legislate on the question of adoption.

Jane Russell traveled to Ireland in late 1951 hoping to adopt an Irish child, after having been turned down in Italy because of her age and non-Catholic religious affiliation. A member of the Church of Ireland Moral Welfare Organisation advised Russell that she would be unable to adopt a child from a Protestant institution without extensive home studies and background investigations, so Russell set her sights on a young Irish Catholic boy who resided with his parents in Britain. The chain of events that led Russell from Ireland to Britain is sketchy at best, but somehow Russell convinced an Irish couple, the Kavanaghs, to allow her to adopt their son Tommy, and within hours the Irish legation in London issued a passport in Tommy Kavanagh's name. This incident prompted a flurry of negative reports in the foreign media, and it sparked a host of questions in the D il (Irish parliament), where members demanded an accounting from government inisters on the practice and extent of overseas adoption.

Once the "secret" was out, lawmakers had no choice but to act to both legalize adoption domestically, and stop the outflow of children for adoption elsewhere. Adoption became a hot political issue in 1952 because a series of embarrassing and highly critical reports in the foreign press about Ireland's overseas adoption practices brought to light by the Jane Russell incident, compelled church and state to compromise to avoid further embarrassment. (Up to this point the Catholic

Church had resisted the introduction of adoption legislation because they feared it would facilitate proselytism.)

Although the Adoption Bill was intended to remedy the defects of the informal overseas adoption, the Adoption Act did not stop the outward flow of children and, in fact, the safeguards established to regulate the adoption of children in Ireland did not apply to overseas adoptions. Neither did the Act implement measures to protect the civil and legal rights of children who were removed from the state. The only change in the overseas adoption practice was the introduction of a minimum age for removing a child from the state. But this was aimed not at protecting the child but at preventing proselytism, as it was based on the assumption that desperate mothers would willingly hand newborn infants over to any individual or organization, including Protestant ones, which offered assistance. The age restriction theoretically reduced the element of desperation that presumably fueled the proselytizing "menace," and attempted to ensure that children sent out of the state for adoption would not lose their Catholic birthright. The overseas adoption practice finally died out in the early 1970s because there was a growing acceptance (or at least tolerance) in Irish society of unmarried motherhood; this, coupled with the introduction in 1972 of the Lone Parent's Allowance, effectively dried up the "supply" of healthy children being offered for adoption both at home and abroad.

See also Russell, Jane; The Catholic Church and Adoption: Lessons from Ireland.

Further Reading

Maguire, Moira J. "Foreign Adoptions and the Evolution of Irish Adoption Policy, 1945–52." *Journal of Social History* 36 (2002): 387–404.

Shanahan, Suzanne. "The Changing Meaning of Family: Individual Rights and Irish Adoption Policy, 1949–1999." *Journal of Family History* 30 (2005): 86–108.

Whyte, John. *Church and State in Modern Ireland*. Dublin: Gill and Macmillan, 1971.

Iroquois Adoption

William Engelbrecht

In the seventeenth century, the Iroquois Confederacy consisted of the Seneca, Cayuga, Onondaga, Oneida, and Mohawk. Iroquois, both male and female, are members of their mother's matrilineage and clan. Clans are large kin groups made up of matrilineages. Since an Iroquois child receives lineage and clan affiliation from his mother, the concept of an illegitimate child did not exist in traditional Iroquois society. As discussed in *Iroquoia: The Development of a Native World*, female members of a matrilineage or clan segment lived together in a longhouse and cooperated with one another in horticultural and household activities, including child rearing.

Members of the matrilineage provided for the care and training of their youngest members. If a child's father died or their parents terminated their relationship with one another, it did not affect the child's social status. If a child's mother died, the mother's female relatives cared for the child, provided the child was old enough to be weaned. No adoption was necessary as long as a child was a member of a local matrilineal kin group.

Adoption was nonetheless important among the Iroquois from at least the seventeenth century. For the Iroquois, it was the mechanism by which non-local individuals or groups were incorporated into Iroquois society. Women made the adoption decisions. Kinship governed both social and political relations and, without kin ties, outsiders were essentially non-persons. Adoption into a matrilineage or clan provided the context in which these outsiders could interact appropriately with other Iroquois.

Many outsiders who were adopted were war captives. An exploration of all the possible reasons for Iroquois warfare is beyond the scope of this article, but Daniel Richter argues that a major reason was the acquisition of captives to replace kinsmen who had been killed in warfare. This motivation led to "Mourning Wars." Women urged young men to bring back captives. The captives were forced to run the gauntlet between rows of hostile villagers who vented their hatred of the enemy. Captives would then be adopted and either ritually killed in revenge or incorporated into a matrilineage. If incorporated, a family might hold a "requickening" ceremony for that individual. This individual then took the name of a deceased person and was expected to behave socially in the same manner as the individual he or she replaced.

Sometimes women and children of a defeated group were incorporated. In 1656, the Onondaga attacked the Arendahronon nation of the recently defeated Huron Confederacy. Most of the Arendahronon men were killed, but the women and children were adopted by lineages, a pattern that appears to have been common according to R. G. Thwaites. As recounted by James Seaver, the most famous captive adopted into Iroquois society was Mary Jemison, a Euro-American girl captured in 1758 at the age of fifteen. Later in life when offered the opportunity to return to Euro-American society, she chose to remain with the Seneca.

Members of a matrilineage exerted pressure on newly adopted members to identify with their new social role as Iroquois. New Iroquois knew that resistance might be met with death so, at least outwardly, they complied. Participation by newly adopted Iroquois in lineage, clan, and community rituals further served to integrate individuals into Iroquois society. For example, the Condolence Ritual is conducted to mourn the death of leaders and to install new chiefs. Today, it still serves an integrative function among the Iroquois.

In the seventeenth century, the Iroquois sustained population loss from warfare and especially from European introduced pathogens. According to George Snyderman, the adoption of non-Iroquois into Iroquois society became an important strategy for maintaining group size. Compared to the fertility of Euro-American women of the same time, Iroquois fertility was relatively low. Adoption, as explained by William Engelbrecht (1987:23) served as an alternative to increased childbearing. Also, as Mary Douglas (1969: 125) noted, matrilineages commonly use adoption as a way of gaining new members.

Sometimes captives were neither killed nor adopted, but instead became slaves or "non-persons" who might be used in future prisoner exchanges or who were put to work doing menial chores. These individuals lived in fear of being killed, but it appears that children of females in this category became Iroquois.

James Lynch distinguishes between assimilative adoption, in which the individual or group becomes Iroquois, and associative adoption. The latter type of adoption facilitated interaction between important outsiders and the Iroquois. Individuals adopted in this manner take on an Iroquois identity, but retain their original identity. Examples of associative adoption in the historic literature include missionaries, traders, and Colonial officials. These individuals were not seen as replacements for deceased kinsmen and no attempt was made to integrate these individuals into a matrilineage. These adoptions facilitated political and economic interactions between the Iroquois and Euro-Americans and were also a way of honoring individuals who had proven their friendship with the Iroquois.

Lynch extends the concept of associative adoption to apply to groups or nations that were brought into the Iroquois Confederacy under the "Tree of Peace." In *The Jesuit Relations*, Thwaites (45:243) describes how a Huron village, when faced with possible annihilation from the Seneca and other Iroquois, moved to Seneca country and lived apart in a separate village as Hurons. They became "children" under the "Tree of Peace" with the Seneca handling their external affairs. In the eighteenth century, the Tuscarora moved from North Carolina to New York seeking refuge with the Iroquois. They were eventually adopted into the Iroquois Confederacy while maintaining their separate identity. The Five Nation Iroquois became the Six Nations with the addition of the Tuscarora. The Tuscarora were referred to as "younger brothers," having a higher associative status than the earlier Huron who joined the Iroquois to escape military defeat. Using the metaphor of a longhouse, these incorporations were referred to as "extending the rafters."

As a consequence of the adoption of diverse individuals and groups, the composition of Iroquois population changed markedly during the seventeenth century. In 1656, according to Thwaites (43:265), the Jesuits noted people from seven different nations among the Onondaga, and eleven different nations were represented among the Seneca. Non-Oneida and non-Mohawk individuals were said to outnumber native Oneida and Mohawk, respectively (51:123, 45:205–9). These newcomers enriched Iroquoia by introducing new ideas and practices.

The Iroquois Confederacy is often given credit for enabling the Iroquois to survive the turbulent seventeenth and eighteenth centuries. While the Iroquois political system was clearly important, the role of adoption in the survival of the Iroquois should not be underestimated.

Further Reading

Douglas, Mary. "Is Matriliny Doomed in Africa." In *Man in Africa*, edited by Mary Douglas and Phyllis Kaberry, 121–136. New York, Tavistock Publications Ltd., 1969.

Engelbrecht, William. "Factors Maintaining Low Population Density Among the Prehistoric New York Iroquois." *American Antiquity* 52 (1987): 13–27.

Engelbrecht, William. *Iroquoia: The Development of a Native World*. New York: Syracuse University Press, 2003.

Lynch, James. "The Iroquois Confederacy, and the Adoption and Administration of Non-Iroquoian Individuals and Groups Prior to 1756." *Man in the Northeast* 30 (1985): 83–99.

Richter, Daniel K. *The Ordeal of the Longhouse: The Peoples of the Iroquois League in the Era of European Colonization*. Chapel Hill and London: University of North Carolina Press, 1992.

Seaver, James. *A Narrative of the Life of Mrs. Mary Jemison*. New York: Corinth Books Inc., [orig. 1824] 1961.

Snyderman, George S. "Behind the Tree of Peace: A Sociological Analysis of Iroquois Warfare." *Pennsylvania Archaeologist* XVIII (1948): 2–93.

Thwaites, R. G., ed. *The Jesuit Relations and Allied Documents*. 73 vols. Cleveland: Burrows Brothers, 1896–1901.

Islam and Adoption

Vern L. Bullough

Even before Muhammad was born, adoption was practiced on the Arabian Peninsula. Adoption of an illegitimate child by its biological father, for example, was a way of making an individual a member of the tribe. Muhammad, who had been an orphan himself, adopted his freeman Zaid who had become a slave through the misfortunes of war. In fact, such adoptions were so widespread in the Arabian Peninsula that it is sometimes not clear who had been emancipated and adopted. Refugees could also be admitted to the tribe of their protectors through adoption.

The *Qu'ran* set specific rules about adoption which, more or less, still prevail. The child's biological family is never hidden, and their ties to the child are never severed. The *Qu'ran* specifically reminds adoptive parents that they are not the child's biological parents:

> Call such as are adopted, the sons of their natural fathers: this will be more just in the sight of Allah. And if ye know not their fathers, let them be as your brethren in religion, and your companions; and there shall be no blame if you err in this matter; but (what counts) is the intention of your hearts. *Qur'an 33:4–5*

The guardian/child relationship has specific rules under Islamic law which makes Islamic adoptions somewhat unique. The Islamic term for what in the West is called adoption is *kafala*, from a word that means "to feed." This seems to imply that Islamic adoption can better be described in terms of a foster-parent relationship than a more formalized adoption process. Adopted children retain their own biological family name. Adopted children inherit from their biological parents, not automatically from their adoptive parents. When the adoptive child is grown, members of the adoptive family are not considered blood relatives and, in a sense, have a unique legal relationship. Members of the adoptive family would be permissible as marriage partners and rules of modesty exist between the grown child and adoptive family members of the opposite sex, as it does not between brother and sister. If the child is provided with property/wealth from the biological family, adoptive parents are commanded to take care and not intermingle that property/wealth with their own.

In Islam in general, the extended family network is vast and strong. It is unlikely for a child to be completely orphaned without a single family member to care for him or her. Islam emphasizes the ties of kinship. These ties are extremely important and sometimes great energy and time is spent locating relatives to care for the child before allowing someone outside of the family to adopt or remove a child. As the *Qu'ran* reminds Muhammad:

> Did he not find thee an orphan, and hath he not taken care of thee? And did he not find thee needy, and hath he not enriched thee? Wherefore oppress not the orphan: neither repulse the beggar: but declare the goodness of thy Lord. *Qu'ran 93: 6–11.*

See also Janissary; Muhammad.

Further Reading

According to Islamic tradition, the *Qu'ran* cannot be translated since it is the Word of
    Allah. Thus, the English versions are paraphrases. There are considerable differences
    among them since there is no official version. The verses used here were paraphrased
    by George Sale (New York: A.L. Burt, 1921). Other versions were consulted but the
    meaning seems to be clear.

Levy, Reuben. *The Social Structure of Islam.* Cambridge; Cambridge University Press, 1965.
Smith, Robertson. *Kinship and Marriage in Early Arabia.* Boston: Beacon Press, 1903.

J

Janissary

Vern L. Bullough

The term "Janissary" is derived from the Turkish *yeni cheri,* literally "new troops." This was an elite military corps within the Ottoman Empire whose members were selected out of the *devshirme*—the levy of boys taken from Christian families in the Balkans who were then raised as Muslims to become Turkish soldiers or officials according to their aptitudes. It was a forced adoption by the state. The system dates back to around 1330 when the Turks first entered into the Balkans in force. The sultan Mural II (d. 1451) modified the system, but it was not until the sixteenth century under the reign of Salim I (d. 1520) that the system was fully organized.

The original purpose of the Janissaries was to serve as an infantry corps for the Turkish army which normally fought on horseback. To ensure their loyalty and reliability, they were taken as children and raised as Muslims. Other Turkish troops were drawn from adult converts but the Turks found such troops less reliable.

The total number of Janissaries at any one time was around fifteen thousand. Their numbers, however, might increase during particularly difficult campaigns such as those against Persia. Originally forbidden to marry, the Janissaries were allowed to do so in 1581 and, increasingly, their numbers were recruited from their own children although the child levies also continued.

The Janissaries were deeply involved in politics and had particular influence on the selection of viziers (governors or close advisers to the Sultan). A new sultan often gave them bribes in order to gain their acceptance of him.

Mehmet II created a new regular force of guards (the *Muallem Eshkinji*) in 1826. Fearing they might lose power, the Janissaries revolted. The Sultan reacted by declaring a holy war against them, surrounding their barracks with troops, and killing most of them in the ensuing battle. The Janissaries' flags and traditional headgear were then publicly dragged through the streets to signify their disgrace. The Bektash religious confraternity to which most of them belonged—an Islamic sect that was a mixture of beliefs and practices including elements from Christianity—was outlawed with their extinction.

Further Reading

Glassé, Cyril. *The Concise Encyclopedia of Islam.* New York: Harper and Row, 1989.

Japan and Adoption

Vern L. Bullough

In Japan, adoption in the past was primarily motivated either by blood or money. Japanese culture places great emphasis on blood relations, and families are viewed as a privileged, almost sacred group. Since extended family ties are strong, relatives care for each others children when the need arises but rarely adopt them. The most common form of adoption in Japan in the past, and still today, is of adults by heirless, elderly couples. The couple gives their adoptee (and they are all men) their family name so that the family will continue. The adopted person, in turn, becomes their heir. Grandchildren are also adopted as a legal way to dodge inheritance taxes.

Adoption is becoming somewhat easier. Every Japanese citizen has a *koseki*, official documents held by the government that mark birth, marriage, death, and similar milestones. Traditionally, divorce and adoption were seen as tarnishing the record and confusing identity, which is one reason most adoptions were informal because they were not then recorded. In 1988, a law was passed allowing young adopted children to have their birth family name erased from their *koseki* and replaced by that of their adoptive family. Even now, adoptions are often done in secret so that only the most intimate family members know an individual has been adopted.

It is not that there is a lack of adoptable children, but there is a lack of parents willing to adopt. At the end of the twentieth century, there were approximately twenty-five thousand children living in Japan's 527 state-run or subsidized children's homes, many of them put there by relatives who preferred such placements over outright adoption by themselves or by strangers. The Japanese, when criticized about this institutionalization, emphasize that there are far fewer children in state care agencies than in most other countries, and they argue that such children are generally well cared for, safe, and guaranteed a high school education. Only rarely do children from such agencies get adopted. Most adoption, which does take place in Japan (officially about six hundred each year but probably higher), takes place through private and somewhat secret adoption agencies or individuals.

In the aftermath of World War II and the American occupation of Japan, many mixed race children were adopted by Americans. Japan still furnishes babies for the international market, but in most recent years, there have been less than a hundred such adoptions per year.

Further Reading

Jordan, Mary. "Japanese Couples' Aversion to Child Adoption Changes Only Slowly." *Washington Post.* June 29, 1999. *The Washington Post* Web Site. http://washpost.com/index.shtml

Judaism and Adoption

Vern L. Bullough

Technically, legal adoption as it is now practiced in the United States did not exist in Jewish law, but adoption was often used in the case of adult converts. In the historical past, adoption into a Jewish family was the only way into guaranteed legal status as a free man for a foreigner or one whose status in the community was unclear. Such an adoption also implied that the adopted person would get a portion of the family's inheritance.

Traditionally, however, the care for a dependent child who did not necessarily have a biological relationship with a family has always been a part of the Jewish tradition, but this charitable act did not necessarily result in adoption. Some of the more ultra orthodox groups still do not believe in adoption. Conversion, however, is allowed since being Jewish traditionally has meant being born of a Jewish mother.

In the United States, where the Jewish community has several different group-ings including Reform, Conservative, and traditional congregations with divisions even within these groupings, it was the Reform movement and the independent Ethical Culture groups (which includes many non-Jews) that pioneered adoption. As in the rest of the United States in the first part of the twentieth century, there was a debate among those concerned with orphans and abandoned children as to whether home care or institutional care was the best for dependent children, and Jewish groups came down on both sides of the issue. For example, the Hebrew Orphan's Society was organized in Baltimore. Similar groups appeared in other large northern cities with large Jewish populations such as New York and Chicago. In Chicago, when money was sought for a Jewish institution for orphans from Julius Rosenwald, the head of Sears, Roebuck and Company, he refused to donate and, with others, founded the Jewish Home Finding Society in Chicago in 1907 to place Jewish children in foster homes or in families. Like many other agencies, ini-tially there was a reluctance for the Jewish agencies to place illegitimate children in adopted homes. Rather, they put them in institutions or had them sent out as foster children, sometimes to non-Jewish homes. Ultimately, as adoption developed further, the Jewish community began to place illegitimate newborns out for adop-tion as well. Only gradually did an increasing number of Jewish families turn to adoption, with the largest increase occurring in the second half of the twentieth century when adoption also expanded beyond infants born to Jewish mothers.

Jews adopting infants or children not born to a Jewish mother usually had the child go through a formal conversion experience. Boys underwent a *brit milah* (cir-cumcision) and a *tevilah* (immersion at a ritual bath), girls a *tevilah* and a naming ceremony at the synagogue or temple. They then follow the traditional path of development through a *bar* or *bas mitzva* and are not distinguished from other Jewish children.

As adoption has become more common, special rituals have been adopted by some rabbis to commemorate an adoption with special prayers and ceremonies for when the child is first brought home. There is even a prayer when an adoption fails and the child is returned.

Further Reading

Carp, E. Wayne. *Adoption in American: Historical Perspectives*. Ann Arbor: University of Michigan Press, 2002.

Diamant, Anita. *Jewish Baby Book*. New York: Jewishlights, 1994.

Jewish Children's Adoption Network, P.O. Box 147016, Denver, CO 80214 7016 (Tel: 303 573 8113; email: jcan@quest.net). Jewish Children's Adoption Network Web Site. www.milechai.com/jewishadoption.html

Stars of David International Inc.: A Jewish Adoption Information and Support Network, 3175 Commercial Avenue, Suite 100, Northbrook, IL 60062-1915 (Tel: 800 STAR-349; email: info@starsofdavid.org). Stars of David International Inc. Web Site. http:// www.starsofdavid.org

K

Kinship Care (Formal)

Mark F. Testa

Kinship care refers to the full-time care of a child by a parental surrogate who has a culturally recognized kinship bond with the child. The bond commonly derives from a relationship by blood or marriage to one of the child's parents, or it can draw from any number of "fictive kin" relationships, such as godparent, family friend, or tribal member.

Historically, the duties and prerogatives of kinship caregivers were defined and enforced by local custom, cultural traditions, and reciprocal-aid agreements among families. During the last quarter of the twentieth century, these informal arrangements came under the expanding purview of statutory law, administrative regulation, and judicial oversight as local and central governments assumed a larger role in the financial support, protection, and placement of dependent, abused, and neglected children with kin.

The categories of informal and formal kinship care are used to distinguish between the different normative frameworks (customary vs. legal) that govern a relative's obligations and rights of custody and control of the child. The categories of private and public kinship care are also used to classify the different funding streams (voluntary vs. tax dollars) that relatives can contribute to, or receive, for the child's support.

In some cultures, private-informal kinship care is interwoven with regular child-rearing practices, accounting for as much as one-half of children's living arrangements in a Polynesian society as discussed by William Donner. With urbanization and industrialization, kinship care devolves into a residual component that compensates for dysfunctions in the nuclear family system. Despite recurring predictions of its demise (see Ann Roschelle for example), communities and government continue to rely on the altruism of kin and the unpaid labor of mostly female caregivers to limit both the scope and costs of public foster care.

For much of the twentieth century, the private-informal mode of kinship care functioned separately from the public-formal mode of foster care that emerged in the cities and emphasized the recruitment, licensing, and payment of non-relatives as foster parents. During this period, it was taken for granted that if birth parents failed to discharge their obligations to care properly for children, then other relatives should voluntarily step forward to assume the responsibilities of substitute care. Only as a last resort would government formally intervene, usually with the understanding that extended kin could still be held liable for some or all of the public costs of substitute care.

The official presumption of relatives' responsibility for supporting and fostering dependent children persisted well into the twentieth century. In Great Britain, it was not until 1948 that Parliament retired the obligation under the Poor Laws to support extended kin. In the United States, as discussed by Winifred Bell, relatives' responsibility laws were still being enforced by the states as late as the1960s. Even after the laws' holding relatives liable for the support of public aid applicants expired, most American states refused to extend to kin, who met foster home licensing standards, the same foster care stipends they provided to non-related foster parents. In 1979, the U.S. Supreme Court rejected in *Miller v. Youakim* the differential treatment of relatives, ruling that kinship was not a justifiable classification under federal law for denying full board payments to extended family members who otherwise qualified for federal foster care benefits.

The U.S. Supreme Court's decision came at a time when child welfare authorities in many countries were finding it difficult to keep separate the spheres of informal kinship care and formal foster care. Shortages in the supply of licensable foster homes, which accompanied the increased entry of women into the paid labor force, prompted child welfare authorities to seek out and license extended kin to become the foster parents of abused and neglected children. Formerly colonized people, who had suffered the loss of children to formal foster care as an instrument of assimilation, sought redress in legislation, such as the Indian Child Welfare Act in the United States and the Children, Young Person, and their Families Act in New Zealand, which gave preference to the placement of foster children with kin, clan or tribal members. As a consequence, the once distinct boundaries between informal kinship care and formal foster care began to blur, giving rise to a mixed form—kinship foster care.

The blurring of boundaries between the two modes of substitute care surfaces latent tensions between the particularistic customs and parochial interests of families, tribes, religious communities, and minority ethnic groups under the older system of informal kinship care and the universalistic standards and bureaucratic procedures of organized charity and the welfare state under the newer system of formal foster care.

Definitions of kin may differ: informal kinship care often acknowledges a wider array of relationships, e.g. second-cousins, godparents, friends, and tribal members, than the narrower range codified in law, which is usually limited to close relationships by blood or marriage. Attitudes toward discipline may vary: informal kinship care mirrors the practices common in the general culture, some of which may be prohibited (e.g. corporeal punishment) under the rules of formal kinship care. The decision-making powers of formal caregivers are more delimited than those of informal caregivers: permissions must first be sought from caseworkers or judges before traveling across jurisdictional lines, obtaining medical care for the child, or even spending a sleep-over at a neighbor's house. Formal requirements for obtaining permanent legal custody of a related child may also run contrary to individual family preferences and cultural norms.

Early investigations had suggested that relatives were hesitant about formally adopting the kin they were fostering because of cultural opposition to the termination of parental rights and resistance to recasting extended family relations into the nuclear family mold of parent and child. Workers and relatives also shied away from the subject because the ages of the children and fertility history of the caregivers deviated from the dominant norm of closed adoptions of infants by infertile couples. A portrayal of the concern at the time spoke of the distortion of family relationships and the risk that the truth will be hidden from the child until it is discovered "under damaging circumstances that his 'sister' or 'aunt' is really his mother" (Rowe, Cain, Hundleby and Keane, 1984).

Subsequent research by Mark Testa and colleagues helped to balance the picture by showing that most relatives were willing to consider adoption after learning that birth certificates did not have to change and that subsidies were available after finalization to support the child adopted from public foster care. Concerted efforts in the late 1990s in the United States to hasten termination proceedings and to get the word out about the importance of permanence for healthy child development helped to boost the number of adoptions out of formal foster care and reduce the backlog of children in long-term, kinship foster care. For other relatives who wished to become permanent custodians but found formal adoption problematic, an alternative permanency option of subsidized guardianship emerged (as discussed by the Children's Defense Fund), which does not require termination of parental rights or alteration of family identities.

Although kinship foster care is now an accepted part of the child welfare establishment, accounting for twenty to thirty percent of all formal foster care in many countries (see Roger Greeff), questions continue to arise with regard to the risks and benefits of placing abused and neglected children with kin. Although the knowledge base is still evolving, research, such as that by Philip Garnier and John Poertner, shows that children in formal kinship care are as safe as, or safer than, children placed in non-related foster family care—a finding that runs counter to the conviction that the "apple doesn't fall far from the tree," i.e. that children's safety is jeopardized by placing them in the same homes in which the parents who had abused and neglected them had been raised. Other critics of formal kinship care welcome the greater governmental support but dispute the necessity of requiring relatives to undergo the same training, fingerprinting, and home inspection that are required of strangers who apply to become licensed foster parents.

Predictions that open-ended stipends to relative foster parents would induce parents to abandon children to formal kinship care in the wake of 1990s welfare reform in the United States failed to materialize. Nonetheless, the prospect of incorporating a larger number of private kinship caregivers into the formal system continues to raise both budgetary and policy concerns. As noted by Robert Geen, the number of children in private kinship care in the United States is estimated to be ten times greater than the number of children in kinship foster care.

Scientific knowledge of kinship care is only now catching up with current policy dilemmas. Except for a few pioneering studies of informal adoption by Robert Hill and child-sharing by Carol Stack among African Americans, little existed prior to 1990 in the social science or social work literature to guide policy and practice. Since that time, studies of kinship care have proliferated. Much more is now known about its prevalence, inter-jurisdictional variation in the formal use of relatives as foster parents, differences between kinship caregivers and unrelated foster parents, and the comparative safety, stability, and permanence of kinship placements. Still, significant gaps remain.

Whether the infusion of public subsidies and bureaucratic standards into family-based patterns of loyalty and systems of reciprocity strengthen or weaken voluntary kinship commitments remains an unresolved issue as noted by Janet Finch. On the one hand, there is the longstanding worry that paid systems drive out voluntary ones by substituting financial incentives for caregiver altruism and family duty. On the other hand, there is the alternative hypothesis that government participation helps to sustain caregiving relationships by generalizing the norm of mutual support beyond individual donor and recipient to the wider society.

The jury is still out on these matters. Considering the enormous emotional appeal of the maxim that children are always better off looked after by family than by strangers, F. Ainsworth and Anthony Maluccio point out that the potential for error in policymaking and decision-making by practitioners is high in the absence of clear decision-making guidelines based on sound research from a cross-cultural perspective. As discussed by Mark Testa and Kristin Slack, theoretical advances in sociobiology, evolutionary psychology, and family sociology are refining our understanding of the motivations, willingness, and capacity of kinfolk to look after dependent family members. More empirical research and better program evaluations will be needed, especially outside of the United States, before an informed verdict can be reached on whether kinship foster care is in the best interest of all children who are placed in substitute care or whether it improves outcomes only under uniquely defined circumstances.

See also Foster Care in the U.S.; Informal Adoption.

Further Reading

Ainsworth, F. and Anthony Malluccio. "Kinship Foster Care: False Dawn or New Hope?" *Australian Social Work* 51 (1998): 3–8.

Bell, Winifred. "Relatives' Responsibility: A Problem in Social Policy." *Social Work* (January 1965): 32–39.

Children's Defense Fund. *States' Subsidized Guardianship Laws at a Glance.* Washington, DC: Children's Defense Fund, 2004.

Donner, William. "Sharing and Compassion: Fosterage in a Polynesian Society." *Journal of Comparative Family Studies* 30 (1999): 703–722.

Finch, Janet. *Family Obligations and Social Change.* Cambridge, UK: Polity Press, 1989.

Garnier, Philip and John Poertner. "Using Administrative Data to Assess Child Safety in Out-of-Home Care." *Child Welfare* 79 (2000): 597–613.

Geen, Robert. "The Evolution of Kinship Care Policy and Practice." *The Future of Children* 14 (2004): 131–149.

Greeff, Roger, ed. *Fostering Kinship: An International Perspective on Kinship Foster Care.* Aldershot, UK: Ashgate, 1999.

Hill, Robert. *Informal Adoption among Black Families.* Washington, DC: National Urban League, 1977.

Roschelle, Anne. *No More Kin: Exploring Race, Class, and Gender in Family Networks.* Thousand Oaks, CA: Sage, 1997.

Rowe, Jane, Hillary Cain, Marion Hundleby, and Anne Keane. *Long-Term Foster Care.* New York: St. Martin's Press, 1984.

Stack, Carol. *All Our Kin: Strategies for Survival in a Black Community.* New York: Harper and Row, 1974.

Testa, Mark, and Kristin Shook Slack. "The Gift of Kinship Foster Care." *Children and Youth Services Review* 24 (2002): 79–108.

Testa, Mark, Kristen Shook, Leslie Cohen, and Melinda Woods. "Permanency Planning Options for Children in Formal Kinship Care." *Child Welfare* 75 (1996): 451–470.

Korea and Adoption

Hollee A. McGinnis

South Korea has the longest running intercountry adoption program, and has sent more children overseas for adoption than any other country in the world. Although the first intercountry adoptions occurred in the aftermath of the Second World War, it was the overseas placement of South Korean children following the end of the Korean War (1950–1953) that initiated the large scale practice of intercountry adoption, currently involving the transfer of an estimated twenty to thirty thousand children from over fifty countries each year. South Korea and the generation of children and families formed through intercountry adoption were pioneers. Understanding the historical, social, cultural, and political forces that shaped the development of intercountry adoption in South Korea provides invaluable insight into the complexities and controversy that continue to shape intercountry adoption practice.

Children of War

The practice of overseas adoption of Korean-born children was virtually non-existent in Korea prior to the 1950s, and the western practice of non-relative adoption was culturally not accepted. Although there is some evidence that adoption of abandoned children did occur, cultural beliefs rooted in Neo-Confucian doctrine since the seventeenth century recognized adoption for the purposes of inheritance and continuation of the paternal blood lineage. Children who were orphaned were traditionally taken care of by extended family, with the first western-style orphanages introduced by missionaries in the late nineteenth century. Ultimately, cultural beliefs in ethnic homogeneity, discrimination toward children born outside of wedlock, post-war chaos, poverty, social upheaval, and decline of traditional Korean society contributed to the development of intercountry adoption practices, establishing it as an important component of South Korean social policy for orphaned and abandoned children.

According to the South Korean Ministry of Health and Welfare records, between 1953 and 2002, a total of 151,697 Korean-born children were sent overseas for adoption and placed in more than twenty Western countries. Some estimate as many as two hundred thousand children have been sent abroad, including unaccounted for private adoptions. During this fifty-year period, two-thirds (a total of 100,858 of those children) were adopted into American families, and 42,231 were adopted into European families, half of whom were placed in Sweden, Norway and Denmark. South Korea remains one of the top three countries sending children to the United States for adoption, ranging from seventeen hundred to two thousand children annually. According to the 2000 U.S. Census data, one-third of all foreign-born children adopted by Americans have come from South Korea.

The first wave of Korean-born children adopted internationally were mostly mixed-race, born to Korean mothers and military fathers from various western countries serving under the auspices of the United Nations during the war. The majority of these children, stigmatized by their mixed-race status and illegitimate births, were abandoned and their plight widely disseminated through Western media. The first formal intercountry adoption occurred in 1953 with the passage in the U.S. Congress of the Refugee Relief Act which granted four thousand special non-quota visas for orphans to enter the United States for the purpose of adoption; although there was evidence that informal adoption, particularly of orphans taken in on military bases as houseboys, interpreters, and mascots, occurred during the war. The South Korean government formally set up an overseas adoption program in 1954 with a presidential order establishing Children Placement Services (presently Social Welfare Society) for the purpose of placing mixed-race children with families in the United States and Europe.

That same year, a farmer from Oregon named Harry Holt watched a documentary presented by World Vision about the plight of mixed-race orphans in

Korea. He and his family were so moved by the predicament of the "GI babies" that in 1955 they adopted eight children under a personal bill passed by Congress. The Holts' efforts inspired others to adopt and, in 1956, Holt Adoption Agency was established, and continues to be a leader in the field of intercountry adoption. By this time, the South Korean government began to allow private adoption agencies to process intercountry adoptions including Catholic Relief Service in 1955, Holt Adoption Agency in 1956, International Social Service in 1957, and Pearl S. Buck's Welcome House in 1958.

A legal and permanent framework for intercountry adoption in South Korea would not be established until 1961 with the passage of the Orphan Adoption Special Law. This law was further amended in 1966 allowing only licensed agencies, working with Western counterparts, to conduct intercountry adoptions. That same year, the U.S. Congress passed the Orphan Eligibility Clause of the Immigration and Nationality Act, which established a permanent provision for the immigration of children for adoption, thereby establishing intercountry adoption in U.S. law.

At the end of the Korean War and because of the division of the country at the 38th parallel, North Korea also faced the problem of thousands of orphaned children. The communist state's response was to designate these orphans as national heroes, establishing special orphanages and schools to help orphans advance in society, and encouraging domestic adoption. Communist ideology that viewed society as a collective family helped to promote domestic adoption despite traditional Confucian beliefs in blood lineage. More recently, information has revealed that, during the war, North Korea also sent war orphans overseas to various Communist countries including Romania, Poland, Hungary, Czechoslovakia, Bulgaria, Mongolia, China, and Russia.

Evolving Practice and Controversy

Throughout the 1960s and 1970s, South Korea began a process of transformation from an agrarian society to a modern, industrial nation. As part of this process, many young unmarried women began working in factories, which contributed to a rise in the number of full-Korean children available for adoption. Many of these children were abandoned as a result of their illegitimate status, with many other children being abandoned as a result of poverty, family break-up, disability, neglect, and prostitution. In addition, the South Korean government adopted a policy to reduce the population through family planning, including a one-child policy, and emigration. As a result, a total of one million Koreans have migrated overseas since the war, of which fifteen percent have been children adopted internationally.

Part of the reason for the abandonment of children was due to social attitudes—including a pervasive stigma regarding adoption, cultural preference for boys, and a belief that abandoning a child would provide a better future—as well as nominal government support for single mothers and perpetuation of patriarchal Neo-Confucian ethics. Under the Family Law of 1960, which codified these beliefs into modern law, a child was legally considered the father's property and women had no rights to inheritance or custody of a child. Hence, intercountry adoption continued to expand in the decades following the war and provided a vital service for thousands of children abandoned due to poverty, industrialization, and discrimination. By the 1970s, only half of the children available for adoption were true orphans, with the majority full-Korean and girls.

In the 1970s, intercountry adoption was also meeting the national need and rising demand in the United States and other Western countries for healthy newborns resulting from declining fertility rates, changes in domestic adoption, and social attitudes. The number of white, healthy infants available for adoption in Western nations had declined as a result of effective contraception, legalized abortion, strengthening of women's rights, and weakening of cultural taboos regarding unmarried mothers and single parenthood. Progressive attitudes regarding racial tolerance contributed to the acceptance of interracial adoptions as a means of removing children from institutions into permanent families, and as a socially responsible way of expanding a family without contributing to population growth. In addition, a perception that international adoption was successful further fueled demand. In 1976, international adoptions of South Korean children reached an all time high of 6,597 children, with approximately four thousand being adopted by American families.

At the same time, intercountry adoption was criticized and utilized as a political pawn in a battle for legitimacy between the two Koreas. During the 1970s, North Korea publicly accused its neighbor of "selling" Korean children for profit as "mail-order babies" to foreigners. In addition, reports of adoption disruption and maltreatment of adopted Korean children in Scandinavian countries were publicized. In response, South Korea temporarily suspended intercountry adoptions to those countries from 1970–1975. In addition, the government revised its adoption law in 1976 and renamed it the Special Adoption Law. It restricted the number of receiving countries to eleven, required adoption agencies in Korea to be run wholly by Koreans, and limited the number of agencies to four: Social Welfare Society, Holt Children's Services, Korea Social Services (established as the first agency to be run by Koreans in 1964), and Eastern Child Welfare Society (established in 1972). The Five Year Plan for Adoption and Foster Care (1976–1981) introduced a system of quotas intended to reduce the number of intercountry adoptions by one thousand and increase domestic adoptions by five hundred annually. Intercountry adoptions, however, continued throughout the remainder of the decade at high levels, and by 1980 the government discontinued the policy as a result of its failure to increase domestic adoption.

In 1981, the South Korean government altered its approach towards intercountry adoption, viewing it as a way to develop friendship ties and "goodwill ambassadors" with Western countries and promote emigration. The quota system was abolished and intercountry adoptions greatly expanded with the largest number of children—66,511—to be sent abroad in one decade. During the 1988 Seoul Olympic Games, however, South Korea again faced massive international criticism of its adoption policies, this time by Western journalists who portrayed the host country as the "leading global exporter" of children. In 1989, the South Korean government enacted a policy to terminate intercountry adoptions by 1996, except for children who were mixed-race or had disabilities. In addition, tax reductions were provided to encourage domestic adoption. This second attempt to phase out intercountry adoption, however, was overturned in 1994 on the grounds that domestic adoption rates remained too low. Instead, an annual flexible decrease of three to five percent in intercountry adoptions was planned with eventual phasing out of the practice by 2015. In 1995, the adoption law was changed to its present name, the Special Law on Adoption Promotion and Procedure with small revisions made in 1999 and 2000.

With the exception of the two years following the 1997 Asian economic "IMF crisis" in which twenty four hundred children were processed, the number of children sent overseas for adoption decreased to a little over two thousand cases a year throughout the 1990s. By the end of the decade, domestic adoptions accounted for one-third of all adoptions and efforts to develop a system of long-term foster care were started. Despite this progress, about seventeen to eighteen thousand children remained in institutional care throughout the decade.

Future Directions

Since the 1980s, South Korea has emerged as a modern democratic nation; however, pervading social attitudes that stigmatize single mothers, out-of-wedlock births, and adoption remain. Although the 1960 Family Law was reformed in 1991 giving women equal rights to inheritance, property, and power to include a child in their own family registry, discrimination towards single mothers and lack of economic support make parenting an extremely difficult option. Thus, since the 1990s, the majority of children available for intercountry adoption were born to young (under twenty-five years of age), single unwed women or widows. These women typically entered maternity homes where they could hide their pregnancy, thereby mitigating the shame of having had premarital sex or a previous marriage, and the potential ruin it could impart on future social advancement.

Despite the commitment of the government to limit the placements of Korean children with families overseas, the reality is that intercountry adoption will likely continue in some capacity. Although the government continues to encourage domestic adoptions by South Koreans, prejudices remain. The number of domestic adoptions still cannot keep pace with the estimated seven thousand children in need of state welfare intervention every year or the nearly eighteen thousand children in institutions. Discrimination towards children who are physically or mentally handicapped, or who are mixed-race prevails, and often for those children there are no alternatives except institutional care or overseas adoption.

As the first generation of internationally adopted Korean children reached adulthood, research has generally found the majority of the children have faired well. Many of these pioneers of intercountry adoption, the vast majority of whom were adopted by Caucasian parents and raised in transracial families, have prospered to become healthy, contributing members of society. But for many it came at the cost of losing connection with their birth country and understanding of their ethnic and racial identities. Since the late 1980s and throughout the 1990s, Korean adult intercountry adoptees have steered adoption practices in new directions. Many have returned to South Korea to experience their birth culture or search for birth family, and have informed practitioners about the importance of maintaining a connection to birth culture. Others have formed organizations and associations to share their experiences, and many are imparting their wisdom—through books, film, music and art—to the next generation of intercountry adoptees and their families.

See also Holt, Harry and Bertha; Transracial and Intercountry Adoption.

Further Reading

Freundlich, M., and J. Kim Lieberthal. "Korean Adoptees' Perception of International Adoption." Evan B. Donaldson Adoption Institute Web Site. http://www.adoptioninstitute. org/ (accessed January, 2005).

Hubinette, Tobias. "Demographic Information and Korean Adoption History." *Guide to Korea for Overseas Adopted Koreans*. Seoul, South Korea: Overseas Koreans Foundation, 2004.

Hubinette, Tobias. "North Korea and Adoption." *Korean Quarterly* Winter 2002–2003: 24–25.

Lovelock, K. "Intercountry Adoption as a Migratory Practice: A Comparative Analysis of Intercountry Adoption and Immigration Policy and Practice in the United States, Canada, and New Zealand in the Post W.W. II Period." *International Migration Review* 34 (2000): 907–923.

Sarri, R., Y. Baik, and M. Bombyk. "Goal Displacement and Dependency in South Korean-United States Intercountry Adoption." *Children and Youth Services Review* 20 (1998): 87–114.

L

Latin America and Adoption

Carol V. Johnson

Adoption was practiced informally throughout Latin America for hundreds of years when children whose parents were deceased or unable to care for them were taken in and raised by relatives. Since the early twentieth century, legal procedures have been established to formalize adoptions. Individual countries have also set requirements for adoptive parents, including age limits, minimum length of marriage, and minimum age difference between parent and child. Most permit adoptions by single and divorced individuals, but do not accept unmarried or same-sex couples. Single men usually may not adopt girls unless they are blood relatives.

Adoption law in Latin America generally does not distinguish between adoptions by citizens and those by foreigners who are permanent legal residents of a country. Since the early 1970s, many countries have permitted international adoptions, but in recent years nearly all have severely restricted or even halted such adoptions to protect children, preserve the rights of their biological relatives, and ensure the countries' own future.

These changes have been made as serious concerns have arisen over adopted children's loss of cultural ties to their native countries. Critics of international adoption see it as cultural genocide. They object to the cultural imperialism they perceive when childless couples from wealthier countries feel entitled to adopt the children of poorer countries. Also, rumors have circulated for years that North Americans have ulterior motives for acquiring Latin American children. These rumors are clearly false, but isolated cases of fraud and kidnapping have led to negative publicity, which in turn has fueled anti-adoption sentiment. Finally, progress has been slow in ratifying the Hague Convention on Intercountry Adoption and implementing its provisions, further complicating adoption policy and practice in Latin American countries.

Social and Cultural Context

In Latin American culture, children are loved and highly valued. However, conditions of extreme poverty and political instability in many countries make it very difficult for parents to raise their children. Fertility rates are high because in poor countries without social security programs and where infant and child mortality rates are high, plenty of children are needed to ensure support for parents in their old age. There are few family planning clinics because the Catholic Church prohibits most forms of birth control. Poor, uneducated women cannot afford contraceptive devices, may lack knowledge of them, or may distrust the government programs that offer them. Abortion is generally illegal, and available only to the wealthy.

Among the lower classes, family structure is loose and common-law marriages are prevalent. A culture of machismo encourages men to father children by girlfriends, then abandon these families when they leave to search for work. Among the upper classes, it is common and even expected for married men to have children by mistresses or domestic servants, but they are not expected to legitimize these children or take responsibility for their support. For women, a stigma may still be attached to unwed motherhood, and it is virtually impossible for a poor, single mother to raise several children alone. All of these factors contribute to the large numbers of children whose parents cannot care for them and who may become available for adoption.

A woman who decides to relinquish her child for adoption may contact an adoption agency or attorney, or choose to leave her infant behind when she leaves a maternity hospital. In some cases, because of their mothers' need for privacy or because the mothers distrust the authorities, children are abandoned, frequently in a safe place such as outside a police station, where they may be found and cared for. Because the culture emphasizes strong ties between mothers and daughters, desperately poor women are slightly more likely to relinquish infant boys than girls. Although private adoptions are sometimes arranged for women of the mostly European upper classes, most Latin American children placed for adoption are from the lower classes and are Amerindians, mestizos, or of African descent.

Relinquished or abandoned children are usually taken into care by government or private social service agencies, often operated by religious groups. Orphanages house many children who have been left there by parents who hope eventually to reclaim them, so not all children in orphanages are adoptable, nor are most street children. Increasingly, private foster care has replaced institutional care. It is usually paid for by adoptive parents while their cases are being processed.

The vast majority of adoptions in Latin America are by relatives or foreigners. Domestic adoptions by non-relatives are rare because it is not part of the traditional culture to adopt an unrelated child and raise that child as one's own. Also, poor families cannot afford to formalize the adoption of an unrelated child or adolescent who is living with them.

International Adoptions from Latin America

The first international adoptions from Latin America to other countries began in the early 1970s, when North American missionary couples serving in Ecuador and Colombia sought to adopt individual children from miserable, understaffed orphanages. They began to assist each other in navigating the complex legal process. During the following decade, South Korea, which had been the original source of children for international adoptions in the U.S. beginning in the 1950s, tightened its policies to discourage overseas placements in favor of in-country adoptions. With the future of adoptions from Korea uncertain, agencies in the U.S. developed contacts in Latin America and began to promote adoptions from South America as an alternative to the long waiting lists for healthy U.S.-born infants.

In the 1980s, as the numbers of international adoptions from all countries peaked, adoptions from Latin America also peaked. Thousands of children were adopted from South American countries through programs established in Colombia, Ecuador, Paraguay, Chile, Brazil, and Peru. Desperate poverty and political violence in Central America led to the adoption of thousands more children from Guatemala, Honduras, El Salvador, Mexico, and Costa Rica. Smaller numbers of children were adopted from the Caribbean nations, especially Haiti and the Dominican Republic. During these years, many of the children adopted from Latin America were taken to Canada, Western Europe, and Australia, as well as to the United States.

Since the mid-1990s, adoption rates from Latin America have plummeted as countries have tightened their regulations and as China and Eastern Europe became open to adoptions by Westerners. U.S. State Department figures show that between 2001 and 2005, Guatemala, Colombia, and Haiti were the only Latin American countries with more than one hundred children per year entering the U.S. on adoption visas. Even so, for all international adoptions, Guatemala was the third most frequent country of origin, behind only China and Russia. Its numbers have increased in each of the past ten years, reaching 3,783 in 2005. Relative to its population, Guatemala places more children internationally than any other country.

Adoption advocates argue that the vast majority of placements from Latin America have been quite successful. The children arrive in their new homes with some lingering effects of malnutrition and the parasites that are endemic to their native countries, but most attain good health within a relatively short time. Serious attachment disorders are rare because large numbers are infants and toddlers at the time of adoption, without the history of neglect and abuse common in older children adopted internationally. Also, foster care in Latin America can be excellent. The standard of living may be low by North American standards, but it is a culture where babies and children are handled with a great deal of warmth and physical affection.

Adoption Procedures

To guard against corruption, virtually all Latin American governments that permit international adoption have included two major safeguards in their procedures. First, they have established strict laws requiring prospective parents to appear in court in person to file the adoption petition. Second, they almost never permit foreigners to take children abroad under a legal guardianship arrangement to adopt later in their home country. No child may leave the country until the court is satisfied that the adoption is in the child's best interest and has issued the final decree.

Because of these laws, most adoptions from Latin America have required adoptive parents to make two trips, once to file the petition and the second to return some months later to finalize the adoption and take the child home. Often, at least one parent must stay in the country while the case is being processed. This stay may lengthen out to many months.

These requirements have discouraged all but the most determined families and dramatically reduced the number of adoptions from Latin America since the 1980s. Adoptions from El Salvador, for instance, have all but ceased under a new family code that prohibits the proxy adoptions that were popular during and immediately following the Salvadoran civil war, which ended in 1992. There is great reluctance to send children out of the country because they are considered its most precious natural resource in its efforts to rebuild.

A significant exception to the travel requirements is Guatemala, where adoptions may be carried out by proxy, and legal guardianships obtained so that children may be escorted by agency representatives to their new homes. In practice, however, most parents prefer to travel to Guatemala to see their child before beginning the adoption process. They realize that it is better for their child to meet them in Guatemala so as not to think an escort is the new parent. Some parents also value the opportunity to see their child's native country and even, in some cases, meet the birth mother. The less restrictive policies, together with the relatively short distance between Guatemala and the United States, help to account for the popularity of Guatemalan adoptions in recent years.

Latin American courts conduct thorough investigations to ensure that a child presented for adoption has been voluntarily relinquished by the birth mother. In Guatemala, where birth mothers may arrange adoptions through private attorneys, the petition cannot be filed until DNA testing establishes the biological relationship between the baby and the woman placing the baby for adoption. In abandonment cases, most countries require that before an adoption petition can be filed, the child's impending adoption must be advertised in newspapers to give relatives an opportunity to claim the child, and an abandonment decree must be issued by the court.

Several Latin American countries have established central governmental authorities to oversee all adoptions. Agencies from overseas must be licensed to work directly with these authorities, and there are no in-country private adoption agencies. Colombia was the first to require that all adoptions be processed through a government agency after a 1982 incident in which an attorney was arrested for kidnapping. These central boards usually keep waiting lists of approved families and assign children to families. It is nearly impossible for families to bypass the official channels and adopt particular children who are not related to them. Other countries that permit adoption only through central governmental authorities include Brazil, Chile, Costa Rica, the Dominican Republic, El Salvador, Haiti, Honduras, Jamaica, Paraguay, and Peru.

Countries without central authorities permit local attorneys and adoption facilitators to arrange adoptions, but generally have strict policies for licensing foreign agencies to operate there. Where private, non-agency adoptions are still permitted, those pursuing them are cautioned that the children may have been obtained fraudulently, raising serious ethical issues and increasing the risk that without clear documentation of their legal status, they may not qualify as orphans under U.S. immigration law.

Finally, concerns about adoption fraud in Latin America have led to strict regulation of the fees that may be charged. Countries with central adoption authorities often do not charge for arranging adoptions. This is to avoid even the appearance of baby selling. Fees for other adoption-related services such as attorneys' services and foster care may be strictly regulated. Parents may be asked to report to local authorities any adoption-related fee that exceeds what is usual and customary. It is illegal in every country and under U.S. immigration law to offer payment or gifts to biological parents. An affidavit may be required stating that the birth mother has received no payment for her child.

Although Latin American adoption processes can be extremely long, complex, and frustrating, an unwritten protocol demands that prospective parents not show any impatience during their wait. The culture is generally less hurried than that of North America, and foreigners are well advised not to do or say anything that would suggest a lack of respect for local laws and customs. U.S.-based agencies also warn that any attempt to circumvent the process could result in sudden termination of the proceedings. Even so, attorneys in the countries sometimes advise their clients to take small gifts such as boxes of candy when they visit governmental offices, hinting that doing so may help move the process along.

As elsewhere in the world, adoption policies in Latin America can change suddenly as a country's leaders change, as economic conditions change, and as rumors or occasional cases of corruption surface. Where international adoptions are legal, they may not be possible because individual judges who disapprove of the practice may simply refuse to process the cases. Finally, Latin American countries that have ratified the Hague Convention may be waiting for potential receiving countries to ratify it, and for both themselves and the receiving countries to finish implementing its provisions before authorizing more intercountry adoptions.

The future of adoptions from Latin America may depend greatly on the willingness of adoptive parents to send frequent updates and photos to reassure officials in the sending countries that the children are healthy and well cared for. Countries may require such reports for a decade or more after an adoption, but these reports are in effect voluntary because the requirements are unenforceable once the children leave for new homes overseas.

Further Reading

Bartholet, Elizabeth. *Family Bonds: Adoption and the Politics of Parenting*. New York: Houghton Mifflin, 1993.

Goldschmidt, Ilse. "National and Intercountry Adoptions in Latin America." *International Social Work* 29 (1986): 257–68.

Latin America Parents Association (LAPA) Web Site. http://www.lapa.com

Los Ninos International Web Site. http://www.losninos.org

Nelson-Erichsen, Jean, and Heino R. Erichsen. *Butterflies in the Wind: Spanish/Indian Children with White Parents*. The Woodlands, TX: Los Ninos International Adoption Center, 1992.

Nelson-Erichsen, Jean, and Heino R. Erichsen. *How to Adopt Internationally: A Guide for Agency-Directed and Independent Adoptions*. Revised and Updated Edition. Fort Worth, TX: Mesa House Publishing, 2003.

Pilotti, Francisco. J. "Intercountry Adoption: A View from Latin America." *Child Welfare* 64 (1985): 25–35.

Register, Cheri. *"Are Those Kids Yours?" American Families with Children Adopted from Other Countries*. New York: Free Press, 1991.

Strassberger, Laurel. *Our Children from Latin America*. New York: Tiresias Press, 1992.

U.S. Department of State Web Site. http://www.travel.state.gov/family/adoption/country

Primary Document

How Did a Rumor Change International Adoption Policy?

During the late 1980s and into the 1990s, rumors swept around the world that adopted or kidnapped infants, often said to be from Latin American countries, were being used to provide body parts for organ transplants in wealthy nations. The gruesome and unfounded rumors provide a case study, not only in the sociology of rumor, but also how such misinformation impacted international adoption policy. The following excerpt from a lengthy report by the United States Information Agency provides an overview of the life of this rumor and its impact.

The "Baby Parts" Myth: The Anatomy of a Rumor

Since 1987, a totally unfounded, horrifying rumor has swept the world press. The ghastly and totally untrue charge is that Americans—or Europeans, Canadians, or

Israelis—are adopting infants or kidnapping children from Latin America or other locations, and murdering or maiming them in order to use their body parts for organ or cornea transplants. This gruesome story has been reported hundreds of times by newspapers, radio, and television stations throughout the world, has won prestigious journalism awards, and is believed by tens of millions of people, if not more. . . .

The Mythical Origins of the Rumor

The "baby parts" rumor probably arose spontaneously as an "urban legend," a false but widely believed form of modern folklore. . . . Experts on popular myths state that the "baby parts" story is a modern adaptation of a centuries-old tale. French folklorist Veronique Campion-Vincent wrote: "The baby-parts story is a new—updated and technologized—version of an immemorial fable. The core of the fable is that a group's children are being kidnapped and murdered by evil outsiders.

Accusations of such kidnappings and ritual murder were made against Christians in ancient Rome [and against] Jews throughout antiquity, the Middle Ages, and up to modern times ... Child abductions in 18th century France were explained by ailing nobility who needed them for medical reasons: the leprous King needed blood baths, or a mutilated Prince needed a new arm which incompetent surgeons were trying each day to graft from a new kidnapped child."

The Rumor Breaks into the World Press

In the modern version of this legend, individuals have reported hearing the "baby parts" rumor as far back as the early to mid-1980s, although it did not appear in the international press until January 1987, when Leonardo Villeda Bermudez, the former Secretary General of the Honduran Committee for Social Welfare, mentioned the rumor during an interview in a way that made it appear as if it was true. Mr. Villeda immediately issued a clarification stating that he had merely heard unconfirmed rumors of such activities. All top Honduran officials, including the President's wife, emphasized that there was no evidence for such allegations, but by this time the rumor had been reported by a wire service and it began to circulate throughout the media worldwide, appearing in Guatemala the next month and soon afterwards in Europe.

In April 1987, the Soviet disinformation apparatus began a conscious effort to spread and embellish this unfounded rumor. . . . The Soviet disinformation campaign in the media ended in late 1988.

Occasional disinformation—deliberate lies or distortions undertaken for a political purpose—still occurs. The Cubans continue to press the child organ trafficking story, having repeatedly tried to introduce resolutions on this issue at U.N. human rights meetings. One formerly Soviet-controlled front group, the International Association of Democratic Lawyers, has continued to try to foster the rumor, particularly through its status as a non-governmental organization accredited to the United Nations. Some anti-U.S. extremists, typically from the far left in Western Europe and the extreme right in Guatemala, have embraced the rumor enthusiastically, apparently because it fits with their anti-U.S. political agenda. Most recently, Iranian publications have begun to propagate the rumor.

Although political motivations have been responsible for some of the more spectacular outbursts of the child organ trafficking rumor, for the most part, the rumor has been embraced and spread by well-meaning individuals who believe it out of naïveté or who worry that it may be true. Tragically, the publicity these well-intentioned individuals have given the rumor by deploring a non-existent crime has inadvertently contributed to its credibility and the resultant damage it has done....

The Impossibility of Concealing Clandestine Organ Transplants

Health and organ transplant officials in the United States and other countries have stated emphatically that it would be impossible to successfully conceal any clandestine organ trafficking ring.

In many countries, the sale or purchase of organs for transplants is expressly forbidden by law, with stiff penalties for violators. For example, organ sales for transplant have been illegal in the United States since 1984.

There are similar statutes in many other countries.

In addition to the legal and moral deterrents to organ trafficking, the technical requirements that would be involved in arranging and operating an alleged murder-for-organ-transplantation scheme are so formidable that such clandestine activities are a practical impossibility...

Repeated Investigations Find No Evidence for the Rumor

In early 1987, when the "baby parts" rumor first appeared, representatives of the U.S. Justice Department, the Federal Bureau of Investigation, the Food and Drug Administration, the National Institutes of Health, the Department of Health and Human Services, and the Immigration and Naturalization Service all investigated their records and stated that they had no evidence that would indicate alleged organ trafficking....

In April 1996, French folklorist Veronique Campion-Vincent completed an extremely comprehensive 285-page study for the French Transplant Organization entitled Transplantation, Rumor, and the Media: Accounts of Organ Theft. Her voluminous and extremely thorough examination concluded unequivocally that organ theft rumors are an unfounded urban legend.

The Rumor's Adverse Impacts

The false "baby parts" rumor has done tremendous damage in a number of different ways.

Most dramatically, it led to attacks on Americans and others in Guatemala during March 1994. On March 8, a mob in a Guatemalan town burned the police station in which an American wrongly suspected of child kidnapping had been held. The mob resisted the efforts of several hundred riot police and was not quieted until army troops and armored vehicles arrived to restore order. On March 29, an American tourist, June Weinstock, was savagely beaten by a mob, which accused her of abducting a Guatemalan child....

In addition to assaults on Americans, Guatemalan media reported numerous attempted lynchings by angry mobs that believed that "strangers" were allegedly stealing their children. A Swiss volcanologist, a Salvadoran family visiting relatives, foreign assistance workers, backpackers, and Guatemalan citizens all reportedly suffered such attacks.

The hysteria generated by this rumor has had an adverse impact on intercountry adoptions in a number of countries, according to adoption groups. In May 1991, the Turkish government announced that it was suspending intercountry adoptions because of the rumor. Adoptions have also been suspended or hindered in Honduras, Guatemala, Brazil, Mexico, and many other countries. As a result, some children who might have found loving homes remain in orphanages. The government of Bulgaria has even gone so far as to require prospective adoptive parents from foreign countries to sign a form stating, "I will not permit my child to be an organ donor nor allow the child to give organs or be a part of any medical experiments."

The rumor has also led to groundless, but widespread fears among parents in Latin America and elsewhere who believe that their child might be kidnapped for the purpose of organ transplantation.

Finally, the rumor is probably also causing an indirect but very real loss of life. Voluntary organ donation is a very altruistic activity, and one that can be adversely affected by any perception of impropriety or illicit behavior. Worldwide, there are long waiting lists for organ transplants that exceed donor supply and, as a result, people die every day because of the lack of sufficient donor organs. To the extent that the organ theft rumor has been believed, it has very likely decreased voluntary organ donation, and thereby caused many premature deaths.

1993: The Rumor is Given Credence in Television Documentaries

In November 1993, two hour-long television documentaries, one British/Canadian and the other French, gave credence to the "baby parts" rumor. Both programs contained numerous errors. . . .

In short, the "revelations" of alleged organ and cornea trafficking in both programs turned out to be groundless.

Prestigious International Organizations Examine the Rumor

In addition to the media attention generated by the British/Canadian and French programs, both the European Parliament and United Nations have issued reports that have given credence to the "baby parts" rumor.

On February 25, 1993, the European Parliament issued a report on prohibiting trade in transplant organs that made many valuable suggestions but also included the unsubstantiated claim that "there is evidence that fetuses, children, and adults in some developing countries have been mutilated and others murdered with the aim of obtaining transplant organs for export to rich countries." The report, drafted by the former French Minister of Health and then-European Member of Parliament Leon Schwartzenberg, claimed that "to deny the existence of such trafficking is comparable to denying the existence of the ovens and gas chambers during the last war." . . .

. . . Mr. Schwartzenberg revealed that the source for most of his information had been an article in the August 1992 issue of Le Monde Diplomatique. . . . The claims in Le Monde Diplomatique, which Mr. Schwartzenberg repeated, were groundless.

A former U.N. Special Rapporteur on the Sale of Children, Vitit Muntarbhorn, also gave credence to the rumor in several reports he issued from 1991 to 1994. The Special Rapporteur depended largely on press accounts, which included many mistakes, and offered no credible evidence of trafficking in children's organs. In the June 26, 1995, issue of Newsweek, Myriam Tebourbi, a U.N. employee who assisted the Special Rapporteur, commented, "We never had any real evidence. He had lots of allegations, but nothing concrete. . . . We had no resources to mount our own investigation."

1994–1996: The Rumor Attains Unprecedented Credibility

On March 7, 1994, Eric Sottas, director of the Geneva-based World Organization Against Torture, repeated various claims of "baby parts" trafficking in a 15-page paper that received wide publicity. Mr. Sottas also incorrectly stated that only one-fifth of U.S. organ transplants are centrally recorded and wrongly implied that organ sales are permitted in the United States. In fact, organ sales are illegal in the U.S. and all organ transplants are centrally recorded and monitored....

On March 18, 1996, a series of articles repeating "baby parts" claims in the Brazilian newspaper *Correio Braziliense* was awarded the "King of Spain" prize for journalism.... The series' author, Ana Beatriz Magno, admitted in the March 20 issue of the Spanish newspaper *El Pais* that "I can only reproduce what the international press has written" on this issue and that she did not seek to verify any of the claims she had repeated....

Conclusion

Despite the fact that it is totally unfounded, the "baby parts" rumor is now perceived as fact and accepted as conventional wisdom in large parts of the world. It has generated hysteria in Central American countries, led to brutal, unprovoked attacks on Americans and others, disrupted the lives of numerous prospective adoptive parents and the children they wished to adopt, won prestigious media awards in Europe, caused major disruptions in cornea donations in Latin America, and is, in all likelihood, causing numerous premature deaths because of its adverse effects on organ donation.

This sensationalistic rumor springs from deep, irrational, but very powerful anxieties stirred by advances in the life-saving process of organ transplantation. These fears have unfortunately been fanned by some who have cynically advanced this rumor for political purposes. The false rumor has also been propagated by many others who genuinely believe it. As a result of this cycle of events, the "baby parts" myth has now attained such widespread currency that it continues to feed on itself and, tragically, is widely believed despite numerous corrective statements, authoritative statements pointing to the impossibility of such practices occurring, and the fact that despite almost ten years of searching, no government, non-governmental organization, intergovernmental body, or investigative journalist has ever produced any credible evidence to support the charges.

Source

Excerpted from United States Information Agency. "The 'Baby Parts' Myth: The Anatomy of a Rumor, May 1996." [Online, January 2006]. U.S. Department of State International Information Programs Web Site. http://usinfo.state.gov/media/Archive_Index/The_Baby_Parts_Myth.html.

Lifebooks

Donna Dea Holland

A lifebook documents foster and adoptive children's social, developmental, educational, and medical history. The purpose of the lifebook is to help children learn about and remember their birth family, reasons for leaving their birth family, and the various placements they experienced since removal from their birth family. The lifebook may be used as a mechanism to document other activities in the children's lives. School reports, homework, report cards, crafts, locks of hair, and various other items should be placed in the lifebook.

There are various approaches to creating a lifebook. Some believe it should be done by the foster parent, while others believe it should be designed and created collaboratively by the caseworker and the children. Still others believe it should be created by several people: foster parents, biological parents, adoptive parents, caseworkers and perhaps siblings and counselors. Generally, when caseworkers and counselors are involved in the creation of the lifebook, it is used as a tool for establishing social bonds with children and to aide in the therapeutic process.

There is also debate about the appropriate format of a lifebook. While most agree that a lifebook is more than a scrapbook, some believe the lifebook should be in paper format and created similarly to a scrapbook. That is, it should contain pictures, letters, notes from family members, and should be possessed by the children. Copies of birth certificates, social security cards, and school records may be contained in the lifebook.

Others argue that the scrapbook approach to lifebooks is inadequate compared to other methods of storing data. For example, videotapes, compact disks and digital video disks are arguably more vivid accounts of history. These are sometimes called "living lifebooks." Proponents of the living lifebook suggest videotaped interviews of biological family members; perhaps a final visit message from the birth family. It may also document children's thoughts and emotions about their removal, their biological family, and placement. This will allow the children to be involved in recording their life stories from their perspectives, which may differ from the perspectives of the foster parents, caseworkers, and biological family members.

The best solution is a combination of both the scrapbook format of the lifebook and the living lifebook. Some records of the past fit more appropriately in one format or the other. For example, a lock of a child's hair is best kept in the scrapbook format of the lifebook while an actual haircut could be nicely documented in a video. Similarly, personal interviews with biological and foster parents allow the children to observe the person, hear the voice, and see various mannerisms, much of which is lost in a photograph.

Lifebooks follow children throughout their placement experience and accompany them through reunification or adoptive placement. However, given that foster care reentry is not uncommon, caseworkers should retain a color copy of the lifebook in the event the child returns to foster care. If reentry occurs, the lifebook process can be added to the copy rather than risk loss of information and continuity in the child's life history. Additionally, children in group homes and residential placement need caseworker involvement to develop the lifebook.

The time children spend in group homes and residential placement should be included in lifebooks. There may be staff members or activity the children want to remember.

Children who experience foster care drift need caseworker support on the lifebook. Many young adults who transition out of foster care at the age of eighteen have little recollection of earlier foster home placements. Some do not even know the names of towns and schools they attended much earlier in their foster care placement. The lifebook may serve as a mechanism for documenting places of living, schools attended, and reasons for foster care drift, and later serve to refresh young adults' account of the foster care experience.

One additional problem can occur. Some children who possess their lifebook may not take proper care of it. Some children have intentionally destroyed all or parts of the lifebook. Occasionally, this is due to an accident but sometimes it is intentional. Thus, it is important the caseworker retain a copy of the lifebook.

The lifebook helps fill the gaps in memory about where the children have been, why they were in various placements, and explanations of absent siblings. The format of the lifebook and the persons involved in creating the lifebook vary. The overall benefit of the lifebook is to provide a source of identity and an accounting of their experiences.

Further Reading

Aust, P. H. "Using the Life Story Book in Treatment of Children in Placement." *Child Welfare* 60 (1981): 535–560.

Backhaus, K. A. "Life books: Tools for Working with Children in Placement." *Social Work* 29 (1984): 551–554.

Clegg, P., and K. Toll. "Videotape and the Memory Visit: A Living Lifebook for Adopted Children." *Child Welfare* 75 (1996): 311–319.

Holoday, R., and S. Maher. "Using Lifebooks with Children In Family Foster Care: A Here-And-Now Process Model." *Child Welfare* 75 (1996): 321–335.

McInturf, J. W. "Preparing Special-needs Children for Adoption Through Use of a Lifebook." *Child Welfare* 65 (1986): 373–386.

Little Orphan Annie

Kathy Shepherd Stolley

"Little Orphan Annie" was a famous fictional orphan who was introduced to Americans in an 1885 poem by James Whitcomb Riley. Published during the period of the orphan trains and alleged to have been based on an orphan taken in by Riley's family, the poem's Annie worked at chores all day and played with the children in the evening. Annie's comic strip life started in an orphanage. Over the years, she survived a range of adventures with her little dog Sandy, many involving "Daddy" Warbucks—a sometimes rich guardian introduced early in the series.

At one point, the comic strip appeared in 500 newspapers. Readers, many of whom were adults, would write the paper with advice or to provide comments on the storyline. Annie was also popular with children, even competing in popularity in a 1937 poll with "The Lone Ranger." She starred in a radio serial, "Adventure Time with Little Orphan Annie," during the 1930s and 1940s. Decades later, Annie became the star of a prize-winning Broadway musical and Hollywood movies.

As noted by Eileen Simpson, the appeal of Annie through her years of heart-wrenching adventures was that Annie reminded families, children, and parents alike, that they had each other. She had "pluck, energy, and resourcefulness ... An indestructible little scapegoat. Annie was an orphan *for* them. Small wonder she was so well loved" (p. 243).

See also Orphan Trains; Popular Culture and Adoption.

Further Reading

Simpson, Eileen. "A Mythic Orphan." *Orphans: Real and Imaginary*. New York: Weidenfeld and Nicolson, 1987: pp. 234–243.

Longitudinal Adoption Studies

Vern L. Bullough

The first American longitudinal study of adoption had its origin in 1934 when the Iowa Bureau of Child Welfare established a policy mandating psychological assessment of children prior to their adoption. The policy led to a longitudinal follow up of children "from the lower social, economic, and educational" levels placed in average and superior foster homes or in adoption at young ages. Though the compilation was conceptualized as a "service project" rather than planned research, it became well-known among social psychologists for the insights it provided into the plasticity of mental growth, developmental changes in age-to-age stability of mental test scores, and the association of children's cognitive abilities with educational characteristics of their biological and adoptive parents.

A sort of follow-up study was the Colorado Adoption Project, a longitudinal study of adopted children, their adoptive parents, and their birth parents. The children were studied at one, two, three, four, and seven years of ages, and results were published of various stages of the research. In general, the results demonstrated a significant, although limited, genetic relationship between infant mental development and adult intelligence. Some relationship was found for environmental influence on mental development, but an even stronger relationship appeared in the control families, which implies a partial genetic mediation of this environmental link. Apparently, adoptive parents have a strong impact on a child's intellectual level in the early years, and genetics "kick in" at a later day.

Other longitudinal studies include the Texas Adoption Project, a study of children measured twice at ten-year intervals, and the Minnesota study of 100 identical twins raised apart. Generally, there has been a strong correlation for intelligence and other traits and biological inheritance, but the value of environment and good parenting are also important.

Further Reading

Bouchard T. J., Jr., D. T. Lykken, M. McGue, N. J. Segal, and A. Tellegen. "Sources of Human Psychological Differences: The Minnesota Study of Twins Reared Apart." *Science* 250 (1990): 12.

Plomin, R., and J. C. De Fries. *The Origin of Individual Differences in Infancy: The Colorado Adoption Project.* Orlando: Academic Press, 1985.

Plomin, R., J. C. De Fries, and D. W. Fulker. *Nature and Nurture During Infancy and Early Childhood: The Colorado Adoption Project.* New York: Cambridge University Press, 1988.

M

Massachusetts Adoption Act (1851)

E. Wayne Carp

The path-breaking 1851 Massachusetts law, "An Act to Provide for the Adoption of Children," is commonly considered the first modern adoption law in American history. It codified earlier state court decisions that had already transformed the law of custody to reflect Americans' new conceptions of childhood and parenthood, which emphasized the needs of children and the contractual and egalitarian nature of spouses' rights of guardianship. Prior to the legislation, adoptions in colonial America and the new nation had occurred mostly for the purpose of name changes and to ensure that adopted children could inherit from their adoptive parents, though many adoptions were formed for more emotional reasons. The total number of adoptions in the period before the Massachusetts legislation is impossible to know, but adoption was becoming more frequent in the years leading up to the 1851 law.

The Massachusetts statute differed from all earlier statutes in its emphasis upon the welfare of the child—it made the adopted person the prime beneficiary of the proceeding. The Massachusetts Adoption Act, as it was commonly called, was the first statute to establish the principle of judicial supervision of adoptions. The law required the judge, before issuing the adoption decree, to ascertain that the adoptive parents were capable of raising, feeding, and educating the child. The concern for the child's welfare drew upon the "best interests of the child" doctrine, which had been evolving slowly in custody cases since the early 1800s, and which would become the cornerstone of modern adoption law. The statute also provided for the written consent of the birth parents, if living, or of the guardian or next of kin if the parents were deceased. Further, it ended the power of birth parents over their children by severing the legal bonds between them and freeing the child from all legal obligations to them after adoption. Finally, the law provided that, for purposes of inheritance, custody, and all other legal circumstances, the adopted child would be considered the legitimate child of the adoptive parents.

The enactment of the Massachusetts Adoption Act marked a watershed in the history of the Anglo-American family and society. Instead of defining the parent-child relationship exclusively in terms of blood kinship, it was now possible to build a family by assuming the responsibility and emotional outlook of a birth parent. In the next quarter century, the Massachusetts Adoption Act came to be regarded as a model statute, and twenty-five states enacted similar laws.

Further Reading

Grossberg, Michael. *Governing the Hearth: Law and the Family in Nineteenth-Century America*. Chapel Hill: University of North Carolina Press, 1985.

Zainaldin, Jamil S. "The Emergence of a Modern American Family Law: Child Custody, Adoption, and the Courts." *Northwestern University School of Law* 73 (1979): 1038–1089.

Primary Document

A Milestone in Adoption Legislation: The Massachusetts Adoption Act (1851)

This milestone law, which as E. Wayne Carp points out in his entry on the "Massachusetts Adoption Act (1851)" is "commonly considered the first modern adoption law in American history." It reflected and codified "Americans' new conceptions of childhood and parenthood," emphasized children's welfare and parental consent, as well as the need for adoption petitioners to be capable and "fit and proper."

"An Act to provide for the Adoption of Children," Acts and Resolves passed by the General Court of Massachusetts, Chap. 324 (1851)

Be it enacted by the Senate and House of Representatives, in General Court assembled, and by the authority of the same, as follows:

Sect. 1. Any inhabitant of this Commonwealth may petition the judge of probate, in the county wherein he or she may reside, for leave to adopt a child not his or her own by birth.

Sect. 2. If both or either of the parents of such child shall be living, they or the survivor of them, as the case may be, shall consent in writing to such adoption: if neither parent be living, such consent may be given by the legal guardian of such child; if there be no legal guardian, no father nor mother, the next of kin of such child within the State may give such consent; and if there be no such next of kin, the judge of probate may appoint some discreet and suitable person to act in the proceedings as the next friend of such child, and give or withhold such consent.

Sect. 3. If the child be of the age of fourteen years or upwards, the adoption shall not be made without his or her consent.

Sect. 4. No petition by a person having a lawful wife shall be allowed unless such wife shall join therein, and no woman having a lawful husband shall be competent to present and prosecute such petition.

Sect. 5. If, upon such petition, so presented and consented to as aforesaid, the judge of probate shall be satisfied of the identity and relations of the persons, and that the petitioner, or, in case of husband and wife, the petitioners, are of sufficient ability to bring up the child, and furnish suitable nurture and education, having reference to the degree and condition of its parents, and that it is fit and proper that such adoption should take effect, he shall make a decree setting forth the said facts, and ordering that, from and after the date of the decree, such child should be deemed and taken, to all legal intents and purposes, the child of the petitioner or petitioners.

Sect. 6. A child so adopted, as aforesaid, shall be deemed, for the purposes of inheritance and succession by such child, custody of the person and right of obedience by such parent or parents by adoption, and all other legal consequences and incidents of the natural relation of parents and children, the same to all intents and purposes as if such child had been born in lawful wedlock of such parents or parent by adoption, saving only that such child shall not be deemed capable of taking property expressly limited to the heirs of the body or bodies of such petitioner or petitioners.

Sect. 7. The natural parent or parents of such child shall be deprived, by such decree of adoption, of all legal rights whatsoever as respects such child; and such child shall be freed from all legal obligations of maintenance and obedience, as respects such natural parent or parents.

Sect. 8. Any petitioner, or any child which is the subject of such a petition, by any next friend, may claim and prosecute an appeal to the supreme judicial court from such decree of the judge of probate, in like manner and with the like effect as such appeals may now be claimed and prosecuted in cases of wills, saying only that in no case shall any bond be required of, nor any costs awarded against, such child or its next friend so appealing. [Approved by the Governor, May 24, 1851.]

Source

As re-printed on the University of Denver College of Law Website. http://www.law. du.edu/sterling/ Content/ALH/MA_adoption.pdf (accessed February, 2006).

Matching

Judith Schachter

"*Matching.* The attempt to select adoptive parents similar to the child to be adopted. The selected parents and children may be similar in appearance, interests, intelligence, personality or other traits. This practice has also become known more recently as trying to achieve a 'good fit' when choosing a family for a specific child." The definition from the 1991 *Encyclopedia of Adoption* reflects a central tenet of child placement practice in the United States. Since the first American adoption law in 1851 until the present, the goal of matching a child with adoptive parents has guided practice and been variously articulated in policy. The traits to match include religion, race, intelligence, and physical features. While interpretation changes, the ideal of "fit" between adopted child and adoptive parent maintains matching in practice.

Matching accompanied the passage of American adoption laws in the late nineteenth and early twentieth centuries. Under the rubric of "the best interests of the child," matching was thought to create a bond between parent and child as secure and as loving as the bond created by birth. During the Progressive Era, social workers defined matching as a best practice in adoption and the profession developed increasingly systematic approaches to discovering similar traits in child and adoptive parents.

Supervised by experts, adoption decisions obey the professional standards set by agencies. These standards are complemented by cultural norms of kinship that assume similarities indicate relatedness. The combined force of "fit" advocated by experts and "resemblance" embraced by participants means matching persists, even as state and federal laws forbid basing placement decisions on race and ethnicity. In non-agency adoptions, adoptive parents reinforce the ideology of matching by choosing children whose traits resemble their own.

Early outcome studies concluded that similarities between parent and child contributed to successful adult adjustment. Subsequent studies of outcome persuaded practitioners to refine the dimensions of matching and to add further characteristics upon which to compare parent and child. From the 1930s through the 1960s, visible traits like skin color and physique were supplemented by assessments of personality, capability, and intelligence. In the following decades, emphasis on infant placement demanded new methods for determining the fit between child and adopting parents. At the same time, identity politics demanded that racial and ethnic factors structure placement decisions. For some practitioners, ignoring the principle of matching put the child at risk in a society in which race and ethnicity are crucial to individual identity.

Many practitioners incorporated race and ethnicity into a growing list of traits upon which to match child with parent. As infant placements increasingly dominate practice, experts evaluate the parents in order to create a good fit. The traits deemed crucial reflect cultural assumptions about person, social status, and achievement. Class status is presumed to correlate with capability; years of education are a measure of intelligence; marriage is a sign of stability. Interviews with parents probe for information that can predict success in the transfer of the child. Genetic testing offers another attribute upon which to match child with parent.

Matching upholds the view that the adoptive family should be a facsimile of the biological family. From its first *Standards for Adoption Service* to the 2000 edition, the Child Welfare League of America grapples with the issue of how to achieve a match that will benefit the child and not jeopardize the search for a family—or violate laws against discrimination. While arguing for practices that speed placement, the *Standards* also assume that sharing race and ethnicity with a parent contributes to the child's well-being.

Since the 1970s, race has dominated the public discourse on matching in the United States. Following the civil rights movement, adoption of black children by white parents raised accusations of racial genocide, of depriving black children of their heritage, and black parents of their children. In 1972, the National Association of Black Social Workers condemned transracial adoption, a position that persists even in the face of two potential challenges: the 1994 federal Multiethnic Placement Act (MEPA) and the growing number of international adoptions.

MEPA mandates that placement not be delayed or denied on the basis of race, color, or national origin. In practice, race can be a factor without violating the law, as long as the child is "speedily" placed. The 1997 federal Adoption and Safe Families Act (ASFA) inadvertently further encourages matching. Designed primarily to move thousands of children out of foster care, ASFA maintains same-race placement by favoring first, family reunification, and, second, long-term foster care or guardianship, and only third, adoption. The first two are likely to maintain the child in a racially "familiar" household, while the latter tends toward transracial adoption, given the proportion of white parents to parents of color in the pool of adoptive parents.

International adoptions, too, reveal the significance of race in decisions about adoption. A miniscule number of children come from African countries, while a large number come from Russia, China, and Latin American countries. Adopted primarily by white parents, these children fall short of transgressing the proscription against white-black adoption. International adoption upholds matching in other ways as well. Traits like intelligence, capability, and physique frame the choice of a child, as does replication of the generational span. Behind these practices lies the "as-if" of American adoption: by law, the adopted child is *just like* a biological child. By custom, this means creating a facsimile of the biological family, in appearance and in form.

Founded on the assumption that a child thrives best in a family whose traits resemble his or her own, matching determines the cultural conceptualization of adoptive kinship as a facsimile of biological kinship. At the same time, by definition, adoption is premised on the conviction that social parenthood, or created kinship, can provide security and well-being to a child. Matching, in American adoption practice, holds adoption to a biological model for permanent ties between parent and child, despite the extension of this form of kinship across diverse individuals.

See also Multiethnic Placement Act (MEPA); Transracial and Intercountry Adoption.

Further Reading

Adamec, Christine, and William Pierce, eds. *Encyclopedia of Adoption*. New York: Facts on File, 1991.

Carp, E.Wayne. *Family Matters*. Cambridge: Harvard University, 1998.

Child Welfare League of America. *CWLA Standards of Excellence for Adoption Services*. Washington, DC: Child Welfare League of America, 2000.

Modell, J. Schachter, with Naomi Dambacher. "Making a 'Real' Family: Matching and Cultural Biologism in American Adoption." *Adoption Quarterly* 1 (1997): 3–33.

Medical Research Involving Orphans and Foster Children

Kathy Shepherd Stolley

A dark chapter in the history of medical research involves the use of orphaned, foundling, and poor children as research subjects. In her review of medical research between 1890–1930, Susan E. Lederer recounts several cases of research involving such children. Beginning in 1801, a series of investigations using children in the Philadelphia almshouses were aimed at producing immunity from measles. The physician involved attempted to inoculate healthy children with body fluids including blood, tears, and even excretions from the skin eruptions of infected children. During the mid-1800s, a Chicago physician conducted research on orphans by inoculating children with blood from those already ill with measles. In 1908, Philadelphia physicians conducted tuberculosis research, primarily using poor and orphaned children living in St. Vincent's Home, by administering tuberculin to them. The early 1900s also saw diagnostic research on syphilis conducted on orphans and hospital patients in New York. The syphilis research resulted in the president of the New York Society for the Prevention of Cruelty to Children lodging charges of battery against the physician involved, charges that the district attorney declined to pursue. Another grievous case of research conducted on orphans involved a New York physician using children at the Hebrew Infant Asylum to test a vaccine for pertussis, as well as conducting invasive procedures to study infant digestion, and withholding orange juice to study the of impact of diet on rickets and scurvy.

Lederer also reports that medical research with child subjects was apparently not uncommon. A study of one pediatric journal, from the years 1911–1916, found eighty-six reports of experimentation involving children. Few of these reports addressed parental approval. However, whether parents were not asked or informed, or the permissions were not reported is unknown. It may also reflect that the children used in these studies were frequently orphans.

The World War II years also saw the use of orphans in medical research. In one case reported by David J. Rothman, dysentery research was conducted by the U.S. government's Committee on Medical Research (CMR) on children in the Ohio Soldiers and Sailors Orphanage. Teenaged boys were injected in various ways with different vaccine suspensions, all of which quickly resulted in serious side effects including pale, ashy skin, temperatures of 105 degrees, severe headaches and backaches, nausea, vomiting, and diarrhea. Further research tried varying doses and injections, all generating less severe reactions, but still severe enough to regard the vaccine as unsuitable for general use. Girls were also used in some of these vaccine studies, with similar results. Mentally retarded subjects were also used for this research.

Why use children in such research? Lederer answers this question by noting several arguments. Physicians felt that, in attempts to develop vaccines against such illnesses as tuberculosis, they needed an uninfected population, more likely to be found among children. They sought comparisons with adult physiology. Some desired medical advancement that could be had by medical discoveries. And, she argues, some performed in the interests of child welfare, although not always in the interest of their individual subjects. Some other commentators have been less generous in their assessments of researchers' motives.

Although ethical review boards are now in place to guard against such abuses, concerns about the use of orphans and foster children in medical research still surface periodically. For example, interest groups have also expressed concerns of potential over-medication of poorly behaved children by overextended staff. In 2004, a news item and a British Broadcasting Corporation documentary entitled "Guinea Pig Kids" raised questions about the involvement of researchers and pharmaceutical companies in HIV-drug trials using children at a New York foster care facility. The controversial story caught the attention of groups such as the Alliance For Human Research Protection (AHRP) that continue to follow it at this writing.

Further Reading

Alliance for Human Research Protection (AHRP). "Promoting Openness, Full Disclosure, and Accountability." AHRP Web Site. http://www.ahrp.org/ethical/incarnation/timeline0805.php

Department of Health and Human Services (DHHS). Office of Human Research Protection (OHRP). "Preliminary Findings RE: Human Research Subject Protections Under Multiple Project Assurance (MPA) M-1356 and Federalwide Assurances FWA-2635 and FWA-2636, May 23, 2005." DHHS OHRP Web Site. http://www.hhs.gov/ohrp/detrm_letrs/YR05/may05c.pdf

Lederer, Susan E. "Orphans as Guinea Pigs: American Children and Medical Experimenters, 1890–1930." In *In the Name of the Child: Health and Welfare, 1880–1940*, edited by Roger Cooter, 96–123. New York: Routledge, 1992.

Pyle, Encarnacion. "Forced Medication Straitjackets Kids." *The Columbus Dispatch*, April 24, 2005. Dispatch.com Web Site. http://www.dispatch.com/reports-story.php?story=dispatch/2005/04/24/20050424-A1-00.html (accessed March, 2006).

Rothman, David J. *Strangers at the Bedside: A History of How Law and Bioethics Transformed Medical Decision Making*. New York: Basic Books, 1991.

Scott, Janny, and Leslie Kaufman. "Belated Charges Ignite Furor Over AIDS Drug Trial." *New York Times*, July 17, 2005, p. A-1.

Medieval Europe and Adoption

Vern L. Bullough

Adoption was little practiced in the Medieval period. Instead, abandoned infants and children were informally taken in by others in the village. As urban centers developed, hospitals appeared which took the sick, the crippled, orphans, and foundlings. Some of these hospitals later developed into orphanages.

In England and in many parts of Europe, abandoned infants were usually relegated to parish care. Some poor parents entrusted or sold their children to noblemen or prosperous burghers who were childless or whose only children had died. Many of these "adoptions" became suspect because they were regarded as an effort to get or maintain a legacy, and both ecclesiastical and secular legislation soon prohibited this. The long-term effect of this prohibition was to discourage outright adoptions.

Some adoptions still occurred. Medieval epic literature describes cases of "illegitimate" infants being abandoned or transferred to relatives for rearing. This was also the case for twins since it was widely believed that a woman could conceive twice consecutively and that, accordingly, twins were not born of the same father. Thus, at least one twin was illegitimate and had to be abandoned or adopted.

Regardless of where abandoned infants ended up, usually in churches or religious institutions, the Christian Church in the West felt a responsibility to keep orphans and abandoned babies alive. This was particularly difficult in terms of infants, who comprised the largest category of these children. The first concern was to see that they were baptized. The chief problem, however, was feeding them. This meant finding a wet nurse since animal products were rarely used.

Some of the institutions kept slave women as wet nurses. Others had local women under contract. Mortality was high among both the natural children of the wet nurse and the others she took in. At the Innocenti orphanage in Florence (founded in 1420) where statistics are available, the mortality rate for the first year ranged between 27–55 percent. In Santa Creu in Barcelona, between 52–67 percent of these children died before they were two years old.

These statistics may seem horrifying to modern readers, but it is estimated that over 50 percent of all children in pre-industrial Europe died before they were five. In the sixteenth century where more accurate data is available, the mortality rate for those under five in England was between 20–30 percent. In France, it was 57 percent. Abandoned infants had far higher mortality rates.

If the child survived past five, there was increasing pressure for him or her to leave the hospital or orphanage and become a valuable member of society. This meant apprenticeship for boys. It meant domestic service for girls, often with a promise of a dowry or marriage after their domestic service was completed. In Florence, this "placement" occurred anywhere between the fifth and tenth years, but even younger children were sometimes apprenticed. In theory, their apprenticeship would last between nine and sixteen years. They learned a trade, received food, clothing, and shelter at the master's home, and were paid at the termination of their apprenticeship. Depending on the master, some learned to read. Girls rarely learned a trade, although, in cities like Florence, many ended up in the cloth industry.

Foundlings and orphans in general were contracted out at younger ages than the children of artisans, who usually started apprenticeships at eleven or twelve. Length of apprenticeship varied by crafts. Some apprenticeships, like those for cooks, were only two years. Apprenticeship was longer for foundlings if only because they entered earlier. Usually their apprenticeship contracts were drawn up either by the orphanage or, in some cases, by the city. Each might receive a monetary payment or a wardrobe, and, in some instances, tools of the trade, at the end of the apprenticeship. Girls received a dowry.

Not all of the children found apprenticeships or domestic service. Any population center usually had small bands of child beggars and vagabonds. These bands were often made up of children of mixed ages with older children supporting siblings or even non-relatives. Many girls ended up in prostitution. Some boys were able to survive as choir boys, an opportunity not open to girls. Adoption remained rare although it occasionally took place within families.

See also Child Donation; Foundry Wheels; Medieval Orphanages.

Further Reading

Brodman, James William. *Charity and Welfare: Hospital and the Poor in Medieval Catalonia*. Philadelphia: University of Pennsylvania Press, 1998.

Brundage, James M. *Law, Sex and Society in Medieval Europe*. Chicago: University of Chicago Press, 1987.

Gies, Frances, and Joseph Gies. *Marriage and Family in the Middle Ages*. New York: Harper and Row, 1987.

Goody, Jack. *The Development of Family and Marriage in Europe*. Cambridge: University Press, 1983.

Shahar, Shulamith. *Children in the Middle Ages*. New York: Routledge, 1990.

Twins and Adoption in Medieval Europe

Vern L. Bullough

Usually, if not always, the birth of twins in Medieval Europe meant the abandonment of at least one. This was because of the popular belief in Medieval Europe, as well as in many other cultures, that a woman could conceive twice consecutively. Accordingly, twins were not born of the same father and were, in effect, illegitimate. In *Le Fresne (The Ash Tree)*, the twelfth century poem by Marie de France, the birth of twins was regarded as a punishment for a mother who had once slandered a pious and chaste woman for giving birth to twins. The birth of twins was often kept secret. One was abandoned, dispatched off to relatives, or put in the hands of a carefully chosen wet nurse. Illegitimate children were treated in much the same way, although some noblemen and prosperous burghers acknowledged their illegitimate children and undertook their upbringing.

Medieval Orphanages

Vern L. Bullough

Parents in early medieval Europe developed various means of coping with the problem of unwanted children. Many were simply abandoned. Some were sold to others, often into slavery. Children could also be surrendered by parents to others to pay a debt or other obligation, but without any formal adoption.

Religious institutions attempting to deal with the problem developed the concept of oblation, a symbolic abandonment of a child in a church or religious institution. The child, in a sense, was regarded as a gift to the institution. The assumption was that such children should remain in their new homes and any attempt to leave their religious home could result in excommunication. Parents of either sex could donate a child up to the age of ten and, though they could not make gifts to the child, they could to the monastery or church. Boys given to the church or monastery were expected to become priests or monks, although at age eighteen they could decline to accept the vows of celibacy of a priest. If they did decline the vows, they were allowed to marry. Girls were expected to become nuns.

Specialized institutions for the care of orphans, the poor, and the ill began to appear in the twelfth century. The original institutions seem to have been associated with the Crusades and were undoubtedly influenced by Byzantine models. The Hospital of Saint John in Jerusalem in 1181 assumed responsibilities for care of orphans as well as pregnant women. By the end of the thirteenth century, a growing number of hospitals in Europe accepted foundlings along with the sick, the dying, pregnant women, and sometimes the indigent. By the close of the fourteenth century, most urban hospitals in southern Europe did so and the numbers of abandoned children grew. Many large German, French, Italian, and Spanish cities established institutions specifically for abandoned children. Some homes would admit orphans but not abandoned or illegitimate children. Some institutions placed children in foster homes and a few paid these guardians a subsidy.

One of the earliest foundling homes was Santa Maria degli Innocenti in Florence which opened in 1445. By the end of the century, it was receiving at least nine hundred children a year, most of them unweaned infants. About 60 percent of them were female. It is estimated that 30 percent of the infants died within a month of their arrival and another 30 percent within a year. Only a minority lived to age six, as few as 13 percent in some institutions. In England as well as elsewhere, abandoned infants were considered a parish obligation and the large foundling homes did not exist. Mortality rates, however, remained high. One of the features in many of the foundling homes was a revolving door in a niche in the wall which allowed a parent or servant to deposit an infant safely without being observed. The same practices applied to the state-run foundling homes.

In sum, as John Boswell has stated, the institutional homes gave a quiet and efficient way of dealing with foundlings who, out of sight, were also out of mind. Let them disappear into social oblivion or, more likely, an early death.

See also Child Donation; Foundling Wheel; Medieval Europe and Adoption.

Further Reading

Boswell, John. *The Kindness of Strangers*. New York: Pantheon Books, 1988.
Trexler, Richard. "The Foundlings of Florence, 1395–1445." *The History of Childhood Quarterly* 1 (1973): 259–84.
Trexler, Richard. "Infanticide in Florence: New Sources and First Results." *The History of Childhood Quarterly* 2 (1975): 98–117.

Mexico and Adoption

Vern L. Bullough

Traditionally, adoption in Mexico is an informal affair. But as with other countries, the process has become increasingly formalized. It currently is regulated by a section of the legal code entitled, "The State System for the Full Development of the Family," which regulates a number of family issues. To qualify for adoption, a child must have orphan status which means that either the parents have died, or a parent (or parents) have released the child for adoption. Abandoned children may also qualify for adoption, but to become qualified the Mexican government has to do a thorough search for any living relatives of the child. The actual procedure for adoption varies among each of Mexico's thirty-one states and their procedures differ from each other.

All orphans in need of adoption are put into orphanages. The government first tries to place them with relatives or, failing that, with a Mexican family. Mexico discourages breaking-up of siblings, and adoptive parents can adopt several siblings together. Children are placed for a trial adoption of six months, before the procedure is finalized. A would-be adoptive parent has to be over twenty-five years old, as well as at least seventeen years older than the child being adopted; if the child is over fourteen years old, the child must also give his or her own consent.

Mexico does allow foreigners to adopt but they have to go through the six month trial period in Mexico itself, although in some cases this requirement can be waived. Because of the rather strict conditions of adoption, a number of adoption agents operate independently of the legal orphanages. Some foreigners wanting a Mexican child run into difficulties because, unless the child is legally adopted, the child does not have a visa. This can cause difficulty for the child later when the child tries to attend school in the new country, or get a driver's license, or a social security number.

Model State Adoption Act

Keith N. Hurley

The Department of Health, Education, and Welfare (HEW) proposed the "Model State Adoption Act and Model State Adoption Procedures" as a result of the "Child Abuse Prevention and Treatment and Adoption Reform Act of 1978." The Act called for HEW to issue the proposed legislation in response to the Congressional panel's need to "facilitate the elimination of barriers to adoption and to provide permanent and loving home environments for children who would benefit by adoption" (Public Law 95-266). This assignment was to be accomplished by promoting the establishment of model adoption legislation and procedures for States.

One of the key requirements of the Act was disclosure of adoption records. This was also a controversial requirement. Congress required that HEW solicit comments from the public after developing the proposed Act. Eighty-two percent of the comments received opposed the Model Act. HEW tried to rewrite sections of the Act, however the proposal never gained support.

Further Reading

Carp, E. Wayne. *Family Matters: Secrecy and Disclosure in the History of Adoption.* Cambridge, MA: Harvard University Press, 1998.

Mormons and Adoption

Gwen Brewer

Mormon Belief About The Eternal Family

Adoption among members of the Church of Jesus Christ of Latter-day Saints (often abbreviated as LDS), commonly called the Mormons, has a unique place in their theology. The concept of adoption, however, fits significantly into the world view of the Church of Jesus Christ of Latter-day Saints. Perhaps "view of the human place in the eternal universe" would be a better way to put it. Mormons believe that God created a universe containing many worlds, at least one of which, our earth, he populated with human beings. The human beings on the earth are the spirit children of God, our Heavenly Father and his wife or wives, our Heavenly Mother(s). These spirits all must come to earth, like Jesus did, to get a mortal body. After experiencing this mortal life, each spirit will obtain an immortal body and eternal life. Moreover, if the spirit/human has lived a good life and performed the necessary ordinances, such as baptism and temple marriage, he/she will become a god and be able to people his/her own world(s). To Mormons, Jesus, our brother, is the model who demonstrates how spirits move from spirit to mortal body to immortal, eternal body. Because he lived a mortal life of moral excellence, he became a god who can now create and people his own world(s).

The nuclear family with father, mother, and children has special status in this world view. The father, who holds the priesthood, is the head of the family. The wife is his helpmeet. Together, they create children, thereby giving waiting, pre-existing spirits mortal bodies. This family unit will be an eternal family unit if the members live good lives and if they participate in all the Church ordinances. Any time after about age eighteen, males and females (if they are in good standing in the Church) are eligible to participate in temple ordinances, including marriage.

Temple marriage to the Mormons is eternal marriage, a marriage for "time and all eternity." Temple marriage contrasts with civil marriage, which is an earthly union—a union for time, but not eternity. Waiting spirits, still living with their Heavenly Father and Mother, are born as children to mortal women. If the woman is joined to a husband in eternal marriage, these children become part of an eternal family. Adopted children can be "sealed" to the family in a special temple ceremony that makes them part of the family for eternity.

Adoption Among The Mormons: 1830–1950

The Mormon history of adoption follows the pattern of adoption in United States history, modified by the Mormon belief system and the environment created by the cohesiveness of the Mormon people. Very early in the Mormon Church, as the concept of temple sealings was made known, many prominent men were adopted and sealed to Church leaders. Both Joseph Smith (the founder of the Church) and Brigham Young (an early Church President) adopted a large number of men as their sons. By 1893, some thirteen thousand adult adoptions had taken place. This policy of adopting unrelated prominent people was changed when Wilford Woodruff became President of the Mormon Church. In 1895, he clarified and modernized the "sealing ordinances," discouraging the adoption of members by prominent leaders, and setting up a system still used today, which seals immediate family members to one another and then seals ancestors to the family. Children are automatically sealed to parents who have been married in the temple. If the children marry in the temple, then the grandchildren become part of the eternal family, and so on. Temple ordinances by proxy are performed for ancestors who lived before temple ordinances were available; that is, living people can perform the necessary rites for people who are deceased. This explains why Mormons have large genealogical libraries. Adoption (sealing) of deceased people through temple ordinances and focusing on ancestors of Church members is a thriving practice.

Adoption of children in the mid- and late nineteenth century reflected practices in the country at large, except the cohesive Mormon community made it easier for motherless children to find homes. Most adoptions were casual, with relatives or friends taking in children of members who had died. But there were formal adoptions as well. For example, Joseph Smith and his wife, Emma, formally adopted twins. During the polygamous period, orphans were often placed in polygamous families where they could mingle with the many children of various wives and either be sealed to their new families or to that of their deceased parents.

After a slow start, formal legal adoption of children by Mormon parents became increasingly common during the twentieth century, usually of children born into other Mormon families. In the early part of the twentieth century, disapproval of the nationwide practice of doctors selling babies led to religious, public, and government action. The Mormons, for their part, turned to the Relief Society, the operant women's organization of the Church, to investigate the matter. The result was the establishment of a special branch for adoptive services in 1923 under the guidance of Amy Brown Lyman.

Lyman, trained in Chicago and Denver, established professional training for social workers, and set forth policies for counseling unwed mothers, placing babies and children needing homes, and processing parents who wanted to adopt children. In accordance with professional opinion at the time, babies and children were placed in homes with similar occupational, economic, cultural, and racial background. Though most of the adoptees were Caucasian, there were some minority children also handled by the agency, which placed them where possible with families of similar background, often among non-church members. This was particularly the case of African-American children, since the Mormon Church at that time did not accept African Americans into full membership. Latino and Indian children were usually placed in Mormon Caucasian homes because of the lack of Mormon Latino or Indian parents wanting more children. Foster care was appropriate in some cases.

Administration of Adoptive Services: 1950 To Present

Many changes occurred in the last half of the twentieth century, both in the administration and the social context. The administration of social services was shifted from the women's Relief Society to a program run by men in the priesthood, now called LDS (for Latter-day Saints) Social Services. The professional framework was maintained but much expanded into a complete, efficient, and concerned child placement agency. On the Internet, LDS Family Services has many entries directed toward pregnant, unwed women and prospective parents—available counseling, videos, articles, group meetings, medical help, legal procedures, bibliography, and available outside resources. Selected adoptive parents must be members of the Church in good standing who were married in the Temple and who have completed a home study by Family Services. The LDS Family Services also supports a rich program for the adoption of children with special needs—older children, those with physical or emotional handicaps, siblings who need to be together, and racially-mixed children. One of the more fascinating aspects of Mormon adoption practices is the increasing number of African American children who are adopted into Mormon families after the Church officially changed its views on race in 1978.

Social Context of Adoption: 1950 To Present

A dominating feature of the LDS Church is the emphasis on family. In a 1995 "Proclamation to the World," the Church Administration stated: "The family is ordained of God. Marriage between man and woman is essential to His eternal plan. Children are entitled to birth within the bonds of matrimony." Adopted children, though not born "within the bonds of matrimony," are legally and sacredly a part of the family unit, sealed in the temple for eternity to the families that adopt them. Mormons have large families by current standards, and one reason for this is that Mormons want to give the waiting spirits in Heaven a mortal body. Many Mormon adoptive parents think that God meant a particular adoption to take place, and tell stories about the spiritual messages they received.

Despite the Mormon emphasis on sexual abstinence before marriage, babies are born to single women who did not want to marry the father nor raise the child. There are, however, not enough babies to give to all the people that want them. The LDS agency, like other agencies, is reluctant to give babies to people who already have children and, as a result, Mormons have entered the national and international adoption market on a large scale through a variety of adoption agencies, adopting special needs children of different races and age groups, especially African American infants, as well as infants and toddlers.

In a study of sixteen adoptive families interviewed by the author of this article in the Salt Lake City area in August 2004, almost all the recent adoptions were of African Americans but others were also included. One childless family adopted five children—three as babies and two as toddlers: two African Americans, one bipolar Guatemalan, and two Caucasians. Many, especially younger couples, wanted more children than the mother felt she could have so they adopted more. Some adopted because they wanted to give orphaned, needy children a home. Seven of the families ended up with five to eight children. One family had twelve. All of the adopted families were conscious of the cultural background of their children and wanted to emphasize and incorporate this diversity. They celebrated holidays such as Chinese New Year and Kwanza, as well as the more traditional American ones. Social groups for the parents of adopted children from various areas of the world have been formed and organizations such as Genesis have been established.

In contrast, American Indians are seldom adopted by Mormons today. For a time in the 1960s and 1970s, the LDS Church set up an Indian Placement Program taking Indians into their homes as foster children. Only about 5 percent were adopted. Most of them were well into childhood when they entered the Mormon homes, and cultural differences made it difficult for many to adjust. With the passage of the Indian Child Welfare Act of 1978, which gave control of placement of Indian children to the tribes (reversing the previous federal policy of trying to assimilate Indians) and emphasized cultural familiarity in the placement of Indian children, the Indian Placement Program was abandoned.

Most of the Mormon adoptions are open adoptions. Adoptive families prepare extensive dossiers to send to the birth mother so that she can choose which family she wants to raise her child. Many of the adoptive families meet with the birth mother, and some have ongoing relationships. Thus, while in Mormondom, adopted children sometimes keep contact with the birth mother; they also become an integral part of a probably large family functioning within a supportive community, and are taught to believe that they will be part of that family for all eternity.

Further Reading

Carp, E. Wayne, ed. *Adoption in America*. Ann Arbor, MI: University of Michigan, 2002.

LDS Family Services. Provident Living Web Site. http://www.providentliving.org/familyservices/strength/0,12264,2873-1,00.html (accessed September, 2004).

Ludlow, Daniel H. "Social Services." In *Encyclopedia of Mormonism*. Vol. 3. New York: Macmillan, 1992.

Miller, Dennis E. "The Indian Adoption Project and the Indian Child Welfare Act of 1978." See article in this handbook.

Woodger, Mary Jane. *Amy Brown Lyman, Mother of the Church of Jesus Christ of Latter-day Saints Child Placement Agency*. Joseph Fielding Smith Institute, Forthcoming.

Woodruff, Wilford. "Discourse," May 28, 1894, *The Latter-day Saints = Millennial Star.* Liverpool and London: Anthon H. Lund, 1894.

The following individuals were interviewed by Gwen Brewer:

Anonymous attorney. Interview with author. Salt Lake City area. August 19, 2004.

Cooley, Jane, former judge's clerk and former volunteer counselor for LDS Family Services. Interview with author. Kayesville, Utah. August 16, 2004.

Dawson, Glen R., Judge, Second Judicial Court of Utah. Interview with author. Bountiful, Utah, August 18, 2004.

Hansen, Klaus, Professor of American History, Queen's University, Kingston, Ontario, Canada. Email message to author. September 14, 2004.

Manscill, Craig, Professor of Church History, Brigham Young University. Interview with author. Provo, Utah. August 20, 2004.

Sixteen adoptive parents. Salt Lake City area, August 16–19, 2004.

Watson, Matt, LDS Family Services. Personal telephone communications with author. Salt Lake City, Utah, August 11, 17, 19, 2004.

Moses and Adoption

Vern L. Bullough

The first reference to adoption in Jewish and Christian scriptures is the case of Moses. The story appears in Exodus 2:11. Because the Egyptian Pharaoh worried about the growth in the number of Hebrews in his kingdom, he ordered midwives to kill male babies delivered to Hebrew women. Moses's mother managed to bear a son without being denounced by the midwives and hid him for three months. Fearing that the baby would be discovered, she made an ark of bull rushes daubed with slime and pitch. She laid the ark in the "flags" by the riverbank and stationed the infant's sister nearby.

A daughter of the Pharaoh came down to the river to bathe and discovered the baby. Although she identified the infant as a Hebrew child, she felt compassion for him. The infant's sister, observing the woman's emotional reaction, stepped forward and asked the princess if she wanted a wet nurse to care for the child. The Pharaoh's daughter paid the infant's biological mother to nurse him.

According to the scriptures, when the child was weaned, the princess made him her son. She gave him the name Moses, meaning "to draw out," because she drew him out of the water. He was raised in the royal household. Moses was, however, apparently aware of his Hebrew background. As an adult, he killed an Egyptian while defending a Hebrew and had to flee the wrath of the Pharaoh, finding refuge in the Hebrew community.

Further Reading

The Holy Scriptures According to the Masoretic Text. Philadelphia: Jewish Publication Society, 1917. (The English Christian version of the scriptures is essentially the same.)

Muhammad (570? – 632)

Vern L. Bullough

Muhammad, the founder of Islam, was born in Mecca c. 570–571 (some sources say as late as 580) to the Hashim family of the Kuraysh tribe. He was given the name Muhammad, meaning highly praised. His father, Abdallah, died before he was born and his mother died when Muhammad was about six years old. As a fatherless boy, and then as an orphan, his lot was not easy. His paternal grandfather, Abd al-Muttalib, cared for and protected him until his death. Muhammad then became the ward of his uncle Abu Talib. Although he was never formally adopted, the story of Muhammad's life emphasizes the kind of informal interfamilial caretaking that later was institutionalized into adoption.

There are differing accounts of Muhammad since no biography of him was written until he had been dead for a hundred years. However, at least four were compiled during the second century after his death. These furnish the traditional account of Muhammad's life. Like the Christian accounts of Jesus, they are selective in what they say, intermixing tradition and fact.

From Muhammad's own statements, it is apparent that his uncle guardian was not very prosperous and that there was little opportunity for Muhammad in any of the businesses of his uncles. Lacking capital from his father, a job had to be found for him outside the family circle. He found work with Khadijah, a widow and a distantly related wealthy family member who had been married twice, and had children from each marriage. According to Muslim tradition, she soon asked him to marry her. We know that he had four daughters who grew to maturity and several sons, all of whom died in infancy or childhood. Khadijah herself died about 619.

Even before she died, Muhammad had begun retiring to a retreat and contemplating the world about him. In 610, while in one of his retreats, he had a revelation that commanded him to preach the Truth to his fellow Meccans. Thus began the series of revelations that came to be called the Koran and led to the founding of Islam, one of the major religions of the world today.

See also Islam and Adoption.

The Multiethnic Placement Act (MEPA)

Joan Heifetz Hollinger

The Multiethnic Placement Act of 1994 (MEPA), as amended by the Interethnic Provisions of 1996, is a federal civil rights law that, along with the Adoption and Safe Families Act (ASFA) and other federal initiatives begun in the 1990s, is aimed at removing the barriers to achieving permanency for the hundreds of thousands of children who are in the public child welfare system, and especially for the African-American children who are disproportionately represented in out-of-home care and who wait much longer than others for permanent homes.

MEPA's specific goals are to decrease the length of time that all children wait to be adopted, facilitate the recruitment of foster and adoptive parents who can meet the distinctive needs of children awaiting placement, and eliminate discrimination in child placement decisions on the basis of race, color, or national origin. To achieve these goals, MEPA imposes two basic prohibitions and one affirmative obligation on all state agencies and other entities that are involved in foster care or adoptive placements, and that receive federal financial assistance, not only under Titles IV-E or IV-B of the Social Security Act, but from any federal program. First, MEPA prohibits these agencies and entities from delaying or denying a child's foster care or adoptive placement on the basis of the race, color, or national origin of either the child or the prospective parent. Second, MEPA prohibits these agencies and entities from denying to any individual the opportunity to become a foster or adoptive parent on the basis of the prospective parent's or the child's race, color, or national origin. Third, to remain eligible for federal assistance for their child welfare programs, states must diligently recruit foster and adoptive parents who reflect the racial and ethnic diversity of the children in each state who need foster and adoptive homes.

As originally enacted in 1994, MEPA prohibited federally funded agencies or entities from "categorically" denying placement opportunities and from delaying or denying a child's foster care or adoptive placement "solely" on the basis of race, color, or national origin. The Act also provided that it was "permissible" to consider a child's "cultural, ethnic, or racial background" and a prospective parent's capacity to meet these needs as among the factors relevant to determining the child's best interests. Prompted by testimony that these provisions harmed African-American and other minority children by implicitly condoning systemic avoidance of transracial placements, Congress amended MEPA in 1996. The Interethnic Provisions repealed some of MEPA's original provisions, including the "permissible considerations," and replaced them with the explicit and broad prohibitions that are now central to MEPA. It is now clear that any actions—not just categorical decisions—that delay or deny placements or opportunities to be a parent on the basis of race, color, or national origin are unlawful. While retaining the affirmative recruitment mandate, the 1996 amendments clarify that children who are in state care are not immune from constitutional protections against racial or ethnic discrimination, and that all child welfare agencies receiving funds from any federal source are subject to the anti-discrimination provisions of Title VI of the Civil Rights Act of 1964.

Can Race, Color, or National Origin Ever be Considered in Making Placement Decisions?

In several Guidance and Information Memoranda issued since MEPA was amended, the U.S. Department of Health and Human Services (HHS) has indicated that "discrimination is not to be tolerated," whether directed at children in need of placement, at prospective parents, or at previously "underutilized" communities. According to HHS, agencies may not routinely consider race, color, or national origin in making placement decisions. Many longstanding child welfare practices are no longer permitted, for example, to set a specific time period during which only searches for a racially or ethnically matched placement will occur; to use lists of placement preferences based primarily on racial or ethnic factors; or to require caseworkers to provide additional justifications for transracial, but not for same-race placements.

MEPA does not prohibit same-race placements; nor does it require transracial placements. It does require individualized assessments of the needs of each child. In explaining that "the best interests of the child" remains the operative standard in placement decisions, HHS Memoranda often invoke the technical terminology of civil rights law. Any consideration of race, color, or national origin must satisfy the "strict scrutiny" test: Does a particular child's distinctive needs require that these factors be considered and is such consideration necessary in order to serve a "compelling state interest"? If "narrowly tailored" to the circumstances of particular children, consideration of "suspect" racial or ethnic factors may, in a small number of cases, be necessary to serve a compelling interest in protecting children's best interests and thus pass the strict scrutiny test.

In Memoranda directed at child welfare agencies, HHS suggests that the strict scrutiny standard requires ascertaining the distinctive needs of each child, determining whether any of them are based on racial or ethnic factors, and then asking whether these needs can be met by a foster or adoptive parent who does not share the child's racial or ethnic background or, alternatively, can be met only by someone from a similar background. For example, in a case involving an older child whose consent to a proposed adoption is required and who has lived exclusively with caregivers who share his racial background, it would be appropriate for an agency to attempt to comply with the child's request for a same-race placement. By contrast, in a case involving a younger child who has been emotionally harmed by ethnic slurs and bullying at her school, it would not be appropriate for an agency to assume that only a caregiver from the same ethnic background could help her deal with this situation. Although this child has a specific need based on her ethnicity, it is a need that can be taken care of by many different prospective parents, not just by someone with the same ethnic background.

MEPA's ban on routine or stereotypical reliance on racial or ethnic factors in placement decisions enables agencies to focus, instead, on a wide range of child-specific factors. These include the length of time a child has been with a caregiver and the quality of their attachment to each other, as well as the child's age, sex, and developmental, cognitive, emotional, educational, physical or mental health needs. Moreover, MEPA does not preclude agencies from complying with federal and state law preferences for placing children with relatives. Nor does MEPA prohibit agencies from taking into account a child's cultural background, including language, religion or other customs, so long as "cultural needs" do not become a "proxy" for racial or ethnic factors and a means for circumventing MEPA's core prohibitions. Agencies are warned against assuming that foster or adoptive parents have to share a child's cultural experience in order to develop the child's awareness and appreciation of that culture.

Some agencies are uncertain about the legal line between efforts to accommodate a child's cultural needs and an impermissible use of culture as a proxy for relying on racial or ethnic factors. Agencies are even more perplexed about how much deference they can give to a biological parent's preferences for where her child should be placed. Tensions have arisen between practices that favor more open placements that take parental preferences into account and HHS's admonition that federally funded agencies can comply with some parental preferences but cannot be bound by a request for either a same-race or a transracial placement. At least one state has been faulted in an HHS Office of Civil Rights investigation for using parental preferences as an unlawful excuse for making race-based selections of foster parents.

MEPA's prohibitions do not apply to foster or adoptive placements governed by the federal Indian Child Welfare Act (ICWA). Because ICWA intends to facilitate tribal survival by preserving tribal ties to Indian children, agencies are bound by ICWA's placement preferences for children who are eligible for membership in, or are members of a federally recognized Indian tribe, unless a court finds "good cause" for departing from those preferences.

Do Prospective Adoptive Parents Have A "Right" To Adopt A Particular Child?

While MEPA expressly prohibits the discriminatory denial of any individual's "opportunity" to become a foster or adoptive parent, and requires that states diligently recruit prospective parents who are as diverse as the children in need of homes, the Act does not guarantee anyone a general right to adopt, nor a right to adopt a particular child.

Agencies retain considerable discretion when evaluating the suitability of applicants to care for the children in state custody. Although they may not rely on generalizations about the abilities of prospective parents to care for children with similar or different racial or ethnic backgrounds, agencies are allowed to discuss an applicant's feelings, capacities, and personal preferences—with regard to caring for a child of a particular race or ethnicity—if the discussion is part of a general exploration with all the applicants about the kinds of children and physical or mental conditions they are willing, or unwilling, to accept. Information about any special needs of African-American or Latino children, for example, has to be presented to all prospective parents, not just to Caucasians. Nonetheless, except in emergency short-term placements, HHS suggests that it would be contrary to a particular child's best interests to disregard the preferences of prospective parents, including racial or ethnic preferences, and risk a later disruption or dissolution because the parents never really wanted that child.

In developing programs to satisfy MEPA's requirement that states recruit racially and ethnically diverse prospective parents, states may target specific minority communities, but must allow individuals outside the targeted communities to participate in all informational or training sessions.

Enforcement Options and Remedies

Failure by a federally funded foster care or adoption agency to comply with MEPA's anti-discrimination provisions is an express violation of Title VI of the Civil Rights Act. A state's failure to engage in diligent recruitment efforts may also violate Title VI. Any individual or group of children or adults who can prove that they have been harmed by a violation of MEPA is entitled to bring a private action in federal district court seeking injunctive relief from the offending state or other entity.

The primary means for enforcing MEPA is not, however, through private litigation but through administrative actions responding either to individual complaints or to violations found by the Office of Civil Rights (OCR) in its own reviews of state child welfare programs. HHS provides technical assistance and encourages voluntary compliance. Nonetheless, if violations are not corrected within an agreed upon time, HHS can seek to have federal funds withheld from the offending agency. Since 1995, HHS has conducted a number of compliance reviews and required some states to undertake corrective actions after OCR found systemic practices that impermissibly denied or delayed placements of minority children by imposing different and stricter criteria for transracial than for same-race placements. These unlawful practices include "cultural competency" requirements that were applied only to prospective parents interested in a transracial placement, evaluations that attached more significance to race than to the specific physical and emotional needs of individual children, and placements of medically fragile young children with same-race foster parents, who were not trained to care for these children's medical needs, instead of with specially-trained foster parents of a different race.

Has MEPA Made A Difference?

MEPA was enacted in the belief that prohibiting the use of racial or ethnic considerations in placement decisions and actively recruiting a more diverse pool of prospective foster and adoptive parents would decrease the time children—and especially African-American children—spent in out-of-home care and increase, as well as equalize, the chances for all children to have a permanent adoptive placement. Yet, a decade later, even though adoptions from public agencies have increased, many tens of thousands of children who are legally available for adoption continue to languish in foster care. In most states, 40 percent or more of these children are African American, a number grossly disproportionate to the percentage of African Americans within the general population of all children. Many of the African-American children in out-of-home care are over the age of eight, are in sibling groups, and have special developmental needs.

Studies by the Urban Institute and for the Donaldson Adoption Institute suggest that, except for a few programs targeted to specific minority communities, most state recruitment and retention programs, including those mandated by MEPA, remain poorly funded and woefully inadequate to generate enough prospective parents willing to care for the children with the greatest needs. Even if many agencies are in compliance with MEPA's anti-discrimination prohibitions, there is credible evidence that placement delays are attributable to a host of factors other than the vestiges of systemic discrimination. These other factors include court delays, high caseloads, inadequate services for children and their biological or prospective parents, and the many exceptions to the ASFA provisions intended to expedite permanency. The prevalence of other circumstances that cause harmful delays is not a justification, however, for reintroducing race-based placement decisions.

In many states, there is a subtle, yet pervasive, resistance to MEPA based on a belief that children do better in same race than in transracial placements. For the most part, however, this belief is not substantiated by longitudinal social science research. Moreover, most child welfare experts do not advocate that MEPA be repealed. Instead, they favor a more flexible application of the "strict scrutiny" standard in order to permit some consideration of racial or ethnic factors in a larger number of cases.

Some child welfare experts complain that a focus on implementing MEPA draws attention and resources away from programs that are needed to address the underlying conditions of poverty, drug and alcohol abuse, housing, education, and job training that would reduce the numbers of families and children in need of out-of-home care or adoption in the first place. Yet, even these advocates acknowledge that, for the children who do need foster or adoptive placements, it is better to base placement decisions on an individualized assessment of the needs and circumstances of each child than on categorical or stereotypical racial or ethnic assumptions. There is also evidence of a greater understanding that children in state custody deserve the same protections from civil rights laws that everyone else is entitled to enjoy.

See also Indian Adoption Project and the Indian Welfare Act of 1978; Transracial and Intercountry Adoption.

Further Reading

Cahn, Naomi, and Joan Heifetz Hollinger. *Families By Law: An Adoption Reader*, Part 6. New York: New York University Press, 2004.

Hollinger, Joan Heifetz. "A Guide to the Multiethnic Placement Act of 1994 as amended by the Interethnic Provisions of 1996. ABA Center on Children and the Law, 1998." Administration for Children and Families Web Site. http://www.acf.hhs.gov/programs/cb/pubs/mepa94/ (accessed February, 2006).

Katz, Jeff. *Listening to Parents: Overcoming Barriers to the Adoption of Children from Foster Care.* New York: Donaldson Adoption Institute, 2005.

Macomber, Jennifer Ehrle, Erica H. Zielewski, Kate Chambers, and Rob Geen. "An Analysis of Interest in Adoption and a Review of State Recruitment Strategies." Washington, DC: Urban Institute, 2005. http://www.urban.org/publications/411254.html.

U.S. Department of Health and Human Services. "Administration for Children, Youth and Families. Information Memorandum: ACYF-CB-IM-03-01. 03/25/2003." http://www.acf.hhs.gov/programs/cb/laws_policies/policy/im/im0301.htm.

U.S. Department of Health and Human Services. "Administration for Children, Youth and Families. Information Memorandum: Guidance for Federal P.L. 104-188 Section 1808, Removal of Barriers to Interethnic Adoption, ACYF-IM-CB-97-04 (June 1997)." Administration for Children, Youth and Families Web Site. http://www.acf.hhs.gov/programs/cb/laws_policies/policy/im/im9704.htm (accessed February, 2006).

U.S. Department of Health and Human Services. "Administration for Children, Youth and Families. Information Memorandum: Questions and Answers that Clarify the Practice and Implementation of Section 471(a)(18) of Title IV-E of the Social Security Act, ACYF-IM-CB-98-03 (May 1998)." Administration for Children, Youth and Families Web Site. http://www.acf.hhs.gov/programs/cb/laws_policies/policy/im/im9803.htm (accessed February, 2006).

Mutual-Aid

Elizabeth M. Tracy

Mutual-aid or self-help groups mobilize relationships among people who share common tasks, goals, or problems. Mutual-aid groups allow members to learn from one another. People in a mutual-aid group may realize for the first time that they are not alone and that they are not fully responsible for their situation. A distinguishing feature of mutual-aid groups is their ability to support people who have personal problems, while at the same time advocating for changes in the larger society.

Mutual-aid groups are based on the following beliefs: 1) people with a common problem or status can best help and support one another; 2) a group is an effective medium for mutual-aid to occur; 3) people gain inner satisfaction and self-esteem from helping others; and 4) help should be available whenever needed. Mutual-aid or self-help groups are often an important factor in a successful adoption.

Principles and Types of Mutual-Aid Groups

Mutual-aid or self-help groups can be made available in a variety of formats: self-help groups, Internet support groups, peer-run or delivered services. They provide social support, which has been shown to help people cope with stressful situations, and also provide specialized knowledge and perspectives. They also provide opportunities for parents to both receive support and give support to other parents who face similar parenting challenges. They are also able to connect parents to new resources and new ideas for solving problems. Adoptive parent support groups serve multiple educational and social functions for the child and family and can lead to the formation of play groups, support for prospective adoptive parents, as well as support for those planning intercountry adoptions (as noted by the National Adoption Information Clearinghouse). Those interested in forming groups can often get in touch with other adoptive parents through their local adoption agency or through the National Adoption Information Clearinghouse.

Parents™ is a national trademarked organization of state networks of parent support groups, which as of this writing, operates in twenty-nine states. It has adopted a series of helpful principles to guide mutual support groups. These include (1) *Trust*: Members of such groups know that all information shared in the support groups is confidential, and within the limits of the law, never discussed outside the group setting. (2) *Reciprocity*: Parents provide non-judgmental support to one another and learn about ways to strengthen their families. (3) *Leadership and Accountability*: The parents' group depends on the efforts of those parents who attend, and it is this group that determines the agenda and defines their own goals in the group. (4) *Respect*: Each parent should have the right to express his or her opinion and also to allow others to speak, rather than allowing one or two people to take over. (5) *Parenting in the Present*: Support groups are urged to focus on what is happening today, rather than spending time on things in the past that cannot be changed. (6) *Shared Leadership*: Parents and professionals should work to build successful partnerships, sharing responsibility, expertise, and leadership. (7) *Responsibility*: Members of the groups hold each other accountable for sharing the values mentioned above. (8) *Non-Violence*: Members should use positive methods of solving problems and realize that violence at any level is not an acceptable form of dealing with problems and issues (FRIENDS, the National Resource Center for Community-Based Child Abuse Prevention program grants).

Benefits and Future Directions

Most research has found few differences between self-help groups, such as FRIENDS, and individual therapists for the kinds of issues that adoptive parents and families might encounter, although all recognize that at times there is a need for professional help. A good self-help group would recognize when an outside professional might be needed for individual members.

The mutual-aid approach is consistent with recent directions in child welfare practice, including: embedding services within communities, involving neighborhood residents and community based networks in the child protection process, encouraging greater community involvement of families, employers, and social and religious institutions, and emphasizing the importance of agency partnerships to coordinate the best possible outcomes and solutions for children and families. There is strong support that all participants benefit from mutual-aid—both for those who provide, as well as those who receive, help. The professional service delivery system also benefits in that more people are reached and there is support for people beyond the formal service delivery period, which is often time-limited. Mutual-aid will continue to be a means to fill in service gaps and complement services delivered.

Further Reading

American Self-Help Group Clearinghouse. "Self Help Group Sourcebook Online." American Self-Help Group Clearinghouse Web Site. http://mentalhelp.net/selfhelp (accessed December, 2004).

Child Welfare Information Gateway. "The Value of Adoptive Parent Groups." Web Site. http//www.childwelfare.gov/pubs/F_value.cmf

FRIENDS, the National Resource Center for Community Base Child Abuse Prevention Program Grants. Friends, the National Resource Center for Community Base Child Abuse Prevention Web Site. http://www.friendsnrc.org/resources/fact-sheets.asp (accessed February, 2005).

Gittterman, A., and L. Shulman, eds., *Mutual-aid Groups, Vulnerable and Resilient Populations, and the Life Cycle*. New York: Columbia University Press, 2005.

Lieberman, M., L. D. Borman, and Associates. *Self-Help Groups for Coping with Crisis: Origins, Members, Processes, and Impact*. San Francisco: Jossey-Bass, 1979.

North American Council on Adoptable Children (NACAC). "Database of Parent Support Groups." NACAC Web Site. http://www.nacac.org/pas_database.html (accessed December, 2004).

Pancoast, D. L., P. Parker, and C. Froland. *Rediscovering Self-help: Its Role in Social Care*. Beverly Hills, Sage, 1983.

Powell, T. J. *Self-help Organizations and Professional Practice*. Silver Spring, MD: National Association of Social Workers, 1987.

Solomon, P. "Peer Support/Peer Provided Services: Underlying Processes, Benefit, and Critical Ingredients." *Psychiatric Rehabilitation Journal* 27 (2004): 392–401.

Mutual Consent Registries

Vern L. Bullough

One of the projects that grew out of the changing views of adoption is the Mutual Consent Registry. As adopted individuals attempted to trace their biological parent(s), and mothers who had given up a child for adoption tried to trace their birth child(ren), it was found that many birth mothers did not want to see or visit their child and many children did not want to see their birth mother or father. In order to maintain privacy when desired, many states established registries that provide information if both the birth parent and the adopted adult are registered. Some states have also required the registration of the adoptive parent.

Over half of the states have adopted mutual consent registries. Other states have enacted what are called "search and consent" laws. These laws allow adopted adults to contact the state social services department or an adoption agency and request that the birth parent be located. If such a search is successful, consent is requested to provide identifying information to the adopted person, and the two parties can then get together. A few states simply have open records that allow both birth parents and adoptees to see the record and do their own tracing.

It should be noted that there are differences of opinion among adoption organizations on open adoption and state registries. In the past, on the one hand, the Child Welfare League of America has argued that state registries do not go far enough. On the other hand, the National Council for Adoption supports confidentiallity and state-level registries when both birth parents and adult adopted persons agree to information exchange. Still other individuals, if not groups, believe registries merely set the stage for intrusion into family and personal privacy. In addition to state registries, there is an international registry, the International Soundex Reunion Registry.

See also Adoption Search Movement; Open Adoption; Paton, Jean; Reunion.

N

Native Americans and Adoption: Defining Who is "Indian"

Vern L. Bullough

For much of the twentieth century, large numbers of Indian children were sent to Indian schools, often located hundreds of miles away from their tribal homes. The concept behind this practice was to "Americanize" the Indian children. Some children were even beaten when they spoke their native language in the schools. The policy was summed up in 1995 by the National Indian Child Welfare Association as a deliberate policy to remove the culture from the child as a way to solve what was then called the "Indian problem." As part of this policy, the Child Welfare League of America in the 1950s and 60s, in cooperation with the Bureau of Indian Affairs promoted the Indian Adoption Project, based on the belief that Native American children were better off in non-Native American homes. Some American religious groups made special recruiting efforts to convince young Indian parents to give up their children for the good of the child.

A congressional investigation in 1978 found that state courts had removed one-quarter to one-third of all Native American children from their families and placed the majority into non-Native American homes. The result of the investigation was the Indian Child Welfare Act of 1978 that mandated special provisions for Native Americans and their placement into foster or adoptive homes. Under the act, an Indian child's tribe or the Bureau of Indian Affairs must be informed if the child is placed for adoption, and preference in placement must be given first to the child's tribe and last to another culture. Even birth mothers who wish to transfer parental rights to an adoptive family fall under this law, and they must first receive permission from the tribe before adoptive placement may occur. However, a family with no Indian ancestry may be able to qualify as "culturally Indian" and hence able to get an Indian child. What is culturally Indian, however, is a rather broad term and might include one Indian ancestor, the adoptive parents living in a state with a large Indian population, the family having Indian friends, and even if the would-be parents read books about Indian culture. The decision is handled on a case-to-case basis. For those Native Americans adopted without going through such a procedure, and where the tribe has intervened to prevent a transracial adoption, the courts have usually decided in favor of the tribe.

The issue is further complicated by the difficulty in deciding who should be classed as Indian. Native Americans total over one and a half million people in the United States belonging to three hundred different tribes in twenty-seven states. About one-half of them live on Indian reservations. Supporters of the new legislation held that as many as 25 percent of the Native American children had been placed into foster homes or adoptive homes because of such reasons as the lack of indoor plumbing, small houses, or other conditions of poverty or social problems. Obviously many such decisions to take Indian children were based on cultural differences.

Some believe that for the Indian tribes to enter the case, the child has to have more than 50 percent Native blood. There is also disagreement about those Indians who do not live on reservations. One of the more troublesome cases involved that of Karen Adams of Long Beach, California, whose son's girlfriend had given birth in November, 1993, to twins whom they turned over to a family in Ohio. Soon after they had turned the twins over, the father decided he wanted them back, and

Karen backed him. They sued to get the twins back under the provisions of the Indian Child Welfare Act. The issue was complicated by the fact that the twins were only one-eighth Pomo Indian, one-quarter Yaqui (a tribe of the southwest that is not officially recognized), and the majority of their ancestors were Caucasian. None of the parents or grandparents lived on a reservation. As a result of the complications, congressional legislators proposed amendments to the Act that would make it more difficult to reclaim children after they had been placed and would weaken tribal court authority in volunteering placement. Both sides in this case agreed to an open adoption so that they could have contact with each other, although they were separated from each other by thousands of miles. Clearly the issue of adoption of Indian children remains somewhat unsettled as of this writing.

See also The Indian Adoption Project and the Indian Child Welfare Act of 1978.

Further Reading

Hollinger, Joan Heifitz. *Adoption Law and Practice*. New York: Matthew Bender, 1988.
Hollinger, Joan Heifitz. "Beyond the Best Interests of the Tribe: The Indian Child Welfare Act and the Adoption of Indian Children." *University of Detroit Law Review* 66 (1989): 450–51.
Plantz, Margaret C., Ruth Hubbell, Barbara J. Barrett, and Antonia Dobree. *Children Today,* (January–February 1989): 24–29.
Smith, Lynn. "A Child's Place." *Los Angeles Times,* November 21, 1995: E1, E4.

Neighborhood Houses

Ginger Hemmingsen

"Neighborhood House" is a term that is frequently used interchangeably with other descriptors, including but not limited to: *settlement house, neighborhood center*, or *community center*. These "houses" or centers are located within a defined neighborhood, and are designed to reflect the unique characteristics, needs, and strengths of the neighborhood and the neighborhood's residents.

Neighborhood houses originated in Great Britain as settlement houses in the late 1800s, and were typically connected with churches or faith-based organizations. In response to the needs of America's increasing numbers of immigrants, settlements soon became an important part of the American landscape. The best known of the American settlements was Hull House in Chicago founded in 1889 by Jane Addams, later a Nobel Laureate for Peace.

The original concept was to have the workers "settle" within the neighborhood and, in some instances, to actually reside within the house, thus the term "settlement." Intended to provide upward mobility for the poor, settlement houses were often at the forefront in social reform and child welfare, including playing a vital role in finding homes for children without families. The United Neighborhood Centers of America, Inc., founded in 1911, has over forty-five hundred members world-wide today.

Neighborhood Houses Model

Neighborhood centers may take many forms and are housed in a variety of locations including churches and synagogues, government agencies, schools, libraries, or not-for-profit agencies. They are often based in low-income neighborhoods and offer a variety of services, or target a specific group such as youth, families with children, or the elderly. However, there are elements that are critical in the development of a center to make it a true neighborhood center.

Neighborhood centers are based on valuing the neighborhood as the core of the city, and affirming that neighborhood surroundings have an impact on the life and livelihood of the residents. Thus, the most critical component in developing a neighborhood center is to ensure that it is reflective of the families and culture of the neighborhood, and that residents have a feeling of ownership and connectivity to it. This can be accomplished in a variety of ways: ensuring that staff and volunteers are comprised of neighborhood residents; involving residents in a center advisory board; or completing an assessment to ensure that the services offered meet the neighborhood's needs.

As neighborhood centers have evolved, they have partnered with residents in building stronger and safer neighborhoods for their children. The second component critical to neighborhood house development is to ensure that the neighborhood residents have the skills, resources, and services they need to provide a safe and successful future for their children and themselves. Thus, neighborhood centers typically offer a wide variety of services and resources that are designed to respond to the unique needs of the residents. Examples may include job training, parenting groups, meals for the elderly, youth groups, day care, etc.

It is increasingly important for neighborhood centers to build partnerships with other organizations based in the neighborhood. This can include other service organizations, the public sector (such as the schools and hospitals), and the private sector through any businesses based in the neighborhood. The neighborhood center can become the hub of building a collaboration that can ensure families have multiple resources to help them address their needs.

Neighborhood centers have some common characteristics and philosophical approaches distinct from other service providers. They tend to focus on the strengths or assets of the neighborhood, as opposed to focusing on deficits or problems, based on research which has shown eliminating problems does not result in long-term change. Taking a developmental approach ensures that the neighborhood and its residents feel recognized and valued. Neighborhood centers are flexible, evolving to meet the needs of the families served. The focus is typically on the whole family, believing that it is critical to develop all family members. By helping the parents succeed, the center is also impacting on their children.

Recognizing the value of the neighborhood in the child's development, neighborhood centers are playing an increasing role in finding families for foster/adoptive placement that will allow the child to remain in their neighborhood or families who will agree to help the child maintain a neighborhood relationship. A neighborhood center can become a tremendous resource for adoptive families, playing a critical role in helping them build connections with families facing similar parenting challenges or issues, and by helping adoptive families access the resources or skills they may need to ensure a successful and permanent placement.

Further Reading

Blank, Barbara Trainin. "Settlement Houses: Old Idea in New Form Builds Communities." *The New Social Worker*. 5 (1998). The New Social Worker Online Web Site. http://

www.socialworker.com/home/index2.php?option=content&do_pdf=1&id=51 (accessed February, 2006).

Downs, Susan Whitelaw. *Neighborhood-Based Family Support*. Detroit, MI: Skillman Center for Children, 1994.

Feldberg, Michael. "Minnie Low and Scientific Tzedakah." *Blessings In Freedom: Chapters in American Jewish History*. Jersey City, NJ: KTAV Publishing House, 2002. American Jewish Historical Society Web Site. http://www.ajhs.org/publications/chapters/chapter.cfm?documentID=227 (accessed February, 2006).

Hirota, Janice M., Prudence Brown, and Nancy Martin. "Building Community: The Tradition and Promise of Settlement Houses." Report Prepared for United Neighborhood Houses of New York. The Chapin Hall Center for Children at the University of Chicago, 1996. International Federation of Settlements and Neighbourhood Centres Web Site. http://www.ifsnetwork.org/uploads/TheTraditionAndPromiseOfSettlement Houses.pdf (accessed February, 2006).

Orr, John B., Grace Roberts Dyrness, and Peter Spoto. "Faith-Based Adoptive/Foster Services: Faith Communities' Roles in Child Welfare." Prepared for Annie E. Casey Foundation and published by the Center for Religion and Civic Culture. University of Southern California, March, 2004.

Rusnock Hoover, Cynthia. "Family and Neighborhood Models Summary Report." *Center on Work and Family*, Publication #770. Battlecreek, MI: W. K. Kellogg Foundation, November, 1995.

Smith, Mark K. "Settlements and Social Action Centres." (January, 2005). The Informal Education Homepage Web Site. http://www.infed.org/association/b-settl.htm (accessed February, 2006).

United Neighborhood Centers of America Web Site. http://www.unca.org

Primary Document

Chicago's Famous Hull House

Today's neighborhood houses, or centers, have evolved from the tradition of earlier settlement houses. Chicago's Hull House, founded by Jane Addams and Ellen Starr Gates in 1889, became one of America's most famous settlement houses. Hull House provided a wide range of services to the poor (for both children and adults) in the largely immigrant neighborhood where it was located. Among its many services, it provided an employment bureau, English lessons, art and music classes, and a theater. Children's services included a kindergarten and day care. The following *Chicago Journal* excerpt describes a tour, provided by Addams herself, through the "Children's House."

"Built for Children: Tour Through the Addition to Hull House"

... The addition to Hull house has been completed and christened the "Children's House," for it was built for the little ones of the neighborhood, through the generosity of Charles Mather Smith, whose daughter is one of the many who have for years taken an ardent and practical interest in Hull house.

The new house is of red brick and stands in the northeast corner of the courtyard, just opposite the picture gallery, so that Hull house and its two additions now form three sides of a hollow square. The "Children's House" is four stories in height and built of red brick. On the first floor are two pretty rooms, which are used for the meeting of clubs in the mornings or evenings, and in the afternoons the back room is used for the "baby kindergarten" of children under 4 years of age, who are too young for the regular kindergarten on the third floor, and the front room for the precocious children of 6 years or thereabout, who are far enough advanced to be prepared for the public schools.

These rooms open off the large front hall, where is a broad staircase with frequent landings, which make it easy for the little feet to climb. The south room has light woodwork, pale yellow walls, pretty rugs on the floor, and comfortable chairs scattered around; the north room is pale sea green, and furnished with small chairs and tables for the baby kindergarteners.

On the second floor are the nursery, kitchen, and sleeping rooms for the "creche" babies. The little ones were taking their tea when Miss Addams showed the rooms to the reporter, but when she appeared in the doorway all the babies who could walk made a rush in her direction and clung to her skirts, while they babbled in unintelligible jargon of their plays and pleasures. She had a kindly word or caressing touch for them all, and showed with pride the cheery room with its bright walls tinted "baby blue" and gayly [sic] colored little chairs and tables. In the adjoining room the walls were buff and a host of little white enameled cots and beds stood in a row, for here the babies take their noonday rest. At the end of the room was an old-fashioned wooden cradle, the "hood" part of wood, too, and here the youngest baby of the "creche" sleeps—"such a dear baby," said Miss Addams, lovingly. A smaller room opening this one is tinted pink, and three white beds are for the use of the older children in the daytime, and of the nurses at night. One side of this room is lined from floor to ceiling with cupboards,

and here are dozens upon dozens of little blue and white and pink and white pinafores, small woolen frocks, and undergarments....

When the children arrive in the morning they are taken to the bathroom adjoining this room and bathed. Then they are dressed again in their own clothes, with one of the "creche" pinafores over all, and taken into the nursery to play. After an early dinner they go into the kindergarten: then at 4 o'clock they have tea, and at 6 o'clock or before their mothers come for them.

The kitchen opens off the nursery ...

On the third floor is one large room for the use of the kindergarten. It is 45×30 feet, and the walls are strongly colored—Indian-red half way up, with the upper half and ceiling in yellow. Still, the effect is not crude, but warm and bright. A piano stands in this room, a few good pictures on the wall, some glassed-in book-cases hold curiosities that are used in object lessons, and the kindergarten chairs and tables are all the furniture of the room, with the addition of chairs for the "grown-ups," when lectures are held there....

The studio is on the fourth floor, a charming room, the walls are covered with gray burlaps draped with fishnet, and the ceiling a pale sea-green. Here Miss Benedict, one of the residents, instructs the children of the neighborhood, who show a marked taste for art, and they make rapid progress, particularly little Italians.

The music room is on the same floor, and it was a pretty thing to see the children practicing their Christmas carols under the guidance of Miss Elenore Smith....

Almost every nationality was represented—the musical Germans, dark-eyed Italians, stolid Swedes, swarthy little Russians, fair-haired Danes, and rosy little Irish and Americans. Mrs. Smith has nearly 100 children in her class and is enthusiastic about her work....

"Playing is sometimes mechanical," said Miss Smith, "but singing is not, consequently

I think that every child that is taught instrumental music should also be taught vocal music. Music has a refining influence, and the songs we teach them have helped to counteract the harm done by the horrible songs they have heard in music halls and bar-rooms. I think nearly every child has, naturally, a taste for music; I have about 100 pupils here, and they are all fond of it...."

Source

Excerpted from "Built for Children: Tour Through the Addition to Hull House," *Chicago Journal,* (December 12, 1895): 5. Full text available online at the Urban Experience in Chicago:

Miss Addams is charmed with the "Children's Home," and is eager to point out the great advantage it is to the children to have larger and more convenient quarters, built with a special view to their comfort.

Charles Mather Smith has bestowed a royal Christmas gift on the Hull House little ones, and one which will do incalculable good.

Hull House and Its Neighborhood, 1889–1963 Web Site. http://tigger.uic.edu/htbin/cgiwrap/bin/urbanexp/main.cgi?file=new/show_doc.ptt&doc=527&chap=32. (accessed June 2006)

Newborn Adoption

Vern L. Bullough

Adoption of newborns in the historical past did not occur frequently. A major factor preventing it was the problem of infant feeding, an issue which orphanages for abandoned infants also faced. Though traditionally large numbers of women in the past have tried to avoid breast feeding, the mortality rate of the infants involved were high. Data from Europe in the sixteenth century, where in some areas it was the custom to feed babies pap meal instead of breast milk, show that mortality rates were extremely high. The bubbly bottle and other similar developments were no less dangerous to the young infants and wet nurses were not that much better. Some evidence for this statement about wet nurses comes from a 1971 study of twins in Senegal where 47 percent of the breastfed twins did not survive beyond their first birthday, compared to 27 percent of the non-twin population. The mother simply did not produce enough milk to keep them healthy. Since the wet nurse of the past usually had an infant of her own to feed, the Senegal figures for twins became relevant, and being a wet nurse for large numbers of women meant that either their own infant or the infant for which they were a wet nurse would die. In some areas in the eighteenth century, infant mortality reached 90 percent among the lower economic classes.

Two developments in the last part of the nineteenth century increased the survival chances of newborns without a mother. The first was the invention of the rubber nipple and the second was pasteurization of the milk. Following the vulcanization of rubber in 1839 by Charles Goodyear, there was an explosion of rubber products. The first patent for a rubber nipple for infant feeding was by Elijah Pratt in 1845; this was soon followed by a series of patents improving upon it. The first seamless nipple, patented by C. B. Dickinson in 1874, was designed to fit over the mouth of the bottle. The development of the nipple coincided with the invention of pasteurization of milk and efforts to improve delivery. In the twentieth century, special infant formulas were developed and a relationship was established between the commercial infant-food manufacturers that began to appear and the medical profession.

The comparatively rapid adoption of the new methods of infant feeding can be demonstrated by the radical drop, and then disappearance, of advertisements for wet nurses such as in the *The Times* of London in the last two decades of the nineteenth century. Abandoned babies had a good chance of surviving in an institutional setting, but they also could be available for adoption and were increasingly sought by would-be parents. The result was a change in attitudes toward infant adoption.

See also Infant Adoption.

Further Reading

Bullough, Vern L. "Bottle Feeding," *Bulletin of the History of Medicine*, 55 (1981): 257–59.

Nineteenth Century Changes in American Adoption

Dennis Miller

In 1800, there were no formal adoption statutes in the United States. By 1900, most states had enacted some type of statute to deal with the adoption of parentless children. This change was necessitated because the traditional measures for dealing with orphans became inadequate in the face of a rapid increase in their numbers. This increase, E. Wayne Carp notes, was principally due to disease, the Civil War, explosive immigration, industrialization, and the social problems that accompanied the growth of cities on the eastern seaboard of the United States. The welfare of dependent children in the nineteenth century would be decided in the context of competition between proponents of the competing theories of institutionalization, foster care, and adoption. The fate of parentless children would be influenced not only by the major events of the century, but by the growing field of social work and the increased professionalism and secularization of those responsible for the care of those children.

No provision for adoption was made in English common law and there was not a great need for it in colonial America. Inheritance was by blood, so there was little reason to formalize adoptions. Children in need of guardianship who could not be cared for by relatives or neighbors were placed in indenture or apprenticeship situations. Carp reports that this practice was most common in Massachusetts and New York. In many situations, younger children were taken in by relatives while older children became indentured or apprenticed. As Burton Z. Sokoloff notes, large plantations in the south, in need of labor, took in large numbers of orphans. The system worked well enough that, in 1800, there were only a handful of institutions for the care of parentless children in the entire United States. By 1880 there were several hundred. Much of the increase was a direct result of the Civil War.

The practice of informal adoption provided guardianship for many parentless children prior to 1900 because a child in need usually lived near a large extended family, which was common in rural societies. In fast-growing industrial cities of the nineteenth century, the bonds with the extended family were stretched and the welfare of parentless children was often left to strangers. Humanitarian and religious reformers turned to the almshouse and the orphanage to reform, rehabilitate, and educate these children. Carp notes that these were criticized as being expensive, rigid, excessively harsh with discipline, and failing in the caliber of the children they produced.

Most working-class children in New York City, as Clay Gish reports, would lose at least one parent before reaching adulthood. The most common solution was to institutionalize them; however, these institutions were overwhelmed by the large number of children who needed care. It is estimated that, in 1852, there were thirty-thousand vagrant children on the streets of New York. Sokoloff notes that the lower east side of Manhattan was the most densely populated area in the world, with a density of two hundred fifty thousand per square mile. Contributing significantly to this situation was the opening of the Erie Canal in 1825, which economically linked New York City to the interior, and immigration after the Irish potato famine of 1846. As it became clear that institutionalization was insufficient to meet the needs of dependent children, "placing-out" became popular.

In early nineteenth century America, child labor was highly prized by farmers who were attempting to transform the western prairie to farmland. This need for labor was partially met by "Orphan Trains" implemented by Charles Loring Brace and the New York Children's Aid Society. Brace was a religiously motivated reformer who believed that children could not develop appropriate character traits while institutionalized, but could do so in a good Protestant home. According to data reported by Carp, from 1853 to 1893, eighty-four thousand children were moved by orphan trains from cities to agricultural areas. In addition to addressing the needs of orphans, the Society also provided both a temporary refuge for children from families in distressed circumstances and an agency for teenage children looking for work. Gish reports that 48 percent of all cases administered by the Society were boys fourteen–seventeen years of age looking for work.

This movement away from institutions and toward "placing-out" was given support by the clearly unsatisfactory conditions that prevailed in many institutions. It was estimated that, in 1844, 15–20 percent of people in almshouses in New York City were children. They were not separated from the other residents and, as Sokoloff reports, often were forced to live among the mentally ill.

The orphan train project was the subject of much debate while it was active and afterwards. Brace and his colleagues believed that Catholics were unworthy parents and saw the orphan trains as vehicles to rescue and rehabilitate children. This attitude was formed in the context of widespread anti-Catholic feelings in America, the result of the arrival of large numbers of Irish-Catholics into what had been a predominantly Protestant country. Alarmed by the placement of their children in Protestant homes, Carp reports that adoption agencies and institutions were founded by both Catholics and Jews to keep children from the grasp of Brace and others.

Many people who had taken in children through informal circumstances wished to legalize the situation for purposes of inheritance. The only recourse in the early part of the century was through individual private bills of adoption. Through this mechanism, a prospective adoptive parent would petition a state legislature to legalize an existing situation. Essentially, these were property transfers whereby a child was deeded to the adoptive parent. This was a time-consuming task that made no inquiry into the conditions in which a child lived or how he or she was being treated. With the increase in children being placed-out, the number of such petitions became unworkable. This procedure was unsatisfactory in both its inefficiency and in its ability to protect the welfare of the children involved. Carp notes that, between 1781 and 1851, Vermont enacted three hundred separate bills of adoption.

Statutes were passed in Mississippi in 1846 and in Texas in 1850 that allowed for the public recording of private adoptions without the need for private bills of adoption. These statutes made the public legalization of private adoptions much easier than private bills of adoption, but did not go beyond that. The first general adoption statute was passed in Massachusetts in 1851. It is considered to be the first "child-centered" adoption statute and the model for those that followed in other states. Sokoloff reports that this was the first statute that placed the welfare of the child first and required judicial acquiescence for the petition to be granted.

For the first time by the provisions in the Massachusetts statute, Carp notes, judges were given the authority to decide if the circumstances of adoption were fit and proper with respect to the welfare of the child. The Massachusetts law provided for: the need for written consent to adoption by the biological parents; consent by the child to be adopted if he or she had reached fourteen years of age; a married adopter had to secure written agreement from his or her spouse on an adoption petition; the presiding judge had to verify that the adopters were suitable; the adopted child would become the legal child of the adopters; and the biological parents would lose all legal rights and obligations concerning the child.

The Massachusetts statute did not address the procedures for determining the suitability of adopters or the welfare of the child directly. Naomi Cahn notes that was addressed the first time by a similar statute in Pennsylvania in 1853. According to Louann Carroll, by 1873, seventeen states had enacted adoption statutes.

Social problems in the latter half of the nineteenth century were exacerbated by the concentration of working poor in slum conditions in large American cities. Orphanages became increasingly filled with the children of single parents. Desertion was the divorce of the working poor and it became increasingly common in cities where anonymity made it easier. Husbands could not simply disappear in sparsely populated rural areas, but they could in large cities. Abandoned women with dependent children became a new class of urban poor.

During the first part of the nineteenth century, child-savers were motivated by a desire to rescue children from poverty; in the latter part of the century, Cahn notes, the motivation changed to one of saving them from neglect and abuse. This was concurrent with the advent of professional child-saving agencies that exercised the oversight required by the general adoption statutes. Informal adoptions, indenture, and apprenticeship had not provided for child welfare to be monitored, leaving the system open to abuse, a circumstance that states attempted to address through legislation. As the Adoption History Project timeline shows, in 1868, Massachusetts began the modern foster care system by paying for children to be boarded in private homes and appointing agents to conduct periodic inspections. In 1871, New York established the New York State Charities Aid Association. In 1891, Michigan was the first state that required a judge to certify the good moral character and material soundness of a potential adoptive parent. In 1898, the

St. Vincent De Paul Society became the first Catholic agency to place children in homes instead of institutions.

While most states had enacted adoption statutes by 1900, many adoptive homes were not subject to oversight or supervision and child-placement was not yet a specialized profession. To address deficiencies in the original legislation, the Massachusetts statute was amended seven times in twenty years. Those amendments focused principally on defining, in detail, the rights and the status of biological parents. As Cahn notes, an additional revision in 1876 increased the definition of parental desertion from one to two years.

Adoption statutes in the twentieth century continued to strengthen the provisions intended to insure proper placement and oversight of the welfare of children. As noted by the Adoption History Project, the 1917 Minnesota Adoption Law provided that a petition of adoption could not be granted until a child had resided in the home of the proposed adopters for a minimum of six months. It granted the adopted child the same rights of inheritance as biological children, including the right to inherit from relatives of the adoptive parents. It also required that adoption records be kept confidential, setting a precedent for "closed adoption" that became customary in adoption proceedings.

The nineteenth century represented significant and lasting changes in the way in which dependent children were cared for. The pressures of population increase in large cities combined with war, disease, poverty, illegitimacy, divorce, and desertion created a large population of minor children who were orphaned, abandoned, or were living in circumstances of poverty so severe that child-savers saw the need to take action.

With the move away from orphanages and toward the placing-out of children, "baby farming," which was the sale of infants for profit by baby brokers, became an unfortunate by-product. This was aided by doctors and midwives in lying-in hospitals where prostitutes, abandoned women, and unmarried young women delivered their babies. Previously, a pregnant girl could place her newborn with whomever she chose. In the late nineteenth century, Carroll recounts, unwed pregnant women were considered immoral outcasts whose newborn children were removed from them and put up for adoption. Children could even be purchased on the installment plan. Baby brokers would sometimes collect from both sides of the transaction, the birth mother and the adoptive parents. Baby farms were unregulated, unsanitary, and disease-ridden. According to the Adoption History Project, when the abuses and living conditions that accompanied baby-farming came to light, public reaction prompted the passage of regulations that helped curtail the practice.

The care of dependent children had been originally left to relatives and neighbors. By mid-century, institutions had been founded by benevolent organizations and were caring for many urban children. By the end of the century, the function was increasingly being assumed by the state. The adoption process had been formalized and legalized, with jurisdiction passing from state legislatures to the judiciary. While the welfare of the child was addressed in statutes by the end of the century, true professionalization of those managing the adoption process would not happen until the twentieth century.

An orphaned child in 1800 could expect to be taken in by a relative or neighbor, apprenticed, or placed in indentured servitude. An orphaned child in a large city in 1850 could expect to be placed in a foundling home or almshouse operated by a religiously-motivated organization. An orphaned child in 1900 could expect to become a ward of the state and "placed-out." In 1910 there were still more than one hundred thousand children in American orphanages, which were drawing heavy criticism in the press, and in the U.S. Congress, for their living conditions. By 1920, orphanages were being dismantled and the placing-out of children into homes became the preferred method of dealing with dependent children as discussed by Melosh.

The twentieth century has seen a continuation of the regulatory processes initiated in the nineteenth century, with all states regulating adoption through the enforcement of standards that protect the welfare of children. It became clear that the abuses that accompanied the placing-out of children could only be curtailed through the vigorous adoption of minimum standards and the replacement of baby farmers by professional social workers. Principal proponents of minimum standards, as noted by the Adoption History Project, were the U.S. Children's Bureau and The Child Welfare League of America.

See also Baby Farming; "Binding-out" Children; Brace, Charles Loring; Child Welfare League of America; Massachusetts Adoption Act (1851); Orphan Trains; Orphanages; Social Work Perspectives on Adoption; U.S. Children's Bureau and Adoption.

Further Reading

Adoption History Project. "Baby Farming"; "Minimum Standards"; "Minnesota Adoption Law, 1917"; "Timeline of Adoption History." The Adoption History Project Web Site. http://www.uoregon.edu/~adoption/ (accessed September, 2004).

Alliance for Non-Custodial Parents Rights. Summary of "The American Invention of Child Support: Dependency and Punishment in Early American Child Support Law," by Drew D. Hansen, *Yale Law Journal*, (108 5): 1123–1153 Alliance for Non-Custodial Parents Rights Web Site. http://www.ancpr.org/american_invention_of_child_supp.htm (accessed September, 2004).

Berebitsky, Julie. *Like Our Very Own: Adoption and the Changing Culture of Motherhood, 1851–1950*. Lawrence, KS: University Press of Kansas, 2000.

Cahn, Naomi. "Perfect Substitutes Or The Real Thing." *Duke Law Journal*, 52 (2003). Duke Law Web Site. http://www.law.duke.edu/journals/dlj/articles/dlj52p1077.htm

Cahn, Naomi, and Joan Heifetz Hollinger, eds. *Families by Law: An Adoption Reader*. New York: New York University Press, 2004.

Carp, E. Wayne. *Family Matters: Secrecy and Disclosure in the History of Adoption*. Cambridge: Harvard University Press, 1998.

Carp, E. Wayne. *Adoption in America*. Ann Arbor: University of Michigan Press, 2002.

Carroll, Louann. "The History of Open Adoption." Adoption.com Web Site. http://e-magazine.adoption.com/articles/430/the-history-of-open-adoption.php (accessed September, 2004).

Gish, Clay. "Rescuing the 'Waifs and Strays' of the City: The Western Emigration Program of the Children's Aid Society." *Journal of Social History* 33 (1999): 121–140.

Hacsi, Tim. "From Indenture to Family Foster Care: A Brief History of Child Placing." In *A History of Child Welfare*, edited by Eve P. Smith and Lisa A. Merkel-Holguin. New Brunswick, NJ: Transaction Publishers, 1996. pp. 155–173.

Herman, Ellen. "The Paradoxical Rationalization of Modern Adoption: Social and Economic Aspects of Adoption." *Journal of Social History* (Winter 2002). http://www.findarticles.com/p/articles/mi_m2005/is_2_36/ai_95829286

Holt, Marilyn Irvin. *The Orphan Trains: Placing Out in America*. Lincoln, NE: University of Nebraska Press, 1992.

Melosh, Barbara. *Strangers and Kin: The American Way of Adoption.* Cambridge, MA: Harvard University Press, 2002.

O'Connor, Stephen. *Orphan Trains: The Story of Charles Loring Brace and the Children He Saved and Failed.* Boston: Houghton Mifflin, 2001.

Sokoloff, Burton Z. "Antecedents of American Adoption." *The Future of Children: Adoption* 3 (1993): 17–18.

Stern, Alexandra Minna, and Howard Markel, eds. *Formative Years: Children's Health in the United States, 1880–2000.* Ann Arbor: University of Michigan Press, 2002.

U.S. Children's Bureau. *Adoption Laws in the United States: A Summary of the Development of Adoption Legislation and Significant Features of Adoption Statutes, With the Text of Selected Laws,* ed. Emelyn Foster Peck. Bureau Publication No. 148. Washington, DC: Government Printing Office, 1925.

Zelizer, Viviana A. *Pricing the Priceless Child: The Changing Social Value of Children.* New York: Basic Books, 1985.

Primary Document

Adoption by Deed in Texas

Adoption by deed predated the earliest adoption acts in the United States. An informal form of adoption—a contract between two parties in which children were deeded like property from their biological to adoptive parents—adoption by deed continued to exist in some states into the 1900s.

Laws of the State of Texas, 1850, Chap. 39[*]

SECTION I. Be it enacted by the Legislature of the State of Texas, That any person wishing to adopt another as his or her legal heir, may do so by filing in the office of the Clerk of the County Court in which county he or she may reside, a statement in writing, by him or her signed and duly authenticated or acknowledged, as deeds are required to be, which statement shall recite in substance, that he or she adopts the person named therein as his or her legal heir, and the same shall be admitted to record in said office.

SEC. 2. Be it further enacted, That such statement in writing, signed and authenticated, or acknowledged and recorded as aforesaid, shall entitle the party so adopted to all the rights and privileges, both in law and equity, of a legal heir of the party so adopting him or her. Provided, however, that if the party adopting such person have, at the time of such adoption, or shall thereafter have a child or children, begotten in lawful wedlock, such adopted child or children shall in no case inherit more than the one-fourth of the estate of the party adopting him or her, which can be disposed of by will.

*Also found in Oliver C. Hartley, *A Digest of the Laws of Texas* (Philadelphia, 1850), pp. 88–89. This act was not repealed until 1931. See *Acts of 1931*, chap. 177, sec. II.172.

Source

"Laws of the State of Texas, 1850." As reprinted in Abbott, Grace. *The Child and the State: Volume II. The Dependent and the Delinquent Child. The Child of Unmarried Adults*, New York: Greenwood, 1968, p. 172. First published 1938 by University of Chicago.

Primary Document

The First Act Requiring Investigation of Adoptive Parents

As concerns grew that children be placed with suitable adoptive parents, legislation was enacted requiring investigations of prospective adopters. As noted by Robert Bremner (1971: 147 and others), Michigan's 1891 Act made it the first state in the nation to require such an investigation.

The Michigan Act of 1891

"An Act to provide for the adoption and change of name of minors, and for making them heirs at law of the person or persons adopting them ...," 1891—ch. 77, *Public Acts of the Michigan Legislature*—Regular Session 1891 (Lansing, 1891), pp. 81–82.

... judge of probate with whom such instrument is filed, shall thereupon make an investigation, and if he shall be satisfied as to the good moral character, and the ability to support and educate such child, and of the suitableness of the home, of the person or persons adopting ..., he shall make an order to be entered on the journal of the probate court that such person or persons do stand in the place of a parent or parents to such child, and that the name of such child be changed to such name as shall be designated in said instrument for that purpose. Whereupon such child shall thereafter be known and called by said new name, and the person or persons so adopting such child, shall thereupon stand in the place of a parent or parents to such child in law, and be liable to all the duties, and entitled to all the rights of parents thereto; and such child shall thereupon become and be an heir at law of such person or persons, the same as if he or she were in fact the child of such person or persons.

Source

As reprinted in Bremner, Robert H. ed. *Children and Youth in America: A Documentary History. Volume II: 1866–1932 (Parts 1–6).* Cambridge, MA: Harvard University Press, 1971: p. 147.